MASTERPLOTS II

POETRY SERIES
REVISED EDITION

MASTERPLOTS II

POETRY SERIES
REVISED EDITION

8

The Translucent Mechanics–Zone
INDEXES

Editor, Revised Edition
PHILIP K. JASON

Project Editor, Revised Edition
TRACY IRONS-GEORGES

Editors, Supplement
JOHN WILSON   **PHILIP K. JASON**

Editor, First Edition
FRANK N. MAGILL

SALEM PRESS

Pasadena, California   Hackensack, New Jersey

Editor in Chief: Dawn P. Dawson

Project Editor: Tracy Irons-Georges *Research Supervisor:* Jeffry Jensen
Production Editor: Cynthia Beres *Research Assistant:* Jeff Stephens
Copy Editor: Lauren Mitchell *Acquisitions Editor:* Mark Rehn

Some of the essays in this work originally appeared in *Masterplots II, Poetry Series*, edited by Frank N. Magill (Pasadena, Calif.: Salem Press, Inc., 1992), and in *Masterplots II, Poetry Series Supplement*, edited by John Wilson and Philip K. Jason (Pasadena, Calif.: Salem Press, Inc., 1998).

∞ The paper used in these volumes conforms to the American National Standard for Permanence of Paper for Printed Library Materials, Z39.48-1992 (R1997).

Library of Congress Cataloging-in-Publication Data
Masterplots II. Poetry series.— Rev. ed. / editor, Philip K. Jason ; project editor, Tracy Irons-Georges
    p. ; cm.
    Rev. ed.: Masterplots two / Frank Northen Magill, 1992-1998.
    Includes bibliographical references and indexes.
    ISBN 1-58765-037-1 (set : alk. paper) — ISBN 1-58765-045-2 (vol. 8 : alk. paper) —
    1. Poetry — Themes, motives. I. Title: Masterplots two. II. Title: Masterplots 2. III.
Jason, Philip K., 1941-   . IV. Irons-Georges, Tracy.

PN1110.5 .M37 2002
809.1—dc21

                                                                2001055059

First Printing

TABLE OF CONTENTS

TABLE OF CONTENTS

MASTERPLOTS II

MASTERPLOTS II

Poetry Series
Revised Edition

THE TRANSLUCENT MECHANICS

Author: George Oppen (1908-1984)
Type of poem: Meditation
First published: 1972, in *Seascape: Needle's Eye*

The Poem

A spare, free-verse poem, George Oppen's "The Translucent Mechanics" comprises twenty-nine lines, four of which contain only a single word. The title invites readers to experience the poet's vision into the tentativeness and transparency of things, revealing them as organic mechanisms, ever in flux.

The poem is written in the third person, as the poet takes on a persona that views things from shifting perspectives. First, he assumes the point of view of the wind, moving through "the clever city"—specifically, the port of San Francisco—penetrating its "hinges," or workings, to discover its "secrets of motion"—that is, its life.

"Flaws" are discovered, as well as "fear," but so is commerce with vital forces. A "message" is "fetched . . . out of the sea again," the sea indicating the primordial matrix of life. "Angel" and "powers," or spiritual voices, now declare the dialectic of "'things and the self.'" "Prosody" that "sings/ In the stones" entrusts to "a poetry of statement" a "living mind." Objects in poetry inhabit both human language, including the poem itself, and the physical, material world—both of which are themselves objects.

The "living mind/ 'and that one's own,'" the individual synthesizing imagination, willing to see things "at close quarters," paradoxically attains the transcendent view of "archangel." Oppen has called this way of seeing existence as one "the imagist intensity of vision"—that is, perception that penetrates the complex interrelationship between language, thought, and things. It perceives the correspondent, dynamic structures of self and universe. Without this unifying vision, "earth crumbles"; the experience of reality deteriorates.

Forms and Devices

Oppen has been associated with Objectivism, a school of poetry that links the structure of objective reality with that of the human mind. The poem mediates the world of things and that of human language; it serves as a nexus of words, images, and things.

Moreover, the poem exists as an object itself, a universe of its own, exemplifying authenticity and coherence. It exhibits organic form, with cadences and contours produced by a particular voice and time. Objectivism's commitment to integrity, to precise articulation of word and event, and to scrupulously rendered experience decries superfluity or ornamentation. To achieve clarity, the poet rejects mellifluousness or melodic flourishes in favor of the pure resonances of well-honed imagery.

The poem's spareness, along with its syncopated rhythm, forces the reader to concentrate on words and images one at a time, necessitating their redefinition. According to Jonathan Galassi of *Poetry*, "Oppen's lines move in fits and starts; they are slowly accrued 'discrete series' of phrases, chains or associations. . . . The lesson, the articulations of a meaning, is what matters." Cid Corman, also a poet, has noted that "Oppen often repeats words . . . as if he were literally discovering the sense in them and he were started by it." The words Oppen repeats—"fear," "say," "what"—suggest the crux of the poem, as symbolized by the wind: a blind groping for definition.

Words that imply communication of meaning dominate the poem: "voices," "murmur," "message," "say," "prosody," "sings," "poetry," "statement." Phrases appear in quotes within the poem—"'things and the self,'" "'and that one's own'"—drawing attention to them as language.

The poet indicates that definition is variously mutable and stable by using imagery linking restless wind and transcendent spirit. For example, both express themselves in sound: The wind "murmurs"; angels and powers "say." This connection harkens back to the Scriptures, in whose original languages the same word signifies both. Significantly, the poem climaxes with an invocation to "Archangel/ of the tide," suggesting the divine spirit that brooded over the waters of creation.

Themes and Meanings

Although Oppen worked as an organizer for the U.S. Communist Party for a number of years, he wrote no verse during that time—nor are his poems overtly political. Nevertheless, his poetry is radical in its focus on the fundamentals of thought, matter, and existence.

"The Translucent Mechanics" articulates the universe of quantum mechanics, which is located somewhere between the sensory mechanism of the observer and the physical properties of the object observed. Each observer, as exemplified by the poet3, creates his or her own world.

Many of Oppen's poems, including this one, explore, according to Galassi, "the nature of the poet's work and his role . . . as a user of language." Language is one way in which human beings structure their world. The "mechanics" of language are transparent, some would argue, as its forms may reflect its effects; syntax is a system of language that indicates how the arrangement of words in a sentence, or sentence structure, conveys meaning. It is theorized, moreover, that the patterns characteristic of language are themselves products of the structure or mechanics of the human mind.

Oppen's poems, as crystallizations of language, betray a discursive, dialectical intellect. Critic Irwin Ehrenpreis notes in Oppen's work "the effort of the mind to reach clarity of vision by turning always upon itself, traveling back and forth between things and words, reconsidering and correcting earlier impressions or ponderings."

Oppen's guide through this odyssey would appear to be a relentlessly probing mind. It penetrates to the organic structure of things, reflecting and readjusting its own image in the process. Oppen has said, "I was thinking about a justification of human life, eventually, in what I call the life of the mind." For the poet, all things are analogues of the mind—systems of meaning animated by dynamic structures that radiate in and through them. Oppen uses poetry, as it illuminates these structures, to reveal the mind.

Amy Adelstein

TRANSMIGRATION

Author: Brendan Galvin (1938-   )
Type of poem: Narrative
First published: 1982; collected in *Winter Oysters*, 1983

The Poem

"Transmigration" is a mid-length narrative poem with irregular stanza lengths and meter. The poem's title suggests the transmigration of the soul, the theological idea that after death one's soul migrates to exist in another creature, human or animal. In the case of Brendan Galvin's poem, the transmigration referred to is of a middle-aged man who jogs to lose a paunch gained from overeating. The jogger has "sat out easy rains" and has not worked very hard at becoming healthier. Ironically, instead of becoming healthier, he dies on the beach, and his soul enters a seagull. The title also introduces the concept of migration, an idea that Galvin plays with throughout the poem. The onset of winter is traditionally associated with death, but it is also the time when birds migrate. Thus, Galvin conjoins the idea of a soul's migration after death with a bird's natural instinct to migrate when the days grow shorter. The poem begins precisely at the moment of death as the jogger's soul leaves his body and reawakens in the seagull.

Much of the poem charts the orientation of the soul to its new body. The man, now a bird, is afraid and lands immediately on a tree, its "new feet gripping." Getting in touch with "instinct," however, he is able to acclimate himself to the new body. The man enjoys the new perspective, which is both visual and spiritual. Visually, the soul sees things differently, looking "for the first time" at the world from above. Spiritually, the soul knows the secret that humans do not, that death is another beginning, though one of a different sort than most suppose.

Although the poem begins with the man's soul entering the seagull's body, there are many retrospective moments within the poem where readers glimpse his previous existence as a human. One poignant example is the memory of Ryder beach, where he and "one summer's girl" were surprised on the shore by a construction crew. However, Galvin reminds readers that "such memories are useless," and the beach holds no nostalgic human associations but has become a place for the bird to hunt for fish. At the end, as the bird flies above the town, he hears the organ playing at his own funeral, though from where he flies it sounds "thin as a harmonica." He follows the cars of the funeral procession, but Galvin tells him that he "can't feel" for what he trails. The bird, or soul, or man experiences the "simple rightness of things" and knows he could never explain it to "that veiled woman/ and downcast kids" he sees below at the cemetery.

Forms and Devices

The most notable poetic device in "Transmigration" is the use of the second-person pronoun "you." Galvin addresses the soul of the man that has entered the seagull, but the effect of the "you" is to position the reader in the man's place. Readers become the "you" that is addressed and see from the bird's perspective, experiencing a "bird's-eye view" of life from the position of a participant. This is the ultimate transmigration of the poem. The poet's task is to cause readers souls to transmigrate from their own bodies to absolute identification with the "you" of the poem. The "vowels of love" Galvin refers to are, in some sense, his statement about poetry. The sound and sense experience of the poem should move one into a direct experience of it, a loving transmigration from reader into participant.

"Transmigration" is notable, as is Galvin's work in general, for a rich use of simile and metaphor. Given the subject matter, it is interesting how human the comparisons are. The poem opens, for example, with the simile "When your bones turn/ loose and light as a deck chair." Like the seagull, the deck chair is part of the seascape, but unlike the bird, it is part of the human world. Galvin compares the hollow-boned lightness of a bird to the tubular construction of a deck chair and, in very human terms, tries to convey what it feels like to suddenly have one's soul reawaken within a bird. As a bird seeing the world from above for the first time, the soul still experiences things in human terms. The runway of an airport, for example, "could be/ a dropped paperclip." The metaphor places readers in the position of the bird, which views the runway from height, but also reminds them of the man's previous life and suggests he may have held a job in an office. Similarly, when he hears, from his position in the sky, "Crackles of speech/ as off a police radio," the simile visually reminds readers not only where and what the man is now but also what he used to be. The police radio and the "money talk" he overhears suggest the complications of human society and contrast with the uncomplicated life he now leads. Conversely, some of the poem's metaphors reflect on how animalistic the man was before his death and how heavy he was compared to the lightness of the bird. He jogs because he has been to "too many troughs" and is "trying to shake off a pelt."

In writing a poem about what it feels like to become a bird, Galvin is forced by human circumstances to rely on metaphors emerging from human experience. Such a move, though perhaps necessary, is also successful and constantly keeps before the reader the transmigration that has occurred from man to bird. Some of the visual imagery places the reader firmly into the position of the bird. Readers see common things in an uncommon way, "from above" like a bird. Simple things that went unnoticed such as the beauty of a plowed field ("the art of tractors") are now seen "for the first time." Above all, spatial orientation has altered dramatically. The bird experiences a different relationship to the sun, moon, earth, sea, and sky. Flying so high he can sense the curvature of the earth, the seagull watches until the "last light/ drops off the planet's/ easy curve."

Themes and Meanings

"Transmigration" first appeared in *The New Yorker* but has been reprinted in three collections. In each case, it occupies a significant position in relation to the collection as a whole. In *Winter Oysters* (1983), for example, "Transmigration" occupies a separate section unto itself; in *Great Blue* (1990), it occupies the final place in the first section. Most significant is its appearance in *A Birder's Dozen* (1984), in which it is the thirteenth and final poem. All the poems in *Birder's Dozen* are about birds: "The Birds," "Chickadee," and "The Grackles" are representative titles. However, "Transmigration" comes last and is about a man's transformation into something that he had previously only observed. Galvin's point in positioning the poem at the end seems to be a desire to migrate, through poetry, from observer to participant. Reading his twelve poems about birds, the reader becomes transformed into one in the thirteenth.

In some sense, however, the poem is not about a man becoming a bird but about what it feels like to become a soul. The contrast between the man's physical heaviness and the bird's lightness is a significant one. The heaviness suggests the burden of being human, of the "weighty" decisions and responsibilities. The lightness of the bird is a removal of those things, and, unchained, the soul is free to fly in a kind of immediate contact with the natural world. The new relation to space and time is part of that contact, as the bird has no real concept of time passing other than flying higher in the sky so the sun will stay out longer. It is no wonder that the poet watches longingly and asks, "What are you, a soul?"

Near the end of the poem, the bird listens and watches as his funeral procession leaves the church and wends its way to Memorial Lawn cemetery. Although the bird knows the "simple rightness of things" the transmigration has caused, he cannot entirely forsake his human life and thoughts. In the dramatic climax of the poem, the soul sees his wife and children below, but they become "that veiled woman" and the "downcast kids." His connection to them is severed, and he knows that he could say no words of comfort to explain the "rightness" of things as they are. Still, though his existence as a bird is liberating, he knows he will never be able to leave his human life behind. He will haunt Main Street "for snatches of the inconsequential/ that bind person to person/ and day to day below." Though liberated, his soul is still bound, and the poem ends with the man/seagull/soul flying with exhilaration and sadness into the night sky.

Joe B. Fulton

TRAVELING THROUGH THE DARK

Author: William Stafford (1914-1993)
Type of poem: Lyric
First published: 1962; in *Traveling Through the Dark*

The Poem

William Stafford's "Traveling Through the Dark" is a short poem of eighteen lines, divided into four quatrains and a closing couplet. The title clearly describes both the literal and the figurative situation in the poem as well as its governing metaphor: The speaker himself is traveling through the dark on a narrow mountain road, and by extension, so is everyone.

The poem is written in the first person, giving an immediacy and directness to the experience; the reader is there with the poet, though he tells the story in the past tense. Many poets choose to speak through a created voice, or persona, but one senses in this poem that Stafford is speaking directly from his own experience. By sharing his personal experience so vividly, Stafford gives it an immediacy, authority, and power that helps one make it a part of one's own.

The first stanza begins with a description of the setting and the context of the events which follow. The speaker is traveling at night on a narrow mountain road and comes upon the body of a dead deer. Because the road is so narrow, he realizes that the dead deer is a hazard to other drivers, who might swerve suddenly to avoid it and drive off the road into the river canyon and be killed.

Stanza 2 shows him getting out of the car to look at the deer; he discovers that it is a doe, only recently dead. As he drags it off the road, he realizes that its belly is unusually large. In stanza 3, he discovers the reason: Inside the dead doe is an unborn fawn, still alive. He hesitates, not sure what to do. Should he try to save the fawn? Is there some way to rescue it, although its mother is dead? Should he be more concerned with the safety of other travelers in the dark and the fact that the dead deer is a dangerous road hazard?

While he hesitates in stanza 4, he notices the car, which seems animal-like to him as it aims its parking lights and purrs its engine. He stands in the glow of the taillights and watches the exhaust of the car turn red. Around him, the car, the doe, and the unborn fawn, he hears nature listen, waiting for him to make a decision.

In the final couplet he makes his decision, the only one he can possibly make if he acts responsibly for all involved; he pushes the doe over the edge of the canyon and into the river. The decision is difficult because he has realized humankind's responsibility for the whole natural world, especially the animal world. It is, however, the only possible decision, because even if he had the instruments to do a cesarean section, he could not keep the fawn alive, and to leave the deer there on the road might cause others to die as well; in their swerving to avoid the deer, they might veer off the narrow canyon road and crash down into the river.

Forms and Devices

Stafford uses poetic form with startling effectiveness in this poem. His quatrains use an *abcb* slant rhyme pattern ("road" with "dead," "killing" with "belly," "waiting" with "hesitated," and "engine" with "listen") with great effectiveness; the slant rhyme undercuts any romanticized notion that being in nature is an unadulterated delight. He also uses the sound reinforcements of assonance and alliteration; in stanza 1, for example, there is "dark," "deer," and "dead"; "river," "road," and "roll"; and "might," "make," and "more." The repetition of sounds, as subtle as it is, intensifies the nuances of the speaker's experience and helps to lead him (and the reader) to the final action, which must be done without any "swerving." Stafford also builds an effective movement from external to internal action, and from physical to moral responsibility; he emphasizes this process with the pause in the middle of the poem (line 12) in which he hesitates in order to decide the best course of action to take. Another important poetic device is the use of puns, or wordplay, here intensely serious rather than comic. Besides the dual meaning of "swerving," for example, there is the dual meaning of "still" (line 11): The fawn continues to live, but it is quiet as well (as is the speaker).

The central device of the poem, however, is the use of action as metaphor. The decision of one person is exemplified and amplified to represent a decision for all people, in any time and place. The decision is also a specific answer in a specific situation to the question of one's individual and communal responsibility to the environment in which one lives. Because Stafford has deliberately understated his case, both through an objective point of view (he tells what he thinks, but not what he feels, about the situation) and a slant rhyme scheme, each of which avoids the obvious in sense and structure, he has allowed readers to make their own emotional responses, without any poetic sentimentality.

Themes and Meanings

"Traveling Through the Dark" asks readers to examine in a profound way the implications of their actions and the connotations of their thoughts and words. To live in the modern world, Stafford suggests metaphorically, is to travel through a variety of physical, mental, emotional, and spiritual landscapes, some of which may be cast in light, but others of which are in shadow. Every individual, at one time or another, will go over (figuratively, at least) narrow and dangerous mountain roads on dark nights, and one must discipline oneself to go as responsibly and self-consciously as one can. How can one prepare oneself to deal with the unexpected? To act rather than to ignore, suggests Stafford—to be a participant rather than merely an observer, because physical situations can provide the context for moral and ethical choices.

"Traveling Through the Dark" focuses on the parallels between physical swerving (line 4) and mental swerving (line 17), between a literal loss of control and a figurative loss of mental control caused by doubt. Coupled with this is the connection between the human (and even mechanical) world and the animal world. In the fourth stanza, for example, the car "aimed" its headlight; its engine "purred"; and "the warm exhaust turn[ed] red," suggesting a mingling of breath and blood. As the speaker expands his consciousness of the world from himself to the doe, fawn, and himself ("our group" in line 16) and then further to all society ("us all" in line 17), he extends his thematic perceptions from the individual to the communal: The reader is asked to make a decision with him. The decision has to do with what is, in any particular situation, the humane act as well as the just thing to do—what it means to be responsible, not only for oneself, but for one another and for the environment.

The questions suggested by the poem are many, and they concern each individual's particular responsibility for the environment as a whole (air, land, and water) as well as for the other creatures that inhabit it. Stafford uses personification effectively to indicate and insist that all creatures are in the world together; human responsibility is finally a communal as well as an individual one.

Clark Mayo

TRAVELS IN THE SOUTH

Author: Simon J. Ortiz (1941-   )
Type of poem: Narrative
First published: 1976, in *Going for the Rain*

The Poem

"Travels in the South" is a three-part poem in free verse, its sections divided by geographical location: "East Texas," "The Creek Nation East of the Mississippi," and "Crossing the Georgia Border into Florida." As the title suggests, Simon J. Ortiz, a member of the Acoma Pueblo tribe of American Indians, takes readers on an emotionally charged journey through several southern states beginning with an early morning departure from the Coushatta people in Alabama and ending in a state park in Florida. Using first person throughout, he skillfully situates these travels within the context of the narrator's heritage, culture, family, and community.

The first part, "East Texas," establishes a warm connection with the Coushatta people who feed and emotionally nourish the narrator on this leg of his journey. While the poem begins here, readers sense that his travels actually began earlier and that this locale is merely where he begins his tale, which is, in essence, a quest to find Native American people. It thus constitutes the narrator's search for identity. A humbling stop at the Huntsville State Penitentiary and a talk with the American Indian prisoners there completes his Alabama trip. When Ortiz turns his attention to Texas, the tone shifts; in fact, the narrator admits he does not want to be in Dallas, Texas, where the Bureau of Indian Affairs relocation official cannot even say how many American Indians live in the city. Witnessing much suffering, including a jobless Navajo and "an Apache woman crying for her lost life," the traveler moves on to Lake Caddo, named, according to the park ranger, for "some Indian tribe." There, much to his delight, he happens upon two seventy-year-old black women with whom he spends the rest of the day fishing and laughing.

Part 2, "The Creek Nation East of the Mississippi," begins at a hot dog stand in Pensacola, Florida, where the narrator asks for the names of local Native Americans. The vendor directs him just across the state border to Chief Alvin McGee's home in Atmore, Alabama, where he is surprised and heartened to recognize McGee as the same American Indian he had seen in pictures in old history books. While the venerable chief reminisces about famous local American Indian leaders and laments the devastating losses indigenous communities have experienced over the years, the two men watch the election news on television. When George Wallace is once again elected governor of the state, they clearly sense another loss for Native Americans as well as other people of color. Attempting to lift the old man's spirits, the narrator urges, "please don't worry about Wallace, don't worry." His words ring hollow, for as he travels on to his next destination, he hears a radio broadcast about the National Guard killing college students at Kent State University and must pull off the road despite, or perhaps because of, a sign that says "NO STOPPING EXCEPT IN CASE OF EMER-GENCY." Tired and depressed, the traveler begins to ponder the demoralizing results of his search for identity and community in a hostile country.

The final section, "Crossing the Georgia Border into Florida," chronicles several difficulties in Atlanta, Georgia, where the young narrator's long hair and dark skin elicit nervous glances and discriminatory practices from local white people. Reeling from such injustice, he empathizes with African Americans who experience abuses regularly but lack the opportunity to move on, which contrasts with his mobility when the American Indian meeting at the Dinkler Plaza ends. Settling finally at a campsite in a Florida state park "noted for the Indians/ that don't live here anymore," he seeks respite in nature. The poem concludes with a surprisingly apt image: The traveler offers crumbs of bread—"white, and kind of stale"—to the squirrels and birds. When they refuse such tasteless and paltry handouts, he understands why.

Forms and Devices

"Travels in the South" is a poem about recovery. It centers on one man's efforts to reclaim his Native American heritage by retracing the steps of his ancestors in the South. Sadly, the reader learns that many American Indians are merely a nameless memory in the minds of white people who now claim the land for their state parks and recreation areas. The American Indians that he does manage to locate still struggle to exist amid hostility. Yet Ortiz retrieves the tribal names—Coushatta, Caddo, Creek, Navajo, Apache, Acoma—and in doing so reclaims for himself an important part of his identity. Language, specifically the power of naming, becomes the catalyst for the poem's powerful message: Native American survival today depends upon a strong link with the past. Herein lies continuance.

By using names from both the past and the present, Ortiz creates a paradoxical mix of traditional Native American and what he calls "Mericano" culture. Each section of the poem and thus each mile of his journey unearths these surprising linguistic juxtapositions. He finds that the dominant culture is killing his people. Instead of living in harmony with the land, they are prisoners in the "State Pen" or unemployed welders in Dallas. He learns of an elder's whereabouts when he buys a hot dog and a beer, and, as they watch television together, they see their civil rights steadily erode. Significantly, however, at each stage of his journey, the narrator is sustained by the rising of the sun and by the language and wisdom of his elders. Two old black women, in a symbolic gesture, teach him about the stubbornness and perseverance of turtles and thus about his and all oppressed cultures' need for resistance and persistence. As he receives a traditional blessing from Chief McGee, he remembers his grandfather and "the mountains, the land from where [the narrator] came."

A final, illuminating mix of the old and new occurs in the third section when the narrator, a modern American youth wearing the styles of the 1970's, worries about the potential harassment he might encounter in the deep South because of his long hair. This concern calls to mind his grandfather, named "Tall One" by the Acoma, who also had long hair. Thus, while Ortiz merges the "Mericano" and Native American cultures, it is not with a sense of despair but rather a conviction that the traditions and heritage provide security in the present and an empowering solidarity with all oppressed peoples.

Ortiz saves the most meaningful situation, which illustrates the chasm between the old ways and the new, for the end of the last section in which the narrator's "brothers," the squirrel and red bird, refuse the crumbs of white bread he offers, a symbolic rendering of the "too little, too late" offerings of white society. The American Indian beliefs that animals are relatives and that their presence in life offers messages humans would do well to heed are instructive: Their refusal suggests that the narrator, too, should decline the "leftovers" of mainstream culture and thereby defy the tacit degradation accompanying such gestures.

Themes and Meanings

Ortiz is a storyteller, a fact to which he alludes in the second stanza: "Once, in a story, I wrote that Indians are everywhere." His travels in the South attempt to prove that Indians do indeed live in every part of the United States and thus debunk the popular "vanishing Indian" stereotype. Growing up in the oral tradition, his commitment to the Acoma tribe is strong. He believes that culture survives because of the story, which in turn generates poetry that tells the life of the people. Yet as a young man he was struck as if by a revelation by the writings of the Beat generation. He recalls being overly impressed by Jack Kerouac's prose. Indeed, many of Kerouac's themes are echoed in "Travels in the South": a focus on struggling people, a search for identity, and an on-the-road experience that ultimately exposes America's rough edges and dark underside.

These motifs are repeated in his books of poems published after *Going for the Rain*, especially *A Good Journey* (1977) and *Fight Back: For the Sake of the People, for the Sake of the Land* (1981). His poetic works chronicle "red power" activism and an awareness of the extended problems created by society's decimation of American Indian lands. Ortiz's poetic vision is clear in this early poem: Society's caretakers of the land, the park rangers in Texas and Florida, lack a basic understanding of its history and significance. This deficit is highlighted further in the second stanza when the narrator meets Chief McGee, who shows him his garden and fields. Speaking of the white oppressors, Chief McGee says, "There ain't much they don't try to take." In the final stanza of the poem, the traveler pays $2.50 to enter the space once owned by his people, a painful and ironic commentary on how successful white society has been in their greedy quest for land.

"Travels in the South" offers readers a series of images that illustrate how one man can feel like an outsider in his homeland. Ortiz cleverly contrasts the deep spirituality of the Acoma tradition with the shallow surface of contemporary society. Pueblo oral tradition includes stories, advice, and counsel, the priceless legacy the narrator inherits from his elders and, in effect, passes on to the readers.

Carol F. Bender

TRAVELS OF THE LAST BENJAMIN OF TUDELA

Author: Yehuda Amichai (1924-2000)
Type of poem: Meditation/lyric
First published: 1968, as "Masot Binyamin haacharon miTudelah," in *'Akhshav ba-ra'ash*; English translation collected in *The Selected Poetry of Yehuda Amichai*, 1986

The Poem

"Travels of the Last Benjamin of Tudela" is a long autobiographical meditation of 1,014 lines divided into 59 unnumbered stanzas of irregular length. It has the thematic score of an epic, but is written with the immediacy and emotional intensity of a lyric poem. The title invokes a recurring figure in Jewish lore: a wanderer who searches for the Ten Lost Tribes—the ancient Hebrew people exiled from their homeland. Translator Stephen Mitchell notes that Yehuda Amichai was living on Tudela Street in Jerusalem when he wrote the poem. Thus the poet himself, writing from the capital of the renewed Jewish state, becomes the final "Benjamin." His comparatively short and tumultuous personal history is played out against the long, anguished history of his people. Late in the poem, there is the suggestion that the speaker may be writing on Yom Kippur, the Jewish Day of Atonement, when Jews are expected to reflect on their past deeds and communal fate.

The poem is in the first person. The specific biographical details, as well as the nature of the self-scrutinizing voice, make it clear that the speaker represents Amichai himself rather than a dramatic persona. The speaker is "in the middle of my life." In the first nine stanzas, he addresses an unnamed "you"—the child he was—and recounts details of the boy's personal history: his arrival, at age twelve, in the port of Haifa in the British-controlled Palestine of the 1930's; his secular education in a Montessori kindergarten; his religious education in the synogogue. Already, however, the regime of "fact" is invaded by something else. The immigrant boy has entered more than "the new kingdom of your life." There is something else that will shape him: "the heart's shoulders carried an anguish not mine/ and from somewhere else ideas entered." That something else is the long, complicated history—both spiritual and secular—of the land he has entered. That land—and especially its holy city of Jerusalem—becomes a central presence in the poem, interweaving its fate with his own.

In stanza 6, the poet introduces the idea of the distance between child and adult, and first uses the pronouns "I" and "me." Beginning with stanza 10, the poet speaks directly to the reader in the present-tense first person. Henceforth, his many subsequent excursions into memory are from the position of a remembering adult, a man who has played many roles: son, husband, father, lover, soldier—and poet. The remainder of the poem deals with all these roles, these different ways of relating to self and others, and the different sorts of pain, responsibility, and desire associated with each. Stanza 14 portrays the poet's inspection of his face during shaving. He sees himself as a "white-foamed clown" and sees those to whom he has been related—"All of them,/ my lovers and my haters"—as "the stagehands of my life." The next stanza deals with his father, and the subsequent ones (through stanza 20) merge memories of his lost religious belief with those of warfare and adult romantic love. The theme of loss—of many losses—gains force. In the twentieth stanza, the poet says: "Sometimes I want to go back/ to everything I had, as in a museum," searching for a woman he loved. Time itself is interrogated—it is inevitably working toward both a mature sense of self and that self's ultimate dissolution in death. The long dispersal of the Jewish people and Amichai's own destiny as a man and a poet come together explicitly in stanza 22. History is portrayed as an enemy seeking to "castrate" him, to silence him, "so that I'll be scattered and dispersed/ so that I won't be like a tower of Babel rising heavenward." The three-line stanza that follows seems to answer the doubts raised by both memory and prophecy: "Not to understand is my happiness."

Such happiness, however, is for "stupid" angels, not men. In stanza 24, the poet questions his own honesty, and in stanza 26 he begins a process of self-acceptance that builds throughout the remainder of the poem ("I can't kick the habit of myself"). Stanza 28, close to the middle of the poem, adopts a playfully dramatized tone, as if the speaker is a tour guide to Jerusalem and Jerusalem herself is a woman, perhaps a lover, of whom the speaker has intimate knowledge. The poet then pictures himself holding his young son in his arms. The subsequent stanzas deal, in part, with his role as father and with the reality of his son's life. The tone is tender yet painful; the speaker appears to have left his son (by leaving a marriage?): "My child blossoms sad,/ he blossoms in the spring without me,/ he'll ripen in the sorrow-of-my-not-being-with-him." The speaker looks at the course of his adult life with an unrelenting eye. In stanza 38, the world-weary figure of the title comes home: "Small, triangular panties on a clothesline on/ a roof in Jerusalem signal to the tired old/ sailor from Tudela, the last Benjamin." In stanza 40, the speaker strikingly equates his own history with that of Jerusalem.

The imagery of a final judgment dominates the last sections of the poem. In the Jewish religious tradition, it is in the ten-day period between Rosh Hashana and Yom Kippur that God judges humanity and seals His final verdict in The Book of Life, symbolized by the blowing of the ram's horn, or *shofar.* The speaker's self-inspection has been brutal, but the plaintive earlier refrain, "Don't see me this way, my son" (line 35), is now replaced by an acceptance of judgment—"The time has come for the canon of my life to be closed" (line 46)—symbolized by the recurring sound of the *shofar.* The forty-seventh stanza compresses several of the poem's major concerns— judgment and responsibility, the sensuous lure of an earthly lover whom the speaker has chosen (a choice for which there appears to be an undercurrent of guilt), and history's destructiveness made vivid by war: "Today is the day of judgment, today you, today war." The powerful forty-eighth stanza recapitulates the tragic history of all the wars the Holy Land has endured, from Roman times to the present, including the biblical war of Satan with God and God's "war" with Job. The imagery is violent, physical, and overwhelmingly immediate. It is a surrealistic collage of suffering that reads, in part, like a frenzied reporter's account of a current war, but it is also a condensation of the horrors of all war, in the face of which even a poet's language breaks down in a catalog of destruction, and words are finally replaced by the acronymns of death: "M.I.R.V., S.W.A.T., I.C.B.M."

After this brilliant nightmare, the final ten stanzas are quieter, as if the poet is exhausted by the effort of his long meditation and is emerging from it. In this final movement, there is a stoical acceptance of his individual life and death, as if writing the poem has helped him "place" himself: "I'm forty-three years old. And my father died at sixty-three." (line 51). The sounds of the *shofar* blast now seem to signal humankind's forgiveness of God as much as God's forgiveness of humankind. After all the struggles of body and spirit, there is "a long cry, a long silence" (line 56). The certainty of death lends an irredeemable quality to "things that can't be changed" and writes an end to all fleshly, as well as spiritual, desires.

The penultimate stanza acknowledges the speaker's replacement by his son, as he replaced his father. In "the sweetness of my son's breath" he senses renewal: "my childhood of blessed memory. His childhood." The final stanza, nine short lines, returns to the opening, the speaker's arrival as a young immigrant, one who bowed not to kiss the ground but to duck bullets. Now he speaks with self-knowledge, no longer at war with himself or others. He expects to be forgotten, and, paradoxically, in this way he will have entered history, become one with the land, like a fruit: "its ripening is its forgetting." The land has laid its claim on him. In the (perhaps tentative) reconciliation of the final lines, he recognizes that, despite everything, it sustains him like a mother or lover, "until the final kiss."

Forms and Devices

"Travels of the Last Benjamin of Tudela" achieves coherence partly through the repetition of key images; like musical motifs in a symphony, they are repeated with variations—sometimes of phrasing, sometimes of context, sometimes both. (Examples are: "I ate and was filled"; "Massada will not fall"; "Today is the day of judgment.") Because this is a poem of intense self-scrutiny, the words "face," "skin," "hair," and "clothing" function as signs of outer identity that may or may not convey inner states (opposed to these is "heart"). Other key words—not precisely images— similarly recur: "childhood," "memory," "forgetting," "prophesy." Often stunningly visual, Amichai's images can appeal to several senses at once: "Angels looked like Torah scrolls in velvet dresses and petticoats/ of white silk, with crowns and little silver bells, angels/ fluttered around me and sniffed at my heart and cried ah! ah!"

The poem is laden with symbolic references to Jewish religious traditions; notable among these are Job, whose earthly sufferings were inflicted as a test of faith, and Yom Kippur, when God is said to seal the fate of everyone on earth. The poem contains numerous fragments of specific prayers from Jewish liturgy, often thrust (sometimes shockingly) into a secular context. Underlying the many passages describing sensual love is the biblical Song of Songs. There are also numerous references to the tempestuous secular history of Israel, such as the fall of Massada, the ancient Jewish garrison that chose suicide rather than surrender to the Romans, and Josephus, the Jewish-Roman historian who chronicled its fall. Such symbolism characteristically collapses many historical events and epochs into a single passage of great emotional force, most notably in the "war" collage that employs the style of surrealism—the nonrational association of images—to create a nightmare "logic" of surpassing intensity.

Similarly, the poet's own past and present are blended throughout the poem—sometimes easily, often jarringly. The central symbol in the poem is Jerusalem itself, uniting both secular and religious history, as well as the speaker's own. Another striking device is personification; the poet speaks of Jerusalem as if the city were a living woman. History is personified as a remorseless enemy. Conversely, the poet often speaks of himself in metaphor, as if his life were a house, a building, or a play. There is also a playful use of onomatopoeia—the reproduction of specific sounds in words; for example, the "Ta-da" of the shofar. All of this is united by a self-conscious "I," which knows it is writing this poem.

Themes and Meanings

"Travels of the Last Benjamin of Tudela" is not only a "Jewish" poem. In the largest sense, it is a meditation on fate, both personal and human. It deals with the poet's relationship to a country whose present is shadowed by the memory of ancient prophecies and by the history of the innumerable wars that have stained its landscape. It is a powerful antiwar poem. It also deals with the poet's relationship to himself. The basic theme is duality, individual identity caught between unrelenting opposites: past/present, body/soul, sacred/secular, war/peace, love/betrayal, speech/ silence. The poet seeks some correspondence—or at least communication—between his childhood and his adult life, between his inner being and the "outer" roles he has played. In the process, dualities expand, the speaker's lived identities multiply or merge. Son becomes father, father becomes soldier who "orphans" his son many times. The macrocosm of Jewish history is reflected in the microcosm of personal fate—and vice versa: "Even the Torah portion for my Bar Mitzvah/ was double, Insemination/ Leprosy."

Jewish history is a history of exile and dispersal, and the poet seems threatened by a permanent condition of disunity and self-exile. The theme of a split self is stated early in the poem. The poet speaks of "all the unreal fathers I've established/ instead of my father, in the soft land of the 'seven kinds'/ not just two, male and female, but seven kinds." Jerusalem, in all its multiple identities, becomes his reflection, and he, in turn, reflects it: "I've been patched together/ from many things, I've been gathered in different times." Like an archaeologist, the poet sifts through the layers of self, trying to weigh consequences, to sort the true from the false in his actions, motives, and desires. Like Benjamin, he has wandered, but his wanderings and his wars have been spiritual as well as physical. The resolution he finally comes to is a harsh one—not self-forgiveness, but acceptance of "things that can't be changed." It is the acceptance of an imperfect, human self, and the acceptance of death. There is also a celebratory note, however: In the persistence of self, in the persistence, too, of the scarred, blossoming landscape—"with wars and with this springtime"—he has come home.

"The Travels of the Last Benjamin of Tudela" bears comparison with other major meditative lyrics. Like Tennyson's "In Memoriam," it weighs the meaning of love and memory against the finality of time and death; like Galway Kinnell's *Book of Nightmares* (1971), it questions what a father can bequeath to a child in a world of evil and betrayal; like Whitman's epic "Song of Myself," it embodies a celebration of being in which self is equated with landscape. There is, however, a crucial difference. Whereas Whitman joyously proclaimed, "I celebrate myself/ And what I assume you shall assume,/ For every atom belonging to me as good belongs to you," Amichai's voice is more muted, lonelier. As if in direct contradiction, he proclaims: "I am a solitary man, a lonely man. I'm not a democracy . . ./ . . . No need to disperse me,/ I'm already dispersed." Amichai's vision is not one of transcendence. His self is something with which he is stuck. There is no question of changing it, only of accepting it. His release from time and self will come with death, "the final kiss," but his son will remain to play out the drama anew.

Stan Sanvel Rubin

TRIBUNALS

Author: Robert Duncan (1919-1988)
Type of poem: Lyric
First published: 1970, as *Tribunals: Passages 31-35*

The Poem

The five poems whose group title is *Tribunals* form part of a much longer sequence called *Passages*. The publication of *Passages* spans several books by Robert Duncan. He began to compose them in 1964, and a considerable number of them can be found in his 1968 book *Bending the Bow*. The poems in *Passages* are open in form, built up of phrasings defined by various lengths of white space, and usually several pages in length. They tend to "cluster," so that, as with *Tribunals*, thematic as well as formal considerations help unite a small group, defining that group as distinct within the entirety of the production. Duncan had been a longtime associate of the poet Jack Spicer, whose five-, six-, and seven-poem clusters came to be called "serial poems," and that term seems to fit *Tribunals*. Although there is no sequential matter that binds the poems together, there are identities of scale and tone.

In *Tribunals*, these identities are grand, making this group perhaps the greatest of the groupings that constitute *Passages*. From the first lines of Passages 31, "The Concert,"

> Out of the sun and the dispersing stars
> go forth the elemental sparks,
> outpouring vitalities,
> stir in the *Saliter* of the earth
> a *living* Spirit,

to the final lines of Passages 35, "Before the Judgment,"

> Children of Kronos, of the Dream beyond death,
> secret of a Life beyond our lives,
> having their perfection as we have
>
> . . . come into these orders as they have ever come, stand
>
> as ever, where they are acknowledged,
> against the works of unworthy men,
> unfeeling judgments and cruel deeds,

the tone is sublime, the scale, large. Duncan had the habit in his compositions of incorporating passages from other authors, and among those cited here is Hesiod, a Greek poet of the Homeric Age, whose *Theogony* and *Works and Days* Duncan had been reading at the time. Other identifiable sources include *Aurora* (1634), by German mystic Jakob Böhme; the essay "Projective Verse," by Duncan's older fellow-poet Charles Olson; works by Antoine Court de Gébelin, Gérard de Nerval, and pioneering American geographer Carl Sauer; the *Inferno* (c. 1320) of Dante; and the Hell Cantos of Ezra Pound. Citation on such a scale, and over such a range, can suggest a whole world, and that is precisely Duncan's intention, although the "wholeness" remains an ideal, and the actuality is rent—two nations riven by the Vietnam War in a world that is filthy with self-interest.

Duncan was among the many who opposed America's intervention in Southeast Asia—the previous group of *Passages*, "Of the War," demonstrates this clearly—so it is understandable that the poems of this group offer glimpses of a nation on the verge of civil war and confront the question of good and evil with an immediacy matched only, in American poetry, by Pound's *Cantos* (1917-1970). The problem for the poet (or anyone) who looks into Hell is the fascination that horrors exert—the hypnotic power of evil. Dante knew this, and he created a Vergil to be his guide through the Inferno, "Dante being so drawn into a fascination by the controversies of that place," as Duncan writes, that he needed the idea and figure of the older poet to remind him to stop staring. Duncan makes use of this recollection to keep his own poem moving, remembering that there could be no evil without a corresponding good. The good entered these passages in various ways: as sensual, essential pleasure (for example, in "Passages 34, The Feast," which consists in large part of a recipe for preparing leg of lamb); as art (as in Passages 33, with its vision of modern art as regenerative even in its dying); and as genetic, a genetically encoded ability to tell evil from good.

There are passages of great sweetness, serenity, and simplicity throughout, providing relief for the darker portions—the denunciations of corrupt public figures, "bosses and war-mongers"; the litany of terrible dreams endured by president, poet, soldier, protestant; the wretched facts of war, with its maimings and wholesale murders. The overall effect, as the reader moves through this "free" yet carefully meted-out verse, with its long, mellifluous or shuddering lines made of aurally precise phrases, is of the mind confronting the worst and surviving, in some essential fashion, unscathed.

Forms and Devices

Robert Duncan spoke of his methods of composition on many occasions, and he was, even among poets, unusually aware of what he called "the adventure of forms." William Carlos Williams, earlier in the twentieth century, scoffed at the term "free verse," pointing out that since verse is always a measure of something, it can never be truly free. Williams labored throughout his life to find a measure that would reflect the realities of the era in which he lived, even as the sonnet had in Elizabethan times. He took the modernist destruction of traditional conventions in poetry not as an end in itself, but as an invitation—an obligation!—to find new forms "more consonant with the day." Robert Duncan was among those poets who took upon themselves Williams's task. The seriousness and meticulousness of his approach is reflected not only in his poetry, but also in his writing about it, and even in his correspondence. In a preface he wrote for an issue of the magazine *Maps* that was devoted to his work, Duncan told of his frustration in endeavoring to persuade the publisher and printer of *Tribunals* to respect the poet's directives, to bring the typeset version into alignment with the poet's typed original. "Faced with the problem presented in . . . page proofs where the measured spaces in which intervals in the poem were articulated were lost where the stanza or section ended at the bottom of a page," Duncan writes, "I saw that a symbol was necessary to make the count clear. . . . I was willing to pay for these symbols to be made; but at the last it was the printer's distaste for how it would mar his typography that carried the day." Duncan decided to circulate photocopies of his own typed, true-to-impulse work among friends and private subscribers. He published no books for fifteen years, and when *Ground Work* (1984) was finally published by New Directions, the text was photocopied from the poet's typescript.

The phrasings of these poems are breath-based, although they are also derived from mental operations, a matter of pauses for judgment and selection; Duncan, who was unwilling to perpetuate the long divorce between mind and matter performed by Western civilization, found that the twin sources of these hesitations were actually one and the same. Duncan was substantially in agreement with Charles Olson, whose essays on poetry had called for the page to reflect the utterance of the poet in the instant it came to him or her, a compositional move intended to cancel the interference of reflective thought: All such thought should precede the act of composition, Olson believed. What he and others were after was a form of presence; they sought some way through or around the remove of the page and the book.

It must be said that Duncan's poetry, while admirable in many respects, does not strike one as being as radical as his poetics. The phrasing, while breathtaking, usually falls into standard syntactic groupings. As he remarked once, talking about his tour-de-force poem "My Mother Would Be a Falconress": "My censor wants to be Modern, but my poor little personality keeps coming out in iambic pentameter!"

The poems of *Tribunals*, however, are far from mere iambic pentameter, for they reveal a master of metrics at his best, capable throughout of wedding matter to rhythm—or, as the poet himself no doubt would have put it, of discovering in the matter its essential rhythm. The attentive reader cannot help but notice that the poem speeds up or slows down, appears to dance, to amble, to parade, or to hover as the requirements of the subject shift. Perhaps most remarkable of all is the stately tone that Duncan sounds in these poems, conjuring an air of majesty and judgment, charitable and severe by turns, that evokes divine intervention, if only in the reader's mind.

Themes and Meanings

The tribunals of the title are conducted by powers of the imagination, although Duncan places them in various locations—in the imagination, in the genetic structure, in the dawn of civilization. "For they go about everywhere over the earth," he writes in "Before the Judgment," "attendants, daimons not only of men but of earth's plenitudes,/ ancestral spirits of whatever good we know," and these spirits, he continues, know the heart's secrets, inhabit memory, enter conscience, and attend every judgment. He quotes from Hesiod, who says that "they are called . . . truly *full of awe*

holy unstaind [sic] by bloodshed/ . . . spirits of earth." Ever the syncretist, Duncan juxtaposes Judaism and pre-Socratic Greek thought: "So there *was* a covenant made with
Good and into its orders I was born." Duncan is seeking authority, in a historical period when consensus is unattainable, for his condemnation of the proliferating ills, if
not evils, to which America is subject. As the corruption reaches into the courts of law
and the Congress, into the heart of the presidency, and throughout the community at
large, and as greed and exploitation threaten the very survival of the earth itself, there
can seem to be no place from which to judge these events, no uncorrupt remove, no
viewpoint that is not merely personal and hence trivial. In such a time, how lovely to
believe the old stories that Hesiod tells in his *Works and Days*: that of the young
maiden called Justice, daughter of Zeus, who reports all attempted violations upon her
person to her father, who straightaway exacts divine retribution—or that of the thirty
thousand immortal spirits who keep watch for Zeus over all humanity's deeds. It is
crucial to an understanding of *Tribunals*, however, and "Before the Judgment" particularly, to realize that for Duncan these are not simply pretty stories one would like to
believe, but actualities, given in the species and fostered by culture, of which Hesiod's
texts are at once evidence and inculcators. It is not merely a matter of language: These
actualities preceded language and thus guarantee its power. Whether in the mind, in
nature, or in the heavens, here they are; people know them, or may recognize and acknowledge them, freely electing so to do, each in his or her own due time. In a shifting
reality, they are to humans as fixed stars are to mariners.

There is a spirit of community in *Tribunals* on whose behalf the poet's sense of outrage operates. This community is historical—that is, part of the past—but it is also
very much a part of the present, since it is made up of the counterculture that opposed
the policies of the federal government and attempted to create another society based
on trust and justice and love. At times, in these poems as in others written before and
after, Duncan appears to be cautioning members of this community against their own
excesses; there may be something of this in Passages 31, "The Concert," in which he
writes of those who "shout, leaping upon the tables, outpouring vitalities, stammer-
ing," and adds, "the isolated satyr each man is,/ severd [sic] distinct thing"—as though
to modify the high, unreal hopes of the enthusiasts. Yet another way of reading this is
that he sees no one as more or less privileged than these people, who at least are doing
something to express the spirit within. They all contribute to the concert.

It is as a concert, too, that Duncan views the various modernisms he celebrates (or
conjures to dismiss) in Passages 33. "Everywhere in life, death is at work": The Greek
tag of the title is extended in this poem to the fate of artworks, which alter as humanity
alters, having their initial conception outdated by the march of events, taking on other
meanings as they enter the museums, the entire process sometimes seeming no more
than an unending exercise of tastes—until one realizes the primacy of the present,
where even the past must come to be heard, and where the seizure that is meaning is
absolute. Only by inhabiting the present fully can one stop the passage of time in its
movement toward death, and one cannot do so until one accepts the presence of death
everywhere. Duncan sees the mystery of eternity in time, with which art deals in its

tense struggle with art history and art appreciation, as akin to the individual life within the diachronic and synchronous whole.

Duncan's yearning to find some belief worthy of himself is everywhere at work within these poems. One wonders whether the poet needs to believe or simply makes use of the structures of belief as so many compositional materials with which to tell stories. It is a skeptic's question, but then, as the poet himself writes in Passages 32, he is the "Child of a century more skeptic than/ unbelieving, adrift/ between two contrary educations,// that of the Revolution, which disowns/ everything,/ and that of the Reaction,/ which pretends to bring back the ensemble/ of Christian beliefs." Clearly, Duncan was interested in returning to humanity many more belief systems than that of Christianity. As he concludes this poem, it is difficult not to feel that the answer to the skeptic's question must be yes:

> will I find myself traind [sic] to believe
> > everything
> as our fathers, the scientists, have
> > traind to deny?

David Bromige

TRILCE

Author: César Vallejo (1892-1938)
Type of poem: Poetic sequence
First published: 1922; English translation collected in *Trilce*, 1973

The Poem

 Trilce is a collection of seventy-seven poems brought together in a poetic sequence. The poems do not have titles; instead, each poem is headed by a Roman numeral. Although *Trilce* was virtually ignored upon its publication, it was later understood to be one of the principal poetic texts of the twentieth century. Its opaque and intentionally contradictory use of language baffled early readers. It remains a difficult, but by no means impossible, work. An awareness of César Vallejo's struggle to create an entirely new poetic language helps the reader to address the difficulty and to begin to make some sense of it. Many critics have noted, however, that *Trilce* is a kaleidoscopic work. It constantly yields new configurations and new possibilities. It is a profound poetic work whose depths are not easily sounded, but whose multiplicity of meanings always yields some treasure to diligent readers.

 The book's title serves as a good introduction to the difficulties and possibilities of *Trilce*'s poetic techniques. The word "trilce" has no exact meaning. It is a neologism, a new word invented by Vallejo, that for English-language readers will recall the invented vocabulary of Lewis Carroll's "Jabberwocky." Numerous interpretations of Vallejo's title have been suggested. It is possible that the word is a blend of the Spanish words *triste* (sad) and *dulce* (sweet). Many commentators, however, believe that some suggestion of *tres* (three) is also intended by the title. Since Vallejo generally chose words with multiple layers of meaning, it is likely that he intended his neologistic title to resonate with any and all possible interpretations; the word "trilce" is probably meant to suggest all these ideas—sadness, sweetness, and the number three. The latter probably implies the trinity, a concept to which Vallejo alludes and with which he tinkers throughout his poetry.

 Trilce does not easily lend itself to outlining. There are no precise thematic divisions in the work. Indeed, the poems, beginning and ending abruptly, read more like fragments of one long poem than discrete units. *Trilce* can be usefully compared to a modernist symphony in words: Themes repeat, words appear again and again, certain linguistic devices guide the work's movement. Sometimes slow and pondering, sometimes playful, sometimes breathtakingly urgent, *Trilce*, like a musical composition, is a work that explores time and even, in a sense, requires simultaneous readings. In other words, whereas a normal text proceeds start to finish, one word following the previous word temporally as well as spatially, *Trilce* is more like a polyphonic performance in which certain themes and sounds (notes) are meant to echo and harmonize with others.

In the first poems, the distant past is recalled as the poet remembers his childhood and replays certain key moments in his past, such as parental abandonment. It is a familiar world that the poet revisits, and he finds himself a bit put off by that familiarity—a familiarity which means that nothing is new. The puzzling nature of time concerns him in these reflections, as does a sense of inadequacy in his sexual relations. In poem XI, these basic themes come together, and from then on the poet's meditations become more obsessive, dark with exasperation and melancholy—not in an affected way, but in Vallejo's own sincere, if almost esoteric, voice, as he explains in poem LV.

Some of the poems are set in Lima, the large capital city of Peru. As the speaker explains in XIV, he has come from his town to Lima only to discover that in the capital "ancient sentiment dies"; a mute outcry seems his only recourse in confronting what translator David Smith calls the abyss. Sentimental views of the past give way to a more ominous present in poems such as poem XV.

Prison imagery also has importance; some of *Trilce* was written while Vallejo spent three months in prison on a false charge. It is clear that the experience informed the already acute anguish he sensed in the human experience. Orphanhood, Vallejo perceived, was a basic condition of that experience. His mother is gone, he laments in XXVIII; life is "mighty with orphanhood." A possible response, he decides in poem XXXVI, is to "refuse symmetry firmly" and attempt a "leap through the needle's eye." These dicta appear initially to be rather recondite, but Vallejo seems to have in mind a rejection of the dehumanizing tendencies of the world he discovered upon moving to Lima. In XXXVIII, the poet speaks, for example, of glass "waiting to be swallowed up," an act that "hurts when they force it." A certain victim's paranoia takes over the text on such occasions, often associated with the prison experience. The sheer weight of living becomes odious as the speaker struggles to stay alive. The urge to return to the past becomes stronger than ever, but home is "locked and no one answers," he discovers in LXI. It is clear that the past is sleeping forever. *Trilce* ends with a realization of—if not a resignation to—the fact that he has been abandoned to orphanhood.

Forms and Devices

Trilce is a formally intricate work; many of its complexities, however, are readily grouped together under the heading "linguistic distortion." One of Vallejo's preoccupations in the poems is to free language from the accepted poetic rhetoric of the early twentieth century, particularly that of the Spanish *Modernismo* movement, a movement that deeply affected the young Vallejo. *Trilce* reveals Vallejo dramatically breaking away from his former influences. In *Trilce*, his second book, Vallejo abandoned the ornamental aspects of *Modernismo* poetics and sought to strip language of its conventions.

Vallejo's rejection of poetic norms is so absolute that even the appearance of the poem is altered. Thus, grammatical parody is evident throughout *Trilce*. One finds, for example, such simple devices as garbled spelling, unusual typography, and interchangeable parts of speech. In this respect, Vallejo resembles the American poet E. E. Cummings, who always played with the visual surface of the poem.

Vallejo, however, extends his challenge to the reader to deeper levels as well. One of the notable features of Vallejo's poetics in *Trilce* is his flair for neologisms. From the first poem on, Vallejo invents words and phrases that disturb the reader's faith in ultimate meaning. He seems to reject the possibility of ascertainable meanings.

Similarly, Vallejo challenges the reader over and over with recondite phrases in which words are put into seemingly impossible combinations. Vallejo's technique is related to catachresis, the rhetorical device which defamiliarizes objects by attributing to them qualities not normally associated with them. Vallejo's version of the device is surrealistic in that he gives voice to the language of the unconscious. Intense emotions and unforeseen relationships are perceived, even when the complete meaning of a phrase is obscure.

Similarly, Vallejo distorts syntactic structures in his poems, making it virtually impossible for the reader to discern logic in the text—at least the kind of rules-based logic to which one is accustomed in language. Vallejo uses words—the tools of language—but not the rules of language. Examples abound in *Trilce*, beginning with the opening line of the first poem—a relative clause that has no referent. On occasion, the fragmentation of syntax reaches a crescendo, as in poem XX. On such occasions, the poems resemble feverish talk. Indeed, they are at that point barely poems. Each stanza, each pared-down, cut-off phrase is like a sudden flash of intuition announced and abandoned in almost the same breath. The point of all this tampering with syntax seems to involve a search for new relationships among words, images, and ideas, and thereby to endow those words with new, multiple—and hence more profound—meanings.

In some ways, Vallejo's linguistic play is similar to the techniques of cubism, an early twentieth century movement in painting that sought to discover new ways of looking at an image. Whereas cubist painters fragmented an image so that it might be viewed from a number of contrasting yet not necessarily mutually exclusive angles, Vallejo fragmented syntax, grammar, and even the words themselves, thus representing and recomposing both the physical and the rhetorical figures that were his subjects. The language is thus presented in its rawest form, disconnected from immediate meaning.

A reader might question all this linguistic sophistication, wondering whether it adds up to anything significant or is merely willful obscurity. Vallejo himself answers this question in poem LV, when he contrasts his poetics with those of the French Symbolist Albert Samain. The delicate melancholy of Symbolism is replaced by Vallejo's exploration of the language of the unconscious. This challenge is intended to wake up those readers who have been lulled to sleep by delicate and decorative poetry. Vallejo thus confounds his readers by unveiling the unexpected and laying it bare.

Vallejo also has a more private purpose: In letting the language of the unconscious speak, he is giving voice to words and imagery buried within himself. Through language, he is calling upon spiritual resources he has not even suspected. The violence of his wrenched syntax is thus a reflection of the violence of his wrenched soul. His violent, internal struggle is literally played out on the page. Therefore, in calling upon this new, elemental language, the poet is also forcing upon himself an exercise in self-discovery. What Vallejo rejects is the poem as simple verbal object, done for its own beauty and without reference outside itself. Instead, he demands poetry that tests limits, that pushes beyond the boundaries of a sterile, empty art, that discovers the real poem behind the ornamental façade and the real poet lurking inside the affected, superficial one.

Vallejo's art is difficult and challenging, but it is not unrewarding. Even when the poetry is random and chaotic, the genius of the poet endows it with uncommon depth and power.

Themes and Meanings

A number of important themes appear and reappear in *Trilce*, but the basic subject, the one upon which all others are grounded, is the poet himself. The separate poems that compose *Trilce* are best understood, at least initially, as statements either about Vallejo or about the human concerns and problems which his own life exemplifies. Vallejo always speaks with a profound urgency; his poems are cries of pain and suffering, voicing his despair upon realizing the meaninglessness of that suffering.

In particular, the *Trilce* poems locate this pain and suffering in the sheer drabness of everyday life and in the same day-in and day-out drudgery that wearies the speaker of these poems. In some of the poems, the drudgery is urban, as Vallejo concentrates on the intimidation one feels upon arriving in the dehumanizing city. In others (poem XVIII for example), the prison setting intensifies the drabness; the obvious and all-too-real walls that surround him physically enforce the limitations of life.

Occasionally in *Trilce*, the poet contrasts these scenes of dreariness with his idyllic memories of a pastoral childhood. The paradise he recalls is clearly a forsaken one, however, and while he seems to hope that he can will a return to the past, the poet is always aware of the impossibility of that hope. There is a strong current of remorse and a sense of loss running throughout the poems. The poet speaks of his orphanhood, and this becomes a prominent theme of the book. This orphanhood is experienced most acutely as the poet endures the hostile environments of city and jail. The security of home becomes more and more remote until the poet feels not merely isolated but abandoned, first by family, friends, and lover, and then finally by God. The finality of this abandonment—and the height of his isolation—is understood in poem LXXV, one of *Trilce*'s central poems. In it, Vallejo experiences an epiphany of sorts as he realizes that his past is dead and he must surrender to the "orphanhood of orphanhoods." To Vallejo, the basic human condition is orphanhood, because humankind, wretched and in anguish, has been left to seek hope in a world bereft of meaning. Bonds between human beings are easily broken. Love is foredoomed, given the conditions of existence.

Vallejo's is a dark and bleak vision of life, but it is not an utterly desperate one. Despite the anguish, despite the foreboding, the speaker has not yielded entirely to despair. There remains for him the slight possibility that language—despite its starkness—can be reconstructed. This attempt at reconstruction results in the poetry of

Trilce. The speaker gropes and grunts his way through the shards of language, grasping and clutching at what he can. The words come in fits and starts. Language is not entirely sufficient, yet it proves to be the only way the poet can test limits and push forward through the darkness.

Testing limits or confronting limitations, then, is another of *Trilce*'s major themes. The limitations the speaker confronts are numerous—some temporal (the past) and some spatial (a jail cell). Often the limitations are interior and spiritual, as Vallejo chips at the façade that keeps him from understanding the truth about himself. Poem XXXVI, one of Vallejo's best, is crucial in this regard. Alluding to the biblical passage about the camel passing through the needle's eye, he speaks of the human struggle to accomplish the impossible and of the inevitable frustration at finding no escape from limitations. Thus, while efforts to break down barriers and exceed limitations often end in failure, they do not necessarily result in despair. Vallejo remains furious and rattled as he yields. The struggle is enacted and reenacted.

The need to understand temporality is clearly involved with this struggle. Hence, another of *Trilce*'s major themes concerns the nature of time. Time is a puzzling phenomenon in the poems. For Vallejo, time seems to pass yet not elapse. In poem II, for example, the past and the future are jumbled to the point of being indistinguishable. Furthermore, time is urgent, incessant in its pressure; it is so insistent that the speaker feels threatened. Time is paradoxical as well. Its passage is certain, yet it also seems to reverse itself sometimes and speed wildly forward at other times.

Trilce is a great work of poetic rebellion. The poet speaks with a powerful, passionate, and personal voice that transgresses the boundaries of syntax, grammar, and logic, yet succeeds in communicating the intense suffering of those who are physically and spiritually downtrodden. Because of its innovations, because it shattered all traditions in Spanish poetry, and because it opened new possibilities for an iconoclastic poetics, it is considered one of the great works of the twentieth century.

Stephen Benz

TRILOGY

Author: H. D. (Hilda Doolittle, 1886-1961)
Type of poem: Meditation
First published: The Walls Do Not Fall, 1944; *Tribute to the Angels*, 1945; *The Flowering of the Rod* 1946; collected in *Trilogy*, 1973

The Poem

Trilogy is a poem in three parts that in the collected edition is slightly more than one hundred pages long. Each of the three parts consists of forty-three poems that are written primarily in unrhymed couplets, though there are occasional stanzas of triplets and single lines. The first part, *The Walls Do Not Fall*, addresses the need H. D. (Hilda Doolittle used these initials rather than her full name) feels to refashion the old myths of monotheistic patriarchy so that they may come to include myths of female creativity and power. Her sense of this need arises from seeing all around her the devastation of World War II. H. D. situates the possibility of transformation away from the routine of war, at the very level of language itself. She sets out to reveal the hidden power of language to make and unmake the way human beings perceive and experience the world. Her tendency to explore the etymological and poetic possibilities in words accounts for her sometimes unfamiliar and arcane choice of words. *The Walls Do Not Fall* opens H. D.'s *Trilogy* in the same way that Dante initiates *The Divine Comedy* (c. 1320)—with a vision of the Inferno. In both poems, the reader experiences the destruction of human community as a result of a spiritual or imaginative failure. Part 2 of *Trilogy, Tribute to the Angels*, opens up the possibility of a new version of Revelation. H. D. requires that the pagan, typically feminine, figures of fertility and generation that Judeo-Christian civilization erased be restored. The transformation, so fully detailed in part 1, begins to take place. *Tribute to the Angels* corresponds to Dante's *Purgatory*. Here H. D. presents the possibility of purification in an alchemical fire. The final part of the poem, *The Flowering of the Rod*, pays tribute to the power of the suffering and pain of war to transform bellicose, masculinized mythologies of the past into the benign and generative possibilities of the procreative and peaceful feminine. It corresponds to Dante's *Paradise* (c. 1320).

The title of the first part, *The Walls Do Not Fall*, refers to the threat against London posed by the German air raids in 1942. The walls of the city were literally at risk, and H. D., who voluntarily spent the war years in London, links the modern city to many ancient cities that were menaced by war. "There, as here," she writes, "ruin opens/ the tomb, the temple; enter/ there as here, there are no doors." The bomb blast tears off the roof of the tomb or the temple. Yes, there is destruction, but at the same time, there is an opening (where there had been a roof), a place where something new enters and the walls do not fall down.

H. D. believes (partly, at least, as a result of her analysis by Freud) that the history of the race is reproduced in the history of the individual, and that the past is contained in an abbreviated and condensed form in the present. "Here," in this case, is London; "there" is Karnak, Troy, or Luxor. While the immediate place of danger is paralleled by other, distant cities, there is a parallel in time as well as space. The events of the past, especially the events that have to do with the creation of consciousness, continue to exist and act in the present.

In the second part of *Trilogy*, *Tribute to the Angels*, H. D. initiates the process of linking the cosmology of the Judeo-Christian tradition with the suppressed fertility goddesses of earlier polytheistic cultures. The poet adds Hermes Trismegistus to the familiar Old and New Testament angels who are the messengers of God. By introducing Hermes, H. D. makes available to her reader both the alchemical power that transforms base material into gold (Hermes is the god of alchemy) and the power of interpretation that sanctions H. D.'s revision of Western mythological thought (Hermes also presides over the specialized science of interpretation that was named for him: hermeneutics). His mythic power gives H. D. permission to "take what the old-church/ found in Mithra's tomb,/ candle and script and bell,/ take what the new-church spat upon/ and broke and shattered." The model of transformation requires that one take the broken ruins of modern culture "and of your fire and breath,/ melt down and integrate/ re-invoke, re-create/ opal, onyx, obsidian,/ now scattered in the shards/ men tread upon."

The third and last section, *The Flowering of the Rod*, is an enactment of the feminization of the historical and traditional masculine mythologies. In this section, H. D. refashions the story of the Nativity from the New Testament; she links Mary of Nazareth with Mary Magdalene. The linking of the Madonna with the harlot is a way of restoring the Scarlet Whore of Babylon—who, H. D. believes, was actually the Egyptian goddess of fertility, Isis—to the central creative act of Christianity. The birth of Christ is described as the "word made flesh," so by implicating Mary Magdalene with that primal act, H. D. is able to introduce a powerful feminine mythic presence at the point of the making of language. Having moved from modern London in *The Walls Do Not Fall* to a medieval city in *Tribute to the Angels*, H. D. concludes *The Flowering of the Rod* in the desert of ancient Israel. In the cradle of civilization in the Near East, where the Christ as child finds himself made flesh, H. D. finds her new beginning in the emblematic gift of the magi: "Kaspar [one of the magi, who figures significantly in the final section of *Trilogy*] knew the seal of the jar was unbroken/ he did not know whether she knew/ the fragrance came from the bundle of myrrh/ she held in her arms."

Forms and Devices

Like the great medieval poem that *Trilogy* resembles, *The Divine Comedy*, H. D.'s meditation on the spiritual and cultural consequences of World War II is imaginatively based on a cosmological vision of analogy. H. D. shares with Dante (and with many more recent and more skeptical thinkers, such as Freud) a view of the world and history as a totality made up of nesting correspondences and interconnections, and a sense that no cultural or spiritual imagining is ever really lost. The potentiality of the past is not only still present but also can be restored or caused to be reborn.

H. D. affirms the interconnectedness of the things in the world by means of what she calls the "palimpsest." A palimpsest is a manuscript or paper on which writing has been totally or partially erased to make space for new writing. It is important for H. D., however, that the old writing is still present as a trace or a suggestion and remains to somehow color one's reading of the new text. A simple example of the palimpsest is the "sword," a weapon or means of destruction that contains within it the "word," which for H. D. is infinitely redemptive. While it is erased by and enclosed within the sword, the "word" is always there, waiting to be reread by the poet. To achieve this re-reading, the poet must "search the old highways/ for the true-runes, the right-spell,/ recover old values."

In her search along the "old highways," H. D. finds "Isis, Asete or Astarte." These are Semitic or Egyptian goddesses of fertility and reproduction who have been diminished by the prevailing monotheism to harlots, deprived of their force and charisma. The trace or palimpsest remains, however, and the goddesses have the power to reassert their power. Those who consign them to the "flesh pots" are speaking, H. D. declares, in the rhythm of "the devils hymn."

Those who have designed the spiritual world in which everyone must live and fight wars write within a destructive context: "your stylus is dipped in corrosive sublimate, how can you scratch out/ indelible ink of the palimpsest/ of past misadventure?" The "devil's hymn" is not itself the final word against the poet, however: "But we fight for life, we fight, they say, for breath." What good are the poet's writings? They can be taken "with us/ beyond death." H. D. calls for a recognition of the fundamental source of language: "Mercury, Hermes, Thoth/ invented the script, letters, palette." The source of language, not only spoken language, but also all the means by which human thought and feeling are inscribed upon the world, is far more complex and diverse than the modern world thinks. The plural divinities to whom H. D. looks are far more powerful than had been realized. "The indicated flute or lyre-notes/ on papyrus or parchment/ are magic, indelibly stamped/ on the atmosphere somewhere,/ forever." Here H. D. returns to her "sword"/"word" palimpsest: "remember O Sword,/ you are the younger brother, the latter-born,/ your Triumph, however exultant/ must one day be over." In the next verse, she indicates by using italics that the erased writing in *sword* is not merely language or language in general; rather, it is the act of incarnation that begins the Christian era: "*in the beginning/ was the Word.*"

Another example of H. D.'s ability to reread—and hence to transform—the language by probing within everyday, feeble, constricted language for something more potent occurs at the end of *The Walls Do Not Fall*. In this final stanza of the section in italics, the poet returns to the walls of the city: "*Still the walls do not fall,/ I do not know why;/ there is zrr-hiss, lightening in a not-known,/ unregistered dimension; we are powerless.*"

This despair must be read against her earlier declaration, "I profit by every calamity." What profit could possible accrue from such calamity? "*The floor sags/ like a ship floundering;/ we know no rule of procedure, we are voyagers, discoverers/ of the not-known,/ the unrecorded.*" The palimpsest is the ideal vehicle for H. D., who sees herself as one of the "*voyagers*." The profit that comes to H. D. in this calamity is the poem, the language itself. She concludes with thoughts that serve to exemplify the possibility that there can be a cracking open to rebirth and restoration that even the most terrible disaster can entail: "*possibly we will reach haven,/ heaven.*"

Themes and Meanings

The integrity of H. D.'s poetics—that is, the fact that the abstract forms that she uses are consistent with the meanings that she wishes to communicate to her readers and audience—is clearly presented in the urgent and historic concerns of *Trilogy*. Like T. S. Eliot's *Four Quartets* (1943), *Trilogy* has always before it, as a source and as an unattainable goal, Dante's *The Divine Comedy*. Unlike T. S. Eliot, however, H. D. reaches beyond the Eurocentric and Anglo-Christian to a larger and more global possibility of meaning.

In this large sense, the central theme of *Trilogy* is the validation of cultural redemption or resurrection. H. D. looks, for example, at the "pyramid of skulls" that represents Golgotha, the site of the crucifixion, and sees it instead as "a flowering cone." It is then "not [simply] a heap of skulls." She insists on its being "no poetic phantasy/ but a biological reality." The narrative line of the last part of the poem, "The Flowering of the Rod," moves from the devastation of the crucifixion to the redemption of the nativity, as H. D. designs a new mythic setting for these events. This is, indeed, the theme of the poem as a whole: The devastation of *The Walls Do Not Fall* foretells and contains within it the implication of recovery and rebirth. "The place of the skulls" is the place where Christ "redeems" the thief suffering beside him on a cross. Thus it is, for H. D., the place where the victims of outrage are somehow redeemed. She writes, "So the first—it is written,/ will be the twisted or the tortured individuals." Moreover, "the first to receive the promise was a thief;/ the first actually to witness His life-after-death,/ was an unbalanced, neurotic woman."

The thief and the unbalanced woman are New Testament figures, linked retrospectively with Hermes and the pagan female harlots of pre-Christian mythology. In the last section of the poem, H. D. makes the link with the character of Kaspar, one of the magi. Kaspar is the one who provides Mary Magdalene with the jar of ointment with which she anoints the feet of Jesus, despite the scorn of those who despise her as a prostitute. In the process of making this gift, Kaspar also renames the goddess: "technically Kaspar was a heathen;/ he might whisper tenderly, those names/ without fear of eternal damnation,/ Isis, Astarte, Cyprus/ and the other four;/ he might rename them,/ Ge-meter, De-meter, earth-mother/ or Venus/ in a star."

H. D.'s poem moves backward in history, from the present catastrophe of war to the moment of redemption ("on the floor of the ox stall," the site of the Nativity), in order that she might, in the poem, project renewal into the future. As a "heathen," Kaspar is able to see "as in a mirror, clearly, O very clearly." What he sees clearly in the mirror he also hears clearly in the spirals of the sea shell: "the echo/ of an echo in a shell." What he sees and hears is "the memory that yet connects us/ with the drowned cities of pre-history." H. D. sees that the memory of the past contains within it a projection that allows one to understand and anticipate the future: "an idea, a wish, a whim, a premonition perhaps,/ that premonition we all know,/ *this has happened before some-where else,/ or this will happen again—where? when?*"

Kaspar is a witness to the crucial event, but he is only a spectator: "he did not know whether she knew/ the fragrance came from the bundle of myrrh/ she held in her arms." The figure of Mary, combining both the virgin and the fallen prostitute, is the concluding image of the *Trilogy*. In her, too, are the many neglected feminine divinities of all mythic systems.

The central event, the utterly transforming event to which these words refer, occurs when an apparently unremarkable woman ("she was shy and simple and young") gives birth to the incarnate word. It is appropriate that this difficult and allusive poem (written in the last two weeks of December, 1944) should conclude with an image of the direct and unadorned event of the birth of a child.

Sharon Bassett

TRISTIA

Author: Osip Mandelstam (1891-1938)
Type of poem: Lyric
First published: 1919; in *Tristia*, 1922; English translation collected in *Modern Russian Poetry*, 1967

The Poem

Osip Mandelstam's "Tristia" is the title poem of a book published in 1922. Told in the first person, the poem reflects the mood of a person leaving his home, city, and possibly, country. The title is taken from Ovid's book of the same name.

The poem opens with the poet's statement that he has learned the "science of parting." The parting is not a joyous one; it is accompanied by the weeping of women after a long night's vigil, by the cock's crow, and by red eyes gazing into the distance. The women's lament mingles with the Muses' song. All these details closely follow Ovid's elegy, except for the cock crowing.

Resemblance to Ovid carries over into the second stanza. The parting is still accompanied by sorrow, uncertainty, and fear, and the departing person watches, like Ovid, the fire burning on the acropolis as he passes by. In the middle of the stanza, however, the poet shifts his perspective somewhat and speaks of the dawn of some new light. This cannot refer to the Ovid poem and is more in line with the cock crowing, which normally heralds a new day, a new beginning. This clearly clashes with the poet's, and Ovid's, mood of sadness at the beginning of the poem. The poet himself questions this change by employing as the antithesis of the image of an ox chewing lazily in his stall that of a cock flapping his wings loudly on the city wall.

In the third stanza, the departing one is preoccupied with fresh memories of home, the peaceful and happy activities such as spinning at the loom, for example, and he recalls a barefoot Delia—a girl from classical mythology but also from Alexander Pushkin—who flies toward him and descends upon him like swan's down. This leads the poet to muse about the fleeting nature of joy and laughter. Life passes in anticipation and rediscovery: What has been before, will be repeated. The only real joy is to be found in the act of recognition.

The final stanza depicts a resigned poet, who leaves worry about the future to women. Men are born to fight battles, while women die telling fortunes. The poem ends on an upbeat note, in direct contrast to the melancholy and sorrow at the beginning.

Forms and Devices

"Tristia" has four stanzas of eight lines each, rhyming conventionally, *ababcdcd*. The verses consist of eleven syllables, forming mostly anapests, each stanza closing with an iambic pentameter.

Mandelstam uses images as the predominant formal device. He is fond of juxtaposing them, or even using them antithetically. The ox chewing lazily in the stall reflect the endless waiting before departure. This is contrasted with the crowing of the cock in the morning, which is loud and ebullient. This antithesis is repeated for emphasis. The other antithesis is found at the very end of the poem, when man and woman are contrasted. Man's role in life is depicted by a metonymy, "bronze," a hard metal used for making arms. Woman is characterized by another metonymy, "wax," indicating the softness of her nature. Wax is also used here as a metaphor for telling the future.

Another image is that of a fire that the departing person sees burning on the acropolis just as he is saying good-bye to his city. Fire being one of the basic elements, this image measures the magnitude of the loss and the injustice inflicted upon him.

The images of spinning (the shuttle and the spindle) underscore the domesticity and tranquillity of a homelife the persona is leaving behind, thus etching in relief once more the depth of his loss. This is reinforced by the image of Delia, a light-footed woman of Tibulus, whose ethereal figure is likened to swan's down.

The most striking images are those of wax figures that are produced by melting candles in a shallow dish of water, resulting in all kinds of shapes which are then used by women for divination. This is found as much in classical literature as it is in Pushkin and other Russian writers.

Finally, a striking image of a distended skin of a squirrel is provided in the form of a simile. It is designed to show the heart of a departing man, stretched to the limits of endurance after being forced to leave his home and his loved ones.

Themes and Meanings

"Tristia" is a poem of parting. This is evident from the very first line, when the poet says that he has perfected the science of parting. The fact that there are so many echoes of Ovid and his poetry in Mandelstam's poem tends to underscore this predominant theme, because Ovid is perhaps the most famous case of a poet banned from his city and forced into exile.

Two questions immediately arise: Why was Mandelstam inspired to write a poem about parting, and how much of the poem reflects his own thoughts and sentiments? The most obvious answer lies in his long interest in antiquity and his fascination with classical writers. Two prominent scholars who have written about Mandelstam, Victor Terras and Clarence Brown, advocate this explanation, especially Terras in his article "Classical Motives in the Poetry of Osip Mandelstam" (1966). Brown, on the other hand, agrees with Terras in his book *Mandelstam* (1973), but he adds that Mandelstam was influenced equally, perhaps even more, by Russian poets, especially by Pushkin and Anna Akhmatova, and that "Tristia" is as much Pushkinian as it is Ovidian.

What these critics seem not to stress enough is the fact that the poem is also Mandelstam's own—much more so than appears at first glance. Not only are the formal aspects—striking images and metaphors, a mixture of lyrical and reflective passages, sporadic departures from the main train of thought, frequent interventions on the part of the poet, the unique rhythm—typical of him, but the mood he imparts to the poem is unmistakably his own. There is in "Tristia" melancholy mixed with stoicism, even defiance, hope always threatened with latent despair, and a tacit understanding of what life is really about; taken together, these belong to no one but Mandelstam.

He has been accused sometimes of living in the past or in the future, certainly in a sphere of his own. Yet he frequently gave expression to his own reactions, in a veiled fashion, to the happenings around him. In "Tristia" he most likely gave vent to his feelings of uncertainty and anxiety amid war and revolution. At the time of the writing of the poem (1918), Mandelstam was subjected to many dangers and had several close calls. It is quite possible that he thought often of involuntary parting, even exile, and that he used his excellent knowledge of classical literature in general, and of Ovid in particular, as an inspiration in expressing his own thoughts and feelings about separation from his dear ones. For that reason, "Tristia" may refer to the atmosphere of 1918 in Mandelstam's Russia just as it may to some other, undetermined time.

Vasa D. Mihailovich

THE TRIUMPH OF LIFE

Author: Percy Bysshe Shelley (1792-1822)
Type of poem: Lyric
First published: 1824, in *Posthumous Poems of Percy Bysshe Shelley*

The Poem

Percy Bysshe Shelley's *The Triumph of Life* is a long fragment of 547 lines (ending abruptly in the middle of line 548) written in terza rima, an interlocking three-line stanza form employed by Dante and Petrarch. The poem's title is taken from Petrarch, who wrote a series of Triumphs, or *Trionfi* (1470), each one presenting the triumph of an allegorical figure. For example, Petrarch's *Triumphus Amoris* celebrates the triumph of love. In Shelley's poem, Life is the triumphant figure, but its "triumph" is far from positive.

The poem begins with a description of the sun rising and nature awakening. The recumbent speaker of the poem, whose "thoughts must remain untold," is turned away from the dawn. As the sun rises behind him, the poet falls into a trance and "a Vision [is] rolled" on his passive brain. In his "waking dream," he finds himself sitting "beside a public way" and watching multitudes of confused people going past like gnats or fallen leaves. A chariot appears bearing a deformed "Shape"; the chariot is driven by a four-faced charioteer who has all of his eyes banded. The "Shape" presides over a triumphal pageant which has enslaved everyone except "the sacred few." This free group is not specified, although Socrates and Jesus ("they of Athens and Jerusalem") are said to be in it.

Dismayed by the sight of the frenetic and helpless captives following the chariot, the poet wonders aloud about the Shape and the pageant. His questions are answered by Jean-Jacques Rousseau (1712-1778), a deformed figure who has holes for eyes. As Vergil guides Dante through the *Inferno*, Rousseau, whose works inspired many of the Romantics, interprets for the poet Life's hellish triumph. It is Life, Rousseau explains, who leads the procession; among his prisoners are bishops, warriors, kings, philosophers, Napoleon, Voltaire, Frederick the Great, Immanuel Kant, Catherine the Great, and Leopold II. According to Rousseau, even Plato was conquered by Life through his love for a young man, and Aristotle fell because of his association with Alexander the Great. The poet asks Rousseau to explain where Rousseau came from, where he is going, and how and why his journey began. Although Rousseau cannot answer all these questions, he tells his own story in the hope that both he and the poet will learn from his experience.

Rousseau's narrative begins with Rousseau asleep in a cavern under a mountain. Through this cavern runs a rivulet whose waters (like those of the river Lethe) induce forgetfulness, so Rousseau has no memory of his life before awakening. As the day progresses, Rousseau rises and sees "A shape all light"—the reflection of the sun in the water of a well. This female shape bears a crystal glass full of the drug nepenthe and her passage through nature suggests "silver music." The shape is associated with nature and represents natural beauty, but her feet blot out the thoughts of those who gaze upon them, an action that seems oppressive rather than inspirational.

Rousseau asks this shape essentially the same questions the poet had asked him: "Shew when I came, and where I am, and why." Instead of answering him, the shape offers him a drink from her cup of nepenthe, and Rousseau's "brain [becomes] as sand." After his lips touch the cup, Rousseau's vision of the "shape all light" is abruptly replaced by the bright, glaring vision of the deformed shape of Life and his triumph. The "shape all light" fades into a dim, glimmering presence. Much of the remainder of the poem is devoted to Rousseau's description of Life's pageant, in which the dancers are phantoms and "dim forms." The fragment ends with the poet's question, "Then, what is Life?," and Rousseau's incomplete response to that question.

Forms and Devices

Much of the ambiguity of *The Triumph of Life* stems from the fact that it is a fragment. Some critics suggest that it would have ended positively if Shelley had lived, or that it would have been followed (in the Petrarchan manner) by another poem in which Life would be triumphed over (perhaps by Love). Other students of the poem have argued that the conclusion would have confirmed its pessimism, or that Shelley would have been unwilling or unable to finish the poem. Shelley's untimely death by drowning make all such theories speculative—readers of the poem can never know what changes Shelley may have intended. The fact that Shelley left the poem in manuscript, with many revisions (and drawings of sailboats), has also created problems for editors of the poem, who must interpret lines which are often close to scribbles.

The structure of *The Triumph of Life* is repetitive: The poet's visionary experience is basically repeated in Rousseau's narrative. At the beginning of the poem the poet faces the starlit night, which is soon obscured by the sun. The next vision that comes is the "cold glare" of Life's triumph which, in turn, overcomes the sunlight. Similarly, Rousseau awakes in the shadows of a cave, but soon the "gentle trace/ Of light" is obscured by the "Sun's image radiantly intense." As was the sunlight of the poet's narrative, the "shape all light" of Rousseau's story is soon erased by the harsh light of Life. Moreover, in both sections of the poem key questions are asked: The poet wants to know where Rousseau came from, where he is going, and why and how his journey began. Rousseau queries the shape all light in the same manner: "Shew whence I came, and where I am, and why." Rather than progressing toward an answer, the poem seems to repeat itself, and the reader is left to wonder if any resolution would have been possible, even if Shelley had lived to "complete" the work. Characteristically, the poem ends with the poet asking yet another question, to which Rousseau only begins to respond: "Then, what is Life?"

The allegorical nature of *The Triumph of Life* adds to its complexity. The shape all light in particular has been interpreted in a variety of ways. Her associations with nature and beauty suggest her potential to inspire, but her effect on Rousseau is to turn his brain into half-erased sand and introduce the glaring vision of Life. Is she, then, a muse or a sinister seductress? In contrast, the allegorical figure of Life is much less ambiguous, although the fact that the poet must ask about Life at the end of the fragment suggests that this abstract personification is not easily defined. Life's deformity and the deforming effect of his cold light are, however, clearly negative, and Life's charioteer, who is four-faced but blinded, guides the car badly. Moreover, the insane dance of the followers of Life's chariot, which recalls the mad festivities of Johann Wolfgang von Goethe's *Walpurgisnacht*, is shown to be compulsive, tragic, and humiliating. Thus the allegory presented in the fragment, in which Life is a deforming force which destroys as it disfigures, portrays the human will as weak and ultimately helpless, for only the "sacred few" can escape Life's complete domination.

In order to emphasize human frailty, Shelley uses historical figures, including men who wielded considerable power in their lives. Napoleon, who was once so powerful that his "grasp had left the giant world so weak," follows Life's chariot tamely, his "hands crost on his chain." Even "The Wise,/ The great, the unforgotten" have been subdued, for "their might/ Could not repress the mutiny within." Life's power dominates everyone, *The Triumph of Life* suggests, except for Socrates and Jesus ("they of Athens and Jerusalem"), who escaped Life through execution. The poem uses allegory and historical personages in order to suggest that only superhuman or transcendent beings can resist Life.

Themes and Meanings

Perhaps the most haunting figure of *The Triumph of Life* is the deformed and eyeless Rousseau, who guides the poet through Life's hellish pageant. To Shelley, Rousseau was a strange, contradictory person, capable, through his political writings, of considerable mischief, but also the author of the idealistic *Julie: Ou, La Nouvelle Héloïse* (1761; *The New Héloïse*), a story of a passion that becomes transformed into a noble and chaste love. It was difficult for Shelley, and many of his contemporaries, to reconcile the high-minded writer of *Julie* with the often immoral figure of Rousseau's *Les Confessions de J.-J. Rousseau* (1782, 1789; *The Confessions of J.-J. Rousseau*, 1783-1790); as a result, the character of Rousseau in *The Triumph of Life* is a complex mixture of idealism and corruption.

Rousseau is initially presented as a rather repellent creature: He has "thin discoloured hair" and tries to hide holes which "Were or had been eyes." Thus one of the ironies of *The Triumph of Life* is that the poet's guide is blind—as blind, perhaps, as the four-faced charioteer who guides Life's car so badly. Rousseau indicates that his state on earth is partly to blame for his decay: "if the spark with which Heaven lit [his] spirit/ Earth had with purer nutriment supplied," Rousseau argues, he would not have fallen into his final state of corruption. Moreover, even if he has been "extinguished," his spark has given rise to "A thousand beacons," including the torch lit by the French Revolution. Later in the poem, however, Rousseau recognizes that his "words were seeds of misery" and that he has created "a world of agony"—some of the beacons he inspired caused suffering as well as enlightenment. Rousseau also suggests that his fall could be explained by his innate self-destructiveness: Rather than being conquered by Life, he was overcome by his "own heart." After the shape all light disappears, Rousseau willfully plunges into Life's pageant, bearing his "bosom to the clime/ Of that cold light." Thus Rousseau becomes an object lesson—endowed by Heaven with a Promethean spark, he fell at least in part because he could not discipline his heart and create works that helped better humanity's condition.

In some ways Rousseau embodies the problem that he is helping the poet understand, "why God made irreconcilable/ Good and the means of good." As a would-be benefactor of humankind, Rousseau certainly intended to do good, but he lacked either the power or the will to accomplish his goals. His search for knowledge from the shape all light in his allegorical narrative leads to his brain becoming like sand, and when Life comes he perversely bears his bosom to Life's deforming light. To resist Life, one would need to have the self-discipline of a Jesus or Socrates, who stoically accepted death. To Shelley, however, Rousseau was ultimately a disappointment. The transcendent mind that created *Julie* was also capable of the follies of the *Confessions* and the political works that led to the destructive and futile violence of the French Revolution. Thus in the poem Rousseau is presented as eyeless, deformed, and "extinguished."

Although one must always allow for the fact that Shelley may have intended to end *The Triumph of Life* in a positive way, it is difficult to determine how he would have dispelled the pessimism that pervades the fragment he left. Rousseau offers the poet knowledge, but this knowledge does not bring the poet peace of mind. The poet's question at the end of the poem, "Then, what is Life?," suggests that the poet has learned very little of importance. The very search for knowledge seems futile and even destructive. Certainly, Rousseau's declaration to the poet does not seem very encouraging: "If thirst for knowledge doth not thus abate,/ Follow it even to the night, but I/ Am weary." In this complex and ambiguous poem little can be known by either the poet or by Rousseau. Both move from one "waking dream" to another, and the reader is left with a vision of Life that appears both hellish and irresistible.

William D. Brewer

TRIVIA
Or, The Art of Walking the Streets of London

Author: John Gay (1685-1732)
Type of poem: Poetic sequence
First published: 1716

The Poem

The full title of this poem is *Trivia: Or, The Art of Walking the Streets of London*, and the word "trivia" here is easily misunderstood. In the modern sense of "insignificant details," it would seem to indicate a poem about a congeries of minor matters. However, to readers of the eighteenth century who were steeped in the classics, it would be understood in the Latin sense of the intersection of three roads or as the plural of *trivium*, the three subjects of traditional education (grammar, rhetoric, and logic). It might even be seen as an allusion to the three-headed goddess Hecate, or Diana, who ruled over day, night, and the underworld and was sometimes referred to as Diana of the crossways. Accordingly, the poem is organized in three cantos, or books. *Trivia* offers a liberal education in urban sociology.

Book I, "Of the Implements for Walking the Streets and Signs of the Weather," is prefaced by an advertisement, or notice to the reader, to the effect that the author owes "several hints of it to Dr. Swift," the celebrated dean of St. Patrick's Cathedral, Dublin, and author of *Gulliver's Travels*. That Swift and the other members of the Scriblerus Club (including Alexander Pope) thought highly of *Trivia* is supported by their letters. Swift's "Description of the Morning" (1709) and "Description of a City Shower" (1710) are clearly models for Gay's much longer compositions; Gay's *Rural Sports* (1713) and *The Shepherd's Week* (1714) were preliminary and highly regarded experiments in the same genre. *Trivia*, *The Beggar's Opera* (1728), and *Fables* (1727) established his fame, and he was accorded a burial in Westminster Abbey beside Chaucer's tomb.

The opening lines of *Trivia* parody those of Vergil's *Aeneid* (transcribed c. 29-19 B.C.E.) and thus set the mock-heroic tone; instead of declaring his subject to be "arms and the man," Gay states that it is "How to walk clean by day, and safe by night." Accordingly, his first substantive stanza is on the choice of shoes, which should not be foreign or fashionable but "firm, well-hammered" ones that will be serviceable in snow, rain, or sleet. Shoes too wide, he says, may cause a sprain; those too short will cause corns or blisters.

Next the poet evaluates various types of overcoats and cautions against Bavarian ones or those with lace; he recommends a simple, inexpensive wool that will allow the wearer to "brave unwet the rain, unchill'd the frost." The potential walker is advised to carry a cane—not like those of the city beaux, which are amber-tipped and used for show, but a practical one—one that, if sturdy, will chase others away and will attract the attention of carriage drivers.

In a long stanza Gay describes the perils of walking in foreign cities and bemoans the increased street traffic in Britain, augmented by "coaches and chariots" as well as sedan chairs so that no longer "Rosie-complexion'd health thy steps attends,/ And exercise thy lasting youth defends." Then he provides a dissertation on the weather, with special attention given to cold, fair, and rainy days and a list of superstitions to be disregarded. This consideration of rainy weather leads logically into a recommendation that ladies should wear pattens (shoes elevated by metal cleats) and carry umbrellas.

The preliminaries of Book I run to 282 lines; Book II, "Of Walking the Streets by Day," is 468 lines; and Book III, "Of Walking the Streets by Night," is 416 lines. Since few walkers ventured onto the streets of London at night, clearly the proportions of the poem are quite appropriate.

Gay recommends the morning for walking: "For ease and for dispatch the morning's best:/ No tides of passengers the street molest." There are dangers, however: Barbers, perfumers, and bakers can soil black clothes; chimney sweeps, coal merchants, and dustmen can bespoil lighter clothing, and tallow men, chandlers, and butchers can spot any clothes. Likewise, the fop with his powdered wig and the miller should be avoided, but the bully should not be demurred to: He may mutter curses, but he will yield. Should the walker lose his way, he should seek directions from a tradesman rather than a boy—and never from a woman, for she may be a pickpocket.

A second edition of *Trivia* (undated, but probably 1717) contains an addition (lines 99-220) on the rise of the shirtless shoe-shine boy, an illegitimate son of the goddess Cloacina, whose image was found in a sewer by Tatius, king of the Sabines. The celebrated Dr. Samuel Johnson judged this addition "nauseous and superfluous." The interpolation contains the memorable couplet, "But happier far are those (if such be known)/ Whom both a father and a mother own"; nevertheless, inorganic and irrelevant, the addition lacks merit.

The remainder of Book II cautions against walking in narrow streets and those that house chandlers, fishmongers, and butchers—or walking where masons are at work or boys are playing football. It reminds the walker that Mondays and Thursdays are "days of game," when bull- and bear-baiting can be seen, and that Wednesdays and Fridays are fasting days so that seafood can be seen in the stalls. The fruits of the seasons are enumerated. Gay reminds the walker to be charitable to widows and orphans, the lame and blind, for walkers are blessed: They are immune to jaundice, coughs, asthma, gout, and stones. Accordingly, they should never envy those in coaches or in fine clothes. To his fellow walkers he says, "give me sweet content on foot."

Book III cautions against walking near noisy crowds, where pickpockets usually congregate—often aided by ballad singers or girls with pretty faces—and offers advice on eating oysters, avoiding cheats, identifying whores and rakes, bribing watchmen and policemen, and avoiding the numerous terrors of the night, including fires. It comprises what Gay calls "Useful Precepts," among which are:

> Let constant Vigilance thy Footsteps guide,
> And wary Circumspection guard thy Side;
>
> . . . .
>
> Though you through cleanlier Allies wind by Day,
> To shun the Hurries of the publick Way,
> Yet ne'er to those dark Paths by Night retire;
> Mind only Safety, and contemn the Mire.

Forms and Devices

The epigraph of *Trivia* is the opening line of Vergil's ninth eclogue: "Where are you off to, Moeris, walking on the road to town?" The quotation illustrates both Gay's indebtedness to the classical tradition and his plan for what might be termed a city eclogue, a poem in which conversation about current matters, spiced with proverbs and advice, takes place between an older, sophisticated person and a younger, inexperienced auditor. The prefatory motto is taken from Vergil also, and it preempts criticism of the poem by addressing any potential gainsayer as "ignoramus as you are." That is, Gay regards himself as *the* authority on walking the streets of London and thus is inhospitable to cavilling criticism. He is the model for modern city tour guides, pointing out buildings, homes, and institutions of interest. He warns his audience against the pitfalls of disregarding his directions and suggests the delights of further exploration and examination. The accuracy of almost all the topics of *Trivia* can be verified by consulting two twentieth century collections of historical illustrations, *The Thames About 1750* (1951) and *Engravings by Hogarth* (1973), which substantiate even the minor details of Gay's remarkably memorable descriptions of persons, places, and practices.

The classical model is borne out by the frequent allusions to Greek and Roman notables, both civil and mythological: Ariadne, Orpheus, Oedipus, Phaeton, Pythagoras, Regulus, Scylla and Charybdis, Theseus, and Vulcan are among them. The comprehensiveness of the guidebook aspect of *Trivia* is impressive: The reader is beguiled by pithy comments on such places as Cheapside, Covent Garden, Charing Cross, St. Clement Danes Church, Drury Lane, Fleet Ditch, Ludgate Hill, and the Thames bridges. Clearly, Gay's apprenticeship to a London silk mercer provided him with the opportunity to see more of the side streets, the fashions, and the employments of London than most poets, so his poem is marked by its social realism and by its frank admission of the unsavory aspects of early eighteenth century British urban life. While many poets painted only the atypical upper social stratum, Gay took as his subject the whole spectrum of London life: prostitution, poverty, pickpocketing, and pilferage as well as fops, fashions, food, and fairs.

Both the comprehensiveness of his overview and its reliability (as tested by more particular contemporary commentaries) are deserving of admiration. All the sounds, sights, and smells of the city are conveyed with verisimilitude. One twentieth century literary critic, George Sherburn, wrote that Gay, "like many realists, stressed the gutter to the neglect of more pleasant prospects; but for his foot passenger, his warnings were vivid and sage. Like Hogarth he paints the grotesque realities of London life." This is high praise, really, because painter and engraver William Hogarth is greatly admired for his penetrating vision of city life in his day, which counterbalanced the misleading representation offered by upper-class artists and writers. Part of Gay's strength is derived from his effective juxtaposition of morning and evening, walking and being carried (in chaise or carriage), males and females, refinement and depravity, bucolic and urban, rich and poor, indolence and industry, beauty and sordidness. He is concerned, it is clear, not with a particularly partisan presentation but with presenting a comprehensive portrait of London. The effect of *Trivia* is comparable to viewing one of Canaletto's panoramic scenes of the Thames and its environs.

In his early poems Gay made frequent use of alexandrines and triplets for variety; these characteristics of verse composition were condemned by Pope, and Gay subsequently abandoned them for the most part, even revising some lines of *Rural Sports* and *The Fan* to eliminate these solecisms. Gay's poetic technique was normally a mixture of the established and the original; he is more rigid in his adherence to the heroic couplet than Pope, yet he uses a more demotic language than his mentor, and his sentence structure is less complex.

Burlesque, a form of parody that imitates the form and style of a serious work but makes the imitation entertaining by the disparity between the subject matter and the method, is basic to *Trivia*, in which many of the aspects of street life are compared to famous incidents in classical mythology. Accordingly, Gay compares the rustic in awe of the city to Theseus in the Cretan labyrinths, horses straining up Ludgate Hill to the Parthians throwing their javelins backward, the walker caught in a street brawl to Laius slain by Oedipus at a crossroads, and moisture on church monuments to Niobe dissolving into tears. Not all these allusions and comparisons are meaningful to a present-day reader, but their force would have been apparent to Gay's readers.

It has been observed that Pope was prepared to sacrifice truth for a brilliant epigram or a brilliant antithesis. Such was not Gay's practice, though his self-composed epitaph indicates that he was as capable as Pope in this most demanding form of composition: "Life is a jest, and all things show it./ I thought so once, and now I know it." Perhaps the best epigram in *Trivia* is the following, occasioned by writing on the great frost of 1715: "Ah Doll! All mortals must resign their breath,/ And industry itself submit to death!" Or this, doubtless written tongue-in-cheek: "Death shall entomb in dust this mould'ring frame/ But never reach th'eternal part, my fame." Even the final line of the poem has the merits of brevity and pithiness: "This work shall shine, and walkers bless my name." In his use of classical allusions, juxtaposition, the many forms of imagery, adherence (but not slavery) to metrical forms, and epigrams within the burlesque form, Gay exhibits enviable compositional skills.

Themes and Meanings

Although Gay was evidently aware of the pitfalls associated with writing a mock-heroic poem on the simple topic of walking the streets of London and entitling it an art—inviting his readers to compare it with Horace's *Ars Poetica* (the art of poetry, c.

17 B.C.E.)—, he clearly saw his endeavor as having some utilitarian value for country folk and others who were less familiar with London thoroughfares than he was. His intent was to be of help to the uninitiated and the inexperienced, and he acknowledged toward the conclusion of his poem, "Yet shall I bless my labours, if mankind/ Their future safety from my dangers find." His didacticism is therefore quite clear: He wants to be a guide, to be helpful—a commendable intention for a poet or a friend when in need. The reader is thus well disposed toward the poet and is ready to accept his guidance and even his predispositions and prejudices.

The issue or concern at the heart of the poem is the safety of a neophyte tourist in London, sightseeing on foot by day or night, in all the seasons. While the subject might seem devoid of poetic possibility, Gay's selection of particular subject matter provides the basis for the poetry—rather than mere verse—to be found in almost all sections. Edgar Allan Poe argued in *The Poetic Principle* (1849) that there is no such thing as a long poem—that in actuality a long poem is a series of minor poems, each deserving that name only to the extent that it excites by elevating the soul. There are numerous exciting and elevating sections in *Trivia* that complement the ironic and bathetic sections, and over the centuries the preponderance of critical reaction has been that the former are the more numerous.

Trivia has been praised as a literary burlesque and as a serious social document, a detailed picture of eighteenth century life in a great metropolis. It was drawn by a writer with considerable life experience at both extremes of the social scale, one acquainted both with life in rural Devonshire and with the manners and affectations of the aristocracy.

It has been declared to be the finest mock-georgic in English and to be the greatest poem on London life in English literature. Perhaps these descriptions are somewhat too generous in their praise, but it must be allowed that Gay's accomplishment is great: He shifted the subject of poetry from the country to the city, from the ancient to the contemporary, from the exalted to the lowly, and he did so with clear-sighted realism, a refreshing cynicism, and a tolerable irony. Moreover, he never forgot that the social classes are interdependent, a theme that pervades his *Fables* and *The Beggar's Opera* as well.

A. L. McLeod

TROOP TRAIN

Author: Karl Shapiro (1913-2000)
Type of poem: Lyric
First published: 1944, in *V-Letter and Other Poems*

The Poem

Karl Shapiro's "Troop Train" is a long lyric poem of five octaves (eight-line stanzas) written in either a nonrhyming or coincidental rhyming pattern. It is one of the principal poems taken from Shapiro's second collection of poems, *V-Letter and Other Poems*, for which he won a Pulitzer Prize. The *V-Letter* collection was written from 1942 to 1944 while Shapiro served in the U.S. Army during World War II. As Shapiro noted in *V-Letter*'s introduction, this poem (as well as the majority of the others collected therein) was written while he was stationed in the war zones of Australia and New Zealand.

Interestingly, "Troop Train" serves as a model of Shapiro's ability to distance himself from his poetic subject. Just as Shapiro was a conscientious objector during World War II, which disallowed him from carrying weapons, he was still a part of the war while he stood apart from it. Hence, while war raged around him, his role as a medic put him unarmed in the midst of the fighting. This detachment is what one finds in "Troop Train." It allows the poet to stand back, as a voyeur, and observe the war's events without unnecessarily romanticizing those events because of his direct involvement. The result, then, is part objective portrayal, part something closer to real truth, and part something that is intensely creative because the poet is able to reshape, redefine, and restructure that reality.

Hence, while Shapiro most likely rode on numerous troop trains and could have easily written only about that personalized experience, he chooses, instead, to observe what impact the train has upon the town through which it passes, upon the townspeople, and upon the troops themselves. This third-person observation keeps his own personal summary out of the poem.

Thus, the train "stops the town we come through." All activity is temporarily aborted because these troops are heading to the battlefront to stop the advancement of the enemy who, if they proceed, will eventually take over the town. The people's attentions are arrested, perhaps in the spectacle of the train itself or in the awareness of the impending battles the troops face. The troop train, here, is an instrument not only to stop the war but also to stop the town. This suggests, perhaps, that the town has a war of its own—its labor, where "workers raise/ their oily arms in good salute"; its inability to preserve innocence, where kids, who should never have been exposed to the criminality of war, "scream," not out of fear but at the train, "as at a circus"; where businessmen "glance hopefully and go their measured way" because life is a set of accounts and ledgers where one hopes to succeed and to not end in the red.

Furthermore, the women, coming out to their "dumbstruck door," are most succinctly aware of the war's impending significance. They "more slowly wave and seem to warn us back/ As if a tear blinding the course of war/ Might once dissolve our iron in their sweet wish."

The soldiers are "clustered on [them]selves/. . . hang as from a cornucopia/ In total friendliness." Ironically, the image is one of the horn of plenty, a celebration of life's sustenance, a Thanksgiving scene. However, how can troops, traveling perhaps toward imminent death, sustain life or, for that matter, be thankful? Shapiro's purpose is understood: All are thankful to be alive, if only presently, and thankful for the community for, once the soldiers arrive to battle, they must ultimately face death alone.

Once the troop train passes the town, Shapiro turns the ride into something of a poker hand, where "luck" determines who wins or loses. No longer the "faces bunched/ To spray the streets with catcalls and with leers," or the "mouths that want the drink-of-water kiss" from "a lady smiling pink," the soldiers are now the "good-bad boys of circumstance and chance." About the ensuing card game, the poet writes, "Dealer, deal me my luck, a pair of bulls,/ The right draw to a flush, the one-eyed jack." Although this may be taken literally, the poet's intent is that one sees this as a request of fate, too. The speaker says, "Deal me winners, souvenirs of peace," but the odds of winning are squarely stacked against soldiers: "Luck also travels and not all come back."

Forms and Devices

In the introduction of *V-Letter and Other Poems*, Shapiro made a disclaimer pertinent to his use of forms and devices. He said that he had not "written these poems to accord with any doctrine or system of thought or even a theory of composition." Further, he stated, "I have nothing to offer in the way of beliefs or challenges or prosody." Nonetheless, despite this self-effacement, Shapiro would become one of America's postmodern experts on prosody and poetic structure. Perhaps much of what he had done in *V-Letter* was successful intuition, yet the best poets premeditate their work through form and craftsmanship. Shapiro's craftsmanship is so sound, it seems unlikely "Troop Train" came from chance.

Specifically, the poem's octave structure is enhanced by a methodical, slow meter. The standard meter of poetry in English is iambic; however, Shapiro manipulates that meter into an accentual verse, with roughly five stresses per line juxtaposed with any number of unstressed syllables. Unlike iambic meter, where unstressed syllables alternate predictably with stressed ones, Shapiro offers no such predictability. While there is a cadence to the poem, it is not the cadence of a metronome; rather, the poem plods along, like a train would, slowly toward its destination, wheels clacking upon the tracks in a haphazard rhythm. Similarly, then, the soldiers are being carried toward their own unpredictable destinations—such is the rhythm of life itself.

One of Shapiro's enduring strengths as a poet is his ability to shape simile and metaphor. Instead of describing the troop train as a train, Shapiro's metaphor casts it as a cornucopia, a horn of plenty. However, the fruits of the harvest, for which the townspeople are thankful and hopeful, are the soldiers; the soldiers, in service to war, are hopeful the harvest of death will not include them—not at this interval, at least. However, the train is not just metaphorically a cornucopia, it is also a symbol for life's passage, moving on "through crummy continents and days,/ Deliberate, grimy, slightly drunk we crawl." As Shapiro writes, "Trains lead to ships and ships to death or trains," and these trains lead "to death or trucks, and trucks to death." The train, like life, is a "march to death/ Or that survival which is all our hope." Nonetheless, the end result of all train rides, all marches is death, the "Nightfall of nations brilliant after war."

Additional metaphors arise in the life-as-poker-game analogy. Shapiro writes that "Diamonds and hearts are red but spades are black." Diamonds are gemstones, precious as life is precious; hearts are the life source and the passion for living. Spades connotes the digging tool used to fabricate not only foxholes but also graves, and in both death resides. "Spades are spades and clubs are clovers," Shapiro adds, repeating the spade image so that the reader does not lose sight of the matter-of-factness of death; the clovers, black like death, become the ground cover of graves grown over.

Furthermore, Shapiro makes fine use of personification and synecdoche. Personification, or the giving of human qualities to nonhuman things, turns the soldier's packs into the "twist" of "murdered bodies." The guns, unlike the nervous and apprehensive men about them, "only seem themselves." Oddly, then, the guns are calm and at ease, aware of their identities and of their purposes; they fear nothing. Conversely, the men have become iron that the women wish to dissolve. The men are not whole, but, as synecdoche commands, they are parts: "faces bunched," "eyes fixed," kiss-desirous mouths that sting. They are "the shoulder" the gun strap "tightens across . . . and holds firm."

Themes and Meanings

Shapiro never intended to be a "war poet." His precise meaning of that statement may be broadly interpreted. War poets tend to either romanticize war or protest war. In Shapiro's case, because he assumes the objective middle ground of the observer, much of an audience's reading will be determined by personal sentiments and agendas. However, one should remember that Shapiro, because of his Judaism, objected in conscience to the war and would not fight in it. This did not disallow him from an active involvement as a medic, however, in the defense and support of his country.

An ongoing theme of Shapiro's *V-Letter* collection and of such poems as "Troop Train" concerns the inhumanity of people. Death is the great equalizer, and all people march onward toward death. With luck, some live a little longer than others. The tragedy of war is that it hurries people toward the permanent conclusion. Death may not be an unfair part of life; however, war commissions death, and anyone who is misplaced into war submits, perhaps, to an unfair policy.

Mark Sanders

A TRUE ACCOUNT OF TALKING TO
THE SUN AT FIRE ISLAND

Author: Frank O'Hara (1926-1966)
Type of poem: Mock pastoral
First published: 1968; collected in *The Collected Poems of Frank O'Hara*, 1971

The Poem

Frank O'Hara's remarkably inventive and characteristically humorous "A True Account of Talking to the Sun at Fire Island" is an eighty-three-line poem written in 1958 but first published posthumously in 1968 and widely anthologized since. In keeping with the idea of a true testimony, the persona is identified as the poet O'Hara himself.

The poem begins (in the first thirteen lines) quite simply but dramatically, with the poet awakened by the sun—who is annoyed because he (O'Hara assigns the sun a masculine gender) has had difficulty awakening O'Hara. The poet attempts to apologize in lines 14-26. He is a guest at the beach house of Hal Fondren, a close friend since college days, and stayed up late the night before talking with his host. This excuse allows the sun to explain why he wants to speak with the poet. Lines 27-56 constitute the sun's primary message, while lines 58-76 represent important advice offered as a sort of valediction, or farewell message. Lines 77-83 function as an envoy or coda, allowing the sun to exit the stage and the poet to go back to sleep.

"A True Account of Talking to the Sun at Fire Island" depends primarily upon whimsical personification for its effects. For example, the sun is described as "petulant" when he compares O'Hara's lackadaisical attitude to the startled attentiveness he received when he last visited a poet, the 1920's Russian avant-garde writer Vladimir Mayakovsky. This playful allusion refers to a poem by Mayakovsky that serves as precursor and model for O'Hara's poem.

The sun points out that ordinary people think O'Hara is crazy, while other poets—who are crazy—think that he is boring. The sun insists that the poet should not let such criticism bother him. The sun, too, is criticized every day by those who are dissatisfied with the weather and, he points out, someone is always dissatisfied with the weather. The sun assures the poet that it is no disgrace to be "different," confiding that he has been keeping an eye on the poet, watching his development, and is now pleased that he is "making [his] own days, so to speak" by beginning to express himself in his own fashion.

It is clear to the reader, however, that the poet has not entirely abandoned being concerned about what other people will think of him. If he had done so, there would be no need for the sun to make this special effort to bolster his courage and self-esteem.

Forms and Devices

"A True Account of Talking to the Sun at Fire Island" is a lyric poem that, because it purports to record a verbatim conversation, can also be considered a mock pastoral.

The pastoral is an ancient form—used by poets writing in English since the sixteenth century but dating back to the Greek poet Theocritus—which presents a dialogue in a rustic setting. Here, however, instead of a conversation on love or philosophy between two shepherds, is a conversation between the poet and the rising sun.

O'Hara employs a comic tone and dramatic form in order to present serious ideas in a pleasant way. The sun's comments are often comedic plays on words. "I can't hang around/ here all day," he tells the poet. Later he claims not to be upset that people do not "look up" to him because it would hurt their eyes. Choosing that colloquial phrase instead of the word "admire" allows O'Hara to depict the sun as a witty, tongue-in-cheek conversationalist. The poem tacitly suggests that ideas presented in this avuncular tone will be much more readily received than advice given in a sternly authoritarian manner.

The sun's valedictory remarks also undermine the traditional pastoral form by acknowledging the fact that O'Hara is an especially urban and sophisticated man. The poet is not at all interested in endorsing a traditional view of nature, nor is he seriously attempting to present his wisecracking sun as the equivalent of a capricious classical deity or the powerful Judeo-Christian God one might encounter in the poetry of John Milton. Nevertheless, the poem's dramatic situation will easily lead readers to at least contemplate (and then discard) such identifications.

Basically, O'Hara distrusts philosophy and metaphysics, preferring to view poetry as pure art or as purely personal communication—as useful as the telephone. One result of this view is the unpretentious colloquial diction of his poems. The model for this poem is the Russian poet Mayakovsky's "An Extraordinary Adventure Which Befell Vladimir Mayakovsky in a Summer Cottage," written in the village of Pushkino in June, 1920. It is further testimony to his deep love of poetry—and art for its own sake—that on July 10, 1958, writing at the beach resort of Fire Island, New York, O'Hara chose to pay homage to his predecessor with his own poem. Similarly, O'Hara wrote a poem every year in commemoration of the birthday of the composer Sergei Rachmaninoff.

Themes and Meanings

O'Hara has been admired as an idiosyncratic and inventive poet, yet his work also contains a sometimes satirical awareness of traditional poetic conventions. On one level, "A True Account of Talking to the Sun at Fire Island" echoes the praise of nonconformity found in Ralph Waldo Emerson's famous essay "Self-Reliance" (1841), but the poem also has additional resonances.

Because O'Hara carefully dated his manuscripts, it is clear that this poem continues to explore concerns recorded in "Ode: Salute to the French Negro Poets," written the day before. Both poems argue that poets may be unappreciated and even disparaged by their fellow citizens; yet they can expect to be praised by future generations if they are brave enough to persist in telling the truth about life as they understand and experience it. To be a poet, in O'Hara's view, is to accept a difficult but vitally important vocation. While much of "A True Account of Talking to the Sun at Fire Island" seems to say that this poetic vocation, or "calling," is ultimately rewarding, the final lines somewhat ominously suggest that reward is beside the point, that the poet is actually the servant of unspecified forces in the universe that he cannot fully identify yet must obey.

"A True Account of Talking to the Sun at Fire Island" seems to confirm what many poets before O'Hara have asserted: that the poet is, in fact, a medium through which cosmic forces speak—and that there is something glorious and personally fulfilling about accepting this misunderstood and often unappreciated role. There is little in O'Hara's purposefully nonchalant tone, however, that urges the reader to think of this as an especially mystical or religious observation.

At first reading, O'Hara's cosmic encounter seems to have a curiously mundane result. The poet in "A True Account" does indeed experience a transcendent moment, but this experience seems merely to arm him with the tools that will allow him to chart an independent, self-assured path in the contemporary urban society of creativity, style, and clever conversation that he ordinarily inhabits.

The poet's tools—or "miraculous arms," to use a phrase from Aimé Césaire, one of the French poets O'Hara admired—are his enhanced perceptions. That fact, and the sun's promise of continued poetic inspiration, reinforce an idea that firmly links the modern urban poet with ancient forebears such as the Greeks, who felt that the human ability to make poetic utterances was an unexpected and undeserved gift from the divine Muses. In "A True Account of Talking with the Sun at Fire Island," O'Hara eschews the supernatural but nevertheless enlists himself in the ages-old struggle by poets to be the truthful witnesses of humankind's fate.

Lorenzo Thomas

TRUMPET PLAYER

Author: Langston Hughes (1902-1967)
Type of poem: Lyric
First published: 1947, in *Fields of Wonder*

The Poem

Originally published as "Trumpet Player: 52nd Street," Langston Hughes's "Trumpet Player" is a literary jazz poem consisting of five eight-line stanzas and a four-line coda. It is one of a body of Hughes's musically oriented poems and is written in the spirit of his jazz poems, such as "Jazzonia" and "Jazztet Muted." The setting is a bar where a trumpeter is on stage playing his instrument, telling his story—aspects of the personal and collective African American experience in the United States. The poem describes the musician, his music, and its meaning, developing the theme of the ameliorative effects of music.

Stanza 1 emphasizes the dark rings of weariness under the trumpet player's eyes. This weariness, deeper than temporary tiredness, is born from the racial memory of the African American slave experience, the slave ships of the Middle Passage, and the whips against thighs on southern plantations to the streets of the urban north. The second stanza describes the musician's hair, which has been "tamed," smoothed down until it gleams like patent leather. In other words, his natural hair has been changed to a slick, processed style popular, especially among musicians, in the 1930's, 1940's, and 1950's.

Stanza 3 is devoted to sound and rhythm, which are described using a metaphor of liquor: the sound is like "honey/ Mixed with liquid fire," a combination of smooth, mellow, bold, and forceful tones; the rhythm is intense "ecstasy/ Distilled from old desire—." That desire, as identified in stanza 4, is a longing for a serene, distant, somewhat romanticized past of moonlight and sea, free from the pain of slave ships and whips. His reality is different: His moonlight is the stage spotlight and the "moons of weariness/ Beneath his eyes"; his only sea is liquor in a bar glass.

As in stanza 1, stanza 5 again describes the musician and his music. Blowing his horn in a one-button jacket, he seems carried away by his music, unaware of what musical riff begins to touch him in a positive way, but touch him it does. The four-line coda explains that he is touched in such a way that the music assuages his troubles. Thus, the poem is a sympathetic portrayal of a troubled musician who finds solace in his music.

Forms and Devices

Hughes's poetry has been influenced by African American rhythms, especially gospel, blues, and jazz; "Trumpet Player" reflects the influence of jazz and blues. The structure, variations in rhyme and rhythm, blues idiom, punctuation, and figurative language identify the poem as a simulation of jazz improvisation, a reflection of the musical motif in the poem. The varied structures of the stanzas are like jazz variations.

The structures of stanzas 1, 3, and 5 are similar, each being basically a sentence written in free verse. Stanzas 3 and 4, though separated spatially, are linked structurally. Stanza 3 is comprised of two parallel sentences, each of which describes the sound and feel of the music; stanza 4 is a continuation of the second sentence with additional parallels contrasting the trumpeter's desired state with his actual state. The fifth stanza mirrors stanzas 1 and 2, except that it continues the thought to the coda, which begins with the word "But," indicating a reversal from a troubled to a peaceful mood.

In jazz compositions, musicians often play basic chords or regular rhythms; one or more musicians then depart from them with myriad variations, at the end returning to some version of the basic beat. In "Trumpet Player," the combination of unrhymed and rhymed lines conveys that sense. Written in free verse, the first five lines of the first five, eight-line stanzas give a sense of the free-flowing rhythms, the swing, of jazz. The last three lines of the stanzas pick up a rhyme but, except for rhymed lines 4 and 8, do not follow a set pattern from stanza to stanza. For instance, in stanza 1, lines 4 and 8 and lines 2, 6, and 7 rhyme; in stanza 2, lines 4 and 8 are the only rhymed lines; in stanza 5, lines 4 and 8 as well as lines 2 and 6 rhyme. Although the free-flowing rhythms of jazz continue, the final four-line stanza brings resolution, as a jazz piece might be resolved, through the two rhymed lines.

Other features locate the poem within the jazz tradition in its integration of the blues idiom. The subject matter is similar to that of traditional blues songs, which recount a problem in straightforward, simple language, but end on a positive note. Although the image of success with his "Patent-leathered" hair and *"fine* one-button" jacket, the musician is weary and troubled, a state reflected in his eyes. Yet, like the piano player in Hughes's "The Weary Blues," he finds solace in his music. The process of this transformation is reflected in the short, one-word third line of the coda, "Trouble," and the elongated, five-word final line, "Mellows to a golden note," which simulates the easing of the troubled mind. Moreover, the repetition of phrases, such as "The Negro/ With the trumpet at his lips," evokes feelings of weariness, longing, and unfulfilled desire, and the structure of the final four-line stanza recall Hughes's blues poems, such as "Miss Blues'es Child" and "Lover's Return."

Punctuation complements structure and meaning. Consistent with the jazz structure, the poet varies the use of the poem's few marks of punctuation. Periods are used to end stanzas, which basically constitute the end of a sentence and a thought. At the end of stanzas 3 and 5, however, a dash signifies continuation of a thought. In stanza 3, the dash emphasizes the word "desire" and links "old desire" with the musician's current desire to connect with the past. In stanza 5, the dash also indicates a continuation, but links the music to his present well-being. In stanza 2, it is used before the last line to introduce an ironic comment about his "tamed down" hair. He describes it as gleaming like "jet" and wryly comments, "Were jet a crown." The final period at the end of the last stanza is consistent with his coming to terms with his feelings.

Traditional poetic devices—descriptive words and figurative language, such as metaphor, simile, and personification—are used within the jazz structure and help to elucidate the theme of the ameliorative power of music. The images of cracking whips and moons under his weary eyes are replaced by images of the moon and sea, natural surroundings that portend tranquility, not unnatural surroundings where spotlights replace moonlight. Metaphors identifying music as honey and rhythm as ecstasy evoke both the sound and the feel of jazz music, which expresses struggle, sorrows, joys, and aspirations and, paradoxically, also liberates one from the mundane world of bars and hypodermic needles, feelings of sadness and worry. Personification is evident in the lines, "the music slips/ Its hypodermic needle/ To his soul—," indicative of an active and meaningful relationship between the artist and his music. This affinity becomes a catalyst for his change of mood.

Themes and Meanings

An obvious interpretation of the poem is that the trumpet player has reached the trappings of "success," yet he is still troubled, perhaps because he feels a sense of alienation from his heritage, as suggested by the taming of his "vibrant" hair, or perhaps because he is burdened by a heritage of oppression. Filling the sucker-sized bar glass with "liquid fire" and distilled ecstasy, however, the music, a glorious part of his heritage, soothes his troubled mind.

The theme also encompasses the collective African American experience apparent in the identification of the musician as "The Negro," whose heritage includes the pains and degradation of slavery as noted in reference to the "memory/ Of slave ships" and the "crack of whips." This heritage is also one of resilience and survival, and music has been one of the means for that survival. It was apparent in the chants of slaves attempting to soften the physical pains of the lash, attempting to cloud the sharp memories of loved ones lost in the holds of ships or on the auction blocks; it was apparent in songs pining or plotting for freedom, an "old desire," still present. The integration of the concrete "trumpet at his lips," the riff, and the hypodermic needle, and of the abstract "soul" and "Trouble/ Mellow[ing] to a golden note," affirms that the music is an integral part of the African American experience. So intertwined, it has a transforming effect both, individually and collectively. In Hughes's philosophy, it is typically a positive effect.

Universal in its appeal, the poem can also be read on a symbolic level. From this point of view, the trumpet player may also be symbolic of the poet and other creative artists. The pen, like the trumpet, has the power to chronicle history and to penetrate humans' innermost thoughts and feelings; the word and the music can also have a positive effect on human emotions. The musical theme and structure also suggest an integral relationship among the artist, the music, and the experience. Such a relationship is apparent in human experience generally, for music is indeed a universal language touching the elemental feelings of all humanity and creating the possibility for transformation.

Hughes's poem embodies a symbiosis between music and poetry, for the poem defines music as the poetry of the soul. The poem's reference to music's soothing of the soul—the essence of the African American experience and the essence of being—identifies art as an expression of human possibility, affirmation, and resilience.

Della Burt-Bradley

THE TRUTH IS

Author: Linda Hogan (1947-   )
Type of poem: Meditation
First published: 1985, in *Seeing Through the Sun*

The Poem

"The Truth Is," a poem in free verse, comprises forty-seven lines arranged in six stanzas of unequal length. It depicts the speaker's conflicting emotions about her dual heritage. The speaker, in this case, is the poet's alter ego and reflects her own background: Linda Hogan's father is a Chickasaw Indian, and her mother is a European immigrant from Nebraska. Hogan uses the first person and, later, addresses herself by name, both of which clearly indicate that the poet is speaking of her own predicament.

The first stanza brings out the conflict. Normally, the two hands of an individual work in harmony to accomplish tasks. In this case, however, her hands, symbols of her ancestry, refuse to cooperate. The left hand represents the Chickasaw part of her heritage and the right that of her white lineage. Their separateness is so distinctive that the speaker needs to reassure herself that both hands, hidden away in each pocket, are indeed hers. She describes herself as a woman who "falls in love too easily" yet "sleeps in a twin bed"—in other words, she maintains her single status. The emptiness of her pockets indicates the absence of material possessions. The fact that she walks with her hands in her pockets further suggests her reluctance to advertise her ancestry. She informs readers that if she ever puts her hands in someone else's pocket, it is "for love not money."

The speaker continues her meditation on her peculiar state in the second stanza. She would like to envision herself as a grafted tree bearing two distinct yet equally appreciated types of fruits—perhaps apricots and cherries. The unfortunate truth, she realizes, is that the grafting, in this case, has not been successful: She finds that both branches "knock against each other," creating unwarranted tension. Yet, this constant warring is not what they desire; they "want amnesty."

The tone changes from reflective to conversational in the next stanza. The speaker admonishes herself—"Linda, girl"—to stop fretting about history. After all, nothing would be gained by going over the record of wrongdoings (by the white ancestors) or of loving generosity (of the Native Americans). The sense of her disharmonious existence is further conveyed by her comparison of herself to an old Civilian Conservation Corps member from the days of the Depression. The phrase "taped together" evokes the image of an object barely held together: She sees herself in a similar predicament. Her empty pockets, devoid of "coins and keys," the accoutrements of modern life, reinforce the absence of tangible wealth. She finds consolation in the fact that since wealth blinds the soul, hers remains unfettered by material bondage.

In the fifth stanza, the speaker recounts further the dangers of being "a woman of two countries." Her hands remain sheltered in the dark, empty pockets; in other words, she remains ignorant of both heritages that they represent. While she pretends to act nonchalantly, she cannot escape the "enemy." She desires to forget the gory history of the relationship between the white settlers and the Native Americans, to stop thinking of "who killed who." However, it is difficult to forget it all when she is constantly reminded of "that knocking on the door/ in the middle of the night"—a reference to the thoughts about continuing acts of violence originating from mainstream society.

Resolution, for the speaker, comes not in achieving a state of amnesty between the warring elements of her being but in the acceptance of her struggle. As she shifts her attention from hands to feet and shoes, the dilemma continues, for the right foot is still white and the left is still Chickasaw. In other words, "the truth is" that she will have to learn to live with this ever-present tension as she journeys through life.

Forms and Devices

Lacking a formal structure, the poem is deftly held together by metaphors, similes, symbols, and imagery. Hogan's use of hands to denote her heritage is a rather unusual metaphor, suggesting the emphasis on actions rather than thoughts. That these hands are hidden away in the pockets is a reminder of the unseen but powerful forces of heritage. Furthermore, the emptiness of the pockets reflects the speaker's state of existence: Her heritage has not, as yet, brought her any material or spiritual riches. Phrases describing the woman, who "falls in love too easily," who "sleeps in a twin bed," and who "walks along with hands/ in her own empty pockets/ even though she has put them in others/ for love not money," evoke the image of a vulnerable woman in search of peace and love.

The metaphor of a grafted fruit tree in stanza 2 is a powerful one. Normally, the process of grafting produces new varieties. If the grafting is successful, it is difficult to distinguish between different branches. In this case, however, this is not so. The grafting of the two cultures has not worked well; the speaker's dream that the tree would bear two fruits, each distinctive in itself, has not been realized. The phrase "It's not that way" tersely reveals the truth. The image of branches that "knock against each other at night" contrasts the reality with the speaker's erstwhile dream of peaceful coexistence. "Who loved who" and "who killed who" allude to the history of relations between whites and Native Americans, which has been dominated by violence.

In the fourth stanza, the use of simile, imagery, metaphor, and symbolism further advances the idea of the failure of an emergent composite identity. The speaker compares herself with an old worker from the Depression era and evokes another powerful image of herself as a "taped together" relic of the past. The pockets are depicted as "masks/ for the soul," serving as blinders that hide the soul. The coins and keys clearly symbolize material wealth and possessions. Their absence leaves the pockets free of jingling elements; their continued emptiness, however, suggests her failure to fill them with other riches.

The next two stanzas draw upon the earlier metaphors and allusions in reiterating the ever-continuing conflict. The pretense of not being concerned or afraid cannot go too far. The line "you better keep right on walking" clearly suggests moving on without being debilitated by the state of inertia. The poem thus succeeds in using these figures of speech effectively in establishing the mood of the speaker.

Themes and Meanings

One's identity is an amalgamation of many ingredients, the most important of these being, perhaps, one's heritage. Harnessing the forces of heredity and environment has never been an easy task. It becomes even more complicated when one does not belong to the mainstream of society. Having a mixed ancestry further compounds the problem, especially when those two elements are derived from a mutually adversarial relationship. Such is the context of Hogan's "The Truth Is."

The speaker's desire to reconcile the Native American and the European parts of her heritage permeates her life. If only she could create a distinctly new identity from this mix, life would be peaceful and simple for her. However, it does not happen this way. She realizes that the underlying, persistent clashes that are revived by the memory of historical wrongdoings, and, occasionally, by interruptions from the present will continue to be a part of her existence. Her reassurance to herself that she should forget about the past and live in the present helps her to accept the situation.

Ignoring the existence of this tension is of no avail; she cannot carry the pretense of being unconcerned for too long. The solution, then, is to acknowledge the truth and keep treading one's path. In her own life, Hogan seems to have achieved that equilibrium. In *Winged Words: American Indian Writers Speak* (1985), she admits that though her mixed heritage creates "a natural tension that surfaces" in her work, she has learned to use it to her advantage to strengthen her imagination.

Discussing Native American poetry, scholar Brian Swann observes, "Most poems reach for balance, for sanity in a mad world, in the face of antagonism, past and present. One sees a desire for wholeness—for balance, reconciliation, and healing—within the individual, the tribe, the community, the nation" (*Harper's Anthology of 20th Century Native American Poetry*, 1988). Hogan's poem reflects this tradition. "The Truth Is," in the end, transcends the speaker-poet's feelings and speaks to all those who share her experience of struggling to reconcile the different strands of their heritage.

Leela Kapai

TRYING TO TALK WITH A MAN

Author: Adrienne Rich (1929-   )
Type of poem: Meditative lyric
First published: 1973, in *Diving into the Wreck*

The Poem

Adrienne Rich's "Trying to Talk with a Man" is a compact and powerful poem consisting of thirty-nine lines arranged in nine stanzas that vary in length from one to seven lines. The poem describes a conversation between a man and a woman who have gone out into the desert where bombs are being tested. As the title indicates, this conversation is difficult: The speaker is "trying" to talk and perhaps not succeeding. Each of the two people in the poem, a man and a woman, sees the other as dangerously threatening; communication has broken down.

Almost all the poems in *Diving into the Wreck* are cast in the form of dialogue. This poem is the first in the volume, and it sets the book's tone. As its title indicates, conversation is a central metaphor. Whereas several of Rich's earliest poems speak about women who are silent and defer to men (such as "Aunt Jennifer's Tigers" and "An Unsaid Word" in *A Change of World*, published in 1951), the woman here is the active initiator of the discussion. "Trying to Talk with a Man" is about the dangers of an accelerating arms race, but its deeper subject is the creation of a real dialogue between men and women. The poet becomes Woman trying to talk with Man, as she calls upon her counterpart to join her in the task of questioning and redefining the habitual thinking about issues of gender and power.

The poem's conversation takes place in a barren desert where bombs are being tested. The location signifies the extremity Western civilization has reached. To be able to speak together, the man and woman have given up the shallow entertainments and trivial luxuries of society:

> What we've had to give up to get here—
> whole LP collections, films we starred in
> playing in the neighborhoods, bakery windows
> full of dry, chocolate-filled Jewish cookies,

The catalogue of civilization's foregone delights contrasts with the desert's stark urgency. The list itemizes the things—possessions, food, status—that tempt people with false promises of happiness, and thus prevent them from solving fundamental societal evils. Nevertheless, the poem's two characters have arrived at the boundary of realization, the desert's barren terrain. They face the likelihood of impending destruction, talking together in an attempt to repair the damaged communication.

Speaking together, they analyze dangers and itemize emergency precautions. However, their conversation evades the real issue, for bombs are a symptom of the problem. The society that produces bombs is the problem. The greatest danger lies in evasion, in the failure to exchange ideas and to admit responsibility for the danger.

Each speaker feels the other is dangerous. While the man regards the woman with suspicion, she believes his "dry heat feels like power." In this poem the two speakers have not yet established a meaningful dialogue. Therefore, the uneasiness persists, and the problems are not resolved. Without dialogue, there is no way to halt the testing of bombs and to defuse civilization's drive to destruction.

Forms and Devices

The poem is written in unrhymed free verse, with approximately half of the lines end-stopped, the other half run-on. The rhythmic base is iambic pentameter with a moderate amount of variation. Iambic pentameter is close to the natural speech rhythms of English and thus complements the poem's formal structure as a conversation. The voice is third-person plural, "we," and the speaker addresses another person, the man in the title, as "you."

Rich's earliest poems (for example, "Aunt Jennifer's Tigers," "The Uncle Speaks in the Drawing Room," and "An Unsaid Word") were statements rather than conversations. They were often more tightly structured, with greater regularity of stanzas and more frequent rhyme. She wrote that her early poetry was "an arrangement of ideas and feelings, . . . and it said what I had already decided it should say." In 1964 she asserted that "instead of poems *about* experiences I am getting [writing] poems that *are* experiences." That is, she was more willing to follow, work with, and learn from ideas, emotions, and images that arose during the writing process. The looser form of the later poems reflects that loosening of the composing process.

Rich has a strong sense of place, and many of her poems start by placing a speaker in a particular locale, often an urban location. This poem establishes a dramatic setting immediately, for the first line stands alone in its own stanza and proclaims: "Out in this desert we are testing bombs." To call attention to place, the word "here" is repeated four times (two of them in the emphatic position at the end of lines) in the space of the poem's thirty-nine lines. Similarly, "this desert" occurs twice, the word "place" appears once, and "locus" once.

Diving into the Wreck is Rich's seventh collection of poems, and, strikingly, it is the first of her titles to use a verb form. Similarly, "Trying to Talk with a Man" makes use of the same verb form, the present progressive tense, thirteen times to emphasize activity that is continuing in the present time. Most of these present participles ("talking," "moving," "playing," "driving," "walking") are at the start of the lines, giving them added prominence. Through its use of devices such as conversation, the inclusive "we," and the present progressive tense, the poem gathers urgency and immediacy, drawing the reader into its social and political critique.

Themes and Meanings

Rich is primarily a political poet, and this poem expresses her critique of a society following destructive paths. She frequently uses her own location and experience as starting points for an examination of social and political issues. At the time she wrote this poem, she had already been active in the Civil Rights movement, the women's movement, and the antiwar movement protesting against American involvement in the Vietnam War. At this stage of the women's movement, feminists had formulated a critique of Western patriarchy. They believed that militancy and disregard of human rights had led Western civilization to the brink of disaster. Their goals included recognition of the rights of women and minorities (including people of color and homosexuals), better social services, day care for children, elimination of the disparities in salaries of men and women, better health care, and, in general, a more compassionate social ethos.

Rich has written both poetry and prose articulating her political concerns. In 1971, the same year that she wrote "Trying to Talk with a Man," Rich was invited to participate in a forum discussing "The Woman Writer in the Twentieth Century." She wrote an important essay, "When We Dead Awaken: Writing as Re-Vision," in response to that invitation. The essay speaks of the exhilaration of awakening consciousness, and of the need for women to reexamine the conditions of their lives. The conclusion argues that "The creative energy of patriarchy is fast running out; what remains is its self-generating energy for destruction." It is up to women to redirect the destructive energy of patriarchy into more constructive channels and to inject a new, more humane, creative energy.

Many of Rich's poems reflect her passionate commitment to these political concerns. Indeed, in the title poem of *Diving into the Wreck* Rich uses the metaphor of a shipwreck to critique a social order that she perceives to be drowning, in need of redirection. In "Trying to Talk with a Man" another extreme setting is used: a desert. The desert indicates the actual physical setting where bombs are tested, but as a symbol it signifies extremity, danger, sterility, and desolation. Reinforcing these ideas, the poem speaks of "condemned scenery" and a "ghost town/ surrounded by a silence."

The word "silence" is repeated twice in this poem. It turns out that the silence is "familiar," and that the two people have brought it with them to the desert. Real communication between men and women is lacking, with potentially dangerous consequences for individuals and for society. At the time she was writing this poem Rich explained her interest in dialogue in an interview published in the *Ohio Review* (1971). She described her obsession with the question of how people could talk with each other and escape from the traps of rhetoric to arrive at real communication.

To counteract the "silence" real communication is necessary. In this poem Rich argues that the redemption of Western civilization is as immediate, as simple, and as difficult as an act of communication between men and women.

Karen F. Stein

TURNING

Author: Rainer Maria Rilke (1875-1926)
Type of poem: Lyric
First published: 1927, as "Wendung," in *Gesammelte Werke*; English translation collected in *The Selected Poetry of Rainer Maria Rilke*, 1982

The Poem

"Turning" is a poem of fifty-four lines divided unevenly into ten stanzas. The title suggests a turn or change in some important issue, and that is, indeed, the focus of the poem: a turning away from the poet's previous vision of the task of poetry to a new phase in his development as a poet. The poem is written in the third person, a device often used to distance the poet from the speaker or subject of the poem. In this case, however, it is clear that the poet is Rainer Maria Rilke himself. He sent the poem to a friend, saying that "it portrays the turning that will certainly have to come if I am to live." This poem can be read as a history of Rilke's poetic focus on observation of the outer world and a transition to bringing his vision inward.

The poem opens with a slightly altered quote from the philosopher Rudolf Kassner, a friend of Rilke: "The way from intensity to greatness leads through sacrifice." The quote is quite appropriate, as the poem represents a time during which Rilke was turning away from his intense exterior observations to look into himself for poetic inspiration. The poem can be divided into two main sections. The first, longer section describes his former way of seeing and creating poetry. The second section, beginning with the sixth stanza, reveals his doubts of his earlier perspective and describes his new intentions for his poetry.

Rilke lets his reader know from the very first line that a change is imminent: "For a long time he had achieved it with observing." The act of *Anschauen* (watching, observing) is now in the past, but, before he lets it go completely, Rilke lists his earlier achievements. The power of his look could force nature and inanimate objects to submit to him: "stars collapsed on their knees," and towers were "filled with terror." This power was not entirely negative since a landscape could "rest in his calm perception," animals and birds trusted him, and flowers returned his gaze as they did to little children. The very rumor of such an observer, a seer, stirred up women. In all these cases, the poet shows, even boasts about, how he could will everything to his unique poetic vision.

The poem then begins its transition from the proud declaration of earlier victories to an overriding feeling of doubt. A lonely, anonymous hotel room is evoked along with an air of depression. This is a scene he has been through many times (in fact, Rilke traveled and lived a great deal abroad, often in difficult financial circumstances). He avoids the mirror, perhaps to avoid looking at and into himself. The bed torments him, due not only to its probable poor construction but also to his own doubting consciousness. He is painfully alone with his thoughts and heart—a heart that still beats painfully, desiring to feel love. The poet can no longer avoid his moment of truth: He does not have love in his heart. The turning point of "Turning" comes when the poet realizes the limits of his former successes. He must go forward with himself and his poetry because the world can only mature and be nourished in love. The "work of the eyes is done," and he must now go forth and "do heart-work" on the very images he had earlier submitted to his gaze but still does not truly know. The poem's last lines are a plea for him to look within and learn from the feminine inside himself to discover her multiple natures so that he might finally learn to love.

Forms and Devices

The structure of "Turning" is more difficult to grasp than Rilke's earlier poems, which had regular meter and rhyme patterns. "Turning" has no rhyme pattern and has a very irregular meter, though iambic meter dominates. The stanzas are divided unevenly, the longest containing thirteen lines and the shortest containing one line. This irregular structure is appropriate for "Turning" when one considers that the poem is a criticism of the unemotional, objective vision that the poet now rejects in favor of listening to his emotional side that is striving to be released. A poem that was highly structured, following a strict rhyme and meter pattern, would betray the very purpose of what the poem is trying to say.

One structure that Rilke does use repeatedly in "Turning" is the present participle. Examples abound throughout the poem, including *knieend* (kneeling), *weidende* (grazing), and *ein Schauender* (one watching). This grammatical form has the same effect in German as it does in English; there is a sense of an ongoing process, a flowing movement both in sound and meaning. That this grammatical structure is used in German much less frequently than in English makes it all the more noticeable in the original. When reading the poem aloud, there is little that is musical or rhythmic due to its lack of rhyme and regular meter, but the present participle slows down the language and softens the proselike effect of the poem's message.

One device used frequently in "Turning" is personification (giving human characteristics to animals, inanimate objects, or abstract qualities). The objects that the poet has conquered through his gift of observation take on human characteristics or actions. The stars he mastered with his look "collapsed on their knees," the towers he stared at were "filled with terror," the landscape "sank to rest" in his calming observations, and the flowers "gazed back into him." During the difficult transition period in his art, the rooms he stays in during his wanderings also take on a personality. They are "distracted, alienated, . . . moody," and the very air in the rooms becomes filled with voices discussing his work and, finally, judging it and him to be without love—a judgment that will lead to a crisis and a turning point in his poetry.

Themes and Meanings

"Turning" is more than a poem; it is Rilke's self-critique of his work up to that time and a declaration or manifesto of how he intended to change his vision of poetry. It marks a new stage in his efforts to combine art and life. To understand the change he desired, one must first understand how Rilke saw the world through his writing. His perception revolved around the idea of *Schauen* (observation, seeing, watching), a skill he consciously cultivated that reflected his personal philosophical view of the world. This perspective developed out of his lifelong love of art.

The interest in pictures came early to Rilke, beginning in his childhood with a love of the visual arts. He later studied art history (among other subjects) at universities in Prague and Munich, traveled to Florence (a city rich in art) in order to develop precise observation skills, and, as a young man, lived in the artists' colony at Worpswede near Bremen, Germany. There he became involved with several artists, befriending the painter Paula Modersohn-Becker and marrying the sculptor Clara Westhoff, and developed his skill of observation. Later in Paris he also worked for the sculptor Auguste Rodin, about whom he wrote a monograph. For most of his life he was interested in and exposed to the visual arts and the theories and techniques of artists. He looked at poetry as a craft to be honed and polished.

This artist's vision is evident in the first part of "Turning" as the poet proudly lists his conquests of animals, buildings, nature, even the cosmos while bending the outer world to his will. Then he begins to doubt himself and his method. Rilke wrote that his "gazing outward" had "eaten him empty" and had no true relation with the outside world. He would have to turn completely away from his earlier convictions, which were cold and impersonal, and make "a devoted effort to achieve inner intensity." In the latter half of the poem, he acknowledges the limits of his method of observation and realizes he must begin on a new journey to find love and "do heart-work" on the images he sees. He has suffered through a crisis about himself and his poetry but has successfully turned to a new, inward-looking direction for his future work.

Shoshanah Dietz

28

Author: Philip Levine (1928-   )
Type of poem: Narrative
First published: 1986; collected in *A Walk with Tom Jefferson*, 1988

The Poem

Based on Philip Levine's own experiences when he traveled to California on a fellowship to study with the well-known poet and scholar Yvor Winters, "28" is a long narrative poem. In the opening line, the poet describes himself as twenty-eight years old and faithless, a statement that will be repeated throughout the poem. No exact meaning of faithless is given, forcing the reader to speculate about the poet's intention. He then describes driving across the country while under the almost hallucinatory influence of a fever, seeing birds appear, then vanish, along the roadside.

Time and place are fluid in the poem. Levine shifts back and forth between the present and various time periods in the past. After setting the reader off on the cross-country trip that took place twenty-eight years ago, Levine moves ahead in time to an unspecified period, when he was injured in a motorcycle accident when a station wagon accidentally forced him off California Highway 168 (Tollhouse Road). The description realistically conveys vivid, fragmentary details remembered from the accident: the children's open mouths, the long slide across the asphalt, the motorcycle tumbling away. A sense of mortality and death, which recurs throughout the poem, is first introduced here. This accident is an image that reappears several times, a warning of death. As the section ends, the poet returns to the present and describes how, even today, the scars on his arm return him to the awareness of life's fragility that he first experienced on Tollhouse Road.

The second section continues the trip, through Squaw Valley to the San Francisco area, where narrative details lead to further speculations on mortality. At the beginning of section 3, Levine again returns the reader to the present. It is a gray day in New England. The poet, looking out of his window, watches children outside; once again, his memories slip back to near death on the road. In the fourth section, Levine resumes the trip with his arrival in California and subsequent meeting with Arthur, who is introduced to the reader as he tends his garden, a place where he is "almost happy." (Arthur is the poet Yvor Winters who was Levine's teacher and mentor in California.)

The next two sections describe details of his life in California, recounting his relationship with Winters. He mentions that he is still faithless, not yet part of a family of five, not having received the lesson of the mountain road. The sixth section, which describes Arthur, is poignant. At fifty-six, Arthur sees the Nothingness that waits ahead and deals with it by reciting French Breton poetry.

The final section begins in April, when Levine is twenty-nine and traveling from place to place throughout California, then shifts to the present and the poet's house in New England. He realizes that he is the same person today as he was twenty-eight years ago. He watches the children outside, filled with poetic images of the past and present. He understands them no more now than he did at age twenty-eight; he doesn't know why the accident happened in the past or the why the small blond girl waves at him today.

Forms and Devices

The poem is told in the first person, and the details are clearly autobiographical. In fact, Levine has written a prose account of the same experiences that inspired "28" in an essay, "The Shadow of the Big Madrone." It has been collected in Levine's memoirs, *The Bread Of Time: Toward an Autobiography* (1994). This essay is extremely helpful in understanding the narrative details in "28"; in addition, it gives a glimpse into Levine's poetic process since he includes his first draft of the poem in the essay.

In "28," Levine combines strong, narrative details, which describe the people he meets and the places he travels, with lyrical, almost mystical, language used to describe nature and emotions. His descriptions of nature are rich with metaphor and simile. One evocative metaphor declares that the sea at Bondy Bay, which runs underneath his house in California, possesses the power to erase the "pain of nightmares." Levine begins section 3 with another vivid metaphor describing nature. The sun threatens to withdraw its affection, a bleak image with which the reader can easily identify. Levine, however, extends this image by adding narrative detail in an extended simile. The pale sky becomes "bored" like a "child in the wrong classroom"— or like a man of twenty-eight, who forgets the names of the trees he has been taught (a reference to another incident Levine mentions in "The Shadow of the Big Madrone"). The connection between nature and the poet's emotional state is clear.

Similar connections between autobiographical, narrative detail and poetic imagery describing emotional discoveries fill the poem. In one long sentence stretching over nine lines of poetry, Levine moves from a factual description of writing to his wife to a metaphor comparing the voice of American writer Kenneth Rexroth to the one God uses to lecture to Jesus Christ. He then switches metaphor and theme as he speculates about "the cold that leaps in one blind moment/ from the heart to the farthest shore." He is amazed that he ever believed allergy pills (or any of man's devices) could be proof against the mortality that comes to all nature, even creatures that he never knew existed. Such dazzling combinations of fact, imagery, and emotion keep the reader moving quickly through the varied times and places in the poem. In fact, these rapid shifts in subject, these unexpected mixtures, help to create the emotional power of the poem.

This emotional power is particularly noticeable in the portrait of Arthur/Winters. Levine recreates Winters's voice, ruined and graveled, for the reader. The garden, where he "was almost happy," is filled with "wounded tomatoes" and "elusive strawberries." Such details lead into the fact that the dying Winters is preparing for Nothingness, while reciting Breton poetry.

In his first books, Levine's poetry was formal and metric. He frequently employed a seven-syllable rhymed line. He later, however, experimented with the length of his line. The poem "28" is written in free verse using the natural rhythms of speech. He uses long poetic lines to bind images together, often creating complex pyramids of images.

Themes and Meanings

As Levine combines narrative and lyricism, he also combines themes, incorporating a number of motifs into the poem. It is impossible to ignore his richly detailed snapshots of American life. Levine has frequently been compared with nineteenth century American poet Walt Whitman for his democratic portrayal of working-class America. Indeed, Levine grew up in working-class Detroit and incorporates those experiences into much of his poetry. Like so many of his poems, "28" presents brief, vivid, instant flashes of Americana: towns such as East Palo Alto, home to "divorcees and appliance salesmen" and people such as the Okie Sunoco station attendant on Pacheco Pass.

Levine also intends the poem to be a tribute to Yvor Winters. In the introduction to his memoirs, Levine expresses his need to honor the memory of those persons who helped make him the writer and thinker he became. Clear, narrative details based on Levine's own experiences provide the vital emotional backdrop for "28." For Levine, these portraits are intimately tied with poem's main theme, the inexorable passage of time and the progression to Nothingness. The poem's title refers to Levine's age when he met Winters. Winters, twice that age, was dying. Now that Levine has reached fifty-six, the same age, he reexamines his life and relationship with both Winters and mortality. As the poem returns to Levine's youth, the reader is also shown Winters's preparations for death, the "final cold, a whiteness like no other."

A sense of mortality fills the poem in many other ways. Even before the reader is introduced to Winters, Levine introduces the subject of death. In the first section, when Levine describes his motorcycle accident, he prefaces it with the line, "I have died/ only twice." Death is a constant motif. The Sunoco station attendant warns him that an entire family had been killed on the road the day before. Nature, too, reflects this sense of inevitability. The sea creatures shudder from the cold that travels outward from the poet's heart; the black roses in his backyard are "battered, unclenched."

However, "28" is not a poem about hopelessness and tragedy. Death is seen as part of the natural progression of life. The last line describing Winters proclaims, "he was dying and he was ready." In contrast to Winters's preparations for death, the poet's third child is about to born. Life and death are both present. In the present, the poet, now fifty-six, watches children from his window. The poem ends with a joyous, graceful image as an eight-year-old blond girl waves to the poet before cartwheeling away. Levine no longer repeats the poem's opening line, "I am faithless." Family, relationships, and memories bring faith.

Mary E. Mahony

TWICKNAM GARDEN

Author: John Donne (1572-1631)
Type of poem: Lyric
First published: 1633, in *Poems, by J. D.: With Elegies on the Authors Death*

The Poem

"Twicknam Garden" is a lyric in three unorthodox nine-line stanzas, with five lines in iambic pentameter and four in iambic tetrameter, rhyming *ababbccdd*. It is essentially a compliment poem, a gift to the poet's (theoretical) mistress. Both the persona speaking in the poem and the recipient are participating in a popular social role-playing game of the period. The poet presents himself as emotionally devastated because he cannot stop loving, although his beloved constantly rejects him and even holds him in disdain. The lady, on the other hand, while possessing all the qualities capable of inspiring love, must remain serenely aloof, arousing passion but in no way obligated to respond or even acknowledge it. This is the standard situation of the conventional sonnet sequence. Since Twickenham Park was the principal residence of the Countess of Bedford, one can assume she was the lady.

The poem begins by establishing the poet's emotional situation—"blasted with sighs, and surrounded with tears." The images are more intense than modern readers recognize: The poet compares himself to a winter countryside, torn by winds and immersed in water. He comes to Twickenham Garden for more than relief; he comes for everything that spring, the restorer of life, implies. Here life is restored through the eyes and ears, by seeing and hearing the lady, but even here the poet is caught in a dilemma: The presence of the lady provokes him to declare his love, and that will arouse her anger and his further dismay. Even the greatest pleasure thus turns bitter. He feels like the serpent in Eden, the contradictory element which makes everything else perfect.

The second stanza returns to the image of health. The persona observes that his situation would improve if winter prevailed at Twickenham; then, the contrast between its wholesomeness and his disease would disappear. Realizing that this could be possible only if the garden were destroyed or he left, he asks to be changed into a part of the garden, or even into a weed or a structure. He would fit unobtrusively into a wintry, desolate, mournful situation. He specifically names the mandrake, a plant with a forked root, popularly believed to resemble a human being and to utter a groan when plucked out of the ground; it also has particular sexual connotations, being used in primitive folk rituals to enhance fertility.

In the third stanza, the persona invites all who claim to be lovers to test themselves against him. They should collect samples of his tears in pure vessels to compare with those of their lovers. If the tastes do not match, their mistresses are false. He goes on to observe that since women can manufacture tears at will, their eyes are not true indicators of the state of their hearts. In fact, he says, you can judge a woman's feelings from her eyes about as well as you can judge her costume from her shadow. Women are simply not reasonable beings. Only one of them remains constant; his mistress, and she is constant only in rejecting him.

Forms and Devices

John Donne, the originator of what came to be called Metaphysical poetry—noted for the complexity and difficulty of its figures—is fairly conservative in his use of devices in this poem. Still, much of the imagery is intricate and multilayered, tying together several levels of meaning, and the diction is equally rich. The rhythm of the lines further reinforces the way several meanings are played with simultaneously.

The most obvious technical aspect of the poem is its irregular regularity, to give it the kind of paradoxical name Donne would have liked. That is, the poem is not cast in a standard pattern: The most popular nine-line format is that of the Spenserian stanza, used almost entirely for long narrative poems. Furthermore, no common lyric format mixes tetrameter and pentameter lines as this does. The poem reads as if it were designed to provide evidence to support Ben Jonson's famous assertion that Donne "deserved hanging for not keeping accent." For example, the opening line, supposed to be in iambic pentameter, reads more naturally—in Donne's pronunciation and ours—as an irregular, four-stress line.

Once he establishes this unorthodox format, however, Donne uses it consistently throughout the poem. That is, he treats his irregular pattern as if it were regular. In fact, he stresses its regularity. All three stanzas have identical rhetorical and dialectical structure; they all divide into a four-line unit, a three-line unit, and a concluding couplet. Further, the opening quatrain in all three units presents a positive situation or topic, the middle triplet transforming it by giving it a negative slant, and the final couplet confirming the dilemma. The structure of the poem thus replicates the dominant image of the poem: The lover's chronic unhappiness results from

> The spider love, which transubstantiates all,
> And can convert Manna to gall.

This clever duplication of effect was known as "wit" in Donne's time and was one of the most prized qualities of poetry. It appears throughout the imagery and diction of this poem. The opening, for example, creates an image of a lover "blasted with sighs, and surrounded with tears"—that is, suffering the kind of wind and water damage brought to the surface of the land by winter. This kind of far-fetched connection illustrates exactly what is meant by Metaphysical wit; it requires imaginative audacity. Donne follows it up by bringing the lover to long for spring, which can be seen on four levels: the season of spring, which restores the damages of winter and renews life out of the death of winter; the spring that flows in this garden, maintaining its vegetal life; a medicinal spring, which produces healing waters; and the metaphorical spring, which is the restorative season for lovers. Finally, it becomes the effect of spring in his mistress's appearance and voice.

Other metaphors show the same kind of multiple reference. It is so pervasive that only a few examples need be given here. The richest lode appears in the opening stanza. There, the lover is called a traitor to himself, for he bears "the spider love"—a spider because it catches everything in its web and transforms everything it catches, and because it changes the living into the dead. His love forces him to seek his mistress, for only there can he live, but, like a spider, this love will bring him to the death of her rejection.

Themes and Meanings

The central theme of the poem emerges from the metaphor of love as a spider, transforming everything and ultimately bringing death. Love becomes the ultimate paradox: The lover cannot survive out of the sight of the beloved, but the only response he gets from her is disdain. Part of this problem is simply the conventional pose of the Petrarchan lover, whose mistress, placed on a pedestal, cannot lower herself to notice him; if she could so lower herself, she would no longer be the perfect woman. The only perfect love is the eternally unrequited variety.

Part of Donne's concept, however, penetrates to a deeper level. The persona concludes the first stanza with this figure:

> And that this place may thoroughly be thought
> True Paradise, I have the serpent brought.

Again, the figure begins simply, then becomes complex. The concept of paradise comes easily to mind. Winter and spring coexist here; therefore, paradise must be timeless, beyond the sphere of the temporal. Therefore, this must be the paradise of yet unfallen humankind. The Garden of Eden—the original paradise—also contained the serpent, however; therefore, the snake has to be here, since this is both the lover's paradise and the place from which he will be driven by the disdain of his mistress.

The serpent here is directly associated with sex, partly because of the phallic associations of the snake, but also because in the popular mind the cause of humankind's Fall was sexual indulgence. Donne's deeper theme thus focuses on the incompatibility of sex and love and on the differences between male and female attitudes toward relationships. The lover brings the serpent of sex into paradise: However pure his love, his body is also engaged in love, requiring satisfaction of its own—except that this satisfaction is impossible. The lady lives, acts, and moves on a higher plane of being; only thus can she inspire love. The idea of her condescending to become sexual is almost sacrilegious. True love is doomed to frustration.

Observing that it would be healthier for him if winter were to take over permanently, the poet-lover muses that he would then not have to endure this constant torture of life in death, this state in which even the trees mock him—for they are fertile and flowering, and, metaphorically, are the trees of life and the knowledge of good and evil, which humankind inherited in the Fall. By the Fall, humankind became aware of sin, and, in Donne's time, sex was considered inherently sinful. The lover could evade this only by being transformed to something less than man—"some senseless piece of this place." In the final stanza, women consequently become the "perverse sex," because they evoke love but reject its basis in sexuality.

James Livingston

THE TWINS

Author: Charles Bukowski (1920-1994)
Type of poem: Elegy
First published: 1960, in *Flower, Fist and Bestial Wail*

The Poem

"The Twins" is a forty-three-line poem written in free verse and loosely divided into four parts, within which there are several stanzaic forms. The title is not intended to help readers anticipate the matter of the poem; rather, it facilitates a moment of unanticipated recognition in the last quarter when one realizes that the twins alluded to are in fact the poet and the poet's father.

Many readers will recognize the familiar division between a parent and child, where, as in this case, father and son rebuke each other for not honoring the other's values. The father wants the son to honor mother, country, and right behavior, and the son wants the father to be less somber and to learn to enjoy life. This state of affairs remains the same until the father dies.

The past tense, used in the first part or stanza, reflects the poet's memory of the problem between them. The rest of the poem is written in the present tense, which supports the "here and now" of his dutiful inspection of his father's personal effects. He sees "dead shoes," "dead cigarettes," and the "last bed he slept in." He is temporarily heartened to see that the manner of his father's death ("in the kitchen at 7 am/ while others are frying eggs") was not such a bad way to go, unless it had been his own death, and the poet then is faced with his own mortality.

That unhappy thought sends him outdoors, and the third stanza finds Charles Bukowski examining life outside his father's house. He picks an orange, notices the growing grass, a barking dog, people peeking at him from behind closed doors, and the life-sustaining sun in the sky. The estranged son's reputation as a scoundrel apparently preceded him, for he finds himself to be a stranger in this neighborhood. He hears that what might have been his own legacy was left to some "woman in Duarte," but Bukowski does not "give a damn" because the undeniable, central point at hand is that his father died. The consequences beyond his own personal grief are of no interest to him.

Faced again with the simple, awful fact of his father's death, his last respects are paid in the fourth section by donning one of his father's coats and "flapping the arms like a scarecrow in the wind." It is a bizarre image that secures the notion of the twins as ironic, for the father and son seem to be more dissimilar than similar. They may have looked "exactly alike," but they were also estranged by virtue of their differences, and now the remaining "twin" is unable to walk in the other's footsteps, or wear his coat. The image of the scarecrow, the surrogate watchman over a field of corn, ushers in the dreadful realization that not even the heartfelt disdain that bound the two together is adequate to keep him alive.

Forms and Devices

Free verse is free in that it does not force the poet's ideas into a prearranged metrical or rhymed pattern, but it is not so free that the poet can forget rhythm and stress altogether. To do that would indeed leave the world with prose. Rhythmic movement either assists or impedes the advance of the narrative. In "The Twins," the uncontrollable nature of grief is reflected in the relatively fluid nature of free verse.

The opening section of the poem depicts a tired argument, one that has been rehearsed over and over, and it is jammed together in a rush of prose. The second and third stanzas consist of long lines, each of which generally addresses advancing points in the narrative: "I move through . . ."; "I go outside. . . ." Images of life (seeds, bulbs) and of death (scarecrow) mingle uneasily; at the end of each of the four sections, the poet sees the stark reality of death, and the verse in each stanza shrinks, leaving death conspicuously alone. "He was my old/ man/ and he died." The line lengths shorten relentlessly until in the fourth section there are three stanzas of progressively fewer lines. The poem ends with two syllables: "to die." This gradual constriction of the line reinforces this inevitable final unadorned act of life.

The figure of the twins, while standing literally for the father and son, also stands for the old and the new, the traditional and the contemporary. The poem is an elegy, a modern rendering of an ancient form. A common characteristic of the elegy is expressions of melancholy at the loss of a close friend, as seen in John Milton's "Lycidas." The Christian elegy often ponders the justice of the loss, the mortality of the poet, and it reiterates consolations, often of a life hereafter, as seen in Percy Bysshe Shelley's *Adonais* (1821) and Alfred, Lord Tennyson's *In Memorium* (1850).

It has already been noted that Bukowski mourns the death of his father and faces his own mortality. What of justice and consolation, though? In this little poem one century later, Bukowski seems to be Tennyson's literary heir. In *In Memorium*, Tennyson consoled himself by maintaining a kind of blind faith in a God who was made less apparent by the advances of scientific knowledge ("believing where we cannot prove"). He saw a clockwork universe running by its own rules and a sun in that universe that was burning out.

There is no God in Bukowski's world, and few illusions, but he finds consolation in life itself, in the bright skin of an orange, growing grass, and any living thing. When he looks up "the sun sends down its rays circled by a Russian satellite." This sun is the life giver and sustainer and is in no danger of diminishing. That satellite, however, was the successor to the great explorations of the past, and it was the product of the industrial and scientific revolutions of the nineteenth century that so dismayed Tennyson. The launch of Sputnik in 1957 fostered the worst fears of the Cold War in America. Amid fears of Russian expansionism, Americans imagined unparalleled terrors with Russia ruling the skys. Given the horrors of modern technology and modern warfare, one might begin to see why listening to Hector Berlioz and drinking could be a less painful alternative.

Themes and Meanings

Bukowski is no stranger to the seamier side of life, in Los Angeles and elsewhere. He has been the familiar of junkies and drunks as well as of many artists of his and later generations. He has said that at one point in his life, he quit writing and stayed drunk for ten years, and it was after that long binge that he started writing poetry. Alcohol is a recurrent motif in his poetry. The poet John Ciardi, while poetry editor of *The New Yorker*, commented that he could detect the ingestion of "a sip of sherry" in any poem. The tone of the fourth part of "The Twins" is just maudlin enough to be motivated, at least in part, by alcohol. Remember that Bukowski advised his father to "learn to paint and drink," and in another poem, "Counsel," he claims that drink maintains continuance because "drink is a form of suicide/ wherein the partaker returns to a new chance/ at life."

No condemnation is intended here, for in every age people look to visionaries and madmen to correct their own vision. One only need point to John Lennon, Timothy Leary, and William Burroughs as examples of men who have taken drugs to cut through the trappings of the routine, anxiety, or pain of modern life. One can be grateful to those who do so and pass on their experiences as poetry or other forms of expression: It shows everyone else how to survive or how to save themselves from the direct experience.

Bukowski readers may never know which came first: the drinking or the pain. They can see a certain delicacy of touch and plain dignity in the raw quality of life he leads. With humor, he realizes, for example, that his father probably "painted" rather well the seedy life of the scoundrel son. If the reader is feeling generous, the analogy drawn between his father's fall bulbs sitting on a screen ready for planting and the son planting his seed with a whore from Third Street may actually be a moment of self-deprecation in favor of the life-giving leanings of his father. In any other context, it simply would be a bad joke. Moreover, the more one is able to see that even though some form of reconciliation was never possible (perhaps never even wished for) between father and son, there was still a basic bond between them that this poem acknowledges: "A father is always your master, even when he's gone." This filial respect is one of the few authenticities in life. "Very well, grant us this moment," Bukowski says to the universe. Looking in the mirror at the twins, the ludicrous image of himself dressed in his father's coat, he too is waiting to die.

Barry Crawford

TWO POEMS ON THE PASSING OF AN EMPIRE

Author: Derek Walcott (1930-   )
Type of poem: Meditation
First published: 1962, in *In a Green Night: Poems, 1948-1960*

The Poem

As the title indicates, these are two poems about the passing of an empire: first the Roman, then the British. For Derek Walcott, the linking of the two imperial powers, however disparate they might seem, stresses the repetitive nature of history; in several other poems, he draws the same comparison, viewing the Roman conquest of the Mediterranean as analogous to the British domination of the Caribbean.

Born on the Caribbean island of Saint Lucia, Walcott grew up during the fading days of the British Empire. Of African descent, he received a British education and learned "the English tongue I love"—as he says in another poem, "A Far Cry from Africa" (1962). In that poem, he asks the question common to postcolonial writers, especially those who are not of British descent but whose language is English: "Where shall I turn, divided in the vein?" A one-time colonial subject himself, Walcott can empathize with those who in earlier days lived under "Rome's trampling feet." Thus the two poems become a single work, for the title does not announce "the Passing of Empires," but "the Passing of an Empire."

Poem 1, when read without the parenthetical statement, simply presents an image of a heron, not a particularly graceful bird in flight, landing on a stump and disturbing the "quiet with a caw"—a hoarse and unpleasant bird sound. Within the parenthesis, the heron is linked somehow to the Roman Empire. Possibly, Walcott had in mind an obscure classical poem that depicts the heron as a traitor bird; according to that tradition, the ancient armies watched for herons feeding in shallow water and thereby determined where the soldiers might safely cross into the city they intended to invade. "Thank God," the poet says, those days have passed.

Poem 2 takes a more concrete approach by presenting a specific example of imperial folly. Although it is only hinted at, it seems that Walcott is depicting a West Indian—most likely of African descent—who had served in the English army during World War I; after all, the mother country relied in both world wars on its far-flung subjects to defend the "Emerald Isle" against the enemy. One-eyed and one-armed, "the pensioner, a veteran," hears a new generation of colonials singing the words of the usurper's anthem; "Rule, Britannia, rule." The old man then wonders whether the boys would believe what he might reveal about the futility of spilling blood for Empire, only to gain "such a poor flag as an empty sleeve."

The two poems blend into one: The herons no longer signal to the "trampling feet," and the arrogant words "Rule, Britannia, rule" diminish in power. The time of Empire has passed.

Forms and Devices

Although didactic in nature, "Two Poems on the Passing of an Empire" avoids the pitfalls of some moralistic poetry by utilizing an indirect presentation of ideas by means of imagistic and metaphoric devices.

The simplicity of the opening image of the heron flying, braking, then decorating a stump, at first belies its importance in the overall meaning of the poem's two parts. Without the five lines in parentheses, the image figures as a pure and striking depiction of this rare bird—and nothing more. Yet the poet's parenthetical interruption cannot be ignored, since in it he links the bird with the Roman Empire. The heron in the completing line no longer serves as the emblem of Rome's conquest, but acts as the harbinger who announces, "underline[s]," the "Passing of an Empire."

In the second poem, Walcott switches technique and draws an extended metaphor riddled with words conjuring up death: first the deathlike existence of the pensioner, then the "passing" of Empire. The old man lives in a house that resembles a "coffin," where the specter of death hovers over him. He is stooped and appears to be "threading an eternal needle." Like a "grave" he is one-eyed. His head is called a "skull," his single eye oozes "balsam" (oily secretions), and his jaw is "doddering" (feeble, senile). The allusions to death continue as he listens to the children singing and thinks of them practicing "to play dead," to "pour their blood out."

The final simile—"such a poor flag as an empty sleeve"—plays first on the veteran's physical state, his arm obviously lost in the war. Then Walcott dares to extend the analogy by suggesting that the British flag is as useless and pathetic as a sleeve hanging empty, purpose and meaning lost in both cases. After all, the poet is speaking here of the hallowed "Union Jack," the cloth symbol of the British Empire on which once the sun never set.

On the one hand, Walcott makes effective use of a number of poetic devices to show that the veteran's ruined life stands for the cruelty and injustice that imperialism dealt its subjects. On the other hand, by introducing the children naïvely singing the conqueror's anthem and by having the half-dead veteran responding negatively to their innocent games, the poet suggests—but does not say—that Empire is dying and young lives may no longer be touched by its excesses. While poem 1 celebrates the demise of the Roman Empire, announced by the raucous shriek of the heron, poem 2 predicts the coming end of colonial loyalty to England, that loyalty symbolized by an empty, dangling sleeve.

This poem is one of Walcott's earlier works. Although lacking some of the elegance, polish, and complexity that characterize the later poetry, it effectively introduces the theme of Empire's sad legacy, a theme to be treated in varied ways again and again throughout Walcott's extensive poetic output over the years. Furthermore, the poem, although an apprentice work, demonstrates the lucidity, the free rhythms, subtle allusiveness, rich imagery, and overall mastery of poetic technique that distinguish all of Walcott's work.

Themes and Meanings

Walcott is certainly no apologist for the history of British imperialism, as this poem and others prove. Still, his stand should not be construed as revolutionary or radical. For example, when his highly successful play, *Dream on Monkey Mountain* (1967), was published in 1970, he wrote in the introduction to it and other plays that he was not advocating a movement back to Africa but considered such political discourse a kind of fantasy. He does not believe that those coming out of the colonial experience should shackle themselves with hatred and bitterness toward their former oppressors.

Walcott considers it wrong to use literature for political purposes or for revenge, because for him such motivation obstructs the art itself. He has criticized some Third World literature for setting out to exorcise the demon of colonial history and to get even with the former oppressor. Needless to say, many radical Third World writers and critics consider Walcott a traitor to their cause. Walcott has argued, though, that mastering the conqueror's language and literary heritage is the greatest form of revenge. Answering those detractors who say that this mastery amounts to nothing more than mimicry, Walcott has pointed out that when victims can name, can express themselves, can reveal their own truths, can establish their identity in the torturer's language and make use of that language's literature, then they emerge victorious. Even more, theirs is an ironic victory.

Certainly, no one will dare to call Walcott a mimic. The descendant of African slaves brought to the Caribbean to work on the sugar plantations, with a British sailor somewhere in his background, Walcott has learned to name in the imposed language, and to do so splendidly and originally. A work such as "Two Poems on the Passing of an Empire" writes back to the imperial center in its own language and makes use of that language's poetic devices to reveal the injustice meted out to colonial subjects.

The poem functions on a larger scale, however, because neither revenge nor revolution motivates the poet. His is a concern with ways in which humankind might save itself from perpetuating its folly, repeating its mistakes, pouring out the blood of its young for a flag that is no more meaningful than an empty sleeve. It is especially significant that Walcott does not treat the British Empire alone but in a historical perspective alongside the Roman Empire. By establishing this analogy, he enlarges the poem so that it transcends the political treatise, the catalog of imperial wrongs, the exorcism of history. Instead, the poem calls for a revolution that will bring about the union of humankind, regardless of origin, color, nationality, religion, and any other irrelevancies the "empty sleeve" of a flag might represent.

Robert L. Ross

TWO TRAMPS IN MUD TIME

Author: Robert Frost (1874-1963)
Type of poem: Lyric
First published: 1934; collected in *A Further Range,* 1936

The Poem

Robert Frost's well-known poem "Two Tramps in Mud Time" is made up of tightly rhymed (*ababcdcd*) iambic tetrameter lines; nevertheless, the nine stanzas sound relaxed and anecdotal. The speaker/poet tells of a moment during the Depression when two tramps caught him in his backyard and challenged him briefly on an ethical point: Presumably, there are needy workers who chop wood for a living, and Frost is "playing" with another person's work. At the very worst, he is stealing a job from someone.

The poem begins with the sudden appearance of the two strangers, who pause to watch Frost at the block; one stays behind a moment and jeers at his efforts. The poet, by his own telling, is not at all awkward with an ax and has been enjoying up to now his own skill and strength. Almost half the poem—stanzas 3, 4, 5, and 6—is devoted to a pastoral diversion from the unpleasant incident as Frost tells with precision how a New England April is really "May" one moment and "March" the next—first lovely and then wicked. Nothing is in bloom yet; a single bird is trying out his first notes, although seeming to use his song to warn the awaiting buds not to be fooled by the temporary warmth. The poet knows what a time he will have come summer, when he will be looking for water with a divining rod, but for right now it is "mud time": Every "wheelrut" is a brook. Whole ponds form in a hoofprint, and when one turns one's back the frost shows its "crystal teeth." This mud-time setting is part of what makes the appearance of the tramps memorable and almost mythic-sounding. "Out of the mud," "Out of the woods," they come—to challenge the speaker's rights.

The speaker clearly knows his rights, but he is rattled, perhaps hurt and angered, at being made light of by a drifter. Most of the issues are in the poet's own mind and soul, because he seeks to know why he feels so strongly. His conclusion is summarizing and aphoristic in a way characteristic of Frost. He concludes that he has hit on a matter vital to everything for which he stands: "My object in living is to unite/ My avocation and my vocation." The poem's last stanza resembles a homily; the sharply worded sentiment seems worthy of one's taking it entirely to heart. Few poets move more fluently between the small happenstances of life and their larger truths.

Forms and Devices

Frost's noted skill is fully demonstrated in the rhymes and the loose yet breathtakingly subtle iambs found in "Two Tramps in Mud Time." So "easy" is the poet with his craft that one can read volumes of his work without ever sensing any strain to make the rhyme and meter work. One need only note here where the four stresses fall in each line to see how free Frost remains within what are tight metrical constraints in the hands of less-deft poets. At a time in modern American poetry when poets such as William Carlos Williams were insisting that poets break free of the tyranny of the iambic foot, Frost set a powerful precedent. He made new discoveries for formal meter precisely when Williams thought it was safe to decry it.

Despite his skills, Frost feared he would never be taken seriously in the academic community. He ended up widely honored and widely read, but he complained, sometimes without strong evidence, that critics thought him an anachronism in the "free-verse" scene. No doubt the break from the iamb changed poetry for all time, but fortunately Frost underestimated the academic community's ability to value him. Important critical work on Frost continues alongside work on poets who for a time were believed to be more important for the second half of the twentieth century. In the time lapsing since Emily Dickinson, none but Frost found such boundless ways of using ordinary American speech, New England vernacular, and formal meter in so fine a poetic outpouring.

Frost was perhaps most fond of the pentameter line. When adopted in blank verse, the pentameter line is thought to approximate ordinary spoken English. In "Two Tramps in Mud Time," Frost shows that he can also make colloquial sounds in the shorter tetrameter line. When rhymed, the four-beat line calls for the rhymed word to appear a stroke faster than in pentameter lines. The shorter the line, the more difficult it is to sound as perfectly natural and at home as Frost does here.

Themes and Meanings

Some might argue that Frost has set up a straw man type of argument in this poem—that he has set up two bitter tramps merely to knock down their position with his own. A quick reading proves the two tramps fairly unimportant figures in the larger poetic narrative. Yet the poem is a great favorite, and it is important to discover the ways this poem extends beyond mere rhetoric.

First, Frost portrays accurately the mixed emotions of both outrage and embarrassment at being jeered at by those at the bottom of the social ladder. Frost's account of himself reminds the reader how shaky the ground can feel beneath one's feet when one suddenly gets a catcall from one's vulnerable, blind side. Nothing shows people exactly how isolated they are from those of other social orders than when sudden, unsociable contact is made. From the point of view of the landed gentry, Frost's poem captures this emotion almost instantly. Another emphasis is set into motion by the third stanza, however, a new emphasis that allows Frost to get somewhere deeper, to matters of the soul.

Frost's long digression about the season of April and its peculiar blend of winter and spring is actually a demonstration of what it is he does in the working world. This piece of pure poetry is Frost earning his keep, so to speak. He splits April as cleanly as anyone splitting a stick of oak, displaying his prowess as a wordsmith. Everything he hits with his ax falls on each side of him—nothing missed and nothing in excess. Readers are asked to judge Frost by his "appropriate tool." Once he is sure that he has shown the reader his skill, he can return to the encounter with the tramp.

Frost alludes to depths greater than those normally plumbed in the matter of the economic depression of the 1930's. Hard times aside, what is truly destructive in a nation's troubles is the undermining of human values. By implication, his original idea of "mud time" expands to include a murky moment in American history. He pleads that citizens not yield to an unnatural split between love and work. "Vocation" should not, by Frost's own logic, have a connotation all that different from "avocation." Each is a calling, and, in Western religions, callings come from outside the self; there are many famous Old and New Testament calls from God. Frost is a secularist of such spiritual heritage. Here, his reference to his two eyes "mak[ing] one in sight" is both spiritual and a completion of a theme begun with himself (two-footed) hitting his single mark. The tramp presents an occasion to state that there are no important deeds done without the unity of love and need. Frost has tried to "prove" himself integrated in love and need by his having forged this very poem out of his experience both with wood and words. He has strived in the poem to hit and expose the "mortal stakes" buried within his brief encounter. Frost knew what the stakes were from the beginning, and his job has been to make the reader believe the stakes are as high as his line "For Heaven and the future's sakes" suggests and to entwine in several ways the ideas of love and need. At the end of the poem, it is difficult to pull those words apart or to give one concept a higher value than the other. The poem is a proving ground for the entwining as well of idea and craft. Idea is carried in the flow of thought, and craft is manifest in the ease of his meter. Readers cannot easily separate them, because each so clearly takes some of its strength from the other. So it must be with the concepts of need and love. A division between them is more rhetorical than real. The division between them disappears when the one finds its beginning in the other.

Beverly Coyle

THE TYGER

Author: William Blake (1757-1827)
Type of poem: Lyric
First published: 1794, in *Songs of Innocence and of Experience*

The Poem

"The Tyger" is a short lyric poem of twenty-four lines that asks, without giving explicit answers, how an all-perfect God responsible for innocence and goodness can be the creator of violence and evil. Its questions are unanswerable, for they search a realm altogether beyond human understanding. Divine creation occurs outside time and place through a being who is, by definition, incomprehensible and worthy of the childlike wonder expressed by the poem's speaker before the terrible beauty of a dark, alien reality.

That William Blake envisioned all reality as a duality of light and dark, peace and violence, good and evil, and innocence and experience is indicated by the full title of the volume in which "The Tyger" appeared: *Songs of Innocence and of Experience, Shewing the Two Contrary States of the Human Soul.* According to Blake's private mythology, the ideal is an artistically and imaginatively unified humanity (or cosmos) harmonizing the contraries, which, in this volume of his poetry, are split into psychological realms of innocence (vulnerable to victimization by a stifling adult world) and of experience (a fallen world of suffering, evil, and division). Thus, instead of an integrated primal human being, there is in this volume a poem of innocence entitled "The Lamb" juxtaposed to its contrary, "The Tyger," arguably the greatest and most cryptic lyric poem in Blake's entire literary canon.

The poem begins with a childlike speaker directly addressing a tiger and receiving no answers to repeated questions about its creation. The first three quatrains describe the beast in terms of a frightening beauty: The tiger is a fiery, luminescent intrusion in the dark forests of the world of experience; it is paradoxically frightening and well-proportioned; its eyes burn ferociously; its heart smoulders with pent-up energy; and its feet evoke dread. The poem asks how a being of divine might ("hand") and divine design ("eye") could create this terrible beauty (lines 3-4). In what primordial deep or mysterious steep (as in the Genesis account of the universe's creation) did the being fashion this fiery beast? Where did the being get the rebellious pride of a Satan, a Daedalus, or a Prometheus to defy the natural order of things and seize the fire engendering this monstrous creature? What kind of strength ("shoulder"), artistry ("art"), and force ("hand") moulded the dreadful beauty into existence (lines 9-12)?

The fourth quatrain depicts the Creator as an omnipotent blacksmith keeping the beast under rein with a "chain" as the Creator fashioned its mind and yet remained supremely impervious to its terror (lines 13-16). The fifth quatrain is the most difficult to decipher and continues to stress the being's transcendent omnipotence through an obscure reference to God's victory over the rebellious angels in John Milton's *Para-*

dise Lost (1667). The defeated rebel angels become transmuted into stars surrendering their spears in shower-producing tears (Blake's contemporaries called shooting stars "angel tears"). The all-powerful being paradoxically created this evil and destroyed it, in the same way that this being made the lamb (see Blake's poem of that title) and its opposite, the tiger (lines 19-20).

How can this be? The final quatrain repeats the first quatrain with haunting effect to deny readers an easy answer to this question, yet it suggests that the creation of evil by the Creator of goodness is true and beautiful, even if the divine paradox is beyond human comprehension.

Forms and Devices

"The Tyger" consists of six quatrains, each with couplet rhymes and a rapid singsong meter of three trochaics and one stressed sound in every line ("Týgĕr! Týgĕr! búrnĭng brĭght"). Consonance and assonance are pronounced, especially in the repetition of *s* and long *i* sounds throughout the poem. The complex sound system has the incantatory effect of a visionary nursery rhyme, with a childlike speaker probing very adult questions about the ultimate meaning of what remains the mystery of reality.

Like other songs of innocence and experience, "The Tyger" is a miracle of compressed metaphor, word usage, and symbol that explode into a multiple suggestiveness helping the poem attempt to perform the impossible, to apprehend the ineffable, and to rest in wonder before the inscrutable spectacle of a Creator of contraries, of unity supreme over dualities and contradictions.

Compressed metaphors equate the Creator to a blacksmith (lines 13-16) and equate the creation of the tiger to the reckless daring of archetypal rebels such as Satan and Daedalus, who stormed the heavens on wings, or Prometheus, who stole fire from the gods to give light and warmth to the human race (lines 7-8). Compressed word usage (in, for example, line 10) generates the double meaning of a Creator fashioning a heart out of twisted sinew and knotting up the heart to produce pent-up energy in the tiger. Blake's ellipsis (the deletion of words to the bare minimum needed for communication) pervades the description of the tiger's traits and the Creator's attributes. Compressed allusions to Milton's conquered rebel angels, to the Genesis account of primordial Creation, and to Blake's "The Lamb" occur in the fifth quatrain to underscore the paradoxical omnipotence of the Creator.

Finally, the tiger itself is a famous example of a compressed and evocative symbol. Blake was a painter-engraver who added colored pictures to accompany the texts of many of the poems in *Songs of Innocence and of Experience*. Since "The Tyger" included a small painted representation of a four-footed "symmetrical" animal, a reader's contemplation of the tiger symbol involved both reading and seeing it. The visual and printed symbol of the tiger has an immense complexity of meaning. The tiger signifies more than evil; it also suggests a mysterious, passionate, and violent beauty at odds with the pat, peaceful innocence of its contrary, the symbol of the lamb in Blake's complementary poem. At the time of the French Revolution, the tiger was popularly conceived as a symbol of revolution. Blake welcomed the French Revolution and might have intended his tiger to be a symbol of something more than repellent evil. The tiger is, although terrifying, part of God's all-beautiful creation, beyond the human ability to comprehend completely.

Themes and Meanings

"The Tyger" is about the divinity and mysterious beauty of all creation and its transcendence of the limited human perspective of good and evil that the miseries of human experience condition one to assume. Divine creation occurs outside time and place through a being who is, by definition, inscrutable and worthy of the childlike wonder expressed by the poem's speaker. Humans see contraries and find evil awful; God created the contraries and pronounced them both beautiful.

"The Tyger" is a Blakean song of experience that is to be contrasted with its contrary song of innocence, entitled "The Lamb." Questions also recur in "The Lamb": "Little Lamb, who made thee?/ Dost thou know who made thee?" That poem, however, answers the questions it poses with a simple, almost pat affirmation that the Lamb of God—the Poet-Christ of the realm of innocence—became an innocent to make all humanity innocent in His own image and thereby made all those who are meek and mild worthy of God's blessing:

> He is callèd by thy name,
> For he calls himself a Lamb:
> He is meek & he is mild,
> He became a little child:
> I a child & thou a lamb,
> We are callèd by his name.

By contrast, "The Tyger" contains no explicit answers to ultimate questions, although some answers are implicit precisely because of the absence of answers. The mystery of reality does not lend itself to simple, pat formulations of everyday statements. If the poem "The Lamb" excludes all terror and complexity from life and finds only gentleness and mildness, then "The Tyger" rejects such simplemindedness and opposes a doubleness under a Creator of mercy and aggressiveness, peace and violence, and good and evil, all of which are subsumed in a divine beauty beyond limited human power to grasp fully as a unity. The very concept of the tiger's "fearful symmetry" is a paradox of terrifying richness and terrible beauty that is difficult for the human imagination to apprehend—but not for the divine imagination to create.

Thomas M. Curley

ULALUME

Author: Edgar Allan Poe (1809-1849)
Type of poem: Ballad
First published: 1847, as "To——. Ulalume: A Ballad"; collected in *The Works of Edgar Allan Poe*, 1849

The Poem

"Ulalume" is a dreamlike ballad of 104 lines. It presents a psychologically divided poet in conflict with his soul over a temptation to escape the memory of his dead lover, Ulalume, by pursuing new love and new hope under the influence of Astarte, the moon goddess. The soul, however, forcibly calling the poet's attention to lost Ulalume, reunites with the poet in rejecting the temptation to abandon sorrow by remaining faithful to the melancholy memory of the dead beauty.

"Ulalume" first appeared in the *American Review* in 1847, two years after the same magazine published Edgar Allan Poe's more famous "The Raven." The two poems together helped to secure Poe's reputation as a poet in his own time and, along with the rest of his poetic canon, had an immense impact on European poets who believed in "art for art's sake," especially his champion, Charles Baudelaire, and fellow French aesthetes. These two poems became standard declamation pieces in American schools in the late nineteenth and early twentieth centuries, and thereby served to introduce generations of Americans to their first sampling of poetry. As W. H. Auden remarked in his introduction to *Edgar Allan Poe: Selected Prose and Poetry* (1966), "Ulalume" is worth reading because it "could have been written by none but Poe," who pours into the verses his typical Gothic subject matter, phantasmagoric setting, and psychological themes.

The poem opens with a male speaker in a state of dreaming akin to sleepwalking. He passes through an autumnal nightmare, the "ghoul-haunted" region of "Weir," by a Lake Auber, just before the dawn, on a very special ("immemorial") October day of his life. Walking beside his female Psyche, or soul, the speaker recalls that his heart was as passionately divided as the lava-flowing ("scoriac") hot volcano on "Mount Yaanek" at the freezing North Pole. Of one mind in their melancholy weariness, they are both too emotionally preoccupied to notice what will turn out to be tragically familiar surroundings.

Suddenly, the new moon of Astarte, a Phoenician fertility goddess, rises splendidly before their sight as it crosses the constellation Leo in its circuit through the melancholy heavens. The teary-eyed speaker prefers this warm moon goddess to Diana, the cold Roman goddess of the moon, who perhaps represents the cold and dead Ulalume subliminally in his grief-stricken mind. Astarte is seductive, because she offers Love and lights a path to the oblivion-giving waters of the River Lethe, which can end his preoccupation with Death by obliterating his obsessive memory of the lost Ulalume.

Psyche, his soul, in an agony of terror that causes her wings to droop, warns the speaker to beware of pallid Astarte (lines 51 through 60). This warning is at first ignored by the speaker, who considers Astarte a welcome escape to Hope and Beauty and a beacon to Heaven, far from the morbid melancholy engulfing his lovelorn life. Just as he thinks himself successful in winning over a doubtful Psyche with his kiss, he and Psyche arrive at Ulalume's tomb: They have returned to the very place where they formerly buried his beloved. As a consequence of this realization, the powers of dream cannot tempt him to forsake his sorrowful fidelity to his lost beloved, and he unites with his soul in resisting the Hell-inspired invitation of Astarte to escape his melancholy devotion to the dead Ulalume.

Forms and Devices

"Ulalume" is a ballad consisting of ten stanzas of varying length, averaging ten lines. The rhyme scheme is not always uniform, but each stanza does concentrate on two rhyming sounds to a hypnotic, incantatory degree. There is also regular use of feminine rhyme, which repeats the weaker sound in a polysyllabic final word of a line ("sober," "October," "Auber").

The prevailing meter of the poem is anapestic trimeter with variations, a sound system that lends rapidity and musicality to a poem heavily dependent on incantatory effects of tone and mood for its success. The lines are filled with alliteration, the repetition of consonant sounds in a line ("The skies they were ashen and sober"), and assonance, the repetition of vowel sounds. Poe was fond of alliterating liquid sounds (*l* and *r*) as well as *m* and long *o* for a trilling and organlike musicality. He also notably repeated words, phrases, and almost whole lines within and between stanzas for the sake of imparting an obsessively incantatory effect. The very name "Ulalume," in itself alliterative, echoes the evocative Latin word *ululare*, meaning "to moan or lament." Such devices seduce the reader's ear into entering the phantasmagoric nightmare region of Poe's hallucinatory poetry.

Poe's vague, fantastic scene-painting cooperates with the poem's musicality to create a dreamy nightmare setting for the speaker's melancholy journey of escape and return to the memory of Ulalume. The place names "Auber," "Weir," and "Mount Yaanek" existed nowhere but in Poe's highly developed imagination, but they effectively suggest a no-man's-land of night and nightmare in which the speaker and his Psyche can play out their melancholy debate and eventual integration.

The speaker and his Psyche are on an archetypal journey of separation and then unification, as the divided self of the poet-speaker searches and finds oneness of artistic being in the melancholy celebration of lost love.

Noting that the only reality for Poe was supernal in character, C. M. Bowra, in *The Romantic Imagination* (1961), singled out Poe's vagueness as the distinctive feature of his artistry: "Poe's belief that vagueness is essential to poetry gave to his work its most characteristic quality. No doubt through it he hoped to hypnotize his readers into a trance, and for this reason he uses words as an incantation."

Pope's love of hypnotic, incantatory effects helps to explain his choice of a ballad form for "Ulalume." A folk ballad is a popular, short narrative poem of a legendary or traditional event in simple stanzas having a repeated melody. Like Samuel Taylor Coleridge's "The Rime of the Ancient Mariner," Poe's "Ulalume" transforms the folk ballad into a preternatural poem describing dreamlike states of mind, but retains the repetitious melodic refrains of the genre to assist in transporting readers to a realm of phantasmagoric beauty.

Themes and Meanings

"Ulalume" is about a poet's divided self wanting to escape from sorrowful devotion to dead beauty, but finding psychic integration in fidelity to the dead beauty that lies at the heart of his melancholy artistic identity.

This theme can be interpreted on several interrelated levels. On a biographical level, the theme reflects a crisis point in Poe's life, a time when he was troubled by illness and alcoholism, poverty, literary quarrels, and the death of his child bride, Virginia Clemm, a first cousin who had married him in 1835 at the age of thirteen and died at the beginning of 1847, shortly before the composition of "Ulalume." The poem no doubt reflects Poe's depression and yearning for his dead wife.

On a deeper psychological level, the theme reflects Poe's characteristic probing of the psychic dynamics of his own artistic creation. Like a psychiatrist, Poe explores a dream state, a nightmare, with all its fantastic symbols of the divided self seeking escape from the melancholy preoccupations of his peculiar artistic identity, and finally accepting this identity through fidelity to the vision of dead beauty and lost love. In resisting escape from the core of his artistic sensibility, the poet-speaker and his Psyche (the Romantic anima, or soul, of the artist) achieve the oneness of being, or psychic integration, necessary for artistic creation. Such psychological probing of the artist's creating mind recurs throughout Poe's canon, including certain short stories, such as "The Fall of the House of Usher." Often, Poe is ultimately writing about himself; he is, after all, a Romantic egotist in his writing.

On a purely literary level, the theme reflects preoccupations of the European Romantic movement, such as a wandering Byronic hero unlucky in love, and an interest in the Gothic supernatural. "Ulalume," in fact, illustrates a Romantic theory of poetry that Poe summarized (in self-defense) in his well-known essay on "The Raven," entitled "The Philosophy of Composition."

In this essay, Poe sets forth the following criteria for effective poetry: It should be original but carefully contrived for maximum effect on the reader's mind. It should be no longer than one hundred lines, readable in one sitting, to produce the maximum effect. It should capture beauty, to elevate the reader's soul, and not aim at truth for the reader's intellect, or morality for the reader's conscience, or mere passion for the reader's heart. As European practitioners of "art for art's sake" would agree later, poetry is the servant of beauty, which to Poe implied a special, melancholy subject:

Melancholy is thus the most legitimate of all poetical tones. . . . Of all melancholy topics, what . . . is the *most* melancholy? Death. . . . When it most closely allies itself to *Beauty*, the death, then, of a beautiful woman, is, unquestionably, the most poetical topic in the world—and equally it is beyond doubt that the lips best suited for such topic are those of a bereaved lover.

"Ulalume" adheres to all these poetic strictures, which Poe had applied to a very similar poem, "The Raven." "Ulalume" is so original as to be bizarre, yet is so fully conceived in its musicality and dreary description as to work its spell on the reader's mind. Its length is approximately one hundred lines, concentrating its haunting effect. Finally, it is not primarily didactic, moralizing, or straightforwardly an emotional love poem. Instead, it is an evocative celebration of melancholy beauty, honoring elegiacally the death of a beautiful woman and attempting to draw the reader into the supernal dream realm of the poet and his poetic soul. "Ulalume" does not mean; it is a mood and an intense state of being.

Thomas M. Curley

ULYSSES

Author: Alfred, Lord Tennyson (1809-1892)
Type of poem: Dramatic monologue
First published: 1842, in *Poems*

The Poem

Alfred, Lord Tennyson wrote "Ulysses" in October, 1833, shortly after the death of Arthur Henry Hallam, his close friend. Ulysses (called Odysseus in Greek) is a mythical Greek king whose story is told in the *Iliad* (c. 800 B.C.E.) and the *Odyssey* (c. 800 B.C.E.) by the epic poet Homer. "Ulysses" is based in part on book 11 of the *Odyssey*, which recounts the adventures of Ulysses on his ten-year voyage home from the Trojan War. During a visit to Hades, the abode of the dead, Ulysses is told by the ghost of the seer Tiresias that after he returns home he will set off on a new journey that will end in a gentle death, possibly far from shore.

"Ulysses" derives in larger part from book 26 of the *Inferno* (c. 1320) of Dante, who placed Ulysses in hell with the evil counselors—those whose sin was abuse of the powers given them by God. Ulysses tells Dante about his last voyage (Dante was a partisan of the Trojans, against whom Ulysses fought; the voyage is purely the invention of Dante). He left Ithaca, he says, because his desire for new experience was more compelling than the attractions of family and friends and the obligations he had to society. After he and his men passed the Strait of Gibralter and were within sight of the Elysian fields, the Greek paradise, they were drowned (a chasm behind The Straits was believed to lead to Hades).

Tennyson altered both versions of the story. Homer has Ulysses return home alone, without his men; the *Odyssey* ends with Ulysses preparing to defend himself against his enemies. In the *Inferno*, Ulysses says that after his last adventure (his escape from the sorceress Circe), he was not interested in retiring to Ithaca (in fact, his language suggests that he did not go home). Tennyson's Ulysses refuses to accept a gentle death: He returns home with his men but becomes bored and leaves again.

Elegiac in mood—Ulysses appears to be embarking on his last journey—the poem resembles a dramatic monologue. Along with Robert Browning, Tennyson developed the dramatic monologue as a poetic form, although the form was so new at that point that initially readers probably thought they were encountering a soliloquy. Because it was a means of imitating William Shakespeare, such a monologue is often in blank verse. As in "Ulysses," a speaker addresses an implied audience, not to be confused with the reader. The speaker is not to be confused with the poet, either, although Tennyson told friends that there was more of him in this poem than in any other he wrote in response to the death of Hallam.

The seventy lines of blank verse in the poem fall roughly into three sections. Lines 1 through 33 are an internal monologue. In lines 1 through 5, a series of generalities, Ulysses expresses his dissatisfaction with his position. Seeing his environment as sterile and stifling and uncomfortably conscious of his age, he disparages his private life, his role as king (he sees himself as reduced to performing mundane administrative duties), and his subjects.

In lines 6 and 7, the tone shifts decidedly. Ulysses announces his determination to quit Ithaca and move on, ready to embrace whatever adventure he might find. In lines 8 through 18, he thinks longingly of his life before his return. His passion was adventure; in the course of his travels, he experienced extreme happiness and extreme suffering, with his companions and in isolation, on land and on sea. He has become famous and respected, he says with some pride. His hunger for experience, his constant searching, has acquainted him with "cities of men/ And manners, climates, councils, governments"; he has become wise in the ways of men. Lines 19 through 32 express Ulysses' conception of life as an unending series of opportunities to be seized. While he does not deny the satisfaction of having made his presence felt among others ("I am a part of all that I have met"), he cannot resist the urge to explore further. For him, idleness is abhorrent.

In the second section, lines 33 through 43, Ulysses shifts his tone again, speaking as a public man in relatively flat, "official" language; the speech sets him apart from his conscientious son, Telemachus, to whom he is transferring his power. This is a revised version, edited for public consumption, of the sentiments expressed earlier; "savage," for example, becomes "rugged." Telemachus, he suggests, lacks his dreams, his aspirations, his restlessness. He does, however, have the wisdom and the ability to transform Ithaca into a peaceable and civilized kingdom. It is appropriate, Ulysses announces, that each does the "work" best suited to his abilities.

The monologue concludes in the evening, curiously, when Ulysses indicates he and his men are about to sail. In lines 44 through 70, he exhorts his companions to make the most of the time left to them. He throws out the possible consequences of their voyage into the unknown, citing the darker alternatives first—they could be swept into Hades. On the other hand, they could reach the land of dead heroes, where Achilles lives (Achilles, the hero of the *Iliad*, died in the Trojan War; his armor was given to Ulysses). In the evening of their lives, Ulysses asserts, they may yet set goals, make discoveries, and savor their achievements.

Forms and Devices

The desire of Ulysses to leave for places unknown symbolizes a yearning for intellectual discovery. Although he speaks of "the Happy Isles," most of his references to the physical world are generalized enough to suggest that his goal is not to find an actual place but to learn what is knowable. He says that he wants "To follow knowledge . . ./ Beyond the utmost bound of human thought."

Ithaca is no place for an active life of the mind, as the solemn, declamatory eloquence of the opening lines indicates. The lack of specificity (he is "an idle king" by a "still hearth," with an unnamed wife), the close repetition of identical forms (six nouns paired with adjectives), and the metaphors for sterility ("still hearth," "barren crags," "aged wife") suggest his sense of dissociation from his surroundings. Ulysses also sees no connection between himself and his subjects, whose needs he describes as solely physical. They are "savages" who do not understand him (they "know not me"), a thinker; the heavy closing iambs of the fifth line announce with resounding finality that Ulysses sees his subjects as animals: They "hoard, and sleep, and feed." Wistfully, he thinks of his fellow sailors, who have shared his work, his achievements, and his thoughts (they "have toiled, and wrought, and thought with me—").

His needs are intellectual, although Ulysses uses images of drinking and eating to express them—he will "drink/ Life to the lees [dregs]," and he has "drunk delight of battle" and roamed the world with a "hungry heart." Throughout the poem, the images reinforce the sense of exhilaration he remembers having derived from battling life head on, in safety and in danger ("on shore" and on rough seas, in "The thunder and the sunshine"). With "Free hearts" and "free foreheads"—metonymies for desires and minds—he and his men gave both adversity and good fortune "a frolic welcome" (lines 47 through 49). In sailing toward the "western stars," "beyond the sunset," he will be sailing into the unknown. Literally, he may sail to a "newer world" because he will be leaving the familiar Mediterranean—the known world—and entering the Atlantic Ocean, the unfamiliar sea beyond The Straits. Symbolically, he will always be pursuing the ever-widening boundaries of knowledge: "all experience is an arch where through/ Gleams that untraveled world whose margin fades/ Forever and forever when I move."

Moving toward the setting sun also symbolizes moving toward death, about which Ulysses speaks in a variety of ways. "To pause"—to live as he has been living for three long years ("suns")—is "to make an end"; apparently, he sees pausing and ending as equivalents. This idea is repeated when he applies to himself the metaphor of rusty armor used by Ulysses in *Troilus and Cressida* (c. 1601-1602). Only perseverance keeps honor bright, says Shakespeare's Ulysses; to become idle is to become dull and lifeless, as unused metal does. Death itself, however met, holds no promise—"Death closes all," and Hades is "eternal silence." One comes alive, however, in a struggle against death. In fact, says Ulysses, his struggle against it—his pursuit of the western stars—may lead him to paradise.

Images throughout the first and last sections of the poem reinforce the idea that unlike Faustus, who also sought the unattainable, Ulysses has a desire for knowledge that will never be satisfied. What attracts him is that "untraveled world" whose bounds are constantly shifting. Beyond "the baths" of all the stars, beyond the setting sun, Ulysses wants to sail until he dies.

Themes and Meanings

The significance of the will as expressed in "Ulysses" has generated some conflicting views. In one sense, in his restless desire to move on and to face new challenges, Ulysses is concerned only with satisfying his own needs. "Life piled on life" has suggested to some experience piled on experience rather than experience leading to wisdom. With his rejection of Penelope, the incarnation of patience, loyalty, and devotion ("Matched" even suggests that Ulysses sees their union as having been imposed on him), and with his rejection of his duty toward his subjects, Ulysses has been seen as a selfish hero, if not an immature, elderly man who refuses to accept responsibility. He exhibits an unattractive self-concern, however characteristic of the hero it may be. His distaste for social and domestic responsibilities, in fact, led W. H. Auden to call him a glorified heroic dandy.

A more common view is the one Tennyson himself supported: The poem is about the need to battle life out to the end. Tennyson can be seen as reflecting the spirit of the nineteenth century in approving the determination of Ulysses to explore the unknown no matter what the consequences; interestingly, the fact that Ulysses abandons his wife and child is not treated as the violation of Victorian mores that it was. In this view, his rejection of Penelope is in keeping with his character. Her faithfulness reflects her will, certainly, but not necessarily his. A refusal to see his return to her as his final goal is consistent with the desire Ulysses expresses throughout the poem to continue his search for knowledge. His needs are not physical but intangible, intellectual; they can never be satisfied.

The message of "Ulysses" is not moralistic, although its last line is among the most stirring and quotable in the works of Tennyson. The focus is not on fulfilling one's duties to others. Expectations are upset: Ulysses leaves the duties to his son and sails with a young man's dreams into the unknown. The poem also explores loss (in part the reason for the additional charge by Auden that the poem suffers from indirection). In the opening lines, Ulysses, the wanderer, finds himself stationary and isolated. He is not living wholly in the present. He is choosing to sail westward rather than eastward, toward the dying sun rather than the rising one. The description of the outcome of the journey, beginning "It may be that the gulfs will wash us down," is far from joyous. So melancholy did Thomas Carlyle find these lines that he told Tennyson that they "do not make me weep, but there is in me what would fill whole Lachrymatories as I read."

The sense of loss the poem conveys suggests a certain weariness with life. The references to himself as old, to old age, and, later, to "old days" rather than to the days of his youth run counter to the spirit of the ringing declarations in the last section of the poem. The cadences of the long vowel sounds in lines 51 through 56, in which Ulysses describes the approach of the evening of his departure, suggest a contemplative stance rather than forward movement. Some have sensed a loss of will toward the end of the poem, even an urge to withdraw from life.

Despite the charges leveled against the poem of confused constructions and intentions, the complexity of "Ulysses" permits it to be read as a stirring affirmation or a poignant rejection of possibilities. As long ago as 1855, Goldwin Smith argued that Ulysses "stands for ever [sic] a listless and melancholy figure on the shore."

C. L. Brooke

THE UNBELIEVER

Author: Elizabeth Bishop (1911-1979)
Type of poem: Meditation
First published: 1938; collected in *North and South*, 1946

The Poem

"The Unbeliever" is a highly condensed poem of five five-line stanzas. It begins with an enigmatic quotation from *Pilgrim's Progress* (1678, 1684), the seventeenth century moral tale by John Bunyan: "He sleeps on the top of a mast." These words are repeated in the first line of the poem, signaling that Bunyan's "he" is the strange sleeper in the poem. While the top of the mast is a strange place for sleeping in any circumstance, in Elizabeth Bishop's poem it comes to mean that sleeping anywhere is uncanny and strange. Sleeping, for Bishop, means being unconscious, unaware, and unthinking in a world of intense visual and emotional realities; by contrast, the moment of awakening is a central moment of poetic vision.

In the first stanza the poet offers a remarkable simile: A ship is like a bed. Indeed, "the sails fall away below him [the sleeper on top of the mast]/ like the sheets of his bed." The sleeper has been transported unaware to this unlikely place, and once on top of the mast he has "curled/ in a gilded ball on the mast's top,/ or climbed inside/ a gilded bird, or blindly seated himself astride." The reader cannot help noticing that the lookout, the one who needs the sharpest eye and the most vigilant mind, is asleep and blind.

There are things to see and hear, and the reader must imagine that when the third stanza introduces a speaking cloud, the cloud must be speaking from within the sleeper's dream. When a gull speaks in the fourth stanza, we are likely to come to a similar conclusion. The cloud begins by announcing: "I am founded on marble pillars,/ . . . I never move./ See the pillars there in the sea?" One explanation for this might be that when the cloud looks straight down to its reflection on the surface of the sea, it appears to the cloud that it is firmly planted in the place it finds itself, just as when one is sitting on one train in motion and traveling alongside another train moving at the same speed, it seems as if both are stationary. The cloud imagines that it is held aloft in this motionless state by a marble pillar—as white and marble-like as the shaded whiteness of the cloud and its image: "Secure in introspection/ he peers at the watery pillars of his reflection." He experiences himself as being stationary, though he is being propelled through the air by the wind.

The fourth stanza begins: "A gull had wings under his/ and remarked that the air/ was 'like marble.'" In this case, the possessive pronoun "his" refers back to the cloud's reflection in the line quoted above. The speaking, reflecting gull is, like the cloud, a part of the sleeper's dream; and again like the cloud, the gull mistakes his reflection for a stable, supporting marble tower: "He said: 'Up here/ I tower through the sky/ for the marble wings on my tower-top fly.'" The gull's marble tower, like the marble pillar "supporting" the cloud, are imaginary echoes of the mast on which the sleeper dreams. The only difference is that the pillar and the tower are "imaginary" and the mast is "real."

In the last stanza, the poem returns to the top of the ship's mast where the sleeper keeps "his eyes closed tight," but here "The gull inquired into his dream." There are several interpretive possibilities that open here at the closing of the poem. Presumably the sleeper is dreaming the gull who is imagining that he is flying through the sky on marble wings. At the same time, the gull inquires as to what the dream means. The dream of the sleeper on top of the mast discloses itself to the reader and to the gull in the final lines of the poem: "'I must not fall./ The spangled sea below wants me to fall.'" The sleeper, it is now understood, is the "unbeliever" of the poem's title. One presumes that within the world of Bishop's poem all statements are, in some sense, projections of an inescapable subjectivity. The gull and the cloud look down and "see" substantial and permanent towers and pillars holding them up in the sky where they appropriately belong. It is in their natures to dwell in the air above the surface of the earth. The sleeper, however, is "on top of the mast" and is only able to project or to imagine from a perspective that carries more than a suggestion of paranoia: The sleeping man is out of his element; he does not belong up in the air. So, while his support is in commonsense terms far more substantial than that of either the cloud or the gull, the fact that he is where he should not be makes his subjective impression of the world one of danger and malice: "'It [the sea] is hard as diamonds; it wants to destroy us all.'" The sleeper is the unbeliever, the one who doubts. His despair is tangible, and the danger of which he dreams is real.

Forms and Devices

As befits a poem that opens with a lean line from the Protestant pen of John Bunyan, Bishop pares her poem down to a bare and unadorned minimum. The diction, or word choice, is as unadorned as William Blake's or as a children's nursery rhyme. Even the rhyme itself is understated: a couplet completes each of the five stanzas.

If Bunyan offers Bishop a plainness of form and prosody, she also adopts from him an allegorical mode of presenting her material. An allegory is a narrative of events on one level, usually literal, that points to another symbolic level, often ethical or moral, where its meaning is found. The form of the parable enables the poet to condense and refine a complex line of thought about appearance and reality, about reality and projection, and about belief and faith into a minute space. In addition to benefiting from the brevity of the allegorical parable, Bishop also makes use of a surface simplicity of reference—a sleeping man, a gull, a cloud—to gain access to very complex and problematic intellectual and psychological issues. The form of the allegory invites the poet's use of "personification," and the three "speakers" in the poem carry in their persons the deeper meaning of which they are probably not aware.

Themes and Meanings

It is characteristic of Bishop's poetry, especially in the early period to which "The Unbeliever" belongs, that acute and detached observation brings with it the possibility of intense and sustained vision. At the same time, Bishop is continually calling into question and interrogating her own gift as a poet. While there is nothing as self-indulgent as autobiography in this cool and detached poem, it must be read as a dialogue between the one who dreams (the doubting, distrustful sleeper or poet) and the product of his or her dreams (the confident and believing gull and cloud). The accomplishment of the poet—the dream dreamt by the sleeper on top of the mast—must of necessity be more confident than the poet or dreamer himself or herself can be.

At the level of allegory, the sleeper on top of the mast is sustained in the air and propelled through the water by the substantial mast and sails. Nevertheless, the sleeper, who is the unbeliever of the poem, doubts and fears the environment: "The spangled sea below wants me to fall./ . . . ; it wants to destroy us all," as the gull discovers when he "inquired into his (the sleeper's) dream." The cloud and the gull—who are both the products of the sleeper's dream and examples of divergent "believers," and who are borne aloft and sustained by seemingly insubstantial thermals and variations in air pressure—see themselves held up by marble pillars and marble wings. There is an allegorical or narrative appropriateness in the cloud and the gull: They are in their element, and their confident belief flows from this appropriateness. On the other hand, the man sleeping on top of the mast is out of his element in an inappropriate place, and his edgy anxiety flows correspondingly from his curious misplacement.

"The Unbeliever" essentially means that belief is the product of unbelief, that allegorical confidence is the product of literal doubt, and that the dreaming poet/ sleeper pays for her or his power by virtue of knowledge of the fragility of vision.

Sharon Bassett

UNCONSCIOUS

Author: André Breton (1896-1966)
Type of poem: Narrative
First published: 1932, as "Sans connaissance," in *Le Revolver à cheveux blancs*; English translation collected in *Poems of André Breton*, 1982

The Poem

"Unconscious," a poem in free verse, consists of fifty-five lines. The title refers to that category of the mind outside conscious experience; the original French suggests both "unacquainted" and "unconsummated" as well. The poem is inexact in its subject matter: The poetic voice moves in and out of the poem with no consistent pattern, and changing points of reference, broken thoughts, and the absence of punctuation further complicate the reader's comprehension. Furthermore, it is unclear whether the protagonist of the poem is the narrator, although both reader and narrator share the experience as more than implicit observers. Such lack of clarity lends itself to the dreamlike atmosphere of the text.

The poem begins by reminding readers that the incident about to be described, whether real or imagined, has already occurred. The first ten lines establish a memory of an "odd attempted abduction" of a fourteen-year-old girl standing in an elevator. Line 3 begins the idealization of the girl ("Hey a star and yet it's still broad daylight") that continues throughout the poem. Lines 4-10 emphasize the early pubescence of the girl that entices the narrator. Her age is described as "Four more years than fingers," and her breasts, which the narrator imagines he sees bared, resemble "handkerchiefs drying on a rosebush." These images are important in establishing the virginal representation of the girl and are contrasted by the reminder that her parents are "firmly" beside her. Lines 11-14 tell of the location of the scene in Paris; it is a place the narrator says he remembers no matter where he is. Line 15 returns to the girl and her predicament. The elevator is stuck between floors. Lines 20-23 describes the array of images occupying the third-floor landing below: "light-colored boards the eel of a handrail" and blades of grass painted on the wall that resemble a man's clothing. In such a state, the girl "compares herself to a feathered jack-in-the-box." From line 24 onward, the narrator follows the girl's eyes, greener "than angelica green usually is," where they meet the eyes of a man, eyes that burn with the yellow flame of boron. Above the landing, he notes her calves under a fine dress from Paris. "That is enough," readers are told in line 28, "for these two creatures to understand each other."

Lines 28-48 provide a montage of images as the backdrop to a sexual encounter. The tentativeness of the situation is overcome as "excitement works wonders." Shadows move around them on the wall, the pendulum of a clock derails, thunderbolts flash from the street, and the girl smiles "between fear and pleasure," her heart skipping a beat like the first bud of spring exploding on a tree. With one word, readers are reminded in line 40, this dream can be undone. As in the poem's introduction, line 49 recalls the conclusion. A gunshot sounds and blood leaps down the stairs, but neither is quick enough to stop the assailant. He vanishes in the night, lighting a cigarette. The poem describes him as a handsome man, "Sweeter than the pain of loving and being loved."

Forms and Devices

"Unconscious" is a Surrealist poem. As a founder and primary theorist of this movement, André Breton typically created works recognized more for their exemplification of his notions of what art should be than for their intrinsic literary value. To the Surrealist, poetry is a way to access the unconscious mind with the goal of reuniting the conscious and unconscious realms of experience, the world of dreams and the world of reason, to create "absolute reality" or surreality. The Surrealist devices employed in the poem include the shocking juxtaposition of conflicting or contradictory images and the constant shifting of mood and color.

The strongest contradiction, perhaps, is that the poem takes place outside social norms as it describes a sexual encounter between a man and a fourteen-year-old girl. The dominant metaphor of "Unconscious," that of the elevator resting between the floors, physically draws the mind's eye of the reader to dichotomize the girl's predicament as the central theme. She is on her way up to the fourth-floor apartment of her parents, although in line 10 their presence seems more immediate: She exists between her father, "a post firmly set in the shadows," and the light of her mother. Below, on the third-floor landing, stands the protagonist. However, as the title indicates, this is not a poem in which conscious choices are made. Such tension, derived as much from the shock of the reader as from the text itself, is a Surrealist construction that deceives the reader into drawing a simple conclusion.

The sexual imagery that makes up the poem is bold and abundant. Line 25 tells the reader how the girl's "calves glisten, they are two dark birds that must be warmer and softer than all the others." The man's "boron" eyes burn with excitement. As line 31 focuses on "a parasol being shut," the phallic image of the closed parasol reveals itself. A rush of adrenalin is illustrated by shadows of charging horses and lightning bolts. In line 39, the girl's heart skips a beat as "the first bud" leaps from a chestnut tree. Allusions to nature abound in the poem: Line 15 refers to the girl as Euphorbia, a large genus of plants that includes several species used in food and medicine; the man's eyes burn like the chemical element boron; and the man's hand moves up her dress, which "rises" like a fuchsia. Although the scene transpires in an elevator, the "two creatures" join in a hut during a tropical storm where "excitement works wonders." This device serves to temper the shock to the reader's sensibilities in an effort to convince the reader that the scene is, in fact, quite natural while at the same time reinforcing the notion that what is taking place is, at its core, sexual. However, readers should not be misled: The primary device remains bound to the title. As the poem mixes and matches these images, they are only natural in combination outside the realm of what is rational.

Themes and Meanings

The main theme of "Unconscious" is the awakening of one's sexuality as a vehicle for exploration of the unconscious mind. In approaching the place where the world of dreams and reality meet, the poem reflects the process as well. This overriding quest of Surrealism reveals a debt to Austrian psychoanalyst Sigmund Freud, who defines the characteristics of unconscious processes to include timelessness, an exemption from mutual contradiction, and the replacement of external reality by psychical reality; all these elements are present in the poem.

Read carefully, this is not a poem about a young girl's sexual awakening but of a man's fantasy of awakening a young girl's sexuality. The girl is an object. Stranded in the elevator, dangling between floors, she is a helpless little bird, a "feathered jack-in-the-box." When the two finally join, line 29 explains the experience as something not only natural and exotic but also deriving from a primal collective unconscious. The experience is surreal not because it takes place outside what is rational but because it does not take place at all. Against a backdrop of rationality, from the "abduction" to the man's getaway, the poem shocks the reader with a rape fantasy. However, the scene occurs in that part of the mind where rationality is displaced by the dream, a key to understanding the process.

One of the most telling references in the poem occurs when the narrator calls the girl Euphorbia. At one time, several species of Euphorbia had medicinal value as a laxative or a vomit-inducing agent. The automatic processes such as free association employed by the Surrealists in an effort to unlock the unconscious mind are akin to a mental regurgitation. Normal poetic conventions such as meter and rhyme only constrain the poet to rational modes; the Surrealist forsakes such conventions to allow what lies deeper in the mind to flow unfettered, just as the presence of the girl, Euphorbia, induces the overflow of primal sexuality. Thus the opening line, "One has not forgotten," refers not to something real that has happened but to what, for the poet, continues to happen in the unconscious mind. What this means is not clear. For the Surrealist, says one critic, there is no message, only an invitation to explore the possibilities. Enigmatic as this is, it assists the reader in understanding the distance between normal poetic conventions and Breton's poem, in which contradiction and the absurd stand on equal ground with reality.

Steven Clotzman

UNDER BEN BULBEN

Author: William Butler Yeats (1865-1939)
Type of poem: Lyric
First published: 1939, in *Last Poems and Two Plays*

The Poem

"Under Ben Bulben" is a long poem of ninety-four lines divided into six movements celebrating William Butler Yeats's vision of an artistically integrated spiritual reality. He exhorts readers and artists to share this vision for the fulfillment of the human race through art.

The poem's title refers to a mountain north of the village of Sligo, County Sligo, in the west of Ireland, where Yeats's maternal ancestors (the Pollexfens) had settled. The area afforded Yeats a principal contact with Irish folklore and with the peasantry, both of which figure greatly in his works, including the masterpiece of his extreme old age, "Under Ben Bulben." When he was a boy, Yeats had often climbed Ben Bulben; nine years after his death in the south of France, his body was brought home to Ireland to be reinterred in Drumcliff churchyard on September 17, 1948, at the foot of the mountain and in the parish where his great-grandfather, the Reverend John Yeats, had been rector of Drumcliff from 1805. By W. B. Yeats's direction, the last three lines of this poem are inscribed on his burial stone. Such was Ben Bulben's importance to his life and his art.

Yeats was also fascinated by the supernatural associations of the mountain with legendary Irish figures such as the Fianna, who were horsemen of Finn, the warrior hero. A second-sighted female servant of his uncle, describing some supernatural women to young Yeats, had compared them to the mythical Fianna horsemen still haunting Ben Bulben: "They are fine and dashing-looking, like the men one sees riding their horses in twos and threes on the slope of the mountains with their swords swinging." In the poem, these mythical women and horsemen become a key symbol of integrated heroic action on a spiritual plane for individuals and artists to imitate in the quest for optimum realization of the self.

"Under Ben Bulben" opens dramatically by exhorting all readers to dedicate themselves to a vision of an artistically integrated spiritual reality apprehended through harmonious heroic action. To this end, Yeats begins, let readers swear allegiance to two symbols. Let them swear a pledge of fealty to Percy Bysshe Shelley's Witch of Atlas, a symbol of timeless wisdom and absolute beauty by Lake Mareotis, near Alexandria, Egypt (geographically associated with Christian monasticism and Neoplatonism), and a pledge to the mythical Irish heroes and heroines of Ben Bulben who ride the air in an ideal immortal state of heroically integrated wholeness (lines 1-11). The rest of the poem is Yeats's interpretation of the significance of those two symbols for humanity.

The second movement affirms an eternal cycle of reincarnation, carrying individual souls from incarnations in this life ("That of race") to spiritual existence ("and that of soul") in the *Anima Mundi* (Yeats's all-encompassing Soul of the World, designated as the "human mind" here), and back again, endlessly. Therefore, death is an illusion, and spiritual immortality is the only reality and destiny of the human race (lines 13-24).

The third movement repeats the wish of the Irish patriot John Mitchel (1815-1875) for cataclysmic times that offer individuals opportunities for heroic actions. Such actions integrate the human personality, generate a vision of ultimate spiritual truth (in the way an actor of tragedy earns his tragic recognition of life's meaning in the artistry of heroic endeavor), and fulfill humanity's spiritual destiny in the harmonizing of life's dualities. The wisest "accomplish fate" and become integrated ("choose his mate") through "violence"—that is, through intense, purposeful action (lines 25-56).

The fourth movement narrows the focus of Yeats's appeal for spiritual insight from individuals generally to artists specifically. Integral to humanity's achievement of spiritual vision is the work of all serious artists who adhere to the great traditions of art, beginning with the mathematical magnificence of Egyptian pyramids and the graceful Grecian statues of Phidias, through Michelangelo's monumentally alive Adam and Eve ("globe-trotting Madam"), to Renaissance and declining post-Renaissance masters. They capture, or at least glimpse, the *Anima Mundi* (the all-encompassing Soul of the World, designated here as "the secret working mind") in its earthly incarnation in great art (lines 37-67). It was, after all, the *Anima Mundi* that governed the "cradles" or "gyres" (Yeats's whirling cone symbols explaining human history and personality) that determined history's cyclical course and recurrent renaissances of high art. Therefore, let modern artists dedicate themselves to reawakening humanity's spiritual vision by producing works that imitate the spirit-inspired creations of past renaissances.

The fifth movement narrows the focus of Yeats's appeal for spiritual vision even further by singling out Irish poets for undertaking the calling of great art by which the modern Irish could be reborn heroically. This program would be a continuation of his own lifelong mission as a patriot, poet, and Abbey Theater playwright of Irish heroic themes to refashion the Celtic populace through art. Unlike voguish modern versifiers, true Irish poets must be polished craftsmen, respect their ancient national myths, and yet be so inclusive in subject matter as to integrate opposite topics into an artistic wholeness ("Sing the peasantry, and then/ Hard-driving country gentlemen"), whereby the reader "completes his partial mind" (lines 68-83).

The sixth and final movement has the narrowest focus of all—on a buried William Butler Yeats. He must depend upon some lowly tombstone engraver to carve a poetry of artistically integrated spiritual reality on limestone for a three-line epitaph that transcends earthly mortality through integration of opposites (*"Cast a cold eye/ On life, on death"*) with a final command for the living to pursue an undying spiritual wholeness of heroic action in imitation of the legendary horsemen of Ben Bulben (*"Horseman, pass by!"*).

Forms and Devices

The stylistic characteristics of "Under Ben Bulben" are typical of Yeats's mature canon and modernist literary conventions that helped to make him what T. S. Eliot claimed was the greatest twentieth century poet in English—or perhaps in any language. Published only months before his death and (until recently) considered to be his personal choice for the final selection in any posthumous collection of his poetry, "Under Ben Bulben" is a magnificent summation of a career fashioned by Ireland and dedicated to art. As John Unterecker commented in *A Reader's Guide to William Butler Yeats* (1959), "It is almost as if Yeats—conscious of his impending death—were calling up characters, ideas, and poetic subjects for a last farewell, a sort of final benediction to his art itself."

What kind of a poet was Yeats? For that question there is no simple answer and no simple label to describe him. He is certainly one of the last major poets in the European Romantic movement. He has been termed "a realist-symbolist-metaphysical poet with an uncanny power over words." Through his Pre-Raphaelite father, he claimed literary descent from early English Romantics such as William Blake, Shelley, and John Keats and from European aesthetes of the late nineteenth century. The French "l'art pour l'art" impulse under Théophile Gautier (1811-1872) aspired to a poetry of highly wrought artifice and impersonality, devoted to artistic beauty for its own sake and devoid of bourgeois utilitarian didacticism. All these traits can be found in "Under Ben Bulben."

Coming slightly later, the French Symbolists cultivated an aristocratic impersonality, intense craftsmanship, an escapism through art, and a preoccupation with the suggestiveness of words as they rub together in a line to give off new sensations and meanings not communicated by the individual words themselves. All these traits also surface in "Under Ben Bulben."

The poem is very much a highly crafted artifice encouraging a sort of escapism through art and celebrating the immortal spirit of art and an artistically integrated life of art with a concentrated suggestiveness of meaning that comes from a repeated juxtaposition of images. Although this modernist technique makes for difficult reading, the concentrated juxtaposition of images lends a mythic richness and range of allusion embracing a broad cross-section of Western cultural experience through the ages. If this compressed suggestiveness is "metaphysical" and epigrammatic in tendency, Yeats's realism is present in "Under Ben Bulben" in his Irish sense of place and national purpose directed at reforming the race through art.

The poem's diction integrates the extremes of usage in language, from the colloquial to the elegant, from the crude to the visionary. The prevailing meter is a chiseled iambic tetrameter with variations (the usual line has seven beats, with one stressed sound and then three iambs—"Swéar bў whát thĕ ságĕs spóke"—until the final stanza of octosyllabic verse). The rhymes are almost thumping. Together, the meter and rhyme impose an artistic order on the chaotic subject matter of human experience and lend an incantatory effect in keeping with the poet's call for spiritual vision in his audience of both laypersons and artists.

Themes and Meanings

"Under Ben Bulben" is about humanity's need for an artistically integrated vision of spiritual reality and is a call for artists to serve humanity by communicating this vision through works of great art. Although the poem embodies arcane ideas of Yeats's esoteric philosophy, described in *A Vision* (1925, 1937), the reader can nevertheless obtain a clear glimpse of the poem's meaning through a careful study of the text and the movement of its motifs.

The poem is Yeats's last will and testament. Speaking as a patriotic prophet-poet about to abandon his career to the young, he exhorts all humanity to follow his faith and all poets to serve humanity by practicing his faith in their art and by providing the necessary images of an integrated heroic spirituality in which humankind can believe.

The poem is organized around a cumulative series of commands for an increasingly narrower audience—for all humanity first, for all artists next, for all Irish poets next, and for Yeats's tombstone engraver last. Each audience, from the masses to the graveyard artificer, is exhorted to be an artist in pursuit of an undying spiritual wholeness of heroic action in imitation of the mythic women and horsemen of beloved Ben Bulben. The epitaph's terse final command to the passer-by epitomizes the poem's entire theme and is an exorcism of mortality for the buried poet and his readers through the art of poetry.

Finally, in keeping with the theme of heroic spiritual integration through art, line after line of the poem embodies dualities and oppositions (Yeats's antinomies) in the process of being harmonized. If, for example, "Many times man lives and dies" between two eternities "of race" and "of soul," then "ancient Ireland knew it all," and its heroes harmonized them both ("A brief parting from those dear/ Is the worst man has to fear").

Yeats exhorted humanity to pursue the life of heroic action and spiritual insight because he had pursued the same path and created thereby his century's greatest poetic art. As Seamus Heaney eloquently noted in a lecture given at the University of Surrey (1978), "What is finally admirable is the way his life and his work are *not* separate but make a continuum, the way the courage of his vision did not confine itself to rhetorics but issued in actions"; his poetry was "the fine flower of his efforts to live as forthrightly as he could in the world of illiterates and politicians."

Thomas M. Curley

THE UNKNOWN CITIZEN

Author: W. H. Auden (1907-1973)
Type of poem: Satire
First published: 1940, in *Another Time*

The Poem

Twentieth century Western authors and poets have often examined the alienation and silence of modern life and the loss of personal identity and autonomy, accelerated by the advent of technology. Sometimes these works, particularly novels and films, project the loss of a total civilization and political system that leaves individuals helpless. Other works, such as poet W. H. Auden's "The Unknown Citizen," are less dramatic but no less telling about the path of the twentieth century, particularly after the introduction of computer-age technology.

The title of the poem itself, "The Unknown Citizen," reminds the reader of the unknown soldiers who followed their countries' calls, who gave their lives in defense of their countries, who died to ensure the continuity of the society for which they fought, and who stood for the bravery of all soldiers. They are honored for their deeds; only their deeds, not their names, remain as silent witness that they lived. The "Unknown Citizen," though not a warrior, also represents the life his society values and records in his "metaphorical" Bureau of Statistics files, files that hold facts but tell only a partial story, leaving much else in silence.

"The Unknown Citizen" is dedicated "To JS/07/M/378. This Marble Monument is erected by the State." Instead of being a monument to a named citizen, the monument is dedicated to the citizen, known to the state by numbers and statistics, not by name; he is a kind of Everyman in general, who is no man in particular. The poem then details all the supposed characteristics that the state finds important to identify JS/07/M/378 and to remember him.

JS/07/M/378 was by all accounts a model, middle-class citizen; he is even labeled "a saint" for his exemplary life, at least according to the state's definition of "exemplary." He "worked in a [car] factory and never got fired," except for the war years when he served his country as expected. He was a union man who followed the rules. He was popular and never expressed "odd" views; he had an occasional drink with his friends. He subscribed to his local paper and bought the products advertised in it, as the paper and advertisers expected. He had health insurance and a normal illness. He bought modern necessities on "the Installment Plan." He had the usual necessities for his time: "A phonograph, a radio, a car and a frigidaire." He held opinions that he was supposed to hold when he was supposed to hold them. He was married and produced the expected number of children and sent them to school. As recorded by the state, he was a stereotypical model for the middle of the twentieth century.

Auden uses terms from this first wave of mass consumption for the middle class; for example, "Frigidaire," a brand name, came to mean refrigerator for the first generation of users. Formerly, citizens may have had iceboxes for food, which looked similar to modern refrigerators, but which used daily delivered ice for food storage. The Unknown Citizen owned a phonograph, or record player, not the compact-disc players of today's age. For him to have a car was a real consumer step-up, but because JS/07/M/378 worked in an auto factory and belonged to a union, he was probably one of the best-paid workers of his day, with all the necessities that his neighbors had or wished they had. He is remembered for what he owned and that he paid for what he owned over time.

He is no longer alive, so the state "Erected" a monument to him, celebrating the aspects of his life that the state values and that keep the state going. These aspects that the state tracks are supplied by various institutions that supposedly tell who an individual citizen is: the Bureau of Statistics, the War Department (now the Defense Department), the corporate employer, the union, the psychologists, the media, the insurance company, the product and public opinion researchers, the population experts, and the educators. Nowhere in the poem does the Unknown Citizen speak; nowhere does he define himself. He is silent.

Forms and Devices

Auden's word choices to describe the unknown citizen—"popular," "normal," "sensible," "proper," "right"—seem appropriate for a man who is considered by the state to be a "saint," a man who lived as the powers wanted him to live, a man whose life spoke of his adherence to his society's values. However, Auden also uses a rhyme scheme that suggests a possible glitch in the state's assessment of the citizen's life. Perhaps the Unknown Citizen is not in exact harmony with the state, as the statistics suggest.

For example, Auden uses rhyming lines, but he varies the rhyme so that the reader is just slightly off-balance. The first few lines begin an *abab* pattern, but by the sixth line Auden fails to supply a *b* rhyme to complement the *a* rhyme in the fifth line. From then on, Auden rhymes in short spurts, such as "retired" and "fired" in lines 6 and 7, "views" and "dues" in lines 9 and 10, and "Plan" in line 19 and "Man" in line 20, yet he interrupts patterns, such as having lines 8 and 13 rhyme rather than 8 and 9 and lines 18 and 21 rhyme, not 18 and 20. Just as the reader is expecting rhymes, Auden puts off the rhyme for a couple of lines. Then he inserts three lines, 25, 26, and 27, that rhyme.

This scheme points to an undercurrent of meaning that is not accounted for in the states' facts that define this model citizen. This undercurrent becomes a flood in the last rhyming couplet, which asks two important questions that go beyond statistical information and are not addressed elsewhere in the poem: "Was he free? Was he happy?" These questions are answered in an official, statistical way: "The question is absurd:/ Had anything been wrong, we should certainly have heard."

Themes and Meanings

In a mild satirical tone, Auden is critiquing the state's determination to define the meaning of a citizen's life in just a few facts collected by technology. He is suggesting that much more important information about a human life is left uncollected and, therefore, unconsidered by the state and society. This determination is made possible by modern technology that can amass this information and by statisticians who can analyze this information. The result of this accumulation of facts is an incomplete picture. These statistics do not get to the essence of the man. Auden, in fact, might well agree with Mark Twain, who is reported to have categorized the various kinds of lies: "There are lies, damned lies, and statistics." This factual picture lacks the human voice, the flesh and blood person. The statistics lie; they separate the facts and possessions of the man from the essence of the man.

Originally, keeping detailed records of citizens such as these was a cumbersome process because of the amount of information to be gathered, the logistics of gathering, and the storage requirements for the information. This whole information-gathering has been aided by computer technology. Many more facts can be gathered, stored, and shared. The computer seems quite normal to today's citizens, at least those under a certain age. It is a technology that can transport its user anywhere to get any information. All this expansion, including personal uses of computers, however, requires user names and passwords that can replace real names and identities. That there was a time when individuals were known by their names rather than by their social security numbers, user names, and passwords seems almost incomprehensible, particularly to students at large universities and to workers in large corporations, confined to cubicles.

All this information storage and transfer that citizens take for granted now began with small punch cards about the size of an airline ticket and extremely large computers. It is this penchant for gathering and storing information on twentieth century citizens that Auden uses for his comments on twentieth century infatuation with facts and its loss of meaning; this profiling offers facts that together add up to nothing. Neither Auden nor the reader has any sense of who this modern man is. He is truly unknown to both poet and reader.

Since Auden wrote this poem about the nameless, middle-class man in the middle of the twentieth century, technology has strengthened its hold on society. No longer are names and faces needed to conduct the normal business of society. Technology can now store even more information, all of the information about the Unknown Citizen that the poem shares and more. Technology can transmit most of what happens every day without people ever meeting. Technology is even now part of the industry where the Unknown Citizen worked; robots perform many of the tasks that he did. Auden's brilliant, yet simply constructed, twenty-nine-line poem rings even truer now than it did when it described life in the mid-twentieth century. In fact, as technology has become louder and more prominent, the human voice has grown quieter; it is true that society has more facts about its citizens, but it does not recognize the silence that accompanies those facts because it cannot compute anything but facts. Citizens remain unknown.

Carol Lawson Pippen

UP RISING

Author: Robert Duncan (1919-1988)
Type of poem: Meditation
First published: 1966; collected in *Bending the Bow*, 1968

The Poem

"Up Rising," in the tradition of all good political poetry, casts its shadow onto public discourse in ways that are both instructive and artistic. The poem extends to slightly over two pages of free verse. In a play on words, the title resembles the single word "uprising"—evocative of political insurrection—yet because it is written as two words, it suggests the ominous emergence of dark, sinister forces in America that are the foci of the poem's meditation.

The first line mentions "Johnson," a reference to Lyndon Baines Johnson, United States President from 1963 to 1969. The poem declares that Johnson will arise "to join the great simulacra"—empty images—of such men as Adolf Hitler and Joseph Stalin, and "to work his fame/ with planes roaring out from Guam over Asia." This reference to America's bombing of Indochina during the Vietnam War is Robert Duncan's rationale for equating Johnson with two of the century's most brutal, prodigious mass-murderers. Duncan's negative reaction to the Vietnam War is the poem's unifying element.

Duncan portrays Johnson as a megalomaniac, with "all America" subjected to his "will," which Duncan labels "a bloated thing," perhaps a tick, parasitically sucking "blood and dreams" from the nation. The poet notes that Johnson's "fame" is such that "his name stinks with burning meat and heapt honors." Duncan also implicates "the professional military," who are said to be "thinking/ to use him [Johnson] as they thought to use Hitler" in their lust for war.

Here begins a long incantatory passage, taking up most of the poem, on "the mania," which Duncan equates with "the ravening eagle of America." In an unfolding chain of juxtapositions, Duncan implies that the national symbol has been transformed into "the ominous roar in the air,/ the omnipotent wings," a reference to American war planes with "the all-American boy in the cockpit."

To show the horrific perversion that he believes "the mania" has wrought, Duncan uses sexual innuendo in his condemnation when he speaks of the pilot "loosing his flow of napalm." The product of phallic weaponry is not a life-giving force but a fluid that sticks to human skin as it burns. Pleasure has become "the torture of mothers and fathers and children,/ their hair a-flame, screaming in agony."

In a long Whitmanesque passage, Duncan speaks of this mania as having "raised from the private rooms of . . . businessmen,/ from the council chambers . . ./ from the fearful hearts of good people in the suburbs . . ./ raised this . . . hatred of Europe, of Africa, of Asia,/ the deep hatred for the old world . . ./ and for the alien world." Duncan's point is that Americans have come to hate the foreigner, the "other," and because of "the mania"—"this black bile" which "takes over the vanity of Johnson"—their solution is to kill the objects of this hatred.

In the poem's final lines, Duncan brings the devil into the equation, stating that "the very glint of Satan's eyes . . ./ now shines from the eyes of the President."

Forms and Devices

Two highly distinctive features of "Up Rising" are its long lines and its declamatory language, both of which locate the poem in the tradition of Walt Whitman and Allen Ginsberg. Whitman was profoundly influenced by the orators of his day, and Ginsberg made a reputation for himself as a spellbinding reader. "Up Rising" is the kind of poem whose cumulative power and effect are significantly magnified by reading it aloud. The reason for this can be summed up in one word: syntax. The poem is written as a single sentence, within which there are four independent clauses that vary greatly in length, from five lines to more than forty. The first spans nine lines, with the subject and verb in the poem's opening line: "Now Johnson would go up to join the great simulacra of men." The ensuing eight lines consist of a series of phrases and subordinate clauses that establish a seductive declamatory rhythm.

After the connective "And," the second independent syntactical unit, six lines long, similarly begins with its main subject and verb, "men wake." Again, several appended phrases follow. With the third clause, however, a long cumulative incantation of argumentative detail that takes up the bulk of the poem, Duncan breaks this subject-verb pattern. The first line of the passage, "But the mania, the ravening eagle of America," contains the subject, "mania," but fifteen lines of verse ensue before the first of the compound verbs, "has raised," is encountered. There follows a series of four long prepositional phrases, all beginning with "from," and an interjected passage of prose, before the verb's direct object, "entity," is reached. The clause continues for ten more lines, using the same pattern of rhythmically interrupted syntactical flow.

The effect of this kind of sentence structure, which Whitman employed, especially in "Song of Myself," and which Duncan has mastered admirably in "Up Rising," is hypnotic. It lends a primal, almost primitive legitimacy to Duncan's political position, as though it were grounded in natural law. This significantly strengthens the poem's argument.

Curiously, as though the poem were becoming too hypnotic, Duncan interrupts the verse with a sizable chunk of prose, striking a kind of rhythmic balance. Coming as it does immediately after Duncan's accusation of America's universities and corporations—whose scientists have developed "the atomic stockpile; the vials of synthesized diseases . . . and the gasses of despair"—the passage is also an appropriately prosaic mirroring in language of the scientific method.

Duncan's single-minded, uncompromising damnation of the Vietnam War builds up to an emotionally cathartic series of images in the poem's last clause. The nation has a "swollen head," and "from the pit of the hell of/ America's unacknowledged, unrepented crimes," Duncan sees the "glint of Satan's eyes"—as riveting and hypnotic as the language and rhythm of the poem—shining out of Johnson's.

Themes and Meanings

"Up Rising" is a poem fixated on America's involvement in the Vietnam War. Yet despite people's forgetfulness and the passage of time, the poem does not exclude readers the way poems reliant on historical fact risk doing. This condition results from the fact that virtually all Americans have heard of the Vietnam War and most understand, at a minimum, that the war was somehow problematic. Duncan's emotional ferocity in "Up Rising" is therefore credible even to readers who disagree with his political stance.

Indeed, the predominant thematic legacy of "Up Rising" may be that the Vietnam War aroused torrential emotional reactions which have been absent in America's brief wars of the 1980's and 1990's. Vietnam was such that it moved a poet capable of writing such lines as "O Swan, the lover has taken away/ your covering cast at the wave's edge" (from "Four Songs the Night Nurse Sang," *Roots and Branches*, 1964) to create "Up Rising," containing such passages as "this specter that . . ./ would corrupt the very body of the nation/ and all our sense of our common humanity,/ this black bile of old evils arisen anew,/ takes over the vanity of Johnson." Vietnam sundered America, and the scars of its wounds show clearly in Duncan's poem.

Being grounded in a particular time, "Up Rising" contains some abstruse historical details, and shedding light on them will allow readers a fuller understanding of the poem. Readers might miss the connotative spectrum of "this Texas barbecue/ of Asia, Africa, and all the Americas" without knowing that President Johnson—a large, gregarious man given to extremes of mirth and rage—was from Texas and enjoyed entertaining enormous groups with lavish barbecues at his ranch. Many readers will recognize "Lawrence" and "Blake"—whose writings on America Duncan quotes in "Up Rising"—as novelist D. H. Lawrence and poet William Blake. Even more will know "Adams and Jefferson" as two of America's founding fathers who, according to Duncan, held higher hopes for America than the reality that Johnson delivered. The name "Goldwater" at the end of the poem, however, needs explanation.

Barry Goldwater ran unsuccessfully for president against Johnson in 1964. During the campaign, he gained a reputation as a dangerous right-wing extremist who would not only intensify the Vietnam War but also risk a suicidal war with the Soviet Union. By default, Johnson became a peace candidate, yet after his landslide victory, he did in Vietnam what many Americans had feared that Goldwater would do. Knowledge of these details allows readers to experience the full meaning of Duncan's climactic assertion that the "glint of Satan's eyes . . ./ . . . that I saw in/ Goldwater's eyes/ now shines from the eyes of the President."

As a political poem, "Up Rising" contains some dated material, but the poem's artful declamatory rhythms, its moving emotional intensity, and its focus on the Vietnam War—an issue that remains potent in America—contribute enormously to the timeless value of "Up Rising."

Jonathan Daunt

UPON NOTHING

Author: John Wilmot, earl of Rochester (1647-1680)
Type of poem: Satire
First published: 1679; collected in *Poems on Several Occasions,* 1680

The Poem

"Upon Nothing" has always been regarded as one of the earl of Rochester's most important poems. Samuel Johnson called it "the strongest effort of his Muse." In seventeen short stanzas, it moves from philosophical satire on the vanity of human attempts to comprehend the meaning of existence to social satire on particular human pretensions to importance. In the end, Rochester implies, nothing means anything, because in the end, as in the beginning, there is only Nothing.

The first seven stanzas offer a brief, difficult account of the process by which the known universe of things came into existence. "Nothing," the primeval reality, is established as a character. Rochester presents three similar, but not identical, descriptions of the emergence of Something: Nothing "begets" Something (stanza 2), Something is "severed" from Nothing (stanza 3); Matter is the "offspring" of Nothing (stanza 5). Stanza 4 focuses on the moment when abstract Something particularizes itself into individual created things: "Men, Beasts, birds, fire, water, Ayre, and land." However, as stanza 3 had asserted, all particular things, like their abstract source Something, are only a temporary aberration in the universe. All must inevitably fall back into their source, "boundless" Nothing. Stanzas 5 through 7 describe the creation process in terms of political revolt undertaken by a new set of philosophical abstractions. Matter, Form, Time, Place, and Body form a conspiracy of existing things united in opposition to Nothing. Then one of the allies—Time—turns against his fellow conspirators. Things require time to exist, but Time also relentlessly measures their progress into disintegration. In the end all things dissolve back into Nothing's "hungry wombe."

The middle stanzas of the poem (8 to 12) "move" from abstract philosophical satire to the personal, social satire that ends the poem. In these middle stanzas Rochester directs his attack upon three types of pretentious thinker: the theologian ("the Divine"), the philosopher ("the wise"), and "the Politician." These are precisely the individuals who hold themselves to be the knowing intermediaries between high abstract truth and ordinary minds. The latter—"Laick Eyes"—remain happily ignorant of the envelope of Nothing that surrounds their existence. The theologian pretends to superior knowledge—which is, Rochester implies, really a knowledge of Nothing. Nothing is the reward of both good and evil; as a result, the virtuous may expect the small consolation of not being punished ("Nothing" will be taken away from them), while the wicked, who might expect punishment, may rejoice at receiving the identical fate. In stanza 10, Rochester turns to philosophers, mocking their methods and terms: "Enquire, define, distinguish, teach, devise"). Nothing, which is the ultimate answer to all questions, repudiates all analyses. Finally, when the most pragmatic of thinkers, the politicians, attempt to apply high-minded philosophy ("Is or is not . . ./ And true or false") to practical matters, they too are frustrated. The "least unsafe and best" solution to these philosophical questions seems to be a nihilistic belief in Nothing.

In the final five stanzas of the poem, Rochester moves to a more familiar Restoration satire of social types. Having established Nothing as a positive character, he can wittily describe the king's counselors as fit for "nothing." Moreover, he notes that "Something" (gold, although he does not use the word) is absent from the king's treasury. (Charles II's exchequer was often in an embarrassing state, and "Upon Nothing" was probably written at the time of a 1672 declaration of bankruptcy.)

England's "Statesmen" also lack "Something"—intelligence. Stanzas 15 and 16 extend the satire beyond the center of the realm to include the categories already touched upon and to expand beyond England. Bishops ("Lawn-sleeves"), noblemen, scholars, and judges ("ffurrs and Gowns") are full of pompous Nothing. The prides of the French, Dutch, British, Irish, Scots, Spaniards, and Danes prove equally vacant. Rochester concludes by leveling three more items, the gratitude of a great man, the promises of a king, and the vows of a whore: All are equally empty. In making the whore his ultimate instance of nothingness, Rochester emphasizes his contempt for all attempts to inflate the importance and the permanence of human achievement.

Forms and Devices

"Upon Nothing" is a panegyric that celebrates the universal significance of nothing. It is composed as an apostrophe, with Rochester addressing the personified abstraction, "Nothing." The character of Nothing is, however, ambiguous; its sex, for example, is uncertain. In stanza 1, it is a "brother" who "begets," but in stanza 7 it has become a mother with a "hungry wombe." The confusion here, like that caused by the three slightly differently phrased accounts of creation in the first seven stanzas, may constitute a deliberate parody of what Rochester saw as the fatal inconsistencies in the biblical account of creation.

There is a paradoxical aspect to the phrase "hungry wombe"; wombs should produce, not consume. Paradoxes abound in the poem. "Fruitfull Emptinesses" (stanza 4) is, in effect, an inversion of "hungry wombe." In another paradox, "Rebell-Light" does not enlighten but rather "obscures" (covers over, darkens) the dark face of Nothing. The phrase "Rebell-Light" also recalls the two most common names of the devil in the Christian tradition: Satan (adversary) and Lucifer (light-bearer). Rochester's satanic Lucifer, however, is the enemy not of the Creator but of uncreative Nothing.

The end of the poem is openly paradoxical, as Rochester ironically praises the empty knowledge of philosophers, the empty treasury of the king, the empty veracity of the French, the empty courage of the Dutch, and the empty content of the king's word. This avalanche of particular paradoxes is rooted in the core paradox of the poem, the idea that "Nothing" is a thing that may act and which may be addressed.

Rochester develops two principal patterns of imagery in the first half of the poem as he narrates the actions of his personified abstractions. The first is the imagery of sexual generation, beginning with the metaphor of Nothing "begetting" Something and a probable obscene pun on "what" (punning with "twat") in stanza 2. It continues with references to Nothing's "offspring," "embrace," and "wombe." The introduction of "Rebell-Light" in stanza 5 begins a pattern of references to politics and revolt: Nothing's "foes" join in "Leagues"; Time is a traitor whom Nothing bribes into betraying his allies back into Nothing.

"Upon Nothing" is composed in rhymed triplets, a relatively rare form in a period when the heroic couplet had established itself as the standard for poetry. Scholars have pointed to the verse letters of John Donne and the *Divine Emblemes* of Francis Quarles as possible sources. Lines 1 and 2 of each stanza are iambic pentameter; with the exception of stanzas 4 and 14, the third line is an Alexandrine (iambic hexameter). The additional syllables of the concluding line emphasize Rochester's use of the stanza as an end-stopped unit of thought.

Themes and Meanings

"Upon Nothing" has been described as one of the most nihilistic poems in English literature. It may well be; it seems to assert that nothing matters because Nothing is the alpha and the omega of the universe. Yet it also illustrates an inescapable paradox of nihilistic art: Is not a work of art in itself an assertion that something—art—does matter? Is not Rochester's intellectual and linguistic cleverness an assertion of some aesthetic value? And does not his disparagement of the illusions promoted by theologians, politicians, the French, the Dutch, and others necessarily imply an assertion of some moral standard?

"Nothing" figures both positively and negatively in the poem. On one hand, "Nothing" acts like a thing: It is "a being"; it can beget and embrace and bribe; it can be described as a "brother" or a "self"; it has a face, a bosom, hands, and a womb. On the other hand, "Nothing" is the absence of all things: It is the formless, substanceless vacuum from which, according to Judeo-Christian tradition, God created the universe. Rochester conspicuously omits God from his account of the creation of the world and of its eventual dissolution. No providential deity plans the lives of humans or the fate of the universe. Creation and destruction are equally self-generated; the first is spontaneous, and the second is inevitable. Rochester deliberately rejects the pieties of his age. Most specifically, he mocks the pious poems "Hymn to Light" and *Davideis* by his celebrated contemporary Abraham Cowley. Until his own conversion to Christianity prior to his early death, Rochester was strongly influenced by the atheistic, materialistic philosophy of Thomas Hobbes.

There is a sharpness to the last lines that is characteristic of Rochester's satire. His reduction of the great man's gratitude, the king's promises, and the whore's vows to equal emptiness is a pointed gesture. The circle of aristocratic wits to whom he circulated the poem—none of Rochester's verse was published by him—might comfortably share his jibes at the delusions of the self-righteous metaphysicians, but even they, as "Great men" themselves, should have been pricked by the sting of these last lines.

J. K. Van Dover

V-LETTER AND OTHER POEMS

Author: Karl Shapiro (1913-2000)
Type of poem: Book of poems
First published: 1944

The Poems

   V-Letter and Other Poems is Karl Shapiro's second major collection of poetry, written from 1942 to 1944 while Shapiro was on active duty in the U.S. Army during World War II. As Shapiro notes in the book's introduction, all the poems except "Satire: Anxiety" were written while he was stationed in Australia and New Zealand. As described in his 1988 autobiography *The Younger Son*, he left the selection, editing, and arrangement of *V-Letter and Other Poems* to his first wife Evalyn Katz because the rigors of serving as a combat medic prohibited much involvement with the actual making of a book. While one might suspect that the war would most definitely shape the poetry, Shapiro states that he guarded "against becoming a war poet.'" Shapiro remarks that he had not "written these poems to accord with any doctrine or system of thought or even a theory of composition." Furthermore, he states, "I have nothing to offer in the way of beliefs or challenges or prosody."

   Despite Shapiro's modest self-effacement, *V-Letter and Other Poems* established him as one of the most important American poets, prosodists, and poetry critics of postwar American literature. He may have been isolated in the small, war-torn terrain of New Guinea for twenty-six months writing his poetry in his more than occasional lonely solitude, but when he returned to the United States after the war he discovered he was famous. *V-Letter and Other Poems* not only won the Pulitzer Prize in poetry, but it also enjoyed a large readership (including being placed on all U.S. Navy ship libraries), and it launched for Shapiro a long, distinguished career in American letters. Ultimately, the book's publication led Shapiro to become the first poetry consultant to the Library of Congress (the position is now titled United States Poet Laureate), the editor of the prestigious *Poetry* magazine, and a tenured professor at the University of Nebraska at Lincoln, where he edited the literary journal *Prairie Schooner.* Thus, Shapiro did indeed have something of value to offer.

   Much of Shapiro's poetry, including the lyrics found in *V-Letter and Other Poems*, tends to cast the poet as an outsider, an iconoclast. As Shapiro once noted in an interview in *The Paris Review*, "The poet is in exile whether he is or he is not. Because of what everybody knows about society's idea of the artist as a peripheral character and a potential bum. Or a troublemaker. . . . I always thought of myself as being both in and out of society at the same time." While *V-Letter and Other Poems* seems to exhibit a poet who embraces the conformity of traditional forms and prosody, the nonconformist vision is certainly most evident. One will notice, for example, that the poet seems more like a voyeur than a participant despite his actual involvement in the war as a medic. Yet this detachment may have arisen largely from his Jewish heritage: He was a conscientious objector and did not carry a gun; therefore, he observed the violence of war firsthand and assisted in rescuing wounded participants, but he did not himself participate in the making of violence. Thus, his poems very often place him outside the scene looking in while the violent world is dropping shells all around him. Additionally, his use of traditional forms and meter might suggest his conformity to past designs; however, close scrutiny of the work reveals Shapiro's innovative departures from poetic tradition. For example, the lead poem of *V-Letter and Other Poems*, "Aside," is a long lyric poem of six sexains or sestets (six-line stanzas). As Shapiro himself notes in his *Prosody Handbook* (1965), "the stave of six is an iambic pentameter or tetrameter stanza rhyming *ababcc*." However, rather than specifically employing the English stanzaic conventions, Shapiro embellishes. He recasts the stanza's first four lines into a brace or envelope quatrain rhyming *abba*, which is then followed by the rhyming couplet. Interestingly, the brace quatrain is rarely found except in the writing of the Italian sonnet octave. Thus, the iconoclastic poet is simultaneously adhering to and departing from tradition.

In "Aside," Shapiro, as an observer, focuses upon the significance of mail day to soldiers who face combat on a daily basis. The poem is not merely a celebration of mail day but an illustration of how mail day is an occasion for renewal, as if the soldiers had stumbled upon an oasis. The "war stands aside for an hour"; as a result, "demobilized for a moment, a world is made human." Peace is renewed in the souls of the men despite the fact the battle rages elsewhere. For the moment, they will "Say no more of the dead than a prayer" because "there is nothing alive/ Except as [mail day] keeps [them] alive, not tomorrow but now." His detachment from the scene allows readers to more thoroughly enter the scene, to know more immediately what it is to still breathe despite the fact that death has been near and will yet be near.

Much of what holds *V-Letter and Other Poems* together is the way Shapiro focuses not so much on the war itself as on what it is that keeps the men alive. While this is surely a thematic concern, it is also consistent with the lyric quality of the collection. Shapiro neither praises war nor casts aspersion toward it. He does not idealize the heroes or make them romantic and, consequently, unreal. When Shapiro utilizes the heroic quatrain (four lines rhyming *abab*), he does so not to invoke the hero of old but to denigrate the nonheroes of his and the soldiers' world. For example, Shapiro prefaces the ballad "The Intellectual" with the line "What should the wars do with these jigging fools?" Clearly, "The man behind the book may not be man,/ His own man or the book's or yet the time's." The intellectual is Shapiro's nonhero. On the other hand, the poet advocates the man, the soldier, or the artist who will "Do something! die in Spain or paint a green/ Gouache." He says, furthermore, that he would "rather be a barber and cut hair/ Than walk with [the intellectual] in gilt museum halls." If the intellectual is Shapiro's nonhero, the detestable man, then clearly his heroes are the outcasts as shown in the poems "Jew" and "Nigger." In the former example, the Jew is one of the world's active people, though despised and destined to die: "The name is immortal but only the name// Our name is impaled in the heart of the world on a hill/ Where we suffer to die by the hands of ourselves, and to kill." The poem "Nigger," on the other hand, explores the prejudices endured by black men, who are admirable in comparison with the intellectual. This particular poem is filled with active verbs, elevating its character above those who do nothing:

> When you boxed that hun, when you raped that trash that you didn't rape,
> When you caught that slug with a belly of fire and a face of gray,
> When you felt that loop and you took that boot from a KKK,
> Are you coming to peace, O Booker T. Lincoln Roosevelt of grape?

Not only does Shapiro show readers the injustice of a prejudicial world in which the black man is punished for crimes he did not commit, in which he has had to fight battles he did not start, but the poet also shows how black men have been killed by the South's cultural politics. What is a black man's peace, perhaps, but death? Even then, however, Shapiro questions peace in death: "Did the Lord say yes, did the Lord say no, did you ask the Lord/ When the jaw came down, when the cotton blossomed out of your bones?"

Readers may wonder why poems such as "Jew" and "Nigger" are included in a collection composed during and written about World War II. Likely, Shapiro intends for readers to see that all soldiers are "Jews" and "niggers." Soldiers are immortal in name only; in "bondage of murder and shame" ("Jew"), they die and fight upon the hills, bringing to mind the famous portrait of the Marines at Iwo Jima. Soldiers catch slugs fired from the gray, ambiguous politics that find wars necessary; they feel the noose about their necks and hope that Jesus will "cut that cord" ("Nigger"). If this is the case, these poems stand as allegories for the soldier's condition and perhaps the reader's as well. If Shapiro's heroes are people such as barbers ("The Intellectual"), if they "do something," are people not, in the majority, "soldiers," "Jews," and "niggers" too?

Granted, darkness frequents Shapiro's lyrics; yet his poems are not mournful songs as one might suspect when reading a volume about war. They are songs that breathe with the experience and significance of the war itself. Take, for example, "Troop Train," a long lyric of five octaves (eight-line stanzas) written in either a nonrhyming or coincidental rhyming pattern. The soldiers are "clustered" on themselves and "hang as from a cornucopia/ In total friendliness." The image is one of the horn of plenty, a celebration of life's sustenance, a Thanksgiving scene. While this image creates situational irony (how can troops, gathered together, perhaps traveling toward death, sustain life or be thankful?), the effect is understood. They are thankful to be alive, if only currently, and thankful for the closeness when, once the soldiers arrive at the battle, they must ultimately face death alone: "Luck also travels and not all come back." Yet while the trains lead "the march to death," they may also lead to "that survival which is all our hope."

Perhaps one of the most engaging and horrific pieces in the collection is "The Gun." The poem personifies the soldier's gun: "You were angry and manly to shatter the sleep of your throat." In this poem, comprising five brace or envelope quatrains, the reader discovers an image of the close relationship, almost worshipful, the soldier has with his gun. "I savour your breath like a perfume," the poet writes; "I grip you"; "Come with me"; "You are only the means of the practical humor of death/ Which is savage to punish the dead for the sake of my sin!" Interestingly, the words chosen almost suggest a sexual bond between the soldier and his gun; if the gun "comes" with the man, both have experienced the simultaneous orgasm of fear and courage, life and death. The soldier persona, who does not wish to place the blame of violence upon the gun, says, "I absolve from your name/ The exaction of murder, my gun. It is I who have killed." Significantly, Shapiro recognizes the human, passionate aspect of warfare and, furthermore, how the soldier clings to the "god" or lover that might save him.

Forms and Devices

Shapiro is a master of poetic form and devices. Much of his professional career was dedicated to studies of poetics and prosody, as found most impressively in *A Prosody Handbook*. In *V-Letter and Other Poems*, Shapiro's ability to manipulate form and reinvent it is unmistakable. His favorite form in this particular volume seems to be the terza rima, as found in "Movie Actress," "Jew," and the sequence "The Interlude." The terza rima is an Italian form composed of interlocking tercets, or three-line stanzas, ending with a couplet. For example, the rhyme pattern for Shapiro's poems is *aba bcb cdc ded gg*. An antique form, it was introduced into English poetry from Dante Alighieri's *La Divina Commedia* (c. 1320; *The Divine Comedy*). Perhaps Shapiro's use of this form is a matter of "form as an extension of content," a design suggested by American poet Robert Creeley. If Shapiro borrows this form from *The Divine Comedy*, he may be suggesting the divine comedy of the war itself.

Not only does Shapiro utilize the terza rima in *V-Letter and Other Poems*, but he also uses the Italian sonnet form frequently, as in "The Sydney Bridge," "Christmas Eve," "Lord, I Have Seen Too Much," and "On Reading Keats in War Time." An Italian sonnet is composed of an octave (eight-line stanza) and a sestet or sexain (six-line stanza). Typically, the Italian sonnet's rhyme pattern runs *abbaabba cdcdcd*. Shapiro, however, makes many adjustments to this basic pattern, sometimes opting to fashion other rhyme combinations. Among other forms are rhymed or unrhymed quatrain or ballad stanzas ("New Guinea," "Sunday: New Guinea," "Fireworks," "Nigger," "Franklin"), sexain stanzas ("Aside," "Red Indian," "The Synagogue"), and cinquain or five-line stanzas ("Jefferson"). Of particular interest, however, is the ambitious form of Shapiro's ottava rima variations ("Piano" and "Christmas Tree"). The ottava rima is a very difficult poem to write, following a standard rhyme pattern of *ababababcc*. Shapiro, however, modernizes the form by displacing the couplet from its final position and embedding it elsewhere. The rhyme pattern of "Piano," for example, is *ababccab*. What Shapiro gains from reinventing the form is displacement of the expected, which is metaphorically equivalent to the displacement of those soldiers from their other lives. In "Piano," the music of both the piano and the poetic form allows the soldiers to "Escape, escape, escape."

Among the more playful forms Shapiro handles expertly is the ballade, as found in "Ballade of the Second-Best Bed." According to Shapiro's *A Prosody Handbook*, the ballade is a "Gallic importation" consisting of "three stanzas and a four-line envoy (a kind of conclusion or dedicatory stanza). The ballade uses three rhymes, and each stanza uses the same rhyme sounds; the scheme is *ababbcbc*. The last line of the first stanza is used as the last line of the other two stanzas and of the envoy." The overall effect is whimsical; so much repetition of sound renders even the most serious of topics humorous. In Shapiro's ballade, the persona, English playwright William Shakespeare, is giving orders for his will. "Good wife," Shakespeare says, "bad fortune is to blame/ That I bequeath when I am dead,/ To you my honor and my name,/ A table, a chair, and the second-best bed." Its place in *V-Letter and Other Poems* is clever and, once the riddle is solved, unmistakable: Just as Shakespeare must prepare his last will, so must a soldier. Furthermore, in reality a soldier's wife is left with as little as Shakespeare's wife; thus, one might as well find humor in the poverty of living. One additional note about "Ballade of the Second-Best Bed" is merited: Shapiro does not ever mention, among the items of Shakespeare's will, a "best bed"; ironically, the best bed is doubtless the grave because it is there that all battles stop.

This discussion about Shapiro's use of poetic form should in no way minimize his other abilities as a poet. He is a master of English metrics, he has a clear eye for imagery, he understands the subtleties of rhythm, and he constructs metaphors that are both startling and exhilarating. As Shapiro once stated in a seminar in creative writing at the University of Nebraska at Lincoln, every poem ought to have an "alligator," something unusual in it that will bite and hold the reader. Shapiro does this without exception in the whole of his work.

Themes and Meanings

V-Letter and Other Poems is a collection of poems about war, written in a time of war by a mind occupied by the effects of war upon his real-people heroes. However, Shapiro's collection neither celebrates war nor condemns it; it is not a patriotic call to arms, and it is not a protest against violence as is so often found in Vietnam War-era poetry. Rather, *V-Letter and Other Poems* examines the human dimension of warfare, from the brotherhood of "Troop Train" and the realization that any one of those friends playing cards may be traveling toward death to the love poem "V-Letter," which clings hopefully and furiously to the security of love.

Perhaps love is a primary theme of *V-Letter and Other Poems*. While the poet may not necessarily love the war, he loves the human aspect of the war: the human isolation, the human discovery of unusual and unnatural relationships ("The Gun"), the human need for pragmatic heroes, the human stage of the movie house and of locale, and the human dignity despite the indignity of death. Shapiro's purpose is to embrace his world and the life in it despite the destruction raining down upon him and his comrades. It also seems to be his desire to use his poems to write home about the war experience. Historically, the "v-letter" was a correspondence mailed home from the front, read and censored by military personnel before being sent to the United States. The actual, graphic details of war never made it across the ocean, locations were never specified, and secrets were kept secret. However, through Shapiro's metaphors and language, his poetic "v-letters," he tells readers more about war and the human position in war than the most realistic account. The war is a mood, a tone, a shadow settled in people's souls. It is a dark humor and a deep, lasting love. In "V-Letter" he writes, "I pray nothing for my safety back,/ Not even luck, because our love is whole/ Whether I live or fail." This is Shapiro's "v-letter" to all of humanity.

Mark Sanders

A VALEDICTION: FORBIDDING MOURNING

Author: John Donne (1572-1631)
Type of poem: Lyric
First published: 1633, in *Poems, by J. D.: With Elegies on the Authors Death*

The Poem

John Donne's nine quatrains of iambic pentameter make up one of the most beautiful love poems in the English language. In the 1675 (fourth) edition of his *Life of Donne*, Izaak Walton claimed that the author gave these lines to his wife in 1611 just before leaving for France. Whether the details of Walton's account are true, the title reflects the content of the piece: a farewell. The poem is thus in the tradition of the *congé d'amour*, a consolation when lovers part.

The poem begins with the image of virtuous men mildly accepting death. The separation of body and soul is so gentle that those friends surrounding the dying cannot tell whether the men are alive or not. So, Donne says, should he and his beloved part, because they do not want to reveal the quality of their love to the uninitiated. Here, then, is the first reason to forbid mourning.

Through a series of elaborate metaphors, Donne offers a second reason. When an earthquake occurs, causing only small cracks in the ground, everyone is disturbed and regards the event as ominous, but when planets move apart, though the distances are great, no harm results. Earthly lovers, Donne continues, cannot accept separation; they fear it as people do earthquakes, because sensory and sensual stimuli make up the entirety of their affection. Donne and his beloved, however, who love spiritually as well as physically, are less troubled by being apart. Their two souls, being one, remain united even when their bodies are apart, just as gold stretches thinly without breaking.

Even if the lovers retain their individual souls, they are divided only like the two parts of a compass used to describe a circle, linked at the top and working in unison. When the compass draws a circle, one point remains stationary in the center but leans toward the other, and by remaining firmly in one place, the fixed point guarantees that its partner will complete its circuit. So the beloved will, by remaining at home, ensure Donne's return; since he will certainly come back, mourning is inappropriate.

Forms and Devices

In "The Life of Cowley," Samuel Johnson labeled the poetry of John Donne and others of his ilk "metaphysical." In such writing, Johnson observed, "The most heterogeneous ideas are yoked by violence together." The images that Donne employs seem removed from the occasion of the lovers' parting: death, celestial motion, twin compasses. All, however, carry within them the promise of reunion, resurrection, and permanence after change. The virtuous man does not fear death because he knows that at the Last Judgment his body and soul will be rejoined forever in bliss. Though Donne and his beloved are "dead" when divided, they may part confident in having a life together hereafter in this world. The comparison of lover and beloved to body and soul is conventional; Donne extends the idea to make it fresh by incorporating religious implications, a technique he uses often in his poetry. Since both love and religion are mysterious and forms of transcendence, the fusion of the two is justified.

The geological-astronomical imagery that introduces the second argument similarly promises reunion. The separation of sensual lovers is like an earthquake in part because these people are "sublunary"; Donne here draws on the belief that everything beneath the moon is subject to mutability and death. Sublunary lovers fear parting because they can never be certain that they will see each other again. Just as the cleavages caused by earthquakes do not necessarily repair themselves, these terrestrial, hence inferior, lovers may not reunite.

Likening lovers to Earth and other planets is typical of Donne and his fellow Metaphysical poets. Yet the metaphors are not mere poetical trickery. The macrocosm of the universe and the microcosm of the individual become interchangeable because the metaphors convey the lovers' feelings. Donne and his beloved are the world to each other.

Donne and his beloved are, like the planets, beyond the realm of change because they are joined spiritually as well as physically. Since their love is not subject to alteration, they need not fear parting. Moreover, medieval cosmology maintained that in 36,000 years the planets and stars would return to their positions at the moment of creation. The completion of this epoch will mark the apocalypse and resurrection. This image thus unites with and extends the previous one anticipating the Last Judgment.

The conceit of the twin compasses, probably the most famous of Donne's metaphors, similarly builds on the previous one. Just as the planets describe a circuit in 36,000 years, so the compasses make a circle of 360 degrees. It is no accident that the poem has thirty-six lines. The circle is a traditional symbol of eternal love, since it has no beginning and no end (hence the tradition of the wedding ring). The completion of the circle once more promises the lovers' meeting at journey's end.

In a curious sexual reversal, Donne likens his beloved to the masculine principle. Hers is the foot that grows erect as his point approaches. Hers is the firmness that, phalluslike, fills his circle and makes it "just"; the word not only implies the completed round and physical reunion but also circles back to the virtuous (just) man at the beginning of the poem, so that the poem, like Donne, ends where it began.

Themes and Meanings

The sexual imagery that concludes the poem does not contradict the pervasive spirituality of the piece, but complements it. John Donne has been called the poet of mutual love, and though he may play diverse roles—the cynical lover of "The Indifferent," the Platonic lover in "The Relic"—he is also the advocate of physical and spiritual love united. "Dull, sublunary lovers" rely totally on the physical, so their love cannot survive absence. Donne and his beloved may "care less, eyes, lips, and hands to miss," but they do care. The need for both types of love is evident in the metaphor of the twin compasses. The circular motion of the compasses, like the circular orbits of the planets in Aristotelian physics, symbolizes heavenly love, since all movement above the moon takes this shape. Sublunary motion is linear, and that is the figure the two points of the compass describe when they move together in a plane. Together, the divine circle and animal line create the human spiral. Donne rejects the duality of body and soul: Love for him is not one or the other, but both—a single, indivisible entity.

Hence, Donne rejects the Petrarchan idealization of the beloved as untouchable and godlike. He employs the imagery of Petrarch in the second stanza when he speaks of "tear-floods" and "sigh-tempests," but in forbidding such forms of mourning the poem distances itself from the philosophy that relies on such metaphors. Donne's love is human, as is his beloved. The opening lines may imply that she is body and he soul, thereby suggesting that he is purer than she; the second stanza dispels such a reading, linking the lovers in the pronoun "us." In the third stanza, each is a planet, and later their souls are one. The twin compasses may be understood as portraying that same fusion, one foot being the will, the other reason. As body and soul require each other for life, so will and reason cannot operate independently. The sexual reversal of the last stanza corresponds to the beloved's assuming the controlling role of reason, which guides the errant will; its fixedness converts the will's centrifugal force into the circle, a pattern of constancy. Love reconciles opposites and accepts no mastery of one party over the other.

In chapter 12 of *La vita nuova* (c. 1292; *The New Life*), Dante writes, speaking as love, "I am as the center of a circle, to which all parts of the circumference stand in equal relation." This passage may have provided Donne with the idea for his famous conceit of the twin compasses; it certainly expresses the same vision of love's unifying and godlike power, of love as the still center around which the world revolves and to which all things return to find that rest that they can experience nowhere else.

The image of the dying men that introduces the piece indicates the fusion of Donne and his beloved as body and soul and promises resurrection, but the focus on death is too gloomy for the purpose the author intends. The planets have much to recommend them as a metaphor: Again the imagery promises return, and the orbits of the planets in Donne's Ptolemaic system describe circles. Yet if the first metaphor falls short because of its rootedness in mortality, the second proves equally unsatisfactory because it divorces itself from humanity. Only with the twin compasses does the poet find that perfect fusion of human and divine, flesh and spirit, line and circle, that constitutes true love. The author has succeeded in his quest for the correct language in which to couch his meaning, and in the process of creating his poem he has moved from death and separation to life and reunion, imitating the experience the verses promise.

Joseph Rosenblum

THE VANITY OF HUMAN WISHES

Author: Samuel Johnson (1709-1784)
Type of poem: Satire
First published: 1749

The Poem

Samuel Johnson's *The Vanity of Human Wishes* imitates, as its subtitle states, Juvenal's tenth satire. The 368 lines of iambic pentameter in rhymed couplets do not claim to provide an exact translation but rather to apply the poem to eighteenth century England. While Johnson therefore feels free to modernize the allusions, he follows his model closely. The poem opens with the proposition that people ask for the wrong things and points out the folly of the first common request, riches. An interlude follows during which the poet invokes Democritus, known as the "laughing philosopher" because of his amusement at human folly. Here Johnson repeats the poem's central idea, the absurdity of people's prayers.

The poem then resumes its catalog of vain desires. Many seek political power, but no one can remain supreme for long (lines 73-90). As proof of this general proposition, Johnson, after attacking parliamentary corruption (lines 91-98), offers the example of Thomas Cardinal Wolsey, the great favorite of Henry VIII. Wolsey enjoyed preeminence in church and state but fell from power and died, abandoned, in a monastery (lines 99-120). Johnson then offers several other, shorter examples of powerful men who have lost their positions, even their lives, in the vain pursuit of political success (lines 129-134).

Wisdom, though one of the four pagan virtues, also yields no joy (lines 135-173). The beginning student confronts many obstacles and distractions: doubts, praise, difficulty, novelty, sloth, beauty, disease, melancholy. Nor does learning guarantee happiness. On the contrary, the rewards awaiting the scholar are "Toil, envy, want, the garret [later changed to "patron"], and the jail." Again Johnson offers concrete examples to illustrate his point: Thomas Lydiat, an Oxford scholar who died in poverty; Galileo, imprisoned and forced to recant; William Laud, Archbishop of Canterbury, executed in 1645.

Greeks, Romans, and Britons have sought military glory; it, too, proves hollow. Johnson's aversion to war informs the opening passage of this section (lines 185-190). The chief emblem of the futility of "the warrior's pride" (line 191) is Charles XII of Sweden, who conquered Denmark in 1700 and Poland in 1704, and sought to place the Swedish flag on the walls of Moscow. At Pultowa (in 1709), Peter the Great, aided by the Russian winter, defeated Charles, who died nine years later by an unknown hand in his attempt to seize Norway. This section concludes with shorter treatments of Xerxes and Charles Albert, Elector of Bavaria, whose ends were equally inglorious.

Like Juvenal, Johnson concludes his list of vain requests with long life (lines 255-318) and beauty (lines 319-342). Those seeking the former discover "That life protracted is protracted woe" (line 258). Even the few who enjoy health in age lose friends and relatives to the grave and see the familiar world disappear, so that death provides welcome release. Anne Vane and Catherine Sedley, mistresses to royalty, demonstrate that beauty betrays its possessors.

Is nothing worth having, then? Here Johnson parts company with Juvenal, offering a Christian response to this question and urging his audience to wish for those qualities that can bring happiness: faith, hope, and love. Armed with these, the mind can rest content in a tragic world.

Forms and Devices

In this philosophical poem, Johnson often relies on that "grandeur of generality" that he said he missed in the poetry of Abraham Cowley. Even in his portraits, where he might detail particulars (as Juvenal does), he prefers to let the reader imagine the specifics. He does, however, employ a number of image patterns—of battles, disease, animals, the flux of time, and fire—to develop his argument. Often, the metaphors are implied; when he writes, "Time hovers o'er, impatient to destroy" (line 259), he is alluding to time as a vulture. This avian imagery is more explicit earlier in the poem when he describes "Rebellion's vengeful talons [that seize] on Laud" (line 168).

Johnson constructs his argument through synecdoche, offering a few examples to stand for the infinite number of wishes one might make. So, too, the few people cited suggest the many others the reader can imagine. Preferring the general to the specific, Johnson finds synecdoche a convenient device for description. He does not paint a beautiful face but offers "rosy lips and radiant eyes" (line 323). The gifts of nature are suggested by "The fruits autumnal, and the vernal flower" (line 262).

Personification abounds from the first line, in which Observation surveys humankind, to the last: "Wisdom calms the mind/ And makes the happiness she does not find" (lines 367-368). Hope, fear, desire, and hate spread their snares. Preferment has a gate, History speaks, "Pride and Prudence take her [Virtue's] seat in vain" (line 336). Like synecdoche, this device keeps the poem at the level of general truth that the author seeks. As he would write a decade later in *The History of Rasselas, Prince of Abyssinia* (1759), "The business of the poet . . . is to examine, not the individual but the species; to remark general properties and large appearances."

Much of the poem's power derives from the strong verbs that Samuel Johnson uses, and many of these emphasize the destructive nature inherent in conventional desires. Thus, "the knowing and the bold/ Fall in the general massacre of gold" (lines 21-22). Those seeking political power "mount, . . . shine, evaporate, and fall" (line 76). Beauty also "falls betray'd" (line 341). All who seek to rise decline instead.

This paradox is reinforced through the use of antithesis. The section on long life concludes with the examples of the Duke of Marlborough and Jonathan Swift, who ended their lives in senility. During the reign of Queen Anne, Marlborough was the darling of the Whigs and bitterly opposed by Swift, strong supporter of the Tories who sought to conclude the war with France in which Marlborough so distinguished himself. Royal favor should have provided protection, but the favor of Charles I led to the execution of Thomas Wentworth. Similarly, Edward Hyde, father-in-law of James, Duke of York, and Charles II's Lord Chancellor, was forced into exile. Writing of the perils that beset the would-be scholar, Johnson includes praise, which should encourage, and beauty, which should stimulate; but in the world of the poem, all things include and produce their opposites. Gold bribes the ruffian to draw his sword, and gold corrupts the judge who will try this criminal.

Themes and Meanings

In the thirty-second issue of his periodical, *The Rambler* (1750), Johnson wrote, "The armies of pain send their arrows against us on every side; the choice is only between those which are more or less sharp, or tinged with poison of greater or less malignity; and the strongest armour which reason can supply, will only blunt their points, but cannot repel them." This same tragic sense pervades *The Vanity of Human Wishes*; indeed, the controlling metaphor of the *Rambler* passage is an elaboration on the poem's central thesis: "Fate wings with every wish the afflictive dart" (line 15). As Johnson implies through his use of antithesis, wealth, power, learning, glory, longevity, beauty—all that this world offers—prove vain because these things deceive. Johnson does not suggest that if they could endure they would yield happiness. The poem recognizes that the things of this world pass away and laments the mutability of existence. Even when these gifts are at their greatest, though, they breed discontent. The more the wealth, the less the tranquillity of the possessor; the more beautiful the woman, the more likely she is to fall "betray'd, despis'd, distress'd" (line 341).

The gifts are flawed, as are those who seek them. At the beginning of the poem, Johnson speaks of "wavering man" (line 7). Human happiness is ultimately impossible, because one always wants more than what one has. Sweden's Charles XII cannot rest until all is his "beneath the polar sky" (line 204). Wolsey gains so much power that "conquest unresisted ceased to please" (line 107). The irony in the poem reflects the irony of the world and its inhabitants.

Although Johnson draws on Juvenal and invokes Democritus, his poem is less satire than tragedy. Whereas the original, for example, mocks the old man with his dripping nose and toothless gums, the one-eyed Hannibal riding his last surviving elephant, Johnson pities his subjects. The characters he paints are heroic, sympathetic though fatally flawed. Satire posits distance from, tragedy identification with, the figures portrayed, and Johnson felt kinship with those in the poem: Reading the section on the scholar at the home of Mrs. Henry Thrale, Johnson burst into tears.

As Johnson parts company with Juvenal in his outlook on the world, so, too, does he differ in his solution for coping with the evils inherent in existence. For Juvenal, a stoic resignation and endurance are the best one can achieve. Johnson had much of the antique Roman in him, but he was also devoutly Christian. The title of the poem suggests Ecclesiastes' pronouncement that all is vanity; the work itself embraces the Augustinian view that while worldly goods cannot bring happiness, religion can. "Our heart is restless until it rests in thee," Saint Augustine wrote in the opening passage of his *Confessions* (397-400 C.E.), and so Johnson concludes. Trusting in divine Providence to shape one's ends, seeking those things that abide—faith, hope, and love— one can achieve the tranquil mind that eludes those who seek happiness in the wrong places.

Joseph Rosenblum

VARNA SNOW

Author: Roland Flint (1934-2001)
Type of poem: Meditation
First published: 1983, in *Resuming Green: Selected Poems, 1965-1982*

The Poem

Roland Flint's "Varna Snow" is a poignant meditation on time, specifically on the fluid continuum of past, present, and future. The poem's dramatic opening sentence alone is composed of a freewheeling tumble of temporal references: "summer," "years," "morning," "hour," and a specific day (namely, the Fourth of July). The poet, now at midlife—he recalls a childhood event now forty-three years past—ponders the implications of being timebound. Aided by the engine of the imagination, every person, Flint finds, can exist at any moment simultaneously at the juncture of three tenses: in the past, the present, and the future. Here, a natural phenomena, specifically the heavy clouds of windblown seeds released in the early summer by cottonwood trees, triggers a series of observations, first about the poet's childhood on the North Dakota farmlands; then about his present moment as a scholar visiting Varna (in the early 1980's, Flint traveled to Bulgaria as part of a project to translate several prominent national poets); and ultimately about the uncertain time ahead, presumably the inevitable experience of death.

The poem begins tied to a specific time and space. It is early June in Varna, the Bulgarian port on the west shore of the Black Sea. For days now, the poet has watched women sweep the fleecy cottonwood seeds that drift like snow along the city sidewalks. That present moment and location are not actually established until nearly two-thirds of the way through the poem, however. Indeed, the poem's opening sentence is a breathless rush back forty-three years to the North Dakota farmland where the poet grew up and specifically to a memory, triggered by the faux snow of the Bulgarian cottonwoods, of an unexpected Fourth of July snow that had lasted only an hour before melting into "the day's parades, fireworks, and speeches."

That memory, in turn, triggers a further recollection of the Dakota cottonwood trees and their annual release of seeds that would lightly silt the summer farmlands in a wintry white. Lovingly, the poet particularizes that memory, recalling the cottonwood seeds as softer than the snowflakes and moving wildly with the "lightest breath of moving air." Abruptly cutting to the present, forty-three years later and a half a world away, the poet in line 19 confesses that he has not been back to his North Dakota home. Aided by his imagination, however, he now feels suddenly close to that distant place and time and decides the drifts of Varna "snow" are quite like the real snows of long-ago North Dakota winters.

The poet, clearly touched by such spontaneous recollection, impulsively gathers three great handfuls of the fleecy seeds and stuffs them into a knothole of a tree. Ruefully, he identifies the three handfuls as representing his past, his present, and his future: "where I come from/ Where I am today, and where I'm headed in the snow." Stuffing the tree, thus, suggests the bittersweet work of the imagination itself as it serves, like the tree, as a repository—for the memories of the past, for the sort of observations that keep the present resonant and unexpectedly suggestive, and ultimately for the unsettling anxieties of tomorrow.

Forms and Devices

The poem is invitingly direct. Although Flint was a career academic, teaching for more than thirty-five years at Georgetown University, his poem is remarkably free of the elevated diction, dense philosophizing, and studied versification that often characterize the work of contemporary academic poets. He often described his poems as "common feelings, captured in uncommon language." Indeed, his diction is deceptively simple, a sort of elegant colloquialism, a style Flint often termed "user-friendly." Language does not call attention to itself. Flint dispenses with the conventions of rhythm and rhyme. The line length undulates in a sort of gentle ebb and flow patterning appropriate to a memory poem. The verse lines themselves are set in a supple free verse pitched to enhance an atmosphere of bittersweet recollection by frequently indulging the sibilant's sound—the first four-line sentence alone contains six such sounds—whose calming hypnotic effect is quite pronounced. When the poem is read aloud, and Flint's poetry is very much pitched for recitation, that soft lilting sound, along with the repeated use of rich, rolling long vowels, slows the poem's lines and enhances the poem's general mood of recollection.

In addition to the language, point of view here is direct. Flint comes to his poem without affectation. The point of the view here is the unmediated first-person—the poem commences and then sustains the vulnerability of the first-person pronoun—an intimacy that helps create a voice appropriate for the poem's confessional mode. It is as if the poet is speaking directly to the reader. Flint was fond of quoting a line from fellow poet Stanley Kunitz that poetry should be an "art so transparent that you look through and see the world." The poem thus relies on direct observation, the intuitive response to an ordinary natural event, the snowing down of the cottonwood seeds.

Until the closing lines, the poem resists indulging any of the intrusive embellishments of figurative language and heavy-handed symbols. The poet records with careful and loving eye and then recollects with similar directness. Like poet Theodore Roethke, whose influence Flint often acknowledged and who was the subject of Flint's doctoral work at the University of Minnesota, Flint here takes as his subject the ability of the unadorned natural world to trigger such a response and, in turn, to reveal modest truths so obvious that they border on cliché—how persistent the past can prove, how stunning the present moment should be, and how uncertain tomorrow must remain. Yet, like the cottonwood trees that every year send out that splendid shower of snowy seeds, such truths are no less compelling for being ordinary.

Themes and Meanings

It is the ordinary, then, that compels the beauty and impact of "Varna Snow." The midsummer snowstorm that begins the poem is one of those entirely natural events that is nevertheless so unexpected, so singular, and so stunning that it becomes a memory, a distinct moment in time preserved in remarkable detail by the imagination. Flint assures the reader that the imagination is not merely composed of such extraordinary events but is as well a storehouse of far more ordinary moments, like the annual hail of cottonwood seeds, moments that, unexamined, seem quite unremarkable and commonplace. Yet when apprehended by the open eye and recorded by the responsive imagination, such events become incandescent recollections still compelling more than forty years later.

If the imagination is the mechanism for preserving the past, it also compels the present. In line 19, amid his nostalgic recollections, the poet moves abruptly to his moment in the present when he has been so taken by the trees in Varna and particularly by the sight of the women sweeping the snowy piles along the sidewalk, another commonplace sight that ignites, nevertheless, a most striking response. Here Flint moves from past to present in a breathless six-line movement (lines 17-22) that is, in fact, three complete sentences uninterrupted even by a period. The ability to respond, this inexplicable ignition of observation occasioned by a thoroughly ordinary event in the natural world, is part of that same imagination that stores memories.

After he stuffs the seeds into the tree, he closes the poem with the intimations of the darkling fears that are also part of the imagination's storehouse: the anxieties over the future, the midlife late-night thoughts over the dwindling of tomorrows. The closing phrase, "where I'm headed in the snow," is literally about his ongoing errands that day along the Varna streets amid the swirling blizzard of cottonwood seeds but is as well a suggestion of the larger future, the larger uncertainties (chilling, as suggested by the wintry imagery) with which every person at midlife must come to face at moments of honest reflection.

Although there hangs about the poem a clear sense of the fragility of the moment and the speechlessly quick passage of time, Flint resists simple despair. After all, the snow imagery that so abounds here, suggestive of the life-stilling wintry bleakness, is supremely metaphoric. The "snow" is actually a storm of seeds, themselves suggestive of defiant fertility and resilient life. Indeed, the Varna "snow" storm engenders the poem itself and in turn inspires the reader to stay alert and to relish the most apparently ordinary moments. So much of life is stubbornly linear: Each day slips by irrecoverable, childhood can never be relived, death presses relentlessly nearer each day, each individual is a fragile, timed commodity. Yet there throbs here a wider energy: The seasons are wonderfully cyclic, and within the grasping energy of the imagination even the distant past can be summoned at a moment's response. It is that sense of stunning fluidity that rescues the poem from the despair necessarily latent in any meditation on time.

Joseph Dewey

VENDÉMIAIRE

Author: Guillaume Apollinaire (Guillaume Albert Wladimir Alexandre Apollinaire de Kostrowitzky; 1880-1918)
Type of poem: Meditation
First published: 1912; collected in *Alcools*, 1913; English translation collected in *Alcools*, 1964

The Poem

Guillaume Apollinaire's poem "Vendémiaire" takes as its title the name of the first month of the new calendar adopted in the wake of the French Revolution. This month, corresponding to September 22 to October 21, was named for the grape harvest (*la vendange* in French, as opposed to *la moisson*, for harvest in general). Thus themes of wine, drinking, and even drunkenness permeate the poem along with the gathering in of the harvest.

"Vendémiaire," the last poem in Apollinaire's collection *Alcools* (alcohols), parallels the opening poem "Zone" and continues the street scenes of Paris that recur throughout the collection. "Zone" began with an image of the Eiffel Tower as a shepherdess of the bleating flock of Parisian bridges. In contrast to the sights of Paris that dominate the earlier poem, Apollinaire turns in "Vendémiaire" to a general evocation of Paris that emphasizes the sounds of voices.

The opening quatrain focuses on the poet himself rather than his surroundings. Apollinaire situates his life "à l'époque où finissaient les rois," at the time when the new calendar of the revolution had replaced the time of the monarchy. In accord with the title, he walks through Paris in late September, where, during nights filled with grapevines, he awaits "the harvest of the dawn." The harvest, however, will be composed not of grapes but of song. One night, he hears Paris sing: "I am thirsty for the cities of France, of Europe and of the world." This thirst of Paris, which all other cities attempt to satisfy, affirms the dominant position of the capital both within France and in the world beyond.

To this initial voice, seven others reply, as other cities respond to Paris. The first to answer are three cities from Brittany—Rennes, Quimper, and Vannes. This choice underlines the identity of this harvest as something other than the literal production of wine. Brittany is the part of France least capable of producing wine, but this maritime climate produces "reason" and "mystery" that satisfy an intellectual thirst.

The next three voices, those of northern cities, Lyon, and southern cities, reply from within France to pay homage to Paris. The industrial north offers the song of its "holy factories," while Lyon and the south make more emotional contributions. Then from outside France come voices from Sicily, Rome, and Koblenz. The song of Sicily draws on pagan mythology, invoking the danger of antiquity with references to Ixion, who earned the wrath of Zeus, and to the sirens tempting sailors to their doom. This threat is in the past, but that of Rome extends to the present, as Rome with its "imperious voice" seems to challenge Paris. Still, the pope's triple crown falls to the floor, allowing Rome to be exploited by enemies. Finally from Koblenz comes only prayerful silence. As the night ends, Apollinaire sees himself as the "gullet of Paris," drinking in the knowledge imparted by the songs that have come from the rest of the world.

Forms and Devices

Several elements place "Vendémiaire" at the beginning of modern poetry. Many of its lines retain the twelve syllables of the classical French Alexandrine form, but some are cut shorter. Many couplets rhyme, but other lines are unrhymed. Also, this was the first poem Apollinaire published without punctuation, a form he continued in his later, freer verse. In keeping with this advent of modern style, the opening section of the poem contains echoes of Charles Baudelaire, who developed a use of imagery that would become modern Symbolism. In his prefatory poem to *Les Fleurs du Mal* (1857; *Flowers of Evil*, 1931), Baudelaire describes a descent into hell, where he sees "Satan Trismégiste." Apollinaire uses the same adjective to describe the "three-times-powerful" kings who were nonetheless dying.

The poet, according to Baudelaire, descends into the sinful temptations of the world seeking the inspiration that will form his poetry, the evil from which he will derive poetic flowers. Central to this experience is drunkenness. Here Baudelaire was continuing a definition established by the Romantic poets, for whom *ivresse* was not mere physical intoxication but any intense experience, physical or emotional, that led to a form of enlightenment.

Apollinaire uses multiple references to this concept as he describes Paris "at the end of September" (the autumnal season Baudelaire also favored) as a place where vines "spread their light over the city," while overhead "drunken birds" peck at the "ripe stars." Baudelaire had also used the flight of the bird as emblem of the inspiration of the poet and described the birds in flight as being drunk. Apollinaire, however, makes these images especially suggestive of poetic productivity because of the light produced and the ripeness of the stars, which parallels that of the grapes.

The wine produced by the harvest of "Vendémiaire" makes the poet drunk with his own inspiration. Thus the birds are "de ma gloire," the talent through which the poet knows that by morning he will reap the harvest of poetic insight. If physical intoxication produces hallucinations, it follows logically that Apollinaire hears voices. The poet's gift, however, calls forth both insightful utterances and voices that "sing" in the sense of providing the material of poetry.

The imagery of grapes and harvest frames the poem. At the end, Apollinaire returns to the concept that he has "drunk the whole universe." The various voices use other images, many of which again recall motifs of Baudelaire's poetry. The cities of the north especially, with their metallic imagery of factories, echo Baudelaire's substitution of urban scenes for rural imagery in lyric poetry. The mythological theme of Ixion, repeated by the northern cities and by Sicily, parallels a similar use of repeated figures in Baudelaire's "Le Voyage" ("The Voyage"), in which the mythological characters, such as Ixion, represent mistaken choices.

Themes and Meanings

A strong religious theme joins the imagery of wine throughout the poem, drawing on the role of wine as the blood of Christ in Communion. The power of religion places the poet in an ambiguous role, for while as a visionary he dominates his world, he must also recognize the superiority of the divine.

Again the poem is divided between the enclosure segments where, with the dominant wine imagery there are references to the poet's authority, and the voices of the cities that advance religious themes. In the opening line Apollinaire addresses "men of the future" who should remember him. The theme of his own poetic immortality continues in Apollinaire's later poetry written on the battlefields of World War I. In the 1917 poem "Merveille de la Guerre" ("Marvel of War"), for example, he leaves his own story as a "legacy to the future" and continues the universal perception he claims in "Vendémiaire," saying that he "was at war but knew how to be everywhere." The poet's vision allowed him to escape the harsh context of battle.

Explicit religious imagery arrives with the songs of the various cities. Though all seem to give a form of tribute to centrally located Paris, they simultaneously lay claim to forms of transcendent power. The towns of Brittany establish the religious theme with the image of hands forming steeples and then refer repeatedly to mystery, culminating in that of "another life," the afterlife that no man can know.

The industries of the northern cities and of Lyon are described as "holy," with "angels" at Lyon weaving the cloth for which the city was famous. The question of religious authority returns, however, in the voices of the southern cities and of Sicily, which resolve the dualism of dominance and submission. The southern cities say that Paris and the Mediterranean should "share our bodies, as one breaks communion wafers." Clearly, with the example of Christ, it is possible for the victim of a sacrifice to retain a dominant position. Similarly, Rome asserts its power through its "vin par deux fois millénaire," which shares the age of the sacrament established by Christ but must also witness the fall of the pope's triple crown.

The end of the poem reasserts the power of the poet. Because he has drunk all the elements of the universe, he has gained universal knowledge. In his confidence in his poetic role, Apollinaire sets aside the biblical prohibition that men must not aspire to the knowledge of good and evil. As he urges future generations to "listen to my songs of universal drunkenness," he affirms his role in transmitting a divine message. The sun rises on a new day as the poet emerges from his night of visions with a new truth.

Dorothy M. Betz

VERSES ON THE DEATH OF DR. SWIFT, D.S.P.D.

Author: Jonathan Swift (1667-1745)
Type of poem: Satire
First published: 1739

The Poem

   Verses on the Death of Dr. Swift, D.S.P.D. consists of 484 lines of jaunty, satirical iambic tetrameter couplets, with strategic footnotes supplied by the poet, purporting to examine the cynical maxim of Duc François de La Rochefoucauld: "In the adversity of our best friends, we find something that doth not displease us" (from *Réflexions*, 1665). The poem may be conveniently divided into three parts. In the opening section (lines 1-70), Jonathan Swift's narrator persona finds that the maxim perfectly describes his own jealousy: "In Pope [Alexander Pope, the outstanding poet of his age and Swift's lifelong friend], I cannot read a line,/ But with a sigh, I wish it mine," declaring himself as guilty of its truth as anyone. Though the maxim was often denounced as immoral and unchristian, the narrator, representing Swift, an Anglican priest, finds it perfectly accurate: "As Rochefoucauld his maxims drew/ From nature, I believe 'em true."

   In the poem's second part (lines 71-298), the narrator imagines how his death will be received among friends, acquaintances, and enemies. His fame will not last a year before his books will be sold as scrap, his friends will shed a tear or two but soon forget him, and enemies will list his faults and resurrect old grievances. Everyone will enjoy his death—the ladies at cards, the gossips at court, and the wits at the tavern. Here the satire is generally bitter, naming names, heaping ridicule, and rehearsing grudges from a generation before—so much so that Pope and others published an abbreviated and censored version of the poem, "The Life and Character of Dr. Swift" (1739), in order to protect Swift.

   Because of its parade of personal references, and despite Swift's footnotes, this part of the poem can seem off-putting. The reader must possess some essential facts of Swift's life in order to understand it. In middle life, from 1707 to 1714, Swift, already a priest, became one of the most important political personages in England. He was a favorite of Queen Anne, the editor of a leading Tory journal allied to Robert Harley's government, and highly regarded for his acid and very partisan pen. Around him was a distinguished group of friends who figure prominently in the poem: Pope; poet John Gay; Dr. Martin Arbuthnot, Queen Anne's personal physician; Henry St. John, Lord Bolingbroke; and Tory leader Robert Harley, the first earl of Oxford. All his life Swift hoped to be made a bishop, a preferment he thought had been promised him. However, the fall of the Tory government and the death of Queen Anne dashed his hopes. With his enemies in power and fearing for his life, he fled to Ireland in self-imposed exile, an Anglican priest among Roman Catholics, far from the seat of power. Though regarded by the Irish as a patriot for his efforts on their behalf, he viewed the Irish as barbaric and never ceased to ridicule them. The poem looks back upon these glory years with a forlorn memory.

Part 3 of the poem (lines 299-484) shows an unexpected shift in tone. The narrator imagines his death being discussed by "one quite indiff'rent in the cause" at the Rose, a fashionable London tavern. In this voice the narrator praises himself in such generous terms that Pope declared the passage "too vain" and allowed it to be altered. Swift answers the critics' objections that he was personally cruel in his satires ("Yet, malice never was his aim;/ He lash'd the vice, but spar'd the name"), too stridently partisan ("But, power was never in his thought,/ And, wealth he valu'd not a groat"), and, as a cleric, unspiritual in his demeanor ("Perhaps I may allow, the Dean/ Had too much satire in his vein"). The poem ends on this apparently positive and non-satirical assessment—although those who are familiar with Swift are quickly suspicious of the self-flattery.

Forms and Devices

Swift's preferred metrical form was the short, four-stress line in couplets, sometimes called Hudibrastic after Samuel Butler's popular satire "Hudibras" (1678). The meter leads to many forced rhymes—"If with such talents heav'n hath blest 'em, Have I not reason to detest 'em?"—and seems appropriate to the gibing, free-swinging narrator found in the first two parts. Swift's lines, however, do not have the subtle internal movement of Pope's. Swift is primarily a satirist, interested in arrranging his subject matter for a contrast of ideas.

Swift's true claim was as the master ironist of the English language, the artist of saying that which is not, a title he claims in lines 55-58:

> Arbuthnot is no more my friend,
> Who dares to irony pretend;
> Which I was born to introduce,
> Refin'd it first, and shew'd its use.

In the ironic method, Swift allows his narrators, even those speaking in his own name, various shades of untruth in order to jar the reader into a new moral awareness. In one of his most famous instances of irony, "A Modest Proposal" (1729), the narrator soberly suggests that the problem of Irish overpopulation can be solved by fattening up its babies and selling them as food—a proposition taken seriously by some of his less sensitive readers. His irony, in fact, can be so subtle and complex as to make the interpretations of his masterpiece, *Gulliver's Travels* (1726), subject to debate after almost three hundred years. The reader should beware of regarding *Verses on the Death of Dr. Swift, D.S.P.D.* as "sincere" and "confessional," even though Swift the historical figure was known to have many of the preoccupations about which he wrote. Even Pope seems to have been "bit, " that is, seduced into taking as true what is strategically untrue, in his interpretation of the last part of the poem.

The poem is best regarded as a composition, consisting of a number of voices played against each other for ironic purposes. *Verses on the Death of Dr. Swift,*

D.S.P.D., far from being "sincere," undermines the premises it asserts. After the narrator declares Rochefoucauld's maxim to be true, for instance, the reader is shown the impartial observer who remembers Swift's virtues and accomplishments. Fame, which in the account of Swift's narrator persona does not last a year, is in no danger, according to the impartial observer; even the footnotes the poet supplies argue that history is in some sense preservable. The proof that fame can be maintained is belied by history itself, for, centuries after the event, readers are still rehearsing the facts of obscure people because of the roles they played in Swift's life. What is one to make of the "indiff'rent" observer's apparently overgenerous account?

Swift was notorious for his scurrilous and scatalogical attacks, a characteristic even his friends had to recognize. In "The Legion Club" (1736), for instance, the Irish senator Sir Thomas Prendergast was described in these vile and highly personal terms: "Let Sir Tom, that rampant ass,/ Stuff his guts with flax and grass;/ But before the priest he fleeces,/ Tear the Bible all to pieces." One is not always sure, in other words, just where and when the joke applies, but the reader should recognize Swift's constant ironic turn of mind.

Themes and Meanings

Verses on the Death of Dr. Swift, D.S.P.D. was written toward the end of Swift's creative life, with almost all his famous work behind him. Despite its irony, it stands as an apology for his life and work, a looking back with various regrets and satisfactions. However personal it may appear, it has models in classical and contemporary literature. Its themes of friendship, death, and the transitory nature of fame suggest the satires of the Roman poet Horace, which both Swift and Pope imitated. A theme more significant to Swift, however, one consistently involved throughout his writing, was his belief that humans are innately sinful and degenerate, the lowest of all God's creatures, a view derived from the religious doctrine of the Fall of Man and one which he found to be true by common observation.

Rochefoucauld's cynicism pales before Swift's savage attacks on human nature. As the king of the Brobdingnagian giants said to Gulliver after European culture had been described to him, "I cannot but conclude the bulk of your natives to be the most pernicious race of little odious vermin that nature ever suffered to crawl upon the surface of the earth." The whole of *Gulliver's Travels* is a violent attack on pride, the deadliest of the seven deadly sins and the origin of all other sins because it is the condition of humans putting themselves above God.

Because of his terrible strictures against human nature, Swift was often charged with misanthropy. A final irony is that *Verses on the Death of Dr. Swift, D.S.P.D.* presents a Swift, who, by embracing Rochefoucauld's maxim, actually moderates his anger toward human nature. As the Latin epitaph he wrote for himself states, in translation, the dean lies in a place "where savage indignation can no longer tear his heart."

Bruce Olsen

VERSES ON THE DEATH OF T. S. ELIOT

Author: Joseph Brodsky (1940-1996)
Type of poem: Elegy
First published: 1970, as "Stikhi na smert' T. S. Eliota," in *Ostanovka v pustyne*; English translation collected in *Selected Poems*, 1973

The Poem

"Verses on the Death of T. S. Eliot" is a poem in three parts modeled on W. H. Auden's 1939 elegy "In Memory of W. B. Yeats." The classic elegy of Western tradition is a meditation on death, be it the death of a particular person or death as the inevitable end of all things mortal. At the same time, it "finds consolation in the contemplation of some permanent principle" (*Princeton Encyclopedia of Poetry and Poetics*, 1974). Joseph Brodsky's elegy, like Auden's, mourns the death of a poet; unlike Auden's, it takes considerable comfort—even exults—in the power of memory and poetry.

Thomas Stearns Eliot, American expatriate and British subject, died in England on January 4, 1965. Brodsky, Soviet citizen in exile in Russia's far north, learned of the elder poet's death a week or so after the fact. Part 1 begins with the flat statement of when and where Eliot died: "at the start of the year, in January" in a city of streetlights, entryways, intersections, and doors inhabited by darkness, cold, and snow. The city seems concrete enough, a real and practical place haunted by eternal but practical concerns. The question of inheritance is raised, but, in a shift to another plane, Eliot's heirs are the Muses, who can hardly complain that he has left them bankrupt. Poetry may be orphaned, "yet it breeds within the glass/ of lonely days," echoing like Narcissus's lovesick nymph and visible in the rhythm of time and the "rhyme of years." Death takes the singer, not the song; it has no need for the fields or seas or well-wrought lines in a poem. Eliot the Anglican convert may have managed to live through Christmas into the beginning of the new year, but the new year itself marks the end of the old year and its holiday; the calendar rhythm of the year, like the rhythm of ocean waves, bears him away from his own high holiday. Time and tides rather than God pull him out to sea, leaving the rest of humanity on dry land.

Part 2 continues in the same meter and on the same vast scale of seas and continents. However, the realistic cityscape is replaced by a funeral tableau, a scene straight from a Greek or Roman bas-relief. Magi, prophets and priests of antiquity, are called in to hold the halo while two mournful female figures stand downcast on either side of the grave (that is, the ocean). They are America, where Eliot's life began, and England, where it ended (in Russian, *Amerika* and *Anglia*, both feminine nouns). The final line of part 2 is a single sentence set apart that acts as a conclusion: "But each grave is the limit of the earth." Part 3 shifts meter and rhyme scheme. The poet invokes the god Apollo to cast down his own wreath at Eliot's feet as a marker of immortality in the mortal realm. The footsteps and songs will be remembered by the trees and the land, by wind, by every sheaf of grain. What he has left behind will be felt, invisibly but tangibly, in the same way that love is felt after the loved one disappears forever. Just as the body recalls touch, memory recalls words.

Forms and Devices

Brodsky's initial and most obvious device is his choice of models: Auden's poem on the death of Yeats. The poem is not a narrative, so the three parts are not chapters forming a beginning, middle, and end. Instead, they vary in formal structure and in tone, changing the stance of the person looking at this poet's life and work. While Auden eschews rhyme and strict meter in the first two parts, Brodsky observes them. (The English translation, though more regular in meter than Auden's poem, is not as traditional in form as Brodsky's original version.) The formal likeness is greatest in part 3, in which the meter (trochaic tetrameter), regular rhyme scheme (*abab*), choice of stanza (quatrain), and use of repetition give the whole section both regular movement and finality.

Yet Brodsky's poem is not an imitation; rather, it uses Auden's reflection on a poet's life, death, and art as a framework for a different sort of monument. For example, Auden's three parts reflect stages in Yeats's poetry, last to first: realistic, sober, and urban in his last years; ironic and emotional in the middle; Romantic, balladic, and folkloric in the beginning. Brodsky uses his divisions differently; they mark not progression but a shift in angle of vision that is linguistically expressed as style. Connecting links are arranged not in time but in space, using imagery often found in Eliot's own work: bleak cities, landscapes, and seas. There are echoes of Eliot's themes, especially the likeness of beginnings to endings and the connections between poetry and death that run through his *Four Quartets* (1943): "the end is the beginning,/ And the end and the beginning were always there/ Before the beginning and after the end./ And all is always now." ("Burnt Norton") and "Every phrase and every sentence is an end and a beginning,/ Every poem an epitaph" ("Little Giddings"). There are also allusions to other poems, including "The Coming of the Magi" and "The Cultivation of Christmas Trees." Aside from allusions to Eliot himself, the poem contains classical pastoral imagery of wood and water as well as allusions to Narcissus and the lovelorn nymph Echo, Aeolus the wind, the Roman poet Horace, and finally, triumphantly, Apollo, god of poetry, patron of the arts. Through the classical allusions, imagery, and rhyme also come echoes of Russian poets Alexander Pushkin, Osip Mandelstam, and Anna Akhmatova.

Themes and Meanings

An elegy, by definition, deals with death and life, the ephemeral and the eternal. It need not deal with anyone famous or powerful, but when it does, it often makes a point of just how fleeting fame and power are. In the case of tyrants and warlords, the elegy may act as a warning that earthly victories and treasures, however glorious, cannot be taken into the afterlife. In the case of poets, the message is a different one: Beginning with Horace and his ode "Exegi monumentum aere perennius," poets have

spoken of the monument that will last as long as art and human memory that other poets have built and that they hope to build for themselves.

At the same time, poets (Eliot included) are mortal, and when they leave this earth
they leave forever. For all the play in part 1 on endings equaling beginnings, on cycles
and rhythms, the living are orphaned, left behind. Part 2 ends with the unequivocal
statement that "each grave is the limit of the earth," and Eliot's departure in part 3 is as
final as the end of love. Still—and this is Brodsky's contribution to the tradition—the
love may no longer be visible, but it is tangible. The body remembers touch, and the
ordinary things of earth—footsteps, grass, wood—remember sound. Words, even if
never carved in stone, have weight and mass and continue to exist as part of this world.

If poets are mortal, poetry is not. Horace's ode was translated by Russian poets
Gavrila Derzhavin and Alexander Pushkin and so became part of the Russian tradition
just as Russian poetry became part of the classical tradition. Brodsky's mention of
Horace automatically brings in Pushkin and Derzhavin, and, by incorporating some
of Eliot's own imagery and sensibility and alluding to Mandelstam and Akhmatova,
Brodsky connects them all and connects himself, in turn, to them. His choice of
subject (Eliot) and his choice of model (Auden on Yeats) brings in English-Irish-
American speech as well, adding another link to the connection or another strand to
the web of association called context. In his famous essay "Tradition and the Individual Talent," Eliot talks about tradition not as "blind adherence" to what others have
done but as a historical sense, a sense that the past is both past and present. "The feeling that the whole of the literature of Europe from Homer and within it the whole of
the literature of his own country has a simultaneous existence and a simultaneous order" is what gives writers a sense of their own time and their own place. Meaning does
not exist in a vacuum but rather in a context. Brodsky both pays tribute to the tradition
and changes it by his presence.

Jane Ann Miller

VERSES ON THE UNKNOWN SOLDIER

Author: Osip Mandelstam (1891-1938)
Type of poem: Poetic sequence
First published: 1967, as "Stikhi o neizvestnom soldate," in *Sobranie sochinenii,* second edition; English translation collected in *Selected Poems,* 1975

The Poem

Described as an "oratorio" by its author, "Verses on the Unknown Soldier" (also translated as "55 Lines about the Unknown Soldier") is a cycle or sequence of eight poems, with the individual poems showing considerable variation in length and stanzaic structure. At 114 lines, the "oratorio" is one of the few longer works in Osip Mandelstam's poetic oeuvre and is closely connected with a looser cycle of meditations on the age and on the poet's place in it, which Mandelstam wrote in the 1920's. The basic meter is an anapestic trimeter but with the many syncopations typical of Russian modernism.

The work can be described as written in the first person, with two qualifications: The second, fifth, and sixth poems in the sequence contain no first-person singular pronouns, and the "I" which appears in the remaining poems has more than one referent.

The first poem of the "Verses on the Unknown Soldier" opens by evoking elemental forces present on a battleground: the air, which the poet calls to witness; the stars, which render condemnatory judgment; and the rains, which remember the forest of crosses commemorating the fallen. In its second half, turning from memory to prophecy, the poem introduces the motif of the tomb of the unknown soldier and predicts a grim future in which humanity will go on "killing, freezing, and starving." The lyric hero first appears in the final two stanzas, in a close identification with the pilot of a disabled and falling warplane. This doomed pilot, who also appears in other poems by Mandelstam in the 1930's, re-experiences, in turn, the fate of a duelist in the nineteenth century poet Mikhail Lermontov's story "Princess Mary," who is shot off a cliff. Through this further regression, the pilot/lyric hero will render an account of what it is like to feel the pull of an "airy chasm."

As the title of Mandelstam's "oratorio" and the imagery of massed graves suggest, the immediate historical reference is to World War I and the Russian Civil War. Weapons of twentieth century industrialized war that bring death from the air are, however, presented in highly metaphorical language. Long range artillery, for example, is transformed into the "far-off heartbeat of the air," while the airplane becomes a "sickly swallow that has forgotten how to fly." Indeed, the entire second poem, consisting of a single stanza and structured as one sentence, is based on the image of a gas attack, metaphorized as a threat from the stars. (In a revision that is typical of Mandelstam's creative process, an explicit reference to the "gas of Verdun" did not make it into the final version.)

While the imagery of air and space dominates the first two poems, the third and fourth are bound by the imagery of light. This light is both the flash of heavy ordnance, the light of a new prophetic revelation, and, as energy moving at the speed of light ("a number suffused with bright pain and a mole of zeroes"), an allusion to an Einsteinian universe in which the sequence of events is relative to the position of the observer. Hence, the war that is remembered is inseparable from the war which will take place in the future. In the third poem, it is the future apocalyptic war which speaks through the medium of light: "I am not Leipzig nor Waterloo,/ I am not the Battle of Tribes. I am the new,/ from me it will be bright."

The fourth poem brings the ray of light, carrying its awful message of millions of deaths, to the eye of a speaker moving his lips in the darkness. Since Mandelstam frequently uses the image of moving lips to signify the poet's work, this speaker is now clearly identified as the poet.

The fifth poem begins with the suggestion of an infantry song. The cannon fodder of the centuries are particularized in Jaroslav Hašek's Schweik and Miguel de Cervantes's Don Quixote. There follows a vision of a postwar world populated by mutilated veterans and victims of battle: "And around the outskirts of the age/ the family of wooden crutches goes knocking. . . ." This grim picture, at once reminiscence and prophecy, is countered in the sixth poem by the image of the human skull. The literal sense of the first line is "Is it for this the skull should develop?" Here, as elsewhere in Mandelstam's writings, the skull is less a *memento mori* than an object of reverence, an emblematic image representing a human-centered universe. Hence, the skull "shines like a sentient cupola/ foams with thought, dreams of itself."

This humanist affirmation continues in the last two poems. Poem 7 continues the "skull" theme implicitly, by echoing the syntax and associations of poem 6. Using the first-person plural, the poet now identifies himself with all of humanity. The theme of "air" returns but with a different emphasis: It is now the life-breath, as well as freedom and a place in history, goals for which one actively struggles in what the poet calls "a glory beyond compare." Having achieved this expression of solidarity and faith, the poet speaks in the last stanza as the biological Osip Mandelstam. Envisioning a roll call (perhaps at the Day of Judgment), he states his date of birth and concludes with another motif that runs through Mandelstam's work, the fire of time: "And the centuries surround me with fire." Here, the image suggests both a field of fire and an aureole of glory.

Forms and Devices

One leading feature of "Verses on the Unknown Soldier" which is much less evident in a translation is the extensive network of allusions to other texts, including the poet's own writings. What does come through in English translations of the cycle are, first, the highly elliptical and compressed style, and second, the ordering of the poems so as to bind and transmit the lyric plot. Both these phenomena give the work sufficient unity so that the reader may, with equal justice, treat it either as a cycle of poems or as a single large poem.

Mandelstam's ellipticism generates a tension-field for the distinctive interaction of metonymy and metaphor. The work is, for example, full of paronomasias—that is, plays on words with a common phonetic core that invite the reader to invent a common etymology: "Austerlitz-oyster," for example, or "nameless manna," or (to give a more literal translation than David McDuff's) a "mole of nulls," that is, a number with many zeroes, which presents the speed of light as if it were a chemical substance.

As this instance suggests, the sound-echoes that link such metonymic fragments give rise to metaphoric associations as well; in other words, one seeks resemblance between what is juxtaposed. Thus, "Austerlitz," the name of a great battle in which the defeated Russian army sustained large losses, is a synecdoche that stands for the Napoleonic era, while the "oyster," which Russian literature marks as a "European" food, is another synecdoche, which stands for the Westernizing current in Russian society. Put them together and one has an associative complex that conjures up the Russia of the Napoleonic Wars.

In context, Austerlitz appears immediately after a series of battles mentioned as inadequate prefigurations of the war yet to come. The paronomasia appears in the couplet "In the depths of a black marble oyster/ the light of Austerlitz died." Hence, the oyster's darkness is also the sky over the battlefield and—via the reference to black marble—the tomb of Napoleon, the victor at Austerlitz and the antithesis of the Unknown Soldier. Along another chain of connotations, the oyster shell in the third poem is contrasted with the human skull in the sixth. The cycle as a whole exfoliates by means of such complexes of associations.

The number and order of lines and stanzas, the relationship of poems within a sequence or a collection—all such considerations were of concern to Mandelstam, who was intensely aware of shape as a bearer of meaning. The ordering of the poems within the cycle can serve to illustrate how the parts of the work develop through a series of contrasts and returns. To give a few examples, the opening poem is echoed in the fifth poem, which opens the second half; both allude to World War I and picture the sufferings which are brought by war on a massive scale: the forest of crosses, the population of cripples. The poison gas (which is also poisonous speech) in the second poem is answered by the poet's affirmation of the human struggle for air in the second-to-last. The third poem anticipates and contrasts with the sixth, with emblems of war giving way to the skull that figures Mandelstam's belief in the sanctity of human life.

The first half of the cycle ends with a poem that represents the poet as speaking in the darkness; the second half ends with him surrounded by the fire of centuries. Overall, there is a development from a vision of humans as cosmic victims to an assertion of positive identity and a claim to a place in history. To put it in terms of echoes, the cycle begins as a requiem for past and future wars and ends as an *exigi monumentum*, a lyric in which the poet, acting as spokesman for all the unknown soldiers, puts forward a claim for the value and permanence of his achievement.

Themes and Meanings

The "Verses on the Unknown Soldier" are the matrix about which grew the "Third Voronezh Notebook," the last part of Mandelstam's final collection of verses, first published nearly three decades after his death. The collection concludes Mandelstam's poetic witness to Russia's historical experience, as viewed from the perspective of a victim of Joseph Stalin's "Great Transformation." The Voronezh poems were written during Mandelstam's exile to that provincial city in 1934-1937 and were followed some months later by the poet's re-arrest and his death, apparently in a transit camp near Vladivostok.

In this context, the ellipticism of the poems, well exemplified by the "oratorio," is not merely a mark of Mandelstam's modernism. It is also a form of what is known in Russian literature as Aesopian language, the use of allusive language to transmit to the reader what must not be stated openly. Thus, in his horror of mass slaughter on the one hand and his subjective attraction to death's "airy chasm" on the other, the poet is not only meditating on modern war past and future, but he is also using war as a metaphor for the experience of the Soviet peoples in the era of the purges and the gulag. The final three poems are exemplary in their solidarity with all the victims and in their refusal to capitulate to a contempt for the human individual, which masked itself as historical necessity.

Yet even these large civic meanings do not exhaust Mandelstam's "Unknown Soldier" cycle, for history has given the poems an additional register of significance. Noting the allusions to Einsteinian physics and the way in which the poet pictures a blinding light from the sky as the carrier of the threatened annihilation of humanity, Russian readers have seen the cycle as not only a meditation on their experience in the poet's lifetime but also as an uncanny prophecy of the terrors of the nuclear age. Reading the lines in poem 3 in which the death-bearing light announces a new illumination to the world, the English-speaking reader may think of both biblical apocalypse and of that other prophetic allusion, from the *Bhagavad Gītā*, which came to the mind of American physicist J. Robert Oppenheimer as he witnessed the first nuclear blast: "I am become Death, the destroyer of worlds."

Charles Isenberg

VIEW WITH A GRAIN OF SAND

Author: Wisława Szymborska (1923-   )
Type of poem: Meditation
First published: 1986, as "Widek z ziarnkiem piasku," in *Ludzie na moście*; English translation collected in *View with a Grain of Sand: Selected Poems,* 1995

The Poem

"View with a Grain of Sand" is a poem of thirty-seven lines grouped into seven stanzas that range from four to seven lines each. In both Polish and English, the poem exhibits occasional irregular rhymes, although these are not the same lines in both versions. (For example, the fourth stanza rhymes the second and fourth lines in Polish and the first and second line in English.) Like much of Wisława Szymborska's poetry, the language in "View with a Grain of Sand" sounds like everyday conversation, differing from prose or ordinary speech only in very subtle rhythms and patterns of sound.

The speaker of the poem may be Szymborska herself, although such an identification does not affect the meaning conveyed or the impression formed by the poem. This speaker pictures a lake and its surroundings, beginning with a grain of sand from the shore. She mentions that the sand is complete in and of itself and that it is not affected by people touching it, talking about it, or dropping it on a windowsill; these things pertain solely to human experience. The speaker then considers the window that overlooks the lake but that has nothing to do with the lake itself except in human perception. The poem reminds its readers that the "wonderful view" exists only in the individual mind, as do colors, sounds, odors, and, most strikingly, pain. Szymborska's speaker goes on to say essentially the same thing about the lake, that it knows nothing of the attributes people associate with it. She adds that the lake lies beneath both a sky similarly unaffected by human thoughts or feelings and the sun that "hides" behind clouds and "sets" beyond the horizon but which, she reminds readers, neither truly hides nor actually sets. By bringing up these two particular figures of speech, common not only in Polish and English but also in many other languages, Szymborska quietly suggests that human perceptions of "reality" often prove to be highly illusory in nature since the sun only seems to behave as human beings describe it as behaving. Citing such a commonly known fact strengthens the message Szymborska conveys: People's ideas are not accurate reflections of the world around them.

Finally, the speaker discusses the passage of time, which seems to rush by as if carrying an important message for someone, but again she points out that such perceptions are the result of human imagination. Time does not rush; it simply exists as do the lake and sun. The personification of time is merely the result of human thought at work. Through repetition, the poem reinforces the thought that it is the human desire to appreciate and understand the world that is responsible for the interpretations people place upon the physical universe. In his afterword to Szymborska's poetry collection *Nothing Twice* (1997), translator and poet Stanisław Barańczak explains that Szymborska is a poet who often asks questions that she does not attempt to answer. Instead, she seems to focus on challenging her readers' assumptions as if the questions themselves are more interesting than any possible answers. In "View with a Grain of Sand," she makes readers wonder if the ideas they associate with the world around them have any meaning at all and ask why humans tend to see only themselves in the rest of the universe.

Forms and Devices

The poem exhibits a subtle musicality of language, as when Szymborska writes of the glass in the window that is "colorless, shapeless,/ soundless, odorless, and painless." Besides an implied pun (in English) on "pane," the repeated syllable "less" provides a rhythmic feel for the reader. This rhythm is further emphasized by occasional rhyme, as in stanza 4, in which Szymborska writes "The lake's floor exists floorlessly,/ and its shore exists shorelessly," pairing not only the final adverbs in each line but also their corresponding nouns "floor" and "shore." The use of sound echoes (not always true rhymes but repetition of sounds within words such as "sky" and "skyless" in the fifth stanza) enlivens what would otherwise seem almost like simple prose. Although there are noticeably more such rhymes and echoes in Polish, where conjugations and declensions provide many words with the same final syllables and thus make rhyming somewhat easier, enough of the strategy survives in English to give a free, almost floating quality to the verse. The diverse lengths of the lines also reinforce this impression: In English, the lines vary from three to fifteen syllables in length (which resembles the original version's range of five to fourteen syllables per line). The unfettered quality of the poetry suggests private reflection or reverie, especially appropriate to the subject of the mind considering its own perceptions.

The subject, beginning with a tiny grain of sand and moving through increasingly large concepts to time itself, creates a perception similar to that established in motion pictures when a camera changes focus from a small detail to a vast panorama in one movement—the microcosm has been replaced by the macrocosm, and the reader is encouraged to reflect that all existence is similar to that of the items, both small and large, that Szymborska has mentioned. What she claims for a grain of sand, a lake, the wind, the sky, the sun, and even time might equally be said of anything in the universe. Just as the casual-sounding language is given shape and rhythm by careful arrangement of sound, the insight into existential philosophy that forms the content of the poem is made far more accessible by Szymborska's use of specific physical objects and places to anchor and clarify what otherwise might be too abstract to present in an effective poem.

Themes and Meanings

In "View with a Grain of Sand," Szymborska stimulates her readers to question their interpretations of the world around them. Viewers of the lake might normally watch the waves lapping at the shore, but readers of the poem are reminded that the waves and the shore in themselves signify nothing except that the wind has ruffled the surface of the lake and that the water ends at a certain point. The refreshment, serenity, or pleasure usually associated with such perceptions have nothing to do with the lake itself but only with the people who view the lake. The poem encourages readers to remember this as they consider their own responses to such scenery. If the water, shore, and wind that humans see as beautiful are untouched by human thought, they also lack any inherent meaning for human beings. The same is true of the sky and sun, which only obey their own natures and do nothing of what humans believe them to do. By implication, the only meaning is that which people make for themselves in their thoughts about the world. Even the passage of time, essential to thought and human consciousness, has no essential meaning for humankind. People may perceive it as purposeful or fast, but that is only because of their capacity to deceive themselves. Time, in the final line of the poem, truly bears an "inhuman" message, one that people could never understand because it is totally alien to them. The human perception of time will always be in human terms. It is as if human nature forever cuts humanity off from the rest of existence because people seek meaning and sense where none exists and find only themselves, their thoughts, and their feelings.

Szymborska's assertion that the human mind's activities and attempted interpretations of the world reflect only human reality resembles some of the insights offered by Buddhist and Hindu doctrines: The world is essentially an illusion, and profound understanding of existence must come through the mind itself. However, Szymborska does not offer teachings about the true nature of knowledge or the mind but only suggests that no one may fully grasp the inhumanity of the universe. She has mused over the emotional implications nature scenes have for many observers and has suggested that there are no meanings or essential emotions to be connected with such scenes. She implies that the human habit of contemplating their place in the world is best answered by suggesting that people may truly have no place in existence except for whatever places they create in their own thought.

Paul James Buczkowski

THE VILLAGE BLACKSMITH

Author: Henry Wadsworth Longfellow (1807-1882)
Type of poem: Ballad
First published: 1840; collected in *Ballads and Other Poems*, 1841

The Poem

Henry Wadsworth Longfellow's "The Village Blacksmith" emphasizes how the life and work of a common working man can provide an example of persistence and accomplishment in spite of trials and tragedies. The poem is developed in eight stanzas of six ballad-like lines of alternating iambic tetrameter and iambic trimeter.

The poem begins by picturing the site of blacksmith's workplace as "Under a spreading chestnut-tree," then specifically describes the smith himself as a man made strong by his work: "mighty," with "brawny arms . . . strong as iron bands." The smith's physical appearance continues to be the focus in stanza 2. He wears his black hair "long." He is "tan" from working outside in the sun. More important, however, his character can now be revealed. He is "honest," willing to do any type of work, and "owes not any man."

The third stanza centers on how important the smith's work is to village society. All year long, people can "hear" the "bellows blow" and the regular beat of "his heavy sledge." The sounding rhythms of his workplace are as central to the villagers as the tolling of the church bell when the "evening sun is low." In stanza 4, even children realize the significance of the blacksmith as they stop to watch the smith work on their way "home from school" and enjoy the excitement of "the flaming forge," the roaring bellows, and the "burning sparks."

The poem moves away from the blacksmith's workplace to the town church in the fifth stanza. With his children, the widowed smith listens to the "parson pray and preach" and to "his daughter's voice,/ Singing in the village choir." Although the service "makes his heart rejoice," in stanza 6 the sound of his daughter's singing reminds him of his wife's "voice,/ Singing in Paradise," her death, and the "grave," which cause him to shed a tear because of life's trials.

Stanzas 7 and 8 summarize the message of the blacksmith's example. His life is a mixture of ordinary human experience: "Toiling,—rejoicing,—sorrowing." Yet he persists, regardless, accomplishing something every day, thus deserving "a night's repose." Just as the blacksmith's life has been shaped by meeting and facing life events, so each person must be willing to continue on with life formed "at the flaming forge" with "Each burning deed and thought" shaped at the "sounding anvil."

Forms and Devices

Although loosely balladlike in form and although included in *Ballads and Other Poems*, "The Village Blacksmith" departs from the traditional ballad in certain important ways, as implied by Longfellow himself when he referred to it as "a kind of ballad." Instead of the traditional narrative or chronological development of the ballad, Longfellow employs descriptive passages of the usual and the commonplace to develop his poem. Like many of Longfellow's shorter lyrics, the poem centers on a single item—in this case, an ordinary blacksmith—and uses description of that item as a means to develop a lesson about life. Although a traditional ballad would ordinarily include some exciting or climactic event or turning point, no such narrative device appears in "The Village Blacksmith." Instead, the poem proceeds in a natural order from a description of the blacksmith and his character (stanzas 1-2) to his importance to the village (stanza 4) to his religious commitment and persistence in life (stanzas 5-6) to the lesson his life provides for the reader (stanzas 7-8).

A second way in which the poem differs from the traditional ballad form is the use of six-line stanzas (rhyming *abcbdb*), rather than the usual four-line approach (rhyming *abcb*). Within this rather unusual ballad stanza length, Longfellow also varies the meter of the individual lines, thus relieving monotony and providing emphasis for the content of the poem. Of the forty-eight lines in the poem, twenty show variations from the expected regular metric system of an iambic tetrameter line followed by an iambic trimeter line. Often Longfellow substitutes an anapestic foot for an iambic foot, as in the first three words of the second line of stanza 3: "You can hear his bellows blow." The most remarkable variation occurs in the first line of stanza 8, when Longfellow departs completely from iambic meter and uses falling rhythm to slow down the line and emphasize the mixture of experiences in the blacksmith's life: "Toiling,—rejoicing,—sorrowing."

Throughout the poem, appropriate images related to the blacksmith's vocation and life are used. Visual images dominate stanzas 1 and 2, beginning with the reference to the "spreading chestnut-tree" (the setting is said to be based on the blacksmith's workplace in Longfellow's own town of Cambridge, Massachusetts) and including the emphasis on the blacksmith's strength and appearance as evidenced in his "large and sinewy hands," "his brawny arms," and his perspiring "brow." Stanza 3, by contrast, is dominated by aural images: the sound of "his bellows blow[ing]" and "his heavy sledge/ With measured beat and slow."

Visual images resume in stanzas 4, 5, and 6, mixing with more sound images. The children "see the flaming forge" and "hear the bellows roar." The blacksmith is pictured at "church," sitting with his sons, listening to the prayer and sermon and "his daughter's voice" in the choir. These sounds and sights remind him of his wife, now dead, and cause him to wipe "A tear out of his eyes." Stanza 7 depends on generalized images of the blacksmith's life routine—his mixed emotions as he "goes" through life, his daily work of accomplishing "something," and his "night's repose."

Besides appropriate images, Longfellow employs a few meaningful similes to develop his poem. Similes are used in stanzas 1 and 2 to fill out the picture of the blacksmith's strength and appearance. He has arms "strong as iron bands" and a face "like the tan." Both features grow naturally out of the blacksmith's occupation, a vocation that centers on working with iron and often performed outdoors, where the flames of the forge are not a threat to buildings. Similarly, the simile in stanza 3 that describes the rhythm of the blacksmith's daily work "Like a sexton ringing the village bell" at sunset is appropriate to the setting of the poem in a small village centered around religion and churchgoing.

The rural simile of stanza 4 is similarly apt for small-town life, as Longfellow describes "the burning sparks" as being "Like chaff from a threshing-floor." The climactic simile in the poem is in stanza 6, however, when both literally and figuratively the daughter's singing sounds to the blacksmith "like her mother's voice,/ Singing in Paradise!" It is this reminder of death and afterlife that causes the blacksmith to weep and consider, at least briefly, the tragedy of his own life.

Helping to redeem the poem's perhaps too explicit lesson-giving is the structuring of the final stanza around the metaphor of blacksmithing. In the final lines of the poem, Longfellow weaves the didactic truth of the need of persistence in life with the daily objects of the blacksmith's trade:

> Thus at the flaming forge of life
> Our fortunes must be wrought;
> Thus on its sounding anvil shaped
> Each burning deed and thought.

The use of the words "flaming forge," "wrought," "sounding anvil," "shaped," and "burning" help to elaborate the message of the poem in figurative language appropriate to the vocation of the poem's title.

Themes and Meanings

"The Village Blacksmith" is an excellent example of how Longfellow, throughout his poetic career, was able to write highly accessible poetry that reflected popular American ideas and sentiments. Like his well-known "The Psalm of Life" (1839), this poem about a blacksmith ties together the need of actively doing something with the inevitability of life's mutability—themes Longfellow would return to throughout his career.

Centering the poem around a blacksmith helped to contribute to the poem's success and made it a mainstay recitation piece for schoolchildren in the nineteenth century. Blacksmithing, after all, was a central part of then-rural American life, necessary for the shoeing of horses—the mainstays of ordinary transportation and farmwork—and the creation and repair of ordinary farm and household implements. Readers knew the importance blacksmithing had and were ready to accept an "idealized" picture of this trade.

By idealizing a blacksmith, Longfellow was also elevating the ordinary laborer, an appealing subject for a society built around the goals of common people hoping to achieve the American Dream through hard work. Importantly, Longfellow made sure that the moral and religious character of the poem's protagonist is above reproach. The blacksmith is not only hardworking and persistent but also honest and pious.

As ideal as the blacksmith's life seems to be, it has also included tragedy. His loving wife is now dead, and he is a single father raising a family of considerable size. The blacksmith is not allowed to dwell on his loss, however, even though he can be shown to shed "a tear" in church. Instead, he faces life's troubles by daily doing his job, accomplishing the small tasks that keep life ordered and worth living, reaping his reward with a good night's sleep. Such is the "lesson" the blacksmith's life "hast taught" every reader.

Delmer Davis

VIRGINIA BRITANNIA

Author: Marianne Moore (1887-1972)
Type of poem: Lyric
First published: 1941, in *What Are Years*

The Poem

The twelve stanzas of this poem focus on the visual aspects of Virginia (the colony and then the state), with an emphasis on the British and Latin origins of its early settlers and nomenclature. The poem's title combines both elements: "Virginia," in deference to England's Elizabeth I (known as "the virgin Queen"), and "Britannia," the Latin name for Britain. Approaching the subject of the poem like an English mariner arriving at the New World, the poet describes the shore of "Old Dominion," Virginia's first name. Natural elements mingle with bits of history and architecture, crowding the poem's stanzas with vivid, evocative details. The new land is seen as a "cedar-dotted emerald shore" (line 3) on which are found the flora and fauna indigenous to Virginia: the redbird, the trumpet flower, the hackberry, the ivy flower, and the sycamore. Into this world came the musketeer, cavalier, parson, and "wild parishioner," who built churches, laid ornamental brickwork, and created the cemetery, where God's natural wonders surround the graves of sinners.

In all stanzas except the first, the poet interweaves religion, history, and nature. "A fritillary zigzags" opens stanza 2, reflecting the design of the poem itself as the poet's eye zigzags through Virginia's history and natural features. The encounter between the early settlers and a well-established native culture and its members results in an odd blend, "We-re-wo/ co-mo-co's fur crown" (lines 16-17) with a "Latin motto" (line 18). In the third stanza, the poet returns to the natural context in which history took place, "all-green box-sculptured grounds" (line 28), for example, and hints at incongruity, "almost English green" and "un-English insect sounds" (lines 29-30). In the next stanza, the "terse Virginian . . . drives the/ owl from tree to tree" (lines 37-39), and the wild creatures mingle with ornamental stone work. The odd mixture proliferates throughout the next three stanzas, which focus on man-made designs among ivy, pansies, and a variety of horses, jumpers, mounts, "work-mule and/ show-mule" (lines 62-63). The presence of the African American is evidenced, his "Black idiom" used to characterize what in Virginia "has come about" (line 64), an "inconsistent flowerbed!" (line 72).

Literal flower beds continue to be described as the metaphorical flowerbed-state takes shape. The seventh stanza is almost wholly a description or listing of flowers, which merges in stanza 8 with a portrait of a Native American princess and the inharmonious mixture that emerged from the combination of land, native, and settler. The disarray is reflected in the state's first flag, a "tactless symbol" (line 99), and in the state's other features, both natural and imported: "cotton-mouth snakes and cot-/ ton fields" (lines 102-103) and "tobacco-crop/ records on walls" (lines 107-108). This serpentine configuration, created as European civilization spread over the state and mingled with the wildlife, has had a deleterious effect on the land itself: The settler has been "Like strangler figs choking/ a banyan" (lines 110-111). The land seems to have suffered the most.

The poem ends on this bleak note. The vision of the green, wild land darkens as man's influence spreads, mixing European with indigenous elements until the cypress is "indivisible" from the English hackberry. The land loses its identity as the atmosphere becomes polluted, "as sunset flames increasingly" (line 138), as the mountains are gouged and blackened, and as the town spreads. Above this evidence of man's "arrogance," however, clouds retain the image of nature's unspoiled condition. The poet suggests that a new generation may see in those clouds "an intimation of what glory is." In the child's vision lies hope of a regeneration of nature.

Forms and Devices

The poem's unity is created in part by the structure of the stanzas, which combines duplicate rhyme schemes throughout with stressed lines to give the poem regularity. Visual clues add to the appearance of sameness—all the stanzas have twelve lines, for instance, and the lines are indented the same way, each stanza having four different left margins. The third, seventh, and twelfth lines are all flush with the left margin, creating divisions of three, four, and five lines, within which groups of lines are given their own indentation. Indentation divides the stanzas into overlapping units of thought and enhances the complex texture of the poem. The rhyme scheme is also complex: *abcdddcefggc*. Within a sequence of triple rhyme (*c . . . c . . . c*), Marianne Moore places three consecutive rhymes (*ddd*) and a pair (*gg*). The rhyme scheme reflects disharmony as well as complexity. The regular rhymes ("shore/-floor" and "flower/tower") mingle with a variety of other kinds, more or less incongruous, including slant rhymes ("has/was") and many others that require some effort to hear or see (such as "prison/and on/Dominion" and "imperialist/deer-/Madeira-").

The lines show a similar complex pattern of stresses, although Moore is much less concerned with regular patterning in this regard. In each stanza, the opening pair of lines (*ab*) generally contains four stresses each, and the pair of rhymes (*gg*) is stressed in a three-two sequence, followed by a long final line. Regularity is therefore only approximate; long lines are combined with medium and short lines in the same order within each stanza. Attention is drawn to line length throughout the poem, particularly in the way some words are broken up: "unscent-/ed, provident-/ly hot." (lines 70-71). In this example, two lines are made to begin with an "ed" and an "ly," respectively. Were it not for the approximate consistency in the pattern of stresses, the poem might be said to contain lines of free verse set within a regular stanzaic pattern.

A variety of sounds also adds diversity, the traditional appearing among the unusual. An occasional line is laden with alliteration—"spotted sparrow perched in the dew-drenched juniper" (line 129)—helping the line move smoothly along, whereas elsewhere, sound and rhythm slow the line: "the one-brick-/ thick serpentine wall built by" (lines 108-109). Many of the lines read more like prose than poetry (those in stanza 10, for example), yet on the whole, the array of sounds and rhythms elevates the tone of the poem, especially in combination with the poem's richly visual features. The lines are densely crowded with colorful details, rare combinations of things, and shapes that create a tapestry corresponding to the poem's subject, Britain Virginia: a garden, a cradle, an exotic blend of geographic and cultural features. The resultant mosaic of imagery, structural design, and sound enables the reader to see, hear, and feel the poem's subject.

Themes and Meanings

The emphasis on disharmony in the poem is unmistakable from start to finish. Virginia, the poem asserts, is a land of diversity. Mention of its origin as a European colony begins the poem, and whatever is said about the land derives from the historical moment when European encountered nature and man in this particular spot. The resulting assortment continues into modern times in the form of Latin mottoes, European architecture, and assorted decorations. The land has suffered from the changes, however. Like the bird's eye that has come to resemble "sculptured marble" (line 43), the imported tree has become indistinguishable from the native one. The land's "lost identity" parallels the encroachment of man on the environment, to destructive effect.

Throughout most of the poem, the poet maintains an objective view of the settlement of Virginia while cataloging its effects on the land and its native culture. The bizarre appearance of a Native American chief "could be no/ odder than we were" (line 18). Although the European settler is criticized for having shown the land no mercy, the "redskin" is no noble savage. He is still "famous for his cruelty," and the best that is said of him is that he "is not all brawn/ and animality" (lines 116-117). The poem's catalog of the natural features of the land—its flowers, trees, and animals, especially the birds—develops into a sympathetic portrait of a land threatened by the changes that settlement brought to it.

All the attention given to the variegated texture of the land and its natural features culminates in the penultimate stanza, where the poet focuses on "The mere brown hedge sparrow," symbol of the persistence of the natural element as well as its vulnerability. The bird's naïveté is both attractive and frightful, for the bird's "satisfaction in man's trustworthy nearness" renders the bird's ardor "reckless." The image of nature celebrating man's presence in the land is shadowed in the final lines by ominous hints. The bird "even in the dark/ flutes his ecstatic burst of joy" (lines 127-128), and the bough of the live oak presents a "darkening filigree" (line 133). The final image of the land shows sunlight flaming against a "blackening ridge of green" (line 140). Though glory-rich clouds hover aloft for the child to see, the poet suggests that in the clouds one sees only an "intimation" of glory, and they are, after all, detached from the land itself, and passing.

Bernard E. Morris

THE VISION OF JUDGMENT

Author: George Gordon, Lord Byron (1788-1824)
Type of poem: Satire
First published: 1822

The Poem

George Gordon, Lord Byron's *The Vision of Judgment* is a special type of satire, a travesty, unique in that its excellence far outweighs that of the original, Robert Southey's *A Vision of Judgment* (1821), which would have remained virtually unread had Byron not satirized it. Byron's travesty was managed with such skill that Southey could not even retaliate without making himself appear more absurd. Southey's lengthy poem extravagantly praised the recently deceased George III (who died January 29, 1820), describing his arrival at the gates of heaven, his response to attacks from enemies, and his triumphant entry into heaven.

Byron's shorter version (106 stanzas) opens with Saint Peter at the gates of heaven, nodding over his rusty keys. He and his fellow saints and angels have little to occupy themselves since so few petitioners for entry have appeared. Only the Recording Angel, busy listing all of humankind's transgressions, has been so occupied that he has stripped his wings for quills (pens) and must be assisted by six angels and twelve saints. The Napoleonic Wars, and especially the battle of Waterloo, created so many casualties that the Recorder is disgusted.

After skipping "a few short years of hollow peace," Byron focuses on the death of George and his elaborate funeral rites and then pauses to reflect on the passing of the eighty-year-old monarch. The narrative returns to Saint Peter, alerted by a cherub to the impending arrival of George III, whom Peter does not recognize (a jibe at the monarch's lack of virtue). Peter remarks that few kings reside in heaven and recalls Louis XVI's arrival, carrying his head; when refused admission, his howls caused sympathetic saints to receive him. As Peter is assured that the puppetlike George will be judged fairly, a caravan of angels escorts George to the gate; in the rear is Satan—aristocratic, disdainful, fierce—reminiscent of John Milton's Satan in the beginning of *Paradise Lost* (1667, 1674), as well as of Byron's own romantic heroes. Satan is so frightening that he terrifies Peter and the cherubs, who huddle together to protect themselves and George.

At this point in the poem, the gates fly open for the great archangel Michael, worthy adversary of Satan. Byron, in jest, withholds further description of Michael, affirming himself unable to match the ravings of "Bob Southey" and Johanna Southcote (religious fanatic and versifier). The confrontation between the fallen angel Lucifer (Satan) and his onetime adversary, Michael, constitutes the great dramatic highlight of the poem. Michael, "the viceroy of the sky," is greeted with respect by the assembled angels. Both Michael and Satan seem worthy combatants as they salute each other politely across neutral space. Like an elegant gentleman, Michael bows to his foe; Satan greets him haughtily but civilly ("He merely bent his diabolic brow"). Both acknowledge "a proud regret" that their destinies have been so different. Byron then digresses to cite authority for Satan's visit to heaven in an allusion to the story of Job. Michael invites Satan to state his claim to George III.

Satan, as "prosecuting attorney," charges George with responsibility for terrible slaughter and strong opposition to liberty. Satan points out that during his reign George had served Satan, and although he exercised some domestic virtues (being a good husband and father), the king's great sins were public, affecting millions. Given the location of this "trial," perhaps Satan's most damning charge is George's lack of religious toleration. Saint Peter is ready to concede Satan's claim, but Michael chides both for lack of discretion and calls for witnesses to prove Satan's case.

At Satan's signal, "a cloud of witnesses" appears, representing such a spectrum of interests that Michael pales, then turns color, and assures Satan that only a few witnesses need to be called. John Wilkes (a controversial eighteenth century politician) and Junius (the author of a series of letters attacking George III, whose identity still remains unknown), both witnesses in Southey's poem, are selected. As in Southey's poem (although for a different reason), Wilkes declines the offer to speak against George, refusing to dishonor the dead. Junius insists that his earlier attacks are still valid. Byron comments that Junius is not merely a shadow but, in his opinion, really no one at all.

The "trial" is now interrupted by the devil Asmodeus, who is carrying Southey himself, snatched from earth to testify. Satan recognizes him readily (expecting him in hell eventually). When Southey begins to review his poetry, he is interrupted by Michael and the general dissatisfaction of the group. The satire here is personal: against Southey's poetry, politics, and even his appearance. Michael silences the murmurs of protest and allows Southey to continue. With brazen effrontery, Southey offers first to write a biography of Satan; upon his refusal, Southey makes the same offer to Michael, before proceeding to introduce his "Vision." As he begins, both angels and the damned vanish: Angels fly away briskly, and devils rush howling back to hell. Michael's teeth are set on edge, and he cannot blow his trumpet. Saint Peter uses his keys to knock down Southey, who falls into a lake and sinks. He is buoyed by his own emptiness (inner corruption), and Byron's telescope, which enabled him to view these events, is withdrawn. In all the commotion, George III slips into heaven, where the reader leaves him practicing Psalm 100.

Forms and Devices

For *The Vision of Judgment*, Byron employs travesty, a type of satire that ridicules by humorous imitation the subject matter of another work. The style of the original is not necessarily employed, but the focus is on the subject matter, which could be rudely treated. The structure was determined by Byron's imitation of the original, particularly two sections describing George III's arrival in heaven. The narrative generally follows Southey's poem until Byron discards the imitation for a frontal attack on Southey when Asmodeus delivers the poet laureate before the "tribunal." Since the attack on Southey and his poem is so concerted, the poem achieves a unity of purpose and coherence denied Byron's masterpiece, *Don Juan* (1819-1824).

As in *Don Juan*, however, the tone is civilized, gentlemanly, and colloquial, as well as sometimes flippant, even irreverent. Byron refers to John Wilkes as "A merry, cock-eyed, curious-looking Sprite" and to the angels as "Tories," saucily using Southey's words against him. The diction and tone of the Satan-Michael episode contrast with the colloquial manner elsewhere. The two address each other with such politeness and respect that they could be opposing members of Parliament discussing some legislation. In contrast, Byron can stoop to diatribe as Satan abuses George III— "this old, blind, mad, helpless, weak, poor worm"—or when Byron refers to Southey's poetry as "spavin'd dactyls." Nevertheless, the general mood of the poem is one of exuberant good humor, impudence, and high spirits.

The verse form is ottava rima, which Byron used so successfully in *Don Juan* that he could claim it for his own. The stanza consists of eight lines, rhyming *abababcc*. The longer stanza released Byron from the confines of the heroic couplet that he tried in earlier satires but found uncongenial. Some of the rhymes are forced, not for lack of poetic skill but to increase the comic effect: "document/saints" and "hexameter/ would stir."

The poem's satire and humor do not rob it of metaphoric language and imagery. Similes are frequent: Angels arrive "like a rush of mighty wind," the corrupt Southey is "light as an elf," and angels huddle "Like birds when soars the falcon." In metaphor, Michael is a glorious "Thing of Light" and "the Viceroy of the sky." Visual imagery provides a heavenly gate with the "flashing of its hinges" creating "a new/ Aurora borealis," "azure fields of Heaven," and Michael changing color "as a peacock's tail." The combination of visual image and simile is brilliant; Byron even provides auditory imagery in response to Satan's signal: "Infernal thunder shook both sea and land/ In all the planets—and Hell's batteries/ Let off the artillery." Such imagery is also found in the murmuring of disgruntled spectators at the trial and in the howling of the agonized audience for Southey's poem.

In addition, allusions contribute to the poem's themes by supporting the message against intolerance. Byron invokes the Christian symbols of the fish and the lamb, evocative of sacrifice and redemption. The story of Job is borrowed from the Bible to provide proof of Byron's description of Satan's visit to heaven. A further reference to the Bible is Junius's statement, "What I have written, I have written," which recalls Pilate's words at the time of the Crucifixion (John 19:22), an ironic contrast when the words are directed toward the tyrannical George. Indeed, irony is an effective tool in the poem, for example, when Byron asserts that men could write letters without hands, since many had written them without heads.

Themes and Meanings

The focus of Byron's satire is primarily Robert Southey, who had provoked Byron's anger by his attacks, especially in Southey's preface to his *A Vision of Judgment*. Byron announced his counterattack in his own preface to *The Vision of Judgment* (originally signed "Quevedo Redivivus," or "Quevedo," a seventeenth century satirist, "Reborn")—personal, political, literary, and "religious." The scope of the ideas in the poem, however, transcends targeting Southey.

Southey had accused Byron of being a corrupter of morals and a "Satanic" poet. He had also spread rumors about the conduct of Byron, Percy Bysshe Shelley, Mary Godwin, and Claire Claremont when they resided in Switzerland. Furthermore, Byron was particularly opposed to Southey's smug righteousness.

Politically, the two were opposed. Earlier, Southey, as well as the other "Lake Poets," William Wordsworth and Samuel Taylor Coleridge, had been more idealistic and radical, turning conservative as they matured. Byron considered them political renegades, apostates from liberalism. As a "turncoat," Southey won government approval and was appointed poet laureate. This appointment helped occasion Southey's writing *A Vision of Judgment*, with its fawning flattery of George III. Byron, in the guise of Satan in his poem, indicts George III for bloody wars fought for evil causes (such as maintaining America as a colony), for intolerance, and for obstruction of Catholic Emancipation (which Byron himself had defended in the House of Lords). Cleverly, Byron allowed George some domestic virtues (he was a good father and husband) so as not to create an unbelievable monster. With great irony, however, Byron draws the contrast between George's elaborate funeral and his obvious unworthiness of such mourning.

In addition, Byron opposed Southey's poetic principles. He and other Lake Poets had attacked John Dryden and Alexander Pope (eighteenth century poets Byron had defended in earlier satires). Byron dismisses Southey as a hack. Southey's glaring error in experimenting with the use of classical unrhymed hexameter in his tribute to George and his glossing over George's obvious faults made him vulnerable to Byron's acerbity.

The attack on hypocrisy extends to the apparent attack on religion. Neither God nor established religion, however, is targeted; Byron challenges the hypocritical cant he found in Southey's poem. Southey was too judgmental in damning fellow mortals; Byron digresses briefly to explain his own position in support of a merciful God. Byron may treat figures such as Saint Peter, Michael, and Satan with levity (as when Peter sweats at Satan's appearance) but only to make them more human and sympathetic. His theme was anti-bigotry and pro-toleration, especially in freedom of religious choice, and he regarded Southey's assumptions about good and evil as impious.

Byron astutely allows Satan to be his spokesman; thus Byron distances himself from retaliation against his own liberal views, and his pose as a civilized gentleman makes Southey more reprehensible. With comic brilliance, Byron advocates tolerance, liberty, freedom of speech, and freedom to worship. The greatest irony of the satire is that Byron used Southey's own words against him, his own ammunition to destroy him.

Elizabeth Nelson

VOLTAIRE AT FERNEY

Author: W. H. Auden (1907-1973)
Type of poem: Meditation
First published: 1939; collected in *Another Time*, 1940

The Poem

"Voltaire at Ferney" is a short poem consisting of thirty-six lines divided into six stanzas. Each stanza contains two or three sets of lines that rhyme. A casual reading of the poem and its title suggests that the author is merely portraying a scene in the life of François-Marie Arouet, better known to history as Voltaire. In fact, W. H. Auden had reviewed books about the famous French philosopher. (He assumed that the reader was familiar with the life and times of Voltaire and therefore did not provide any background information.) A thorough reading of the poem reveals that Auden essentially constructed an epigram in which he attempted to develop a psychological profile of Voltaire. His approach is analytic and conceptual, and there are no dramatic scenes. The poem, however, takes on additional meaning when one considers the period of time in which it was written as well as the changes that were taking place in Auden's own life.

In the beginning of the poem, Voltaire is surveying the ancient estate of Ferney, located in the county of Gex, which borders on Switzerland. In 1754 he had settled in Geneva, being *persona non grata* in both France and Prussia. In 1758 he had acquired Ferney when his relationships with the leaders of Geneva were becoming strained. (Voltaire's friend and associate Jean Le Rond d'Alembert had published an article on Geneva that revealed the personal failings of its Calvinist clergymen.) Ferney was in France, but it was only three miles from Geneva, thereby allowing Voltaire to avoid its Calvinist leaders—or flee to Switzerland should the Catholics in Paris (re)issue orders for his arrest. To safeguard his investment against confiscation, he purchased the estate in the name of his niece. Shortly thereafter, Voltaire added, by a life purchase, the neighboring seigneury of Tournay and could legally call himself a lord and even display a coat of arms. As the first stanza indicates, Ferney was a working estate employing eight hundred people in agriculture, weaving, and watchmaking.

The blind old woman of the second stanza is Marie de Vichy-Chamrond, Marquise Du Deffand. The greatest minds in Europe came to visit her salon in Paris. She liked Voltaire as much for his fine manners as for his great mind, and their correspondence remains a classic of French literature. The marquise lost her sight in her mid-fifties but heeded Voltaire's advice to go on living to a ripe old age because "nothing is better than life." At the very least, she could enrage those who paid her annuities. Voltaire ultimately concluded that life is worth living in order to fight "against the false and unfair" as well as to garden and to civilize others. In Voltaire's 1759 novel *Candide*, Professor Pangloss, Voltaire's parody of the philosopher Gottfried Leibniz, tells his young pupil how the unfolding of tragic events clearly proves that this is the best of all possible worlds. Candide agrees, but she insists on cultivating their garden, if only to protect them against the three great evils—idleness, vice, and want. To Voltaire culti-vating one's garden could only be considered a beginning when so much was amiss in the world.

Forms and Devices

To Auden ideas were not vague abstractions of the mind. They were real things that shaped the terms and conditions of the unending struggle for democracy and social-ism. Auden's affectionate portrait of Voltaire attempted to capture both his relatively unimportant personal failings as well as his larger contributions to the important causes of reason and justice. It was at Ferney that Voltaire learned of the arrest, tor-ture, and murder of the Huguenot Jean Calas by the Catholic authorities in Toulouse and began his struggle against the abuses and ineptitude of France's *ancien régime*.

In the third stanza Auden assumes a subtly critical attitude toward the motives, methods, and character of Voltaire and his philosophical contemporaries by describ-ing them as a group of rebellious schoolchildren who want to defeat "the infamous grown-ups." Voltaire is presented as "the cleverest of them all," who does not hesitate to lie when necessary and is willing to bide his time until the moment is right. In the fourth stanza Voltaire reflects upon those who might have been effective allies in his crusade. These include d'Alembert, who compromised himself by drawing a pension from the court, the "great enemy" Blaise Pascal, the "dull" Denis Diderot (who es-poused an unacceptable system of materialistic atheism), and the weak and sentimen-tal Jean-Jacques Rousseau.

Voltaire did not seem to care if anyone took offense at his scandalous conduct. He carried on a scientific partnership and openly adulterous affair with Gabrielle Émilie Le Tonnelier de Breuteuil, Marquise du Châtelet, who is mentioned in the fifth stanza. His relationship with his niece, Marie Louise Mignot Denis, can only be described as disgraceful even by the standards of the court of Louis XV. Yet Auden is not entirely without sympathy for Voltaire's desire for the more sensual pleasures. At the end of the fifth stanza, he writes that Voltaire had "done his share of weeping for Jerusalem" and that "it was the pleasure-haters who became unjust." However, Auden may also be suggesting that Voltaire was too confident about his chances for success and that his lack of humility and sense of propriety detracted from the larger causes.

Themes and Meanings

Auden wrote "Voltaire at Ferney" during what he described as the third period in his career, which covered the years between 1939 and 1946. During this time, Auden underwent profound changes in his religious and intellectual perspectives. After an earlier visit to Spain during its civil war, he became disillusioned with the political Left and began his return to the Anglican faith. In 1939 he settled in New York City and eventually became an American citizen. His works from this time often raise questions concerning the nature of existence, thereby suggesting his reaffirmation of Christianity. They also contain lighter and more romantic verses, some of which lack the unusual style and vigor of his best earlier works.

In one sense the poem is autobiographical. Auden, like Voltaire, had wandered from one country to another and had finally settled down in a distant part of the world. Both men had made personal and intellectual mistakes in their lives. Both had matured and retreated from the more radical ideas of their respective youths. However, maturity did not mean that they had abandoned their most cherished beliefs. Now, both men must gear up for the most important struggles of their lives. Both will use their talents of the pen to further their causes. Many of Auden's poems from this time express strong antiwar sentiments.

The parallels between the situation in Europe before the French Revolution and the outbreak of World War II are obvious; large-scale violence and bloodshed were about to be unleashed, changing the face of history. In the last stanza, Auden states that "the night was full of wrong,/ Earthquakes and executions." In Voltaire's time, an earthquake on All Saint's Day in 1755 had destroyed Lisbon. Christians wondered how God could have permitted this disaster to happen at a time when so many people were praying in the churches. One Jesuit priest proclaimed that the earthquake was God's punishment for the vices that were permitted to flourish in the city. Rousseau, however, argued that fewer people would have been killed had they not abandoned the more natural life of the villages. He added that people must remain optimistic and continue to believe in the goodness of God; everything in the end would be right. The only alternative was suicidal pessimism. These kinds of explanations seemed absurd to Voltaire, and they helped prompt him to write *Candide*. Likewise, a series of miscarriages of justice in France resulted in the execution of several men accused of crimes against God—as well as in the burning of books written by Voltaire, Rousseau, and other philosophers—and persuaded Voltaire to declare war on the Church.

Auden's final remark about "the uncomplaining stars" appears to acknowledge a certain futility. There are limits to what one person can do to advance the causes of reason and justice. He, like his eighteenth century counterpart, had hope—if little reason for optimism. Nevertheless, they "must go on working." At that time Auden could not foresee that he, like Voltaire, would return to his native land at the end of his life and be showered with honors.

Peter A. Schneider

VOWELS

Author: Arthur Rimbaud (1854-1891)
Type of poem: Sonnet
First published: 1883, as "Voyelles"; in *Reliquaire*, 1891; English translation collected in *An Anthology of French Poetry from Nerval to Valéry in English Translation with French Originals*, 1958

The Poem

Arthur Rimbaud's sonnet "Vowels" follows the standard Petrarchan form of octave and sestet, in Alexandrine lines. While Rimbaud's use of imagery was highly experimental, he retained traditional verse forms.

The opening line, which gives the sonnet its name, has caused considerable critical comment and interpretation. Rimbaud simply names the five vowels, linking each to a color: "A black, E white, I red, U green, O blue: vowels." Questions immediately arise concerning why he links certain vowels to certain colors.

Rimbaud seems quite aware that his arbitrary assigning of colors to vowels will mystify the reader when he continues in the second line, "I will some day tell of your latent birth." Subsequently, in his work *Une Saison en enfer* (1873; *A Season in Hell*, 1932), Rimbaud would write, "I invented the color of vowels! . . . . I withheld the translation of it." Despite this mocking refusal to explain, the balance of the sonnet presents a series of images that do suggest reasons for these associations.

The images of the octave contrast with those of the sestet in that all are fairly specific references to living creatures. The letter *a* suggests a "corset black with flies." The basis for this association seems questionable, for while flies do appear black, they have no clear link with the letter *a*. Critics have suggested, however, that a source for Rimbaud's images may lie in children's alphabet books, which at the time showed *a* for *abeille*, or a bee, a flying creature easily assimilated with a fly.

Once this technique of positing a word beginning with the requisite letter is established, the next two vowels become easily intelligible: *e* for *esquimau* and *i* for *indien*. The latter is not so clearly spelled out in the text of the sonnet as are the ice and "white kings" that represent the Eskimos, but critics have noted the parallel allusion to American Indians as *Peaux-Rouges* in Rimbaud's poem "Le Bateau ivre" ("The Drunken Boat"). These two evocations of peoples of distant North America introduce an element of exoticism into this poem written, as was all of Rimbaud's verse, before his departure for the travels to distant lands that consumed his later years.

In the sestet, the imagery becomes more expansive. In addition, here, as in the initial line of the poem, the alphabetical order of the vowels is reversed, with *u* before *o*. The "cycles" and "final bugle" suggest alliterations for these vowels with *univers* and the last word supplied by Rimbaud himself, "Omega." Thus the reason for the deviation from alphabetical order becomes clear. What began with the alpha of *a* must end with omega, the *o* capitalized to emphasize the letter's cosmic significance, a vision of

"His Eyes" seen in a context of "silences crossed by Worlds and Angels." The poem has progressed from the minute and repugnant image of the flies through the realm of humankind, the extent of which is suggested by the examples of distant peoples, and the wide vision of seas and fields, to a final transcendent invocation of divinity, consistent with the reference to alpha and omega.

Forms and Devices

Many explanations have been offered for the source of Rimbaud's linking of colors to vowels, ranging from the child's alphabet book to the color variations that base metal is supposed to undergo as the alchemist attempts to change it into gold; the latter explanation draws upon the "alchemy" mentioned in the sestet. One important influence on Rimbaud's imagery was the work of Charles Baudelaire, who, in his sonnet "Correspondences," defined synesthesia—the linking of sensations of two different senses—as a source of poetic inspiration.

Baudelaire's fusion of senses relies heavily on perfumes, while Rimbaud's linking of vowel sounds to visual colors retains the single link of eye and ear. Still, his imagery becomes more coherent when read in the context of the dual world of good and evil Baudelaire posits in *Les Fleurs du mal* (1857, 1861, 1868; *Flowers of Evil*, 1909). The moral dualism within the poem coincides almost perfectly with the contrast between octave and sestet.

The octave presents the repugnant imagery of an imperfect world. Just as the boat in Rimbaud's "The Drunken Boat" had to traverse polluted waters before arriving at the sea, the progression of "Vowels" begins with the image of flies surrounding cruel, stinking objects. In this context, the "gulfs of shadow" that begin the second quatrain appear to be an emblem of death.

The second vision, that of the Eskimos, seems initially less repugnant than the first. The frozen landscape may be preserved from the corruption of death (though in Baudelaire's imagery, polar areas are linked with the spiritual death of the poet). The shivering flowers that end the sixth line eloquently reflect this linkage. Flowers, an emblem of poetry from *The Flowers of Evil*, cannot flourish in such a hostile climate.

The images of blood and drunkenness that close the octave return to the repugnant elements of "The Drunken Boat," the link with this poem reinforced by its reference to *Peaux-Rouges*. After the harsh octave, the repeated references to "peace" in the first tercet, along with the pastoral image of grazing animals, turns to a homely, European context, much as Rimbaud at the end of "The Drunken Boat" sought to return to calm "European water."

The image of the alchemist's wrinkled forehead abandons the essentially geographical motifs that have dominated the poem to this point. Given Rimbaud's own interest in alchemy and his concept of the vocation of the poet, the reader may take this figure to represent the poet himself. The proximity of the alchemist to the figure whose eyes alone are revealed in the last line conveys Rimbaud's sense of the importance of the poet. The final tercet, with its sounding horn seeming to call the world to judgment and its multiple capital letters, invokes the image of God. The poet, godlike in his inspiration, has arrived through permutations not unlike those of alchemy at a transcendent vision.

Themes and Meanings

Rimbaud not only believed that the poet was destined for greatness by a gift for revealing ideas previously unknown, he also saw the process through which the poet would gain this enlightenment as extraordinarily painful. In a letter he wrote to his friend Paul Demeny on May 15, 1871, Rimbaud described the process of creation thus: "The Poet makes himself into a *seer* by a long, immense and reasoned *disordering* of *all his senses*. All forms of love, suffering, and madness." The poet must undergo the great pain of this process because of his duty to fulfill the poetic potential he senses vested within him.

Descriptive elements throughout "Vowels" recapitulate this creative process. In the first quatrain, the adjectives parallel the first efforts of the poet, with *latentes* and subsequently *éclatantes* suggesting first the latent nature of his talent and then its bursting forth; *cruelles* ("cruel") brings him to the suffering of disordered senses that must accompany this birth. The *sang craché* ("spit-out blood") and the *ivresse* (drunkenness) of the second quatrain echo the letter to Demeny in which Rimbaud wrote that the poet "uses up all poisons within himself."

While poets at Rimbaud's time sometimes sought inspiration in hallucinogenic substances, his biographers have indicated that Rimbaud found more physical sickness than mental exaltation in these experiences. Thus the "penitent drunkenness" of the octave seems closer to his actual experience than the "divine vibrations" to which he sees the poet progressing in the sestet. Throughout the agitated questing of his life, Rimbaud never reached the peace of pastoral tranquillity he posits in the "pastures sown with animals." Perhaps this choice of image for that peaceful state, a land rich with animals but devoid of human beings, hints at Rimbaud's flight in later years to isolation in Africa, far from his countrymen.

Yet perhaps Rimbaud himself offers a better explanation. His desire was not so much to flee humankind as to approximate the experience of the animals. In *A Season in Hell*, he describes at considerable length his own evolution as a poet. Once he began to discover the "hallucination of words," he wrote, "I was lazy, prey to a heavy fever: I envied the happiness of beasts." The peace of the animals may then be linked to their absence of language. The poet, arriving at this stage, must evolve beyond the use of words or, if he is "lazy," refuse to use them at all.

This discomfort with words may offer a clue to why Rimbaud abandoned poetry in his final years. Sound, even that of the *Clairon*, becomes strange and strident (the dual suggestion of *étrange*), incorporating an element of foreignness as the music of poetry grows ever more remote from the poet. Rimbaud has not, as it turns out, freed himself from the menace of death suggested in the octave. Like Hamlet at the end of his life, Rimbaud finds that "the rest is silence."

Dorothy M. Betz

VOYAGES

Author: Hart Crane (1899-1932)
Type of poem: Poetic sequence
First published: 1926, in *White Buildings*

The Poem

"Voyages" is a lyric sequence composed of six love poems that the poet wrote to his absent lover, a merchant seaman named Emil Opffer. The shortest of the lyrics, part 1, runs a mere sixteen lines; the longest, part 4, thirty-two lines. The majority of the 146 lines that constitute the entire sequence are in blank verse, but there seems to be no sustained effort at any measure of formal consistency. For example, lines yield to free-verse rhythms, and the five five-line stanzas of part 2 employ occasional rhymes. The eight four-line stanzas of part 6, meanwhile, follow an irregular rhyme scheme.

Part 1 describes children playing at the seashore, "[g]aily digging and scattering" while "[t]he sun beats lightning on the waves." For all the elevated use of language—"contrived a conquest," "treble interjections"—there is nothing unusual going on here. It is a typical, childhood day at the beach, but the speaker says that if the children could hear him over the sound of the "waves [that] fold thunder on the sand," he would impart a dire warning to them: Play as you might on the safety of the shore, "there is a line/ You must not cross," for "The bottom of the sea is cruel."

Part 2 continues in the spirit of the observation with which part 1 ended, but now the sea is like a woman whose "undinal vast belly moonward bends,/ Laughing the wrapt inflections of our love." If she is a jolly and motherly figure in the first stanza, in the second she appears more like a tauntingly pitiless queen or judge—"scrolls of silver snowy sentences,/ The sceptred terror of whose sessions rends"—whose cold vastnesses sunder all things except the "pieties of lovers' hands."

Now the scene changes to the Caribbean, to images of tropical flowers and wandering seafarers—"O my Prodigal"—and the reader learns why the speaker sees the sea as cruel—his lover is the voyager who is away at sea. The speaker cannot blame the sea for this painful state of affairs, but he does contend with the sea almost as if she is a woman who is alienating his lover's affections. He reminds his lover of time's passage, which the sea, with her tides, herself measures, and urges a speedy return because "sleep, death, desire" are all one in his absence. Thus there can be no resolution to this deeper, emotional "voyage"—"bequeath us to no earthly shore"—until the lovers are reunited.

In part 3, the speaker imagines another possibility to sustain him through the pain of their separation. Because all earthly seas are one and the night sky is a common, starry sight, the act of gazing upon the sea at night, its blend of light and darkness hardly separable from the sky's in their "infinite consanguinity," unites him with his lover; only at dawn, when the demarcation of sea and sky is clarified, can the illusion of union be broken.

In part 4, the speaker continues the idea that he can imaginatively share his lover's presence by contemplating the marriage of sea and sky, which the lover must also have in view, albeit in other climes—"Blue latitudes and levels of your eyes." So too, a faith in the power and truth of love sustains him now, for he can—must—imagine that his lover is feeling and doing likewise.

Part 5 continues in the same vein as the speaker contemplates the bay into which his lover's ship will eventually sail on its return. It is night once more, and the sea is moonlit. It is as if the speaker can see his lover, "too tall here," both in the sky and in the moon's reflection in the bay waters, for the moon, as it blends both a promising light and an emptying void into itself, reminds him of his lover's blond hair and then of his lover's absence.

In part 6, the speaker can no longer bear imaginatively projecting himself into his lover's presence by contemplating the sea and sky. Now, like the tidal currents that wend their way across the ocean surface, the speaker seeks such actual proximity as might be his if his "eyes [were] pressed black against the prow." Thus he achieves the resolution of his agony. For, blinded by his love and his longing, he accepts their physical separation at last for exactly what it is and can recognize that the basis of their love is a transcendent devotion, a "fervid covenant." It becomes for him "Belle Isle," the journey's true end, wherever it might be in time and space. So too, inasmuch as he holds him truly in his heart, the lover has indeed become the incorruptible and ubiquitous "imaged Word . . . [w]hose accent no farewell can know."

Forms and Devices

Hart Crane was convinced that language is the cornerstone of both approximating and explicating human experience. It is no accident that his poetry employs a heightened language as it explores intense states of awareness, emotion, and thought. Certain of his devices are not difficult for the reader to understand, and the innovations that he and his contemporaries advanced are now familiar.

When in part 1 the "brilliant kids" on the shore "fondle [their] shells and [their] sticks," an interpretation that sees phallic and masturbation imagery in such an apparently innocuous statement does not sound farfetched, because readers expect poets to work layers of textured meanings into the surface. Crane can fall victim to such textures. "Adagios of islands," for example, with its musical connotation of a slow, graceful movement, borders on mere verbal adornment; this is a risk that Crane is willing to take.

An extreme devotion to an intricate architecture of words is no vice in a poet, but in Crane's case it did occasionally lead to verbal excesses. Even then Crane was eventually vindicated. "The seal's wide spindrift gaze toward paradise," an image of the ultimate blankness with which any living being confronts the abyss of eternity, was originally described as "spindrinny" until a friend, Malcolm Cowley, convinced Crane that no such word existed. Crane substituted the also somewhat obscure "spindrift." Years later, Cowley discovered the word "spindrinny" in Herman Melville's classic, *Moby Dick* (1851).

Themes and Meanings

"Voyages" is a sequence of love lyrics, and there is no literary theme more universal than love; neither is there one more fraught with bewitchment, bother, and bewilderment. For purely autobiographical reasons, Crane also made this love sequence a commentary on man and his relationship with the sea. The irony is that depicting the separated lovers as individuals between whom there is an unbreachable barrier of time and space was not only true to biographical detail but also added to the metaphorical dimensions of the love theme.

The pain of separation is so immense that it can seem to be akin to, if not a species of, death. Thus love poetry finds in the lover's separation from the object of affection a deeper meaning: the individual's sense of separation from his Creator and from some primordial sense of innocence and union with the external universe.

"Voyages" develops and explores all these themes. The children who play upon the shore are any innocents who do not yet know the perilous nature of the voyage, life, that is awaiting them. That the sea is presented in images of both mother and tormentor, lover and rival, reflects on the individual's inability to reconcile the notion of a loving Creator with fears of an indifferent or malicious universe.

In such an existential maelstrom, it is no wonder that the requited love of a fellow mortal who is equally estranged and alienated yet still willing to cast his fate with his lover's is a balm, a boon, and—when there must be separation—a bane.

Crane carries this notion through to its logical conclusion, and that is what makes "Voyages" a consummate achievement. Even when there is physical presence, all human beings are separate entities, able to sympathize but incapable forever, at least in this world, of the total and complete union that the human soul seems to crave. Part 6 of "Voyages" confirms this truth and then goes on to posit a larger one: It is in the spirit that all people are already joined; therefore, there is no such thing as separation. Consequently, each person is, for every other, "the imaged Word . . ./ Whose accent no farewell can know."

Russell Elliott Murphy

VRINDABAN

Author: Octavio Paz (1914-1998)
Type of poem: Meditation
First published: 1969, in *Ladera este*; English translation collected in *The Collected Poems of Octavio Paz: 1957-1987*, 1987

The Poem

Ladera este (1962-1968) (*East Slope*, 1987), in which "Vrindaban" appears, represents Octavio Paz's attempt to come to grips with the bewildering sights, sounds, and smells of India, where he served as Mexican ambassador from 1962 to 1968. In a note to the poem, Paz says that Vrindaban is one of the sacred cities of Hinduism. According to legend, Krishna, one of the chief Hindu gods, spent his youth in its forests, playing on his divine flute to entice the milkmaids to dance with him.

The poem develops its 163 lines of free verse through the parallel depiction of two experiences. Against the night and the curtain of the forest, the poet is writing. (The reader recognizes at once a recurrent Paz theme: poetry about the act of writing.) The narrative thread switches to the poet being driven in a car at night among darkened, "extinguished houses" that contrast with his "lighted thoughts," which momentarily led him to believe that he was a tree covered with leaves. He is returning from a trip in which, as the reader will see, he has had a disturbing experience.

The poem switches back to the poet planting words in a garden, that is, writing under lamplight on a piece of paper. By now the reader notes that Paz inserts his description of himself writing in parentheses in order to set it off from the racing car and the sights of India that will soon appear.

Meanwhile, his thoughts race like the car in a kind of free association that quickly culminates in a rhetorical question about belief that receives the ambiguous answer "I believe," which, says the poet, should be followed by a series of dots which will allow the reader to supply the missing words. India now intrudes with its misery and stench, its ecstatic combination of sublime colors and suffering, putrefaction alongside the peacock's tail.

On his trip, Paz has met with an unsettling sight. The "saddhu," a Hindu holy man, takes the stage covered with ashes, his eyes an expressionless glint, his bowels rumbling at the narrator. The phrase "Gone gone" refers to a famous passage in sacred Hindu writing that describes the saddhu as having left the world of phenomena and crossed over to the other shore. After another brief parenthesis about writing, Paz reveals some of the ambiguity he feels toward the holy man with the juxtaposed nouns: saint scoundrel.

The sight of the saddhu leads Paz to make an important declaration. Despite his interest in visions and epiphanies, absolutes are not his theme. He is too hungry for life to cross to the other shore, and he willingly accepts life's corollary, death. In its last lines, the poem celebrates the act of writing ("a memory inventing itself"), awaiting the dialogue with readers who will speak with him always.

Forms and Devices

As is often the case with the work of Octavio Paz, the visual impact of the poem is calculated. The absence of punctuation, the columnar structure, the ambiguous placement of words contribute effects of openness, free association, parallel happenings, and special emphases on meanings by location.

Paz uses parenthetical expressions for the description of the writing process. Nearly all matter within parentheses begins with the pronoun "I," followed by "write" or "set down." This device situates the act of creating poetry apart from the flow of thoughts and impressions, to highlight the solitude it demands and ultimately to contrast it, in this case, with the profoundly disturbing reality of the saddhu, who as a visionary is also a kind of poet. The one exception to this practice occurs when the narrator recalls the holy man with the phrase "Gone gone." Here the saddhu momentarily enters the space reserved for the description of the poetic act.

Paz has mixed feelings about the saddhu that he cannot, or perhaps does not wish to resolve. He resorts to the juxtaposition of contraries to bring out his dilemma. The absence of connectives (for example "or") helps heighten the opposition. "Saint scoundrel saint," and again "Saint clown saint beggar king damned," the narrator will not make a choice for himself or for the reader.

Paz abstains from using end rhymes in his poetry, but that does not mean he is unaware of the musical nature of verse. Alliteration (the repetition of initial and internal sounds in a line) is one of his favorite stratagems. In the original Spanish for example, the words *Ido ido* ("Gone gone"), emphasized by their placement, receive an echo in *Idolo podrido* (rotted idol), which the English translation cannot exactly render.

Successful metaphors add to the poem's impact. The opening "forest of breathing" refers to the night sounds that the poet must banish from his lamplight. Often one metaphor suggests another: the quiet garden that is the stars leads to the garden of letters, which then suggests the notion that the words the poet writes are seeds (germs) ("I plant signs"). An interesting personification takes place in the description of the holy man, whose odors are so strong that they come and go as if they were concubines. The "cowering pot hook" refers to the saddhu's physical shape, but *garabato* (pot hook) in Spanish can also mean "scribblings," so the word could refer as well to those signs the poet is planting.

The image of the saddhu is so potently drawn that both the reader and the poet have difficulty shaking it off. Filthy, foul smelling, smeared with ashes, flinty-eyed without the gaze of love that produces beauty, he sits on the ghat (the steps leading down to the river) like a pot hook and bedevils Paz with contradictions. The image will not leave the poet and contrasts with the protected lamp glow in which he plants his words.

Themes and Meanings

Two strong oppositions run through "Vrindaban." The first of these is the contrast between the poet and the saddu; the second, the distinction between the ego and consciousness on one hand and the concept of nirvana, the cessation of individual existence, on the other. In a broad sense these oppositions may be seen as part of the contrast between East and West (the Orient and the Occident). On a personal level, the poet Octavio Paz, concerned with the poetic process and the insights it affords to beauty, the moments of transparency with their sense of unification between the writer and the world, must reconcile his strongest inclinations with a tradition and a culture that is at once attractive and repulsive. The quandary is accentuated by the fact that Paz's Mexican heritage also has roots in an Indian civilization that at first glance appears to be divorced from the western tradition brought by the Spaniards to Mexico.

The saddu disturbs the poet Paz because, as one concerned with poetic states of consciousness, he has respect for the ancient tradition of the Indian seers. Nevertheless, his own background is deeply involved in what might be called the Western European intellectual practice. East meets West in this poem, and it is unsettling. West sees the putrefaction, the drug-induced stare. Perhaps the saddu did see Krishna, the blue-black god, but the gaze that Paz encounters is different from the power of the visionary eye in "Same Time." Instead of conversation or the advice given to the young poet in "Same Time," Paz hears the rumblings of the seer's bowels. Meanwhile, East laughs at West. In Paz's memory, the mountebank continually watches from the other shore.

During the time of *East Slope*, Paz fell under the influence of the controversial American composer John Cage, and his poem "Reading John Cage," published in *East Slope*, contains the following quote in English: "(The situation must be Yes-and-No,/ not either-or)." What Cage taught Paz comes out in "Vrindaban." There is no need to choose. Instead of the typical western cultivation of ambiguity, or the search for deeper meaning in paradox, the matter can be best understood in terms of both yes and no. It is this insight that underlies the following lines in which the list of nouns maintains strict neutrality with regard to value: "Saint scoundrel saint" and "Saint clown saint beggar king damned."

Still Paz appears to make a choice. The tradition of the West hung too heavily upon him. That is the meaning of the lines "The absolute eternities/ their outlying districts/ are not my theme/ I am hungry for life and for death also." Indian mysticism, as deeply as he admired it, is not for him. He loves the world of phenomena and does not desire to be "gone" across to another shore in which his consciousness is lost, even though he accepts the fact that some day through death, a corollary of life, his consciousness too will disappear.

Howard Young

WAITING FOR THE BARBARIANS

Author: Constantine P. Cavafy (Kōnstantionos Petrou Kabaphēs, 1863-1933)
Type of poem: Narrative
First published: 1904, as "Perimenontas tous varvarous"; in *Poiēmata*, 1935; English
translation collected in *Collected Poems*, 1975

The Poem

Constantine P. Cavafy's "Waiting for the Barbarians" is a thirty-five-line poem composed of questions (in fifteen-syllable lines) and answers (in twelve- and thirteen-syllable lines). Although the speakers are not identified, they are clearly citizens of a city in the Roman Empire speculating on a public event and trying to assess its importance by observing the behavior of their public officials. Each stanza of the poem contains one or more questions, followed by a brief answer.

The first question about why people have gathered in the forum is given a precise reply: Today the barbarians are expected to arrive. Puzzled by the inactivity of the senate, the first speaker is told that law making has been suspended because of the imminent arrival of the barbarians. It seems futile to continue legislating when the barbarians will surely want to make their own rules.

The first speaker's focus then shifts to the emperor, who has risen early and sits on his throne at the city's main gate, wearing his crown. The first speaker is told that the emperor is waiting to welcome the barbarians' leader and has even prepared a scroll of the most important names in the city.

Then the first speaker notices the consuls and praetors, officials appearing in their finest public dress, adorned with various items of dazzling jewelry. He is assured that the barbarians are impressed with such displays of wealth and power. The first speaker also notices that the city's "distinguished orators" make no show and present no speeches. He is informed that barbarians find "rhetoric and public speaking" boring.

Then the public mood shifts, and the first speaker is bewildered by the sudden seriousness of the people, who are now leaving for home and seemingly lost in reverie. The second speaker answers that it is because "night has fallen" and the barbarians still have not arrived. Indeed, word has come from "the border" that the barbarians no longer exist. The first speaker ends the poem wondering what will happen without the barbarians, since they were a "kind of solution."

Forms and Devices

The poem proceeds by asking what seem like simple-minded questions that are put to a well-informed authority on the significance of public events. Yet the rudimentary quality of the questions enables Cavafy to describe the setting with maximum objectivity, since the questions are based purely on observation and on a desire to understand events, without interpreting too quickly. Each answer to a question thus elaborates some aspect of the setting, of what it means to wait for the barbarians. By asking questions, the first speaker is able to lay bare the assumptions of the second speaker, the public officials, and the populace. As a result, the dramatic impact of the scene is enhanced: It comes alive by the gradual revelation of details and explanations.

The major device of the poem is irony. Although the first speaker seems naïve, and the second, by comparison, sophisticated, in fact, no one in the city (as the conclusion implies) is acting on solid information. Instead, they are all behaving according to their expectations of what they think the barbarians will be like. At the same time, the populace and their leaders are exposing their own sense of futility. Neither the senate nor the emperor provides any positive action. In their passive roles they are like the people they lead—waiting for the intervention of an external force.

The dialogue form of the poem also enhances its irony, since the format of questions and answers would seem to provide some resolution of certain issues—or, at the very least, a full exploration of the issues—as in Plato's dialogues. Yet, just the contrary is true: No matter how many questions are asked, the same answer is always given, which makes a mockery of the dialogue form, since no new knowledge is acquired.

The imagery of the poem enforces the notion of a complex civilization, wealthy and cosmopolitan, that has stagnated. It can dress itself up to awe the barbarians, but it cannot act for itself. Nowhere does the poet explicitly state his opinion. On the contrary, he prefers understatement and irony, allowing adjectives such as "embroidered," "magnificent," and "elegant"—used to describe togas and jewelry—to convey the grand, yet inert, quality of this civilization, which at this point in its development can do no more than display itself.

Themes and Meanings

As the last line of the poem suggests, "Waiting for the Barbarians" is about a state of mind as much as it is about an actual event. Although the setting would seem to be in a later phase of the Roman Empire, the city is not identified, the emperor is not named, no specific historical event is evoked, and the speakers themselves are less individuals than they are the voices of a civilization, of a certain habit of mind, of what might be termed decadence.

The civilization described in the poem is obviously in decline, no longer having the energy to renew itself. Not only does the senate not meet, not only does the emperor take his position at the city gate and function as no more than a figurehead, but even the orators (who merely have to create speeches, not perform deeds) cannot arouse themselves, rationalizing their inactivity by claiming that the barbarians are bored by speeches. Such lack of faith in the power of words is the ultimate in decadence, in an attitude that suggests nothing is really worth doing.

The barbarians, then, hold out a kind of solution to the decadent, for the barbarians are presumed to be energetic, to prefer action over talk. The irony is that this conception of the barbarians is itself a projection of a decadent civilization, which imagines that a more primitive people will provide a vitality that the civilization lacks. The barbarians, notice, are presumed to be somewhere beyond the borders of the city, comfortably far enough away so that the populace can imagine being saved (rejuvenated) by an outside force, untainted by urban corruption.

The odd thing about the poem is that there seems to be absolutely no fear of the barbarians. If they represent all that is antithetical to this well-developed city, why is it that an invasion does not provoke anxiety, at the very least? It seems clear the citizens and their leaders have nothing to lose, that the very trappings of civilization mean nothing to them in a state where neither individual nor collective achievement is possible any longer. What the barbarians are being offered, in other words, is the shell of a civilization. It is a community weary of itself that has lost any sense of purpose and awaits a new force to give it direction.

Without barbarians, the first speaker finally realizes, the city must confront itself and find its own solution. The real anxiety the poem expresses, therefore, is internal. The city has exhausted itself and seeks an external means of revival. As long as it can project beyond its limits to the barbarians, it can defer admitting its sense of self-defeat. The people's faces turn serious and they are confused when they realize that this relatively easy answer to their problem has evaporated. The barbarians, in fact, have been no more than a rumor, a figment of the imagination, greedily grasped by a desperate populace and its leadership. Elaborately primed to receive their conquerors, the people are in doubt as to what to do next. Ironically, the one public event that has brought everyone together has been predicated on welcoming the very forces that would destroy civilization as they know it. So hopeless have they become that they would accept any order except their own.

The structure of the poem reinforces its meaning by making all the answers to the first speaker's questions end in a reference to the barbarians, for this is a civilization that has stopped thinking for itself and that has lost faith in its own institutions and people. Because there is no answer to the first speaker's questions other than that the barbarians are coming, when the barbarians do not come, the civilization is revealed as utterly bankrupt, literally empty, and incapable of conceiving of another "solution" to its problems. It is, as both the questions and answers imply, a civilization without alternatives.

Carl Rollyson

WAKE UP

Author: Raymond Carver (1938-1988)
Type of poem: Narrative
First published: 1988; collected in *A New Path to the Waterfall*, 1989

The Poem

"Wake Up" is a narrative poem divided into six sections. Most of the poem is narrative, but in section 5, the poet records a brief dialogue between the speaker and his female companion. The setting of the poem, Kyborg Castle, in Zurich, Switzerland, provides an occasion for the two speakers to contemplate human suffering and death.

The first section of the poem introduces the spatial setting: the dungeon of a medieval castle. There the speakers observe an executioner's block, which sits near an iron maiden, one of a number of instruments of torture used in the Middle Ages, which was, curiously enough, in the shape of a female. Also in the dungeon is a rack, used for stretching criminals. The poet notes that at times the torturer would have to awaken his charges by throwing water over them. This was done so that the prisoner would feel the effects of the torture to the utmost.

In contrast to the images of torture is "an old cherrywood crucifix," which hangs on the wall in the chamber's corner. Section 3 questions the suitability of the image of crucifixion in a room noted for punishment. Moving almost to the level of sarcasm, the poet suggests that the "criminal" would, almost at the point of death, possibly receive religious conversion. This section hints at the horrible punishments often associated with the Inquisition, which claimed to be acting with God's inspiration.

At this point, the poet begins to move toward the central concerns of the poem. Having looked at the objects, he sees some paradoxical connection between the medieval past and the present. Section 4 expresses the poem's thematic concern with universal human suffering and raises questions about the ways humans often attempt to experience and to tempt life "without fear of consequence," drawing back from life-threatening experiences just at the moment when mortality seems likely. Also in this section, the first (primary) speaker acknowledges the presence of a woman, and, playfully, they pretend she is his executioner. In the posture of someone about to be beheaded, he places his head on the block, preparing for imaginary death by breathing deeply. The speaker is so involved in the experience of the moment, he does, in fact, say that he feels he "could almost drift off" like the many others who were awakened by their torturers.

Section 5 records a dialogue between the primary speaker and his companion as she, like the real torturers, tries to get him to "wake up" from his imaginary death. For the time being, he does not do so; he wishes to continue his near-death experience. Realizing there would be little time, when this close to death, for prayer, he attempts to embrace the experience of death as the prayer "drops unfinished" from his lips and his companion moves to touch him with her imaginary ax ("the idea-of-axe"). Pretending to be beheaded, the male speaker imagines what will come after death: ". . . I tilt, nose over chin into the last of sight, of whatever sheen or rapture I can grasp to take with me, wherever I'm bound."

The poem ends as the speaker and his companion discontinue their game of executioner-victim. Recognizing they have just undergone an experience that differs only imaginatively from the reality of death, they leave "just shaky and not ourselves" and seek the "light" from the dark dungeon they have just exited. When they finally leave the castle, however, they find themselves still in need of light even though they are "outside" and "in the open."

Forms and Devices

For the most part, "Wake Up" is more like a story than a poem. Although the poem contains a few poetic devices, the poet relies primarily on conveying the experience through portraying the emotional effects of imagining death and using symbolic language. The poem was inspired by a trip Raymond Carver and his second wife, Tess Gallagher, who is also a poet, took shortly before Carver discovered he had lung cancer in the fall of 1987.

Except for a few lines (particularly those in section 3), the poem reads like a narrative, which perhaps suggests that it can be labeled a "prose poem." A prose poem conveys the poet's feelings about one experience in a concentrated manner like that of a poem, but it does not follow poetic conventions with regard to form, rhyme, and meter. Even though the poem is very proselike, the author does use figurative language. Most frequently used are parallelism and personification. A series of parallel prepositional phrases opens the poem, giving a rhythmlike effect and suggesting the poem's almost ritualistic reenactment of the tortures of the Middle Ages that will be applied to the speaker's present life and, by implication, the universal human misery with which the poem is concerned.

The poem's use of traditional poetic devices, however, is minimal. The poet describes the iron maiden, which is in the shape of a woman, as possessing an "iron gown" and as having "serene features . . . engraved with a little noncommital smile." Such personification ironically parallels the later incident of having the speaker's companion, a woman, play the role of executioner. A simile is used as an extension of the personification when the poet writes that the "spiked interior" of the iron maiden could close on one "like a demon, like one possessed." The iron maiden becomes a symbol of death, which possesses one and takes away all the light, with iron representing the strength of death from which there is no escape. This image is therefore a springboard for discussing torture, which is portrayed throughout as a symbol of the human need for control over destiny, particularly mortality.

Other notable symbols and poetic devices in the poem occur in sections 2 and 3. The rack suggests, once again, the human need to control destiny through exerting control over another person. The crucifix, in itself a symbol of human suffering, death, and destiny, represents a paradox to the poet. The torturers themselves were, like Christ and those who crucified him, "human, after all"—thus connecting the need for human control with death. Perhaps the poet is also suggesting that Christ, as according to Christian mythology, died for humanity in order for human beings to overcome death.

In section 4 the speaker describes himself and his companion as "the North Pole and the South." In this metaphor he hints at a conflict between the two, who seemingly are polar opposites. Also in this section, he describes the groove into which he places his head as "pulse-filled"—another example of personification with symbolic significance. Since the poet has suggested the eternal and universal quality of human suffering throughout the course of history, to describe the groove as "pulse-filled" suggests that it has a life of its own, with many stories to tell. Furthermore, the groove, a seemingly dead object, is full of life even though it is ironically associated with deadness and decapitation.

The last two sections, characteristic of the minimalism with which the prose of Carver is often associated, have no significant poetic devices. The poet, however, does call the imaginary ax his companion holds "the idea-of-axe"—perhaps indicating his playfulness while simultaneously suggesting that imagining a near-death experience brings about central questions about life and mortality. Carver closes his episode as the speaker and his companion leave the dungeon and seek light, a metaphor for life, hope, spirituality, and purpose, but they find little promise of the "chink of understanding" he mentions in section 3.

Themes and Meanings

Since the poem was included in Carver's last collection of poetry, which he completed in the last months of his life, it is difficult not to see the personal meaning the poem must have had for him. The poem concerns two primary, interrelated themes: the meaning of human suffering and death.

Both themes are carefully woven into the images of the poem and the experience Carver records. The poet's ambivalence toward the female (the iron maiden and the companion) may be rooted in personal conflict between Carver and his wife over confronting the mortality of a loved one. Both speakers seem to have been affected by the close resemblance of their game to their own lives as human beings who must die and come to terms with the meaning of death.

At first glance, one is tempted to give the poem a Christian reading. Section 3 does, after all, connect Christ, humanity, and state. The poet also implies that the victim of an execution, perhaps like the victim of a terminal disease, would have sometimes found faith, "light," or "even acceptance of his fate." In section 5, the speaker, while acting out the ritual of execution, says he is seeking "whatever sheen or rapture I can grasp to take with me, wherever I'm bound"—in other words, he is seeking a light to explain the mystery of life to him as he confronts his own mortality. Both sections indicate that the speaker is contemplating his own death and searching for something to give his own suffering existence some meaning. Because the poet introduces the idea of religious faith, which was so much easier to believe in during the Middle Ages, the poem may be read as a commentary on postmodern humanity's need for faith in Christ, or, more broadly, for religious faith.

The poem itself, however, seems to undercut such an interpretation. On the one hand, the poem may concern the need for a reassuring faith that explains human destiny and mortality for both the dying (the speaker) and the living (his companion). On the other hand, the poet indicates that no such explanation is to be found. The images of waking throughout the poem may be read as metaphors for awakening one's consciousness to the inexplicability of death and human suffering; the poem may thus be suggesting that religious faith is rooted in unrealistic hope.

In several places, Carver uses images of sleeping and waking, and in every case the images of sleeping are associated with attempts to escape from the pain of the moment, and the images of waking are used to bring the victims of execution (those from the past and himself) back to the reality of their own (human) suffering. These images could be interpreted as an ironic commentary on the almost universal assumption that death itself enables one to escape suffering and that sleeping and daydreaming are themselves forms of escape from the pain of everyday existence. Though the poet is seeking this form of escape (saying in section 4 that he "could almost drift off"), his companion will not allow him to do so. Furthermore, though the poet is hoping for a "sheen" or "rapture" to comfort him on his journey into death wherever he is bound, he is apparently unable to discover one.

The poem ends with the recognition that the light he has been seeking is not present. Although escaping the "dungeon" of human life through either death, the imagination, or religious faith may be attractive, no real explanation for the torture and meaning of existence can be found. Nevertheless, the speaker does suggest that the universal and eternal quest for "light" is never completely given up. The two visitors to Kyborg Castle have found that the mystery of human life is never fully illuminated.

D. Dean Shackelford

THE WAKING

Author: Theodore Roethke (1908-1963)
Type of poem: Meditation
First published: 1953, in *The Waking: Poems, 1933-1953*

The Poem

"The Waking" is the final poem in the collection *The Waking* (1953), for which Theodore Roethke received the Pulitzer Prize in poetry in 1954. In a departure from the free verse of much of his earlier work, this poem is composed in the form of a villanelle, a nineteen-line closed verse form consisting of five successive tercets rhyming *aba* followed by a closing quatrain rhyming *abaa*. Two key lines that contain the theme of the poem are repeated alternately at the end of each stanza and then again together in the last stanza. The title suggests the central idea of the poem: a discovery of the fundamental paradox of human life. The "waking" to which the poet refers involves the broad assertion that life leads to death. More precisely, the poet has grasped the insight that living (waking), which involves coming to new awarenesses, ultimately leads only to dying (sleep). By using several examples, the speaker reveals that this truth is not overwhelming or even essentially negative. Rather, "The Waking" describes the poet's revelation of life as an organic and somewhat mysterious process; the poem portrays the refinement and gradual confirmation of this truth. Hence, for him life is a process in which individuals move unhurriedly ("waking slow"), trusting nature to take them through the seemingly contradictory processes of coming to life and moving toward death. The poem is written in the first person, and the poet speaks to readers directly about his own experience. In this way, Roethke makes use of a rich tradition in lyric poetry in which the poet speaks on his own authority and in his own voice directly to the reader. The poet also employs another tradition, an old American penchant for the slightly didactic voice of the "seer" or "visionary" who has seen, who now knows, and who wishes to impart his understanding.

In the first stanza, the poet speaks from within the darkness (as readers learn by the third stanza) as he chants his awareness that life leads to death: "I wake to sleep, and take my waking slow." He ventures to say (in lines 2 and 3) that this fact cannot make him afraid because he is aware these are the necessary processes of nature. In the second stanza, he amplifies the idea that abstract knowledge is not frightening but is even irrelevant because he, like the Metaphysical poets of the seventeenth century, would rather "think by feeling," basing his life upon the stream of experience rather than abstract ideas. The third stanza presents a vivid example that illustrates why he is unafraid of the awareness that life leads to death: When he senses the presence of someone he cannot clearly see (perhaps, for Roethke, his dead father), he feels the holiness of nature and the rightness of nature's plan.

Two more examples are offered in the fourth stanza: "Light takes the Tree" and "The lowly worm climbs up the winding stair." Both examples depict the miraculous and wonderful growth in nature. These two examples of life processes are contrasted to the central idea in the fifth stanza that nature has "another thing" to do to human beings (death). Thus in stanzas 4 and 5 he exemplifies the two processes that he has set out in the first stanza—growth and decay, or living and dying—and challenges the listener with the *carpe diem* theme to "take the lively air," to live fully in the time remaining. In the sixth and final stanza, the poet sets forth the justification for his trust in nature's plan: Whatever seems to die still remains. He says, "What falls away is always," and so the reader sees the poet's vision: Life does indeed lead to death, but death does not entail a complete severance. Rather, everything (and everyone) abides.

Forms and Devices

The form of the poem is the villanelle, a verse form that can be traced back to Italian folk songs of the late fifteenth through the early seventeenth centuries. In the sixteenth century, French poet Jean Passerat gave the poem its current form. One distinctive quality of the Roethke villanelle is the contrast between the precision of this complex, closed form and the loose process of association that so clearly marks the poem.

The poem contains two central metaphors—waking and sleeping—and connotations hovering around these two metaphors express much of the ambiguity of the poem and the richness of the poet's vision. In a narrow sense, the antithesis of waking/sleeping suggests gaining consciousness and losing it, growing and diminishing, and living and dying. The poem's title itself suggests another meaning of "waking": the dawning of the idea that the process of waking/sleeping does not involve a horrible reality. That is, the metaphors of waking and sleeping describe the life cycle, and the waking that the poet wants to describe for the reader is the new awareness that this life cycle is to be feelingly lived and loved rather than feared.

Every metaphor in the poem—the light, the tree, the air, the worm, and the winding stair—plays a part in clarifying the poet's vision. The light taking the tree and the worm ascending the stair represent two images of growth. The suggestion to "take the lively air" presents a direct invitation to the reader to enjoy life, particularly the things that bring great pleasure and joy, while the time remains to enjoy them. A final, important image of things "falling away" contains the fundamental reason for the poet's acceptance of and trust in life. He avows, "What falls away is always." Hence, what dies only seems to pass away from human presence at times, for the poet senses the presence of absent things and people even though they cannot be clearly apprehended by the senses. The atmosphere of this poem is celebratory as the poet paints a backdrop of night, loss, and death only to lead readers to an awareness of the presence of departed friends and an ultimate acceptance and trust in nature.

Themes and Meanings

In simplest terms, the poem's theme is acceptance of nature's cyclical and seemingly contradictory plan for the living. Seen in this way, life is a natural, organic process of growth and decay, perhaps recalling for some William Cullen Bryant's poem "Thanatopsis." Related to this view of life is the invitation to enjoy life while one has it, to make use of the limited amount of time one has to grow. However, the poem suggests much more about the nature of the actual experience of this life. Human beings "think by feeling"; that is, their lives begin in feelings and senses, and all thought and knowledge naturally follow from and are intertwined with feeling. Armed with this awareness, the human being is free to "dance from ear to ear." In other poems, Roethke centers on what he suggests here: the divine, mad dance of the person/poet who is in love with this brief, contradictory life.

Life, then, is not a problem to be solved or a process to endure; rather, it is a mystery, a paradox to which people must open their trust, for "What falls away is always. And is near." In this poem, Roethke speaks from within the idealist American Romantic tradition of Bryant and Ralph Waldo Emerson and the English Romantic vein of William Blake, William Butler Yeats, and even William Wordsworth. This poem does not spiritualize the poet's grounded experience; it does not take readers beyond the natural world. Rather, it describes the holiness of the "eternal now" as it teaches readers what Roethke himself declared during a panel talk on the poem "Identity" at Northwestern University in 1963: "'We think by feeling. What is there to know?' This . . . is a description of the metaphysical poet who thinks with his body . . . and it is one of the ways man at least approaches the divine . . . for there is a God, and He's here, immediate, accessible."

Jeffery Galle

WAKING EARLY SUNDAY MORNING

Author: Robert Lowell (1917-1977)
Type of poem: Lyric
First published: 1967, in *Near the Ocean*

The Poem

"Waking Early Sunday Morning" is a long lyric poem, a meditation on mortality in fourteen eight-line stanzas. The title invites comparison with Wallace Stevens's poem "Sunday Morning," and indeed the poem may be read as Robert Lowell's pessimistic, Puritan-tinged reply to Stevens's celebration of an earthly paradise. Stevens evokes a lushly fertile world in which the "balm and beauty of the earth" is heaven enough, but, in Lowell's vision, the earth is no longer a garden but an exhausted volcano, its violence all but spent, "a ghost/ orbiting forever lost" in a universe empty of meaning. The poem is written in the first person, both singular and plural, so that the speaker is sometimes "I" and sometimes "we." The speaker, implicitly Lowell himself, moves from the personal to the prophetic, expressing first a desire for freedom, then a wistful longing for lost religious faith, and finally regret for the doomed planet and its children fated to fall "in small war on the heels of small/ war."

"Waking Early Sunday Morning" is an internal journey through the thoughts of the speaker as he awakens. The poem begins with a dreaming image of freedom and escape, the wish to "break loose" like a salmon swimming against the current, leaping and finally clearing the waterfall to reach its native stream. Yet the image carries its own darkness: The salmon braves the current only to "spawn and die." The second stanza finds the speaker waking from his dream and feeling the childlike joy of a Sunday morning's leisure ahead, "squatting like a dragon on/ time's hoard before the day's begun"—a line that echoes seventeenth century English poet Andrew Marvell, whose "The Garden" is also recalled by the rhymed octosyllabic couplets of Lowell's poem.

The poet's awareness moves from himself to his surroundings, from mice and termites in the walls to the harbor view outside his window, from a glass of water at his bedside to the "new electric bells" calling worshipers to Sunday church service. Through several stanzas, the poet explores this lost connection to the "Faith of our fathers," to the white steeples of New England now reduced to "vanishing emblems" of a salvation no longer assured. This Puritan faith, recalled in the lines of hymns still sung but not believed, was not without its own terrors, yet it gave to its followers a sense of order and a chance for redemption, a "loophole for the soul."

In the closing five stanzas, Lowell explores the condition of a people whose only god has become the god of war, of the United States as a Philistine empire of excess and military might without true direction. Again, in stanza 12, there is the longing to break free, to find redemption in some pastoral summer. However, the poet allows no return to innocence, no escape from this wounded earth: "Pity the planet, all joy gone/

from this sweet volcanic cone." Humanity is left forever in the ruins of the paradise it has destroyed.

Forms and Devices

"Waking Early Sunday Morning" uses a relatively strict and demanding metrical form: the iambic tetrameter or four-beat couplet. Each of its fourteen stanzas contains four couplets or eight lines. Though the form and meter echo Marvell's "The Garden," Lowell's poem is modern in its diction and subject matter, and the regularity of form is varied by Lowell's use of off-rhyme. In stanza 3, for example, Lowell rhymes "night" with "foot" and "sun's" with "dawns." These slight irregularities, together with Lowell's use of three seven-syllable lines in the last stanza, give the poem an edge that keeps the reader from being lulled by its musicality.

The word pairs Lowell chooses for rhymes, and even his line breaks, often challenge the reader's expectations. "Waking Early Sunday Morning" does not actually break poetic rules, but it defies poetic conventions, as when the speaker, in the midst of a visionary exhortation ("O to break loose"), suddenly breaks in with "Stop, back off." The voice abruptly becomes more casual, more intimate. There are similar shifts in diction throughout the poem. Sometimes the speaker is musing, personal, and introspective; sometimes he is almost biblically oratorical; and sometimes he is almost comradely or Whitman-like, addressing readers and pulling them into the "we" of the poem. These shifts in rhetorical style reflect the speaker's shifts in perception from dream state to consciousness, from casual observation to philosophical speculation, and from wry amusement to despair.

Language in the poem is playful yet precise. Lowell delights in using words that resonate with other poems he has written, with works of other writers from Roman poet Horace to Marvell to Stevens, and with figures and events from history. Thus the description of the nocturnal animals in the third stanza—"obsessive, casual, sure of foot"—recalls Lowell's own "Skunk Hour" and its mother skunk and kittens searching for food in the moonlight. The "rainbow smashing a dry fly" in stanza 2 is clearly a trout but also calls to mind the last line of Lowell's poem "The Quaker Graveyard in Nantucket," which in turn refers to the biblical story of Noah with its comforting story of God's covenant. That comfort is subverted in "Waking Early Sunday Morning": There is no promise that the world will not be destroyed; what God may not do, humanity will.

Biblical imagery and literary allusions abound in "Waking Early Sunday Morning." The glass the poet gazes through in stanza 5 and the line "Each day, He shines through darker glass" in stanza 9 echo the biblical metaphor "For now we see through a glass, darkly" (I Corinthians 13:12). Elsewhere in the poem, U.S. military forces are seen in terms of an army of elephants, recalling Hannibal, whose exploits are recounted in Lowell's translation of Roman poet Juvenal's tenth satire. Other phrases suggest events from more recent history: The reference to chance assassinations is surely the poet's response to the violent events of the 1960's. "Waking Early Sunday Morning" is a poem that seems constructed in layers, broadly referential yet personal, dense with many meanings yet still accessible on an immediate, physical level.

Themes and Meanings

A descendant of Puritans who at one point converted to Catholicism, Lowell was a student of the classics who was fascinated by ancient Rome. He saw history as a continuing process; *Near the Ocean* (1967), the collection in which "Waking Early Sunday Morning" first appeared, contains original poems by Lowell as well as his translations of works by Horace, Juvenal, and others. In an introductory note, Lowell speaks of "the greatness and horror of [Rome's] empire," then adds, perhaps slyly, "How one jumps from Rome to the America of my own poems is something of a mystery to me." Actually, there is little mystery in the metaphorical connection Lowell draws between Rome near the end of its empire and the United States in the latter half of the twentieth century. In "Waking Early Sunday Morning," Lowell evokes a sense of living in "fallen" times, referring to both the fall of an empire and humanity's original fall from grace. The poem is thus one observer's reflections upon a particular time and place as well as a metaphorical recasting of ancient myth.

Lowell was not only a poet steeped in history but also a poet of his times. During the 1960's, much of his work reflected his political concerns and moral beliefs; poems in *For the Union Dead* (1964) touch upon ethnic segregation and nuclear war, and *Near the Ocean* continues this mingling of public issues with the exploration of private concerns Lowell had pioneered in his autobiographical *Life Studies* (1959). He opposed the Vietnam War and, in 1965, refused an invitation to read at a White House arts festival as a protest against President Lyndon Johnson's Vietnam policy. Certainly Lowell had Vietnam in mind when he wrote of "man thinning out his kind" through a succession of small wars in "Waking Early Sunday Morning," and certainly Lowell's public repudiation of Johnson echoes in the poem's portrait of the president "swimming nude, unbuttoned, sick/ of his ghost-written rhetoric"; yet the image also recalls Lowell's father singing in his bathtub in "Commander Lowell." By showing these figures of authority literally stripped naked, Lowell at once satirizes and humanizes them. They are flawed, perhaps even destructive, but they are not monsters.

"Waking Early Sunday Morning" has something of the mood of an elegy. The voice in the poem is not that of a thunderous Jeremiah of the Bible or the fierce Puritan Jonathan Edwards preaching doom but rather the quiet voice of a rueful observer who hopes for the best even as he expects the worst. Understanding of human weakness and compassion for the troubled human species permeate its melancholy yet often lovely stanzas. The personal despair and loss of faith treated in Lowell's earlier, more explicitly "confessional" poems such as "Skunk Hour" are transmuted in "Waking Early Sunday Morning" into a gentle pity for all humanity and for the fate of the earth itself.

Kathryn Kulpa

WAKING IN THE BLUE

Author: Robert Lowell (1917-1977)
Type of poem: Lyric
First published: 1959, in *Life Studies*

The Poem

"Waking in the Blue" consists of forty lines divided into six uneven verse paragraphs. Though essentially free verse, the poem contains remnants of the rhymed couplets Robert Lowell used for the poem's original composition (as he did for many poems in *Life Studies*).

The title points, first, to Lowell's autobiographical experience of awakening at daybreak in a mental institution—a memory Lowell presents through a surrealistic metaphysical conceit in which he and his fellow patients are sea creatures swimming in the "agonized blue" of the institution. The title also hints at the poem's class conflict in which the mental ward's Roman Catholic attendants function in a "sea" of "Mayflower screwballs" wearing the "blue" of French sailors' jerseys.

The poem begins with one of those night attendants rousing himself "from the mare's-nest of his drowsy head." As the poet (who seems to be the speaker in the poem) "catwalks" through the institution, he awakens with tensing heart to the bleakness and "Absence!" of his surroundings.

In the second and third verse paragraphs, Lowell presents satiric vignettes of the institution's "thoroughbred mental cases": Stanley, the former Harvard all-American with "kingly granite profile in a crimson golf-cap"; and "Bobbie," the "roly-poly," swashbuckling member of Harvard's Porcellian club. Lowell portrays himself in the poem's final verse paragraph as a strutting "Cock of the walk" only to discover in "the metal shaving mirrors" a reflection, not of himself, but of his own "shaky future" in the "pinched, indigenous faces" of his older companions.

Wedged between the vignettes of other mental patients and Lowell's self-portrait is the next-to-last verse paragraph in which the poet presents the contrasting Roman Catholic attendants (who attend Boston University instead of Harvard). For this segment, at least, the poet assumes their perspective ("hours and hours go by under the crew haircuts"). Even when Lowell seems to judge these nonaristocratic interlopers and their "slightly too little nonsensical bachelor twinkle," the reader may find their seriousness and intellectualism (with the "B. U. sophomore" dozing over literary theorist I. A. Richards's 1923 *The Meaning of Meaning*) superior to the backward-looking antics of the "Mayflower screwballs."

The poem concludes with Lowell's resigned assessment of his social class, and himself in particular, as "ossified" artifacts unable to change even through self-destruction: "We are all old-timers,/ each of us holds a locked razor."

Forms and Devices

Lowell uses a cluster of metaphors to achieve both of his purposes in "Waking in the Blue." These purposes are his desire to "confess," through the therapy of his poetry, his terror about insanity and his suicidal tendencies, and his critique of New England social pretense.

The central cluster of metaphors functions as a metaphysical conceit. Throughout the poem, Lowell extends the metaphor of the asylum as an ocean and its inmates as either sea animals—a seal and a sperm whale—or crew members "swashbuckling" or strutting in "turtle-necked French sailor's jersey" aboard a ship. In this surrealistic network of images, the blue outside the institution's window makes bleaker the agony of the oceanic asylum. Despite Lowell's attempts to console himself with the confident swaggering sailor-figure, he identifies with the seal and whale confined within the claustrophobic blue. This anxiety is most explicit at the poem's beginning when, according to the logic of the conceit, he becomes a whale waiting to be a harpoonist's victim: "My heart grows tense/ as though a harpoon were sparring for the kill." This same anxiety resurfaces as a fear of impotent self-destruction at the end of the poem when the harpoon is transformed into the "locked razor" that "each of us holds."

The same extended metaphor of sea animals swimming in the ocean and seamen swaggering above it introduces Lowell's critique of Bostonians circulating in a common blue-blood milieu. A related cluster of images allows the poet to make his social commentary more explicit. Lowell uses a number of images of corpulence—"a ramrod/ with the muscle of a seal"; "redolent and roly-poly as a sperm whale"; "After a hearty New England breakfast,/ I weigh two hundred pounds"—to suggest aristocratic satiety. These images and an accumulation of mineral images—"the petrified fairway," "A kingly granite profile," "metal shaving mirrors," "a locked razor"—anticipate Lowell's claim that "These victorious figures of bravado ossified young."

In "Waking in the Blue," Lowell asks, "What use is my sense of humor?" The answer is that Lowell (much like Sylvia Plath and John Berryman) uses humor throughout the poem as a defense against the confusion and terror evoked by such painful memories. Lowell includes absurdly incongruous details to mask his terror and save himself from his own confessions, juxtaposing Stanley's "kingly granite profile" with his "crimson golf-cap," and "Bobbie's" Louis XVI appearance with his swashbuckling dance in his "birthday suit."

Lowell also uses an unexpected rhyming couplet in the first verse paragraph for comic effect: "My heart grows tense/ as though a harpoon were sparring for the kill./ (This is the house for the 'mentally ill.')" The pairing of "kill" and "mentally ill" lends the final line a comically macabre, almost camp, effect. Significantly, this comic use of rhyme occurs in the verse paragraph that contains Lowell's most concentrated use of other formal techniques such as assonance ("Azure," "agonized," "Absence") and alliteration ("blue" and "bleaker"; and "heart," "harpoon," and "house"). It is at this moment in the poem when Lowell directly reveals the agony that underlies the rest of the poem, that such formal defense mechanisms are necessary.

Themes and Meanings

Lowell obliquely announces the two central themes of "Waking in the Blue" in the seventh line of the poem when he creates a pun on the word "petrified" ("Crows maunder on the petrified fairway"). Through one sense of the word ("terrified"), Lowell introduces the poem's confessional theme: the poet's wrestling with insanity and potential suicide. The other meaning of "petrified" ("made rigid like stone") announces Lowell's critique of the inert, ossified aristocracy of New England.

Lowell's confession of his anxiety over his weaknesses and failure, though held at bay somewhat by his subtle use of form and humor, pervades "Waking in the Blue." Even when Lowell and the reader chuckle at an insane inmate's cavorting in the nude or soaking in a "urinous" Victorian bath with golf-cap intact, they sense the poet's discomfort at his own ineptness and absurdity. At the poem's end, reader and poet reel first from the knowledge that "metal shaving mirrors" are necessary to prevent the poet from committing suicide and then from the even more dismaying realization that he is too paralyzed to attempt even this most desperate of measures.

In the context of the poem, neither nature nor the past offers the poet any refuge from his unhappy self-knowledge. Objects in nature that might have provided John Keats and his negative capability with escape from the sad truths of the self only become objective correlatives as Lowell projects his quiet despair and resignation onto the "petrified fairway," "agonized blue window," and "maundering" crows. The past (which for a poet such as William Wordsworth might sustain one through a crisis of self-recognition) only leaves Lowell with reminders of a vacuous heritage, in which a "Harvard all-American fullback" is an oxymoron and the "Mayflower" heritage of his Winslow and Lowell families produces a "screwball" disposition.

In contemplating his fate as one of the ossified "figures of bravado," Lowell seems quite comfortable in seeing himself as a representative figure for the Brahmin class he attempts to parody in the poem. He attempts to stretch beyond his personal battle with failure to examine his entire class's struggle by publishing "Waking in the Blue" in the historical context of *Life Studies* (a monograph in which he includes such history-minded poems as "Beyond the Alps" and "Inauguration Day: January 1953").

For much of the poem, Lowell attempts through parody to distance himself from the "thoroughbred mental cases" he describes. By the end of the poem, however, he is forced to resign himself to being one of them. Even in his moment of victorious bravado, in which his strutting as "Cock of the walk" echoes the swashbuckling dance of the Mayflower "Bobbie," Lowell must recognize that the "pinched, indigenous faces/ of these thoroughbred mental cases" are his "shaky future." When he finally resorts to the inclusive pronoun "We" at the poem's end, his pun on "oldtimers" suggests that he, like the other blue-blood crazies, is an ancient malfunctioning timepiece, an ossified relic that marks the passage of time by its own inability to change, even through the ultimate change of death.

Janice Moore Fuller

WALES VISITATION

Author: Allen Ginsberg (1926-1997)
Type of poem: Meditation
First published: 1968, in *Planet News, 1961-1967*

The Poem

"Wales Visitation" is written in free verse and divided into nine stanzas. As is usual with Allen Ginsberg's writing, the poem uses the convention of cataloging, begun in American poetry with Walt Whitman, the American poet who has most influenced him. Originating with a visit to Wales that Ginsberg took in July, 1967, the poem records his response to this visit and describes some of the beautiful scenery in Wales that he, as had so many earlier poets, admired. The poem was also inspired by an LSD experience, during which Ginsberg was trying to move beyond his earlier tendency to reflect haunting visions within his consciousness; instead, he wanted to record with concrete detail the outside, the particular, world. As a result, the poem is a series of concrete descriptions of the Welsh landscape.

Highly personal in tone, the poem falls in the tradition of meditations initiated in the English Romantic period and particularly seen in William Wordsworth's "Lines: Composed a Few Miles Above Tintern Abbey," to which Ginsberg refers in his poem. The first-person point of view and the references to self in "Wales Visitation" suggest that the poet's concern is with a subjective response to the outside world.

As the poem begins, the speaker, Ginsberg himself, sets a tone of awe at the beauty of the Welsh landscape and refers to trees as "mountain-brow" covered with "white fog," to clouds rising "as on a wave," and to "mist above teeming ferns" on the edge of a "green crag." He immediately lets the reader know that the poem is about his response to and interaction with the glory and beauty of the natural world.

That the poem is also about the creative process of the poet-self becomes clear in the second stanza, in which he focuses on the subject matter of poetry: a vale in Albion (the Latin name for England), people in general, the "physical sciences," language, thistles, and green daisies. Referring to the poet as "Bardic, O Self, Visitacione," Ginsberg focuses on the poetic visionary's response to the external and the eternal in nature and in self.

The next stanza sets up a contrast between the scenic beauty of the Welsh landscape and the urban setting of London, a city full of such images of modern progress as towers and television. The poet opts for the beauty of nature and its eternal qualities as opposed to the transient symbols of material progress. He refers to William Blake, of whom he is a disciple, and to Wordsworth, both British poets of the Romantic period who observed and reflected on the natural beauty surrounding them. When Ginsberg, the present poet, sees and hears the same visions, he becomes one with all other poets: "Bard Nameless as the Vast, babble to Vastness!"

The fourth and fifth stanzas further reflect on Ginsberg's surroundings, with the poet cataloging the movement of the wind, the valley, the hills, the leaves, and the grasses. The movement is "Nebulous upward" to Heaven, and the poet wonders at the vastness and immensity of the natural world, suggesting Heaven is apparent even in a "grassblade." All the natural world, the universe, is "One Being."

Stanzas 7 and 8 celebrate the perfection and the vitality of the external world, even going so far as to suggest that every living thing, be it valley, mountain, or human, breathes and is in constant motion. Ginsberg makes references to daisies, vegetables, sheep, horses, canals, pheasants, green buds, and hawthorn—all of which he describes as part of "One being so balanced, so vast, that its softest breath" is responsible for the movement of all living things. Although inhabited by a variety of forms, the natural world has a "Buddha-eye."

The final two stanzas bring the meditation to a close, as the "high" point of the drug experience begins to lose momentum. Stanza 8 describes the poet's response as a great "Oh!" bringing together all the elements of nature through the senses. Here, Ginsberg suggests that there is no secret to the universe, that the spirit behind it all is visible in the particulars he sees. Proclaiming the constant movement of the spirit once again, the poet reiterates his belief that in the particulars, he has seen "myriad" forms of "the great One."

Forms and Devices

Ginsberg's free verse employs cataloging so as to saturate the reader's mind with emotion and images. The most frequently used poetic devices in the poem are imagery, simile, metaphor, and personification. The poem consists of a series of images of the natural world to which the poet is responding and by which he is being inspired.

Almost all the poem's concrete imagery evokes positive responses from the reader, as it did, one can assume, for the poet himself. The well-known Welsh fog and mist are symbolic of the spirit within the natural world, and all the poem's images of the natural world are described as being in motion, suggesting their vitality and spirit. Ginsberg is noted for a style in which few pauses occur between ideas and images. Imagery as a poetic device is seen when the poet describes the mist as "gigantic" and "eddy-lifting," the ferns as "teeming" and exquisite, and the "satanic" and symmetrical thistle as "sister" to "green-daisies' pink tiny/ bloomlets." In the last image, Ginsberg is trying to exorcise the demons of his inner consciousness and move beyond the poetry of merely inner vision he had written earlier.

More particular types of poetic devices in the poem are simile and personification. The speaker compares the rising of the clouds "as on a wave" (a simile), and another striking simile is the second stanza's description of the "pink tiny/ bloomlets angelic as lightbulbs." These and other similar images appeal to the senses, suggesting a speaker who is inspired by the glory and beauty of nature and enabling the reader to visualize the Welsh landscape.

Other images in the poem are similar. The remainder of the poem continues the descriptive listing of natural beauty set forth in the first stanza, and near the end of the second stanza the poet introduces the idea that the natural world is connected to the world of the spirit. The natural elements the poet sees are the same visions seen by all other poets and visionaries, even the "folk." Ginsberg is suggesting that everyone is capable of the same delight in and visionary appreciation of nature.

By far, the most frequently used poetic device in the poem is personification. The poet, in trying to show that all elements of nature are one with humanity and the divine spirit, characterizes the natural world as both humanlike and symbolic of the divine spirit running through all life-forms. The orchards are of "mind language manifest human," suggesting that the elements of nature communicate through a language of their own and that thus there is no difference between human and nature. The thistle is "sister" to "grass-daisies." The trees have "arms," the valleys "breathe," the vegetables "tremble," and the meadows are "haired" with ferns. Even the ground is "vagina-moist," the mountainside's grass is "wet hair," and the vale is "bearded." Ginsberg's use of personification recalls Whitman's "Song of Myself," in which Whitman, like Ginsberg, is trying to show that all the natural world and the human world are one and animated with the same spirit.

Themes and Meanings

"Wales Visitation" is a poem about poetic inspiration, the oneness of all in the universe (humanity, nature, and God), and an appreciation of the natural world. All three issues are intertwined in this experience, inspired by Ginsberg's LSD experimentation, in which he was trying to enhance the visionary experience through the use of hallucinatory drugs.

The poem suggests that the poetic imagination can be inspired by the external world, and in this regard Ginsberg is moving away from poetry reflecting his own inner experience as a visionary to a poetry that records the poet's response to the external "particulars," as he calls them. The art of poetry enables one to see as Blake, Wordsworth, and all other poets—and God—can see. Like his predecessor and inspiration Blake, the poet assumes the role of godhead in Ginsberg's vision. Through the use of LSD, the poet believes that he has enhanced his acute perceptions of the world outside himself and recognized the oneness of all spirit. That is, Ginsberg holds the Eastern idea that all the universe makes up "One Being" and that the role of the poet is that of prophet-inspirer who enables readers to see connections with this spirit emanating from all. Note particularly the images of breath and breathing, which Ginsberg takes as evidence of the oneness of all spirit.

Some of the most important lines in the poem occur in stanzas 5 through 9. In stanza 5, Ginsberg introduces the idea of "One Being on the mountainside stirring gently," a line suggesting the oneness of all the universe and the Eastern concept of the godhead. Ralph Waldo Emerson's poem and figure "Brahma," a symbol of the oversoul according to transcendental philosophy, strikes comparison with Ginsberg's vision since Ginsberg has been heavily influenced by transcendentalism and those influenced by it (American poets Whitman and William Carlos Williams, among others). Calling the earth his "Mother," Ginsberg reflects on the idea that the natural world is the origin of all being, and each flower is described as "Buddha-eye, repeating the story,/ myriad-formed—." Buddha is the incarnation of the divine according to the Buddhist religion, of which Ginsberg has been a practitioner since the 1960's, and the meditative nature of the poem originates in part with Ginsberg's frequent practice of Zen meditation.

Perhaps the most important line in the poem refers to "Heaven balanced on a grassblade," suggesting the essential spirit and divinity of all living things. Within the microcosm of the individual blade of grass is all being itself, including the godhead. God, self, and nature are all inseparable. The poem concludes with a reiteration of this same concept: "What did I notice? Particulars! The vision of the great One is myriad" (stanza 9). The constant movement observed in this experience in Wales reflects the life and spirit within all and thus explains why the natural scenery is personified: The life of all, human and natural, is apart from and at the same time one with God.

D. Dean Shackelford

WALKING TO SLEEP

Author: Richard Wilbur (1921-   )
Type of poem: Meditation
First published: 1967; collected in *Walking to Sleep: New Poems and Translations,*
  1969

The Poem

At 143 lines, "Walking to Sleep," the longest of Richard Wilbur's poems, is the title
poem of *Walking to Sleep,* 1969, in which it was first collected. As the third part of
that book, it concludes the section of original poems, with a number of translations
following. In an interview with William Heyen (*Conversations with Richard Wilbur,*
1990), Wilbur confesses that the book represents eight years of work. Because poets
give a great deal of thought to the placement and arrangement of poems, the placement of this poem implies that its ideas embody a sense of finality which transcends
mere bodily sleep. The poem is written in the first person, and the speaker is barely
distinguishable from Wilbur himself. The speaker assumes an air of authority and sea-
soned wit as he addresses the reader.

"Walking to Sleep" opens on a note of grave confidence which the speaker establishes and continues throughout the poem. Suggesting that the reader step off into the
"blank of your mind," he assures the reader that such confidence is absolutely necessary for the journey—which will be both imaginary and real. The journey begins in
the realm of the imagination as shaped by the real. The speaker warns the reader, however, that frustrations occur, especially if the reader attempts to control the direction
and outcome of the journey. What follows is an interplay of images and specific directions.

As if the speaker becomes aware that he may be frightening the reader, and finding
the reader still awake, he suggests that the reader forget all that the speaker has said
and begin again. The poem itself seems to begin again at this point; this time the
reader starts in the real world, allowing the imagination freedom to shape experience.
Finally, Wilbur ends the poem by averring that the most fruitful journeys are those
which remain open to the real and the imaginative experience, with no attempt at control.

Forms and Devices

By using direct address as the vehicle for advancing the poem, the poet establishes
an intimate relationship between the speaker (essentially the poet himself) and the
reader, involving the reader in the argument of the poem. The reader mentally hears
the speaker, reacting as if the reader and the speaker were in close communication, indeed, in the same room. Wilbur reinforces this tone by stepping outside the flow of
images to ask questions, give advice, or warn the reader. The effect of direct address is
to strengthen the conversational resonance.

Wilbur is the master of the iambic pentameter line, which is composed of five poetic feet—an unstressed syllable followed by a stressed syllable. The lines "Detach some portion of your thought to guard/ The outside of the building; as you wind," taken from well within the body of the poem, seem to sing with the strength of the iambic beat. Through the use of the five-stress line, the poem emphasizes the walking pace which the reader and speaker assume. To avoid a sing-song effect, Wilbur varies the placement of the stresses. For example, the first two lines of the poem end with an unstressed syllable, while the third line ends with a stressed syllable: "Step off assuredly into the blank of your mind." By emphasizing "mind," the poet underscores the role that the mind plays in this journey, which the poem elucidates.

A formalist poet, Wilbur uses form adeptly, not as adjunct to the poem, but to emphasize the meaning of his lines. The long lines stretching across the page shape the poem into one stanza with no break, except for the slight pause implied by the indentation of "What, are you still awake?" Wilbur therefore controls the pace at which the reader reads the poem, drawing similarities to both a leisurely reading and taking a walk.

Characteristic of a poem by Wilbur, the images are intensely beautiful and sensual. After the poem takes the major twist when the speaker tells the reader to forget everything he has said, the speaker conveys the great possibilities that nature provides for helping the reader to understand the journey through a series of images. He advises the reader to rub his or her eyes as if waking up and to see: "The phosphenes caper like St. Elmo's fire,// Let all things storm your thought with the moiled flocking/ Of startled rookeries, or flak in air,/ Or blossom-fall." In such lines, Wilbur's poem recalls the iambic lines that William Wordsworth uses as he walks through the English countryside. These and other images reveal the order in disorder which the poem seems to defend.

Themes and Meanings

In a conversation with John Graham (*Conversations with Richard Wilbur,* 1990), Wilbur states that this poem speaks about someone giving advice to someone else about how to get to sleep. The first line, "As a queen sits down, knowing that a chair will be there," provides an image for the confidence with which a person should enter the land of dreams. Although such an idea may have provided the impetus for the birth of the poem, its singularity gives rise to the idea that the poem is uncharacteristic for Wilbur, as suggested by its length. The poem reads as if the poet would make his readers understand, once and for all, his writing process as well as its effect on him. The use of vivid, almost surreal imagery mimics the fragmentation that the personality undergoes as it yields control of the journey to the process of journeying itself. Thus, while the poet's interpretation sheds light on the poem, there are other ways of reading it.

Another possible way of understanding the poem "Walking to Sleep" is understanding "sleep" as a metaphor for death and the journey as the process of dying. Certainly the fact that the poem is the final one in the volume's section of original poems suggests that possibility, as if the author were telling his readers that death is the end of the journey for everyone. Such an interpretation would suggest that the interplay between the imagination and the real world culminates in the release of control, which the speaker calls for, leading to the acceptance of the inevitability of death. Indeed, such undertones exist in the poem, but another interpretation arises as well.

The poem also seems to speak of the poet's own struggle with the sources of the creative process itself. When the poet, in creating a poem, steps off into the "blank" of his mind, anything can happen. No one can maintain a blank mind for very long; consequently, the poem begins a catalog of dreamlike images that occur to the poet. Just as a queen risks falling when she "sits down, knowing that a chair will be there," the "Potemkin barns" in eighteenth century Russia existed in a village of facades erected to deceive Empress Catherine II. Such images may emerge from dreams, hallucinations, or other subconscious sources.

The poet allows that such sources are most fruitful when there is little attempt to control them. If there is too much control, "what you project/ Is what you will perceive; what you perceive/ With any passion, be it love or terror,/ May take on whims and powers of its own." The poet, then, must allow the process to take him where it will.

The poem continues to intersperse guidelines and vivid imagery as if to suggest a cause and effect relationship. Sometimes the warnings take on the tone of a governmental official: "Should that occur, adjust to circumstances/ And carry on, taking these few precautions." The reader learns that there is nothing that can be done to foresee with any accuracy what will happen as the mind journeys. Whether the reader seeks shelter in the Great Pyramid that Cheops erected or in an iron shed in a military barracks, both are temporary and subject to invasion, whether by grave robbers or enemy soldiers.

The poet suggests that even pleasant images can distract the reader from the journey. Thus the poem counsels the reader to avoid beautiful rooms with beautiful women in them and to continue doggedly in pursuit of "The kind assassin Sleep." At this point, the poem twists as the speaker asks "What, are you still awake?/ Then you must risk another tack and footing./ Forget what I have said." Instead of using the imagination as the vehicle for travel, the poem suggests that the reader look closely at the ordinary things in ordinary life. At this point, the poem celebrates nature as revelatory of whatever truth the reader seeks.

The final image, that of Vishnu sleeping by a pool, alludes to the story told about Vishnu, the Preserver, the chief god worshiped by the Vaishnava as the second member of the trinity in Hinduism, which includes Brahma, the Creator, and Shiva, the Destroyer. As Vishnu slept, wrapped in "maya," the illusions of the flesh, the images that crossed his face contained all of history—past, present, and to come. Yet he received these "as they came," with no particular importance attached to or difference made among them. Wilbur suggests that the poet should imitate such receptivity.

Martha Modena Vertreace-Doody

THE WALL

Author: Eugenio Montale (1896-1981)
Type of poem: Lyric
First published: 1925, as "Meriggiare pallido e assorto," in *Ossi di seppia*; English translation collected in *Selected Poems*, 1965

The Poem

"The Wall" is a short poem in irregular verse, its seventeen lines divided into four stanzas. The author believed that titles often mislead or constrict the reader's understanding of poems—thus this poem has no title in the original Italian. In being untitled, it is like most of the other poems in *Ossi di seppia* (1925; *Bones of the Cuttlefish*, 1984); it differs from the majority of Eugenio Montale's works, however, in that it is written from an impersonal point of view.

"The Wall" opens with a situation common in the sunny Mediterranean: the search for repose during the hot noon hours. Although lethargy and sleep are common in this oppressive period, the anonymous observer is paradoxically attentive. The narrator's sense of hearing is abnormally heightened in spite of his "lazying" beside the orchard wall, and he is acutely aware of the wild, harsh surroundings. Instead of dismissing as unimportant background noise the "crackles" and "rustles" of nature, the poet makes them the central focus of stanza 1.

The next stanza shifts this focus to the sense of sight. The narrator watches, as if through a magnifying glass, columns of tiny red ants in the nearby cracks and brush. The ants become a significant presence in the dry wasteland, keenly observed as they scurry in their frantic, often contradictory motion atop their minuscule mountains.

In the third stanza, as if using a motion-picture camera, the poet replaces extreme close-up with its opposite, the distant vista. The observer's attention moves quickly from foreground activity to background scenery, where "through leafy branches the distant/ throbbing" of the glittering sea can be seen. This panorama has as accompaniment the "tremulous creaks of cicadas" rising from nearby hills. Elements originally introduced separately—sight and sound, near and far, vast and tiny—are here combined for a comprehensive landscape.

Thoughts, feelings, and associations unexpectedly crystallize and unite in the final stanza as the narrator again begins "moving in the dazzling sun" beside the garden wall. The harsh and barren landscape, the distant vastness of the sea, the travail of ants, and the strident sounds of life all suddenly come together in a significant pattern. The familiar rural wall becomes a looming symbolic presence. Suddenly perceiving a parallel between personal and universal reality, the narrator experiences the revelation that "all of life and its labor" can be summarized in "this following alongside a steep wall/ topped with sharp bits of broken bottle."

Forms and Devices

Montale uses two formal devices—omission of a title and refusal to specify the "voice" of the poem—to help immediately immerse readers in his poetry so they can experience its unique vision as fully, directly, and intimately as possible.

Another device he uses is imagery, the most famous aspect of his poetry. Taking as his source the commonplace realities of nature and daily life, he presents sharply etched details with spare, economical description. These carefully delineated images are radiant with life; like the glaring midday landscape of "The Wall," their concreteness creates a multifaceted significance which pervades the poem.

When images have such an extensive influence on the poem, they can be said to provide its basic structure. This is certainly the case in "The Wall," as the poem's English title attests. Of major importance to its setting and action, the image of the wall both opens and closes the poem. The wall, the physical reality of which is expressed first in terms of simple description, is later treated as complex metaphor. This metaphor simultaneously symbolizes the narrator's perception of existential reality while it embodies the pessimistic vision of life itself, for it is through "this following alongside" the orchard wall that the narrator progressively perceives the wholeness—both physical and metaphysical—of life.

Although the poem has many such concrete images, it is the way they are related which breaks the poem into two equal sections. The first half of the poem centers around the notion of division or separation, which is communicated through the poet's apportioning attention between two different senses. In stanza 1, the narrator relates things as they are heard (indicated by the verb "listening"), while in stanza 2 they are related as seen (indicated by "spying"). The third stanza has images presented through both sight and sound, thus signaling the beginning of the second section, which focuses on the notion of combination or integration. The joint or simultaneous perception (synesthesia) illustrated in this stanza is physical, while in stanza 4 it is metaphysical. The former combines sensations drawn from different physical senses, while the latter integrates perceptions derived from physical and mental or spiritual experience.

The language communicating these images, sensations, and thoughts is of great importance in creating the poetic integration of the vision, for its sound and sense influence the reader. While assonance, dissonance, onomatopoeia, and parallelism all play their parts, rhythm is language's most imperceptibly affective quality. Understanding this, Montale uses rhythm to make the reader actually "feel" what the poem says. For example, the still atmosphere of noon and the seeming suspension of time itself are conveyed through the poet's careful selection of individual words. Emphasizing the easy flow or harsh stops of sound, the smooth current or rough eddies of syntax, sensitively positioned words cause the reader, like the anonymous narrator of "The Wall," to teeter between everyday reality and the brief "instant of forever" the poet seeks to capture.

Themes and Meanings

A rich melding of keen observation and metaphysical insight, "The Wall" is above all a poem about the nature and complexity of life. It takes as its point of departure the realities of the physical world: stifling heat, blinding light, barren surroundings. Within this predominantly hostile environment life continues, persevering and sometimes even flourishing, as the poet's abundant references to wildlife indicate. Recognizing in nature's lesser creatures life's blind instinct to persist and endure even in adverse conditions, the poet further conveys this idea by suggesting a parallel between the ants' futile striving and the person's dogged following along the forbidding wall.

Even such humble everyday objects can demonstrate life's basic truths, for Montale believed that all reality is intimately connected with the spiritual realm. Because of this connection, the attentive and open-minded observer may unexpectedly experience a revelation of the larger realities of life, as does the narrator. Even inherently insignificant details such as a barren landscape can reveal not only objective reality, but personal, moral, and spiritual reality as well.

The concept of synesthesia, or simultaneous sensory perception, also evidences this relationship between tangible and intangible. For example, in stanza 3, the remote vision of the Mediterranean is presented first in visual terms ("the distant/ throbbing of sea-scales") and then in auditory ones ("while tremulous creaks of cicadas/ lift"). In this translation of sensory data, even the bright, shifting motion of the sea finds its aural correlative in the shrill, ceaseless notes of the insects. All of these elements subtly evoke the vast, impersonal, all-engulfing rhythm of nature. This additional theme—already implicit in the poem's circular structure and its generalized existential message—becomes an important part of the poem's overall meaning through the poet's reliance on synesthesia.

Montale's vision of the meaning of life would not be complete without the idea that a commitment to living (represented symbolically in the scorching, glass-topped wall and by one's following it) is itself an act of faith. Through this faith a glimpse of the larger reality infusing the concrete, tangible one may unexpectedly appear. According to Montale, such revelations are not necessarily accessible only through the grand traditional symbols of religion, but may also be manifested through the modest and incidental realities of daily life. Just as the lazing but observant narrator received enlightenment through mundane actions and events, so may others glimpse meaning in the material world. The most important thing for Montale, however, is not necessarily the occurrence of a revelation, or even the actual contents of the vision; rather, it is the idea that such a sign may occur at all. Anything which takes individuals out of their self-limiting reality and joins them with the essential truths of existence is significant in and of itself, and is therefore to be cherished—perhaps the most basic message of the poem.

Terri Frongia

WALT WHITMAN AT BEAR MOUNTAIN

Author: Louis Simpson (1923-   )
Type of poem: Lyric
First published: 1963, in *At the End of the Open Road*

The Poem

Louis Simpson's Pulitzer Prize-winning poetry collection *At the End of the Open Road* includes the poem "Walt Whitman at Bear Mountain." This verse contains twelve stanzas, which are uncontrolled by rhyme, meter, or specific divisions. Two topics—the poet Walt Whitman and the United States—bring the only order to the forty-four lines of poetry. In the verse, Simpson celebrates Whitman, bemoans a nation of self-seekers who have forsaken the American ideal, predicts the nation's demise, prescribes a remedy—confusing though it is—for the loss of the American Dream, and leaves the reader with a sense of optimism.

The initial twenty-five lines of the poem center on Walt Whitman, who had an impact on Simpson's life and work but did not determine his writing style. The first five lines describe the bronze statue of Whitman. Located at Bear Mountain State Park in New York, the sculpture is a realistic representation of the poet. As the self-sufficient poet had often done, the statue stands "squarely on two feet"; the form is "Neither on horseback nor seated." The figure "Loafs by the footpath . . . looks alive/ . . . And he seems friendly." In the next five lines Simpson asks Whitman several questions: "'Where is the Mississippi panorama/ And the girl who played the piano?'" The poet wonders where Whitman and his promised nation are.

In lines 11-15 Simpson laments the national preoccupation with transient, material goals, the general neglect of Whitman, and the lack of emphasis on nontangible things. The figure of Whitman responds in lines 16-25 to Simpson's queries and denies ever having made prophecies or offered prescriptions. Whitman admits that he, too, tried to advance or advertise himself and is "vastly amused" to be found out; he freely and humbly confesses to being "wholly disreputable."

Simpson uses lines 26-35 to unveil some professions that are, in his opinion, deceitful. The poet contrasts the hypocrisy and deafness of many Americans—particularly those in jobs that ignore the American Dream—with the honest occupations of housewife and storekeeper. He notes the difference between the self-aggrandizement of selfish Americans and the humility of the common folk who take no thought for upward mobility.

Simpson gives dire predictions for the nation in lines 36-38. In fact, the poet compares the probable fate of America with the actual outcome of ancient Greece and Rome. The last lines (39-44) prescribe a remedy for the nation's crisis. The creative imagery of the closing words brings the reader a sense of hope for the future.

Forms and Devices

Simpson is a poet of emotion and imagination. Meter, rhyme, and stanza do not direct his "Walt Whitman at Bear Mountain." Rather, the poet uses feeling and intellect to bring about the reader's understanding. His loose style and natural voice, not a formal structure, help Simpson to achieve one of his major objectives: to make his writing sound like speech, not rhyme.

It is not surprising that Simpson begins his own thoughts about the United States with references to the American bard Walt Whitman. He addresses Whitman also in "In California," another poem in *At the End of the Open Road*. Like Whitman, Simpson focuses on the United States; unlike Whitman, however, Simpson seems less satisfied with the nation.

In "Walt Whitman on Bear Mountain" Simpson employs metaphors effectively. He uses "The poet of death and lilacs" to refer to Whitman and his poem "When Lilacs Last in the Dooryard Bloom'd," an elegy for U.S. president Abraham Lincoln. Through it all, however, Simpson depicts Whitman as remaining quietly on the sidelines. Simpson calls Whitman, in his "wrinkled metal," a waiting "crocodile" that is all-seeing but seems to be "loafing."

Simpson uses contrasts effectively when citing occupations. He suggests in stanza 4 that "Only a poet pauses" to read the words at Whitman's statue. Those in many other careers—"all the realtors,/ Pickpockets, salesmen, and the actors performing/ Official scenarios"—appear to have discarded the American ideal; they are a stark contrast to "the man who keeps a store on a lonely road,/ And the housewife," whom Simpson venerates for their humility and their failure to seek upward mobility.

Simpson uses other stylistic devices in the poem. He makes use in the first stanza of personification when he describes the bronze as looking "alive/ Where it is folded like cloth." He continues this personification when he says the sculpture stands on two feet, loafs, and answers the posed questions.

Allusions to sickness, death, and cemeteries effectively command attention and denote the misplacement of the American ideal. Simpson mentions that "the light above the street is sick to death" and that the general public has "contracted/ American dreams." He emphasizes the illness of society by his use of "a deaf ear" and the word "grave"—with its double meaning—in the tenth stanza. The words "used-car lot," "ruins," and "unbuilding" create images of and feelings associated with wrecks, rubble, and remains.

Simpson's vivid imagery is evident when he describes the "Colossal snows" that the houses of wood endure; these physical structures survive pressures from outside—but not from within. Simpson's continued negativity is in direct opposition to Whitman's optimism.

In conclusion, Simpson offers his reader a sense of hope after the ruin and devastation. His four final lines present images of clouds lifting, mists clearing, plums flowering, people dancing, and an "angel in the gate." The ambiguous angel also appears in Simpson's "In California"; in both poems the angel seems to be observing from afar and distancing itself from the actions of humankind. The angel is suggestive of those guardians of the Garden of Eden, a utopia that could await the nation in the future.

Themes and Meanings

"Walt Whitman at Bear Mountain" employs a travel or journey theme. Like the trip itself, the poem initially has no apparent order. The leaps at first seem illogical, but the sights along the way eventually bring meaning to the verse tour. Simpson moves the reader from New York, to "the Mississippi panorama," to "[t]he Open Road," to "the high Sierras," to the "lonely road," to the ruins of ancient societies that decayed from within before being destroyed from without, to crumbling structures, and finally to the bay, another allusion to Simpson's "In California."

The statue of Whitman that introduces the poem actually exists; it is one that the American sculpture Jo Davidson (1883-1952) designed at the request of Averell Harriman. Harriman, U.S. ambassador to the United Kingdom, secretary of commerce under President Harry S. Truman, and governor of New York from 1954 to 1958—wanted to commemorate his mother's gift of ten thousand acres and $1 million for the creation of Bear Mountain State Park and the adjacent Harriman State Park; he commissioned Davidson to design the statue. The first exhibit of the sculpture was at the 1939 New York World's Fair; the formal dedication was in Bear Mountain on November 17, 1940.

Across from the statue and carved into a granite ledge are stanzas from Whitman's "Song of the Open Road." The first line reads, "Afoot and light-hearted I take to the open road." The statue depicts Whitman walking surely and confidently, as if down an open road. Simpson makes reference to the sculpture and to these lines of Whitman when he pessimistically tells his audience that "The Open Road goes to the used-car lot." Simpson is suggesting that cars in American society in the post-World War II period are more than just a means of transportation; they are his symbols of the class system, of speed and motion, of the abandonment of the American Dream by many in the country, of the impermanence of material goods, and even of a person's worth—by society's faulty measure.

Simpson notes in the poem that American visitors usually do not wait to read the words of the bronze figure; he laments the fact that the people "neglect [Whitman]!/ Only a poet pauses to read the inscription." This speed and lack of concern for ideals are abhorrent to him. The last four lines seem to call for slowing down the too-fast tempo of life and for appreciating the world.

Simpson seems to have three goals in this poem. He honors Whitman, clears the bard of charges that he was a false prophet, and cautions the nation to pause, to consider its path, and to return to the American Dream. Simpson effectively uses contrasts to stress the needed, significant changes. He suggests that the "sickness" and "death" of standards are rampant throughout the nation; for instance, Simpson uses the words "sick," "contracted," "deaf," "grave," and "used-car lot." Even "cathedrals/ Unbuilding" implies the death and decay of the American Dream. The references to illness, imperfection, death, and spoils continue as one reads of Greece and Rome "in ruins"; this mention of past civilizations is reminiscent of Simpson's poem "In California," which mentions ancient Babylon and Tenochtitlán.

By contrast, rebirth and rejoicing are still possible, the poet reminds the reader. He urges the general public to find again the Garden of Eden with its "angel in the gate" and "flowering plum." He suggests that his audience can enjoy the intellectual joy ("imagining red") and dancing if they refocus their sights on something other than selfish concerns. Simpson offers to those who will listen his full vision: the promise, the betrayal, and all that is still possible.

Anita Price Davis

THE WANG RIVER SEQUENCE

Author: Wang Wei (701-761)
Type of poem: Poetic sequence
First published: wr. c. 740's, as *"Wangchuan ji"*; collected in *Lei jian Wang Youcheng quanji*, 1557; English translation collected in *Poems of Wang Wei*, 1973

The Poem

The Wangchuan (literally "twirling stream"), or Wang River, is a river at the foot-hills of the Chung-nan-shan mountain range in Lan-t'ien, about thirty miles south of the capital Ch'ang-an (now Xi'an, Shaanxi Province). The range has long been a cele-brated sanctuary for recluses. Wang Wei lived there on and off for more than two de-cades in an estate that he called the "Twirling Stream Country House."

The estate became the favorite subject of Wang Wei's painting and poetry. Not long after the acquisition, he and his good friend P'ei Ti collaborated on a series of poems. Each was to write a quatrain for each of the twenty attractions around the Twirling Stream area. The poems were then put together into the collection "The Wang River Sequence," which attracted many imitations. Some scholars speculate that the se-quence corresponds to a long scroll by Wang Wei, depicting the same scenes. The scroll no longer exists, though a seventeenth century reproduction thought to be based on a tenth century copy survives.

The twenty attractions described in the poems are named for a variety of geograph-ical, architectural, or vegetational features. The sequence is replete with pictorial sights, but in addition it possesses qualities that are more than visual. It is a testimony to "poetry in painting and painting in poetry," a phrase critics often use to praise Wang Wei's achievement.

The sequence essentially deals with thoughts and feelings arising from interactions between the recluse and the landscape. The scenery, which serves as the setting for the mind to operate, allows the poet's ethic and aesthetic consciousness to unfold at a lei-surely pace; in the process, the scenery also metamorphoses into a poetic "atmo-sphere" that transcends the physical world. Although the sequence follows this over-all pattern, there are different points of interest in the twenty individual poems. Some of them ("Meng Wall Hollow" and "Huatzu Hill") focus on associations and senti-ments induced by the scenery. Others seem to be purely descriptive and devoid of hu-man presence, suggesting that the landscape alone will emanate qualities worthy of poetry. Examples for this category include "Deer Park," "Rapids by the Luans'," "Magnolia Park," "North Hill," and "Magnolia Slope." A third group, which is more preponderant, treats human beings either as in harmony with nature (for example, "Dogwood Bank," "Lake Pavilion," and "Bamboo Grove House"), or as a coexisting but unobtrusive presence in the landscape (for example, "Bamboo Hill," "Sophora Walk," and "White Stone Shallows"). In these poems, the relationship between humans and nature is often reversed, to the effect that the latter becomes the subject of the universe.

Forms and Devices

All the poems in "The Wang River Sequence" are "recent-style" quatrains known as *chüeh-chü*, with five characters to each line. Because the poet is given a mere twenty characters to maneuver for each poem, it is interesting to find out what kinds of devices he employs to maximize his expressive capabilities. In terms of prosody, other than following the tonal pattern (which also includes one rhyme) required for each poem, the poet deliberately seems to be using as few devices as possible. Couplets, constructed according to grammatical and semantic parallelism or antithesis, occur sparingly (in "Apricot Wood House," "Magnolia Park," "Rapids by the Luans'," "Gold Dust Spring," and "Pepper Garden"). The motivation could be to avoid artificiality. Even though historical allusions are used in some of the poems, one has the general impression that Wang Wei's major concern in the sequence is to make language, rhetoric, and prosody function at a minimal level, so that a sense of immediacy and transparency can be achieved. In spite of the apparent simplicity, however, the sequence as a whole is endowed with a rich diversity thanks to the variety of poems assembled.

Two basic approaches are adopted in the composition of the poems. The first is a cinematic perspective, akin to the nonfocal or multiple-perspective vista commonly found in Chinese landscape painting. In "Deer Park," for example, the scene shifts from the empty mountain to the sunset, from the sunset to the deep forest, and from there to the green moss. A similar series of shifts is also found in other poems, especially "Magnolia Park," "Rapids by the Luans'," "North Hill," "Bamboo Grove House," and "Magnolia Slope." These shifts, analogous to a sequence of camera shots, correspond to the scenery that unfolds when a scroll of painting is unrolled or when one looks at the scenery from one point to another on the scroll. This cinematic or painterly approach encapsulates the practice (and notion) of *yu*, that is, "traveling" in the landscape with the intention of "play" or leisurely appreciation. By unfolding the scenery portion by portion, the approach recreates the vitality of the landscape and the continuity of the natural order. The leaps and gaps between individual scenes, analogous to montages in a film or blank spaces on a painting, are also highly suggestive because they leave room for the reader's imagination.

The second approach is that of interfacing, or juxtaposing, human responses with the natural scenes, so that the two become interrelated and, eventually, fused together organically. Thus, the ceaselessness of migrating birds and the endlessness of hue-changing mountains are not only comments on the poet's boundless sadness but also subjects commented upon by the latter ("Huatzu Hill"). Lotus flowers blooming in the lake, and the host and the guest drinking in the lake pavilion, are not separate events since they also blend into a unified condition ("Lake Pavilion"). Other examples abound. The basic pattern is a description of the scenery in the opening lines, followed by an explicit or (more often) implicit thought or feeling. The approach is similar to that of the objective correlative, in that the world outside (scenery) and the world inside (the poet's mind) are intricately related; yet it goes one step further in that the two worlds interact and, as it were, melt into a new world of aesthetic harmony in which the landscape is "personalized" and the poet is also "naturalized." In traditional literary criticism, the technique is known as *ch'ing-ching hsiang-sheng*, or "the mutual generation of scenery and sentiments"; the new "world" of aesthetic harmony resulting from it is commonly called *ching-chieh*.

Themes and Meanings

As Marsha L. Wagner points out, the arrangement of the sequence is thematic rather than geographic. It is possible, therefore, to view the poems as individual segments woven together into a matrix of meaningful motifs, which eventually combine into the main themes of the sequence.

There seems to be a thesis in the sequence taken as a whole, which can be seen from the general movement of the poems. In "Meng Wall Hollow," which serves as an introduction to the sequence, ancient trees decaying on the poet's new homestead remind him of the past owner. The idea that he too will be replaced by another saddens him. The elegiac tone continues in "Huatzu Hill," where the ceaseless migration of birds and the autumnal hue of the endless range again sadden the poet. Significantly, however, the cheerlessness of the two opening poems dissipates quickly and disappears from the rest of the sequence. This change of mood is the unifying spirit of the collection as a whole.

In the remaining poems, three themes can be singled out. The first is the pastoral landscape as a self-contained and self-maintaining entity. There is a conspicuous absence of hubbub from the picturesque retreat. Human activities are restricted and minimal. Where human beings appear, their presence has no consequence to the serenity of the setting, because their activity is peripheral or incidental to the natural course of action of the landscape. Not even the woodcutter knows where the dense bamboos and shrubs are taking him on the off-track trail ("Bamboo Hill"). In the empty mountain, where one can hear voices but not see those to whom they belong, the setting sun's stray rays light upon the green moss ("Deer Park"). Nobody is aware of a man sitting alone in the bamboo grove, singing and playing the lute, while the moon comes along, shedding its light ("Bamboo Grove House"). Magnolia flowers bloom and fall by the brook, where a house stands deserted ("Magnolia Slope"). In these poems, human action—even if allowed—is thus reduced to the level of nonintrusion. Guaranteed to act out its own drama without being disturbed, the landscape unfolds itself as a self-sufficient phenomenon ("Magnolia Park," "Rapids by the Luans'," and "North Hill"). Even human beings living in this world become part of the landscape, as "White Stone Shallows" suggests.

While the landscape continues to dominate the rest of the sequence, a theme focusing on the human condition begins to develop from "Dogwood Bank" through "Willow Waves." The six poems, which can be regarded as a miniseries, are devoted to the pleasant experience of having a friend come for a visit in the congenial retreat. Although visitors seldom arrive, the gatekeeper sweeps the mossy bypath just in case a mountain monk chances by ("Sophora Walk"). The dogwood will provide "dogwood cups" when a guest comes ("Dogwood Bank"). The lake pavilion, which lotuses bloom all around, is an ideal place to drink with a friend ("Lake Pavilion"). Perhaps the friend would find it enjoyable to play the flute on a boat while cruising around the lake, which is so large that one hardly knows the people on the other side ("South Hill," "Lake I"). Even the willow trees (commonly associated with parting) here are different, for unlike those by the palace moat, they do not grow for the sake of making farewells unbearable ("Willow Waves"). In this group of poems, readers, like the visitor, are invited to witness the possibility of a peaceful life in which one's well-being is nurtured by nature. "Willow Waves," in which the poet uses willows at the palace moat to hint at separations brought about by war or demotion, highlights the difference between the life of the recluse and that of the civil servant. In a world where the order of things is ecologically arranged and where human activities are sanctioned by natural elements, existence acquires a special meaning.

Finally, the sequence also contains a mytho-philosophical discourse based on allusions to history and the Taoist classics. The Twirling Stream retreat possesses the power of nature to effect a fundamental change in the course of human action because it stands for an entire *Weltanschauung*. This theme, hinted at early in the sequence, begins to gather momentum roughly at the middle and culminates in a triumphant conclusion at the end. In "Apricot Wood House," the poet imagines that the unusually precious—almost godly—material (apricot wood and fragrant reeds) used to build the roof will bring about something auspicious ("rain among men"). The lake area in which neighbors do not know one another is reminiscent of the agrarian utopia propounded in the sixth century B.C.E. *Classic of the Way of Power* by Lao-tzu ("South Hill"). "Gold Dust Spring," which seems to be associated with Taoist alchemy, has longevity and immortality to offer to its drinkers. The last two poems concluding the sequence indicate tellingly that the retreat is opposed diametrically to the mundane world. In "Lacquer Garden," Wang Wei alludes to the Taoist mystic Chuang Tzu's contempt for the position of prime minister offered to him while he was the garden-keeper. The allusion intimates that the poet would act similarly, not out of arrogance but out of "incompetence." As a result of the denial of worldliness, something is gained. In "Pepper Garden," Wang Wei's allusive imagination turns to *Songs of the South* by the banished poet Ch'ü Yüan. In his frustration, Ch'ü Yüan often referred to himself in terms of fragrant herbs being mistaken for weeds. Just as Ch'ü Yüan is befriended by the gods in his poetry, Wang Wei imagines that one could also become a host to the gods in the arcadia of the retreat. Together, these poems give one the impression that the Twirling Stream Country House is an incarnation of the Taoist utopia on Earth.

Balance Chow

WANTING TO DIE

Author: Anne Sexton (1928-1974)
Type of poem: Lyric
First published: 1964; collected in *Live or Die*, 1966

The Poem

"Wanting to Die" is a short poem in free verse that divides its thirty-three lines into eleven tercets (three-line stanzas). Because it is written in the first person and is conversational in form, this poem has been described as one of Anne Sexton's literary suicide notes. Because it presents a speaker attempting to explain to a sympathetic listener why she wants to kill herself, some critics have also suggested that it reads like a discussion between Sexton and her psychiatrist. The use of the first person in a poem often causes readers to assume that the poet's voice and the speaker's voice are the same—an assumption that, while often erroneous, holds true for this work. Besides being suicidal herself, Sexton often used letters or personal reminiscences as the foundations for her writing. "Wanting to Die," in fact, was initially a free-association addendum attached to a letter written to her friend Anne Wilder when Wilder had asked Sexton why she was attracted to suicide. Knowing that Wilder was a psychiatrist and was, therefore, unlikely to overreact to even strong imagery, Sexton addressed Wilder's very real question in poetic form.

In the opening lines of "Wanting to Die," Sexton's speaker chooses to respond honestly to the question posed to her even though the hearer may find the topic repellant. "Since you ask," she says, she will tell. The speaker describes herself as walking unconsciously through life, unimpressed and unaffected by the world around her. The only passion she feels is "the almost unnameable lust" for death. In the next two tercets, she explains further that she has "nothing against life" and no hatred for "the grass blades" that symbolize the vitality of the living world; she simply loves death's promise more. "[S]uicides have a special language," she says, and "like carpenters, they want to know *which tools.*/ They never ask *why build.*"

So far Sexton's speaker has simply discussed her life in a detached, calm manner. At this point the speaker tries to explain the attraction that death holds and to translate her concept of death into words that the hearer can understand. The next two tercets describe in brief the speaker's previous two suicide attempts; she has "possessed the enemy," death, "taken on his craft," and "rested."

The question remains, however: Why does she want to kill herself? The last six tercets seem to provide an answer, however unsatisfactory it may be to others. The first three describe a suicidal person's perception of life as a kind of "drug." Although its pleasures are "so sweet," life keeps the "body at needlepoint"; an addiction to life, like an addiction to drugs, prevents a person from seeing life's bitter reality. Living an illusion has, the speaker asserts, made her "already [betray] the body" even before she attempted suicide. Further, death has been waiting, "year after year," to "undo an old wound" and release the speaker from the body that has become a "prison." Life is a kind of suffering (the "wound") that only suicides recognize when they are "balanced there" between life and death. Even love, the ultimate reason for living, cannot provide the suicide with sufficient reason to stay alive; love is "an infection" that keeps them sick with life.

Forms and Devices

In writing "Wanting to Die," Sexton rejected the strict formal patterns that permeate her earlier volumes of poetry. Although they are occasionally present, rhyme and meter in *Live or Die* are coincidental—the most important poetic devices of the volume are intense, compelling imagery and suggestive metaphor. Many critics have observed the strength behind Sexton's creative vision; "Wanting to Die," like most of her other suicide poems, is about a woman driven insane by the intensity of her emotions. Not surprisingly, then, other critics are repulsed by the immediate anguish and intimacy of Sexton's confessional lines. They suggest that reading Sexton's poems sometimes seems like a tour through her personal hell. Sexton's imagery does tend to be repellant. The picture of the happy suicide having "rested, drooling at the mouth-hole" has a strong impact. Yet it is also a true picture of the complete "rest" that death brings. Drooling, lack of eye response, and incontinence (the image created when the speaker says, "the cornea and the leftover urine were gone") are the realities of dying, however disgusting they may seem.

"Wanting to Die" is also a highly metaphorical poem. For the suicidal speaker, the desire for death is not easily explained to outsiders. The metaphor of the carpenter (with its suggestion of Christ, who himself could be seen as a kind of suicide in that he willingly chose to die) is used to describe why suicides do not seem to consider the impact of their actions before they act. Carpenters do not ask why they build—they presume that the act of building has a purpose. The carpenter's only concern is which tools to use. Similarly, suicides do not ask why they wish to die; they, too, only need to know which "tools" to use.

For a normal person, death is tragic, even repugnant—the typical reader may not really want to know how the most disgusting qualities of death can be so compelling. Only the careful use of metaphor can overcome repulsion's barriers by comparing what is visually acceptable and understandable to what is gross and incomprehensible. When the poem compares life to an addictive "drug," the use of metaphor effectively explains why the suicide does not want to keep on living: He or she wants the power to choose life or death rather than be compelled to live by an addiction to the pleasures of living; "dazzled, they can't forget a drug so sweet." "Wanting to Die" may not make this rationale acceptable to normal readers, but its use of metaphor makes the suicidal person's obsessions more understandable.

Themes and Meanings

Sexton's major accomplishment in "Wanting to Die" is how clearly and powerfully she expresses the feelings of the emotional suicide. Unless one has faced the miasma of emotions that cause one to consider suicide, one may have difficulty in understanding how someone can choose to commit suicide. Sexton makes this choice comprehensible when she presents the reader with the suicide's view of life as being spent facing trivialities and making no impression upon the world: "I walk in my clothing, unmarked by that voyage." Life under these conditions is meaningless and full of pain. Suicidal people's "clothing," their way of thinking and reacting, does not cover their emotional nakedness. Without the normal person's psychological strength, suicides are vulnerable to the smallest hurts; "something unsaid, the phone off the hook" are witnesses to the suicide attempt as well as goads that drive one to suicide. Most painfully, the relationships of the suicidal person seem unreal and unreliable: "the love, whatever it was, an infection."

For normal people, life is to be enjoyed. For suicides, death is a rest from the constant trivialities that stab at them. Anne Wilder's letter to Sexton celebrated the fact that life abounds in the world—even the life within the blades of grass was to be wondered at and cherished. Human companionship, as represented by the "furniture . . . under the sun"—lawn chairs, perhaps—is treasured by those who love living. "Wanting to Die" acknowledges the attractiveness of these things; it is not the pleasures of life that she cringes from, but rather the fact that these pleasures pale in comparison to the restful cessation of "raging" and sorrow that death provides. Suicides, Sexton seems to suggest, are born with the tendencies that they will act upon later in life. The fact that they are alive rather than dead does not negate their essential morbidity; "Still-born, they don't always die."

Although this way of thinking, like Sexton's imagery, may be repellant to the average reader, it is an accurate reflection of suicidal thinking. Most seriously depressed people think of their lives as a meaningless struggle that they are incapable of changing. Others, suffering from long-term depression, report that they have always been depressed and have thought of death as a comforting option.

Julia M. Meyers

WASHING DISHES LATE AT NIGHT

Author: Kathleen Norris (1947-   )
Type of poem: Lyric
First published: 1981, in *The Middle of the World*

The Poem

"Washing Dishes Late at Night" is a poem in free verse consisting of just seventeen lines, only three of which contain more than five words. The setting is the poet's home, and the title further limits the action to the kitchen. The title also indicates the time, "late at night," when it is natural to be tired, to have one's defenses down. The speaker is busy washing dishes, a task so routine that it leaves her thoughts free. There is another person in the room, whom she sometimes addresses. Since both the poetry and the prose that Kathleen Norris writes are highly autobiographical, one can be fairly certain that her companion, who is described as living with her, is her husband.

Although the poem is divided into three parts of almost equal length, it does not develop chronologically or even logically. Each section provides more information about the action while, at the same time, interpreting it.

Thus, after beginning with a simple, factual title, the author, in the first section of the poem, turns subjective, asserting that a "room tips." This comment is followed by some relevant facts: The room about which the poet is thinking has just been "re-arranged." A logical explanation for her unease could be that, looking at the new arrangement, she feels that it has some aesthetic defect, perhaps a lack of symmetry or balance, which would, indeed, make one feel that it was tipping. On the other hand, the poet might just need time to get used to the changes. After this down-to-earth reference in the second line of this section, however, the present disappears and, with it, the real world. In the last three lines of the section, the poet harks back to a time that she admits seems like a "fairy tale." The use of the past tense is significant; evidently, that golden age is now no more than a memory.

The second part of the poem begins with explicit references to sensual experiences. Now, however, there is a conflict: While the room clings to these memories, the man addressed is eliminating them by hanging "new pictures." Meanwhile, the poet is working at her own chore.

In the first line of the final section, there is a dramatic change of subject. It now appears that the writer's primary concern is not furniture arrangement but the creative process. The poem about "faith" that she was trying to write has been blocked, evidently because of something in the atmosphere. The poem ends with the husband and wife again together, but what they share is uneasiness and fear.

Forms and Devices

"Washing Dishes Late at Night" is written in a terse, uncluttered style. The words are simple and commonplace. Norris uses nouns such as "room," "lovers," and "arms and legs," and verbs such as "tips," "rode," and "dip." Because so many of her words are monosyllabic, the poem has a terse, even an abrupt, quality. In the first line ("The room tips"), for example, two of the three syllables are stressed. Although there is more of a lilt in the occasional longer lines in the poem, such as "Where we have rearranged it" and "Their unencumbered arms and legs," most of the lines resemble the initial one. The last three lines of the poem are heavily stressed: Out of eleven syllables, six, perhaps even seven, are accented, and of ten words, all but one are single syllables. As a result, although the poem concludes without a solution, it does end with a strong statement. There is no question about the doubt the two characters are experiencing at the end of the poem.

Similarly, there is nothing unclear about Norris's images. The dirty dishes, the pictures, and the "pale light," as well as the room, whose importance is indicated by the fact that it is referred to in each section of the poem, are all, quite evidently, drawn from the poet's own everyday experience. Even the "arms and legs" of the naked "lovers" and the fairy tale "dragon" or "horse" are hardly obscure. It is important to note, however, that while all of the images are concrete and familiar, some of them represent the world of the here and now, and others represent the realm of memory and imagination.

Another stylistic device that has thematic implications is the frequent shifts from one personal pronoun to another. "Washing Dishes Late at Night" begins with a reference to the couple's uniting: "[W]e" worked together on the room. Then, in the second section, there is a rather surprising shift. The "lovers" of the preceding stanza are spoken of in the third person, not once, but twice. The poet immediately proceeds to a description of the present, with "You" (presumably her husband) involved in one activity, "I" in another. The final section brings them back together, with "our," "we," and "Both of us." It is evident that the pronouns in this poem were not selected by accident. Instead, they are clearly meant to serve as directional signals, signifying the development of thought and feeling from line to line, section to section.

In prose works such as *Dakota: A Spiritual Geography* (1993) and *The Cloister Walk* (1996), Norris has emphasized one of the important lessons she has learned during her own spiritual awakening: If life is understood as being, above all, a matter of one's relationship with God, everything in this world is significant. This faith is reflected in Norris's poetry. One should never think that her imagery and syntax might be merely incidental or ornamental. For Norris, the purpose of form is to illuminate theme just as the purpose of everything in God's creations is to demonstrate his goodness and power.

Themes and Meanings

Though, at first glance, "Washing Dishes Late at Night" appears to be a poem about change, loss, and alienation, the primary theme of the poem is, in fact, religious doubt. However, the poet does not indicate her subject until the final section of the poem, and, even then, she does so obliquely. Up to that point, she has set up a pattern of contrasts, whose real purpose does not become evident until the very end of the poem.

Dominating the poem is a sense that none of the changes that have taken place is for the better. The new arrangement of the room makes the poet uneasy. Moreover, much has been lost, not only a sense of stability, for one assumes that, in the past, the room did not seem to "tip," but also the kind of magic that made the lovers, presumably the poet and her partner, feel that they lived in a fairy-tale world. There is also the suggestion of a loss of innocence. In the past, even a "dragon" was tame enough to be ridden, but that time has vanished. It is also pointed out that all traces of the lovers' sensual activities, which, in an unfallen world, have their own kind of innocence, are being eliminated.

Although the couple, at first, joined in making changes, it is significant that the two are now separated. The poet's partner is energetically eliminating the past, replacing it with something new, while the poet stands alone, washing away the remains of a communal meal, symbolically washing her hands not only of the past but also of her own unhappiness.

As soon as Norris explains that she had intended to write about faith, however, it becomes clear that this is not merely a poem about change and the loss of stability or about alienation and the loss of love but about something more basic, the source of all uncertainty: doubt of God's presence in the world. The alienation between the lovers, as well as between them and the past, is both a metaphor for a spiritual malaise and a symptom of it. Again, one is reminded of the Fall: After they became separated from God, Adam and Eve immediately turned on each other.

Nevertheless, "Washing Dishes Late at Night" does end with a degree of hope. The poem does not end in total darkness but in a "pale light," though not in the full radiance of God's presence. Moreover, the fact that it is night implies that morning will eventually come. Most important of all, the couple is once again together, though, at present, all they have in common is their sense of instability and a common fear.

It is a mark of Norris's stature as a religious poet that she does not take refuge in easy answers. She writes about temptation, as in "The Monastery Orchard in Early Spring," which refers to Saint Augustine's boyhood sin and to the allure of sensuality; she writes about the ever-presence of death, as in "The Blue Light" and "Desert Run Scenario"; and, as in this poem, she writes about the terror of doubt. However, the dawn does break; the desert does bloom. In many of her poems, Kathleen Norris voices a faith that is even stronger for having dealt with darkness.

Rosemary M. Canfield Reisman

THE WATCHERS

Author: W. H. Auden (1907-1973)
Type of poem: Pastoral
First published: 1945, as "Not All the Candidates Pass," in *The Collected Poetry*; collected as "The Watchers" in *Collected Shorter Poems, 1927-1957*, 1966

The Poem

"The Watchers" is a short, forty-line poem in eight five-line stanzas reminiscent of the medieval French form known as a cinquain, which used a five-line stanza with a variety of meters and rhyme schemes. It was written in February, 1932, but not published until 1945. The speaker or persona of the poem is an observer who is watching a sleeping world from his window late at night. A yellow clock face and a green pier light eerily illuminate "a new imprudent year" as the night's silence "buzzes" in the poet's ear. Except for the clock, the light, and the buzzing silence, the poet is alone in his window; "The lights of near-by families are out."

The speaker then observes various objects and phenomena in the night, describing them in a manner that invokes a feeling of watchfulness and apprehension. He describes a dormant lilac bush as being "like a conspirator" that "Shams dead upon the lawn." The "Great Bear/ Hangs as a portent over Helensburgh," and the "influential quiet twins" (a reference to the Castor and Pollux constellation) "look leniently" upon the sleeping populace.

The scene becomes more ominous when the speaker describes the "keepers of a wild estate" as stocky men carrying guns. On the surface, these keepers are there to ensure the safety of the town's estates, yet they keep the peace "with a perpetual threat" to any intruder. The unknown intruders are given the characteristics of moles that burrow in the earth, peacocks that transform themselves from plain to proud, and rats possessed of "desperate courage." The intruders need these characteristics to trick the keepers and escape detection; the reader may well wonder why people would be forced to escape detection in their own world.

The answer comes as the year moves "Deeper towards the summer" and the poet poses the question of what would happen if "the starving visionary" were to see "The carnival within our gates." Describing the "wild estate" as a carnival suggests a scene of wild riot and unrelenting chaos, and the reader sees that the estate keepers must watch for human intruders who would report on the carnival—the chaos that has taken over the pastoral world where peace and tranquillity should reign. The last two stanzas reinforce this point when the poet implores the estate keepers to use their power: "We need your power still: use it, that none,/ O, from their tables break uncontrollably away." Fearful of uncontrolled behavior that would bring danger and damage, the poem abruptly ends by depicting the carnival of intruders "Mopping and mowing through the sleepless day."

Forms and Devices

"The Watchers" is based on the medieval French cinquain form, which originally had a variety of meters and rhyme schemes. Auden's rhyme scheme varies from stanza to stanza, and he uses both exact rhyme and slant rhyme effectively. The rhyme scheme of the first stanza is *aabbc*, for example, and the second stanza rhymes *abccd*. The rhyme scheme for the third, fourth, and sixth stanzas is *aabba*. In other stanzas of the poem Auden uses slant rhyme, or near rhyme. Slant rhyme uses assonance (repeated vowel sounds) or consonance (repeated consonant sounds) to produce an end rhyme. For example, in the second stanza the poet creates a slant rhyme with "stir" and "conspirator." Slant rhyme is also employed in stanzas 2 and 7. Stanza 7 uses consonance to repeat the closing *ts* sound in "gates" and "streets."

Beyond such recognizable formal devices as rhyme, Auden imbues the poem with a quality of mysterious ambiguity. The watchers—the "stocky keepers" of the estate—are never clearly defined or described, and in fact the speaker notes that they are not exactly real; they are his thoughts about "forms" he saw in a dream. The watchers, then, these shadowy, unseen forces, may reflect a paranoia within the speaker as much as anything in the outside world. They seem like soldiers or sentries, posted in doorways or atop ridges, yet they also have an aspect of ambushers ("'Of late/ Here . . . They lay in wait'"). The precise meaning and boundaries of the "wild estate" itself are also left open to interpretation. The speaker's attitude toward the watchers is also ambiguous, ambivalent. They keep the peace, but only by being armed with guns and carrying a "perpetual threat." The speaker is alternately trying to trick them himself and urging them to use their power to keep order. In the last lines they take on a particularly oppressive cast, protecting the status quo against minor transgressions: one person lunging dangerously about a room and another "out wild-/ly spinning like a top in the field." The first may pose some momentary danger, but the second, although perhaps eccentric, would seem to pose no real threat. As is true in Auden's other works, the very obtuseness or obscurity of the poem adds to its feeling of indefinable unease and apprehension.

Themes and Meanings

"The Watchers" is a poem about contradictions, about the appearances of things and their realities. Auden contrasts pastoral images—the lilac tree, constellations, the seasons—with mechanical images, such as the yellow clock face, the green pier light, the estate keepers' guns, and the carnival, which intrude upon nature's peacefulness. Mechanical images are characteristic of Auden's poetry and identify him as a member of a 1930's group of young, liberal poets called the Pylon School; this group also included Cecil Day Lewis, Louis MacNeice, and Stephen Spender, all of whom used mechanical images.

As a pastoral, the poem describes a rustic setting, including the estate keepers and references to a copse, a bridge, and animals. However, because Auden wants to depict contradictions, the images take on extra meaning. The opening stanzas show the opposition of the quiet night to the intrusion of the light and the clock face, both of which are mechanical objects that impart contrived sequences upon nature—the glowing clock measures artificial hours, and the light artificially lights the darkness.

An estate keeper's job is to maintain the land, yet these keepers carry guns, mechanical objects that can inflict injury and death. Because nature is pastoral, and because Castor and Pollux, the "influential quiet twins," are looking "leniently upon all of us tonight," the intrusive keepers are particularly jarring to the scene. Although the person at the window and the constellations looking down are watchers, the estate keepers are the most significant watchers in the poem, and their guarding is not reassuring but threatening, even dangerous.

Through images containing contradictory meanings, Auden presents worlds in conflict with each other. One is natural and filled with pastoral images, while the other includes humans who come as intruders to subvert pastoral nature into a violent and mechanical environment. Humankind, intruding upon nature, is watched in its watching, a situation that lends irony to the poem. "The Watchers" reflects the uncertainty of England and Europe in the 1930's, with fascism on the rise.

Dennis L. Weeks

THE WAVE

Author: Michael Collier (1953-   )
Type of poem: Narrative
First published: 2000, in *The Ledge*

The Poem

"The Wave" by Michael Collier is a nine-stanza narrative poem consisting of un-rhymed trochaic hexameters. It describes the ritual of a wave during a baseball game, the way fans stand up, block by block, to demonstrate support for their team. The setting is an unspecified town or city in the United States on a cool summer night.

The poem opens with an overview of the baseball stadium, as vendors of cotton candy, soft drinks, beer, pretzels, and hot dogs parade up and down the stands plying their trade. Panning the crowd like a camera, the poet's eye sees birds "attracted// and repelled" by the lights on the field, trapped under the overarching dome as they flit back and forth above the stands. Caught by a glimpse of an anomalous "skinny kid sitting between two fat parents," the poet's vision finally hones in on the home team's mascot taunting the visitors with "oversize antics" above the dugout.

About halfway through the game, as the fifth stanza explains, two slightly drunken soldiers walk to the front of the stands, strip to the waist, lift up their arms, and exhort the crowd, section by section, to stand up and raise their arms in a wave of movement. The aim of these leaders of the crowd, says the poet in the last stanza, is to keep the wave going for as long as they can, for their own sake as well as that of the players and "all of us."

Apart from the final stanza, in which the "us" may include the reader, the poet neither acknowledges nor addresses the reader, except to remark casually, as to a fellow fan, that the night is "cool." That is, the poet offers the reader no unified perspective or central reference point with which to interpret the poem. For example, Collier himself appears only as an impersonal witness to the action. Seated next to the soldiers, he is a spectator, one among many. In addition, the game itself is never described. As a result, both poet and reader become, in effect, voyeurs at a distance, spectators of spectators. As for the significance of the ritual of the wave, if it has a reason or cause, it is that the soldiers who lead it have "paced each other with a beer an inning" and "kept/ their buzz buffed with a flask." Like many other postmodern artists, Collier does not interpose himself between the reader and the scene he depicts. Apparently he deliberately leaves to the reader the job of teasing out the meaning.

Forms and Devices

Collier's modernity in this poem lies in his reliance on a fast-moving sequence of images rather than on the direct expression or argument of abstract ideas that some other contemporary writers have found necessary. His emphasis on fast-paced imagery at the expense of rhetorical persuasion also links this work with the visual arts, especially films. The result is a poem that largely consists of a catalogue of phrases, a tour de force of linked images depicting items ranging from brightly colored cotton candy to the gaudy wrappings of ice cream, from money fanned out in green spokes to dark earth hosed by groundskeepers. All these visual details climax in the vigorous exertions of the sweating soldiers motioning the obedient onlookers to rise from their seats.

Collier also combines this fast-moving sequence of cinematic images with traditional poetic devices, especially enjambment, a technique utilized to split up phrases. In enjambment, the last segment of a group of words spills over into the next line and sometimes even the next stanza, as in "palettes/ of cotton candy" and "two soldiers sitting next to me, who// have paced each other." Breaking up grammatical units creates a sense of continual thrusting forward, a propulsion that powers the poem with dynamic progression toward a conclusion fittingly stated as the necessity for keeping movement going for as long as possible.

Collier also employs such devices as metaphors and similes to explore the tension between natural or religious values and commercial interests at a game, in which the devotion of the fans is exploited for purely monetary purposes. Blades of grass on the field become green dollar bills held up in fingers, the hot dog man "anointing" a weenie with mustard genuflects as he bends to pass it down to a customer, while the groundskeepers care for the infield as carefully as a priest guards the host at a communion rail. The effect of these similes is clearly ironic: The enthusiastic fans think they are participating in a sports event, whereas in actuality they are being duped into the role of passive consumers, not just of sports but also of food and drink.

In the face of this perversion, in which the human need to participate in something greater than the self is contradicted and frustrated, the potential unifying and involving force—the game itself—recedes into the distance, leaving each person trapped within his or her own experience. In this way, as the poem articulates it at the end of the seventh stanza, the poem becomes a kind of "orison," or prayer, for salvation from solipsism.

Reinforcing the way natural and religious symbols such as grass, holy wafers, and orisons integrate concrete images with abstract ideas, Collier also exploits the tension between the visual and the unseen. As the poem progresses, he allows visual elements to be transformed through dramatic, auditory analogies. For example, the poet's most notable use of simile occurs in the seventh stanza, where he utilizes a powerful, accelerating triple comparison between the wave and "quickening" molecules, then "cells dividing," and, finally, "herds stampeding." The increased intensity and movement of this sequence combine with its developing sound effects to culminate in the onset of the wave, which in this context becomes as natural and basic an occurrence as a wave crashing on the beach. Here in the poem, the action of the wave allows the subdued, static audience at the game to be released from passive viewing, which, as Collier himself comments, "changes nothing."

Themes and Meanings

As in his other works, in "The Wave," Collier subtly and cannily uses ordinary objects and events as a point of departure to reveal invisible undercurrents. These hidden forces act both to constrain and to facilitate the possibility of human release. For example, since the ritual of the game becomes more important than the game itself in this poem, crude commercialism appears to stand in the way of the audience's direct participation in and appreciation of baseball. Second, just as it is manipulated into consumerism so, initially at least, the audience seems to express freedom merely mechanically and physically, through merely raising its arms.

On the other hand, in that he deliberately places himself in the same role as that of the fans, that of an onlooker rather than a seer apart or alienated from the rest of humanity, presumably the poet himself participates along with the others in the wave induced by the exhilarated solders. Perhaps he even allies himself as poet with the power of their leadership, their "urgings" and their "sweat." Evoking the childhood games of Simon Says and Mother May I?, Collier may also sense that in some ways participating in the wave involves a return to childish games. Does it possibly also imply obedience to the authoritarianism of childhood? Is the possible complexity of Collier's response to both the soldiers themselves and the wave confirmed in his pinpointing of the ambiguous reaction of the birds, which, swooping under the dome, are both attracted and repelled by the arc lights?

The complexity of the whole poem, including Collier's relationship to his audience, is further developed through the subtlety of the comment he splices into his penultimate analogy between the human activity of the wave and the primitive stampeding of cattle. He terms it an "orison" answered by "unison." Collier seems to be saying that a prayer for union with others can be answered no matter how tawdry the atmosphere of the ballpark or how crudely mechanical the origin of the wave, which now becomes not just a matter of physical movement but also a means of human communication, as in the gesture of waving to another.

From the abundance of details that evoke the culture of the ballpark, from hot dogs to park organ, the reader can deduce a possible final reading of Collier's poem, one in which the wave becomes a celebration of human life, or, at least, of American life. Depending upon the reader's own interpretation of this poem, the soldiers' desire to keep the wave "going for as long as they can" comes to reflect the poet's (or the reader's) optimism or pessimism regarding American culture, or a position somewhere between these extremes.

Susan Tetlow Harrington

WAVE

Author: Gary Snyder (1930-   )
Type of poem: Meditation
First published: 1968; collected in *Regarding Wave*, 1969

The Poem

"Wave" is composed of twenty-four lines in roughly four sections. The poem considers the essence of energy in the universe: The title refers to energy as it is manifested through the objects and forces in nature, for example, in a wave on the ocean. The poem also contains a central image of woman as a primary source of energy or life force in the universe. Beyond that, "Wave" is a meditation on the wonder of spiritual energy as it flows through and manifests itself in the poet's own mind.

The poet begins by describing the various ways the effects of energy can be disclosed in the forms of natural objects such as clamshells, the wood grain of trees that have been cut in two by saws, and "sand-dunes, lava/ flow." As the poem continues, the poet seems to be seeking to understand the very source of all energy.

The second section begins with the lines, "Wave wife./ woman—wyfman," which are a reference to energy as mother or as female force, the sacred source of being in the universe. "Wyf" is an Anglo-Saxon word that is the root word for both wave and wife. Woman is described in the third line as "veiled; vibrating; vague." The words "veiled" and "vague" refer to her mysterious nature. "Vibrating" refers to the kinetic power of natural forces, which in the following line, set "sawtooth ranges pulsing."

Images of energy as manifested in the natural world continue. The poet enumerates: "great dunes rolling/ Each inch rippled, every grain a wave." It is as though the existence of each grain of sand were a confirmation of the creative energy that formed it and placed it in the rippled dune.

Gary Snyder continues in the poem to consider natural forces and their effects on objects in the world. The wind, a force with metaphorical even spiritual associations, blows through thick, thorned shrubbery, shaking the same branches, which at times, catch and trap the poet. The thickets described may refer to the tangle of thoughts in the poet's own mind.

In the final section, which is itself almost a poem within the poem, Snyder addresses the "radiating wyf" as a primal source of energy linking all of the images in the poem. The poem concludes with a prayerlike request for the primal energy of the universe (nature) to catch and "fling" the poet free to ride the unique waves of his own consciousness. As a result, the poet will be opened to the dance of the "things," ideas, and poems of his mind, and will merge with the energy of the universe.

Forms and Devices

"Wave" is written in free verse with no regular metrical pattern. Instead, the poem depends on shifts in cadence and concrete imagery for its effects. The poem is structured to seem unstructured. The first section begins with a stream of words and phrases, which via concrete images, delivers a flow of realizations about the nature of energy.

"Woman," "wyf," "wave," is the image that unites and gives a focal point for the manifestations of energy. "Wave" or "wyf," as radiating power and as the female principle, is both life-giver and unifier. The effects of energy can be seen in marble streaks, pine bark, and solidified lava. In fact, the essence of energy is itself invisible unless felt or manifested through the movement or transformation of matter. Thus these images give testament to the mysterious power of energy and serve to organize the poem.

The unexpected line breaks and the way the poem leaps about have the effect of arousing the reader's curiosity. There is no monotonous plodding verse form to slow one down. At times, "Wave" almost seems like an uncontrolled, stream-of-consciousness reverie. The line, "sometimes I get stuck in the thickets," reads like a casual off-stage remark, as if the poet were talking to himself.

Snyder's use of woman as the unifying metaphor in "Wave" affirms his devotion to the female as sacred life-giver. In fact, he dedicates the collection *Regarding Wave* to his wife, Masa. The energy-as-female principle is not only the woman-wife of the poem, but more deeply the origin and impetus of everything, including the poet's voice.

Themes and Meanings

A wave is a visible manifestation of energy or power in action. The wave that rolls in from the sea and crashes on the shore is energy in motion. Wind blowing across a wheat field and causing it to ripple and undulate is evidence of energy, though the wind itself is invisible. The surge of inspiration that overtakes a poet, a musician, or a dancer is also a manifestation of energy; but what actually is energy? In "Wave," Snyder contemplates the subject but gives no definite answers.

Though Snyder is not a scientist, his approach in "Wave" demonstrates his interest in physical science, specifically the subject of energy. Certainly, he has the perceptive eye of a scientist and the keen, analytical mind of a physicist. The way he describes the delicate striations on the surface of a clamshell and the veins on the back of his hand are proof enough. Though these images are immediate and true, Snyder is looking much deeper beneath such surfaces in an attempt to understand the nature of energy.

In a previous collection, *The Back Country* (1967), Snyder, through his poetry, paid homage to the value of the wilderness experience. His experience as a practicing Zen Buddhist and his knowledge of Native American myths and traditional beliefs in the interrelatedness of man and nature shaped his understanding of the wild territories.

This understanding was grounded in a sense of the interdependence and interrelatedness of all life. In "Wave," Snyder examines the phenomenon of energy not only as the elemental unifying force in nature, but also as the source and fountainhead of life, and thus consciousness—the ultimate mystery.

In seeking deeper penetration into the grainy essence of existence, Snyder wants to be open to the "radiating wyf" (or wave) that is his muse and the source of his poetic vision. In "Wave," the poet searches for spiritual understanding—without the restraints of institutionalized religion—by contemplating natural processes both externally, in nature, and internally, in the mind. By showing the connection between the outer physical manifestations of energy and the poet's muse, the poem points the way toward an understanding of the essence of being, a puzzle shared equally by the scientist, the clergyman, and the poet.

Francis Poole

WE ARE SEVEN

Author: William Wordsworth (1770-1850)
Type of poem: Ballad
First published: 1798, in *Lyrical Ballads*

The Poem

"We Are Seven," written in 1798, is a short poem of sixty-nine lines divided into seventeen stanzas. It relates the story of a narrator meeting an eight-year-old girl who tells him about her family. (According to William Wordsworth, the poem was suggested by a real child he had met near Goodrich Castle in Wales five years earlier.)

Stanza 1 asks a broad question that points to the theme of the poem: What can a lively child "know of death"? In stanzas 2 and 3, the narrator sets the scene. He is presumably walking in the country when he encounters an eight-year-old "cottage Girl," the kind of ordinary lower-class child he might have expected to meet there. He is struck ("made . . . glad") by her beauty, in particular by her thick curly hair and "very fair" (blue?) eyes, by her strange clothes ("she was wildly clad"), and in general by her rural "air." He pauses and, in order to make conversation with her, asks ordinary questions: How many sisters and brothers do you have? Where are they?

The girl gives him an extraordinary answer: How many siblings? "Seven in all." There are herself, two living in Conway (a seaport in Wales), two at sea, and two others who "in the church-yard lie." In short, of the seven, two are dead. She and her mother live in the churchyard cottage near the two dead children—a sister and a brother. Even though it is obvious to the narrator (and to the reader) that these two are dead, the girl tenaciously insists that "Seven boys and girls are we."

The narrator seems amused. He points out gently that the two who are buried in the churchyard are significantly different from her: "You run about" and live, whereas they simply lie. In sum, he concludes, "ye are only five." The child is obstinate and describes how she frequents the two graves near the cottage door. She knits and sews by the graves; she eats her supper there; she sings songs to the occupants of the graves. She tells the narrator how she had played with her sister and brother and describes the days when they were laid side by side in the churchyard.

What had first seemed a pleasant chat with a pretty child has turned into a contest of wills. "But they are dead; those two are dead!" cries the narrator, but he concludes that he is only "throwing [his] words away" when the girl willfully insists: "Nay, we are seven."

Forms and Devices

Wordsworth wrote most of this poem during the spring of 1798 while walking in a grove of trees near his rural home in Somerset. He composed the last five-line stanza first, beginning with the last line. After he had composed most of it, he recited it to his friend Samuel Taylor Coleridge and remarked that it needed an opening stanza.

Coleridge then improvised what is now stanza 1. (Coleridge's first line was "A little child, dear brother Jem," later changed to "Jim"; the first line was changed and shortened in 1815.)

Except for the last five lines, "We Are Seven" is written in standard ballad stanzas in which the lines are alternately eight and six syllables long and which usually rhyme *abab*. This is the stanza of many anonymous oral folk ballads, a kind of poetry that began to be written down, collected, and imitated in the eighteenth century, even though most major poems of that age employed heroic couplets. So when Wordsworth elected to write in the ballad form, he labeled his poem as different from those written during the age that preceded him.

Because "We Are Seven" is written by a single poet, it is a literary ballad, not a folk ballad. Nevertheless, it shares many characteristics with folk poetry: Ballads tell simple stories of uncomplicated characters with straightforward emotions; when they speak, they speak simply and often repetitiously. A ballad's rhythm is marked and fairly regular, for many ballads are meant to be sung. Not only is Wordsworth's little girl a representative of the rural lower class, but the form of this poem is also a literary version of the form that poetry coming from her class was thought to take.

In poems such as "We Are Seven," Wordsworth consciously presented to British readers a new kind of poetry. Its language was to be simpler than that of previous poetry, stripped of poetical terms and circumlocutions until it resembled what he termed in his Preface to *Lyrical Ballads* (1800) "the real language of men." In this poem, one can see how much he simplified. There is only one metaphor, and that is a conventional one ("throwing words away") employed by the narrator when he is most exasperated. The little girl personifies God, but this is hardly a figure of speech to her. The poem's syntax is marked by simple balanced phrases, pairs of words, and parallels. Although its language is somewhat general, it becomes more specific and more touching toward the end of the poem. The reader discovers then how very close the graves are to her cottage door, that she is by them when she eats her supper out of her porringer, that she and her brother would "run and slide." The poem then shifts from being rather matter-of-fact to deeper emotions: The narrator implies his exasperation while the reader responds to the little girl with pity. The last stanza, marked as conclusive by having the weight of an extra line, in fact seems not to conclude at all: Neither the narrator nor the child has begun to convince, let alone understand, the other.

Themes and Meanings

The poem may seem simple at first reading, even childish and laughable. It is true that Wordsworth has not availed himself of many of the resources of impressive poetry, but the dramatic confrontation of the narrator and the little girl is not merely a conversation at cross-purposes. The poet raises important questions to which several answers have been given.

What is one to make of this confrontation? Wordsworth himself gives an opening to an interpretation in the Preface. He says that "We Are Seven" shows "the perplexity and obscurity which in childhood attend our notion of death, or rather our utter inability to admit that notion." This passage has meant to many readers that one should sympathize with the girl because she is blind to the reality that her brother and sister are dead; one should pity her benignly for her childish ideas but reflect sadly that time will teach her the lesson that everyone must learn about death.

Wordsworth's Preface was intended, however, to ease the reception of his poems, not to engage the reading public in specific interpretations. In reality, the poet's (and the poem's) sympathies may have been profoundly with the girl. Late in his life he quoted part of "We Are Seven" to a friend and said that "Nothing was more difficult for me in childhood than to admit the notion of death as a state applicable to my own being." He went on to say that, unlike the little girl who displayed such vitality, his own difficulty in accepting death resulted from "a sense of the indomitableness of the spirit within me." It is not unreasonable, however, to see something of the young Wordsworth's indomitable spirit in the girl as well.

Her visions of the continued life of those who lie buried in churchyards and those who are associated with specific places are lifelong themes in Wordsworth's poetry. He translated and wrote epitaphs, and wrote a long essay on them; many of his finest passages have to do with the spirits of places; his last long poem, *The Excursion* (1814), evokes at great length how the lives of the dead linger on after their burial. Moreover, many readers have noted that Wordsworth often implies that children live closer to God than adults, who have been corrupted by society, especially urban society, and by rational educational schemes.

Even though the first interpretation is favored by many readers, the second may be more true to Wordsworth. The little girl possesses a truth about how her brother and sister live on, perhaps in a place, at least in her memory; the death of the body is not final. The older narrator, schooled in conventional and reasonable notions, is cut off from her vision.

George Soule

WE MET FOR THE LAST TIME

Author: Anna Akhmatova (Anna Andreyevna Gorenko, 1889-1966)
Type of poem: Lyric
First published: 1914, untitled, in *Chetki*; English translation collected in *The Complete Poems of Anna Akhmatova*, 1990

The Poem

Through twelve lines forming three stanzas, the speaker recalls a final meeting between herself and a man, perhaps a lover, someone with whom she had previously had other meetings, implied in the second line, "where we had always met." The place where the meeting took place, the embankment, is clearly recalled, and she remembers of what the man spoke: summer and the absurd idea of a woman being a poet. In her mind's eye, she can "still see" the palace and fortress, she can still imagine the air itself, "so miraculous." The friend, or lover, however, remains anonymous, a suggestion, a reference to summer, an attitude toward women as poets.

The poet remembers setting, mood, feeling, whereas the former acquaintance has faded into a memory of significant details, a voice in spring mentioning summer. The recollection creates an evocative scene in which the natural setting and architecture take on greater clarity than the companion himself, who all but disappears from the poem half way through. It is as if the speaker, hearing him ridicule women poets, turns away to the past, recalling the palace and fortress, symbols of imperial strength, historical continuity, and grandeur. The image of stately buildings diminishes the momentous "absurd." Whatever pain his ridicule may have caused is thus deflected. Then the poet shifts suddenly in the final stanza to the air, contrasting it with the grand buildings and suggesting her own wafting moods, once majestic then as insubstantial as the air.

As the poem advances, however, the poet's vision broadens. It rises from the embankment and the threatening river—the Neva—from the acquaintance and his insulting remark, passes through the pomp of regal power, and comes to God, the ultimate authority and giver of life-giving air, everything. The small talk about summer, the sexist remark of one no longer seen—perhaps because of his prejudice—the grand architecture, all are diminished by the "miraculous" gift of God, which is followed, in the concluding two lines, by the poem's ultimate revelation: In that moment of vision, seeing that the air is God's gift, the poet received another gift, another mad song. The poem rises to this liberating perception—that her poetic gift mingles with the air itself—which is the medium through which God sends the gift of poetic song.

Forms and Devices

"We Met for the Last Time" is a spare poem, lacking metaphor and the conventional decorations of the lyric, but its symbolic overtones are potent nevertheless. Without human characters described and set in motion, although the poem is about two people meeting in a park, the drama unfolds in other ways, through other "characters," the Neva, which, by threatening the city, represents a vaguely hostile force, not unlike the male acquaintance in the abstract sense. Nature, however, is not to be feared for long, for "summer" is mentioned, possibly as a mitigating presence, one that diminishes the threat of the river. The palace and fortress stand like sentinels, stern reminders of man's authority, dominant presences in a natural world of graceful beauty and delicate breezes. From heaven comes the messenger, air.

The movement of the poet through the poem suggests her shifting moods and the course her vision takes as it leaves the embankment, sees the palace and fortress, and discovers the air, transformed into song. It also suggests action in a poem that is but a static memory. The poem actually works like the song the poet says the situation presented by the poem has afforded her: It is set in words but, when sung, is transformed into life, motion, beauty, a moving vision, or a vision of moving things.

The language is simple in both the original and translated versions, and the stanzas in the original are rhymed (*abab, cdcd, efef*—the first and third lines of the last stanza contain slant rhymes). Rhyme would reinforce the poem's final statement, drawing attention to the artful decoration of song without spoiling the simplicity and naturalness of the poet's voice. The subtle grace of the lines is somewhat deceptive in that it makes a very artful and complicated poem appear natural and simple. A considerable amount of tension is created by what the poet does not say directly. One expects conventional expressions and reactions but gets irony and surprise. For example, the beginning lines suggest a mournful recollection of a departed lover, yet the poem by the second stanza is attentive to something else, a critical remark made by a male acquaintance. The final stanza shifts further, from the negative middle to a perception that suggests a consummation. The poem's "action" is created by these shifts in the poet's remembrance—it moves, rather than anything or anyone in the poem— and as it moves, it seems to rise from the embankment, to the stately architecture, and toward the higher realm, where "mad songs" are created, in the "miraculous" air, with God.

As the poet's memory spans the scene from a future time, moving from place to palace to epiphany, so does the poet's attitude shift. The man's casual remarks about the summer are recalled before the pivotal remark about the absurdity of her poetic commitment, a remark delivered without direct comment and left to echo through the rest of the poem. One might think the poet is too hurt to comment, too taken aback; perhaps she is too imperial and dignified, like the buildings of which she is reminded; or she knows the understated report of the remark is condemnation enough. In the final stanza, however, the poet has taken flight from the embankment, the man, the remark, their relationship perhaps. Deeply offended by the remark, she withdraws into an almost religious stoicism, leaving the reader with an ambivalent reference to "mad songs." The conventional regret of lost love has been replaced by a much deeper pain, that of ridicule, and the poet suggests that her mad songs have come from men like the one who cannot see the poetry, only the woman.

Themes and Meanings

The poem weaves among suggestions of romantic love, separation, and bittersweet remembrance while doing something else, perhaps something very dangerous in times of war and social upheaval. It dares to allude to czarist Russia, to the woman's role in modern Russia (in 1914), and to religion in ways perhaps unflattering to temporal authority, critical of prejudice against women poets, and supportive of a power above man and his rulers. It develops three relationships at once: between the poet and her male acquaintance, between the poet and the setting itself, and between the poet as a Russian citizen and the political power structure. Much more than a graceful lyric recollecting a parting by two people, the poem constitutes a polemic, and its essential nature is ironic suggestion.

"We Met for the Last Time" may be read as a parable in which the city, St. Petersburg, is threatened by some kind of flood. Perhaps nature is angered by the way humans are behaving themselves. Part of the problem seems to be prevailing prejudice against women poets, expressed by the man. Rigid authority hovers in the background in the form of a czar's palace and a fortress. The beginning of the third stanza hints that the Russian people, symbolized by the two friends, do not even own the air they breathe. The air is "like" a gift from God, not actually a gift. Perhaps the powers that be allow them to breathe it. In such social and political conditions as these, the poet can only sing "mad songs."

The poem is also about the locale, the park, the buildings, and the nature in which God's generosity is felt. God's grandeur is placed above that of czars and prejudiced men. It celebrates, not the temporal powers but the heavenly ruler. Only a cursory understanding of the conditions in which Anna Akhmatova lived and wrote is necessary for one to sense political overtones in the poem. Her poetry was frequently denied publication and heavily censored when its publication was permitted, and when she received a standing ovation in Moscow at a poetry reading, she feared the authorities would think of her as a political threat. Meeting the American poet Robert Frost reminded her of her own inability to write and publish freely. A deceptively simple lyric speaks of frightened people, it records social prejudice, it alludes to symbols of czarist rule in a way that suggests subordination to the God of religious faith, and it appears to assert that in such circumstances, poets sing mad songs. Love lost does not drive the poet to make a romantic gesture, bemoan her fate, or cry out in self-pity. This poet looks about herself, feels a kinship with the "mad" Neva, hears a former acquaintance ridicule her very essence, glimpses the pompous forms of power, realizes that even the air is not theirs, and recognizes that only in making mad songs can the spirit find release.

Bernard E. Morris

WE MUST LOOK AT THE HAREBELL

Author: Hugh MacDiarmid (Christopher Murray Grieve, 1892-1978)
Type of poem: Lyric
First published: 1955, in *In Memoriam James Joyce: From a Vision of World Language*

The Poem

Hugh MacDiarmid's "We Must Look at the Harebell," a forty-one-line free-verse lyric, makes a curious circle. The opening sentence, "We must look at the harebell as if/ We had never seen it before," directs attention to a particular flower. The poem ends with the general statement that "The universal is the particular." The opening sentence is not as specific as it appears, calling attention to a species rather than a particular flower. Meanwhile, the final sentence asserts the particularity of the universal. The poem thus manages to move from particular to general and general to particular at the same time.

Although MacDiarmid at first points to a specific type of flower, the harebell, he veers off to discuss in parenthesis various types of sheep and, after the parenthesis, various other kinds of flowers: white bedstraw, pinguicula, bog-asphodel, sundew, parsley fern, and Osmunda Regalis (Regal Fern). After the first sentence in the poem, the harebell is never mentioned again. MacDiarmid wants to give a sense of the abundance and beauty in universal nature represented by sheep and flowers one might find in the Scottish landscape. He seems less interested in nature, "flowers, plants, birds and all the rest," than in words and ideas.

The poem is filled with seemingly miscellaneous details to back up or illustrate the assertions in the first eight lines of the poem. Those assertions are: Pay attention to the harebell; memory offers "an accumulation of satisfaction" and therefore an apparent escape from change; "change is in itself a recreation," both a relaxation and a re-creation, and looking at the harebell would be a change; and "An ecological change is recreative," which moves toward the particular. Yet rather than next giving an example of a particular ecological change, MacDiarmid inserts a parenthesis (lines 8-21), followed by a more general statement, "Everything is different, everything changes."

The long parenthesis is not a closer look at the harebell but a disquisition on sheep, who are "different/ And of new importance." The point of the digression seems to be that even the most ordinary things, such as sheep in Scotland, "change" when you take the time to look at them. MacDiarmid then mentions several types of sheep: the Herdwick, the Hampshire Down, the Lincoln-Longwool, the Southdown, "and between them thirty other breeds." The punchline of the parenthesis is the caustic remark that in England, "the men, and women too,/ Are almost as interesting as the sheep." MacDiarmid, an ardent Scottish nationalist, thus takes a jab at the enemy.

The last part of the poem returns to flowers, enumerating and briefly describing several kinds of flowers and ferns. The penultimate line of the poem offers an enthusiastic summing up to reassert that the sheep and flowers he has described exemplify change. By generalizing that "The universal is the particular," the last line reminds readers of the particular flower with which the poem began.

Forms and Devices

"We Must Look at the Harebell" is extracted from the verse essay "The Snares of Varuna," which is part of the extended essay and poetic sequence *In Memoriam James Joyce*, which is in turn part of an uncompleted four-volume project under the working title *A Vision of World Language*. "The Snares of Varuna" refers to the Hindu scripture *Rigveda* (c. 1500-1000 B.C.E.; Eng. trans., 1896-1897), where it is stated that the snares of the deity King Varuna catch one who tells a lie but let the honest person pass. Straightforward truth-telling is MacDiarmid's overarching goal. The method Mac-Diarmid uses in "We Must Look at the Harebell" is consistent with the method of the larger work, but the excerpted section stands alone effectively as a lyric poem.

"We Must Look at the Harebell" is written in fluent, conversational free verse. The vocabulary of the poem is relatively ordinary English. The meanings of unusual words—names of sheep and flowers for the most part—can be deduced from the context. MacDiarmid's style seeks to be as transparent as possible. After the first sentence, the beginning and ending of the poem rely on abstract language, such as "Remembrance gives an accumulation of satisfaction." The abstractions are counterpoised by concrete details about sheep and flowers.

Lines in "We Must Look at the Harebell" break in terms of syntax rather than rhyme or meter. When MacDiarmid uses poetic effects such as alliteration, as in "The Lincoln-Longwool, the biggest breed in England," the effect seems incidental and artless, which is to say "natural." The form of the poem seems less important to MacDiarmid than the ideas the poem develops.

MacDiarmid suggests the universal by mentioning particulars, though they are particulars of type rather than individual examples. He does not describe an individual example of a harebell in sensory detail. In fact, from the poem, all the reader knows of the flower is its name. Similarly, for all but botanists, "a pinguicula" seems to hide the flower in its Latin name, but MacDiarmid goes on to describe the "purple-blue flower" in more detail, mentioning "its straight and slender stem," much more description than he ever gives of the harebell, though that description might equally well describe the harebell, whose bluebell-shaped flowers hang from thin stalks. The nature in the poem is more from books than from experience: "It is pleasant to find the books/ Describing" the regal fern as "very local."

"We Must Look at the Harebell" can be read as a meditation on language and representation. The long middle part of "We Must Look at the Harebell" is an abstracted walk in nature, but a domesticated nature populated with wool-producing sheep as well as wildflowers. The sheep and flowers in the poem are subtly metaphorical, like the words from numerous languages *In Memoriam James Joyce* is peppered with, some natural and some bred by humans.

Themes and Meanings

To judge from the opening sentence, the theme of "We Must Look at the Harebell" is a version of the biblical line "Consider the lilies of the field. They toil not, neither do they spin." As a communist, MacDiarmid was committed to the idea of freeing workers from the drudgery of labor for capitalist factory owners. Harebells or lilies, which "toil not," offer an alternative to the alienation of labor in freedom and the "recreation" that comes from reimmersing oneself in ever-changing nature.

"We Must Look at the Harebell" represents a shift in tone from what comes before it in "The Snares of Varuna" and seems to suggest the results of freedom from the effects of capitalism and English domination. If the tone of the poem is taken to be optimistic (with the exception of the one caustic line about the English sheep being more interesting than English people), MacDiarmid seems to be calling for a recognition of the healing powers of nature. In fact, MacDiarmid is more interested in people than in sheep.

The whole collection in which "We Must Look at the Harebell" appears is a meditation on language, praising what James Joyce accomplished with his linguistic experiments in *Ulysses* (1922) and *Finnegans Wake* (1939), but also striking out in a different direction to create a work on the scale of Joyce's masterpieces. Like Joyce, who was an Irishman living in exile in Europe, MacDiarmid saw himself as a member of a culture at odds with the dominant English culture of the British Isles. MacDiarmid's uncompleted four-volume magnum opus, *A Vision of World Language*, is an exposition of the possibilities of what is true of language in general and of the particular languages MacDiarmid had access to through his voluminous reading.

By examining particular details, poets often express universal truths. At first glance, MacDiarmid's assertion that "The universal is the particular" seems more problematic. If one starts with "the universal," the whole is so general that one cannot possibly see particulars. However, on second glance, if one can find the universal in the particular, one must also be able to find the particular in the universal. Indeed, in both the vast sweep of *In Memoriam James Joyce* in general and in "We Must Look at the Harebell" in particular, MacDiarmid attempts the linguistic magic trick of focusing on particulars without losing sight of the whole. Near the end of *In Memoriam James Joyce* he says, "The supreme reality is visible to the mind *alone*," a reflection of the fact that the mind can hold general and specific, universal and particular at the same time: "An intricately-cut gem-stone of myriad facets/ That is yet, miraculously, a whole."

The voice in MacDiarmid's poems can be by turns brilliant and maddening. Sometimes *In Memoriam James Joyce* seems little more than loosely stitched-together collection of paraphrases and quotations from MacDiarmid's astonishingly vast reading—a deluge of erudition, including snippets from many languages, and footnotes that reveal even more erudition. In the midst of all this verbiage, passages and even whole poems of great beauty appear. "We Must Look at the Harebell" is one of these, a microcosm of the larger work, but with the focus and control the larger work sometimes lacks.

Thomas Lisk

WE SHALL MEET AGAIN IN PETERSBURG

Author: Osip Mandelstam (1891-1938)
Type of poem: Lyric
First published: 1922, as "V Peterburge my soidiomsia snova," in *Tristia*; English
translation collected in *Tristia*, 1973

The Poem

   Osip Mandelstam wrote "We Shall Meet Again in Petersburg" in 1920 and published it in his collection *Tristia* in 1922. In the title, the persona addresses unnamed friends, vowing to meet them again in Petersburg, a former capital of Russia. (Originally Saint Petersburg, the city was renamed Petrograd during World War I, Leningrad after Lenin's death, and Saint Petersburg again in the 1990's; popularly, it has always been known as Petersburg.) Mandelstam spent the best years of his youth in Petersburg, publishing his first poems there and making several close friends among the poets, primarily the Acmeists; it is these poets Mandelstam addresses as "we." During the Bolshevik revolution, Mandelstam was forced to lead a turbulent life, often changing his abode but returning to Petersburg whenever he could. After the revolution had uprooted thousands of people, the poet was confident that he and his fellow Acmeists would renew their friendship in Petersburg. "We Shall Meet Again in Petersburg" is his nostalgic anticipation of that meeting.
   The poet envisions his joy at seeing his fellow poets again, but the meeting acquires the sense of a mission. It is as though they had buried their sun there and they will now do what they had always wanted: utter for the first time their "blessed and meaningless word" so that the "black velvet of the Soviet night" and the resulting emptiness will not stop the women from singing or the everlasting flowers from blooming. They will not be deterred by the oppressive mood of the capital, "arched like a wild cat," by the ubiquitous police patrols, or by an angry car echoing frighteningly through the desolate night. The poet does not need a pass, and he is not afraid of the sentries. Instead, he will courageously pray in the Soviet night for the sake of that "blessed and meaningless word."
   The poet further imagines how the ugliness of the present is overcome by a theater performance during which beautiful female voices and Aphrodite's roses inspire the art lovers, so that they warm themselves by a bonfire (the flames of the revolution) instead of being consumed by it. In such bliss, ages will pass and "the beloved hands of blessed women will gather the light ashes" of the sun they had buried in Petersburg. Amid the sweet-sounding choirs of Orpheus, the radiant dark eyes of the singers, and programs fluttering down from the gallery like doves, the poet once again expresses his defiance in defense of more exalted things in life. He ends his poem by warning the powers of darkness that they will not succeed with their sinister designs. They may extinguish the candles, but they cannot stop "the blessed women" from singing. The unshakable truth is that those dark forces are incapable of seeing "the night sun" and are therefore destined for ultimate defeat.

Forms and Devices

"We Shall Meet Again in Petersburg" is written in one of Mandelstam's favorite forms, the eight-line stanza (*vosmistishye*). The poem has four stanzas of varying meters rhymed *ababcdcd*. Images and metaphors are the main vehicles of Mandelstam's poetic craft, as seen in his other poems as well. From among his most striking images, a buried sun in line 2 and the night sun in the last line both refer to the great Russian poet Alexander Pushkin. The repeated image of "blessed women" engaged in artistic performances with their kindred eyes and rounded shoulders adds an almost religious quality to the poem. Immortal flowers and Aphrodite's roses represent love and beauty expressed through arts. The poet uses all these images to emphasize the beautiful, harmonious, and healing power of the arts.

These positive images are contrasted to the negative ones culled from everyday reality. An arched cat expresses anger and the unfriendliness of life in Petersburg during the revolution. A ubiquitous patrol stands on the bridge as if inhibiting the passage from one part of the town to another, thus underscoring the loss of freedom. An angry car speeds through the gloomy night and cries like a cuckoo in eerie silence, a sign either of terror or of mourning. The "black velvet of the Soviet night" not only expresses the dark, oppressive atmosphere of Petersburg in 1920 but also symbolizes the life-threatening effects of the revolution, recalling an executioner's block draped in velvet. The bonfire itself represents the flames of the revolution; the opponents of the Bolsheviks use it, ironically, to warm themselves despite their opposition, as if to say that the arts conquer all evil. Finally, the image of the candles that the dark forces may extinguish symbolizes life and the enlightenment of the arts threatened by "the black velvet of the world's emptiness."

These powerful images are reinforced by equally striking metaphors. The metaphor of the buried sun representing Pushkin has already been mentioned. Toward the end of the poem, the "blessed women" are gathering the ashes in an almost religious ritual, as befits the burial of the great poet. Women are playing the role of beauty enhancers and peacemakers. Mandelstam extends that metaphor by imagining a theater performance in the twilight of civilization brought on by the revolution. The theater itself, as Steven Broyde remarks in his *Osip Mandel'stam and His Age* (1975), separates with its curtain the world of art and beauty from the real world that has turned ugly. The theater motif is frequent in Mandelstam's poetry, but he uses it in "We Shall Meet Again in Petersburg" to counteract the destructive force of the revolution. Additional metaphors are to be found in the use of Aphrodite as a goddess of love and beauty, who stands for the beauty of the arts pining against the world of drab reality and cruelty. Orpheus is also used as a metaphor for an archetypal poet, specifically for Russian poets endangered and threatened with oblivion.

Themes and Meanings

The basic theme of "We Shall Meet Again in Petersburg" is the mortal clash between two worlds: the world of beauty and artistic freedom and the world of everyday reality and coercion. The poet's firm declaration at the outset that "we shall meet again" implies certain disruption. Mandelstam summons his fellow poets, presumably Nikolay Gumilyov and Anna Akhmatova, with whom he had formed, at the beginning of the twentieth century, the powerful poetic movement known as Acmeism. Being apolitical and nonutilitarian in their poetic creed and devoting all their attention to the purely artistic aspects of poetry, they were branded by the revolutionaries as being antisocial and inimical to the revolution. (Gumilyov was executed during the revolution and Mandelstam himself was executed twenty years later.) The revolutionary chaos disrupted these poets in their favorite activity and, in effect, rendered them useless. Despite all this, Mandelstam promises his fellow poets that they shall meet again and speak "the blessed and meaningless word"—a reference to the unfounded pillorying of their poetry on the part of the Bolsheviks, who advocated engaged, useful, tendentious, and politically oriented poetry.

Mandelstam characterizes the reunion in the poem as a solemn burial of their favorite "sun" (Pushkin), who he considered to be their teacher and poetic God, since Pushkin was also wronged by the society (he was killed in a senseless duel that should have been prevented) and was buried in Saint Petersburg on a winter day similar to the one depicted in the poem. However, the invocation of Pushkin's name is not limited to him individually; it applies to the entire Russian cultural heritage, which, to be sure, is often personified best through Pushkin. By identifying himself and his fellow Acmeists with the great Russian poet, Mandelstam does not so much intend a comparison with Pushkin as he does an avowal of their alliance with true artistic creators and against the destroyers of art such as the Bolsheviks. Mandelstam uses the theater performance not only to glorify the intrinsic value of the arts but also to contrast them with the destructive force of those who are either indifferent or inimical to them or want to use them for their own purposes.

The strongest statement in the poem is contained in Mandelstam's determination to meet again with his fellow poets despite all the dangers and obstacles. Considering how difficult it was for the Acmeists (as well as for other poets not sympathizing with the Bolsheviks) to exist in the midst of revolutionary turmoil, let alone write poetry according to their own creed, Mandelstam's defiance and his nostalgic belief in something that seems to have vanished forever are courageous indeed. By defying the revolutionaries and the prevailing spirit of the time and by declaring that the poets shall meet again, he is saying prophetically that artistic beauty will triumph over the forces of the "velvet night," thus ending the poem on a highly optimistic note.

Vasa D. Mihailovich

WE WEAR THE MASK

Author: Paul Laurence Dunbar (1872-1906)
Type of poem: Verse essay
First published: 1896, in *Lyrics of Lowly Life*

The Poem

Paul Laurence Dunbar's "We Wear the Mask" combines salient features of verse essay and poetic meditation as it examines the need for a special kind of social dissembling in the world in which the author lived at the end of the nineteenth century. The poem presents readers with a speaker who speaks in first-person plural, as "we" and never simply "I." This clearly indicates that the speaker should be regarded as representing a particular or special segment of society. The opening stanza of the poem indicates that the group represented by the speaker pays a "debt" to "human guile" by wearing a "mask that grins and lies." This does not provide any indication that the speaker is not simply speaking for all human beings who have at some time engaged in pretending to be happy when they really are sad.

However, in the second stanza, the idea that the speaker is representing a particular segment of society becomes clearer when the poem indicates that "the world" need not be aware of the true feelings of the sufferers. Indeed, the speaker suggests that the world should only be allowed to "see us, while/ We wear the mask." This suggests something beyond merely dissembling for the sake of duplicity or dishonesty.

This mask that "grins and lies" is hiding the existence of excruciating misery and suffering. The speaker says, "We smile, but, O great Christ, our cries/ To thee from tortured souls arise." There can be no doubt that these people are enduring overwhelming hardships. There is also no doubt that they are determined not to let "the world" know about the true nature of their feelings. This sets up an ironic emotional contrast between what the people are experiencing and what others are witnessing while observing these people.

The speaker says, "We sing, but oh the clay is vile/ Beneath our feet, and long the mile." This brings to mind the concept of pretending to be happy when one is sad or the practice of whistling a happy tune to conceal one's fears. Yet, the image of these "tortured souls" slogging through long, weary miles of vile clay presents a picture of people enduring hardships far beyond anything that might be induced by ordinary fear or sadness.

The poem closes with a repetition of a sentiment stated earlier: "But let the world dream otherwise,/ We wear the mask!" The people show a dogged determination to keep the true nature of their sufferings to themselves and to present to others an outward show of happiness and lack of care. Surely, such insistence on deception must be motivated by powerful feelings resulting from terrifying experiences. Such were the experiences of many people enslaved in the United States before the birth of this poet.

Forms and Devices

Paul Dunbar's "We Wear the Mask" is sometimes referred to as a "muted protest" poem. It is frequently discussed in connection with another poem of his, entitled "Sympathy." Any protest in "We Wear the Mask" is vaguely implied and never openly stated. Instead, the poem informs readers that what they might see and hear might not be the whole truth, or even an accurate partial truth, about a group of humans who might appear on the surface to be quite simple and totally lacking in any complexity of emotion or thought patterns.

The thematic statement "We wear the mask" begins the opening line of this fifteen-line poem. It is repeated as a refrain at the ends of both the second and third stanzas. The final time, it is followed by an exclamation point, which emphasizes the essential importance of this idea. Thus, the reader is being told to keep this masking practice in mind while reading the poem and while attempting to evaluate an outwardly simplistic group of people.

Dunbar makes use of only two rhyme sounds in this solemn meditation. While the word "subtleties" at the end of stanza 1 does not actually rhyme with "lies" and "eyes," it provides an example of eye rhyme. That is to say, it looks as if it could rhyme with those other words. The poet's use of "myriad" and "subtleties" together might send younger readers scurrying for the dictionary. At the same time, it sends to readers already familiar with Dunbar as a writer of poetry in so-called "Negro dialect" the message that this poet can be effective in Standard English and can use "mouth" as a verb without seeming pretentious.

Dunbar's reputation as a dialect poet was not without some justification. Although he wrote in many different dialects, his poems in plantation dialect were particularly popular. Most readers and listeners tended to miss the serious messages in the dialect pieces, concentrating more on how things were said than on what was actually being said. Therefore, Dunbar wrote the majority of his poetry in Standard English. The diction and style employed in "We Wear the Mask" never stray from deadly serious and consistently solemn. Readers are constantly reminded to look beyond the surface if they would like to get at the truth and not be satisfied with stereotypes.

The poet himself had to battle against stereotypes in his life as a professional writer as well as in living as a black man in a country that did not accord much merit to black people. In poems such as this one, he could give literary expression to thoughts and feelings which some readers might have considered inappropriate for such a person as Dunbar. The poet knew not to push the subject-matter boundaries so far as to prevent his writings from being published, but he also felt an obligation to give a voice to the ideals and aspirations of a people who had been denied an effective voice for so long.

Themes and Meanings

Dunbar was born in Ohio, a "free" state, after the conclusion of the American Civil War. Thus, he was never legally enslaved; however, both his parents had been. The young poet heard plenty of information about the lives of enslaved people from his parents and others who had lived through slavery. Many of his poems deal directly with such experiences. This particular poem deals more specifically with continuing racism, which persisted in overt forms long after the abolition of legal slavery. The author himself endured it while attempting to gain employment befitting his background as president of his high school senior class, editor of the school paper, and a member of the literary society. Some would-be employers told him frankly that his race was the only reason they would not hire him. Therefore, he worked as an elevator boy and wrote poems and stories when he found the time. He learned the value of smiling politely and not doing or saying anything that might displease people who could make his life even more miserable than it already was.

This routine of getting along by pretending to go along provides the thematic basis of "We Wear the Mask." This is not simply dissembling; it is a social survival skill that African Americans developed to avoid drawing unfavorable attention to themselves. A smiling person was presumed to be contented; a singing person was deemed happy. Poet Dunbar knew that a caged bird did not sing because it was happy or free, but rather because it longed to be free, as poet Maya Angelou would later write. The singing of the people in stanza 3 of this poem is obviously a prayerful plea rather than evidence of jubilation. Other African American authors who have written about the singing of oppressed people include Frederick Douglass, W. E. B. Du Bois, and Countée Cullen. This singing is part of the art of masking for survival on the part of oppressed people in a hostile societal climate.

All readers of Dunbar's poem may not have experienced the necessity of masking for social survival, but all have probably felt a need to put on a happy face while not feeling happy at all. Thus, while the poem relates to specific groups in American society and history, it transcends particular times, places, and persons, reaching out and including all segments of society and human history. In this poem, as in most of his poetry, Dunbar does not use specific racial or ethnic labels. Still, readers familiar with the poet's life and experiences should have no difficulty determining who the "we" and "they" are in the poem. The poem is specific and particularized in that way, and yet its appeals are ultimately universal, as is the case with so much of Dunbar's poetry.

William Carroll

THE WEARY BLUES

Author: Langston Hughes (1902-1967)
Type of poem: Lyric
First published: 1923; collected in *The Weary Blues*, 1926

The Poem

"The Weary Blues" is a lyric poem with two voices. The central narrative voice describes an African American (or Negro, in this 1923 poem), in Harlem, New York, who is observed singing and playing a blues number. The poem provides a sample of the blues as well as an observation of the blues tradition from an outside source. As the title of the poem indicates, and the narrator suggests (with "droning" and "drowsy"), the musician is literally weary; the setting is late at night. Although the singer is weary, as his physical action, "a lazy sway," implies, he has enough stamina to sing "far into the night." The tone of both the narrator and the singer, with his "melancholy tone" and his playing that comes "from a black man's soul," indicates depression or sadness. Blues singers themselves identify melancholy and misery as the major themes of the blues. The blues, however, serves as more than a method of complaint: The very act of writing or singing the blues provides an antidote to the pain the songs express.

As the poem progresses, the narrator describes the singer/player expressing his loneliness, displeasure, and uncertainty about his present and future. It is in his singing that his inner self, his melancholy "soul," is revealed. In singing the blues, the Harlem man transforms or releases his pent-up emotional burden into musical expression. He receives solace after his trials and tribulations from singing his secular song, much as others have from singing religious songs such as spirituals.

The narrator describes the musician's emotional condition as he performs; it takes a downward direction from producing a "mellow croon" to making "that old piano moan." Balancing the downward movement of the musician's "sad raggy tune," however, is his ability to make "that poor piano moan with melody." He finally makes the piano become his soul mate: "that old piano moan[s]" just as he is doing. The lamentation is turned into a cathartic release: To sing and play the blues is to escape the blues. This link between the instrument and the musician is comparable to the link between the narrator of the poem and the musician.

The piano player's psychological state parallels the sound he produces on the piano. He is moaning or lamenting his existence: "I ain't happy no mo'." He wishes that he "had died." Significantly, his statement is of a previous condition—he does not say that he wants to die. Such an ambiguous ending to his lament suggests a continued resilience as he turns his despair into song instead of suicide. This ability to overcome his emotional circumstances parallels his ability to sing and play while sitting on a "rickety stool" with an old piano in front of him. Despite his age and weariness, the singer/player has momentarily put his "troubles on the shelf."

The poem's descriptive and interpretive voice ("I heard that Negro sing, that old piano moan—") is that of an observer who makes little attempt to explain, intellectually, the causes of the piano player's condition. Rather, he or she describes the events impressionistically, as one would any musical concert. It is through this voice that the significance of the blues and the ambiguity of its meaning are projected. As Hughes writes in "Evenin' Air Blues" (1927):

> But if you was to ask me
> How de blues they come to be,
> Says if you was to ask me
> How de blues they come to be—
> You wouldn't need to ask me:
> Just look at me and see!

As the persona describes the scene and the "syncopated tune," he or she provides images of instability or precariousness, such as "swaying," "rocking," and "rickety stool"; inversion, such as "ebony hands on each ivory key" and "dull pallor of an old gas light"; and ambiguity: "He slept like a rock or a man that's dead." The precarious scene as described is a reversal of traditional imagery of whiteness (light) being superior to blackness (dark). The setting takes place at night rather than during the day, significantly continuing until "The stars went out and so did the moon." The so-called raggy tune is regarded as "Sweet Blues!" suggestive of the narrator's attitude toward the music, musician, and topic. The description of playing—the ebony hands (black) over the ivory keys (white)—further implies inversion, just as the singer sleeps during the day rather than during the night.

Although the mood of "The Weary Blues" is one of resignation, as sung by the singer, the persona's narrative extends it to one of uncertainty: "He slept like a rock or a man that's dead." Implied in the equivocal statement is the question of whether the singer, with "the Weary Blues echo[ing] through his head," has resolved his melancholy and is able to sleep soundly, "like a rock," or is sleeping like a man whose spirit is dead. The narrator's description and commentary, like the blues, do not provide a resolution. Thus, singing and playing "The Weary Blues" can be seen as a means of either revitalizing oneself or resigning oneself to one's condition.

Forms and Devices

The poem utilizes the traditional musical structure of the blues and incorporates actual blues lyrics. In "Note on the Blues" (1927), Hughes states that "the *Blues*, unlike the *Spirituals*, have a strict poetic pattern: one long line repeated and a third line to rhyme with the first two. Sometimes the second line in repetition is slightly changed and sometimes, but very seldom, it is omitted." The repeated line adds emphasis to the intensity of a thought or feeling:

> "I got the Weary Blues
> And I can't be satisfied.

> Got the Weary Blues
> And can't be satisfied—
> I ain't happy no mo'
> And I wish that I had died."

In most blues lyrics and blues poems, the last word rhymes (or off-rhymes) with the last word of the first line, as "self" and "shelf" do. Rhyme is determined by the particular speech patterns of the singer or local community. Since this is a syncopated tune and poem, there is a shift in the regular meter, from iambic to trochaic. There also is a shortening of words ("mo'"), as well as the dropping of sounds or syllables from the middle of a word. Like singing the blues, in which a musician uses gesture and intonation to convey a particular impression, the formal poetic structure of this poem's rhythm is best achieved by reading the poem aloud.

The language used by the narrative voice and the language of the blues present a formal pattern of contrast. The former is primarily educated and in standard American English. The latter, with negatives such as "ain't got nobody" and nonstandard pronunciation and sound ("I's gwine to quit ma frownin'"), reflects the urban, uneducated, working-class person. This contrast in language aids in the development of the themes, since the blues originally was regarded as a lowly art form, not suitable poetic material.

The interjection of exclamatory phrases such as "O Blues!" and "Sweet Blues!" is used to indicate the narrator's acceptance of the art form and to emphasize that the poem is not merely about the blues singer but also about the singing of the blues as a means of overcoming the blues. Such exclamations in the blues, having evolved from "Negro" spirituals, also establish a literal musical link to the African American (and American) musical tradition.

Themes and Meanings

The combining of formal and traditional poetic devices with the idiomatic blues lyrics of "common" folk is suggestive of the fusion of sound and sense the poem achieves—high art with low art. It also is a fusion of the oral and written traditions. "The Weary Blues" is intended to be read aloud, as any musical composition is intended to be performed. In order to understand it, one must react to it emotionally as well as understand the contrasting movements that enhance its contrast of images and meaning.

The central theme of "The Weary Blues" concerns the resilience of the archetypal "common" person who has times of despair or despondency. Music serves as a means of relieving pain or anxiety. The poem transcends the limitations of race, as all people have used music and poetry as a means of getting through bad times. The cause of the blues singer's sense of isolation, loneliness, pain, and trouble is deliberately vague. His inability to identify the exact cause of his trials and tribulations, or the narrator's unwillingness to speculate upon it, enhances the universality of those feelings. The unspoken but evident complexity of the interrelationship between the player and his piano and the narrator and the musician corresponds to the complexity and interrelatedness of musical and poetic traditions. The poem, in its unconventional thematic and formal structure, advocates an equal acceptance of the two.

Norris B. Clark

WHAT THE DOCTOR SAID

Author: Raymond Carver (1938-1988)
Type of poem: Meditation
First published: 1989, in *A New Path to the Waterfall*

The Poem

In "What the Doctor Said," the speaker is recalling the most traumatic experience of his life. His doctor tells him he has terminal lung cancer. The fact that it is inoperable is indicated by the doctor's statement that he quit after counting "thirty-two of them." Twice the doctor refers to "them" as if avoiding calling "them" what they really are: malignant tumors. He does not suggest any treatment such as radiation or chemotherapy, nor does he suggest, as doctors often do, that his patient seek a second opinion. The doctor is trying to be kind but wants to make it clear that there is no hope for a cure. Both doctor and patient feel awkward, and the speaker is more aware of the doctor's feelings than his own. He will have plenty of time to experience his own complex feelings when he is alone with the grim, inescapable fact that he is very gently being handed his death sentence. The doctor quite understandably asks the patient if he is a religious man, presumably hoping he has some faith in a higher power that will give him consolation. This question, however, only makes the patient's grim fate more certain because it is as if the doctor is saying, "There is nothing medical science can do for you; you had better prepare to meet your maker."

The poem ends with a very puzzling statement. The speaker seems almost grateful that the doctor has just given him "something no one else on earth" has ever given him. The speaker deliberately terminates the interview by jumping up and shaking hands with the doctor. Realizing that there is no more to be said or done in that claustrophobic office, he wants to get away. The awkwardness of the interview is underscored by the fact that the speaker recalls that he may have even thanked the doctor—although under the circumstances it would be nearly as inappropriate to do so as for a prisoner to thank the judge who has just sentenced him to be executed. The reader can relate to the patient because it is force of habit to say something such as "Thank you, Doctor" at the conclusion of an office visit. The speaker is obviously experiencing a wild mixture of feelings. What is so strange is that these mixed feelings seem to include gratitude and relief. He regards the doctor's fatal pronouncement as a gift, "something no one else on earth had ever given [him]." The reader is left wondering how such a diagnosis could have any mitigating overtones. It would seem that the speaker sees some ray of hope when the doctor alludes to religion and love of nature. Apparently the speaker feels that although he has only a short time to live, he may still be able to achieve spiritual enlightenment.

Forms and Devices

"What the Doctor Said," a poem of only twenty-three lines, is typical of a popular school of modern poetry. Its members have abandoned all traditional poetic devices, including rhyme, meter, and "poetic diction," and write in a simple, straightforward, conversational manner. The poem is also completely lacking in punctuation. Raymond Carver has even departed from the convention of capitalizing the first letter in each line. There are no quotation marks around the words spoken by the doctor or patient, and there is no question mark at the end of the sentence in which the doctor asks if the speaker is a religious man who prays for spiritual guidance. There is not even a period at the end of the last line. The elimination of conventional punctuation marks makes "What the Doctor Said" seem like a stream-of-consciousness narrative and makes readers feel as if they are eavesdropping on very private thoughts and feelings. A longer example of this kind of interior monologue can be found in the last chapter of James Joyce's famous novel *Ulysses* (1922), often called "Molly Bloom's Soliloquy," which consists of one sentence running for forty-five pages without a single punctuation mark.

It is especially noteworthy that the poem is factual and prosaic except for lines 7-11, in which the doctor appears to be using poetic imagery and metaphysical terminology. These lines stand out in sharp contrast to the others in the poem. The speaker's recollection is sketchy: It seems likely that most of the words he attributes to the doctor in those lines (especially "mist blowing against your face and arms") are not really part of "what the doctor said" but rather thoughts and images aroused in the speaker's own mind. The device of having a few lines of vivid imagery stand out against a backdrop of deliberately prosaic utterance can be found in some of Shakespeare's sonnets. It always has the effect of making the imagery more intense by contrast. A good example for comparison with Carver's poem is William Shakespeare's Sonnet 29, which contains the famous lines:

> Yet in these thoughts myself almost despising,
> Haply I think on thee, and then my state,
> (Like to the lark at break of day arising
> From sullen earth) sings hymns at heaven's gate.

Themes and Meanings

Carver's poems, like his short stories, are usually personal and autobiographical. "What the Doctor Said" deals with an actual incident. In September of 1987, Carver, who had been a heavy cigarette smoker for many years, was diagnosed with lung cancer. Two-thirds of his left lung was removed, but, in March of 1988, the devastating disease recurred—as it often does—as a brain tumor. He underwent seven weeks of full-brain radiation, but by June the doctors found many more new malignant tumors in his lungs, and he knew he had only a short time to live. He died on August 2, 1988.

The most unusual statement in the poem comes as a surprise ending. The patient acts grateful for the bad news. He jumps up, shakes hands, and perhaps even thanks the doctor. The reader is left wondering what priceless gift it is that the speaker feels he has just received. There is something very strange about this deceptively simple, factual poem. The doctor should be offering consolation, but it seems that the patient is more sensitive and aware than the doctor, who is a sympathetic but unimaginative man of science. The speaker realizes that the doctor feels uncomfortable in that awkward situation. The patient actually ends up comforting the doctor, trying to make his ordeal easier. This subtle reversal of roles is a Carveresque touch of humor that gives the poem an added dimension. It is also ironic that while the patient uses only the most prosaic language, the doctor uses "poetic diction" and metaphysical concepts when he speaks of forest groves and blowing mist and asks for understanding of the meaning of life and death.

The idea that death can be a blessing has often been expressed in literature. For example, in the famous soliloquy that begins with the words "To be, or not to be" in Shakespeare's play *Hamlet* (1603), Hamlet says that death is "a consummation devoutly to be wished." In one of Emily Dickinson's best-known poems, she says: "Because I could not stop for death/ He kindly stopped for me." Algernon Charles Swinburne, in his poem "The Garden of Proserpine," writes:

> From too much love of living,
> From hope and fear set free,
> We thank with brief thanksgiving
> Whatever gods may be
> That no life lives forever;
> That dead men rise up never;
> That even the weariest river
> Winds somewhere safe to sea.

What Carver means by the doctor's "gift" is susceptible to multiple interpretations. Perhaps the only person who can be sure of understanding the multifaceted emotion in question is one who, like Carver, knows that his or her own death is imminent and inescapable.

Bill Delaney

WHEN I HAVE FEARS

Author: John Keats (1795-1821)
Type of poem: Sonnet
First published: 1848, in *Life, Letters, and Literary Remains of John Keats*

The Poem

In the sonnet "When I Have Fears," John Keats gives expression to his fear that his young life may be cut off before he has a chance to experience the love of a woman and to develop and complete his calling as a poet. These feelings leave him with a forsaken sense of the vanity of love and fame. The very first line, "When I have fears that I may cease to be," captures the reader's attention at once, for the fear of premature death is universal. Especially when the potential of a richly productive and rewarding life is anticipated so intensely, the threat to its realization is all the more dispiriting.

The first quatrain focuses on the fear that early death will cut off the poet's life of writing. His brain is teeming with subjects, ideas, and inspirations for his work, enough to fill the bookshelf above his writing desk as a legacy of his art. It is a typical human emotion to want time for the ripening and harvesting of one's gifts. Death at a young age would preclude one's lasting significance.

Focus in the second quatrain is related to the first: the fear that early death will kill the imagination, the essential resource of his writing life, before it has had a chance to mature. The poet looks at nature, at the stars and clouds as vital sources of romantic inspiration. He thinks of not living long enough to exercise and develop his imagination as an artist, that would equip him to render human experience deeply imagined and felt.

The third quatrain considers the death of romantic love. In this quatrain the poet expands his thoughts from himself and his potential fame as artist to his desire for love. It is not just the quest for beauty and inspiration in nature, but also his wished-for relationship with a beautiful young woman, that is threatened by death. Not to have the chance to fulfill oneself as an artist or to experience human intimacy as a lover is to feel one's humanity fade into insignificance.

The concluding couplet expresses that sensibility of inevitability: a recognition of universal mutability. Human needs and aspirations confront mortality. The poet's fear that his life may soon cease and with it the magic moments of "high romance" that inspired him both as poet and as lover leaves him defeated. He sees himself as exiled, cut off from all human endeavor and love, a lone figure on a forsaken shore, lost in thought. The inspired, feeling poet and lover has been diminished into a thinker, assaulted by fears that transform "Love," "Fame," and even self to "nothingness."

Forms and Devices

Keats's studied reading of William Shakespeare, especially of the songs and sonnets, inspired him to pursue the perfection of his own poetic skills, including the mastery of the sonnet form as a supreme challenge to his artistry as poet and his mastery of its technical demands. This was his first but impressively successful attempt at a Shakespearean sonnet, with its four divisions of three quatrains, each with a rhyme scheme of its own and a rhymed concluding couplet.

The three quatrains of this sonnet are perfectly parallel, shaped as they are by their rhetorical and grammatical structure. Each refers to a different aspect of the poet's confrontation with his own mortality, introduced by the subordinating conjunction "When": "When I have fears," "When I behold," "And when I feel." In characteristic Shakespearean-sonnet fashion, these three quatrains lead up to the "then" of the last two lines: "then on the shore." Here the main clause of the poem counterbalances the three subordinating ones that precede it by expanding the personal pain to a universal lament. The solemn tone and heavy funereal beat of the couplet underscore the poet's sense of desolation.

That sense of desolation is wrought especially through the cumulative effect of the poet's choice of imagery and analogy. In the first quatrain, his choice of words such as "glean'd," "garners," and "full-ripen'd grain" obviously refers to harvest. Thus, the growth of his poetic genius is like the growing seasons that lead up to harvest time. The seasons are needed for poetic powers to grow and for the "pen" to glean such growth into "books," as granaries store the harvested grain. Hence, the poet's fear that there may be no time for developing his gifts, no time to produce what he is capable of, is like the farmer's fear that what has been sown will never come to fruition—a terrible sense of dread that something of great value will be lost.

Reference to nature's fecundity in the first quatrain shifts to nature's "high romance" in the second. Nature becomes not a source of sustenance but of inspiration. The poet thinks of "sky," "stars," clouds and "shadows," the "Huge cloudy symbols of a high romance." To a romantic poet like Keats, these serve as vital wellsprings to his imagination and his art, essential to the fulfillment of what he has embraced as his poetic calling. An early death would make a mockery of that calling.

The poem is not only about the beauty and mystery of nature; it also discusses human beauty and love, the subject of the third quatrain. Now the poet does not "think," as he did in the preceding quatrain; he says, "I feel." The need for the love of a woman—for the "fair creature of an hour"—and the fear that this need will go forever unmet are emotions of the heart. Both his heart and mind are now in the grip of fears that life will cease and cut him off from all that is most important. The imagery in the closing couplet reflects his utter desolation: a lone figure "on the shore/ Of the wide world," the waters of an endless ocean swallowing "Love and Fame," his passionate hopes for a remarkable life.

Themes and Meanings

The theme of human mortality runs strong in poetry, especially in the poetry of the Romantics. Still, to feel personally the specter of death stalking when one is twenty-two is not common. Keats had reasons for this fear, however. At age eight he had lost his father to an accident. A year later his grandfather and male protector died. While he was in his early teens, his mother died from tuberculosis. Exposed to so much death at so young an age, Keats was attuned more keenly than most to the transience of life. This sonnet poignantly gives expression to a very personal fear of his own early death, which would forever doom to oblivion his human longings and artistic ambitions. In retrospect, the quatrains tremble with prophetic import. In less than a year, Keats's younger brother Tom would be dead of tuberculosis, and shortly after that Keats learned that he himself had contracted the dreaded disease. In little more than three years after writing this sonnet, Keats succumbed, his fame not yet realized and his love of a beautiful young woman never requited.

That Keats had been reading Shakespeare may be reflected in his choice of the Elizabethan words "charactery" (characters, or printed letters of the alphabet) in line 3 and "garners" (granaries) in line 4. In any case, the sonnet form clearly suited his poetic skill and purpose, for he wrote more than sixty poems in this form. As in many of Shakespeare's own sonnets, so also in Keats the themes of love, fame, and death figure prominently. When he wrote "When I Have Fears," Keats had not yet met the young lady, Fanny Brawne, with whom he would become so hopelessly infatuated. The "fair creature of an hour" in line 9 most likely refers to a young beauty Keats had observed in Vauxhall Gardens, an amusement park, a few years earlier and whom he addressed in another sonnet as "a Lady Seen for a Few Moments at Vauxhall." In his imagination she had become the embodiment of absolute feminine beauty and loveliness, everything Keats longed for, simply to "have relish in the faery power of unreflecting love."

As to fame, Keats knew that fame, should it come at all, would be directly dependent on the quality of his art. To develop his potential as poet, to ripen his poetry into a mature poetry of power, beauty, and significance, he would need time. In this sonnet, more directly and personally than in any other, Keats expresses his fear that he may not have that time, and therefore "Love and Fame to nothingness do sink."

Henry J. Baron

WHEN LILACS LAST IN THE DOORYARD BLOOM'D

Author: Walt Whitman (1819-1892)
Type of poem: Elegy
First published: 1865, in *Sequel to Drum-Taps*

The Poem

"When Lilacs Last in the Dooryard Bloom'd" is a long poem in free verse divided into sixteen numbered sections. Written shortly after the assassination of Abraham Lincoln, the poem expresses both Walt Whitman's grief and his effort to incorporate the president's death into an understanding of the universal cycle of life and death.

The first two sections are devoted to lamentation, to the poet's sense that he will never be able to overcome his despair over the loss of the one he loved, and to the pre-monition of catastrophe he had experienced in his observation of the drooping west-ern star. Nature itself seems obliterated by the "black murk" hiding the star.

In section 3, the poet shifts his attention to the lilac bush blooming in the dooryard. The tall lilac bush, with its heart-shaped leaves, is a natural symbol of the human heart and its capacity to mourn but also of its capacity to renew itself, as the lilac bush is re-newed each spring. The flower's powerful scent stirs the poet's memory of the contin-ual cycles of nature and stimulates both sadness and delight, which he expresses in breaking off a sprig of lilac in tribute to and memory of Lincoln.

Section 4 introduces the image of the solitary warbling thrush, which the poet later associates (in section 10) with his own warbling for the dead. Not only is grief natural, it is also what unites human beings and nature, and it is what allows the poet to see in the cycle of the seasons a reason for the coming of death. Sections 5 and 6 describe the procession of Lincoln's coffin, the spectacle of a whole society mourning its loss and acknowledging the presence of death, an inescapable fact that leads the poet (in sec-tions 7 through 14) to merge his individual sorrow with that of society and with the ev-idence that nature presents of birth, growth, and death.

Section 14 intensifies the poet's identification with death; he creates a lyric of wel-come to "delicate death," calling it a "dark mother," a "strong deliveress" from the struggle of existence, a peaceful release into the elements of the universe. Section 15 takes this more assured feeling about death and suggests that the horrible suffering of the Civil War battlefields, the grief of mothers and children for those who were slain, has become transformed into a vision of men at rest, enjoying relief from the agony associated with the memories of the living.

Summing up in section 16 his visions of the lilac blooming in the dooryard, the re-ciprocal song of poet and thrush, and the governing image of the drooping western star, the poet has found a way both to contain his anguish and to find its expression in the natural and human elements he has described: "Lilac and star and bird twined with the chant of my soul,/ There in the fragrant pines and the cedars dusk and dim."

Forms and Devices

Because Whitman feels so strongly that human grief must be understood as part of the recurrent cycle of nature, of the change and the return of the seasons, he relies on the simplest of all devices: repetition. Thus the lines of the first section are repeated in several sections, especially at the end of the poem, which focuses on the images of lilac and star and on the bird's song, which echoes and evokes the poet's own song. Indeed the poem has an echoing effect, as if the poet's first choice of words in sections 1 through 4 must be given similar answering words in subsequent sections.

In another kind of repetition, the poet takes a word such as "warble" and applies it both to the bird and to himself, making the word stand for the identity between himself and nature. Similarly, his precise observation of the "delicate-color'd blossoms" of the lilac later merges (in section 14) into his ode to "delicate death." By offering a sprig of lilac to Lincoln, in other words, the poet is signifying his understanding of this individual instance of death, which then becomes linked to his expanded awareness (later in the poem) of how all death is figured in Lincoln's loss.

What often seems to be merely reiteration of detail—as in the poet's description (in section 13) of the thrush singing in the swamps and out of the dusk, the cedar, and the pines—is repeated at the very end of the poem, suggesting that what the poet observes in nature is what he becomes; it is all "twined" together in his nature as a poet. Only by the repetition of images does the poet gather his data, so to speak, his rich, deep, absorption of the meaning of the universe. This absorption is first signaled to him by the drooping star, which, he implies (several times in the poem), provides a clue and is itself a marker—as are the poem's repeated words—of the necessity, indeed the desirability, of death. Consequently, the poet makes of death a common, even a comfortable experience rather than the aberrant, shocking event presented in the first section.

By the device of repetition, the poet accustoms himself to the manifold manifestations of death. Each recurrence of images such as the "delicious" coming of evening (section 12) and the "mastering odor" of the lilac (section 13) builds up a body of sensuous experience, of sight and smell, that in itself excites a desire for repetition, a longing to see and smell the lilacs bloom again; it also imparts a realization that this very joy cannot be attained without a participation in the rites of death.

Themes and Meanings

"When Lilacs Last in the Dooryard Bloom'd" never mentions President Lincoln by name, nor does it mention the Civil War directly; Lincoln's death and the war are the occasion for the poet's meditation on death and its place in the human and natural universe. The poet knows that his personal grief is a national grief—he admits as much in his references (in section 6) to the coffin passing through the streets—and his task is to transform his individual mourning into an evocation of feelings that can be universally shared.

The response to Lincoln's death is so overwhelming that the event is like the death or fall of a star—a momentous occurrence that demands the poet's fullest measure of understanding. Nowhere does he explicitly connect the drooping star and Lincoln, but in the first section the two are joined by proximity, and later they are joined by the poet's tendency to interpret his feelings in terms of what he sees and absorbs in nature. Lincoln is to his society as the star is to the heavens—an analogical view of existence that the poet pursues in the bond he feels with the solitary singing bird.

Implicit also in the poem is Whitman's assertion that the true significance of Lincoln's death can be grasped only by poetry—not by rational, logical thought, but by the rhythmical organization of sound patterns and images that is identical to the repetitive patterns of life. The poet strives for the presentation of a whole experience, not merely a description of his feelings toward Lincoln's death or toward death itself. Instead, the poem is meant to be an experience, a dramatization of the natural cycle, a piece of an ongoing phenomenon to which Whitman alludes in his references to "ever-returning spring" and his insistence that "I mourn'd, and yet shall mourn," as though he is still present, speaking now and not at some point in the past.

The poet's frequent use of the present tense, as though the experience he describes is happening "now," is his way of intensifying an identification with the poem itself that transcends the occasion of its composition—Lincoln's assassination—in order to explore the human reaction to death and the growth of the poet's own perceptions, as evidenced in his last two lines. In them, his sensibility unites the human and natural realms, thus creating the very form and meaning of the poem (the poet's "chant") out of "the dead I loved so well." Reading the poem, like smelling the lilacs or hearing the bird sing again, recalls death, summons it to full consciousness, and makes it a part of the present, like the "ever-returning spring."

Carl Rollyson

WHEN THE LAMP IS SHATTERED

Author: Percy Bysshe Shelley (1792-1822)
Type of poem: Lyric
First published: 1824, in *Posthumous Poems of Percy Bysshe Shelley*

The Poem

"When the Lamp Is Shattered" is a poem of thirty-two lines expressing the loss of ecstatic poetic creativity in response to the loss of a beloved woman's affections.

The poem was written at the height of Percy Bysshe Shelley's poetic powers, in the last year of his short life, after he had anchored his restless exile from England in Pisa, Italy. There, in 1820, he at last found the semblance of contentment with his troubled wife and a group of close friends. Among Shelley's friends were Edward Williams, a retired lieutenant of a cavalry regiment serving in India, and his charming common-law wife, Jane, with whom Shelley carried on a flirtation and to whom he addressed some of his best lyrics. Whether or not Jane Williams was the inspiration for "When the Lamp Is Shattered" remains a matter for conjecture. It was Jane's husband who was to drown with Shelley when a violent storm swamped their boat off the Leghorn coast on July 8, 1822.

The poem opens with a catalog of images expressing the shattered poetic creativity of the lovelorn male speaker made desolate by the loss of a beloved woman's affections. The desolation oppressing his creative imagination is like a broken lamp robbing the mortal poet of his vital genius ("The light in the dust lies dead"), like a dispersal of clouds breaking up a brilliant rainbow, or like a shattered lute unable to produce sounds to revive the memories of past love songs already forgotten by the lady of his hopeless affection (lines 1-8).

The second stanza elaborates on the images of the first stanza to explore the failure of the poet's joyous creativity in response to his failure in love. When lute and lamp cease, the inspiration for poetic sound and rhetorical brilliance ceases, and the poet's broken heart and desolate spirit have no creative resources left to produce soaring, joyous verse (lines 9-12). The desolate poetic imagination, capable of only grief-stricken songs of death, is like a cramped ancient apartment in a wrecked monastery or like the doleful sea-wind and crashing waves that sound the death knell for a drowned sailor (lines 13-16).

The third stanza takes a new metaphoric and thematic tack and reviews the events of the romantic breakup by personifying Love as an eagle that bemoans the frailty of the heart's affections and yet perversely inhabits the nest or heart of the poet-speaker, the weaker of the two lovers (lines 17-24). He is left to lament his heart-sickness and to wonder why Love made his heart its place of birth, development, and demise ("For your cradle, your home, and your bier"), whereas the still beloved lady, who no longer cares for him, escapes from being so enthralled.

The fourth stanza, continuing the personification of Love as a nesting eagle, warns that his heart will be an inhospitable domicile for Love. His lovelorn passions will act as a tempest blowing against nesting birds of prey (lines 25-26). His disenchanted intellect, like a brilliant wintry sun, will see through Love's tortures and delusions. The poet's embittered being will be but a rotting nest in the cruel winter season, exposing Love to the harsh elements of derisive disillusionment (lines 29-32).

Forms and Devices

"When the Lamp Is Shattered" is a delicate and melancholy lyric poem consisting of four stanzas, each with eight lines of alternating end rhymes. Shelley composed each stanza out of two sets of quatrains and made sure that weak, feminine end rhymes appeared in each stanza to capture the fluttering, evanescent quality of lost love through sound effects (for example, "shattered" and "scattered").

The poem's metrical system wavers between iambic tetrameter and iambic trimeter, both with many variations. The musical irregularity—the abrupt use of stressed sounds breaking, at intervals, the harmony of the iambic beat—works with the feminine rhymes to convey through sound the discord of romantic bereavement. Shelley also made heavy use of consonance and assonance (as in "The light in the dust lies dead") throughout the poem.

Shelley was a master of rhetorical fireworks, so much so that he has been criticized (often unfairly) for overdoing the artistry of poetry and for lapsing into incoherence and obscurity. Desmond King-Hele, in *Shelley: The Man and the Poet* (1960), adjudged "When the Lamp Is Shattered" to be too "trite and trivial" for its repeated appearance in anthologies of poetry; he was perhaps overly influenced in his severe verdict by F. R. Leavis's jaundiced opinion of the poem's diction and overall worth. Such criticism is excessive. Although "When the Lamp Is Shattered" may not rank with Shelley's greatest performances, it is an authentically desolate Romantic lyric on a typical Shelleyan theme of love and poetic creativity. The poem is not overly incoherent or obscure in its piling on of evocative images of his lovelorn state.

Cooperating with his complex sound effects is a series of metaphors and similes that are at the heart of the poem's achievement in communicating vividly the loss of love and ecstatic poetic creativity. The metaphors of the broken lamp, lute, and rainbow in the first stanza are implicit comparisons to the poet-speaker's lovelorn state of melancholy poetic inspiration in the second stanza, which concludes with two similes—explicit comparisons of his muted melancholy powers of imagination to narrow, wrecked cells and to doleful, death-dealing waves.

Finally, a new metaphor, comparing a personified Love to a nesting eagle, is central to the last two stanzas in describing the utter desolation of the romantically thwarted poet-speaker, who is still possessed by a strong emotional attachment. Stanza 4 employs two similes of storm and sun that are integrated with the pervasive eagle metaphor in order to communicate the poet-speaker's wintry embitterment with his failure in love.

Themes and Meanings

"When the Lamp Is Shattered" is about the loss of ecstatic poetic creativity in response to a failure in love. This is a theme close to the deepest concerns of Shelley as a radical thinker, artist, and proselytizer of love as the liberating force for an imprisoned humanity.

As Shelley wrote in his essay "On Love" (1815), "This is Love. This is the bond and the sanction which connects not only man with man but with everything which exists." A major vehicle for releasing an oppressed humanity from the chains of political tyranny and personal insecurity and hatred was the poet's imagination creating liberating visions of love in poetry that would inspire the human race. Shelley was not certain that poetry could accomplish this reformist goal, but he was certain that the artistic effort was worthwhile, if humanity was ever to progress and forsake a hopeless, self-created, and socially conditioned lethargy of spirit. As M. H. Abrams noted in the second edition of *Natural Supernaturalism: Tradition and Revolution in Romantic Literature* (1973), "the imagination for Shelley is the faculty by which man transcends his individual ego, transfers the center of reference to others, and thus transforms self-love into, simply, love."

If the great secret of moral good is love and the great instrument of moral good is the imagination—and if the great strength of the imagination is poetry—then "When the Lamp Is Shattered" is a despondent exploration by Shelley of the dissolution of his noble vision of love and poetic creativity. The poem is a beautiful statement of what happens when love fails, when the imagination cannot transcend self-absorption and sing a joyous love song for another, and when poetry must rest, not in an affirmation of universal love, but in a proclamation of disillusionment and a promise of bitterness.

Thomas M. Curley

WHEN WE WITH SAPPHO

Author: Kenneth Rexroth (1905-1982)
Type of poem: Lyric
First published: 1944, as ". . . about the cool water," in *The Phoenix and the Tortoise*; collected in *The Collected Shorter Poems*, 1966

The Poem

"When We with Sappho" is a poem of 126 lines, divided into a four-line epigraph and six stanzas of varying length. The poem is unrhymed and written in a loosely syllabic form. Most lines have seven to nine syllables, but the number varies from two to fifteen. The title refers to the Greek lyric poet who lived in the seventh and sixth centuries B.C.E. Lines of Sappho's poetry are quoted in the epigraph and read by the lovers in the poem. In the epigraph, the description of wind blowing through an apple orchard inducing sleep links her poetry to what occurs in the poem.

The first stanza introduces the subject of the poem, the poet and his lover spending a summer's day in an abandoned apple orchard. The situation is typical of many lyric poems celebrating the pleasures of love. The poem is written in the first person; the speaker addresses his love directly. He tells her to put down the book of "this dead Greek woman" and love him.

The scene shifts in the second stanza from the New England orchard to the Greek islands where Sappho once lived. Reflecting the title of the poem, the personalities of the lovers merge with that of Sappho.

In stanza 3, a thunderstorm forming in the distance encourages the lovers to undress. The description of the storm parallels the desire building in the lovers. Lines such as the "virile hair of thunder storms/ Brushes over the swelling horizon" foreshadow the lovemaking soon to come.

The lovers pause in stanza 4 to read again Sappho's poetry. Just as the few surviving fragments exist separated from the original contexts, the lovers are isolated in this moment. This is a common lyric theme: that in order to be preserved, love must be protected from the outside world.

In the fifth stanza, the lovemaking has ended, excitement replaced by "stillness" and relaxation.

In the last stanza, the lovers begin to fall asleep, as fulfilled in their love as the year that reaches its peak and "moves to autumn." The significance of the poem's title now is clarified, as the lovers, "with Sappho, move towards death." Rather than end on this somber note, however, Kenneth Rexroth echoes a phrase from stanza 1. Celebrating the beauty of his love, the speaker holds her as if he held "the bird filled/ Evening sky of summer."

Forms and Devices

Repetition of sounds and words is a key device in "When We with Sappho." The frequent repetition of the sibilant *s* sound is well illustrated by the epigraph. The words "sounds," "sprays," "leaves," "slumber," and "pours" imitate the noise of the wind in the trees and invoke a feeling of drowsiness in the reader. Many uses of this *s* sound can be found throughout the poem. Using the sounds of words to suggest their meanings is called onomatopoeia.

The repetition of words is meant to be not only hypnotic but seductive. The speaker repeats phrases to persuade his companion to make love: "Lean back," "Take off," "Kiss me." Similarly, Rexroth seeks to bring the reader under the spell of his strong, commanding voice. Adding to the imperative mood are the repeated references to death: "this dead Greek woman," "dead tongues," the "ruinous/ Orchard," and the "ancient apple trees." The lovers' own mortality is thus gently but insistently emphasized.

Rexroth also uses repetition to guide the reader through the changing stages in the poem. When the lovers pause in the fourth stanza, he twice repeats the request "Read to me again." In stanza 5, the desire to remain quiet, prolonging the ecstasy, is signaled by the repeated command "Do not," and by the repeated words "still" and "stillness."

In the last stanza, repetition serves two purposes: to emphasize the theme of mortality, through the use of words such as "move," "autumn," "sleep," and "death," and to return to the beginning of the poem, completing the circle and mirroring the natural cycles.

Some of the formal devices of the poem are subtle. In the final two stanzas, Rexroth reduces the number of lines in the stanzas and syllables in the lines so that the form corresponds to the experience. The poem builds and lengthens toward the climax of the lovemaking in stanza 4, then shortens as the day moves to an end.

Themes and Meanings

"When We with Sappho" is an intensely lyrical poem celebrating the pleasures of life. The poet praises the beauty of nature and the joy of making love. Like the surviving poetry of Sappho, the poem is frank, sensuous, and erotic. The height of the couple's bliss occurs in stanza 5. Immediately after making love, the lovers seem enveloped within the cloud created by their love, and by (in highly alliterative lines) the "awe filled silence/ Of the fulfilled summer."

The speaker at times describes his lover as if she were a product of nature. He tells her: "I will press/ Your summer honeyed flesh into the hot/ Soil." "Let your body sink/ Like honey through the hot/ Granular fingers of summer," and "Press your bruised shoulders against/ . . . my body." By blending the descriptions of lover and nature, Rexroth indicates another theme. The lovers are as much a part of the natural process of coming to be, flourishing, and decaying as the apples in the orchard. When Rexroth says in the first stanza, "Summer [is] in our mouths," he suggests that the mouths that read to and kiss each other will pass away as quickly as the summer's season.

The poem thus recognizes the inevitability of death. The shortness of life, in fact, is one of the lover's arguments. Since time eventually will wear down their bodies, they should get pleasure from the process: "Let our fingers run like steel/ Carving the contours of our bodies' gold." Other poems illustrating this timeless, universal theme are

Robert Herrick's "To the Virgins, to Make Much of Time" and Andrew Marvell's "To His Coy Mistress."

Rexroth is able to sustain his poem, as simple as its main theme is, through 126 lines. He does so in part by skillfully introducing references to Sappho, celebrating an artist who is a part of this tradition of erotic lyric poetry. In addition, the references delay the poem's climax. The second stanza is for the most part a journey to Sappho's homeland. In stanza 4, the lovers pause to read her verse, and, after the ecstasy in stanza 5, they, too, "with Sappho, move towards death."

The poem is about the power of literature, as well. In the greatest works of literature, the emotion of the author can be recreated in the reader despite the passage of many years. Through the splendor of Sappho's poems, ancient and fragmented as they may be, the lovers can identify with the passion of the long-dead poet. This provides one of the few temporary triumphs over death. The title thus has an added significance. During the time presented in the poem, the lovers are "with Sappho" in the intensity of their emotion. If the reader, in turn, can identify with these lovers, then the reader can be with them.

A final theme is the immortality of art. The second stanza notes how little, if anything, remains of Sappho's world. The almost chance survival of bits of her poetry, however, keeps her alive. As the speaker says in the poem, "Her memory has passed to our lips now." The poem's title also relates to this theme. Even after the poet and his lover have moved "with Sappho" to death, they will live on through this poem, sharing the destiny of all artists whose work endures.

Samuel B. Garren

WHERE

Author: Wendell Berry (1934-   )
Type of poem: Pastoral/meditation
First published: 1975; collected in *Clearing*, 1977; revised in *Collected Poems: 1957-1982*, 1985

The Poem

"Where" is a long pastoral meditation on the history and uses of the fifty-acre farm (Lane's Landing) in Henry County, Kentucky, which Wendell and Tanya Berry purchased in parcels between 1965 and 1968. The poem exists in two forms: a longer, didactic form originally published in *Not Man Apart* (1975) and *Clearings* (1977), and a shorter, revised, more lyrical version that appeared later in *Collected Poems: 1957-1982* (1985). The two versions are so different that they could almost be considered as separate poems.

The original, longer version of "Where" shifts between an impersonal, historical, third-person point of view and a more distinct first-person poetic voice (it is the dominant voice of *Clearings*, the Wendell Berry persona of the farmer-poet). The revised, shorter version of the poem retains more of the impersonal third-person perspective and lacks a clear persona except for an occasional personal pronoun, so that the speaker's presence is merely implicit in the poem.

The original version of "Where" addresses the general questions: "Who owned this land before me?" and "What was its history?" Berry traces the previous ownership of the fifty-acre farm back almost two hundred years to the original land survey by two Scots-Irish settlers, Thomas and Walker Daniels, when it was part of a thousand-acre tract on the Kentucky River. Then he recounts how the land was successively subdivided and sold for profit by subsequent owners, none of whom ever kept it long or passed it on to his or her children.

Part 1 deals with the ten-acre Lane's Landing tract—composed of a steamboat landing, general store, and garden plot—purchased in 1894 by Beriah Tingle, who kept it until 1919. It passed through four more owners before Wendell and Tanya Berry purchased it on February 7, 1965.

Part 2 meditates on the confused factual history of the land that is recorded in dusty deedbooks on the courthouse shelves. The poem draws some cultural lessons about the consequences of poor husbandry and neglect of the land for quick profits: the lessons of greed, laziness, and indifference. Standing in contrast is the character of John R. Tingle, brother of Beriah, who successfully farmed the adjoining forty-acre tract from 1904 until 1954.

The third part of "Where" recounts the history of that forty-acre tract, which passed into the hands of an absentee owner, a Louisville developer, who misused the land and held onto it for speculative purposes until the Berrys were able to purchase it in 1968 at an exorbitant price, extending their farm to fifty acres.

Forms and Devices

The original, longer version of "Where," which seems more coherent, is divided into three parts: Part 1 contains 115 lines, part 2 has 202 lines, and part 3 has 60 lines. Each part of the poem is divided into stanzas that are a sentence or two in length. Part 1 contains eight stanzas, part 2 has six stanzas, and part 3 has three stanzas. The meter is free verse with approximately three stresses per line, which resembles a blank verse trimeter but is looser in form.

The revised version of "Where" eliminates parts 1 and 3 entirely and retains only the first 140 lines of part 2. It contains five stanzas. All specific references to the names of previous owners are dropped, creating a more generalized lyric meditation on the fate of the land. What is lost is the sense of a specific place and historical record. The theme of the poem—the consequences of poor husbandry—becomes more generalized, and the sharpness of the specific references is lost.

The style of "Where" is deliberately terse and understated: images of silence, decay, and ecological degradation predominate. Images of lost primordial richness—clear creeks, tall hardwoods, and black topsoil—contrast with the washed-out gullies, eroded furrows, and scrub growth of the present. The land has been despoiled, and the original settlers are gone, leaving little tangible evidence of their presence beyond their gravestones, silent "as fossils in creek ledges."

In the revised version of "Where," the poem's apparent persona—"the watcher"—is thoughtful and meditative. He notes the quick scurry of a field mouse, the clear notes of a redbird (cardinal) in the top of a sycamore, brief interruptions in "the one/ silence that precedes/ and follows us." The poem proceeds through a series of absences and negations—"no one remembers;/ there is no language here"—because too much of the land's history has transpired elsewhere, in the halls of the state capital, where the fate of the land was brokered by the rich and powerful. The tangible, local, cultural memory is gone, except for the old property deeds on dusty courthouse shelves, which are as useless as "old/ boundary marks." Yet the watcher affirms that "the land and the mind/ bear the marks of a history/ that they do not record."

This elegiac tone is somewhat tempered by the cautious affirmation of the third stanza: "the mind still hungers/ for its earth." Somewhere, the agrarian dream of "an independent/ modest abundance" survives, though haste, indifference, restlessness, and careless husbandry have discouraged the growth of a prosperous, local, rural culture. People do not yet understand the land well enough to create a sustainable, independent local culture.

Stanza 4 rehearses an ecological myth of a fall from innocence and primeval abundance and offers a muted hope for eventual redemption through wiser, less destructive patterns of land use. From primeval forest, to rich farmland, to eroded gullies, "The land bears the scars" of heedless use. Through images of erosion, floods, tree stumps, and silty creeks, the narrator laments the wasted legacy left by the early settlers and their descendants. "A mind cast loose/ in whim and greed makes/ nature its mirror," the narrator affirms, "and the garden/ falls with the man." The oblique allusions to the story in *Genesis* of man's creation and fall reinforce the implicit judgment of environmental destruction. The ruin of the land resulted from the wrong vision—a vision of greed and quick wealth. "Such a mind is as much/ a predicament as such/ a place," the narrator concludes.

Like Adam and Eve expelled from Eden, the narrator is left with the dilemma of trying to recover what has been lost. Like Adam and Eve, he is left with a hard-won moral understanding, but he may also claim the legacy of those few who came before him and loved the land, seeing the possibility of a good life there.

Themes and Meanings

"Where" is a mythic poem about a "paradise lost" and the possibility of regaining that lost Eden. It is a parable of the American frontier and an indictment of the cultural habits and attitudes that resulted in massive environmental destruction. It is an exploration of the cultural mind-set that heedlessly exploited and wasted the natural resources of the land. The history of the narrator's farmland has been one of neglect and misuse. Yet there is some reason for hope. The narrator has chosen to return here, he has laid his claim to this land, and he is in a position to benefit from the mistakes of the past. The knowledge he carries with him is reason for song. Like the clear song of the redbird—"*Even/ so. Even so.*"—there is reason for hope in the narrator's stubborn loyalty to his native land.

Elsewhere, in the autobiographical essay "The Long-Legged House," Berry has written about how hard it is to acquire a genuine sense of place. "Where" describes in part the process of assimilation to a place, an important theme in Berry's work. The poem chronicles his return to the region where he was born and where both sides of his family had lived for generations. For him, buying the Lane's Landing farm meant establishing himself in the region where he could be in touch with the "profound and mysterious knowledge that is inherited, handed down in memories and names and gestures and feelings, and in tones and inflections of voice."

According to Berry, one learns to belong to a particular place through the power of silence—the silence that permits one to be present as if absent—and through the attentive observation through which a place begins to reveal its life in moments of deep intimacy and beauty. This kind of attentiveness permits people to live in the world almost as though they were not in it, so that they will not harm it in any way. It also permits people to view human life as only a small and superficial part of the larger life around them. Thus "Where" is both a personal credo and a contemporary ecological statement of what needs to be done—of people's responsibility to leave a particular place in better condition than they found it. It offers a new vision, a promise of wise husbandry and conservation practices, based upon a sense of permanent allegiance to a particular place.

Andrew J. Angyal

THE WHIP

Author: Robert Creeley (1926-   )
Type of poem: Lyric
First published: 1957, in *The Whip*

The Poem

Many of the poems Robert Creeley wrote in the 1950's concerned some intense moment or passage in a man/woman, often husband/wife, relationship. Woman appears in several guises in these poems—sometimes, as here, in two (at least) in the same poem. The reader finds the woman who is in possession, so to speak, possibly the wife, asleep. The man, her lover, perhaps her husband, tosses and turns, unable to rid his mind of its preoccupations, particularly with another woman, to whom he has also apparently made love, and who is even now not far off. Finally, he complains of his anguish out loud, and this stirs the wife figure beside him into semiconsciousness—she utters a muffled sound and puts her hand on his back.

Transformed by this touch of the real, the man appears to calm down and to view the woman he is with in a light different from that in which he viewed her at the outset. Then, she was "a flat, sleeping thing"—somewhat insubstantial to him, unholdable, removed. This remove stirs the embers of his yearning for the other woman, the one "on the roof"—literally so, perhaps, a houseguest in the poet's Mediterranean villa—metaphorically so, surely, since she is "on his mind." His longing increases until he groans audibly, which causes his companion to hug him. This in turn changes his feelings toward her and toward the other woman, which makes him think that he has uttered this poem "wrongly," because he had been misrepresenting his companion to himself.

One must allow that the woman on the roof could be solely a figment of the poet's imagination, an ideal figure of compliant passion who is liable to spring into (mental) life whenever her "host" feels lonely. The "whip" of the title might be something with which the poet is beaten, or with which he beats himself—guilt, remorse, desire—but it also describes the way the phrases whip around as the poem abruptly shifts emotional direction. "Whip" can also have the sense of "spur": to urge someone onward. Here, the chain of events whips the poet toward a conclusion.

Forms and Devices

It was Creeley's practice at this time to use old measures in new ways, to use, as here, the couplet as a frame for free verse. From an outset at which the first two lines have an identical number of syllables, the poem proceeds through variations upon this measure, ringing telling changes upon the count initially established. For example, in the second stanza or couplet, "sleeping thing. She was," with its five syllables and three or four stresses, is played against the next line, "very white," to render the latter slower, more emphatic. The ear, without necessarily becoming conscious of the fact, allots a certain duration to each successive line, which is based upon the units of time (sound) that immediately precede it. Expecting four beats, five syllables, one tends to draw out a shorter line, giving more duration to fewer syllables. In such ways, meanings arise throughout the poem from various speedings-up and slowings-down, which, together with the hesitations of the end-stopped lines—always end-stopped by Creeley in reading—provide an impression of language under the pressures of actual speech, of a thinking that is feeling/sensing its way through a difficult territory or tangle of human predicament, seeking some enlightenment by way of surcease from troubling thoughts.

Rhyme also comes and goes, surfaces and submerges, throughout "The Whip." While it is seldom found at the line ends, it crops up in several telling series: bed, feather, very, addressed, myself, returned, encompasses, yelled, said, in which the assonantal sound *e* connects its words into an extrasyntactic unit of associational meaning; or night, flat, white, quiet, fit, That, it, but, what, that, put, act, in which the consonance of the final *t* sound performs a like function. One notes too the hand/ back/act sequence that helps connect that particular action, and the night/white/ quiet trio: white night, the whiter for being so quiet?

Creeley's poems of this period derive great energy from the tension between the sentence and the end-stopping of the lines. What will he say next? The reader may wonder, waiting for the corner to be turned. It will often be a surprise. "[A]ddressed" and "encompasses" are two such surprises, as is the final word (and line), "wrongly." About this word there is an aura of ambiguity. Does it modify "think" or "say"? Grammatically, it could be either; syntactically, it should not be both; poetically, surely it *is* both. He thinks—that is his mistake; he says—that too is an error.

Creeley, here as ever, makes masterly use of his vocabulary. Most of the words are short—monosyllables or disyllables—and therefore usually of Anglo-Saxon derivation, carrying with them that sense of the common and down-to-earth that such diction communicates so well (for sound historical reasons). It is against this background that "encompasses" stands out, lengthy and Latinate, and it is this distinction that accounts for the slight shock one feels when one encounters it. The tone of the poem moves back and forth between a demotic American and a slightly Frenchified courtliness. It is somehow a poem of courtly love, in the troubadour tradition, and such phrases as "my love" and "very white"—even "a fit," in its older sense—coupled with "addressed," encourage one to read it in that tradition. It moves matters ahead quickly, however, with what feels like a contemporary, American speed; it does not shy away from the right word, even if that word is an ugly exclamation: "Ugh." In this way, Creeley can suggest the persistence into the present of past manners, and something of how, in the present, these traces may be met and dealt with.

Themes and Meanings

The persistence of the past into the present is often the burden of Robert Creeley's song, as is underlined by his very forms—contemporary versions of traditional conventions. First appearing in book form in *The Whip*, "The Whip" was printed next in

1962 in *For Love* (Creeley's best-selling book—within ten years, some forty thousand copies were in print). "Love" itself is the big question: Is it still (was it ever really) possible? Is there more to it than words? What can a pair of lovers share—beyond "uninteresting weight"? Ultimately, Creeley plumps for love, but only while admitting to the leap of faith such a conclusion demands. Creeley was among those who, trying to rid humanity of those portions of the past that are no longer (if they every were) life-enhancing, cultivated the present, the Here and Now. Thus love could best be known, he thought, through its various instances—all else was vain rhetoric, dubious assumption. Of importance to love, however—to lovers, certainly—is continuity. Can there be a continuity free of damaging or even insupportable assumptions? Can there be a continuity that will enhance and not destroy its instances?

For Creeley, as for some other poets, these questions were not a matter for lovers alone, but for writers, too. Because writing commits a continuity, what one writes today will persist for ten, twenty, fifty years or more. Speaking surely is more "natural," more immediate, truer to the moment. There is a tension, then, between speaking and writing; Creeley, who followed Charles Olson's theories of the written poem as score for the spoken word, often sounds hostile to writing, or at least to that aspect of it that freezes the momentous and fixes the transitory.

Sometimes, the various women in Creeley's poems appear to do double duty as actual (autobiographical) personages and as metaphors for the mind's workings. In Creeley's poem "The Wife," for example, there are two women in opposition to each other, but one is "tangible substance,/ flesh and bone," whereas the other is an idealized, imaginary woman who occurs only in the mind and "keeps her strict/ proportions there." "The Wife" is a lesser poem than "The Whip," being too stately in tone and wooden in movement, but—as duller works sometimes do—it sheds light on other poems by its author. In "The Wife," there is no hint that the "other" is actual, an actual houseguest on the roof, possibly lusting for her host even as he lusts for her. The poem presents a different problem: As long as a man cannot rid himself of an imaginary creation, the actual persons he encounters will eventually prove inadequate. Yet if he succeeds in banishing the ideal from his mind, what measure will remain whereby to judge the actuality of experience?

There can be no enduring solution to this dilemma, but in certain moments, a humanness is suddenly possible, as when, in "The Whip," the woman puts her hand on the man's back and he changes his mind.

David Bromige

THE WHITE MAN'S BURDEN

Author: Rudyard Kipling (1865-1936)
Type of poem: Lyric
First published: 1899; collected in *The Five Nations*, 1903

The Poem

The poem's full title is "The White Man's Burden: 1899, The United States and the Philippine Islands." Written at the end of 1898, it contains an exhortation to Americans to pick up the burden of Imperialism and to take over from Spain the rule of the Philippine Islands, which the United States had just captured in the Spanish-American War. Many Americans intensely disliked the idea of an American empire. Imperialism was associated in many American minds with the corrupt politics of European nations such as Great Britain, France, and Spain; to such minds the United States represented a new start in human history—"the last, best hope of man," as Lincoln had said—and therefore the United States should not make the same mistakes that other nations had made. Mark Twain, for example, declared that if the United States took over the Philippines and suppressed native independence movements there, the American flag's colors should be changed from red, white, and blue to black and white, and the field of stars should bear instead a skull and crossbones.

There were, however, a number of Americans, Theodore Roosevelt most prominent among them, who believed that it was America's obvious fate, its "manifest destiny," to take up responsibility for less technologically advanced peoples, to help them progress to a higher stage of civilization. Rudyard Kipling, a friend of Theodore Roosevelt, wrote for these Americans "The White Man's Burden." Roosevelt received an advance copy of the poem and sent it on to his friend Henry Cabot Lodge with a note calling the poem "rather poor poetry, but good sense for the expansionist standpoint."

In the first stanza, white men are advised to send their best sons to serve the "new-caught, sullen peoples,/ Half devil and half child." The entire emphasis in the stanza is on service to others: "To wait in heavy harness." The second stanza expands on this theme and advises the servants of Empire how to behave to those they serve, with "patience" and open, simple speech. White men are also advised to "veil the threat of terror," that is, to make it clear that they have many dangerous weapons to enforce their will. Nevertheless, it is not polite to insist in a bullying manner on power; Theodore Roosevelt's famous version of this advice was "to speak softly, and carry a big stick."

In the third stanza, the theme changes slightly. The task is again defined as curing famine and disease, but Kipling makes it clear that those who benefit from the Empire will ultimately ruin anything that is done for them. The fourth stanza continues the theme of service, the humble serving of others: "No tawdry rule of kings,/ But toil of serf and sweeper." Kipling asserts that the accomplishments of the white builders of ports and roads in the hot lands will not provide benefit to the white men who oversee the building: "Go make them with your living,/ And mark them with your dead!" He strikes a note curiously like self-pity in the fifth stanza. The Bible is also evoked: the behavior of the Hebrews in the wilderness after the Exodus from Egypt, the complaining of the freed but hungry hordes as they reproach their leader, Moses: "Why brought ye us from bondage,/ Our loved Egyptian night?"

It is in the sixth and seventh stanzas that Kipling finally declares what the real purposes of Empire are: the honor of God, self-testing, rites of passage, and the ordeals of manhood. The white man's acts will be weighed by the "silent, sullen peoples," he states, as will everything the white man cries or whispers. In the seventh and final stanza, Kipling exhorts his audience to "Have done with childish ways"—"search your manhood," he says, and the poem's final line declares what the result of taking up the "White Man's burden" will be: "The judgment of your peers!"

Forms and Devices

The rhythm throughout "The White Man's Burden" is what is called in hymn writing "short measure"—that is, iambic trimeter. All the odd lines have feminine endings; all the even lines end with strong stresses. There is no enjambment in the poem; all the lines are heavily end-stopped. In fact, as many critics have insisted about most of Kipling's poetry, the rhythm is "jingly." Although this charge is not entirely fair—Kipling is sometimes a master poet capable of producing haunting lines and subtle rhythms—Kipling quite frequently tried consciously to write "jingly" poems. He once said that when he started to write a poem he would sing a lively hymn tune or a music-hall song to himself and then try to fit words to the melody and the catchy rhythm.

In the poem, the reader finds the constant use of biblical diction, especially the archaic personal pronoun "ye" throughout, nine times in all. The use of "ye" also makes it clear that the speaker of the poem is addressing an audience or, at any rate, more than one person, since "ye" is the archaic second person plural. For modern tastes there is too much use of exclamation points, which in contemporary English are kept usually for screams of surprise or terror. It is employed in hymns quite frequently, which may indicate Kipling's source for the use of this device.

There is an artful use of inverted syntax in the last stanza:

> Comes now, to search your manhood
> Through all the thankless years,
> Cold-edged with dear-bought wisdom,
> The judgment of your peers!

It is almost as if the postulant for manhood honors sees something approaching, strains his eyes to determine what it might be, and finally perceives it looming up, in sentence-final position, as "the judgment of your peers!" This use of syntax is effective both as a dramatic postponement of an important element and as a forceful ending for the poem.

Themes and Meanings

The phrase "the White Man's burden" is more often on the lips of people who have not read the poem than on the lips of those who have. More damage has been done by the careless invocation of Kipling as an example of vulgar racialism than by the careful examination of what the poet really said. The notion that the Empire-builders are supposed to think only of the service they may render to the "silent, sullen peoples" is not an ignoble one, and indeed many useful projects were created by these empire-builders, very often at the cost of their health, as Kipling insists. Many older residents of former colonies assert that the British did provide better political guidance and more lasting material assistance to their countries than their own rulers have succeeded in providing since freedom came after World War II.

Yet even with all this said in defense of imperial endeavor, there is something radically wrong with Kipling's view of Empire. For one thing, it has often been said that people would rather be ruled badly by themselves than well by others. In this light, Empire is really little more than an impertinence, and when the British realized that, after World War II, they quietly dropped their imperial pretensions. After all, even stronger than the British desire for a sense of gratification at the extent of British power in the world has been the British horror of bad manners—and after the war, imperialism suddenly seemed like the height of bad manners.

Yet there is something even more radically wrong with Kipling's view of Empire, something wrong with Kipling's soul, something that keeps him from ever telling more than half of the truth about anything (though sometimes it is the half that is not often heard). Both in this poem and in the even more famous "Recessional," the poet makes it quite clear that he did not think that the Empire set up and ruled by the British would endure, or even that the achievements of the Empire-builders would prove permanent. He had too much of a sense of history to think that any empire lasts more than a limited amount of time; the Book of Ecclesiastes in the Bible would inform him of this fact. So why encourage the growth of Empire? It is here that one comes upon the ethnocentric core of Kipling's thought: Empire is a test for white men, an ordeal. They are to benefit from their ultimately meaningless activities in the colonies to win the approval of their peers and the moral advancement that accompanies hard work courageously undertaken and carried out. In other words, the people of the colonies are merely the terms of the test for white men. In this respect, the colonial peoples and the ice and snow of the polar regions serve the same function and are, correspondingly, equally inhuman.

Kipling should not be regarded as a vulgar racist; he grew up in India, spoke Hindi almost before he spoke English, had a real sympathy for Indians (mainly Moslems), and had a keen eye for certain aspects of life in India. His only successful novel, *Kim* (1901), is regarded in India as articulating important though limited concepts about life on the subcontinent. Kipling was a man of giant talents; anyone sensitive to literary history will acknowledge that his works are a permanent part of English literature. It is also true, however, that Kipling provides a classic example of the strange distortion of the soul that results when full human status is reserved for a small part of the human race.

Edmund L. Epstein

WHITE NIGHT

Author: Anna Akhmatova (Anna Andreyevna Gorenko, 1889-1966)
Type of poem: Lyric
First published: 1912, as "Belaia noch," in *Vecher*; English translation collected in
Way of All the Earth, 1979

The Poem

"White Night" is a short poem of twelve lines in three four-line stanzas. The title, an oxymoron, seems to bear little upon the drama of the narrative, but can be explained symbolically in terms of "white," often associated in Anna Akhmatova's writing with winter snow, which brings with it a meaning of loss of memory or death, and "night," a reference point to both time, another of Akhmatova's recurrent themes, and the oncoming fall of night for the speaker. "White Night," then, would be a time of loss, of a remembrance of a reality fading into the darkness imposed by time's unstoppable march.

The poem, which begins with "I," does not simply share a personal experience with the reader. "You" is introduced in the third line of the first stanza, along with the speaker's speculations about how the person the "you" represents feels. The continuing presence of both "I" and "you" affects the poem's interaction with the reader, making it appear that the reader is eavesdropping on an intimate dialogue between an abandoned lover and the one who has done the abandoning.

The collection of poems in which "White Night" first appeared is recognized as novel-like in its structure—a series of scenes that together tell a story—and is also considered to be indirectly connected with biographical episodes in Akhmatova's life; thus the spurned lover is identified both as a woman, in keeping with the other poems in *Vecher* (evening), the book of poems in which it was first published, and as Akhmatova's lyrical ego. During most of 1911, she was separated from her husband, Nikolay Gumilyov; shortly after their 1910 marriage (which was strained from its inception and ended in divorce), he decided to visit Africa for an extended period.

The poem's stage is furnished with props constructed from the speaker's emotional state. She is caught between hope, shown in her refusal to lock the door, and despair, shown in her refusal to light the candles, since doing so would signify that everything is normal. Her exhaustion is emphasized in her own admission of tiredness, but so is her depression, which is implied by her inability to face her aloneness in the penultimate testing ground: bed.

She has been watching the light disappear, and the details of the landscape outside melt into the dusk, a parallel to the disappearance of her lover's features, both in the lack of his bodily presence and in the fading of his memory over time. All of this serves to feed her self-pity, to rob her of faith in life's overall goodness.

Complications arise in the poem's action in the complexity of the confessional phrase "I've got drunk on your voice in the doorway." Is the woman wallowing in pity, giddy with a false joy based on desperate wishful thinking, or could she actually be intoxicated from literally drowning her sorrows in strong drink? The poem leaves room for all three interpretations in the first stanza's tension between despair and hope, as well as in its reference to tiredness, which is often used euphemistically to describe a drunken condition.

It is the woman's last declaration, however, her final reflection on her own foolish optimism, that defines the poem's tone. The reader can almost see the woman shaking her head in self-reproach over her own part in her current misery—a first step toward reconciliation with circumstance.

Forms and Devices

While Akhmatova's Russian poems are written in strict meters and exact rhymes, it is her straightforward narrative and logic steeped in elegant aestheticism that distinguish her style and place her in the stream of Acmeism (a movement that arose in 1912 in response to the crises of Symbolism, of which she was a leading exponent) along with other Acmeists such as Osip Mandelstam. Her work is especially noted for its synthesis of the serious and the popular. "White Night" demonstrates this blending even in translation. The moment of absolute blackness that accompanies the sense of being forsaken in love is communicated by means of casual language—contractions such as "haven't" and "don't," and clichés such as "all is lost" and "life is a cursed hell"—in a setting softened by the presence of unlit candles and fields fading in the soft hues of sunset, so that the melodramatic potential of the theme is thoughtfully kept in check.

Almost every word of the poem can be explored through myriad perspectives. The door left unlocked can be a symbol of possible reconciliation as well as a means by which the past (symbolized by the missing lover) can find its way into a future moment. The candles left unlit are objects that define the lodging as primitive, but they also can be a symbol for the wounded heroine's refusal to face a painful truth, a romantic notion proved false.

"Don't care" following "don't know" adds a note of self-pity that is important to the poem's tone, and "tired" does not allow "strength" to be merely a physical disability, especially since it is at the poinit of having "*to decide* to go to bed" (emphasis added) that the woman is frozen by her forlornness.

"Fields," "sunset," and "pine-needles" are additional examples of words laden with symbolic possibilities. Earth, the harvest cycle, and the freedom associated with wide open spaces are all suggested by "fields." "Sunset" brings with it the heavens, and the daily cycle of night and day, which by implication suggests an ending. Those "pine-needles" draw together complicated connections. Pine, an evergreen, can symbolize the realm of the eternal. Individual needles, however, as part of the natural cycle, turn brown and fall, making way for new growth.

An eclectic collection of details is another Akhmatova trademark. In the first sentence of the poem, which extends into the second stanza by means of enjambment, she gathers three images: the unlocked door, the unlit candle, and the unused bed. This series of negative images, which is further reinforced by the two negatives contained in the opening sentence, is associated with the missing lover. Another pattern of twos and threes, which are common in Akhmatova poems, occurs in the repetition of "don't" in line 3 of the first stanza, together with the grouping of "to decide to go" and "to bed" in line 1 of the second stanza.

The structure of the poem is itself a collection of threes that can be classified in a typical Akhmatova arrangement of major-major-minor. Of the three sentences that make up the poem, the first two are complex and the last is simple. Such attention to syntax demonstrates the careful crafting that underlies Akhmatova's poetry.

Themes and Meanings

Twentieth century literature has been shaped by certain recurrent themes, one of which is the theme of time. "White Night" is one of a small number of Akhmatova's earliest poems in which the workings of time relationships—the possibilities of the past, present, and future converging like chemical elements in constantly changing hybrid combinations with unpredictable properties—as the basis of human experience are explored as an important corollary to the theme of tragic love. In her later poems, written after 1940, the theme of time consciousness takes center stage, and other leitmotifs become supporting players, merely different aspects of Akhmatova's main obsession with time.

"White Night" weaves an awareness of time throughout the strains of its melancholy song. Temporal time is shown in the betrayal of the heroine through her separation from her lover, and in the symbolism associated with images such as candles and fields. The past intrudes in the world of memory, in the missing lover's reflected existence playing in the heroine's mind, and in the point of time of the poem: sunset, a vivid reminder of the passing day. It is the anxiety caused by this intrusion, fused with the heroine's vision of hearing her lover's voice signaling his hoped-for return, that feeds her loneliness.

The primary theme of the poem, the theme that is expressed by the messages of time in "White Night" and is common to all the poems in *Vecher*, is the emotional dimensions of love. Akhmatova was a Russian Orthodox Christian, whose philosophy was rooted in "Judeo-Christian values" and who saw art and culture as part of God's hand in the world. Acmeism was, in essence, a religious approach to poetry, in which even ordinary, everyday occurrences had metaphysical significance: The Acmeist's responsibility was to fuse the finite and the infinite, not to escape into spiritual transcendence (the Symbolists' purpose), but to build beauty out of natural materials as a means of revelation. For Akhmatova, love was the conduit.

Virginia Starrett

THE WHITSUN WEDDINGS

Author: Philip Larkin (1922-1985)
Type of poem: Lyric
First published: 1964, in *The Whitsun Weddings*

The Poem

"The Whitsun Weddings" is a deceptively leisurely sounding poem in eight ten-line stanzas. The title refers to the British tradition of marrying on the weekend of Whitsunday or Pentecost (the seventh Sunday after Easter) to take advantage of the early summer "bank holiday" or long weekend. The rhyme scheme (*ababcdecde*) and meter (the second line of each stanza has four syllables; all the others have ten syllables each) are highly structured but unobtrusive.

The first-person speaker, who seems to be identified with Philip Larkin himself, is on his way by train from Lincolnshire to London for the weekend. He has no apparent connection with or interest in weddings at the outset. The first two stanzas describe a normal journey through the countryside on a hot afternoon. The train is nearly empty, and the speaker watches the landscape indifferently, happy only to be on his way "away."

In the third stanza, the speaker begins to notice "the weddings." He admits that he misunderstood the noise at first, taking it for "porters larking with the mails," but as the train pulls out of the station he watches the wedding parties left behind, the brides and grooms having boarded the train. The fourth, fifth, and sixth stanzas turn to the details of those groups that are left behind. They are clearly identified as lower-middle-class, presenting simultaneously funny and poignant appearances: girls in "parodies of fashion" and "jewellery-substitutes," "mothers loud and fat." The speaker becomes more and more interested, and he keeps seeing "it all again in different terms." In stanza 6, he moves from the surface details to the significance of the weddings for the fathers, women, and girls. The train, "Free at last," "hurrie[s] towards London."

In the last two stanzas, the speaker watches the newlyweds inside the train and again assumes his superiority by noting that "a dozen marriages got under way.// . . . and none/ Thought of the others they would never meet." The speaker, however, despite his sense that he is the only one to notice the connections among all the couples, sympathizes strongly with them. He attributes to them the potential "power/ That being changed can give," and he himself has also been changed.

Forms and Devices

This poem relies upon the careful development of the speaker's personality, with very little figurative language until the last two stanzas. As the reader travels with the speaker, the speaker's stance in relation to his country, the wedding parties, and the newlyweds both develops and changes. By participating in that development, the reader comes to share a delicately balanced view of tradition and change.

The details early in the poem establish the speaker as an almost stereotypical businessman-or professional man on his long weekend "getaway." He is aware of the time ("I was late getting away," the train leaves at "one-twenty") and at first wants only to ignore the noise of the weddings and continue his reading. In these same stanzas, however, the details of the scenery hint at the timeless and timely landscape of the poem. At the end of the first stanza, the three elements of sky, land ("Lincolnshire"), and water "meet," establishing a sense of unified, timeless beauty despite such counterdetails as "floatings of industrial froth" and "acres of dismantled cars." These paradoxical elements prepare the speaker and the reader for the similarly mixed view of the wedding parties and newlyweds in the next five stanzas.

As the speaker begins to pay attention to the wedding parties in stanzas 3 and 4, he assumes a superior, almost satirical tone: "girls/ In parodies of fashion," and, at the next stop, fathers with "seamy foreheads; mothers loud and fat;/ An uncle shouting smut." Yet even in this context, the speaker begins to notice some deeper significances, especially for the females. Although the girls wear "nylon gloves and jewellery-substitutes," they are nevertheless "marked off" and participating in something that is especially significant for them.

The speaker moves from his satiric mood to a more sympathetic view in stanzas 5 and 6. In stanza 5, he steps back from the details and realizes that everywhere in England "the wedding-days/ Were coming to an end" as "all down the line/ Fresh couples climbed aboard." In stanza 6, he notices, instead of the cheap clothing and unattractive bodies, "each face" and its ability "to define/ Just what it saw departing." Watching these faces, the speaker imagines what those definitions might be and arrives at some sense of the meanings of weddings: "children frowned/ At something dull; fathers had never known/ Success so huge and wholly farcical." The females, however, have more poignant and ambivalent definitions:

> The women shared
> The secret like a happy funeral;
> While girls, gripping their handbags tighter, stared
> At a religious wounding.

As stanza 7 begins, the speaker is watching the couples on the train: "A dozen marriages got under way." The significance of the changes in their lives is summed up in two key similes reinforcing the paradoxical nature of marriage and its promise of fertility. First, the speaker thinks of London with "Its postal districts packed like squares of wheat," using a traditional symbol of sustenance and fertility as that toward which "we were aimed." Second, at the conclusion of the poem, the brakes slow the train, giving "A sense of falling, like an arrow-shower/ Sent out of sight, somewhere becoming rain." This simile, too, suggests aiming at something unknown and unknowable—such as the future—yet, somehow, leading to the life-giving "rain." These gentle and generous similes demonstrate how far the speaker has come from his initial indifference. As the poem ends, he realizes, and brings the reader to realize, the immense importance of marriage, with its continuity and fertility, and the value of the traditional rites and customs within which those marriages begin.

Themes and Meanings

This poem invites the reader to learn along with the speaker about the depth and value of what may appear to be trivial and even outmoded ways of doing things. What the speaker first found ludicrous about the wedding parties—their predictable sameness—becomes for him an important indication of the continuity of the process by which individual humans are changed but the human race goes on. Ironically, the speaker of the poem is changed along with the newlyweds as he gradually modifies his initial satirical condescension and recognizes the importance of tradition.

The traditions in the poem include not only the wedding days and the general roles played by family members but also the particular poignancy of marriage for women. Throughout the poem, females appear most affected by the weddings. They especially experience the "religious wounding" (both sexually and psychologically) because, as at a "happy funeral," the bride dies (losing her name and, in the Renaissance sense of the word, her virginity). The women especially impress the speaker with their knowledge of "the secret" and seem to sum up within their experience much important knowledge of human life and value. Through their "deaths," they are reborn as wives with new names, and with the potential for renewing the race itself by bearing the next generation of children.

These specific traditions and continuities also form a part of a larger web of meaning in this poem. An entire land and culture—"sky and Lincolnshire and water"—is the setting of the poem, and the title, by placing the poem in the cycle of the year without specifying a particular year, gives the poem a sense of timelessness. Just as the natural world renews itself every year, so does the human race change and renew itself. For the detached, cynical nonparticipant in the rituals, recognizing and appreciating them brings salutary change and a deeper understanding of the world.

Julia Whitsitt

WHO LEARNS MY LESSON COMPLETE?

Author: Walt Whitman (1819-1892)
Type of poem: Lyric
First published: 1855, untitled in *Leaves of Grass*; "Lesson Poem," in *Leaves of Grass*, 1856; "Leaves of Grass No. 11," in *Leaves of Grass*, 1860; "Leaves of Grass No. 3," in *Leaves of Grass*, 1867; "Who Learns My Lesson Complete?" in *Passage to India*, 1871 and in *Leaves of Grass*, 1881

The Poem

Because "Who Learns My Lesson Complete?" appeared in the first edition of *Leaves of Grass* (1855), underwent numerous revisions, assumed its final form in 1867, and remains in the final edition of *Leaves of Grass* (1892), it is safe to say that Walt Whitman placed considerable importance on this poem. "Who Learns My Lesson Complete?" is a short poem in free verse with twenty-six lines of varying lengths divided into nine stanzas. The title asks a rhetorical question that may be simply paraphrased as "Who are they who are most likely to master the lesson taught throughout *Leaves of Grass*?" or perhaps, more cogently, "Who stands in greatest need of the lesson taught pervasively throughout *Leaves of Grass*?" The answer to the rhetorical question is, as is to be expected, contained in the body of the poem itself: Readers—whoever they may be—are likely to learn, and stand in need of learning, the "lesson complete."

After asking the introductory rhetorical question, the poet immediately welcomes all of humanity to "draw nigh and commence": "Boss, journeyman, apprentice, churchman and atheist,/ The stupid and the wise thinker, parents and offspring, merchant, clerk, porter and customer,/ Editor, author, artist, and schoolboy." The reader will note the paired opposites included in the invitation that suggest that all humanity has been summoned to hear the "message complete" to be announced by the poet.

Ironically, however, the "message complete" is ultimately beyond the ability of the poet to communicate to others: "I cannot say to any person what I hear," the poet says, adding that "it is very wonderful." What he has heard are "beautiful tales of things and the reasons of things" that are "so beautiful" he nudges himself "to listen." Though the poet tells readers that he lies "abstracted" (that is, intellectually focused and emotionally intent) upon these beautiful tales, it quickly becomes apparent that the poet sees nature and the universe not as phenomena to be explained but rather as wonders to be celebrated.

What exactly, then, is the "lesson complete" that the poet attempts to communicate to the reader of this poem and to the student of *Leave of Grass* in general? The lesson, readers are told, is "no lesson—it lets down the bars to a good lesson,/ And that to another, and every one to another still." If the lesson is not really a lesson but a removal of obstacles to the reception of a lesson, of many lessons perhaps, then the brunt of the message is that all of humanity can be students of nature and learn the "lesson complete" while free of the usual impediments to knowledge associated with conventional learning experiences. The fundamental lesson transmitted by the poet is quite simply the experience of wonder—hence the recurrent nouns "wonderful" and "beautiful." However, wonder and beauty lie quite beyond explanation; they are emotions to be experienced, not phenomena to be explicated. Who, then, learns the "lesson complete"? The poet has already supplied the answer to the rhetorical question: "The stupid and the wise thinker, parents and offspring, merchant, clerk, porter and customer,/ Editor, author, artist, and schoolboy," that is to say, all of humanity can learn the "lesson complete" if they approach nature in the right spirit—the spirit of wonder.

Forms and Devices

Whitman's poem essentially has a question and answer structure. The question announced in the title "Who Learns My Lesson Complete?" is answered throughout the remainder of the poem. As a writer of free verse, Whitman avoids rhyme and regular meter, preferring the parallel structures observable in the King James Bible and the persuasive prose of the New England Transcendentalists (Ralph Waldo Emerson and Henry David Thoreau, for example). The persuasive nature of the poem makes these repetitious structures quite viable. One might observe the first four words of the final five lines of the poem as a lesson in parallelism: "And that my soul," "And that I can," "And that I can," "And that the moon," and "And that they balance." The student learns to look, in other words, not at the ending of lines for rhymes but at the beginning of lines for emphatic repetitions.

It may be that Whitman had an ironic pun in mind when he titled his poem "Who Learns My Lesson Complete?" The word "lesson" is pronounced identically with the word "lessen." In brief, the poet announces a lesson that lessens the work normally expected of the student; it is the assumption of a sense of wonder, not a scholarly absorption in facts, that will constitute "the lesson complete." This ironic lessening is in reality a mystical increase in the student's appreciation of natural phenomena.

Themes and Meanings

The central theme of the poem is the understanding of the most important type of knowledge, that is, knowledge that cannot be communicated except through a shared sense of wonder. The "lesson complete" is the lesson felt, experienced, and endured; it is not a lesson learned in textbooks or in lectures. The most important kind of knowledge is gained through a relaxation of the soul, making possible the understanding of the wonderful nature of natural phenomena.

As the poem's title suggests, the great poet functions as a great teacher. The poet as teacher is a common nineteenth century figure. The poet does not instruct so much as he shows the way through his own example. Readers of *Leaves of Grass* will recognize the theme of the difficulty of communicating the sense of wonder as pervasive in Whitman's work. The short poem "When I Heard the Learn'd Astronomer," to cite a familiar example, narrates two scenes: The first scene shows the poet attending an astronomy lecture, while the second scene relates the narrator's departure from the lecture to stare "in perfect silence at the stars." The lecture leaves the poet "tired and sick," but he is refreshed when he looks up at the stars, having escaped "the charts and diagrams." The relief from such depression consists in the sense of wonder awakened by simply staring up at the stars. True learning comes about as a result of the sense of wonder rather than formal education.

The theme of equality, of the essential nobility of all human beings whatever their occupation, educational level, economic status, or location is, again, one that all readers of *Leaves of Grass* have come to expect from the great poet of democracy. Another theme, the assertion of immortality and the sense of wonder associated with the belief in immortality is, to most critics and scholars who have commented on this poem, insufficiently developed. As one of the most important doctrines of *Leaves of Grass*, it is more satisfactorily treated in poems such as "Song of the Rolling Earth" and "Salut au Monde!"

James T. F. Tanner

WHOROSCOPE

Author: Samuel Beckett (1906-1989)
Type of poem: Dramatic monologue
First published: 1930

The Poem

Whoroscope is exactly one hundred lines of rambling monologue supposedly mouthed by the famous seventeenth century French philosopher and scientist René Descartes while waiting to be served an egg which he might consider sufficiently mature to be eaten. There is no rhythmical pattern, and the poem's mannered colloquialisms and oratorical informalities give it an aura less of poetry than of desultory chatter. Samuel Beckett uses minor and sometimes intimate details of Descartes's life that he found in a biography of the philosopher written by Adrien Baillet. Beckett entered a poetry contest sponsored by Nancy Cunard's Hours Press in Paris; entries were to relate in some way to time, and this was Beckett's hastily written entry. After winning the contest, Beckett provided notes to explain the poem; his notes, although helpful, are not sufficient for most readers, and *The Norton Anthology of Modern Poetry* (1973) has added to Beckett's notes further information that clears up most of the allusions.

Descartes evidently had an aversion to fresh eggs, and he demanded that his omelette be made from eggs at least eight to ten days old. In the first sentence, he rejects an egg for being clearly too fresh for him; immediately the erudite connections begin, since the expostulation that accompanies the rejection of the egg refers to "the brothers Boot"—two Dutch doctors who had written a book attacking Aristotle. From this moment on, the poem is a supposedly accurate rendering of Descartes's conversation, a combination of associated ideas and stream-of-consciousness maunderings. He thinks next of Galileo, who had musical interests (hence the reference to "thirds") and whom he dislikes, possibly because he was once accused of stealing Galileo's ideas. Galileo used a pendulum in his experiments on the earth's movements about the sun, and he illustrated the enigma of feeling stationary while on a moving object by using the examples of a boat ride or a load on the back of a horse. It is this density of witty allusion that gives the poem much of its aesthetic piquancy.

The next section returns to questioning the omelette, with a mixed Italian-English pun on "prostisciutto," a jamming together of the English word "prostitute" and the Italian word for smoked ham, *prosciutto*. The scientists named in this section all came to Descartes for solutions to difficult mathematical problems. The idea of someone trying to give him a fresh egg seems to lead at line 21 into a memory of how his brother tried to swindle him. He fuses that idea with his memory of being a soldier, earning a few pennies, and repudiating Jesuit thinkers.

The action seems to be taking place at the time when Frans Hals, the famous Dutch painter, is waiting to paint a portrait of Descartes (a painting that still exists). Descartes remembers a cross-eyed girl he played with as a child, and that leads him to a series of other memories, including the death of his own child from scarlet fever. The problem of a suitable egg appears again, and he is still not satisfied. The sad memory of his own child's death has depressed him, and it leads him into the memory of three dreams he had in one night in 1619: In the first one he is blown against the church at La Flèche, and the dreams in total convince him that he had been given important philosophical insights.

He remembers going to the shrine of Our Lady of Loretto to thank the Virgin for showing him in his dreams that his future lay in science rather than the Church. Reference is made to his past interest in the Society of Rosicrucians, whose emblem includes a yellow key. The rest of this verse is a demotic version of his denial that his theory of the nature of matter is inconsistent with the Catholic doctrine of transubstantiation, which deems that in Communion the wafer and wine become the blood and flesh of Christ. He seems to be saying that all things are possible for God, and he ends by mocking Antoine Arnauld, who had attacked him on that point.

Again the problem of the egg comes up, comically enough and appropriately so in conjunction with Francis Bacon, the great English philosopher, who also favored reason over theological superstition and conservatism. The "cave phantoms" is a reference to a Bacon metaphor about humankind's tendency to prefer to believe in accumulated superstitions. He returns to his own troubles with the Church establishment, remembering Anna Maria Schurmann, a scholarly supporter of Descartes's enemy, Gisbert Voet, who attacked a book containing some of his ideas. "Leider! Leider!" (meaning "too bad" in German) was obviously her feeling about Descartes's work.

In the next section, he mocks his own most famous saying, "I think, therefore I am," fusing it with Saint Augustine's "Si fallor, sum" which means "If I err, I exist." He goes on to mock Augustine's repudiation of the pleasures of the world, calling him a "froleur," a teaser. All quarrels aside, Descartes accepts God's existence, and his own—not as a god, or as anything less than a part of the perfection that is God's creation, symbolized by the rose. It is the one moment of lyric seriousness in the poem.

Then Descartes returns to the egg, a double-yoker, which he relishes before going off to Sweden to teach Christina, the Queen of Sweden. She is "murdering" in the sense of insisting that Descartes join her early in the morning; his last illness was blamed on that rigorous practice. The poem ends with Descartes rejecting the suggestion of Weulles, a Dutch doctor who proposes to "blood" him to bring down his fever. The "bitter steps" are an allusion to a line in Dante's *Paradiso* (c. 1320), in which exile from one's native land is described as the painful descending and climbing of foreign steps. He asks to die, and in doing so reminds himself and others of his refusal to reveal his birthday to any astrologer in order to avoid having his future life and death predicted: "my second starless inscrutable hour."

Forms and Devices

In *Whoroscope*, Beckett was looking back with some admiration to two major experimental authors as the inspiration for this poem. The most obvious influence was

James Joyce, with whom Beckett had close personal connections throughout the 1930's. Joyce's deep knowledge of theology and his Roman Catholic education did not deter him from using Roman Catholic doctrine without much concern for good taste; that carefree and careless attitude pervades Beckett's poem, together with a joyful, playful, and somewhat sophomoric enthusiasm for religious jokes and vulgarities. Much of the roughhouse pleasure of the poem lies in its schoolboy tastelessness and a kind of self-congratulatory smartness. Like Joyce, Beckett was not inclined to be deterred by considerations of propriety, and this poem is proof of their mutual belief that more sauciness makes for better art.

The poem's form, however, comes from a poet whose temperament artistically was entirely different from that of Joyce and Beckett. It is T. S. Eliot who contributes the idea of the monologue cluttered so densely with scholarly allusion that the ordinary reader would find the material impregnable. Eliot's work in poems such as *The Waste Land* (1922) and "The Love Song of J. Alfred Prufrock" is, actually, perfectly understandable if all the allusions (historical, literary, religious, and social) are known, and footnotes can provide that knowledge. The experience of reading such poems is, in a sense, a necessarily double one for most readers, who must accumulate all the necessary facts concerning the allusions. Once these are intellectually ingested, the poem makes sense, and much of the aesthetic and intellectual pleasure comes from recognizing the aptness of the references. This is clearly a large part of what is going on in *Whoroscope*, which does, in the main, however, confine its footnote materials to three areas of special knowledge: religion (particularly Roman Catholic), philosophy, and biographical aspects of Descartes's career and personal eccentricities.

The other matter to be met is the way in which Beckett uses or misuses (however one sees it) the Eliot version of the dramatic monologue, developed to its finest point in the nineteenth century by Robert Browning and refined by Eliot, particularly in the two poems mentioned above, to meet the social and psychological problems of early twentieth century man. Beckett adapts it for his own purposes, which are clearly less ambitious than those of either Browning or Eliot, who took the idea of the single figure contemplating his or her life quite seriously. Beckett seems most interested in piling on the gnomic allusion for the sheer fun of it, so much so that the poem is not so much an exploration of a serious moment in the life of the main character who seeks to find a solution through the process of talking about it in a kind of self-analysis session as it is a framework for the improvisatory exuberance and extravagance of the poet's imagination. It is an example of imitating a form (much admired in its original state in the hands of Eliot) by cheerfully mangling it and changing it into what might be called, as in the mock epic, the mock dramatic monologue.

Themes and Meanings

Beckett was a serious student of seventeenth and eighteenth century philosophy, which put a heavy emphasis on epistemology—that wing of philosophy which concerned itself with theories of knowledge, with how things are known. It was legitimate for him to be interested in not only the theories of Descartes but also the minutiae of his life. The interest in philosophic ideas about humankind's relation to the universe and to God pervades Beckett's texts, although the position he espouses in his work is generally so pessimistic and negative that he became the finest representative of the "absurd" in the literary arts. He explored, over and over again, in his plays and novels, the simple proposition that life is meaningless in any spiritual sense. That idea is not quite clearly formed in his early work, and it must be remembered that *Whoroscope* is his first published work.

In the first place, the poem can be seen as a repudiation of the idea implicit in Eliot's use of the dramatic monologue that sense can be made out of life in the process of the making of the poem itself. Nothing is, in fact, solved in *Whoroscope*, if indeed there was anything of serious moment to be concerned about. Descartes has an eccentric attitude toward breakfast omelettes, which it was his practice to eat every morning. Getting the eggs sufficiently mature for his consumption is the obvious problem in the poem, and it might be argued that the problem is eventually solved, and Descartes is then free to go on to his fate in Sweden, dying of a chill. It has, it might be argued, a kind of mildly comic biographical structure. That might be misleading, however, because there are forms of the dramatic monologue which do not necessarily require the movement from inertia to action. If the tradition is traced back to Browning in the nineteenth century, it can be seen that the "problem" structure which Eliot uses in his poems is only one of the kinds of dramatic monologue. There is another kind, represented by Browning's "My Last Duchess" and "Fra Lippo Lippi," in which the main character does not have any particular problem, but in the telling of the tale reveals hidden aspects of character.

Observers of the Descartes of *Whoroscope* may come to their own conclusions as to who he is and what he knows by the end of the poem, and they may not be much impressed by his vulgarity, self-praise, and derisive attitude toward his enemies. If the poem is seen as tonally comic, however, Descartes may get off lightly as a somewhat foulmouthed but charmingly witty manipulator of his life and his conflicts therein. In the widest sense, the poem is a kind of mocking of the usually portentous exposure of character that is a mark of the dramatic monologue, and the piling on of recondite allusions—quantitatively excessive, qualitatively clever, and sly beyond measure—may be seen as "meaning" in itself, as a good-natured, stunningly confident *jeu d'esprit*, using an imploded version of Descartes's life and a respected literary form to prove how well Beckett could play his instrument.

If meaning of somewhat more substantial weight is needed, it is possible to argue that it is quite sneakily an attack on Descartes and the presumption of thinking that human beings can know anything—or, indeed, that there is anything to know. If that is how the poem is read, it can be seen as clearly presaging the things to come, the works that would make Beckett one of the great writers and one of the most influential thinkers of the last half of the twentieth century.

Charles Pullen

WHY THE CLASSICS

Author: Zbigniew Herbert (1924-1998)
Type of poem: Dramatic monologue
First published: 1968, in *Selected Poems*; as "Diaczego Klaysycy," in *Napis*, 1969

The Poem

"Why the Classics" is a thirty-four line poem divided into three parts. It is characteristic of Zbigniew Herbert's free verse and economical use of language. As the final poem in *Selected Poems* (1968), it is, so to speak, the poet's signature, a justification of his classicism which attempts to put the present in perspective by invoking historic events, myths, and works of art.

The first part recalls the Greek historian Thucydides (c. 460-400 B.C.E.), who participated as a general in the Peloponnesian War (431-404 B.C.E.), the great conflict between the Athenians and the Spartans. Although Thucydides deals as a military historian with the whole war—including its politics, battles, and diplomacy—the poet is struck by the historian's account of his failure to relieve Amphipolis, his native city under attack by the Athenian enemy, Brasidos. It is a minor moment in the historian's narrative that the poet points out in comparing the episode to "a pin/ in a forest." Yet to Thucydides, his failure is of such importance that he pays for it by exiling himself from Amphipolis. Exiles "of all times" know what this separation cost Thucydides, the poet remarks—without, however, spelling out the meaning of exile.

In the second part, the poet turns to the recent past, noting the refusal of generals to take responsibility for their defeats, preferring, instead, to blame subordinates and to champion their own virtues. It is circumstance, not human character, that is to blame for these failures, these generals claim—citing "envious colleagues/ unfavorable winds." Thucydides, on the other hand, engages in no special pleading for himself, merely noting the number of his ships and the season in which they quickly sailed. Again, as in the first part, the poet does not explicitly say what he makes of Thucydides' account.

The third part shifts the apparent subject matter of the poem from war to art, making no overt reference to the content of the first two stanzas. Instead, the poet makes an explicit statement, a value judgment, suggesting that if art is to pity a damaged world ("a broken jar") or the defeated self ("a small broken soul"), then it will leave a pathetic legacy, comparable to lovers waking up in a squalid hotel and weeping over the shabby conditions of their affair.

Forms and Devices

Herbert employs two of his characteristic devices in this poem: understatement and irony. Indeed, these two devices are linked together to achieve the meaning of the poem. Thus Thucydides seems to be described merely as a historian who minimized his own part in a great war. That he is admired by the poet seems apparent in the last two lines of the first part, although exactly how exiles of all times feel is not made clear. Presumably, however, their exile causes them great pain, and presumably Thucydides similarly suffered from this sacrifice. In the second part, the poet again implies admiration for Thucydides because the historian does not excuse his failure; he only describes his military effort, which is in great contrast to the complaining generals of the recent past.

The structure of the poem's argument in the first two parts sets up the expectation that this contrast between the ancient and more recent past will be resolved in the third, concluding part—and so it is, except that the poet's subject matter has changed abruptly, necessitating a re-evaluation of what the poem has been about. The understated quality of the poem's first two parts is a clue to the fact that the poet has actually been using the example of Thucydides to think about art, about what the poet is supposed to make of life.

The irony is complex: The poem is about something more than war and the generals' attitude toward it. By refusing to rationalize his own failure, Thucydides was able to show the intricacy, the greatness of the war, and yet by saying no more about himself, Thucydides proved, in the poet's view, his greatness. The lesson for the poet is clear: Eschew "self-pity," the efforts to vindicate the self, and size up the world for what it is. Otherwise, the poet's vision is like the weeping lovers in a "small dirty hotel"—it is trivial and self-involved and unable to come to terms with reality.

One other formal device is essential to grasping the significance of the poem: It is written without punctuation, or capitals at the beginning of sentences. In the first two parts, each stanza forms a sentence, a natural unit of meaning that is meant to be open-ended, subject to revised interpretation, a dangling and modifiable statement that depends on the unpunctuated statements which precede and follow it. Only in the last part, with its two stanzas divided between "if" and "what," does the poem come to a kind of closure, a definition of what it is about—although the last stanza's lack of a period leads it back to the first sentence of the poem, linking the image of the present with an image of the past, and art and the lovers with the Peloponnesian War, the initial stimulus and now confirmation of the poet's view of art.

Themes and Meanings

The poem is a statement of why the classics mean so much to the poet and should mean as much to the present reader. A classic, in Herbert's view, is a work of art that contains a meaning that is true in all times and places—not merely in its account of a specific subject matter such as war. The Greeks, who are often praised for their development of the classical ideal, believed there was an order in nature that should be imitated in the order of human affairs. A belief in order meant a sense of proportion, of the individual finding an appropriate place in the community, the *polis*. Individuality per se was not a value, though individuals had a value, which was determined by examining, as Thucydides and the poet do, the nature of things and of humankind's place in them.

For Thucydides, the paramount value is his native city, not himself. Failing to save it means to him a life of exile, for only in this way can he assert his subordination to the very thing for which he fought: his land and people. Yet the irony of the poem is that Thucydides becomes a great individual precisely because of his sacrifice and loyalty, because of his sense of place, his subordination to an ideal greater than himself. That, in essence, is classicism and why the poet accepts it. If the poet, like the "generals of the most recent wars," only serves himself, then he leaves nothing for the future, for his present has shrunk in significance.

The poet, disenchanted with his present, speaks as an exile. That is why he identifies with Thucydides and knows how "exiles of all times" feel. The classical point of view is out of fashion and individuality reigns supreme, with generals being simply the type of leaders who put themselves, not their cause, first. The cause for the poet is his art, and the poem therefore is a kind of declaration, his avowal that his art—all art—should serve a greater purpose than the self. Self-love leads to self-pity and to a breakdown in the belief in universal values that the poet finds in the classics.

The poem recognizes that individual failure is inevitable. That it was winter and that Thucydides sailed quickly suggests that there could have been extenuating circumstances that the historian/general might have used to absolve himself of blame. Did the fact that he had seven ships mean he was well- or ill-prepared? The poet does not say, but he seems impressed with Thucydides' classic response, putting his fate second to that of Amphipolis. In another sense, then, his individual story has been like a "pin/ in a forest" because it must, in the classic view of things, be regarded as an infinitesimal part of the war. Hence the historian was right in allotting so little of his narrative to it.

The poet implies that there is an objective way of viewing history and that the classics provide examples of it. To think otherwise is to limit the self and art to the "small dirty hotel" of the imagination, a pathetic image reflective of the anticlassical tendency to create an artificial inner world, in which it is not the sun that "dawns" and awakens human sensibility but "wall-paper," a false subjectivity that shuts out reality and humanity's connection with its past and future.

Carl Rollyson

WICHITA VORTEX SUTRA

Author: Allen Ginsberg (1926-1997)
Type of poem: Mock epic
First published: 1966; collected in *The Fall of America: Poems of These States, 1965-1971*, 1972

The Poem

"Wichita Vortex Sutra" is a long poem (690 lines) in free verse that is divided into two main parts. Part 1 (156 lines) was actually written the day after part 2 (534 lines); the poem was written on February 14 and 15, 1966. The word "sutra" in the title is the Sanskrit word for thread, connective cord, or rule, and is used in a religious context to denote any of the sermons of the Buddha. Situated near the geographic center of the continental United States, Wichita, Kansas, is, for Allen Ginsberg, also the cultural heart of the country. Overwhelmingly white, Christian, and conservative, Wichita is the quintessential expression of mainstream America, the metaphoric axis of its violently whirling vortex. In terms of sound sense, Wichita (though an Indian name) evokes the word "witch," thus conjuring images of sorcery, witchcraft, evil portents, and America's Puritan heritage. So, taken as a whole, the title employs alliteration as it ironically juxtaposes Buddhism and Christianity, order and chaos, prayer and violence, and suggests an incantation or sermon meant to admonish, and possibly even exorcise, America.

Written in the first person, the poem describes a 250-mile bus ride (south on Route 77) from Lincoln, Nebraska, to Wichita, Kansas, on a bleak Sunday afternoon in midwinter. (Indeed, the route from Lincoln to Wichita traces a kind of sutra—a thread or connective cord—between the two cities.) In terms of narrative strategy, the poet shifts between vivid descriptions of the rural midwestern landscape, quotations from contemporary newspaper reports, free-associative meditations on the Vietnam War then raging, the larger history of the Cold War, and the state of America's soul. The form of the poem, philosophical meditation thinly disguised as travelogue, may owe something to "Travels in North America" by the Nebraskan poet Weldon Kees, a native of Beatrice—one of the towns that the bus passes through on its way to Wichita.

Rife with hyperbolic, angry, and plaintive exclamations arranged in uneven lines spread over long, loosely structured stanzas, the poem does not offer a concise or neatly defined argument. Nonetheless, it does manifest a coherent polemic. As is characteristic of so much of his poetry, Ginsberg starts out by lamenting the sexual and emotional repression that is at the root of the terrible loneliness of American life: "to speak my lonesomeness in a car,/ because not only my lonesomeness/ it's Ours, all over America." He then echoes his hero, Walt Whitman, in calling for a renaissance of joyful feeling: "No more fear of tenderness, much delight in weeping, ecstasy/ in singing, laughter rises that confounds/ staring Idiot mayors/ and stony politicians eyeing/ Thy breast,/ O Man of America, be born!" Ultimately, though, the poet's main concern is with language, particularly its grotesque misuse in the service of militarism: "I search for the language/ that is also yours—/ almost all our language has been taxed by war." Much of the poem is concerned with exposing and denouncing "language abused/ for Advertisement,/ language used/ like magic for power on the planet." However, the poem also envisions positive alternatives. Counterpoised against the distorted language of the media, politicians, and "U.S. military spokesmen," the poet offers as exemplar the visionary language of his friend, Bob Dylan: "His youthful voice making glad/ the brown endless meadows/ His tenderness penetrating aether,/ soft prayer on the airwaves,/ Language, language, and sweet music too."

Forms and Devices

Ginsberg's poetic approach might be best described as historical stream-of-consciousness. Like Whitman, Ginsberg starts with the consciousness of the individual self and expands its purview to encompass the putative consciousness of American society as a whole—and, by extension, of the entire universe ("I am the Universe tonite"). As a poem ultimately about the United States, much of the imagery of "Wichita Vortex Sutra" consists of precise and telling descriptions of the American landscape: "Prehistoric excavation, *Apache Uprising*/ in the drive-in theater/ Shelling Bombing Range mapped in the distance,/ Crime Prevention Show, sponsor Wrigley's Spearmint,/ Dinosaur Sinclair advertisement, glowing green—." Here and elsewhere, the scenery is charged with metaphoric significance; seemingly banal landmarks act as synecdoches for American commercialism, militarism, police repression, and the exploitation of resources and other peoples.

As Ginsberg gets closer to Wichita, "the heart of the Vortex,/ where anxiety rings," his concern with the degradation of language becomes more urgent. Accordingly, he summons his bardic powers to effect a ritual transformation of the language through his own utterances: "I call all Powers of imagination/ to my side . . . to make Prophecy . . . Come to my lone presence/ into this Vortex named Kansas/ I lift my voice aloud,/ make Mantra of American language now,/ I here declare the end of the War!"

As it nears culmination, the poem gathers momentum and takes on aspects of a shaman's chant as the word "language" is more frequently interjected: "U.S. Military Spokesman/ Language language/ Cong death toll/ has soared to 100 in First Air Cavalry/ Division's Sector of/ Language language/ Operation White Wing near Bong Son/ Some of the/ Language language/ Communist/ Language language soldiers/ charged so desperately/ they were struck with six or seven bullets before they fell." Thus, the poet uses the very word "language" as a kind of linguistic solvent to destabilize and overturn that which the word (self-reflexively) denotes. False, degraded language must be deconstructed and banished before a more truthful language can be uttered in its place.

Themes and Meanings

Though on one level it is certainly an antiwar poem, "Wichita Vortex Sutra" transcends both its genre and the specific historical circumstances that occasioned its creation. A fundamental premise of the poem is that language, though a simple tool, is also a tremendously powerful and potentially dangerous tool, much more powerful and dangerous than is generally assumed. More than merely expressing consciousness, language shapes consciousness and therefore controls history.

As an example of the reality-transforming power of language, Ginsberg cites an utterance by President John F. Kennedy's secretary of defense, Robert S. McNamara, who "made a 'bad guess'/ 'Bad guess?' chorused the Reporters./ Yes, no more than a Bad Guess, in 1962/ 8000 American Troops handle the/ Situation.'" McNamara's sloppy and infelicitous use of language may or may not actually have helped to precipitate the disastrous U.S. involvement in Vietnam. Ginsberg dramatizes McNamara's statement because he sees it as typical of a chronic pattern of U.S. government deceit, exaggeration, misapprehension, and misstatement that marked the entire history of the Cold War: "Communism is a 9 letter word/ used by inferior magicians with/ the wrong alchemical formula for transforming earth into gold." In the mouths of such men, language ceases to have any mimetic significance; it is reduced to gibberish, an abstruse and secretive currency of power. Indeed, as if language were not debased enough, new terms are coined to obscure reality further: "General Taylor *Limited Objectives/ Owls* from Pennsylvania/ Clark's Face *Open Ended/* Dove's *Apocalypse.*"

Ginsberg also asserts that America's corporate media is ideologically all of a piece, and is at one with the government, in the creation and dissemination of lies and distortions that further oppression and war: "N B C B S U P A I N S L I F E/ Time Mutual presents/ World's Largest Camp Comedy:/ Magic in Vietnam—/ reality turned inside out." Yet against such concerted and powerful forces of mystification, the lone poet also has enormous power: the power to name evil. The evil that Ginsberg identifies as underlying America's war on language, on nature, on its own and other peoples, is a Puritanical, life-denying strain that is integral to the American character.

Engaging in the sort of instructive hyperbole that marked his treatment of the McNamara statement, Ginsberg closes the poem with an arresting assertion: "Carry Nation began the war on Vietnam here/ with an angry smashing ax/ attacking Wine—/ Here fifty years ago, by her violence/ began a vortex of hatred that defoliated the Mekong Delta—." The idea that Carry Nation (the famous midwestern temperance advocate who marched into barrooms and smashed bottles and fixtures with a hatchet) somehow instigated the Vietnam War is not literally true. What is true is the *spirit* of the statement—its equation of prohibitionist fervor with interventionist arrogance. To Ginsberg's way of thinking, both events come from a characteristically American intolerance of difference, an insatiable desire to control or to destroy.

Robert Niemi

THE WIDOW'S LAMENT IN SPRINGTIME

Author: William Carlos Williams (1883-1963)
Type of poem: Elegy
First published: 1921, in *Sour Grapes*

The Poem

William Carlos Williams's "The Widow's Lament in Springtime" is a twenty-eight-line, free-verse lyric in which a widow expresses her grief over the death of her husband as she looks at the growing plants and flowers of spring that remind her of her loss. It is a modernist version of a pastoral elegy that uses images of nature to lament the death of a loved one. Unlike earlier elegies such as John Milton's seventeenth century "Lycidas" or Walt Whitman's nineteenth century "When Lilacs Last in the Dooryard Bloom'd," there is not the usual coming to terms with the fact of mortality—no consolation, no hope, nor even resignation hold out in the end. Instead, the poem uses the dramatic interior monologue of the widow to express her sorrow as she looks at the trees, bushes, and flowers, ending with her final suicidal wish to be immersed in the marsh, and so be with her husband in death.

The poem begins with the widow thinking, "Sorrow is my own yard/ where the new grass/ flames as it has flamed/ often before." Yet this year, rather than a sign of springtime joy, it is a "cold fire" that surrounds her and reminds her of her deceased husband and bereavement. Lines 7-8 jump suddenly into the past tense to explain, tersely, that she has lived for thirty-five years with her husband.

Lines 9 –19 come back to the present to describe the springtime growth: First, the white plum tree with its "masses of flowers," and then the cherry branches and the yellow and red "masses of flowers." However, the beauty, color, and vitality of these spring trees and flowers, rather than symbolizing the usual ideas of joy, newness, birth, growth, and development, now represent grief, the past, death, loss, and deprivation. In a flat tone, she notes that her grief in her now colorless world overpowers any joy or beauty they once held for her. In fact, they are now only a source of sorrow. She observes, "today I notice them/ and turn away forgetting." In lines 20-24 the widow mentions that her son has told her about "trees of white flowers" in the distant meadows.

In the last of the six, flowing sentences which often use enjambment and run on to the succeeding line, lines 25-28 give her final death wish and a sense of the sensual, seductiveness of death to her: "I feel that I would like/ to go there/ and fall into those flowers/ and sink into the marsh near them." In later years Williams described the poem as his "imagination of what mother would be thinking" after his father died of cancer on Christmas day, 1918.

Forms and Devices

Without using any pattern of rhyme or rhythm, the poem concentrates on an objective, flat, and unemotional description of the springtime images, emphasizing the sharp contrasts, anthitheses, and inversions of standard symbols initially with striking figures of speech (metaphors such as "Sorrow is my own yard" and "the new grass/ flames," as well as the oxymoron "cold fire,") and several proximate repetitions ("flames" and "flamed" in line 3, "year" and "years" in lines 6 and 7, "masses of flowers" in lines 10 and 11, and "today" in lines 18 and 20).

The unusual metaphor "new grass flames" creates both a visual comparison of brightness and shape and a kinetic one of a flame flickering and grass blowing. The title itself seems to foreshadow the tension between a flat, prosaic, objective description—an almost deadening, hypnotic, unemotional effect heightened by the nearly continual enjambment and simple conjunctions and prepositions that string the phrases together—and an overwhelming, inescapable grief in the widow's dramatic monologue, where one seems to overhear the speaker's thoughts, rather than be directly addressed. The title describes a detached viewpoint from outside the widow, whereas the poem itself is in the first person and completely interior.

In addition to this flat tone, the widow's voice is somewhat halting and disjointed, sometimes abruptly shifting focus without logical coherence, as if her mind, numbed by grief, is flitting from image to image and conjuring up its inevitable associations. For example, the only two relatively short sentences, which parallel each other (lines 7-8 and lines 9-10), shift to the past tense and then back to the present again with the first sentence inverted ("Thirtyfive years/ I lived with my husband"), highlighting the disconnectedness of each sentence with the previous one in terms of subject matter. Thus, the repetitions, including the repeating of "flowers" four times, serve as not logical but rather associational links in the widow's bereaved mind to stitch together discordant, discrete images and thoughts.

Since earlier published versions of the poems also changed the verb tenses to past—"load" to "loaded" in line 12 in *Selected Poems* (1949) and "turn" to "turned" in line 19 in *Collected Early Poems* (1951)—one may surmise that Williams was quite conscious of the tense shift when he let the one in line 8 stand. The running together of "Thirtyfive years" may signal that disintegration of the "unit" which was her marriage and perhaps the irrevocable break between the discrete past and the sorrowful present. For the first seventeen lines, the widow uses mostly simple verbs that do not state she is initiating an action in the present; beginning in line 18 the active verbs of the present ("notice," "turn away," "feel," "fall," "sink") show her wish for initiating actions that eventually lead to the idea of commiting suicide.

Themes and Meanings

As a member for a while of the Imagists and Objectivists in the modernist movement, Williams was, at this early stage in his career, following the model of his friend and fellow poet Ezra Pound. Williams was striving for the simple, clear, concise, sharp image, presented as objectively as possible, with virtually no editorializing or commentary. In several ways "The Widow's Lament in Springtime" anticipates this strategy, seen in slightly later Williams poems such as "The Red Wheelbarrow" and "Spring and All" (both published in the 1923 collection *Spring and All*). For Williams, the poem was both a picture and a "machine made of words," and, as he famously said in his long poem *Paterson* (1946-1958), there are "[N]o ideas but in things." That is, the abstract concepts in poetry are to be derived from, or couched in, concrete particulars. Like those two later short poems, "Widow's Lament" creates a series of sharp images in free verse and, for the most part, in unadorned, simple language, inverts the usual symbolism of spring and utilizes continual enjambment, connecting short phrases of sentences that run down the page.

Several elements foreshadow the widow's suicidal impulse at the end. One is the gradual movement of the four locations in nature—from her yard, to the meadows and woods, and finally to the swamp. Another is the symbol of the white flowers, mentioned immediately after (and associated with) the previous line about her years with her husband. The symbol of the white flowers on the trees appears again in line 24, which immediately triggers her desire to "sink into the marsh near them," and so be in death with the white flowers that remind her of her lost husband. Her immersion into the former "joy" of the springtime flowers and into the oblivion of the reunion with her dead husband demonstrate the seductiveness, sensuousness, and escape from grief her death wish promises.

This motif of enclosure, entrapment, and engulfment—the inability of the widow to "turn away" and escape the "cold fire/ that closes round" her—encircles the poem as her grief encircles her. Her own yard, once a source of joy, surrounds her, and the new grass "closes round" her. At the end, her son's attempt to distract or cheer her by pointing out the beautiful white flowers on the distant trees becomes counterproductive, since she merely formulates the desire to submerge herself in the marsh, a suffocating engulfment that attempts to escape her grief. The repetition of the phrase "masses of flowers" in lines 10 and 11 and the dual connotation of "masses" underscore both the heaviness and the abundance or omnipresence of her grief. These elements, coupled with the connotation of heaviness in the verb "load" in the very next phrase, suggest the flowers represent a kind of funeral wreath to her.

Joseph Francavilla

THE WIFE OF BATH'S TALE

Author: Geoffrey Chaucer (c. 1343-1400)
Type of poem: Narrative
First transcribed: 1387-1400, in *The Canterbury Tales*

The Poem

Geoffrey Chaucer's romantic narrative "The Wife of Bath's Tale" is one of *The Canterbury Tales* told by the pilgrims during their journey to visit the shrine of Thomas Becket, the Archbishop of Canterbury who was murdered in his cathedral in 1170. After the "General Prologue," in which the Wife of Bath mentions that she has been married five times and would welcome a sixth husband, and that she spends her married life pursuing power over her husbands, she tells a tale about a knight who must marry; dominance in a romantic relationship becomes an important theme in the poem as it does in the Wife's prologue and in her personal life.

The plot begins when a knight encounters a maiden and rapes her. Initially, King Arthur decides that his punishment should be death. The queen, however, intervenes on the knight's behalf, asking the king to spare the man's life. Arthur decides to leave the knight's fate in her hands. The queen decides to send the knight on a quest; he must search throughout the land to determine what women most desire. The knight reluctantly embarks on his quest and asks countless women what they want most, only to receive as many different responses as possible. Distraught, the knight encounters some women dancing in the woods; as he approaches, they disappear, leaving him only with a hideously ugly old woman who seems to know about his quest. She promises to tell him the correct answer provided that he subsequently grants a request of hers. After he agrees out of desperation, she whispers the answer to him, and he then returns to court.

The knight tells the queen and her ladies that women most desire sovereignty over their men and that if the ladies at court do not approve of the answer, they can take his life. The women approve of his answer, thus saving his life. The old hag then appears and demands that her request be fulfilled—to marry him. Shocked, the knight refuses, offering the woman his money and everything else if only she will let him out of the bargain; she refuses, so he, with great reluctance, marries her.

The marriage begins poorly, with the knight refusing to consummate the marriage because he considers her extremely ugly and far beneath him socially. She then embarks on a long speech about *gentilesse*, which means nobility of spirit. The knight listens to her oration and starts to relent in his loathing of the woman. The hag then makes the knight an offer: She can be either beautiful but unfaithful to him or ugly and faithful. Instead of making this choice, the knight decides to allow her to choose which she would prefer. Delighted that her new husband has passed her test by permitting her the power to choose, she will be both beautiful and faithful to him.

Forms and Devices

"The Wife of Bath's Tale" is a medieval romance in the chivalric tradition. Chaucer's tale, a poetic narrative, is typical of medieval romances in that it contains a knight on a quest, mercy, honor, and the royal court. The supernatural and magic also play a major role in the tale, as in most medieval romances. The supernatural manifests itself when the knight is lured to the dancing women who magically disappear, leaving him alone with the old hag; she demonstrates her magical abilities when she transforms herself into a young and beautiful woman.

In "The Wife of Bath's Tale," as in "The Miller's Tale," the pilgrim undercuts the majestic and noble action of "The Knight's Tale." In "The Wife of Bath's Tale," the narrator portrays the knight as an arrogant and class-conscious rapist, quite different from the noble knights who appear in "The Knight's Tale." This tale is told by the feisty, aggressive, and lustful Wife of Bath immediately after she concludes her prologue. The reader should note that the tale is not only told by the Wife of Bath, but also told from her feminist point of view.

It is essential that readers understand the correlation between her prologue and her tale. Both concern marriage and the desire for the wife to acquire dominance in relationships. The tale is told in heroic couplets, a form that Chaucer inaugurated into English poetry. Heroic couplets are lines that contain ten syllables, with the stress being on every even-numbered syllable. The rhyme scheme is *aabbccdd* . . . and so on; in other words, the second line rhymes with the first and the fourth with the third. The fact that he employed heroic couplets rather than the majestic seven-line rime royal (*ababbcc*) suggests that he did not consider the characters and the actions to be noble and grand.

Themes and Meanings

A significant theme in Chaucer's poem is marriage, which is the Wife of Bath's hobbyhorse. The romance is also about domination in regard to gender roles. The romance begins with the Wife of Bath mocking friars, claiming that they are too dishonest; this satire serves as an act of vengeance because the Friar has previously interrupted her prologue. The Wife's satire of friars manifests to Chaucer's readers that the woman hates to be controlled by others (in the second interruption of the prologue, the Friar attempts to terminate the extensive and rambling monologue of the Wife, a chatterbox). Her mockery demonstrates her anger at the Friar for trying to harness her voice, to dominate her verbally. She also claims that women need to be careful of friars, for these supposedly holy men have been known to sexually assault females. Thus, the Wife of Bath, in her quest for revenge, suggests that the Friar is a rapist—"he ne wol doon hem but dishonour"—linking her adversary with the protagonist of her tale, the lecherous knight.

When the knight rapes the maiden, he physically dominates her, controlling her as he shames her. When Arthur transfers his authority to his queen, she then governs the knight's fate. After dominating a woman, now another woman controls him and can either take or spare his life. He then sets out on a quest—which the queen herself chooses—regarding the question about female desire. If he does not find the answer, he will die, so he finds himself totally at the mercy of the queen and her ladies. The fact that every woman he encounters provides him with a different answer suggests Chaucer's gentle mocking of women: They cannot reach a consensus. However, the question is open and broad, allowing for many different valid answers.

The knight then finds himself at the mercy of the old woman, who knows the answer and will tell him, provided that he puts himself solely in her authority by granting her desire. When the knight returns, he gives his answer, declaring that women desire sovereignty over their men. He then adds, "This is youre moste desir though ye me kille./ Dooth as you list: I am here at youre wille." The knight has perhaps learned something from this quest because he puts his life completely at the mercy of the women. He declares that they may kill him if his answer does not satisfy them, allowing them to decide whether his response is worthy of preserving his life.

Although the women declare that he may live, he then is forced to marry the hag, a decision enforced by the queen and her court. The knight begins his marriage as the dominating spouse, informing his elderly bride that she is unworthy of him because of her ugliness and her low social class. Her eloquent but long-winded speech—the hag, like the Wife of Bath, talks incessantly—impresses the knight.

When she provides him with the choice, beautiful and unfaithful or ugly and faithful, he decides not to make a choice. Specifically, he chooses to let her decide, which is actually a decision in itself. By permitting his elderly wife to decide, the knight endows her with power, indicating that she alone will govern her own life without an attempt by him to control her. Instead of making such a significant decision about her physical appearance and her loyalty, he entrusts her with autonomy. His actions suggest that he has learned a great deal through his quest and his wife's oration. As a reward, she transforms herself into a beautiful *and* a faithful wife. By allowing her to have control in their marriage, he thus benefits from both aspects of the bargain.

It might be troubling, however, to some readers that this knight rapes a woman and eventually is rewarded with a young, beautiful, and loyal wife. The old hag's transformation into a gorgeous woman represents the narrator's (the Wife of Bath's) wish fulfillment. The Wife was a beautiful woman who became ugly as she grew old; she laments the loss of her beauty and youth in her prologue. Because there is unquestionably a close connection between the narrator and the hag, the readers can perceive this transformation as something the Wife of Bath wants for herself. The old hag marries, which the Wife also wants; perhaps her reason for embarking on the pilgrimage in the first place is her search for husband number six.

Eric Sterling

THE WILD COMMON

Author: D. H. Lawrence (1885-1930)
Type of poem: Lyric
First published: 1916, in *Amores*; revised in *The Collected Poems of D. H. Lawrence,* 1928

The Poem

"The Wild Common" is, in D. H. Lawrence's own terms, "a good deal rewritten." Among his earliest writings, it was composed in 1905 or 1906 at a time when he was "struggling to say something which it takes a man twenty years to be able to say." Lawrence finally got that said when he published his extended version of the poem— twenty percent longer and with more than fifty percent of the original reworded—as the opening poem in his *Collected Poems* of 1928. The forty-two-year-old poet changed little of the basic scenario, or even of the rhyme scheme and rhythm, of "The Wild Common" from the version he wrote at nineteen. The content of the poem, however, matures markedly.

Critical consensus prefers the revised poem, with its increased detail and clarified focus. The earlier version is almost never anthologized. Some commentators consider the improvements over the first version as substantive as William Butler Yeats's sweeping revisions of his poems. Whereas the original is more of a personal effusion on the beauties of the English countryside, the later poem zeroes in on issues of substance and shadow, celebrating the corporeal present in an exultant "I am here! I am here!"

"The Wild Common" in its final form consists of ten four-line stanzas, each stanza following a regular *abab* rhyme scheme. The rhythm is irregular, and that prosodic irregularity is compounded by alternating short and long lines. The title aptly prefaces Lawrence's paean to life's natural beauty, beauty both physical and spiritual. This English "Wild Common" fairly bursts with warm sunshine and inviting water, with ecstatic larks and rejoicing peewits (birds also known as lapwings), with blossoming shrubs and lively flowers. The poem is written in the first person, a perspective that helps sharpen the poignancy of the poet's personal encounter with the natural world.

On its most fundamental level, the poem is an ode to nature's beauty. Lawrence writes simultaneously as an observer from the periphery of the natural world and as an active participant in nature. The speaker is at first an observer, content to paint impressions of the common, but as the poem progresses he becomes a participant, immersing himself in the inviting atmosphere of the common. Lawrence's description invites the reader to accompany him in that rich sensory immersion.

It is in the second stanza that the poet first enters the wild common. He interrupts a tranquil scene of rabbits resting on a hill. Questions in rapid succession—"Are they asleep?—are they living?"—move the poet to startle the rabbits into motion. Lawrence's excitement pulsing through these images charges his punctuation, where the sparks of exclamation points begin to fly. Though the third stanza returns the poet to passive observation of the common, he manages even in quiescence to enliven the ordinary with crackling details, with kingcups (buttercups) that "surge to challenge the blossoming bushes" and a "streamlet" that, however lazy, "wakes again, leaps, laughs, and gushes."

The beginning of the fifth stanza marks a crucial shift in the poet's thought, raising philosophical issues that broaden the significance of "The Wild Common." Observing his own shadow on the common turf triggers for the speaker crucial questions about the meaning of his life. He ponders the significance of death, which causes him to wonder how physical realities relate to spiritual ones. That thought in turn raises for the speaker the question of how consciousness and unconsciousness interact.

In the final five stanzas Lawrence explores possible answers to those questions. He finds his most satisfying answers in his plunges into the sensuous delights of the wild common. Lawrence makes it clear that the physical and spiritual interweave as thoroughly as the landscape knits together the plants, the birds, the weather, and the light of the common. The poem's climactic concluding image interweaves at deeper levels the sensual and the metaphysical: The poet immerses himself in the common's pond to find in its waters answers to his deep questions from stanza 5.

Forms and Devices

That experience of integration, like most experiences in D. H. Lawrence's poetry, is richly physical. The reader can taste in this poem the sweet substance of felt life and relish Lawrence's incomparably responsive eye for natural detail. It seems significant that Lawrence in his revising of this poem shapes the sensuousness away from the erotic toward the religious. The earlier poem featured a central image of "soul like a passionate woman," with close-ups of intimate love running "ecstatic over the pliant folds rippling down to my belly from the breast-lights."

The images that replace those erotic visions in the final version are, in contrast, strikingly incarnational, even liturgical. Lawrence sees a beatific sun whose "substance" transubstantiates into "yellow water-blobs." He makes simple peewits angelic, "wings and feathers on the crying, mysterious ages." The climax of the poem is explicit incarnation: "All that is God takes substance!" A rabbit stands in for the priest at this "confirmation," while in the background lark songs—a decidedly liturgical seven lark songs—are "pealing" like church bells. The underlying emphasis on religious ceremony consecrates the youth's dive into the pool as emblematic baptism into life.

It is intriguing that the question of Lawrence's materialism is so much debated among critics. Some readers see him as limited by his focus on natural phenomena to the exclusion of spirit. Perhaps that perception of materialism is more a response to Lawrence's insistence on the personal. Lawrence's ultimate poetic technique goes beyond religious emblem and even sensory detail to insistence on personal presentation.

Lawrence wrote frankly from his own experience. What many readers admire in Lawrence's poetry is not so much the poetry as Lawrence himself; they are drawn to the human feeling rather than the sometimes awkward phrasing. His poetry in general, and this early poem in particular, has been condemned by critics for inept phrasing and frowned upon as imperfectly articulated. Lawrence came out of the Georgian era at the beginning of the twentieth century, sharing with other Georgian poets habits of stodgy syntax, heavy rhyme, and predictable subjects taken from nature. Yet Lawrence also came out of that era in a different sense: His reaction to the natural world seems more deeply felt than that of the usual serene Georgian; it is both emotionally and prosodically more intense.

"The Wild Common" is central to Lawrence's poetic canon; he comes close in his essay "Poetry of the Present" to suggesting it as a kind of exemplum of the essence of his poetic statement. The poem speaks to the heart of Lawrentian concerns, returning the reader—through the plunge of the speaker into the water and the immersion of the reader into the countryside—to a sense of the divinity inherent in life, to a feeling of the divine nature in all things. Even those who dislike "The Wild Common" think that it has affinities with the best in Lawrence. A companion poem of shared theme and similar method, "Red Moon-Rise," is seen by many as the finest poem in Lawrence's volume *Love Poems*.

Themes and Meanings

Appropriately set in late spring or early summer, "The Wild Common" is an effusion of life, which explodes everywhere in its vivid imagery—light "leaping" from the bushes, birds "sweeping" above the "turf" while water "gushes" from the gorse. The overflowing of life approaches resurrective proportions. Rabbits quiescent as "handfuls of brown earth" on the "mournful turf" come to dramatic life when the speaker lifts his arms in blessing and "the hill bursts and heaves under their spurting kick!"

All that fecund life stirs the urgent question: "What if . . . I were gone?" Behind that poetic pondering on death lies the deeper question of how to be sure that one exists in the first place. Amid the teeming life of the common the speaker sees his own "white shadow." It is that uncertain "quivering" reflection of himself in the waters of life that makes him aware "how splendid it is to be substance." Outer reflections can be key to inner identity.

Burgeoning life becomes in the poem a kind of revelation of personal being: "You are here! You are here! We have found you!" shout the peewits and the rabbits and the "seven larks singing at once." The "naked lad" dives into the fertile water and merges with that oxymoronic white shadow which is his own soul, finding himself, body and soul, in nature. He is integrated, whole, "No longer shadow!" The poem's ultimate affirmation—"All that is right, all that is good, all that is God takes substance"—is not only the central theme of this poem but also the underlying theme of Lawrence's *Collected Poems* as a whole.

Steven C. Walker

WILD NIGHTS—WILD NIGHTS!

Author: Emily Dickinson (1830-1886)
Type of poem: Lyric
First published: 1891, in *Poems: Second Series*; collected in *The Poems of Emily Dickinson*, 1955

The Poem

"Wild Nights—Wild Nights!" contains no narrative plot to report; there is no story to tell. The poem is sustained exclamation, an extended expression of agitated yearning for reunion with a lover. In the first stanza, a storm seems to be raging, the seas in ferment from the winds. Were the speaker with her lover, there would be stormy nights of their own making, born of passionate indulgence and privilege ("Our luxury").

In the second stanza, the persona remarks that the winds cannot avail against "a Heart in port"—that is, a lover can transcend life's buffetings, given the stability provided by love. As a parallel to this thought, no longer does a lover require compass or chart on troubled seas, since in finding love, the voyage is done, the "port" reached.

In the third stanza, where Emily Dickinson typically employs ellipsis (word omission), she compresses her articulation sharply. Consequently, readers must fill in the missing thought, which seems to be that love's formulative power makes everything like "rowing in Eden," or into a paradise where life's swells are leveled. The allusion to Eden turns menacing, however, reminding the persona of the tossing sea of the present night and propelling anew an anguished longing for the anchorage of her lover's presence on this night of storm.

"Wild Nights—Wild Nights!" may come as a surprise to readers who have thought of Emily Dickinson as the Amherst recluse, purposely rejecting life, including thoughts of romance, for the "higher calling" of art. Moreover, the poem proves decidedly up-to-date in its erotic celebration of love by way of imagery easily understood by a generation exposed to Freud. Even at the time it was published, Dickinson's friend and editor, Thomas Wentworth Higginson, expressed anxiety lest unscrupulous minds should read into the poetry more than the sexually innocent Dickinson had intended. Yet the fact is that "Wild Nights—Wild Nights!" is but one of many poems Dickinson composed on the subject of love, several of them equally explicit.

Forms and Devices

"Wild Nights—Wild Nights!" (poem 249) begins with the unusual rhyme scheme of *abbb*, only to abandon rhyme altogether in the second stanza, then assume it again in the final stanza, though in a pattern differing from the initial stanza. Throughout there is a heavy employment of trochees and a sustained pattern of dimeter line length, an unusual feature in a poet greatly indebted to the quatrains of alternating iambic tetrameter and trimeter lines of the church hymnals of her day. Clearly,

Dickinson appropriates rhythms conducive to the persona's anguished mood in the poem.

This poem shows a fierce independence of conventional norms typical of all of her poetry, whether in form or subject matter. There is a fondness for the dash to isolate words and to imitate oral language. Here the dashes halt the pace of language and suggest the mind's tendency to redefine continually. Concurrently, the resulting interruptions coerce readers into a more diligent reading and pursuit of interconnection.

Capitalization of nouns occurs similarly as a typical Dickinson feature. This makes one note the "thingness" of life around one (by definition, a noun is whatever exists), or the individuality of what one often takes for granted or sweeps away with abstraction. Throughout, the style is a plain one, nearly all of its diction stemming from the Germanic roots of the language.

Except for her biblical reference to Eden, there is an absence of reference to the world of conventional society. In style as well as outlook, Dickinson was determined to assert her own identity.

The poem shows affinity with a type of poetry practiced in seventeenth century England and later dubbed "metaphysical" by the renowned Samuel Johnson. In this kind of poetry, startling analogies, often highly extended (and therefore called "conceits"), were the hallmark of an intensely intellectual argument set in a dramatic context. Metaphysical poetry became the staple of Puritan poetry in the New World. Among its chief practitioners were Edward Taylor and Anne Bradstreet.

Dickinson exhibits ties with her Puritan antecedents, whatever her troubled relationship to their faith. She employs the same tight construction, love of ellipsis, preference for the meditative, and striking employment of analogy, as in the subtle association of the stormy sea with tumultuous passion and the juxtaposition of the stormy sea voyage and the port of love where compass and chart are no longer needed. This analogy continues into the last lines, in which the persona exclaims, "Might I but moor—Tonight—/ In Thee!"

Themes and Meanings

One of the many enigmas surrounding the life of Emily Dickinson concerns her relationships with the opposite sex. It is commonly held, despite scant evidence for it, that Emily Dickinson fell in love with a married clergyman, Charles Wadsworth, pastor of Arch Street Presbyterian Church in Philadelphia. At the time, he was forty and she was twenty-three. In 1862, Wadsworth announced that he was assuming a church in California. According to the tradition, this news came as a lifelong blow to Dickinson and in her loss, she turned to poetry as her consolation.

This is speculation only, however, for there were a number of men in Dickinson's life. One can reasonably assume that in the years 1859-1860 she had indeed fallen in love. It is known that toward the end of her life she had passionately fallen in love with Judge Otis Lord. What is important is that Dickinson celebrates love and its consummation as one of the few glories in a world replete with God's indifference and the specter of mortality. In Dickinson's life there seems always to have hovered the fear of abandonment, most likely a legacy of her childhood experiences with a passive mother and overbearing father. Consequently, she clung to her friends and sometimes employed exaggerated language, adopting the pose of Romantic dreamer. Still, there is no reason that one should doubt the genuineness of the love spoken of here. The poem speaks universally for lovers, whose security is their love for one another.

There is more than meets the eye in "Wild Nights—Wild Nights!" In its impassioned tones, the poem fantasizes sexual abandon when lovers are present again and are joined. Few poems have captured the power of anticipatory love as well as this one. As if to make no mistake about her meaning, Dickinson repeats the phrasing and assigns an exclamation mark. "In Port" in stanza 2 is similarly replete with the hint of physical intimacy, as is the reference to mooring.

In another ironic undertone providing tension within the poem, there is a hint that love may be a beautiful illusion. The reference to Eden in the last stanza represents the transfigured state of love's fancied weaving, its ability to transcend the banal opposition. Yet Eden is only the projection of fantasy—hence the Fall from Paradise in the following line, with its return to the sea of this world, where drowning threatens. Yet love has not lost its wager. Whatever love cannot do to render a genuine return to Paradise, it does offer sanctuary to its exiles.

Ralph Robert Joly

THE WILD SWANS AT COOLE

Author: William Butler Yeats (1865-1939)
Type of poem: Lyric
First published: 1917, in *The Wild Swans at Coole*

The Poem

"The Wild Swans at Coole" consists of five six-line stanzas rhymed *abcbdd*. The meter is iambic, but loosened to accommodate the irregular cadences of speech. Odd-numbered lines have four stressed syllables, even-numbered lines three. The stanza, then, is a modified ballad stanza plus a rhymed couplet. Although William Butler Yeats uses six-line stanzas in many other poems, nowhere else does he employ exactly this stanza, which is stately but not stiff, well-suited to the poem's reflective tone and melancholy mood.

It is a lyric poem both because of its musicality (in the oldest sense of "lyric") and because it is a direct expression of personal feelings, which may be identified as the author's. It is a dramatic lyric in that the poem's physical setting, particularly in the opening stanza, serves as an objective correlative to these feelings—representing, reflecting, "dramatizing" them.

"Coole" in the title refers to Coole Park, the estate in Ireland's County Galway of Lady Augusta Gregory, Yeats's friend, collaborator, and benefacter. Yeats spent a considerable part of each year there for many years, beginning in 1897; he often walked paths through the woods on the estate and to Coole Lake, with its swans.

On its first appearance, the poem was dated October, 1916, a time when Yeats's spirits were at a low ebb. Still unmarried and childless at age fifty-one, he felt that life was passing him by. Over the years, his friend Maud Gonne had rejected several proposals of marriage from him, and in 1916 she had done so again; even her daughter Iseult had declined a proposal from him that summer. (In 1917, Yeats would marry Georgia Hyde-Lees; their daughter would be born in 1919, their son in 1921. This poem, then, unknown to Yeats, was a farewell song to lonely bachelorhood.)

The speaker in the poem draws two contrasts: On the one hand, between himself now and himself when first he walked "on this shore"; on the other hand, between himself and the swans. "All's changed," he says, since first he came there; and the change is in him: He walks with a heavier tread and his heart has "grown old." This sets up the second contrast, for the swans—energetic, "Unwearied," passionate—exhibit the very traits that he finds diminished, or lacking, in himself. The apparent lack of change in the swans underscores the changes that the poet feels, at age fifty-one, recollecting himself at age thirty-two.

Forms and Devices

The poem's opening lines describe a scene of "autumn beauty" and also objectify Yeats's depressed state of mind. "October twilight" establishes at the outset a sense of things—a day, a year—coming to an end. Yeats's mood, as it emerges over the course of the poem, is correspondingly autumnal, reflecting his awareness of the mortality he shares with everything terrestrial and temporal. That the "woodland paths are dry" is significant because Yeats characteristically associated dryness with physical and imaginative sterility. No less than "water/ Mirrors a still sky," landscape mirrors mood.

Yeats often thought in terms of the four traditional elements: earth, air, fire, and water. (See, for example, "The Song of Wandering Aengus," 1897, and "Sailing to Byzantium," 1927.) "The Wild Swans at Coole" omits fire but makes conspicuous use of the other three, particularly by associating air with water and by distinguishing the two of them from earth.

Water mirrors sky (air) not only literally but also figuratively. In the Yeatsian cosmology, air and water are spiritual, earth is physical. "What's water but the generated soul?" Yeats would ask in "Coole Park and Ballylee, 1931"; and "spirit" means breath (or air). Earth is solid, shaped, fixed—hence (paradoxically) mortal; air and water are amorphous, unstable—hence (paradoxically) immortal. Earth is temporal; air and water are eternal. There is no "autumn" for air or water, as there is for earth and terrestrial organisms, such as trees and poets. Swans hold dual citizenship of the spirit: "They paddle in the cold/ Companionable streams or climb the air" with equal ease and grace. At a practical level, Yeats's inability to complete his count of the swans enables him to sustain the illusion that the ones he sees now are the same swans, unchanged, that he saw nineteen years earlier.

The most profound paradox relating to the swans, which makes them "Mysterious" indeed, is how they can be so completely engaged in life yet not subject to mortality. The solitary man wistfully watches the paired swans, still passionate, "lover by lover," and wonders why he is alone and feeling his age. The poem does not attempt to resolve this paradox. It remains an enigma, like the "still sky" and the "still water," their surfaces smooth and untroubled, with no indication of what might be beneath or beyond them. "Still," though unobtrusive, is one of the key words in the poem. Not only does the word describe the two spiritual elements—tranquil, apparently motionless— in the opening and closing stanzas (thus again mirroring each other), but it also appears twice in the penultimate stanza, in a different sense: "Unwearied still . . . Attend upon them still." Here "still," meaning "now, as before," refers to duration in time. The swans are at once in and out of time. The paradox deepens.

Themes and Meanings

A word often overlooked in discussion of this poem, perhaps because it appears only in the title, is "Wild." Yeats called the swans wild, first of all, to indicate that they are in no way domesticated. They do not nest at Coole; thus, as the poem's ending suggests, they may fly away at any time. Yeats also called them wild because of a set of admiring associations he had with that word. He habitually called all manner of flying things wild, and he had done so since he began publishing in the mid-1880's.

He associated the quality of wildness with the power and freedom of flight, and he recognized it in certain people—rebels, for example—who led active, independent lives. In "September 1913," he applied the traditional Irish term "wild geese" to exiled heroes from history. Although he did not always approve of Maud Gonne's firebrand political activities, as early as 1910 he compared her with Helen of Troy, offspring of Leda and Zeus-as-swan, thus one of the "daughters of the swan." Yeats also associated the quality of wildness with passion and mating, and in this respect too Maud Gonne came to his mind; passionate herself, the object of his passion, yet unwilling to mate with him.

The wild swans at Coole are independent, vigorously active, and passionate. The second stanza provides a powerful image of the whole flock of swans taking off in unison:

> I saw . . .
> All suddenly mount
> And scatter wheeling in great broken rings
> Upon their clamorous wings.

The verb "mount" does double duty, clearly referring to the swans' ascension into the sky, but also bearing with it overtones of its other meaning: to copulate. The verb pulls together—admirably, for Yeats's purposes—his main associations with wildness: power, freedom, and passion.

The power and passion that Yeats finds wanting in himself are imaginative as well as physical. He was in a dry spell as a poet in 1916-1917. Of the 374 lyrical poems in Yeats's *Collected Poems of W. B. Yeats* (1956), only ten (totaling 273 lines of verse) were composed during these years. In contrast, twenty-three poems (963 lines) come from the following two years. While two or three of the 1916-1917 poems could be considered major poems, as many as eight or nine poems from 1918-1919 could be placed in that category. "The Wild Swans at Coole" reflects Yeats's discouragement as a poet as well as a lover. He was shrewd enough, however, in uncreative periods of his life, to write poems about the difficulties of writing poems. It was a good strategy, for it helped Yeats get through dry spells with something to show for them.

Richard Bizot

WILDFLOWERS

Author: Richard Howard (1929-   )
Type of poem: Dramatic monologue
First published: 1973; collected in *Two-Part Inventions*, 1974

The Poem

With the publication of *Untitled Subjects* (1969) and *Findings* (1971), Richard Howard was acknowledged as a master of the dramatic monologue, a one-sided verse conversation during which the reader gains insight into the character of the speaker. With "Wildflowers" and the other five lengthy poems in *Two-Part Inventions*, however, he explores the possibilities of a new form: the dramatic dialogue. "Wildflowers," for example, attempts to render a conversation between two great figures of nineteenth century literature: the American poet Walt Whitman, author of *Leaves of Grass* (1855), and the Irish-born poet and dramatist Oscar Wilde.

Subtitled "Camden, 1882," the poem purports to re-create what was said when Wilde first visited Whitman in the latter's residence in New Jersey. However, Howard takes certain liberties with historical fact. Although he did seek out Whitman during his 1882 tour of the United States, Wilde actually visited the American poet twice, the first time with his friend, the Philadelphia publisher J. M. Stoddart, and the second time alone. Howard makes Wilde's second visit his first and sets the confrontation in Whitman's Mickle Street residence, a home that he did not purchase until two years later in 1884. Wilde actually visited Whitman in the Stevens Street home of Whitman's brother George. Probably, for dramatic purposes, it suited Howard better that Wilde meet Whitman in the home he lived in by himself except for his housekeeper Mary Davis, a sailor's widow who worked for the poet in exchange for a rear apartment. Over the course of his long literary career, Whitman was the center of a considerable circle of discipleship, and many of his readers made pilgrimage to Camden after he retired from a series of federal government positions in 1874.

As the poem begins, the sixty-three-year-old Whitman is preparing to meet his twenty-eight-year-old admirer from across the ocean. He puts on a red tie and rereads the letter from his Canadian follower Dr. Richard Bucke that first brought Wilde to his attention. Fresh from his tour of the American West, "*dashing between/ coyotes and cañons*," Wilde has come to pay homage to a man whom he sees as "America's great voice." They talk in Whitman's "ruin" of a room, made infamous by his biographers for its disorder. The far-ranging conversation between these two poets is the substance of the poem.

Forms and Devices

The title of the collection *Two-Part Inventions* is a reference to the fifteen keyboard pieces written by German composer Johann Sebastian Bach in two-part counterpoint, a technique of combining two individual melodies to make a harmonious texture.

Similarly, the poem "Wildflowers" takes two very different perspectives and weaves them into a unified dialogue. On one hand is the young, Old World poet who speaks of "form" and artifice in poetry and in life; on the other hand is the elderly New World poet whose gospel is natural freedom. Yet during the course of their exchange of ideas, they reach a level of mutual understanding. Whitman realizes that Wilde really needs an answer to the question of his place in the scheme of things, and Wilde believes that Whitman has provided that guidance in his assertion that a person finds himself by giving himself away. Thus real poetry is deemed sacrificial. In this regard, Whitman's self-confessions in *Leaves of Grass* prefigure Wilde's in *De Profundis*, the latter's 1905 letter from prison.

As the title indicates, one of the poem's unifying image patterns involves flowers. In addition to the pun on Wilde's surname, there is the tributary visit that provides the basic situation of the poem and the floral offering that Wilde makes to Whitman at the end. Known for holding a flower in his hands while lecturing, Wilde presents the older poet with a heliotrope, a small, fragrant, purple flower that turns toward the sunlight. In this case, it is Wilde himself who turns toward Whitman as his guide and prophet.

There is also the comparison that Wilde makes between Whitman's *Leaves of Grass* and French poet Charles Baudelaire's *Les Fleurs du mal* (1857; *The Flowers of Evil*, 1931). He calls both works his "sacred botany," the sacred texts of his time. Baudelaire has taught Wilde the lesson of the artist who suffers for his art; Whitman will teach him the lesson of the artist whose art transcends suffering. Also providing a subtext for the conversation between these two poets is the story of the fisher king. In medieval legend, a desert land is ruled by the fisher king, made sterile by a curse. The king will be cured and his land made fertile only by the sacrifices of a hero who is brave and pure of heart. Prior to Wilde's arrival, Whitman thinks he hears "something like rain, off in the distance." Wilde tells Whitman that he comes to him as one who consults a man *"whose twig bends near water."* Both Wilde and Whitman look to each other for redemption of a sort. Identifying with Wilde's quote from Baudelaire ("I am even as the king of a rainy country, rich but impotent"), Whitman laments the defection of some of his young disciples who grow "old and cold" and looks to Wilde, "a great boy," as a promising acolyte. For his part, Wilde hopes to find in the older poet a key to his destiny.

The poem is also marked by a wealth of historical detail. Howard is noted for his ability to make the nineteenth century come alive through his engagement with the principal artists of the period. One good example is Whitman's reference to the dismissal from his job at the U.S. Department of the Interior after Secretary James Harlan, a Methodist layman and former professor of mental and moral sciences, found a proof copy of some of the poet's work. This rifling of Whitman's desk by his supervisor underscores Whitman's warning to Wilde that "It will not do to fly in the face/ of courts and conformity." To this admonition Wilde, with some of his characteristic wit, replies, *"I shall cross that bridge/ after I have burned it before me."* This well-turned epigram foreshadows his three public trials for homosexuality and his eventual imprisonment.

Themes and Meanings

During the course of this imaginary conversation between two poets, there is much talk of the meaning of their craft. Wilde espouses the aesthetic approach of art for art's sake, and he cites the verse of Baudelaire as part of his contention that literature need not serve a moral or didactic purpose. Whitman, on the other hand, sees himself as a teacher of young men, as the proponent of such concepts as wise passivity, physical and spiritual nakedness, and the primacy of sex and manly love; all of these values he advocates through natural rhythmic cadences. In response to Wilde's recitation of one of Baudelaire's poems, Whitman recoils. To him, it is sickly self-pity organized according to "mathematical principles." This proponent of free thinking and free verse asks, "Is it not a machine,/ a kind of enslavement?"

As he would not be a slave to meter, Whitman chafes at the restraints of illness and old age. For him, his partially paralyzed body confined to a chair by the window is a kind of prison. This central image is part of a larger theme of incarceration. Wilde, for example, speaks of confronting a novel-reading inmate at a "model" prison in Idaho; Whitman terms his age and infirmity "another kind/ of model prison." For one who exalts the life of the senses and the transforming power of touch, it is a tragedy to have to admit that one's "fingers are dead."

This theme of imprisonment is naturally linked to the issue of identity. According to Whitman, one finds oneself through sacrificing or surrendering oneself to others. For Whitman, the working-class boys he nursed in military hospitals during the Civil War were the principal audience he had in mind for *Leaves of Grass*. For his self-expression he was censured by the reading public: "I expected hell./ I got it." In the context of the poem, however, Whitman's scandal is a matter of the past; old age has brought him a modicum of respectability as the "Good Gray Poet." For Wilde, scandal is still to come. His great sacrifice will be his loyalty to his lover, the unworthy Lord Alfred Douglas, and his subsequent public trials and his years at hard labor for acting on his physical affection for other men. In prison, Wilde will drop the mask of art that he donned under the tutelage of Baudelaire and discover for himself "*how a desire becomes a destiny.*"

In a very basic way, Howard is the third part of his *Two-Part Inventions*. Because of his own homosexuality, he understands the position of the gay artist as outsider. In this regard, both Whitman and Wilde reach a shared recognition of their status as sexual outlaws whose desires diverge from the norm. They also realize that to give expression to these desires in the nineteenth century means scandal and censure. Yet pain can be a bridge to insight and suffering can be transcended by transforming life into art.

S. Thomas Mack

WILDPEACE

Author: Yehuda Amichai (1924-2000)
Type of poem: Lyric/elegy
First published: 1971, as "Shalom-bar," in *Ve-lo 'al menat lizkor*; English translation collected in *The Selected Poetry of Yehuda Amichai*, 1996

The Poem

"Wildpeace" is a free-verse denunciation of war in elegiac mode. It is one of several poems pleading for peace by a poet who fought in two major wars and survived a bloody century. His fate was to always be in the location of some of the most violent conflicts. Though "Wildpeace" is one of Yehuda Amichai's shorter poems, it is direct and pungent.

The poem is divided into two stanzas; the first has eighteen lines, and the second, no more than a coda, which reiterates and punctuates the larger statement, has only four. Without any tricks of rhyme or confining meter, impact is achieved by graceful rhythms. Some are the simple cadences of everyday life, while others echo stately pronouncements from antiquity. Likewise, words and images of both secular diplomats and holy prophets intermingle.

The poet's cynicism is clear but never harsh. He distrusts the usual mechanics of peace: cease-fires that are often broken before the ink on peace documents is dried; the grand visions of ancient prophets whose knowledge cannot possibly encompass the modern apparatus of warfare; the platitudes of duplicitous statesmen. Eloquent words from Scripture about beating swords into plowshares are often quoted, even while a perverse society sends a message to the young, still in their playpens, that it is manly and commendable to murder for one's country.

While Amichai has little use for the platitudes and clichés of the official peacemakers, and no faith in their lasting success, he still expresses the wistful hope that eventually the world will be exhausted with carnage and nauseated by the endless parade of orphans all wars leave behind, orphans who provide an unbroken line of desolation from antiquity into the modern age. At that time, finally, on fields formerly saturated with blood, peace may descend like the unpremeditated wildflowers of the field, which no one plants or tends. While the poet's experiences in battle may have exhausted him, they have not yet led him to abandon hope. The life force that runs through nature may succeed where the words of prophets, messiahs, poets, diplomats, and statesmen have failed.

Forms and Devices

Amichai, a strong poetic voice in the latter half of the twentieth century, came to Israel from Germany as a youth. His first language was German, though his poetry was written in modern Hebrew. The American poet Robert Frost observed that poetry itself is what is lost in translation, and the philosopher George Santayana believed no poet could be great who did not write in the language of his mother's lullabies. It is extraordinary that, despite these seeming obstacles, Amichai's poetry has been enthusiastically translated into over thirty languages, and Israelis themselves have regarded him as a national treasure.

Growing up in an Orthodox Jewish family, Amichai learned biblical Hebrew at an early age. He also read medieval mystical poetry, along with Jewish writings from the Diaspora in modern European languages. Later he discovered the major British and American poets, who expressed themselves in contemporary idioms. With this cultural backdrop, he came to his own writing with capable equipment.

Because modern Hebrew is a resurrected language developed from an ancient tongue previously preserved only in religious and scholarly usage, its words have connotative strata reaching back thousands of years. Contemporary referents are constantly playing themselves off against ancient associations. Biblical refrains, Talmudic allusions, and lamentations from the Diaspora still lurk behind modern Hebrew words. Much ironic tension in modern Hebrew poetry results from the historical and sacred associations of a Hebrew word confronting its now secular usage. For example, in Amichai's poetry a lamb is never simply a farm animal providing wool for clothing or food for nourishment. It is the metaphor of biblical poets for all gentle creatures brutally slaughtered.

Even while regarded as one of the most accessible of the major poets of his time, Amichai occasionally resorts to an old rabbinical trick of employing ambiguity to provoke deeper thought in his readers. His reference in "Wildpeace" to "the heavy rubber stamp" lends itself to several interpretations. Yet he has never required an elaborate set of footnotes to be understood.

There are several reasons Amichai's poetry has survived the perils of English translation. The poet himself sometimes assisted in the task, and he was fortunate in his translators, among them the British poet Ted Hughes and the American academician Chana Bloch. The major translators have found corresponding rhythms appropriate to Amichai's tones and humors. His poems abound in metaphors and images from almost everyone's daily experience. He may ironically or sardonically employ a newspaper headline, a slogan from a billboard, a truism, or even a fragment from an old but familiar religious liturgy. Like other Israeli poets of his generation, he was influenced by the lively inventiveness of late twentieth century American poetry.

Even so, the prosaic words and images, even when used with whimsy, are not the primary appeal of this poetry. Its power derives in considerable degree from its juxtaposition of the traditional with the modern. Though he departed early on from the orthodox religious practice of his parents, Amichai always unmistakably remained both a Jewish and an Israeli poet. Like the Irish novelist James Joyce, whom he admired, Amichai never rejected the language and symbols of the faith of his childhood, though he could no longer accept the dogmas. Even when they are most identified with his own time and place, his verses constantly interact with the Bible, the Talmud, and the synagogue liturgy.

In "Wildpeace" a crucial line declares that it is not "a cease-fire/ not even the vision of the wolf and the lamb" that will bring the peace the poet desires. "Cease-fire" is a favorite jargon word of contemporary bureaucratic diplomats and peace negotiators, while the image of a peaceable kingdom, where carnivorous beasts will lie down harmoniously with their prey, comes from the Hebrew prophet Isaiah. Yet Amichai made a subtle shift in the image; instead of the lion, the regal beast of the prophet's vision, the poet has substituted the wolf, a chief emblem of the Nazis, evildoers who, even in a messianic kingdom, would make unacceptable bedfellows.

Children's toys seem comfortable objects, and child's play is practice for adulthood, though blessedly still free of responsibility and cloaked in fantasy. Yet the poet's picture of a boy with toy gun merges disconcertingly into the figure of a girl's doll, which the vendors have promised is so lifelike it will open and close its eyes and say "Mama." "I know that I know how to kill, that makes me an adult," writes the poet. Yet even from childhood the boy is being conditioned to look ahead to the day when he will prove his courage and manhood by killing the human beings that little girls, with their own playthings, are preparing to love and nourish.

Themes and Meanings

As in all genuine poetry, it is impossible to separate meaning from the language that expresses it in "Wildpeace." This poetry, whether in Hebrew or good English translations, is truly "realized content." Amichai is not an ideological poet. Though he had affinities with the European postwar existentialists, especially with Albert Camus, he was a member of no philosophical school. He had no plan for saving the world through programs such as those propounded by Marxists, socialists, or social Democrats. Zionism and representative democracy have failed to bring peace. Neither do divine promises and biblical covenants provide relief from the cycle of destruction. Long ago Amichai rejected intellectually, if not fully in his heart, the God of the chosen people. If God exists, other poems by him have suggested, He is a toothless spirit, either too old to care or too young to understand, for whom Torah scrolls, phylacteries, and menorah candles are shining playthings.

"Wildpeace" is more a poem of gentle yearning and of wishful expectation than of affirmation. If peace eventually comes to a weary world it will not be from prophets, messiahs, diplomats, or statesmen. It will not even come from a divinity that has finally had its fill of the wickedness of humankind and decided to intervene. It will come without flourish, without premeditation, like "lazy white foam." No image more fully suggests that which is commonplace, yet beautiful and beloved, than the wildflowers Amichai envisions suddenly blanketing a field.

While he is neither philosopher nor statesman, Amichai's poetic voice speaks passionately and consistently. It also speaks with the authority of a man who knows war intimately and has always lived in communities on the brink. Against all evidence, and claiming no ready answers, he continued to hope for peace. This is a personal voice speaking from individual experience, but the response seems universal, as his readers in languages as diverse as Arabic and Catalan affirm.

Allene Phy-Olsen

WILLINGLY

Author: Tess Gallagher (Tess Bond; 1943-   )
Type of poem: Narrative
First published: 1980; collected in *Willingly*, 1984

The Poem

Tess Gallagher's "Willingly" is a poem in free verse with forty lines divided into four stanzas. The title suggests the cheerful act of giving one's self or doing a task voluntarily; its function, however, is to establish an ironic mood. While most people would be quite pleased to wake up to the sight of their homes being freshly painted, the speaker is anything but happy. She feels violated and erased by the very action that would bring so many other people joy. Just as her house is inanimate and unable to stop itself from being painted and therefore manipulated, the speaker is just as passive and is unable to exert any will over her life at this time. The title is ironic because to give something willingly one must own and control that which is to be given.

In the second stanza, the narrator's home is bathed in a strange "new light." She reflects that even in her sleep she felt the strokes of the painter's brush, or "the space between them," bearing down on her. The poet compares those ominous strokes with "an accumulation/ of stars" that arrange themselves "over the roofs of entire cities." By equating the power the painter wields with every stroke of his brush to the unyielding strength of the universe, the painter becomes godlike. Under the incredible force of the painter's "steady arm," both the speaker and her house begin to disappear, to become changed by an immutable force.

The third stanza again shows the painter as an agent controlling the destiny of the speaker. The narrator watches helplessly as the painter's "careful strokes whiten the web" of the poet's very complicated disassociation from herself. The painter's elevated status is made clear by the fact that he is standing on a ladder far above the poet's head. On a deeper level, when the poet stands by the painter's ladder "looking up" at him, "he does not acknowledge" her. This lack of response to her presence further strengthens the speaker's feelings of uncontrollable invisibility. By the fourth stanza, the speaker has completely relinquished her house to the painter. Smelling the strong odor of the paint, she thinks, "This is ownership." The speaker did not paint the house, and therefore, in her mind, she can no longer lay claim to it. After this painful revelation, some paint falls onto her shoulder, and it feels as if it passes right through her. In the pain of feeling as if she has no control over her house or her existence, the poem concludes with the speaker trying to convince herself that she has "agreed to this," that the path her life has taken has been taken willingly.

Forms and Devices

The first nine lines of the opening stanza are written in the first person. The first-person point of view allows readers to feel as if they are eavesdropping on the speaker's thoughts and allows them to feel the poet's presence intimately. It is important to note that the last line of the first stanza and the remaining three stanzas are written in the second person. The second person is used in this poem to make the reader take the place of the first-person narrator. Readers who compare the lines "I look back on myself asleep in the dream/ I could not carry awake" to "Some paint has dropped onto your shoulder" will notice that this removal of the first-person speaker who drew them into the poem leaves them with the rather surreal feeling that the rest of the narrative is unfolding in their own minds. With each stroke of the painter's brush, the person who spoke to the readers from the perspective of the first-person point of view becomes an increasingly distant memory until she is finally erased altogether. This switch reflects the major theme of self-erasure in "Willingly."

Enjambment (the running over of the meaning from one line into the next line) is used effectively to emphasize the way the speaker interprets the events in the poem that cause her to feel as if she is a nonentity in her own front yard. For example, as the painter's careful strokes "whiten the web" of turmoil in the third stanza, the speaker "faithlessly" says that "Nothing has changed." However, the fifth and sixth lines of this stanza assert, through enjambment, that "something has/ cleansed you past recognition." These lines eloquently say that the new coat of paint on the poet's house has cleansed her to the point of invisibility and that the way she views her life has been radically changed. Also in the third stanza, the painter blots out the swirl of the house's wood grain "like a breath stopped/ at the heart." The effect that enjambment has here is to create an urgent pause. By ending the line on the word "stopped," an auditory image is created. The reader is compelled to imagine the haunting sound of a last gasp before the silence of death. If the lines were simply end-stopped ("the swirl of woodgrain blotted out/ like a breath stopped at the heart"), much of the dramatic tension the poet has created would be lost. When the paint falls onto the narrator's shoulder in the fourth stanza, the reader is told, "You think it has fallen through/ you." The pause that is created by this enjambed line allows readers to reflect on the importance of its meaning. Symbolically, the paint passing through the speaker reemphasizes that she has disappeared.

Themes and Meanings

"Willingly" is a poem about erasure. What can make people feel as if they do not exist? Lack of control? External powers that seem overwhelming? Change? Gallagher's poem implies that all these things can make a person feel as if life is nothing more than a series of inevitabilities. "Willingly" resonates with truth because it documents the way many people act when their lives take unexpected turns. They withdraw in the same way that the speaker in this poem withdraws: quietly yet tumultuously. Tortured and alone with their pain, these sufferers often see their circumstances as much larger than themselves. The speaker of this poem certainly seems helpless in the presence of the painter whom she elevates into an almost celestial being. The saving grace of this poem, which seems so utterly depressing, is that like most successful poems, it is about the survival of the spirit. "Willingly" manages to transcend the pity that readers seem to be asked to give to the speaker. What is most important is that the creation of this poem, of any poem, is an act of grace in and of itself. Rather than wallow in sorrow, the narrator not only writes of her pain but also shares it with the world. In doing so, she rises above her circumstances and attempts to inspire her readers to do the same.

Paula Hilton

THE WIND INCREASES

Author: William Carlos Williams (1883-1963)
Type of poem: Lyric
First published: 1930; collected in *An Early Martyr and Other Poems,* 1935

The Poem

"The Wind Increases" is a short lyric poem in free verse composed of twenty-eight lines. All the lines of the poem are arranged in such a way as to suggest the motion of wind. In this sense, the poem could be said to be a shaped verse, a type of poem in which the typographical shape of the words on the page represents some part of the subject. Because the overall structural pattern of the poem is so loosely arranged, the poem has no set stanzaic form. In fact, Thomas R. Whitaker, in *William Carlos Williams* (1968), states that the way that the lines are organized encourages the reader to "not think of line-ends"; rather, the set of lines as a whole "dissolve and reconstitute the poetic line as they seek immediacy." Based upon its content, however, the poem can be divided into five parts. In the first seven lines, the poet describes an approaching storm and tells about the "harried earth," the trees, and "the tulip's bright/ tips" being tossed around by the increasing wind. The second part of the poem changes abruptly from this rather literal description of the coming storm to an admonition to the reader: "Loose your love/ to flow." This sudden shift is made all the more emphatic because it and the third part of the poem are in the form of a command. Moreover, this third part is composed of only the single verb "Blow!" At this point, the reader may believe that the poet is referring to the blowing of the wind, that he is perhaps commanding the stormy wind to blow. Undoubtedly, this is one meaning of the line, but the line also suggests that people, after "loosening their love," should allow their love to "blow" or be distributed more freely to their fellow human beings as well as to the world of nature.

The fourth and fifth parts of the poem also seem to involve an unexpected change because they are not directly concerned with describing a storm or with love. Instead, the fourth part asks a question: "Good Christ what is/ a poet—if any/ exists?" The rest of the poem is devoted to answering this question. The reader may also wonder at the quick shift in tone, for the phrases "Good Christ" and "if any exists" imply that the poet himself is both exasperated and frustrated with the difficulty of responding to his own query. There is even a hint of skepticism about whether or not poetry and poets can be developed and created. This irritation and doubt following the poet's comments about the storm and love are surprising. However, after readers finish reading the poem, they see how and why all of these parts fit together to convey the messages that a poet must produce living, moving, fresh ideas just as nature produces new growth each year and that in order to be original and creative, a poet must "loose" his love "to flow." That is, a poet must be full of love—for his craft, for his fellow humans, and for the world of nature—in order to create great art.

Forms and Devices

References to nature abound in "The Wind Increases." The word "wind" is even in the title of the poem. The picture that the poet paints of the increasing wind as well as the other images of nature found in the first seven lines serve to describe literally, albeit somewhat dramatically, the beginning of a storm. In fact, after reading such vivid descriptions of the wind and storm, the reader may wonder about the use of the verb "increases" in the title. Such a word, which is usually used in a precise, mathematical sense, lacks the immediacy and the power of phrases such as "harried earth" and "tulip's bright tips." However, Williams's choice to use the verb "increases" in his title is actually consistent with his style and form. He believed in experimentation in poetry and was not bound by the conventional rules of style or content. Thus, for him to use a word that often has a mathematical connotation in a poem about nature and the philosophy of poetry is not unusual.

Williams does not refer to nature in the middle section (lines 8-13); rather, it is here that he most openly reveals his overriding concern in the poem. He wants to address the same issue that many other poets have contemplated: What is poetry? In order to explore this topic, the poet uses a question-and-answer format. In lines 11-13, he asks what a poet is and then immediately starts to supply an answer. The first part of the answer (lines 14-17) makes no references to nature. Instead, a poet is described as "a man/ whose words will/ bite/ their way/ home." That is, a poet must seek depth of experience, symbolized by the word "home," for people's homes are usually thought of as places where they can expose their "depths." In the last part of the middle section (lines 17-19), the poet emphasizes that the words must be "actual" and yet have "the form/ of motion," that the language of the poet must be abstract yet concrete and vivid.

In the last eight lines, the poet again returns to the use of nature imagery in order to answer his question about the nature of poetry. In these final lines, the poet's essential message concerns his belief that poets must produce their own answers to the age-old questions that have perplexed and "tortured" humans throughout time. However, in order to illustrate this concept, the poet creates a metaphor about a tree: A poet must add new words to each "twigtip" and yet use words that, like the roots of a tree, "grip the ground." These words must also extend all the way "to the last leaftip." That is, a poet should use words that describe even the outermost reaches of thought and feeling just as a tree must extend nourishment to all of its parts, including its most remote leaves on its highest branches.

Themes and Meanings

The central issue of "The Wind Increases" is the subject of poetry itself. In lines 11-13, the poet very directly and almost bluntly asks, "Good Christ what is/ a poet—if any/ exists?" Throughout the course of the poem, the poet replies to his own query, ultimately concluding that there are six essential qualities that a good poet must possess. First, a poet must have an imagination that is "open to the weather." Just as a storm may arise suddenly and without warning, a poem may also arise and come unexpectedly to the poet's consciousness. The poet, however, needs to be open to such an experience in order to produce art. Second, poets must "loose" their love and allow it to flow freely if they are to fully understand and participate in life. Without permitting one's feelings to surface, a person cannot live well or write a good poem. Third, the poet must discover and use words that will "bite their way home" and express the heart and the essential truth of the human condition. Fourth, these words—which must be actual, concrete words—must also be able to capture or emulate the form of fluid, invisible motion. Thus, the language of poetry should be concrete yet capable of describing intangible feelings and ideas. Fifth, a poet must fashion and invent new ideas to add to the already existing body of knowledge. Sixth, in addition to being original, the poet must be rooted in reality and willing to explore every aspect of life and the world.

Thus it requires a combination of vital abilities and talents to become a great artist. If poets do possess all these necessary qualities, they will be able to create their own unique artistic works. According to Whitaker, Williams believed that being an artist was a high calling. Whitaker states that Williams thought that "art itself [was] important because, inviting and refreshing our attention, it [helps] to awaken us from our ordinary sleepwalking—from those habits, blockages, and illusions that produce and perpetuate man's inhumanity to man."

Jo K. Galle

THE WINDHOVER

Author: Gerard Manley Hopkins (1844-1889)
Type of poem: Sonnet
First published: 1918, in *Poems of Gerard Manley Hopkins, Now First Published, with Notes by Robert Bridges*

The Poem

Gerard Manley Hopkins himself thought that "The Windhover" was his best poem, and generations of readers have agreed with him. The poem, composed on May 30, 1877, contains the account of the flight of a falcon, as observed by the poet in North Wales as he attended religious studies at St. Beuno's seminary. The poem ends with a meditation on the activity of God in the world, as evidenced by the activity of the bird.

A windhover is better known as a kestrel, a type of falcon. The octave of the sonnet, the first eight lines, describes the flight of the windhover and its great skill in riding the currents of air. The narrator of the poem catches sight of the falcon at dawn, as the bird hovers and swoops in its hunt for prey. The different maneuvers of the bird in its flight are vividly described.

The first three lines describe the falcon's uncannily steady flight forward: "his rid-ing/ Of the rolling level underneath him steady air." The fourth line describes how the falcon pivots around from his forward flight: "how he rung upon the rein of a wim-pling wing." To ring upon the rein is a term from horse training: A young horse has a long rope attached to his bridle, and the trainer makes the horse trot around him in a large circle. In exactly this manner does the falcon swing around from his level flight forward to sweep into a circle. "Wimpling" means that his wings, to perform this ma-neuver, swing up into a curve that is like the wimple on a nun's headdress.

In the fifth line, the falcon suddenly swings around in the opposite direction. The poet compares the swing to a skater's motion in skating around the curve on a frozen river, "a bow-bend." The sixth and seventh lines describe the falcon coming upright into the wind; the wind comes up against the feathers with a puffing sound: "the hurl and gliding/ Rebuffed the big wind." In the seventh and eighth lines, the poet reports his exhilaration at the skill of the falcon: "the achieve of, the mastery of the thing!"

The action of the falcon reported in the ninth and tenth lines is not clear: "Brute beauty and valour and act, oh, air, pride plume, here/ Buckle!" The word "buckle" is used to describe either an action of the bird or the excitement caused in the poet by a mental assessment of the talent of the bird—or possibly both. The bird may here be diving down onto his prey; falcons and hawks accomplish this action by folding their wings and falling, often at speeds exceeding one hundred miles an hour, onto the backs of their prey. Buckle could describe the sudden folding back of the wings at the beginning of the "stoop," the technical term for the descent of the raptor onto its prey, a buckling as of a metal plate.

In the tenth and eleventh lines, the mental excitement in the viewer's mind produced by the meditation on the ability of the falcon is described as fire: "AND the fire that breaks from thee then, a billion/ Times told lovelier, more dangerous, O my chevalier!" The reference in the word "thee" is ambiguous; it may refer to the falcon, but it may also refer to "Christ our Lord," to whom the poem is dedicated. The fire would come from the bird's actions, or possibly from the action of Christ incarnated in the bird. (If the reference was to Christ, however, and not the falcon, the word "thee" would have a strong accent, by virtue of the rules of syntax—"AND the fire that breaks from thee then"—and there is no special accent.)

The twelfth, thirteenth, and fourteenth lines contain a short meditation by the poet on the way even things much less impressive than a falcon can show "brilliance," can excite sensitive viewers with their otherwise hidden abilities. A plow that has rusted in the barn for a whole winter can be scoured clean and shining merely by the action of plowing a furrow (a sillion is a furrow), and embers from a fire that seem to be entirely cold and dull can crack open and reveal a heart of glowing gold and red.

Forms and Devices

The poem rhymes like a sonnet: *abba, abba, cdcdcd*; however, the lines are not in iambic pentameter, the conventional meter for a sonnet. Instead of the orthodox ten syllables per line, there are in this poem lines from nine to fifteen syllables, so that instead of the normal 140 syllables in a sonnet, there are 177 in "The Windhover."

Hopkins himself described the rhythm of the poem as "falling paeonic . . . sprung and outriding." A falling paeonic meter is ordered as strong-weak-weak-weak, but only eight falling paeonics can be identified in the poem (nine if one can count as a foot two stresses on one line and two on the next line). In fact, the identification of the rhythm of the poem as "sprung" provides an explanation of the irregularity of the poem; sprung rhythm adopts the rhythmic variety and flexibility of prose, and allows each poem to have a characteristic movement expressive of the individual occasion that gave it birth. It is therefore unlikely that any regular rhythm, orthodox or Hopkinsian, will be found in the poem.

In other respects, however, the poem resembles conventional sonnets. A Petrarchan or Italian sonnet, which is what "The Windhover" is as far as its rhyme scheme is concerned, is usually divided into an octave of eight lines and a sestet of six lines. Hopkins follows this pattern in the poem's organization.

The first eight lines describe the flight of the falcon in a generally objective fashion (except for the line "My heart in hiding/ Stirred for a bird"), and the last six lines launch into subjective generality as they describe the conclusion of the flight of the bird and conclude in a meditation on the whole experience.

There are many linguistic devices that add to the impressiveness and vividness of the poem. Hopkins uses syntactic ambiguity in the second and third lines to convey a feeling of level flight. The phrase "dapple-dawn-drawn Falcon" could mean two things: "dapple-dawn drawn Falcon"—the falcon is drawn to the dappled dawn, or "dapple dawn-drawn Falcon"—the dappled falcon is drawn to the dawn. The intonation of the phrase differs depending on which interpretation the reader gives the phrase. If the reader cannot decide which structure is correct, there is a tendency to pronounce the phrase as if it were a string of unconnected words: "dapple dawn drawn falcon," which enforces an "unnatural" steadiness of intonation, which is exactly what the meaning requires—the steady flight of the bird.

Hopkins employs ambiguity of the same sort in the third line, in "rolling level underneath him steady air." Is the phrase to be read as "rolling, level-underneath-HIM, steady air," or as "rolling, level, underneath-him-steady air"? Again, the reader cannot resolve the ambiguity, and again an unnatural stiffness of intonation conveys the uncannily steady flight of the falcon.

Another aspect of the poem's technique is the deliberate use of medieval military and governmental terms from French—*minion* (from *mignon*, "darling," "favorite"), *dauphin*, *valour*, *plume*, *chevalier*, and *vermilion*. The military imagery could derive from Hopkins's training as a Jesuit. The Society of Jesus, founded by a soldier, Ignatius Loyola, features much military imagery in its training of priests. Even the term "dangerous" has a medieval French overtone; in medieval French, *daungier* had the significance of "awe-striking" as well as its modern meaning.

Themes and Meanings

Hopkins was extremely sensitive to natural beauty. In addition to his innate sensitivity, however, he also had theories on the place of natural beauty in God's world. He thought that all individually beautiful things had within them a principle of growth by which they developed, which he called "instress," a curve of stress that entered matter and transformed it into an individual creation. Therefore, the fire that "breaks" from the windhover is not actual flame but the impression made on the viewer when the instress that made the bird what it was suddenly flashes into the viewer's mind. Since the instress is a formative stress, it then begins to shape the mind of the poet as it had shaped the bird. The instress then travels down the arm of the poet and enters the language of the poem, whence it flashes to the mind of the reader. The traveling of the instress is like the path of an electric current, from object to viewer to language to reader.

The instresses that form the physical universe are not, however, merely natural forces. For Hopkins, each of them represents the activity of Christ in the world, since Christ is the principle of the Incarnation, the entry of God into matter. So each time the instress of an object or a creature blazes into Hopkins's head, he is also seeing the proof of the presence of God in the world.

Edmund L. Epstein

WINDOWS

Author: Guillaume Apollinaire (Guillaume Albert Wladimir Alexandre Apollinaire de Kostrowitzky, 1880-1918)
Type of poem: Lyric
First published: 1918, as "Les Fenêtres," in *Calligrammes*; English translation collected in *Calligrammes*, 1980

The Poem

A casual glimpse of Guillaume Apollinaire's "Windows" is enough to reveal its modernity: The thirty-seven lines are of widely varying lengths and are not divided into stanzas. Still, the title is fairly traditional; windows are an age-old symbol of the human eye, the link between the inner world and the world outside. Similarly, the opening verse is reassuringly musical, with careful rhythms and long vowel sounds in the French; it is, however, also enigmatic.

"From red to green all the yellow dies"—the phrase may allude to colors on a canvas, to the colors of the spectrum, to a sunset, or to something else altogether. In spite of the later reference to "sunset," the rest of the work does little to clarify this statement; in fact, at line 2, the poem seems to splinter into a bewilderingly random set of fragments, apparently generated by a process of free association.

Sights, sounds, thoughts, comments, events, memories, snatches of conversation, and rare poetic images are presented to the reader without any indication of their function. The impressions simply sit side by side, and it is up to the reader to work out the connections. For example, the primary colors of the first line may suggest the colorful macaws seen singing in the primitive ("native") forests of the second line; these macaws, perhaps, then generate the "pihis"—mythical one-winged birds—whose "giblets" are presented, without commentary, in the third.

As if recalling Apollinaire's earlier use of the "pihi" in his most famous poem, "Zone," the fourth and fifth lines step back from sound and vision to talk about poetry: There is a poem to be made about this bird, says the unidentified speaker, and "we'll send it by telephone," the new world-linking technology seen so powerfully in "Liens" ("Chains").

These first five lines contain the themes for the whole poem: color, exoticism, the bird's-eye view of the world, and universal connections. After that, the confusion seems to increase, another powerfully suggestive verse (verse 6) contrasting sharply with the most crudely realistic line of the poem (line 9). Yet just as it seems as if all coherence has been lost, the spiderlike hands at the window gradually begin to weave the threads together again, as S. I. Lockerbie has shown. The disruptive snatches of conversation slowly fade out, the links between lines become stronger, and when the tour of the world has gathered speed—allowing the reader to see ever further, ever more distinctly—the train brings the reader back to Paris, back to the first line.

Yet the reader has not simply gone round in circles. The poem began with a death, a sunset, and it continued, with a "shock" and with tears, into the pale colors of night and winter; now the train brings the reader into spring, and the repeated first line seems to suggest a new dawn, the orange implying a bright new day, the word "fruit" a new birth. A flat window, a lifeless palette, metamorphoses into a three-dimensional object of nature. The poem thus ends on a triumphant note of unity.

Forms and Devices

"Windows" was originally written for the 1913 exhibition in Berlin of the cubist painter Robert Delaunay, Apollinaire's favorite artist after Pablo Picasso. Delaunay's preoccupations with color, with windows, and with the Eiffel Tower are all evident in the poem; more important, the poem has strong affinities with cubist techniques of collage.

Like a cubist painting, "Windows" mixes purely abstract elements (the colors) with an artistic representation of reality ("unfathomable violets") and with directly presented reality ("towers"). The tone fluctuates between seriousness and flippancy, the poetic and the colloquial; the vocabulary is sometimes prosaic (the ironically capitalized "Codfish"), sometimes exotic ("pihis"); there are lines of sixteen syllables and lines of one syllable, as well as lines of conventional length. Logical connections between words and lines are removed; there is not even any punctuation or spacing between groups of verses to give clues as to the relationships involved. Legend has it that Apollinaire and some friends wrote the poem together at a café, each adding a line in turn; at first reading, that seems highly credible.

Nevertheless, this collage is skillfully handled, blending experimentation with tradition. Generally speaking, each element is coherent in itself and is confined to one or two lines. Thus the problem is merely one of unexpected combinations and the lack of an overall context into which to fit them. In some ways, that does not so much imitate cubism as anticipate Surrealism; indeed, Apollinaire invented the term, and the most famous Surrealist image, "the earth is blue like an orange," may owe something to this poem.

What is typically cubist in the poem is the juxtaposition of different perspectives. Just as a cubist portrait might show a nose in profile next to the front view of an eye, so in "Windows" the towers are viewed from the side, becoming "streets," and the squares from above, gaining depth by comparison with the surrounding houses. This use of perspective, which may also derive from the then newly fashionable cinema, has two effects: It reproduces the "simultaneity" of modern life, the sensation of multiple impressions striking the viewer all at once, and it suggests that there are numerous ways of looking at the same thing.

There is no identifiable speaker in the poem, no "I" to give a single point of view; the closest the speaker comes to that is in a vague "we," and in the French, an even vaguer *on* ("one," "we," "they"). The poet's place is usurped by anonymous, disembodied voices and by colors and objects—like the window opening by itself—which have a life of their own. The individuality of the poet comes through only in the choice and combination of elements; although there is plenty of sensation, personal emotion seems rare. Keeping the poet out of the poem also means letting the reader in. The ambiguities—do wells look like squares, or do squares look like wells?—force readers to read actively, to add their own associations and attempt to find meanings in the carefully arranged elements of the poem.

Themes and Meanings

Amid the rapid development of technology and with the dawn of a new century, artists partly envisioned and partly effected a departure from old ways. Cars and especially airplanes, whose praises are sung in "Zone," surpassed trains in expanding horizons and in creating new perspectives. For many artists, that strengthened the impulse toward objectivity, in order to cater to the subjectivity of the reader or viewer. This impulse is present in "Windows."

The sprawling modern city can only be perceived in pieces. In the increased pace of daily life, several sensations strike the individual at once: Apollinaire, like the Futurists, revels in this "simultaneity" and attempts to reproduce it in writing, although he himself concedes that painting captures it better.

In the poem, the window "opens" in line 11 and again in line 35. It has not closed in between; rather, the suggestion is that all the sights and sounds of the intervening verses are perceived at once. Lines 10 through 12 move from present to future, a logical sequence, then suddenly back into the past—as if past, present, and future were somehow interchangeable. Like the cubists, however, Apollinaire does more than merely present the fragmentation. Out of the chaos of modern life, he fashions a new unity, linking all of space and time; it is not by accident that "when" and "where" are, with "and," the major linking words in the poem.

Line 35 sums up this movement. Six place-names are juxtaposed in a typically elliptical list; they are pulled together in the mind of the poet. At the same time, "Hyères" sounds like *hier* (yesterday) and "Maintenon" like *maintenant* (now), so the verse also links past, present, and future once again. All places are unified, all times are coalesced, and space and time themselves are linked through the pun.

This vision of unity is very different from that of previous poets. Dissension is not excluded: The "diamond," a prism refracting light, breaks up the climactic flurry of the last eight lines to remind the reader of that. It is as if the light were being broken up into colors, by a window or a diamond, and woven back together simultaneously. It is a new dynamic unity that can incorporate fragmentation.

Paradoxically, it is Apollinaire's inability to capture the whole of the city that allows him to encompass the whole of the world. Unable to represent reality as traditional artists sought to do, he *re-creates* it; death leads to rebirth. "Painting," he writes, "is no longer the art of reproduction, but of creation"; the artist "puts order in the universe." Various forms of human control over the outside world are alluded to: hunting, technology, poetry. In fact, it is almost as if humanity were taking on the role of nature—the hands are "spiders"—in restoring harmony to the cosmos.

Joshua Landy

THE WINDOWS

Author: Stéphane Mallarmé (1842-1898)
Type of poem: Lyric
First published: 1863, as "Les Fenêtres"; in *Les Poésies de Stéphane Mallarmé*, 1887; English translation collected in *Poems*, 1936

The Poem

"The Windows" is a short poem of forty lines that are divided into ten four-line stanzas of Alexandrines. The poem divides exactly into two sections; in the first half of the poem, an old man makes his way slowly toward a window of the hospital in which he is dying. The second half of the poem presents a vision of the old man's dreams that have been occasioned by the warm sunlight filtering through the panes of glass.

Stéphane Mallarmé used this poem, with its almost commonplace title, to introduce a series of poems in *Le Parnasse contemporain* (1863), one of the early collections in what has come to be recognized as the Symbolist style, which coalesced officially following a published manifesto in 1886. (Other poets who eventually produced poems in this style include Charles Baudelaire, Paul Verlaine, and Arthur Rimbaud.) Mallarmé is designated as one of the masters of this style primarily for his extensive use of images that evoke a type of sensuous reverie; these images are, however, frequently difficult to decipher. This difficulty in decoding demonstrates one of the essential paradoxes of the movement: A symbol, by definition, calls attention to something else. When that "something else" is vague or difficult to discern, however, the symbol begins to take on more power in and of itself, not simply as a referential device.

"The Windows" demonstrates this technique initially in the apparent simplicity of the title. Hardly anything could be less unusual than a window; everyone is surrounded by dozens of them every day. In this poem, however, Mallarmé asks the reader, initially by means of a type of omniscient narration of the old man's feelings, to consider windows in a new way. Mallarmé suggests that these windows are, rather than simply vehicles through which light and vision are transmitted, in fact gateways through which individuals might gain access to memories and desires thought to have passed away long ago. The narration of the poem shifts abruptly in line 25 from the third person to the first person in an effort to reinforce the power of the despair the narrator feels at having lost access to such a realm as the old man has dreamed of beyond the window.

Forms and Devices

The dominant metaphor of the poem is simply a window; Mallarmé is asking the reader to consider a familiar object in a new light. He wishes to emphasize that even the simplest objects by which people are surrounded can take on an almost spiritual meaning when considered through the lens of poetic technique. As the old man of the first half of the poem "Shuffles, less to warm his rotting body/ Than to watch the sun on the stones, to press/ His ashen gaunt and skeletal face/ To the panes which a clear beautiful ray attempts to tinge," the reader understands the window initially as a medium through which light, heat, and the old man's vision are transmitted. The old man longs to be outside, away from "the rank fumes" of the hospital where he can hold his "eye on the horizon gorged with light." The use of the word "gorged" (*gorgé*) indicates another use of the metaphor of the glass through which light, heat, and vision move. The old man certainly relishes what is on the other side of the window, but he is also definitely aware of the sensuous quality of the window itself. After he shuffles to the window, "his mouth, feverish and greedy for the azure,/ As when young, he breathed his prize,/ A virginal cheek! soils/ With a long bitter kiss the warm golden panes." In other words, the old man's kissing of the glass indicates an awareness of the sensual pleasure of the symbol, of the gateway through which his own perceptions, and those of the reader, are led back to an era that cannot, apparently, be recovered.

The metaphor of the window is far from exhausted in the old man's lingering kiss that indicates that he is wallowing "in contentment, where only his appetites/ Devour him." As soon as the reader has accepted the use that the dying old man is making of the window, Mallarmé introduces another dimension into the poem by entering in the first person. He notes, "I flee and I cling to all those windows/ From where one turns one's back on life." These windows, then, are not the personal gateway to the past dreams of the dying old man, but poetic gateways through which "I see myself and I brag I am an angel! and I die, and I long/—Let the glass be art, let it be mysticism—/ To be reborn, wearing my dream as a crown,/ In a past heaven where Beauty flourished!" These windows, which are the operation of poetry itself, promise to allow the poet access to a heaven of pure poetry "where Beauty flourishe[s]."

As the final two stanzas of the poem indicate, however, even though one's passions, vision, and understanding can readily pass through such windows, one's body cannot. The speaker of the poem realizes finally that "Here-below [*Ici-bas*] is master; its curse/ Sickens me . . ./ And the foul vomit of Stupidity/ Makes me stop up my nose in face of the azure." That is, the pane of glass remains firmly fixed between the dying old man and his dreams, and between the poet and his. Poetry, like a crystalline pane of glass, presents the illusion of allowing access to another world, but that illusion ultimately shatters because the glass does not.

The speaker finally muses despondently, "Is there a way for Me who knows bitterness/ To shatter the crystal insulted by the monster/ and to escape with my two featherless wings/—Even at the risk of falling in eternity?" Having exhausted the poetic means available to help him escape the "Here-below," the speaker wonders whether death itself, perhaps in suicide, might be a way to escape the reflection of his own image in the window, the monster of line 38.

Themes and Meanings

"The Windows" is ultimately a poem about the relationships between poetry, life, and death. Poetry, like a crystalline window, may allow an individual to gain access to once-forgotten dreams or realms of experience that defy the usual laws of human existence. Therefore, poetry can be a useful crutch for those who are approaching their own death. The old man "straightens his old spine," moves his "rotting body," and presses his "ashen gaunt and skeletal face" to the pane of glass, seeking the warmth of his youth that has been lost. Evidently, however, Mallarmé feels that such a personal use of poetry is inappropriate, since the narrator of the poem is disgusted with the old man's behavior, but Mallarmé also insists that the old man's behavior is unavoidable, that humans need poetry as much as they despise its artifice or its use of symbols to convey worlds long past. By shifting the perspective of the poem from the old man, blissfully unaware that the narrator is watching his reverie, to the poet-narrator himself, who loathes his own inability to see more than his own image in the glass, Mallarmé suggests that perhaps taking pleasure in the symbol itself, be it the poem or the window, might be the best that one can hope for and all the passion that one can need. Therefore, even though one might initially scorn the use of such a commonplace image as a window to introduce a collection of poems, Mallarmé leaves one feeling that even such commonplaces contain a capacity for passionate understanding that is barely concealed within the unbreakable shell of their opaque transparency.

Peter D. Olson

THE WINE MENAGERIE

Author: Hart Crane (1899-1932)
Type of poem: Ode
First published: 1926, in *White Buildings*

The Poem

"The Wine Menagerie" is a convoluted and disjointed attempt to describe the generative capacity of alcohol to spark creativity. It is divided into eleven stanzas of somewhat irregular rhyme; the final three form a kind of self-colloquy.

Hart Crane begins the poem on an almost fatalistic note coupled with an illusion about the redemptive quality of liquor (Crane was himself an alcoholic). When he gets drunk, the same things "invariably" happen. Wine gives him a fresh vision, he claims. He perceives an image of poetic feet in the line of mustard jars facing the bar, while a leopard of creativity hunts through his mind. The leopard image might also be a symbol of fraud; the poet's creative visions, then, may be only an illusion.

The poet now fixes on the wine decanters and sees his image in their glittering bellies; they are a "glozening" glossary flowing into "liquid cynosures" that conscript him to the shadows and degrade him to a stupor. A fantasy of applause is attributed to the expansiveness of his wine-soaked visions.

He scrutinizes the onyx wainscoting and painted emulsions on the saloon wall. His revulsion is further expressed in the descriptions of the people who populate the speakeasy. He describes the "forceps" smile of a woman, her destructive, mallet eyes, and the fearful clatter of sweat on the man with whom she argues.

The poet fixes on a reptile image with octagon skin and transept eyes; he perceives both its fraud and its transforming guile and poison. His mind jumps irrationally to thoughts of arrows and the possibility of superhuman artistry that surpasses all moral limitations. He proposes shedding his skin while a new thought speeds arrowlike to feathered skies. He feels unskeined and transposed into a new identity.

A little boy, an urchin of guile, buys some beer in a canister as the characters in the saloon mutate into grotesques. The poet's flight to creative ecstasy begins to turn back on itself. He perceives a set of black tusks embracing a bouquet of shining roses. The roses seem to promise new heights of creativity, but they are surrounded by an image of terror. Even so, he insists that his creative "talons" will seize vaguely described new purities; he will search out new thresholds and new entities; he yearns to travel in a tear and sparkle in martyrdom. He vows he will distill his competence in human weeping; his creative persona will snare new purities and transmit his energies so that he can become a poetic bird of prey.

Fear then overwhelms the poet. The wine has become a dangerous ally, and his illusory joys begin to dissolve. His wine-soaked visions have become a cage. His search for beauty capitulates to the grotesque and repulsive, and he feels stuck on the ruddy tooth of reality. His mind returns to the saloon and the relic inhabitants of the wine world. He rises from the bar stool to escape the speakeasy with its crumbs of emotional dissolution and fear, but his exile folds back on itself as he is forced to stumble over the remnants of a horrific vision beneath his feet: the severed heads of Holofernes (murdered by his wife Judith) and John the Baptist. The whispering of those Old and New Testament grotesques who were undone by passion floats by his stupefied mind and mocks his pretensions. As he enters the street, he spins drunkenly and pivots like "Petrushka's valentine."

Forms and Devices

The poem was first submitted to *The Criterion*, which was edited by T. S. Eliot. Eliot rejected it, so Crane then sent it to Marianne Moore, editor of *The Dial*. Moore revised the poem—so much so that Crane felt it was hardly recognizable—and published it under the title "Again." It was not to appear in its original form as "The Wine Menagerie" until its 1926 publication in Crane's own book, *White Buildings*.

The poem is divided into stanzas of mainly four-and five-line groups. The final three stanzas are set in quotation marks and constitute a kind of self-colloquy. The rhyming is somewhat irregular. There are some couplets, but most of the lines rhyme *abcb*. A few are *abca*. The poem has a number of off-rhymes, such as "snow/brow" and "eyes/gaze."

The poem has a plodding rhythm and relatively little continuity between the stanzas. Lines within the stanzas are sometimes enjambed. The entire effect suggests a kind of arduous self-consciousness in which images and rhythms are both confused and concentrated.

Crane draws his imagery from the Old and New Testaments, ancient mythology, folklore, Freudian psychology, and even the graphic arts. He jumps sickeningly and carelessly from object to object, from saloon arguments to streaked bodies and stigmas, to the urchin, to black tusks and shining roses. When his hope of transcending earthly limits collapses into crumbs, he is left to stumble over the grotesque, relic inhabitants of his wine world. He spins dizzily out into the street like the pathetic marionette in Igor Stravinsky's ballet, *Petrushka* (1911).

Themes and Meanings

"The Wine Menagerie" shows how creative genius necessarily dissolves into fear when it is contaminated by the effects of alcohol. To put it another way, the poem demonstrates how alcohol fails dismally in powering the creative process. As such, it is a remarkable description of the insanity of chronic drunkenness and how that drunkenness is controlled by an element of trickery and illusions of grandeur. The poet does not simply perceive his world from a weird perspective; he is enveloped by it and condemned to wander among the lowest common denominator of humanity and alcoholic degradation—a grimy saloon of dissipation, fraudulent perceptions, and broken relationships.

Fear is the poet's insatiable companion, and it is pervasive to the degree that it colors his every perception and misperception. He makes no distinction between delusion and reality; because of his self-involvement and narcissism, he becomes enveloped in a terrifying drama in which he becomes the axis of a self-created world gone mad. He does not achieve an intensified and clarified vision, as he seems to hope; rather, his perceptions are dulled, and his metaphorical juxtaposition of opposites becomes absurd and fatalistic. He elevates the trivial into the extravagant, mistaking pretentious drivel for linguistic elegance. The wine is not so much redemptive as it is reductive, reflecting the poet's all-consuming self-obsession and his alcoholic imprisonment in the very bottles that he hopes will provide creative release. Although the poet has tried to generate something profound, he is by the very nature of his experience conscripted to mediocrity. His mind jumps from one absurdity to another; while he seeks a new identity, he remains confused and restricted by his alcoholic confusion. When the caricatures in the saloon mutate into grotesques, they amplify his paranoid isolation from himself and hence from other human companionship.

"The Wine Menagerie" shows that alcohol is not the father of insight. Alcohol provides no profound metamorphosis into creative genius or extra-logical truth. Instead, Crane admits that he is both imprisoned and strained by inflated emotions and by an extreme of drunkenness that can only lead to collapse. Ultimately, he is compelled to flee the debris of the speakeasy and its ugly apparitions. The poem is a remarkable portrait of the confusion, the narcissistic depression, the insanity, and the self-deception characteristic of the alcoholic perspective. As such, it is astonishing in its accuracy, as it demonstrates how a wine-soaked attempt at illumination and self-transcendence can become overcharged and lead to disorientation. The allure of loneliness, the intolerable soul sickness, and the hunger to translate insanity and unintelligible drivel into art are molded into a senseless yet stunningly accurate portrait of the irrational priesthood of an alcoholic writer who wavers between terror and self-sufficiency.

Matts Djos

WINTER HORSES

Author: Barbara Guest (1920-　　)
Type of poem: Lyric
First published: 1991; collected in *Defensive Rapture*, 1993

The Poem

"Winter Horses" is a poem in four short sections of thirteen, eleven, nine, and eight lines, respectively. The first and last sections' lines are left-justified, whereas the middle sections' lines are scattered on the page. The poem's title provides a useful index to the poem as a whole: "Winter Horses" juxtaposes the idea of winter (stillness) and the idea of horses (motion). Readers can fruitfully consider the poem a meditation on the results of this juxtaposition. Seeming paradoxes are linked through logical associations which lead them to be viewed as complementary ideas instead of contradictory ones.

The first section catalogs the effects of winter on the land and the people. The first line, "placed two sticks upon a dazzling plate," suggests the movement of the poem: How will readers reconceive the ordinary (the "two sticks") on the "dazzling plate" of winter? Abruptly the poem moves from the landscape to people, invoking wars, memory, hearsay, and treachery in only two lines; apparently the emotional landscape of winter is neither still nor dazzling but turbulent and pained. The second stanza implies that readers remember the "tawny . . . splendor" of summer in glorious winter sunsets, despite the freeze that "shut[s] the moat."

The next two sections, with their lines shifting on the page, work even more associatively. The conflict between winter (bearing cold stillness) and horses (living motion) persists but now appears to operate by an associative logic rather than by seeming contradiction. Further, the details begin to probe the greater emotional depths of the connotations of these ideas. For example, as the second section's first stanza turns "sea grey cold" into "a door" and then "one boulder," the cold and the forbidding size of a boulder suggest a closed door and thus the emotional connotations of such a door. The poem thus invites the reader's fuller participation as the reader essentially rewrites the poem in trying to create a personal understanding of the associations. The emotional landscape darkens in the third section as the lines approach a more regular spacing, with some lines indented about half a line while others are left-justified. When an unidentified "they" bring the reader, posed as "you," "a fig dish," it appears as a luxury, but the next line offers a corpse. The winter appears increasingly menacing and powerful, despite its designation as *la gloire* (French for "the glow" or "glory") at the beginning of the section; hence the closing lines, "the cramped space ran/ out of breathing." Winter's compass, left unchecked, would deny life to everything that breathes.

The poem's last section brings readers to the start of the spring thaw as winter still clings. Though snow may "lance" the brightness, winter's last attempt to reign over nature will surely fail. The sun, warm enough that windows are "flung" open, will soon dominate again. This moment between seasons, during which both show their force, creates a sense of awe, a "dazzlement" that urges new life. Yet this life arises from death, for the people who come out in their boots necessarily step on the invisible creature of the air, the sylph. Poet Barbara Guest suggests that the cycle of seasons is not pure; one cannot merely associate winter with death and spring with life. Rather, Guest evokes a far more complex layering of the promise and the threat of a season in the world and in the mind.

Forms and Devices

Guest builds the poem through an accumulation of fragments, of striking phrases that might be disturbing in their incompleteness for the reader of traditional poetry. In an interview, Guest described another one of her poems as working "on several levels and [moving] back and forth . . . between levels as reality does." In Guest's poetic vision, reality is fragmented rather than unified. This is not to say that Guest does not believe there is any coherence but that coherence arises between the levels, between the fragments, in a process of association and accumulation. Guest's fragmentary style urges a high level of participation from the reader. Readers cannot simply accept a given narrative or linear logic; rather, they bring their own associations to the poem and hence find the silence on the page (what Guest does not say) as the place for their participation and understanding. This does not mean that the poem can mean anything the reader wants it to, but that the fragments allow both a greater range of interpretation and any interpretation to remain subject to reconsideration by a different reader.

Guest's use of capitalization and punctuation provide further guidance. There are no capitalized words, placing the reader *in medias res*. This evokes questions about the poem's temporality: Is the poem going on now? The alternation between past and present tense suggests some narrative progression, some relation between what has passed and what is happening now, but the fragmentary nature of these phrases leads more to suggestions than to specific answers. Guest's punctuation operates more definitively: Periods organize the fragments that came before it into a unit, and semicolons link fragments to evince a relation. At the beginning of the third section, the exclamation point at the end of the second fragment suggests that the "it" refers to winter, as the section's beginning and the exclamation point enclose what comes between them and thus relate the two fragments to each other. Guest offers *la gloire* as the reader's preconception of winter: "winter/ you know how it is *la gloire!*"

Guest's fragmented imagery provides something similar to a kaleidoscopic effect in the shifts of light, color, shape, and mood. Readers appear to view a medieval scene composed of "feudal wars," "fortifications," and a "moat" that represents the winter while being situated in it, and yet that scene constantly shifts as it accrues more detail. Some of the images require the reader's invention, as when the reader, described as remembering feudal wars, appears to have not only a historical memory but also a historical imagination; for Guest, these may well be one and the same.

Themes and Meanings

The title of the book in which "Winter Horses" is collected suggests a provocative theme for this poem in particular: *Defensive Rapture*. Where does this poem reach for rapture, and where does it appear to defend against or temper it? Is it the rapture itself that menaces, or does something else underlie and necessarily disrupt rapture? Can a defensive rapture be called rapture at all? The answer might lie in the word "rapture" itself. While the word bears the generally positive definition of "transport to ecstasy," its original Latin root, *raptus* ("to have been seized"), is a form of the verb *rapio* ("to seize"), which is the root of the word "rape." Someone experiencing rapture has been seized, and while this feeling brings the pleasure of ecstasy, it also takes possession of one's mind. A mind as aware of *la gloire* as of fortifications and wars might well find rapture impossible to maintain. Indeed, reality offers both fragments of rapture and menace, and a defensive rapture brings one not so much safety as a steady awareness that can recognize and experience both pleasure and pain, particularly through the vehicle of the imagination.

This leads to a second key theme in the poem: the relationship between reality and the imagination. People generally do not consider reality to be as fragmented as Guest presents it, which raises the question of the role of the imagination. In the poem, the reader's imagination creates coherences between the fragments. Is this also how imagination works with reality? The poem highlights the ability of the mind or the imagination to connect seemingly disparate objects and ideas and to devise meaning, revealing what might be the mind's partly conscious, partly unconscious work. Yet this does not imply that the poem ever loses its ability to disturb by the gaps that it leaves; one cannot merely connect the dots. Readers can make easier connections between some fragments than others. Some fragments contain more of a sense of emotional connotation than a precise interpretation. The poem's incompleteness continues to resonate because that incompleteness produces the necessity to rewrite or reconnect with the poem with every new reading. The period that concludes the poem might well serve as an arrow redirecting readers back to the poem's beginning to read that beginning anew in light of what the "end" has provided. As poet Tom Clark has commented, Guest's work "mimes the tenuous, evanescent sense of shimmer or mirage that life's splintered transparencies present us." Readers may revel in that shimmer, recognizing Guest's "splintered transparencies" as the view from their own lives.

Carrie Etter

WITH A COPY OF SWIFT'S WORKS

Author: J. V. Cunningham (1911-1985)
Type of poem: Lyric
First published: 1947, as #42 of "Epigrams: A Journal," in *The Judge Is Fury*

The Poem
"With a Copy of Swift's Works" is a short poem in couplets, totalling twelve lines. It is divided into two sentences; the first is a couplet, and the second is a single thought elaborated over ten lines. The title refers to the occasion of the poem. The speaker is looking at the literary works of the Irish author Jonathan Swift (1667-1745), who was best known for such satirical prose works as *Gulliver's Travels* and "A Modest Proposal." Swift also wrote poetry, contributed essays to literary periodicals, and authored a fourteen-volume *History of the Reign of Queen Anne.* The initial reference in the poem to the pseudonyms of two of Swift's female friends, "Stella" and "Vanessa," suggests that the speaker is thinking of Swift's poetry. Swift helped several eighteenth century Irish women authors, using his editorial, critical, and business skills to connect Dublin-based women writers with publishers in both Dublin and London. He also wrote poetry to Esther Johnson and Esther Vanhomrigh. Johnson was Stella, and Vanhomrigh was Vanessa. Swift's poems on "Stella's" birthdays are very well-known. The use of pseudonyms was common in verse written by both men and women in the eighteenth century.

Cunningham's poem was written in Palo Alto, California, on May 20, 1944. It became one of the forty-three poems that comprise the "Epigram Journal" of his 1947 book, *The Judge Is Fury.* Swift, too, wrote epigrams, which are short, witty poems, often satirical in tone. The Greek and Latin root words mean "to write on" or, as it is commonly taken to mean, to write an inscription. "With a Copy of Swift's Works" is an epigram which serves as an inscription to an edition of his works—akin to something that the giver of a gift might write in a gift book.

"With a Copy of Swift's Works" begins with the presentation of the book to the reader with the cheery explanation, "Underneath this pretty cover/ Lies Vanessa's, Stella's lover." The poet is making two points here. The first is that all that is left of Swift's talents and genius is bound in this book. The second is about the speculation that Swift was secretly married to Esther Johnson (Stella). There were rumors circulating in both Dublin and London society during Swift's lifetime that he was sexually involved with both women; the rumors have never been proven. In the eighteenth century, "lover" was the term for a fiancée or someone who was dating. To say Swift was a "lover" as Cunningham does here is to play off the older and the modern meanings of the term, indicating sexual involvement.

The next ten lines of the poem are its second sentence. The poet instructs the reader not to be saddened by Swift's life or death. Cunningham assumes the reader is familiar with Swift's life: He had hoped for a job in London but was rejected and thus entered the ministry and became Dean of St. Paul's, the most important Anglican church in Dublin. He was rumored to have been very bitter about having to live in Dublin, and some of his earliest critics pointed to his dissatisfaction as the reason he was attracted to satire. The poet's view of Swift is objective and practical. It is by his success as a writer that the person to whom the gift is given or the poem is addressed should know and appreciate him. Swift was unsympathetic in his handling of satiric subjects, even tactless, and he would neither want nor deserve sympathy, states Cunningham.

Forms and Devices

The poem is written in couplets. This form is particularly suitable for writing about Swift, as most eighteenth century poets wrote in couplets. The meter of the poem is the trochaic tetrameter, a popular alternative to iambic meters. The trochee is a syllable pattern that goes from unstressed to stressed syllables, while the iamb is a stressed-to-unstressed pattern. Tetrameter has four accented syllables per line. The third couplet, which marks the second part of the poem, demonstrates the technique of catalexis—omitting the stress on the last syllable of the line to create variety in the trochaic line.

"With a Copy of Swift's Works" employs philosophically based imagery. Cunningham's construction is dependent on several strains of late seventeenth, mid-eighteenth and nineteenth century thought. "Absolute" and "Motion" are the richest words of the vocabulary and are the keys to comprehending the balance of the poem. The third couplet states: "Who the Absolute so loved/ Motion to its zero moved." Swift's satirical vision, and why he came to write what he did, are being described. "The Absolute" was brought into philosophical vocabulary in Germany at the end of the eighteenth century. The concept had been in existence since the mid-sixteenth century in the work of Baruch Spinoza. The phrase "the Absolute," as Cunningham uses it, can be interpreted as a manifestation of God, defined as the creative source of everything real in the world. As an essence or primary source, the existence of God is known through the activities of artists, writers, and musicians, who reveal "the Absolute" to humanity. Humans, then, although mortal, are divine by nature. "The Absolute" was eventually characterized by philosophers between 1803 and 1893 as possessing freedom, reality, truth, and harmony. It is likely that Cunningham was as well acquainted with Samuel Taylor Coleridge's use of the term in his literary periodical *The Friend* (1809-1810) as he was with the work of Georg Wilhelm Friedrich Hegel, James Frederick Ferrier, and Francis Herbert Bradley, all of whom contributed to defining "the Absolute."

The depiction of "Motion" in the poem has its origins in Aristotle, Galileo, and Thomas Hobbes. Cunningham uses "motion," "moved," and "immobile" to relate the action that "the Absolute" takes in relation to Swift. The progress of the remaining couplets is Aristotelian. Aristotle defined the idea of the "Absolute," when he wrote of the unmoved mover. Motion actualizes potential which creates a form which can change in quality, size, and location. Aristotle's idea, as it regards humans, is usually taken to include his idea that humanity could achieve perfection. In the poem Swift is put into action by "the Absolute," which allows him to realize his potential as a writer; then, because he is mortal, he dies.

Galileo's (1564-1642) theory of uniformly accelerated motion adds the element of evolution over time to the poem. Galileo was interested in the description of motion based on geometric axioms, not in trying to determine the cause of motion. Hence motion moves to its "zero," and fury freezes as the anger that motivated Swift's satires diminishes. Finally, Hobbes's (1588-1679) theory of motion is based on the premise that without force or impetus there can be no motion. He posits that movement happens when the body acted on by the force resists it. At the first push of force, however, the body will yield, no matter how hard or solid it may be. Hobbes's theory, when applied to the poem, introduces the concept of tension between the external source of the force and the body it moves. Cunningham uses this notion to symbolize the power of death in life, Swift's mortality, and the reader's love-hate reaction to satire.

Themes and Meanings

The reader's satisfaction with "With a Copy of Swift's Works" depends on prior knowledge of Swift's life and works. Cunningham presumes a reader who knows Swift and would want his works. This reader is acquainted with the rudiments of Swift's life, Swift's own unpublished "Verses on the Death of Dr. Swift, D.S.P.D." (1731), his epitaph, and the philosophical theories of the mover and the moved, developed in Swift's life and expanded upon after his death.

The principal theme of the poem is that Swift's works represent him well. The "pretty cover" of the volume is deceptive, as many of his works were intended to expose the "ugliness" or vice-ridden aspects of human nature. The poet is suggesting that there is no need to feel sorry for this writer, who achieved what he intended.

Cunningham previously alluded to Swift in a 1932 poem, "The Wandering Scholar's Prayer to Saint Catherine of Egypt." In this poem, collected in *The Helmsman* (1942), Cunningham evokes Swift as a specter of death to describe the hobos in the train yards who are dying of starvation and neglect as "Swift in idiot froth." Swift was declared insane and therefore mentally incompetent in 1742 when the symptoms of Mèniére's syndrome had debilitated him beyond his ability to care for himself. He died a painful and miserable death, and his illness caused his reputation to suffer and created a lack of compassion among the public.

Cunningham, like Swift, uses the glib briskness of the satirist's stance to appear lighthearted about serious matters. "With a Copy of Swift's Works" addresses the theme of the relationship between a writer's life and the work produced. When the figure is one of the stature of Swift, it is easy for the reader to misinterpret his motives in writing satirical works and compassionate poetry. Cunningham, while relying on the reader's knowledge of Swift, implies that Swift was acting out the will of a higher power or force in his writing. His satires were not motivated by bitterness about a life that could not be, but by a soul tormented by the realization that perfection is within the grasp of humanity, which is too weakened by vice and self-interest to attain it. When Swift realized that he had accomplished all he could with his work, fury froze within him and he died in harmony with "the Absolute," which had directed his actions to its satisfaction. When fury's force was silenced, the writer ceased to move.

Beverly Schneller

WITH ALL MY THOUGHTS

Author: Paul Celan (Paul Antschel, 1920-1970)
Type of poem: Meditation
First published: 1963, as "Mit Allen Gedanken," in *Die Niemandsrose*; English translation collected in *Poems of Paul Celan*, 1988

The Poem

"With All My Thoughts" is a poem of nineteen lines broken up into four stanzas. The first three stanzas are of four lines each, while the last stanza, breaking this pattern, is seven lines long. The poem does not follow a set rhyme scheme or syllabic pattern, either in the original German or in the English translation. Rather, the music of the poem arises from the sense it creates of being a transcription of the poet's inner thoughts.

The poem's title is incorporated into the opening line of the first stanza. Much of Paul Celan's earlier poetry is titled in the conventional way, but as his work progressed he increasingly shifted to this other mode of presentation. Incorporating the title directly into the poem makes it seem more immediate and strangely anonymous, like a message found in a bottle or an inscription on a monument overgrown with weeds.

In keeping with this sense of anonymity, the poem is written in the first person and addressed to some other, although the poet never makes entirely clear who this other is. Equally strange is the poet's declaration in the first stanza that in order to meet this "quiet . . . open one" he had to go "out of the world." Immediately, it becomes clear that the poet is not concerned with presenting a concrete depiction of a "real-life" event. While the situation of the poem is deeply dramatic, the drama occurs on some level beyond that of strictly representational action. The enigmatic relationship between the events of the external world and the content of the poem is further developed in the second stanza. There, the poet refers to some unidentified past crisis in which both the speaker's and the listener's "eyes broke" (literally but not figuratively impossible). Paradoxically, however, this crisis did not result in tragedy but in a sense of awakening, in a sense of the world becoming new.

While up to this point the poet has claimed to speak "outside the world," stanza 3 charts the entrance of the sun into the poem. The sun is the external world's most visible and obvious emblem, and it is strange that the poet should draw a connection between the inner silence of the soul and the path of the sun. For if, on the one hand, one might think of the soul as a small, focused thing, on the other hand, little could be vaster than the sun's orbit.

Celan further develops this mysterious connection in the final stanza, where "With All My Thoughts" seems most clearly a love poem. For once the soul and the sun have come into contact, the lover's "lap open[s], tranquilly," and a "breath" (the poet's? the lover's?) rises up into the sky, where "clouds" are formed. The poem up to this point has been reluctant to speak of a particular person or situation, but the breath that turns into clouds brings with it the possibility of forming itself into a "name," though the name is never specified.

Forms and Devices

Paul Celan was born in Romania in 1920 and as a young man, lost both of his parents at the hands of the Nazis, a fact that it is always necessary to bear in mind when reading his work. In some of his earlier work—most notably "Todesfuge" ("Death Fugue")—he attempted to deal with the Holocaust directly, but when such poems came to be famous and were anthologized he began to be bothered by them, as though such direct presentation inevitably trivialized the sense of tragedy he had meant to convey.

This biographical fact alone does not fully account for the feelings of anonymity and mysterious crisis present in "With All My Thoughts," but it does help the reader to understand the complex interplay of spiritual and physical realities in Celan's work. The lack of an offset title, for example, is consistent with a poem that refuses to provide some clear referential handle that will allow one to read it in terms of distinct characters involved in a specific situation. The poem reads like a message that has arrived out of nowhere. Its asymmetrical appearance on the page, jagged line breaks, and abrupt pauses push the reader's attention toward the blankness of the surrounding page, as though the poem were merely a crack in the silence there. As stanza 3 makes clear, it is the lovers' silence that "map[s] out/ an orbit for the sun."

Similarly, the sequence of pronoun references and the relationship between pronouns and events in the poem seem purposely obscure. Leaving the world, the "I" in the first stanza encounters a "you" who "received us." In the third stanza, the sun appears, "bright/ a soul and a soul confronted it." Again, the sequence of events does not seem logically ordered as it might be in a straightforward narrative; rather, as might be appropriate to religious meditation, everything seems to happen at once.

This rich confusion helps to reinforce the theme, central to the poem, that the inner "soul" and the external world coexist in mysterious relation. When the poet states in stanza 2 that "our eyes broke," this literal impossibility makes perfect figurative sense, much as it makes perfect sense to speak of silence as "breaking." Consider, too, that eyes "breaking" might simply refer to two lovers gazing at one another, then turning away. Yet for the poet, at this moment of "breaking," "everything began." This curious interplay between the utterly simple and the utterly mysterious is at work on every level of the poem.

Themes and Meanings

"With All My Thoughts" becomes most accessible if one thinks of it, first of all, as a love poem. Certainly, nothing within the poem contradicts this interpretation. Celan's strange mixing of the inner world of the soul and the outer world seems perfectly understandable, for example, if one thinks of how the external world mysteriously and wonderfully seems transformed when one falls in love.

Stanzas 2 and 3, for example, seem to establish a connection between the sun and the eyes of the lovers. One of the most common and traditional associations made in love poems, it occurs frequently in the poetry of the English Renaissance (Celan translated some of William Shakespeare's sonnets into German). For example, the metaphysical poetry of John Donne commonly draws a connection between the inner moods of lovers and the movement of vast cosmic forces.

Yet to read "With All My Thoughts" solely as a love poem in the conventional sense would be to limit it unnecessarily. Further reflection might lead one, for example, to consider how themes of language and love are intertwined in the poem and how both language and love are related to silence. The poem's nonrepresentational language tends to "leave the world" much as the poet claims to have done in the first stanza. In the final stanza, the relationship between language and love seems most explicitly developed, when the breath of the lovers rises to "that which made clouds." One might consider, for example, that the word "spirit" is derived from the Latin *spiritus* ("breath") and that language, too, is a product of the breath.

Language, the breath, the spirit, and clouds are similar in that each seems to exist on some border between being and nonbeing, between substance and emptiness. "With All My Thoughts" is at least in part a poem that attempts to walk that border where language attempts to become real. One thinks of King Claudius in *Hamlet* (c. 1600-1601) who, praying, states "My words fly up, my thoughts remain below./ Words without thoughts never to heaven go." Celan's poem similarly might be considered a kind of prayer, though he is too fastidious as a poet, too aware of the power of words, to declare his intentions blatantly. There is no way of knowing if his word-thoughts arrive; it is enough for that to remain suspended in possibility.

Vance Crummett

WITH OARS AT REST

Author: Boris Pasternak (1890-1960)
Type of poem: Lyric
First published: 1918, as "Slozha Vesla"; collected in *Sestra moia zhizn': Leto 1917 goda*; English translation collected in *Fifty Poems*, 1963

The Poem

Boris Pasternak's "With Oars at Rest" is a part of a collection with a unifying theme, *Sestra moia zhizn': Leto 1917 goda* (*My Sister, Life*). The entire book was written in the summer of 1917, as the Russian subtitle implies, but it was not published in Moscow until 1922. It was received well by critics and readers, and it established Pasternak's reputation as a leading Russian poet. Many critics consider *My Sister, Life* Pasternak's best poetic work.

"With Oars at Rest" opens with the metaphor of a boat beating against the breast of an unnamed person, who is describing the scene. The beating of a boat against the part of a body where heart is located suggests an emotional agitation. The spirits of the agitated person are low, hinted at by the willow branches hanging low and kissing his collarbones and the oarlocks. The persona then tries to alleviate the sad situation by advising that it "can happen to anyone."

The soothing attempt is carried over into the second stanza by a suggestion that since everybody partakes "in this song" sooner or later, they may as well rejoice in it, despite the resulting "lilac ashes" and "crushed daisies." The kisses, seen here as "lips," can be exchanged for the stars, thus making the sad situation almost joyous.

In the final stanza, the strength of emotion acquired through such optimism is enough to embrace the firmament held by Hercules, even though it may mean squandering centuries of nightingales' song that way. The most important thing is to experience love, no matter how difficult, painful, and transient it may be. Also, by placing oars at rest, as the title implies, the speaker is suggesting that even genuine feelings of love cannot be experienced with full intensity all the time and that they may need a rest every now and then.

Forms and Devices

The poem "With Oars at Rest" consists of three four-line stanzas. They are rhymed somewhat irregularly in the Russian, with only the first and third lines in each stanza being rhymed. The main figure of speech is metonymy, the use of an object to represent an idea. A boat, a lake, willows, lilac, daisies, stars, heavens, nightingales—they all serve the poet to reflect human actions and feelings. Thus, the beating of a boat against the breast indicates the turbulence of love emotions, which "can happen to anyone." As it happens so often, the turbulence in love feelings can bring heartache— "lilac ashes" and "crushed daisies"—as well as bliss. Love is so universal that centuries have been "squandered" on the song of nightingales, that is, on love songs.

The use of metaphors is also prominent. They include a boat signifying a man's journey through life; the fragrant lilac that can turn to ashes; daisies that, even when crushed by unhappy love, remain splendorous; lips standing for kisses, which in turn shine like stars; Hercules denoting the strength of the love experience; and nightingales, whose song equals the beauty of love. Pasternak's syntax is elaborate, and his vocabulary startlingly rich. Although the complex syntax can be, and often is, approximated in translation, the rich vocabulary can be transferred with greater difficulty.

"With Oars at Rest" reveals clearly Pasternak's style and his approach to poetry in general: It is complex, intricate, unique, impressionistic, cryptic, and at times obscure to the uninitiated. Throughout his poetic career, his poetry was so advanced that he was sometimes criticized for its "hermetic" quality. Pasternak was little concerned about it, as he explained in his autobiography, *Okhrannaya gramota* (1931; *A Safe Conduct*, 1945): "When *My Sister, Life* appeared, expressing completely uncontemporary sides of poetry . . . , I did not care at all what the power was called to which I owed this book, because it was immesurably greater than me and the poetic theories surrounding me." The following statement by the poet underscores again the elemental force of revolution that inspired him: "In 1917 and 1918 I wrote down only what by character of language or turn of phrase appeared to break from me entirely of its own accord, spontaneous and indivisible, surprisingly beyond dispute." This is a perfect example of Pasternak's ability to sublimate the external stimuli into a unique poetic expression, as in "With Oars at Rest" and in other poems.

Themes and Meanings

"With Oars at Rest" is best interpreted as an organic part of the collection *My Sister, Life*. Pasternak wrote it after the February Revolution of 1917, when the czar was overthrown and democracy instituted for the first time in Russian history. It was short-lived, however. The second revolution, in October of 1917, brought about even more fundamental changes in Russia. Even though *My Sister, Life* was finished before October, drastic changes were already in the air during the summer, which did not leave any one in Russia indiferent. As it turned out, the interval between the two revolutions transformed everything and energized everybody, especially the intellectuals, even those who were not engaged in politics, such as Pasternak.

Pasternak himself commented on those fateful days and on *My Sister, Life* in a letter to a fellow poet, Valery Bryusov. He had defended himself against Leon Trotsky's criticism of his aloofness from social themes by saying that *My Sister, Life* was

> revolutionary in the best sense of the word. That the phase of revolution closest to the heart and to poetry—the *morning* of the revolution, and its outburst, when it returns man to the *nature* of man and looks at the state with the eyes of *natural* right . . . are expressed by this book in its very spirit.

On another occasion, he elucidated further and more directly, "I saw a summer on the earth which seemed not to recognize itself—natural and prehistoric, as in a revelation. I left a book about it. In it I expressed all the most unprecedented and elusive things to be known about revolution." This attitude is similar to poet Aleksandr Blok's likening of revolution to music. Neither Blok nor Pasternak were sympathizers of the Bolshevik Revolution, yet they felt its elemental force and used it as an inspiration for some of their best lyrics.

Pasternak's linkage of revolution (not in political sense) to nature is worth noting. "With Oars at Rest" has no direct references to revolution, but the intensity of emotions expressed in the natural setting of the poem is akin to that of a revolution. The beating of a boat against the breast of a lake is, metonymically, the breast of a human being. The intensity of agitation results in "the lilac ashes" and "crushed daisies" reaching up to the firmament held by Hercules, which is another reference to the strength of a revolutionary turmoil.

A further linkage of revolution to love is a unifying theme that runs throughout the collection. Although the poem is not a narrative in the true sense of the word, a love story can be discerned. It concerns a love affair of the poet with an unknown woman. References to her are made directly but without naming her, or obliquely, through allusions and metonymies. The references are not as direct in "With Oars at Rest" as they are in other poems of *My Sister, Life*. Here, by way of metonymy, the beloved is seen through the effects she has on the poet. He uses this setting to tie his feelings to nature, as he has done thruhout his poetic career. References to nature not only are plentiful but also indicate that the connection between humanity and nature is nearly unbreakable, even when the most intimate feelings of love are concerned. "With Oars at Rest," as a building block of the edifice of Pasternak's understanding and acceptance of nature, love, and revolution, can be seen as the epitome of his general worldview as well as of his powerful poetic craft.

Vasa D. Mihailovich

WITH THE GRAIN

Author: Donald Davie (1922-1995)
Type of poem: Meditation
First published: 1959; collected in *New and Selected Poems*, 1961

The Poem

Donald Davie's "With the Grain" is a meditative lyric of sixty-three lines divided into three sections, each with three seven-line unrhymed stanzas. The poem ponders the applicability of certain aspects of carpentry and painting to fundamental elements of romantic love and literature. The general, alternating contrast between long and short lines in each stanza as well as the lack of uniform line pattern within or between stanzas (line length varies from five to fourteen syllables) echoes the contrast between regularity, or order, and irregularity, or "cross-graining," in the poem's extended metaphor of the effects of the grain in wood on carpentry and other forms of expression.

In stanza 1 of section 1, the speaker moves from particular to general, or concrete to abstract, in a series of third-person questions about the metaphoric applicability of specifics in carpentry (graining) and gardening (tilling) to those endeavors as a whole and, more broadly, to all mental activity or thought. From musing about the application of the idea of the wood's grain in carpentry to human behavior, inherent in proverbial expressions such as "with the grain" or "ingrained," the speaker compares, in stanza 2, the carpenter and his work to romantic lovers by personifying the woodworking: "the irritable block/ Screams underneath the blade/ Of love's demand." In stanza 3 of section 1, the speaker introduces first-person references and addresses the issue of attempting to communicate through the use of various media: carpenters through wood, painters through color, and romantic lovers and poets through language. This stanza thus commences the correlation developed in the poem between lovers and literary authors, who both use language to communicate.

Section 2 moves from a comparison between communication in romantic love and communication in the "decorative arts" (especially carpentry) to a comparison between communication in romantic love and communication in the visual art of painting. Just as wood resists carpenters' blades and hue and light may affect or impede painters' perceptions and renderings of the color of their subjects, so too may the primary medium of communication between lovers (language) resist precise expression. As the painter should find an "equable light" that would not distort hue or color, so, the speaker says to his romantic partner, "we should say, my dear,/ Not what we mean, but what/ The words would mean." That is, the speaker goes on, "We should speak,/ As carpenters work,/ With the grain of our words." Nearly all people have had the experience of having something to say but not being able to find the words to precisely express it, sometimes because the words have meanings that pull in different directions from people's original intentions. The concept of undistorted color in painting (found, according to the poet, in the light of the town of Saint Ives, England) leads the speaker to the idea of a fixed color in love (mauve) that, like the white robes of the Druids in Cornwall or the blue robes of the bards in Wales, would signify devoted, undeflected constancy and commitment.

The association of lovers with bards and Druids in section 2 leads the speaker, in section 3, to call lovers a kind of "fourth estate" that is "hieratic." The imagery of carpentry and the imagery of painting are combined in section 3 in the speaker's references to lovers with true communion of emotion and language who are able to "chamfer away/ A knot in the grain of streaming light" and to the poet as the "carpenter of light" who may "work with the grain henceforward." The repetition of the first three lines of the poem in the first three lines of the last stanza gives the poem a circular or spiral structure, helping to round off the idea that the "colorful trades" of artisan, painter, lover, and poet all aspire, like Icarus, to triumph over elements of the real world that are unruly and a hindrance to their endeavors.

Forms and Devices

In addition to the striking extended metaphors drawn from carpentry and painting that are used to explore interconnections among artisan, painter, lover, and poet in how they deal with the surrounding world, Davie makes repeated use of allusion, pun, and inverted syntax. Stanza 2 of section 1 contains a humorous allusion to William Shakespeare's *Hamlet* (1603) in the speaker's recognition that the expression "ingrained habit" is metaphoric or "fanciful": "And there's the rub/ Bristling, where the irritable block/ Screams underneath the blade/ Of love's demand." Counterposed to the moody, doubtful, and philosophically contemplative Hamlet, who worries about what really may follow death ("To die, to sleep;/ To sleep: perchance to dream: Aye, there's the rub"), Davie's speaker is wittily inquisitive and philosophically contemplative about love and art. In stanza 1 of section 3, Davie alludes to a famous passage in French historian Jean Froissart's *Chronicles* (1373-1410) that vividly and poetically describes a jousting tournament during which two knights strike each other's helmets so forcefully that sparks fly from their lances. Davie's point is that lovers and poets, preferring the "equable light" of Saint Ives to alluring but misleading and sparkling words, would not succumb, like Froissart, to special effects. Indeed, the range of allusion in "With the Grain," including the history of modern painting (the Saint Ives movement), ancient Celtic lore (Druids, bards, Tristram and Iseult), medieval French literature (Jean Froissart), and classical mythology (Icarus), helps add to the philosophical breadth and scope of the poem.

The multiple puns and inverted syntax in the poem not only add to its meaning but also help convey its theme of the waywardness of words. Repeated color references in section 2 suggest a pun on "philtre" as not only the vial that might change perception but also the "filter" that might change the color of one's outlook. In stanza 2 of section 3, the "refractory crystal" that the poet attempts to ignore is "reluctant" to allow its allure to be disregarded. In stanza 3 of section 3, the "colourful trades" are "distinctive" and literally "full of color" as depicted in the poem; the "High lights" into which the colorful trades climb are simultaneously lights that are high up, brilliantly lighted areas in a painting, and distinctive features; the reference to how the ideal sun reached by the colorful trades "Dyes only more intensely" has an overtone of death through a lurking pun on "dies" since the trades have risen like Icarus, who not only rose toward the sun with Daedalus's wings but also plunged to his death because of them and his aspiration.

Following the grain of language is suggested immediately in the poem by the syntax of its first four lines, echoed in the first four lines of the final stanza. This repetition is slightly less exact in the 1990 version of the poem through Davie's change of "elevate" in line 1 in the 1959 and 1961 versions to "deviate" in the 1990 version. However, in all versions the syntax is inverted, suggesting that language, like the grain in wood, cannot always be planed into simple straightforwardness; not all sentences or thoughts begin with a subject only to be followed by a verb and then a direct object. Rather, as in the openings of the first and last stanzas of the poem, the idea has to be found by following the grain of the sentence to discover that the subject is delayed, preceded by the verb: The activities deviate into their own ideas, and the colorful trades elevate into the light of ideas. This inverted syntax is also required by the linguistic requirements of forming a question sentence that begins with the word "why," which emphasizes the poem's contemplative quality.

Themes and Meanings

Davie's interests in literary criticism and aesthetics are reflected in many of his poems, including "With the Grain." The poem reminds readers that language, literature, crafts, art, and romantic love or interpersonal relationships may be, and have been, interconnected. Because of the world's complexity, principles from any one of these areas may cross over into principles of the others; thus, a correlation is revealed in the development of proverbial metaphoric expressions, the shaping of a carpenter's block, the filling of a painter's canvas, the evolution of a romantic couple's relationship through dialogue or argument, and the unfolding of a poem's—including this poem's—form and meanings.

A crucial premise of the poem, in accord with Davie's early reputation as a modern neoclassicist, is that principles of order do indeed underlie the apparent meandering diversity of people, activities, and material objects in the world. These principles allow the poet's recognition of reflections and connections among the disparate data of experience, ranging from modernity to antiquity. The modern romantic partner addressed by the speaker in section 2 is assumed to have the wit and intelligence of the addressees of love poems in the bygone neoclassical and Metaphysical periods of English literature, who could understand and appreciate the artistry and thought of Alexander Pope, John Dryden, and John Donne. These poets, like Davie, could contemplate and find the surprising resemblances between romantic love and planing a block of wood.

Norman Prinsky

WITH TRUMPETS AND ZITHERS

Author: Czesław Miłosz (1911-   )
Type of poem: Meditation
First published: 1969, as "Na trabach i na cytrze," in *Miasto bez imienia*; English translation collected in *The Collected Poems, 1931-1987*, 1988

The Poem

"With Trumpets and Zithers" is an extended meditation on physical being and on the relationship of the particular to the abstract. It is divided into eleven sections, each of which consists of an irregular number of long lines of free verse.

The title invokes musical instruments of a biblical origin. Trumpets and zithers are found both in books of prophecy, such as Isaiah and Jeremiah, where they signal outbursts of energetic vision or ecstasy, and in books of hymnal praise, such as the Song of Solomon or Psalms, where they serve as sweet musical accompaniment to rhapsody. A trumpet blast also marks, in the New Testament book of Revelation, the onset of apocalypse, the fulfillment of divine justice and the end of time.

Czesłsaw Miłosz's poem is difficult to describe sequentially or in summary because it lacks a single, coherent narrative. It is certainly rhapsodic, visionary and, in a sense, apocalyptic, but there is no one action or directed argument that can be said to unify the poem. Indeed, one of Miłosz's aims is to emphasize the particular and the individual over and above any general sense of unity. There is, however, clearly an overarching emphasis in this poem on the interrelated issues of poetic expression, the function and shape of divinity, and humanity's relationship to the natural world.

The poem begins with a "gift." Miłosz praises the variety and energy of life and creation, kneeling to "kiss the earth" with gratitude for having received consciousness and breath. That "gift," he says, "was never named." To name a thing is to comprehend it. Like Adam, Miłosz can assign a catalog of names to objects and beings in the world around him—as he proceeds to do, poetically, in this first section—but he cannot name or identify exactly the essential primal impulse that allowed him to perceive, to know, and to be. Creation, at its heart, escapes the limited capacities of human language.

In the second section, the reader discovers the poet aboard a descending airplane at night. Afforded a panorama of creation below, a kind of God's-eye view, he reflects on his ability to perceive and to know the whole. He addresses his own consciousness, an offshoot of that power which, miraculously, has escaped naming. He finds himself momentarily lifted out of time, without an immediate past or future. He wonders how, without memory or desire, he can still be overtaken by "blame and merit," by the responsibilities of life and knowledge, even when he is attuned ecstatically to the ethereal and the ideal.

The third section is a scene in Mesopotamia, often called the cradle of civilization. Miłosz envisions a "beauty"—an erotically charged image of woman—who stands among animalistic, lustful "grey beards" and represents an eternal principle of order, culture, and motherhood. The whole scene is surrounded by a dark, ecstatic music like that of the preceding section.

Miłosz next finds himself pulled into that music, that frenzied dance of flesh and blood. He tastes in rain a sexual, animal energy. "In the darkness," the physical world as opposed to the pure, divine "light" of creation at the poem's outset, he hears beating "the heart of the dead and the living," a percussive music like that of the drums and strings of the previous section. He sees life as part of an eternal musical cycle, forever breathing in and out, weaving and unweaving itself.

The sixth section is the thematic heart of the poem. "What separates," Miłosz begins, "falls." Whatever resists the unifying drive of the human mind, focused on the eternal and the "crystalline," falls away for Miłosz from ecstasy and the purity of knowledge. Yet he screams "No!" as soon as he makes this statement, resisting the movement that he detailed in the second section to forget "who I am and who I was." Only what separates, he reveals paradoxically, "does not fall." Against his excited disappearance into "architectural spirals," the dervish dance of the mystics and the whirlpool of the cosmos, Miłosz welcomes in his poetry the particular: "this, not that, basket of vegetables." Rather than be lost in generalities, he maintains his individuality. In effect, he wants to make the abstract grammatical forms of his language suit the singular and the unique, but he finds himself thwarted by the generalization inherent in words themselves.

In the seventh section, he has the mute and the animal aspects of existence, those that seem to have an essence prior to any words or names, "testify" in vain "against the language." Particular cases and physical being, he realizes, cannot be "distinguished" in common speech.

In the eighth part, he returns from abstract images and archetypes to the present reality of the United States and modern civilization, to the blur of present-day urban life. Even here, at the end of night, however, Miłosz finds himself still amazed by the incontrovertible fact of his individuality and conscious existence: "this place, this time . . . this particular body."

In the next two sections, Miłosz looks for some form of redemption ("forgiveness") in the music both of human and nonhuman creative labors. He recognizes his memory and his "naming" of the world in poetry as dishonest and as a betrayal of the individual. Yet, he wants to redeem himself and his work by locating in the sensual, sexual, and physical aspects of his experience a spark of divine energy.

The poem concludes with a constellation of images designed to reflect Miłosz's preoccupations. The coelentera (from the phylum name for anemones and jellyfish) is completely physical, sexual, and animal, "all pulsating flesh," yet its energy ties it directly to "the center of a galaxy," to the overarching, spiraling order of the cosmos. The abstractly spiritual and the particular are joined in the vital pulsations of life. Miłosz's "terrestrial homeland" turns round "with the music of the spheres," and he discovers a bond between the physical and the ethereal in his own humanity. He also recognizes, however, that now he can only be certain of his own "unknowing," that, in attempting to bridge the gap between abstract forms and the concrete world, he has forgone the possibility of definitively formulating that bridge in words. As in his other poems, he pursues a vital energy but acknowledges his ongoing failure ever to complete his mission.

Forms and Devices

Miłosz himself translated this poem from Polish into English, capturing much of the original's imagistic density. "With Trumpets and Zithers" takes the form of a mosaic. A mosaic consists of particular objects or fragments of a given color or texture which, when fastened together, yield a larger pattern which no one object could supplant but to which each contributes meaning. Most of the poem's lines are closed, end-stopped grammatical units, and a given line describes a discrete image, thought or action. The connections between successive lines and among those images, thoughts, and actions are difficult to establish. Even within the scope of a single line, Miłosz may introduce several units of meaning that are disjunctive or opposed. For the most part, each line is unique, and when the lines are combined in a series of ninety-five verses, an extremely complex, interlaced web develops. Formally, in Miłosz's poem, one can sense the tension between the particular and the abstract, between the discrete line or image and the variegated whole.

The leaps undertaken from line to line and from image to image give the poem a wild, ecstatic energy. The poet's mind seems to be moving at an incredible rate, his imagination and memory fired either by visionary insight or by the sexual, sensual impulses that he describes throughout the text. "With Trumpets and Zithers" is a dithyramb, a form of poetry which dates to the ancient Greeks, whom he invokes in the first section of the poem. This form embraces extravagant cadences and images and was derived from religious chants or songs. Miłosz's unmetered, extended lines give the impression of a mind unfettered and wildly inspired by some otherworldly presence.

Yet, each line is carefully limited by syntax and ends with a definite period, which suggests that Miłosz also recognizes the bounds of speech and human intellect. The poem has no argument, no readily discerned progression from section to section. He cannot expound with any logical clarity the inspired vision that seems to have overtaken him. Miłosz can only go so far, he himself suggests; others may even come to write about this ecstasy in a better, more fulfilling fashion. Throughout the poem, Miłosz formally counterbalances his divinely inspired frenzy with a recognition of his earthly limitations.

Themes and Meanings

In "With Trumpets and Zithers," as in the other poems of the volume from which it is taken, Miłosz is preoccupied with a specific metaphysical problem, a philosophical opposition. He wonders how anyone, through poetry or otherwise, can look for meaning through the veil of the actual to the *esse*, the core of existence itself, without leaving behind the particular, physical nature of that existence. In other words, Miłosz wants to understand the meaning of his own presence and consciousness, but he cannot attain a vantage point from which a God's-eye view of creation is actually possible and which would permit him to see the whole shape of the cosmos and of his life as a human being. Such a vantage point must, by logical necessity, lie outside the bounds of that life and that consciousness. This is a problem which has troubled mystics and philosophers from ancient times to the present, and it is certainly one of the great unanswerable questions of practiced thought.

Miłosz's own response to this question comes in the form of what he calls, in another poem from this collection, "ecstatic despair" ("The Year"). He recognizes the impossibility of fulfilling his desire for absolute knowledge, or of sustaining the visionary ecstasy that "With Trumpets and Zithers" describes. Nevertheless, he values highly the vital energy of his poetic endeavor, of striving toward the "essence" that forever escapes him, and of the sensual, particularly physical aspects of that vision. If he must despair at never finding a pure, "crystalline" form in which to express himself or escaping the trappings of past and future, of memory and desire, that underpin his consciousness, he nevertheless finds meaning and worth in the dithyrambic fervor of poetry itself.

Miłosz's poems are often dense and complex, but they contain a constant, sustained inquiry into human understanding and the nature of existence. Miłosz is a dualist, always opposing to the apparently fallen world of everyday life a hidden realm of spiritual and ontological wholeness. Recognizing that he can never reconcile these two ethoi in his poetry, he continues his struggle with language and with concept, uncovering value and beauty in the human effort to come to terms with life itself.

Kevin McNeilly

WITHIN THE CIRCUIT OF THIS PLODDING LIFE

Author: Henry David Thoreau (1817-1862)
Type of poem: Lyric
First published: c. 1842; collected in *Excursions*, 1863

The Poem

Henry David Thoreau's "Within the Circuit of This Plodding Life" is a one-stanza meditation of thirty lines in which the poet recalls specific moments in his life when natural phenomena—the icicles of winter, the "shimmering noon" of summer, the recently plowed fields covered in a blanket of snow—renewed his spirit. Such a renewal offers him the courage to move on with the business of living.

The speaker fortifies the idea by establishing a contrast between the "circuit" of his ordinary, "plodding life" and the cycle of nature represented by the round of the seasons. Such a progression, beginning in winter, moving through summer and coming around again to winter, convinces the poet of the shallowness of "the best philosophy," which seeks only to console humanity rather than enlighten it with the "azure hue" of "untarnished" insight. The poet, in other words, finds peace not in a formal philosophical system of objective truths, but in an intuitive grasp of reality as afforded through an observation of and communion with nature.

His observations, as he recalls them, are both poetic and startling in their accuracy. His description of icicles, elongating as they melt against the sun's heat, is a reminder of Thoreau's ability as a keen, accurate naturalist, as his later prose writings, particularly *Walden: Or, Life in the Woods* (1854), published more than a decade later, attest. He remembers observing one winter how these "icy spears" formed on trees, fences and the "jutting spouts" of human-made things. Thus humankind and nature are united in a kind of ironic bond, one made of ice. He remembers also the play of light and shadow at noon in summer, "some unrecorded beam" that shone across the upland pastures "where the Johnswort grew."

In his mind he also hears the humming of the bee and the "purling" play of the brook as it winds along the slopes and meadows. The contrast and the seasonal images come full circuit with the poet's final recollection of a winter scene, the look of the lately plowed fields, a thrush hovering, as all lay covered in an "integument" of snow. Once again, both humankind and nature are bound, as if by the same skin—"integument."

The poet is enriched by his memories, which have connected him with nature. The recollected scenes are part of what he calls "God's cheap economy," that is, a divine manifestation of the truth, simple—"economical"—but effective. In the closing lines he finds the resolution to "go upon [his] winter's task again," going on with living in a world not always congenial to his comfort.

Forms and Devices

Despite the fact that Thoreau gave up writing poetry early in his career, regarding it as distinctly inferior to his prose, his poems show a sense of technical craftsmanship, which he was later to perfect and rework in his prose. "Within the Circuit of This Plodding Life," for example, opens with a simile that at once establishes a connection between the natural progression of the seasons in chronological time—something he was to do in *Walden*—and the poet's recollections in psychological time. Just as the "violet/ Or anemone" is carried along the gentle current of a stream, so the poet's thoughts are whirled along the stream of time to memories of winter and summer scenes that bore meaning in his life.

Though the poem is in the form of a lyric, it is really a kind of meditation in which the internalized action—the poet's recollections—is presented by images and language suggesting an active though pastoral life. A moment of insight for the poet becomes "an azure hue"; the frosty winter night is alive with almost warlike images: the "icy spears" melting against the "arrows" of the sun.

The structure of the poem is simple but carefully wrought. Seemingly random in its movement, the poem is built in a pattern of threes—three scenes, each described in multiples of three: the winter observation unfolds in three lines; the summer scene is itself divided into three sections, the first two having three lines, the last, five. The third scene returns to winter and completes the "circle" with six lines.

Classic nature poetry is often built upon a three-tiered structure comprising the stages of the poet's understanding of his experience: observation, contemplation, revelation. The poet first observes and describes the physical aspects of his experience, usually a natural object or phenomenon, then proceeds to a contemplation of its meaning, finally grasping its truth or significance. In this poem Thoreau revises the format. Beginning with contemplation, suggested by the simile, he proceeds to observations, through his memories, and concludes with an apprehension of their meaning, his intention to go on with his winter task.

The poem's structure is further tightened by the interplay between the rhythm of the seasons and the rhythm of the verse. The thirty-line meditation is conveyed in only three sentences. The first sentence, establishing the simile of the violet in the stream, runs through the first seven lines. The recollection section, containing the three seasonal scenes, is the longest, running twenty-one lines, many of them enjambed—one line running into the next, as in the manner of thought. The final section, containing the poet's resolution to go on, emphasizes the importance of the revelation by a mere couplet—abrupt, final, conclusive.

Finally, though the poem does not feature end rhyme, it does make use of internal rhyme: "nights" at the end of line 9 and "light" in the middle of line 10; "moon" at the end of line 10 and "noon" in the middle of line 14. Examples of consonance (repetition of initial consonants) are also found at the end of line 19, "rill"; line 26, "rear"; and line 29, "rich."

Themes and Meanings

"Within the Circuit of This Plodding Life" can be appreciated on its own terms as a fine example of a nature poem, the product of a young man still under the creative influence of the great English Romantic poets such as William Wordsworth (1770-1850). Much of Thoreau's poem is derivative of Romantic poetry insofar as it postulates the renewal of the spirit as a consequence of the mind's direct apprehension of nature's power to cure humankind's moral ailments. Echoes of John Milton's (1608-1674) famous pastoral elegy are heard in the closing lines, although the poet here, now renewed, does not proceed to "fresh woods and pastures new," as in Milton's "Lycidas" (1638), but decides rather to "go upon [his] winter task again." Thus Thoreau revises the standard elegiac conclusion, insisting that winter, not summer, is the proper season for renewal, a season of hardship and discomfort rather than ease and solace.

More important, however, the poem can be seen as an early statement of the principles of Transcendentalism, which Thoreau's mentor, Ralph Waldo Emerson, had first set out in his essay "Nature" in 1836. The essential idea of Transcendentalism is based on the Romantic belief in the primacy of the self: Every human being carries his or her own divinity. The intuitive is thus more to be trusted than the reasoned, the spontaneous more than the deliberate, the personal more than the social. Personal experience, purified through the proper communion with nature, is thus the sole arbiter of truth. "Within the Circuit of This Plodding Life" reaffirms this conviction.

It is interesting that Thoreau uses the word "economy" in the closing section of the poem. Thoreau constantly reworked his poems. In fact, "Within the Circuit of This Plodding Life," like many of his others, was composed in stages. Lines and phrases were found, for example, in his manuscripts and journals, later to be reworked and appearing as prose in such books as *Walden*. In fact, the word "economy" was used as the title of the first chapter of *Walden*, where, calling himself a "self-appointed inspector of snowstorms," Thoreau pointedly scolds all humans for their plodding lives, worrying about making a living and about money and posessions.

"Within the Circuit of This Plodding Life" ends with the image of a snow-covered landscape, whereas *Walden* opens in winter, almost as if the book begins where the poem ends. Given what is known of Thoreau's methods of composition and of his habit of reworking his material, it is possible to see "Within the Circuit of This Plodding Life" as an early source of, or at least a germ in the development of, his later work.

Edward Fiorelli

WITHIN THE VEIL

Author: Michelle Cliff (1946-   )
Type of poem: Lyric
First published: 1985, in *The Land of Look Behind: Prose and Poetry*

The Poem

"Within the Veil" is composed of twenty-one six-line stanzas. The title suggests that certain conditions are being concealed, as if under a veil, and that they are not being addressed. The first line of the poem, "Color ain't no faucet," establishes that the poet is addressing racism. The poet invites readers into the poem by addressing them directly as "you." By doing this, Michelle Cliff establishes a direct dialogue between herself and readers. She also implicitly makes her readers accountable for the issues she addresses, partly through the casual, intimate tone that she employs throughout. The most immediately noticeable aspect of the poem is that it is written in blues form, with the blues' typical repetition of lines.

"Within the Veil" is a biting commentary on race relations, sexism, and social injustice. Each stanza recounts historical events or phenomena that have adversely affected black people, not only in the United States but also in the Caribbean and on the African continent. The tone of the poem is matter-of-fact, and the poet implies that readers are in the know, indicating that the poem is directed specifically toward black readers. This becomes clearer in stanza 2 and is further developed in stanzas 3 and 4, in which Cliff sets up an oppositional relationship between herself and her readers on one hand and the "whiteman" on the other, advising readers that "We got to swing the thing around." Here, as throughout the remainder of the poem, the reader is co-opted into a collective "we," implying agreement with the poet. From this point on, Cliff speaks not only for herself and about her own experience but also for the reader who supposedly shares her perspective.

Cliff explores many of the major issues that African Americans have confronted since the great migration from the South to the North after World War II. The use of "ofay," a derogatory term African Americans used when referring to Caucasians, further signifies that the poem is aimed at a black audience. Words such as "sisters" and "mama" indicate that Cliff is speaking specifically to black women. However, the poet's criticism is geared not only toward the way white people have treated blacks but also toward African American homophobia (stanzas 6 and 10) and the different hairstyles they have used to divide themselves (stanza 8). When she states, "How dare anyone object/ Tell me I had better not exist," Cliff is both speaking of white attitudes and pointing out that black people must accept one another's differences.

The first ten stanzas draw a historical line from African American migration from the South, to the Harlem Renaissance, and on to the 1960's. The persona of the poem functions as a historian as well as a praise singer who recounts African American achievements. In stanza 5, for example, readers learn about Zora Neale Hurston, a Harlem writer and friend of poet Langston Hughes. Hurston was severely criticized by many male writers, notably Richard Wright, for her work. Hurston focused primarily on all-black communities, specifically her hometown of Eatonville, Florida. Hurston's classic novel *Their Eyes Were Watching God* (1937) has been widely taught since Alice Walker unearthed Hurston's works in the mid-1960's. Cliff alludes to Hurston's seminal anthropological work, *Mules and Men* (1935), to defend Hurston's credibility. In stanzas 8 and 9, two other archetypes are revered. The first is Madame C. J. Walker, the first black female millionaire, who invented the hot comb to press hair. The second is Lorraine Hansberry, the first African American to win the New York Drama Critics Circle Award for the best play of the year, *A Raisin in the Sun* (1959).

Forms and Devices

"Within the Veil" fits into a genre known as blues poetry. The blues is a distinctly African American form of music and poetry that is said to have its roots in Africa, specifically Senegal. There the *griot* (*griots* are performers whose songs and stories keep the oral history of their people alive) tradition is best represented. Blues lyrics generally recount personal stories, and the most popular blues focus on love, heartbreak, and hard times. "Within the Veil," however, fits into another category of blues, one that emphasizes sociopolitical implications. In this type of lyric, although the poem or story may seem to be about an individual's personal problems, the implication is that the seemingly isolated situation is applicable to the group.

Lyrically, the blues form consists of three-line stanzas (musically it is most often in a repeating twelve-measure or "twelve-bar" pattern). "Within the Veil," although it appears as six-line stanzas, adheres to the blues format. Generally the first line of a blues states the problem or situation, and the second line repeats it for emphasis, sometimes with a variation or twist. The third line then resolves the stanza or provides some concluding commentary on the situation. In Cliff's poem each of the standard three blues lines is written as two lines on the page, but the stanza can nonetheless be sung over the rhythmic framework of a twelve-bar blues:

> Gold chains are love-symbols
> You tell me where they are found
> Yes, gold chains are love-symbols
> You tell me where gold is found
> There are mines in South Africa
> Where our brothers sweat their lives underground.

The blues typically maintains a rhyme pattern in which the last line rhymes with the concluding word of the first two lines ("found"/"underground"). Another important element of the blues is the use of vernacular or slang and intimate references. Throughout the poem Cliff uses words such as "ain't" and adopts a casual style of speech: "We got to figure what we can do." Some of the intimate, familiar words that Cliff uses are "baby," "sisters," and "brothers," which are terms of endearment implying that all black people are connected by a common ancestry.

Another technique that Cliff exploits in the poem is the shifting of pronouns, as from the first-person singular "I" to the plural "we." She moves among pronouns, including "I," "you," "we," and "they," to emphasize inclusion or division as it suits the individual stanza and the poet's purpose. In stanza 4, for example, she says that "we" (African American women, "sisters") can call "them" (whites) names, but that "you" (listeners or readers, part of the "we" but here being directly addressed) "lie if you tell me you don't know." Furthermore, by citing concrete examples— whether of famous historical individuals, a police shooting in Boston, or the work of miners in South Africa—Cliff not only establishes credibility for the claims she makes in the poem but also presents herself as a voice of authority and a keeper of tradition.

Themes and Meanings

"Within the Veil" calls for social justice for blacks throughout the African diaspora. Cliff reveals how all black people, regardless of whether they live in the United States, in the Caribbean, or on the African continent, are connected by oppression and should therefore, as a group, be committed to a singular freedom. The poet states the importance of black people not allowing themselves to be divided by sexual orientation ("Your best friend's a bulldagger") or ethnic makeup ("Some of us part Indian/ And some of us part white"). Cliff suggests that ultimately it does not matter what an individual black person's orientation or ethnic background is; in the final analysis, all blacks are subject to the same treatment.

The poem, not unlike the protest poems of the 1960's by Nikki Giovanni and Amiri Baraka, is a call to action. By playing on the sentiments and victimization of blacks, Cliff seeks to motivate black people to act on their own behalf. However, "Within the Veil" does not have a seditious or violent tone that pits blacks against whites as opposing groups. The focus is wider, and the poem's political agenda is to end social, racial, and sexual imbalances. Cliff makes it clear than she is not calling for upheaval: "If we say Third World Revolution/ The white folks say World War III." She states her desire for freedom rather than Armageddon. This biblical reference to the end of the world as a result of the final battle between nations (Revelation 16) is intended as a caution to both black and white people.

In the opening line of the last stanza, Cliff clearly states her position: "It's all about survival." The stakes are high. If black people are to persist and conquer institutional injustices, they must come together and "do it better," or they "might as well lay down and die." Although these are the closing words of the poem, the ending is not a pessimistic one. The tone throughout the poem is guardedly optimistic, its optimism accentuated by the use of the blues form, which is well suited for storytelling, social commentary, and exhortation. By citing several atrocities that have occurred to black people throughout history and around the world and showing their parallel relationships, the poet attempts to galvanize the community to act in its own defense. In the tradition of the blues, the process of identifying, naming, and sharing pain is believed to help abate it; recovery and healing can then begin. "Within the Veil" uncovers—it lifts the veil—so that constructive changes can occur.

Opal Palmer Adisa

WODWO

Author: Ted Hughes (1930-1998)
Type of poem: Narrative
First published: 1967, in *Wodwo*

The Poem

"Wodwo" is a poem of twenty-eight lines written in free verse. The poet is writing in the first person but in the persona of the Wodwo, which he describes in his essay "Learning to Think" (*Poetry Is*, 1970) as "some sort of goblin creature . . . a sort of half-man half-animal spirit of the forests."

The Wodwo is not addressing the reader. Rather, the poem shows the stream of consciousness of the Wodwo. It mumbles to itself in the way that very young children or old people sometimes do, talking themselves through the processes of living and thinking. The poem begins with the Wodwo asking, "What am I?" The question is central to the poem and recurs in various modifications throughout. The reader sees the Wodwo rooting through leaves and following a scent to the river. It dives in, and one gains the first sense of how its exceptionally primitive consciousness experiences the world around it.

When it dives into water, it is actually upside down looking at the river bed, but it can only conceive that it is the river bed which is upside down above it. It is unable to connect the way things appear with the vantage point from which it is looking at them. As soon as it is under water, it forgets that fact and asks what it is doing "here in mid-air." The Wodwo notices a frog and asks itself why it finds the frog interesting "as I inspect its most secret/ interior and make it my own." This may be a chillingly intimate reference to the Wodwo's eating the frog. It asks whether the weeds have seen it before. Unlike them, it is "not rooted but dropped/ out of nothing casually": It knows neither where it comes from nor where it belongs.

As the Wodwo picks bits of bark off a rotten stump, it questions why it does so, since the act gives it no pleasure and is of no use. Its own action seems to have happened to it at random: "me and doing that have coincided very queerly." This brings it again to the question of self-identity; it wonders what its name is, whether it is the first of its kind, and what its shape is.

After walking past the trees, the Wodwo sits still. It assumes in this moment, with childlike perception, that everything stops to watch it, inferring that "I am the exact centre." It cannot sustain this reflection for long. Its attention is taken up again by the masses of roots before it and by the water, though it seems baffled as to how the water has appeared once more. In stream-of-consciousness tradition, the poem has an open ending: "I'll go on looking," says the Wodwo—though for what, it does not know.

Forms and Devices

Many of the poem's verbs are in the present continuous form—"Nosing here, turning leaves over/ following a faint stain on the air"—conveying the Wodwo's limited perception, confined to the object right in front of its nose at any point. The run-on lines, in which a sentence or phrase runs from one line to the next without significant pause, as well as the lack of punctuation emphasize the stream-of-consciousness form of the poem. The bewildered Wodwo's impressions follow one after another without reflection other than its bewilderment at what it is.

It is significant that the only form of punctuation is the question mark, as the Wodwo questions its own nature and the reasons it does what it does. It never gives itself time to find any answers, however, as immediately after it has asked the question, its attention passes back to a frog or to the roots or weeds in its environment.

Ted Hughes acknowledges the influence of Anglo-Saxon poetry on his work. "Wodwo" is a typical example, both in terms of its language—short, concrete words of one or two syllables are favored above longer, abstract, Latinate ones—and in terms of its patterns of alliteration (repetition of initial consonants). The Anglo-Saxon poets divided lines into two parts, with one pair of similar sounds in the first half and one pair in the second. The result was a vigorous narrative style that carried the listener along for substantial periods of oral recitation. Hughes often uses alliteration in "Wodwo" to tie a phrase together and to enrich the sound qualities of the verse, as in "coincided very queerly," "the glassy grain of water" and "know me and name me."

Repetition of words or phrases is another common device in the poem. Lines such as "if I go/ to the end on this way past these trees and past these trees" and "but there's all this what is it roots/ roots roots roots" emphasize the Wodwo's manner of perception, a disconnected series of sensory impressions. The repetition of "very queerly" in the last line's "very queer" almost renders the phrase a motto for the Wodwo in its wonder and bewilderment.

For the most part, the language of the poem is straightforward and colloquial. The poem's few metaphors are typical of Hughes's style in that they are precise concretizations in simple language of more intangible experiences. Describing a smell as "a faint stain on the air" gives it a visible quality. The Wodwo's splitting "the glassy grain of water" adds a solidity to this liquid element. His observation that he has no threads fastening him to anything directly conveys his lack of connectedness with his world.

Themes and Meanings

In "Learning to Think," Ted Hughes wrote of the Wodwo, "I imagine this creature just discovering that it is alive in the world. It does not know what it is and is full of questions. It is quite bewildered to know what is going on. It has a whole string of thoughts, but at the centre of all of them . . . is this creature and its bewilderment."

The Wodwo is reminiscent of the creatures of Anglo-Saxon mythology, such as the marsh-living monster Grendel in *Beowulf* (first transcribed c. 1000 C.E.). Hughes's device of having the reader perceive the world through the Wodwo's awareness exemplifies his belief that poets have a shamanistic nature. Their small, individualized self is unimportant; they can enter the awareness of another creature at will. The poem gives a glimpse into the very primitive consciousness of the Wodwo. The lines "I've no threads/ fastening me to anything I can go anywhere/ I seem to have been given the freedom/ of this place what am I then?" hint that the Wodwo is on the brink of beginning the journey to a human type of self-awareness. Since it is not tied to the earth as are the plants, it has freedom to pursue answers to its endless questions.

The Wodwo exists at a primeval level of evolution. Its powers of reflection are minimal; it can only focus on its immediate environment in the present moment. Everything it encounters—the weeds, the stump, the roots—is chaotic, mysterious, and random. The Wodwo's bewilderment at why it finds itself picking bark off a rotten stump gives a humorous picture of the Wodwo's lack of self-awareness. It fails to make the connection between itself and the actions it performs. One may find humor in this episode if one has also caught oneself performing some unintelligent and pointless activity "on automatic pilot," through no conscious intent.

One can also recognize the pathos of the Wodwo's confusion as to what constitutes itself. For all it knows, it is the only one of its kind. It has no frame of reference by which to measure or define itself. Its observations that it seems "separate from the ground and not rooted but dropped/ out of nothing casually" and that "I seem to have been given the freedom/ of this place what am I then?" are amusing but at the same time strangely moving in their plain understatement. It shows a being completely unaware of its origin or purpose yet attempting to establish connections with the world around it.

In the midst of the Wodwo's busy stream of impressions is one moment of stillness: "if I sit still how everything/ stops to watch me I suppose I am the exact centre." Though on one level this interpretation of perception is amusing in its naïveté, it nevertheless resonates with a profound poetic truth: Many people have had similar feelings when stopping to rest in a forest or in any natural place seldom disturbed by humans.

The power of this poem lies in its ability to take the reader inside the primeval awareness of the Wodwo. As one perceives the world through the Wodwo's senses, one is taken on an adventure in discovery. Such familiar objects as roots, weeds, and the bed of a river take on the fascination of something seen for the first time.

Claire Robinson

WOLF

Author: Osip Mandelstam (1891-1938)

Type of poem: Lyric

First published: 1964, as "Za gremuchuyu doblest' gryadushchikh vekov," in *Sobranie sochinenii*; English translation collected as "For the sake of the future's trumpeting heroics" in *Selected Poems*, 1974; as "Wolf" in *The Eyesight of Wasps*, 1988

The Poem

"Wolf" is a short poem of sixteen lines divided into four quatrains. It is one of several poems written in the spring of 1931 on the same theme; they are considered by some literary historians to be variants of the same poem and are therefore known as the "Wolf cycle," "Wolf" being the central poem. Written in the first person and in the present tense, it is, like many of Osip Mandelstam's verses, highly autobiographical. In order to interpret the poem correctly, circumstances of Mandelstam's life in the late 1920's and early 1930's must be taken into account. From the events of Mandelstam's life at this time, it is certain that the poet and the persona are identical.

The title suggests a predator and, consequently, a danger to the persona. The poem opens with an assessment of the poet's position in society and history. He avers that for the sake "of the future's trumpeting heroics" and of "that exalted tribe," he has deliberately deprived himself of the merriment and honor at his "fathers' feast." Without specifically naming the "exalted tribe" or his fathers, he dwells on the degree of and reason for his sacrifice. This becomes clearer in the second stanza, in which he complains that "The wolfhound age" has jumped on his shoulders, thus introducing a feeling of mortal danger to the poet. In the next line, he hastens to add that he is not a wolf by blood, indicating that he is not in the same league with the forces oppressing him. Instead, he pleads for understanding and compassion, suggesting that he would wish to be tucked into the sleeve of a Siberian fur coat like a hat. However, the warmth and security of a fur coat are not the main reasons for his wish to be transported far away.

In the third stanza, he openly says that he does not want to witness "the snivelling, nor the sickly smears," or, more ominously, "the bloody bones on the wheel." Thus, another motif is introduced, that of the cruelty and inhumanity of man to man. Rather than witnessing all those undignified acts or, even less, participating in them, he would prefer the serenity of the Siberian nights and the blue foxes shining all night as they did in primeval times. In the last stanza, the poet pleads again to be taken to a distant region where a peaceful river, the Yenisey, flows and the pines reach to the stars, avowing again that he is not a wolf by blood. The repetition reinforces the importance of the statement to the poet. At the very end, he declares defiantly that only an equal can kill him, specifically introducing the final motif of death. The last two statements disassociate him from the events around him and express defiance, even courage, in the face of mortal danger.

Forms and Devices

The poem is written in a conventional style typical of Russian poetry of the nineteenth and twentieth centuries. It is rhymed *abab* with twelve-syllable lines alternating with nine-syllable lines, resulting in a distinct, strong rhythm and a highly musical quality, which, unfortunately and perhaps inevitably, is not fully reproduced in translation. The two most striking devices used by Mandelstam are images and metaphors. The first image that strikes the reader's eye is the cup at the feast. Although the image itself is not ambiguous, its significance is somewhat unclear. It is also not clear of whose glory the poet speaks or to what "exalted tribe" he refers. Yet there is no doubt that a feast is taking place. Speaking of his preferences, Mandelstam uses a powerful image of a hat tucked into a sleeve of a fur coat of the Siberian steppes, which suggests warmth, security, aloofness, and beauty. The beauty of a peaceful river flowing through the steppes of Siberia is enhanced by the images of blue foxes shining in the night amid primeval snow by tall pine trees reaching out to the stars. These beautiful images are contrasted to "the snivelling . . . sickly smears" of the poet's surroundings, which he is forced to endure and from which he would rather escape.

There are fewer metaphors, but one of them occupies a central position. It is the so-called mother metaphor: the wolf. It stands not so much for a wolf in nature as it does for a bloodthirsty predator underlying the beastly nature of modern existence in the persona's society. This is clear from the word Mandelstam uses, *volkodav*, which does not mean simply a wolf but a wolf-dog or wolfhound, corresponding to the nature of the times depicted. Mandelstam extends the metaphor by refusing to identify with it, thus placing it in a sharper focus. Another metaphor, "bloody bones in the wheel," is even more drastic. It stands for the oppressive, torturous age in which the persona lives and for the force of a turning wheel that grinds on inexorably and, like fate, cannot easily be stopped or escaped. Thus, by reinforcing the metaphor introduced in the second stanza ("wolf") and by repeating the salient phrase ("I'm no wolf by blood"), Mandelstam creates a powerful sequence of images and metaphors that support and sharpen the quintessence of the poem.

Themes and Meanings

The main theme in "Wolf" is a defiant resistance to the persecution of humanity. On the basis of the circumstances surrounding Mandelstam's life as attested most forcefully in *Hope Against Hope* (1970), the memoirs of his widow Nadezhda Mandelstam, it is certain that his own experience, or a premonition of it, inspired the poem. The persecution of Mandelstam by the Stalinist authorities began in the late 1920's, gathered steam in the 1930's, and culminated in his death in a concentration camp in Siberia in 1938. At the time this poem was written, he was obsessed by the distinct possibility that he would be arrested, which indeed he was a short time later. Images and metaphors in the poems of the Wolf cycle hint time and again at that possibility. The use of the main metaphor, the wolfhound, for the name of the period (*vek-volkodav*, "the age of the wolfhound") unmistakably defines the poet's understanding of the period. He strengthens that definition with frightening images of "the snivelling . . . sickly smears" and "the bloody bones on the wheel" in order to castigate cowardice and sycophancy among those helping the operation of the bloody wheel.

The poet is determined not to give in to the threats. His defiance is prefaced by a declaration of his sacrifice "For the sake of the future's trumpeting heroics,/ for that exalted tribe" at his "fathers' feast." Although these references are ambiguous, it is possible that Mandelstam is willing to forsake his Jewish ancestry for the sake of a better life for all. Perhaps he refers to the brotherhood of fellow writers, many of whom are unwilling to join the "new age," or perhaps he has in mind his own spiritual and artistic values. What matters is that Mandelstam is willing to sacrifice his future for all the lofty causes he enumerates. That the wolfhound jumps on his back just the same, eliciting a bold cry of defiance, should not be blamed on the poet. At the same time, Mandelstam expresses his yearning for peace and serenity in a distant place such as Siberia. There is a hint of resignation in his plea to be left alone and allowed to find peace far away from predators. As Nadezhda observes in her book, the use of the image of a fur coat recurs in Mandelstam's work as a symbol of the Russian winter and a cozy, stable existence. It is clear that the poet desires security, which is quite understandable under the circumstances.

While the ending of the poem remains inconclusive and the reader is left wondering what happened to the poet and whether his defiance was strong enough to overcome all the perceived threats, the real-life drama supplied the answers, attesting once again to the poet's clairvoyance. That Mandelstam finds security in Siberia is both ironic and sad, for it was in Siberia that his life ended prematurely under the most tragic circumstances. Siberia has been a place of punishment and exile throughout Russian history, but Mandelstam's premonition is nevertheless uncanny. The irony is that instead of blue foxes, he was met by the wolfhound again. Yet his defiant statement that "only my own kind will kill me" turned out to be true: While he has been physically killed by the "wolf," as a poet he remains very much alive.

Vasa D. Mihailovich

A WOMAN

Author: Robert Pinsky (1940-   )
Type of poem: Lyric
First published: 1984, in *History of My Heart*

The Poem

Robert Pinsky's short lyric poem "A Woman" begins "Thirty years ago" when the speaker in the poem is a child. The scene is set, probably in the New Jersey town of Long Branch on the Atlantic coast, where Pinsky grew up. That oceanside community, with many gulls, pigeons, and chickens, succeeds in "forming a sharp memory" for the child, who walks along beside the "old, fearful" grandmother figure in the poem. Their walk together is a ramble through history, featuring characteristics of both the grandmother's older world ("Panic of the chickens" awaiting slaughter) and the child's modern world ("a milkshake"). "A Woman" also contains the accumulated suspicions and terrors of that older world in which the grandmother figure lived her childhood: "Everything that the woman says is a warning,// Or a superstition."

The child feels the conflict of his clear-eyed observations and her ominous interpretations. He sees the natural world with its "measured rhythm" of wave motion and seasonal change, "booths and arcades/ Still shuttered in March." For the grandmother this ordinary boardwalk landscape symbolizes "Tokens of risk or rash judgment—drowning,/ Sexual assault, fatal or crippling diseases." She knows too much and cannot forget; he knows too little and cannot understand. The attempts that the grandmother makes to impart her own fears do not fall on deaf ears, but this child's ears are filled with wonder, with the emerging awareness of the world around himself, of its possibilities, and of his place in it.

In the middle of "A Woman" the tone of apprehension is underscored by an image the grandmother recalls from a dream: "a whole family// Sitting in chairs in her own room, corpse-gray/ With throats cut." Though this is a family of strangers, people she only imagines and does not recognize, her fear is real. The child, feeling her helplessness along with her, turns abruptly outward to the natural world again, to its reassuring list of names for things like rivers and inlets, and to features if not altogether without violence at least not sinister or criminal : "waves crashing over the top" of a seawall.

Finally their walk ends in a common solution to trouble: "the old woman has a prescription filled,/ And buys him a milk-shake." Yet rather than find that bit of the ordinary reassuring, the child remembers another event and time when the ancient fears held him back from a simple excursion "and he vowing never,/ Never to forgive her, not as long as he lived." As the protection of the old ways becomes rigidly stubborn, the warnings have become ineffectual. The child's vow expresses a fundamental recognition of more satisfactory alternatives to fear.

Forms and Devices

"A Woman" contains multiples of Pinsky's favorite kind of loosely iambic pentameter line, in which a short phrase is followed by a colon that introduces an extended series of descriptive clauses full of observations and of images. In short, Pinsky writes a discursive poem with distinctly narrative features to organize and impel the action forward. "A Woman" opens in the past, "Thirty years ago," but "gulls keen in the blue," as indeed they do still. The past and the present exist side by side in the language and in its underlying meaning. "Pigeons mumble on the sidewalk" in precisely the way one might encounter them on a boardwalk in the 1940's or in the present time. Word choice such as "mumble," simple enough in its general definition, augments the activity of the pigeons so perfectly that Pinsky might have reinvented the word for his own use.

Observations are essential to Pinsky; "monotonous surf," "gusting winds," and "high bluffs" contribute to the colloquial, predictable language in the poem. Yet when his memory is most intense the images become entirely unexpected, such as "a house-cracking exhilaration of water." Pinsky wants these images to seem both very ordinary and very special—a powerful reminder that daily pleasures can enrich poetry as well as lives.

Pinsky's short lyrics often have a meditative force that is due partly to tone and partly to the arrangements of sounds and of images. The simple images that sustain the poetic meditation in "A Woman" are typical of Pinsky's emphasis on the significance of casual events that people encounter in their lives. There is boldness of enjambment, where lines do not respect their boundaries, and caesuras, where boundaries are imposed within the lines, as the three-line phrases that constitute "A Woman" build through the progress of the poem. The poet uses colons and hard stops (periods) in the middle of lines, adjectives dangling between lines, and adverbs poised between stanzas.

If Pinsky meant to reinforce ordinary events and an everyday atmosphere with an informal line structure, he also conveys the quality of memory with its disjointed and disjunctive impressions. Pinsky moves in "A Woman" from the vague expressed fears of the grandmother figure to quite "Vivid" (for both child and reader) images that would strike fear into most hearts. Yet he is also capable of describing a familiar event with great playfulness; thus the child remembers himself on the previous Halloween "In his chaps, boots, guns and sombrero," dressed (as were so many children in the 1940's and 1950's) to imitate cowboys and American Indians seen and envied in films.

Themes and Meanings

One can scarcely be surprised that the larger, general theme of "A Woman" is childhood. So many of Pinsky's poems in *History of My Heart*, by their expressed intent, are about the early sources of his feelings and being. At first glance, the theme of "A Woman" appears to be conventional, with its focus on the dawning awareness of the child that he is a separate person and has a history separate from the old woman. The poem may be autobiographical and narrate a simple memory drawn from Pinsky's childhood. Yet there is a mystery about what compels humans through life, which is equally important to the thematic development of "A Woman." The transcendence of action as a wonderful irony in the natural world occurs again and again in Pinsky's poem. The child on his walk becomes, in the most graceful way, the subject of a poem. "Stopping at the market/ to order a chicken" provides a series of tactile and sensory experiences (or feelings) that have a far greater impact on maturity and understanding than the activity itself.

This poem also demonstrates the very vicissitudes and difficulties of human life that the child will eventually distinguish and comprehend: the frustrations of youth, the fearfulness of age, the enjoyment of play, the inability to engage with the natural and the impossibility of ignoring it. Pinsky's predisposition to organize poetic themes by utilizing features of past and present—so that explanations from the past illuminate or reveal the meanings in the present—demonstrates a capacity to recognize, to understand, and to process those objects and feelings of the ordinary world into a celebration of the truths they reveal. His insight is timeless, since feelings can and do outstrip events as great motivators. Feelings are dynamic, while actions tend to remain static and fixed in the place (whether real or ideal) where they occurred.

When *The Figured Wheel: New and Collected Poems, 1966-1996* appeared in 1996—with reprinted poems of *History of My Heart*—a review by Katha Pollitt lauded Pinsky's ability to be "autobiographical without being confessional." Pinsky revives the ancient art of "storytelling" and of that humor without which the stories would be impossibly bland. Pollitt claims that "A Woman" is a muse for Pinsky. If this is accurate, then the poet draws as easily from the appalling as from the thrilling features of human experience. The "strangers" that the grandmother sees are terrifying for her, but for Pinsky the "stranger" is himself in masquerade as "Trundled by, the strangers invite him up" to share their delight.

Kathleen Bonann Marshall

WOMAN AT LIT WINDOW

Author: Eamon Grennan (1941-   )
Type of poem: Lyric
First published: 1991, in *As If It Matters*

The Poem

"Woman at Lit Window" is a reflective inquiry in which poet Eamon Grennan considers the possibilities of accurately rendering the details and nuances of a woman he is observing from outside her window while assessing the factors that make it impossible for him to ever quite capture the full dimensions of his vision. The poem consists of three stanzas of roughly equal length (ten, eleven, and twelve lines) divided by a partition of blank space but joined by the continuation of a statement after the line break. Its mood of quiet reflection is established by the contemplative tone that the poet employs in the first line—"Perhaps if she stood for an hour like that"—which creates a feeling of extended time and suspended motion. However, in an almost immediate introduction of opposing impulses, the poet mentions that he would also have to "stand in the dark/ just looking" at the woman, something he doubts he could "stand" to do. The lure of precision carries his thoughts toward a contemplation of the possible components of his verbal portrait, details of such exquisite precision ("etch/ of the neck in profile, the white/ and violet shell of the ear") that he is held in a kind of rapture of meditation before he considers how his subject might react if she became aware of his presence.

Although he knows that he is invisible to the woman's gaze, his curiosity about what he would do "if she starts/ on that stage of light/ taking her clothes off" unsettles him as the barrier that has kept them physically separate is breached by the power of a creative imagination. At this point, the poet is unable to retain objectivity as an observer concerned only with an accurate rendition. The relationship between them— even if in his mind—has been altered so that even though she "frowns out at nothing or herself/ in the glass," totally oblivious to the observer, he cannot quite return to the mood that initiated his desire for a perfect portrait. While he still believes that given sufficient time and a lack of distraction he might be able to "get some of the real details down," he is now aware of the inevitable intrusion of some distraction that will make this impossible. As he continues to muse about the ideal conditions that would permit him to approach his goal, the woman "lowers the blind," cutting off his actual view of her in the window. As the second stanza ends, the woman is "turning away" and "leaving a blank" that is accentuated by the space between the stanzas.

The third stanza fills in the blank space, denoting it as an "ivory square of brightness," an empty frame glowing with potential. This shifts the focus of the poem, which has been wavering between the poet and the woman in the window, entirely to the poet. The energy released by the image of the woman charges the poet's mind so that everything around him is transformed by the power of vision. The poet, now the primary subject of his own contemplation and illuminated by a "half moon" that casts his shadow on the path to his home, moves amid a glow of cosmic radiance. Its source is in the natural world ("a host of fireflies"), but its impact is considerably enhanced by the exultation of his creative consciousness, which sees in the features of the landscape a miraculous essence that defies description but compels an effort to convey its beauty.

Forms and Devices

In "Woman at Lit Window," Grennan moves between moments of reflection and contemplation, in which he considers the possibilities of capturing the essence of the striking image he is observing, and moments of lyric effusion, in which he is reacting directly to and then is almost consumed by the transformative power of the image itself. The poem is structured by the modulation of moods, beginning in a mood of meditation and concluding in an ethos of ecstasy, and is controlled by the alteration, juxtaposition, and intermixture of images of luminescence and darkness. The pattern of imagery is set at the start, with the poet "in the dark" and the woman in the window on "a stage of light." The woman then moves out of the spotlight, leaving "a blank ivory square"—that is, illumination without definition. This is a pivotal point in the poem, a moment of pause and a turn away from the poet's contemplation of the woman and toward a sense of himself as an illuminated object. The light that lingers flows beyond the "stage," less intense but equally captivating, a natural light issuing from the moon and from the pinpoint flashes of fireflies.

The psychological mood of the poet corresponds to the changing light, and Grennan expresses these changes by controlling the tone of the poem, beginning with a meditative, tentative utterance and finishing with a flourish of lyric exuberance but mixing both the lyric mode and the more reflective, philosophical one throughout the poem. The language that he employs at the start is conditional, his ambition qualified by words such as "Perhaps" and "might" and phrases such as "I think I could." His course of action is speculative ("I stand wondering what I'll do"), but, amid this uncertainty, his responses to the image are already vibrant, the description he envisions (and actually offers) vivid and evocative: "I might get it right, every/ fine line in place: the veins of the hand/ reaching up to the blind cord." In this description, there is a sense of subdued excitement mingled with an air of expectancy and then tinged with mild regret and disappointment at the woman's disappearance. As the poet becomes the central subject of the poem, the meditative mode is eventually submerged in the lyrical one. The philosophical cast of the poet's mind is still apparent in his cautious return through the shadowy darkness, but the ecstatic, elevated condition of his spirit is revealed by his fascination with the soft but significant light generators (the half moon and the fireflies). His sensory description of the "fragrant silence" that surrounds him, his identification with the fireflies in their "native ease," and his response to the heartbeatlike "pulse of light" produced by these fireflies illustrate the extent to which the hesitancy of the opening lines has been superseded by the light-generated powers of vision and inspiration. Grennan's description of his shadow—a projection of the self "skinned with grainy radiance"—suggests that he feels his place is still "to stand in the dark"; this darkness, however, is not total, and a keen eye can register gradations that are as interesting in the muted natural light as they are in the artificial blaze emanating from the window.

Themes and Meanings

Throughout his work, Grennan has explored the range of light across a continuum from its absence in total darkness to its fullest manifestations, both in poems written prior to "Woman at Lit Window" and in subsequent ones such as "I Lie Awake Each Morning Watching Light." Although it is not an exact equivalency, light, for Grennan, is often conceived as an analogue for artistic vision. Its occurrence affords the opportunity to see an object or subject with an exceptional clarity. In "Woman at Lit Window," Grennan is transfixed by the illuminated image he sees and is then characteristically inspired to try to capture or convey its essence in language. The persistent problem he faces is that there are always impediments to the ultimate completion of his conception, including the circumstances of his observation, the elusiveness of his subject, and perhaps most significant, the complex of personal responses that occur beyond his ability to predict or restrain them. This is what makes the situation so challenging and, sometimes, so frustrating.

In addition, the title of the collection in which the poem appears, *As If It Matters*, is an expression of one of Grennan's fundamental tenets. He is plagued by a sort of hovering uncertainty about the importance of his work and perhaps even the direction of his life. This is not an overwhelming obstacle, but it affects his attitude toward the world and is a factor in many poems. The title is not taken from any of the individual poems in the collection and has therefore been chosen specifically to apply to all the poems in the book. It implies that the struggle to find the language and form for what he sees is not only likely to be difficult and frustrating but also might not even be worth attempting. In "Woman at Lit Window," Grennan resists this position by proceeding as if it does matter, even if his efforts are inevitably going to come up short of his ultimate intentions. As a demonstration of the validity, or at least the usefulness, of this approach, Grennan concludes the poem with the poet suffused in a light as energizing as that which lit the woman in the window in the first stanza. The striking image of his shadow "skinned with grainy radiance" offers a complicated texture as compelling as the pure light on the woman. The effort to "get it right" has given him an opportunity to share or enter the "radiance" accompanied by the almost magical "host of fireflies" that endow the light with spiritual grace.

Leon Lewis

THE WOMAN AT THE WASHINGTON ZOO

Author: Randall Jarrell (1914-1965)
Type of poem: Dramatic monologue
First published: 1960, in *The Woman at the Washington Zoo*

The Poem

Randall Jarrell's "The Woman at the Washington Zoo" is a free-verse monologue of thirty lines that reveals the alienation and frustration of an isolated speaker. Indeed, since the "woman" is so detached, the words of the poem are no doubt simply thought rather than spoken aloud. Composed when Jarrell worked in Washington, D.C., as poetry consultant for the Library of Congress, the poem is set at the national zoo in Rock Creek Park.

The female speaker is an anonymous clerk in the massive, impersonal federal bureaucracy. In an essay about how he composed this poem, Jarrell described her as "a kind of aging machine-part" and said she is "a near relation" of countless women he observed on the streets and in government buildings of Washington. The zoo suggests both sharp contrasts and revealing parallels with the woman's condition. In a place that is colorful, exotic, and teeming with energy, she sees herself as drab, plain, and lifeless. Like the once-wild animals, however, she too is imprisoned behind bars.

Although the poem has no regular stanza pattern, several line breaks do indicate the progression of the woman's thoughts and feelings. The poem proceeds from calm description to an outburst of fervent desire. It begins with deprecation but becomes a prayer.

In the first three lines she notices other visitors at the zoo—women in saris whose intense colors make the speaker appear even more bland and unappealing. These saris "go by" the speaker, and their purposeful movement is a foil to her physical and emotional stagnation. In lines 4-18 she describes her own dull clothing, laments the monotony of her thankless job, and compares her situation to that of the trapped animals. However, her metaphorical cage is even more onerous than the literal animal cages because she is her own trap, and she must also cope with the distinctly human knowledge of aging and death.

Lines 19-23 descend to an image more ominous and distasteful than that of the caged animals. Now the woman—unnoticed, unappreciated, unloved—sees herself as the leftover food ("meat the flies have clouded") ignored by the zoo animals and now consumed only by scavengers. Near the end of line 23 the woman begins a passionate apostrophe. Addressing the vulture, she implores that he pay her as much attention as he does the white rat left uneaten by the foxes. Desperate for affection, she asks that the bird step to her as a man. Having fantasized a dramatic metamorphosis of the vulture, she begs for an equally miraculous transformation for herself. The reiterated imperatives of the final line ("change me, change me!") reveal her desperation to discard her old self and embrace a new identity.

Forms and Devices

The power of this poem (described by one critic as Jarrell's most visual) derives mainly from its rich images and metaphors. First, the poem uses clothing images as correlatives for the people inside. As viewed by the speaker, the colorful saris are not merely fashions from a foreign country. In contrast to her mundane clothing, they seem like garments—and lively people—from a completely different world. The speaker's whole wardrobe is mentally reduced to one drab navy dress because both her attire and her entire life are so morbidly uniform. Line 11 confirms that the speaker's dull dress is perfectly analogous to her vacuous body and soul. No sunlight dyes her pale body; "no hand suffuses." Presumably, in the right context, light could animate and a loving touch could fill the empty container.

Along with this image of lifeless clothing, Jarrell uses several other images to suggest the woman's diminished status. Since this is a poem of self-examination, the speaker repeatedly studies her reflection in mirrors. Looking into fountains, she sees an evasive, wavy image. Furthermore, that image is not on the surface but beneath the water, suggesting that she is drowning. Later she observes her reflection in the eyes of caged animals and, like her self-image, it is small and far-off. Such simulacra show that the woman is far removed from real life. Her failed attempts to engage it produce images that are shimmering, miniature, and remote.

Although many images in the poem connect the speaker with caged animals, one line may reduce her state to that of a vegetable. Shadowed by the many domes of Washington and "withering among columns," she is like a helpless plant that cannot flourish amid marble and granite. The architectural grandeur of the city overpowers its human inhabitant.

The poem has no regular rhyme scheme, but Jarrell uses occasional repetitions and rhyming words to emphasize the oppressive monotony of the speaker's situation. According to Jarrell, such echoes and verbal duplications imitate the condition they describe. Note, for example, the internal rhyme that describes the woman's dress as "dull null." Continuing to stress negativity, lines 4-18 display frequent repetitions of "no," "neither," "nor," and "not." In lines 5-7, reiteration of the word "so" underscores the sameness of the woman's routine.

In spite of its bleak imagery and deliberately monotonous sound effects, the poem does exhibit brief flashes of humor. The official title of the speaker's supervisor, "The Deputy Chief Assistant," is delightfully oxymoronic. His "no comment" response to her work is perhaps a parody of the bureaucrat's mechanical reply to an unwelcome question. Such fragments of levity may actually reinforce the grim atmosphere of the poem, since neither the woman nor anyone else in her office is likely to perceive any comedy in those circumstances.

Themes and Meanings

"The Woman at the Washington Zoo" is one of many poems by Jarrell that portray depersonalization and loss of identity. For example, "The Death of the Ball Turret Gunner" (1945) is probably Jarrell's best-known poem and his most emphatic depiction of the impersonal government at war. In only five lines the speaker describes his abrupt transition from a child protected by a loving mother to a mere cog in the machinery of destruction. When the speaker is himself destroyed, his bloody remains are simply washed with a hose from his station in the airplane.

Several other poems focus more specifically on the plight of isolated women. Jarrell identifies the woman at the zoo as a distant relative of other women he has described in such poems as "The End of the Rainbow," "Cinderella," and "Seele im Raum." While most of those poems offer third-person depictions of alienation, "The Woman at the Washington Zoo" allows the speaker to voice her own despair. In doing so the woman may seem like a female counterpart of the main character in T. S. Eliot's "The Love Song of J. Alfred Prufrock" (1915). Unlike Prufrock, however, the woman moves beyond passive self-pity. The final sections of the poem focus not on isolation but on the possibility of transformation. If loss of identity is a persistent problem in Jarrell's poems, some dramatic transformation is the elusive solution. Jarrell was fascinated by the magical shifts and mutations in fairy tales, and he translated or imitated several poems by Rainer Maria Rilke that focused on this motif.

At first the woman's appeal to the vulture appears bizarre, but on closer examination its symbolism becomes apt. In consuming carcasses of dead animals, a scavenger clears away the old. By performing this essential function, the vulture enables the cycle of life to continue. Since the speaker sees her own condition as deathlike and desires an infusion of new life, her invocation to the vulture is fitting. Identifying herself with the leftover white rat, the woman takes on the pallid hue of illness and lack of vitality. The vulture, in sharp contrast, displays the colors black and red. Its black wings obviously connote death, but the bright red helmet (suggesting animation and sexual energy) may be a harbinger of rebirth. The woman wants her old self to be consumed so that a new self can emerge.

Since Jarrell stops with her plea rather than its consequence, he leaves the poem open-ended. As time proceeds, she may experience nothing more than continued loneliness and aging. Even if the vulture cannot change her, however, the intensity of her plea may suggest sufficient motivation to change herself.

Albert E. Wilhelm

THE WOMAN HANGING FROM THE
THIRTEENTH FLOOR WINDOW

Author: Joy Harjo (1951-   )
Type of poem: Narrative
First published: 1983, in *She had Some Horses*

The Poem

Joy Harjo's "The Woman Hanging from the Thirteenth Floor Window,"with its reference point in the contemporary urban environment, mourns the sense of desolation, marginalization, and individual loneliness that arises when women are displaced from their spiritual home. At the same time, the poem encourages readers to acknowledge the lives of those individuals living in poverty in a racist culture who somehow survive despite incredible odds. The poem begins with a description of a woman's hands pressed to the concrete window moulding of the tenement high-rise where she lives in Chicago with her three children, Carlos, the baby; Margaret; and Jimmy, the oldest. Birds fly overhead like a halo or a "storm of glass waiting to crush her." With this startling introduction, the poem compels the reader to hear the story that has brought this woman to a devastating point in her life.

The second stanza, merely one short line, attempts to explain her reason for wanting to jump—"She thinks she will be set free"—and thus deftly leads the reader to the woman's memories about family and home recollected in the third stanza. She thinks of herself first as a mother, but also as a child, "her mother's daughter and her father's son." She has been a wife, with two marriages in the past, and, significantly, has an inextricable and strong connection to all the women in the building who watch her at this crucial juncture in her life. Moving from a specific woman's predicament to a more general and widespread human condition, Native American writer Harjo establishes the idea of communal misery and hope as the women watching from the ground also see themselves hanging from the window.

In her youth, as the fourth stanza explains, the woman had enjoyed a sense of belonging, a security and comfort at her home along the shores of Lake Michigan in northern Wisconsin. She was nourished there by meals of wild rice, nurtured in physically and spiritually warm rooms, rocked lovingly in the arms of family. Ironically, the very lake whose shores lulled her as a child now pound relentlessly and viciously against the concrete breakwater on the "Indian side of town" in Chicago. From her precarious place on the window ledge, she can see other tenements and women like herself hanging from windows there. The following stanzas reflect her thoughts about the ways her life has changed in Chicago's alien and hostile environment, or as she thoughtfully describes it, "the lost beauty of her own life."

The final stanza presents two contradictory images, thereby leaving the reader to finish the story. In one scenario the woman lets go of the window ledge and falls to her death from the thirteenth floor; in the other she "climbs back up to claim herself again." With this painful ambiguity Harjo's powerful poem thus speaks for all the women who have survived and for those who have not.

Forms and Devices

For Muscogee Creek writer Harjo, poetry is not so much visual or descriptive as it is evocative. Her gift lies in the transformative expression of feeling and thought, and while at times she cleverly creates a series of complex and conflicting metaphors, she wants her poetry to be clear and alive, to not add to what she calls the confusion of life. Even when writing about painful subjects, Harjo carefully and consciously presents language in a beautiful way, making frequent use of repetition, like a chant, so that ideas enter the reader like a song: "She thinks of all the women she has been, of all/ the men. She thinks of the color of her skin, and/ of Chicago streets, and of waterfalls and pines." Repetition, with its time-honored place in Native American life and literature, is used most often in storytelling as a way for listeners to enter the spiral of meaning and emerge changed. It is a way too for the narrator, the woman hanging from the thirteenth floor window, to revive the memory of herself as she was before the urban destruction of her life.

In the tenth stanza Harjo repeats the refrain "she thinks of" on six occasions, each time ending the phrase with a concrete image of important people and places: her children, Carlos, Margaret, and Jimmy; her father and mother; and "moonlight nights" and "cool spring storms." As the woman visualizes the beloved faces and enriching landscape as she re-creates them, the reader believes she will not let go of the window ledge and life. Yet in the final stanza of the poem the refrain takes a sharp turn: "She thinks she remembers listening to her own life/ break loose." The displacement and removal from her tribal community is achingly real: "She thinks of the 4 a.m. lonelinesses that have folded/ her up like death." She is aware that the knowledge of her physical roots implies a recognition of a spiritual belonging. To call it forth at this time becomes a lifesaving effort.

The story of the silent and tormented woman effectively enters the reader's heart and mind as a song. Harjo's own musical influences, a combination of country western, Creek stomp dance songs, jazz, and blues, infuse the poem with a rhythm and cadence that appeal to its audience, whom she envisioned as women, mostly American Indian women who might be dancing the stomp dance in "worn levis" or swinging on the dance floor in "northside bars," remembering the ballads of their youth, the old love songs, and the heartbreak of the blues. Hers, then, is not a new song. In an interview, Harjo remarked that readers may feel they know this woman. She is not one woman but many women, with a story that happens over and over like the sad chorus of a country ballad.

Themes and Meanings

A 1982 trip to Chicago and a visit to the Chicago Indian Center with its one small room and an old battered rocking chair triggered the poem "The Woman Hanging from the Thirteenth Floor Window" and its sad story. The image of the rocking chair stayed with Harjo, who imagined a woman, rocking for her life. She said, "I kept feeling her there, standing behind me urging me on. . . . She sat down on the edge of my memory and refused to move."

The poem's ambiguous and open ending reflects the poet's belief that women, perhaps especially Native American women, must always retain hope. Despite the ravages of patriarchal oppression over hundreds of years, these dislocated and lonely women are, in Harjo's words, "alive and precious." As she hangs from the window, some voices from the sidewalk scream for the woman to jump. Others cry, sympathetic with her tortured life and current dilemma. She sees women "pull their children up like flowers and gather/ them into their arms" in a protective gesture of family unity. Whether this sustains her or only makes her long for her own community, readers cannot be sure.

In a radical move toward breaking the silence about dislocation of Native American women, Harjo skillfully invites the reader to face the chaos of displacement, spiral down into its center, and emerge transformed by the experience. Recognizing the healing qualities of memory, the poet describes its gifts well for those who may not have the vision to realize and embrace its power. Yet readers will never know how the poem ends. Thus, one singularly haunting woman represents both the women who climbed back up and claimed life for themselves and those who fell, for whom Harjo now must speak. This startling and moving poem uses storytelling to keep their memory alive, to keep women alive insofar as possible in a racist and uncaring society. In "The Woman Hanging from the Thirteenth Floor Window" the message is compelling: Individuals who work to understand the connections between heritage and the world today, who seek to call up what is important beyond this hostile society, may survive. Yet readers can never be certain.

Harjo both frightens and encourages the reader with this poem, which explores the power of language and memory as a way to move into another space, a timeless place that is not simply today's world but a layering of many worlds. She describes this act as tapping a river within that most humans rarely visit despite its life-sustaining potential. Her job as a woman and a poet is to give voice to the stories and to acknowledge the lives, those lost and those saved.

Carol F. Bender

WOMAN ME

Author: Maya Angelou (Marguerite Johnson, 1928-   )
Type of poem: Lyric
First published: 1975, in *Oh Pray My Wings Are Gonna Fit Me Well*

The Poem

"Woman Me" is a short poem consisting of three stanzas and twenty-two lines; it is written in free verse. The title is significant in that there is an absence of punctuation between the noun and the pronoun. That the words "woman" and "me" are not separated by a comma indicates that the poet wishes to underscore the fact that her gender is inseparable from her identity as woman. In addition, the poet identifies herself with the female gender as a whole; she is everywoman.

In the first verse, the unidentified speaker of the poem addresses one woman, although the woman addressed represents all women. Cataloging the physical geography of woman/women in history, the speaker begins with a description of her smile. In this feature is discerned a "delicate/ rumor of peace." Unlike the passive smile of the stereotypical woman as portrayed in American literature written by males, however, the smile of the woman in Maya Angelou's poem represents anything but passivity. Instead, it is an external reflection of a peace found within. Yet in the next line, paradoxically, this peace is mingled with "deafening revolutions" that also lie within. The images of male power and authority that follow, "Beggar-Kings and red-ringed priests," depict men who are powerful in themselves but who also seek woman's power—specifically, woman's sexual power. Woman is portrayed as being in the "grasp of Lions," yet these lions rest in her "lap of Lambs."

In the second stanza, the woman's tears are compared to jewels in a crown. These tears, which caused "Pharaohs to ride/ deep in the bosom of the/ Nile," most likely allude to those of the powerful queen of Egypt, Cleopatra. Woman is represented as a force so monolithic and intense that doors must be bolted shut in order to keep the "winds of death" from taking her.

Woman's laughter, her joy, rings out in the final stanza. Like her tears in the previous stanza, her laughter is so strong and deafening that it overpowers even "the bells of ruined cathedrals." Woman is portrayed as a being who is capable of strong yet contrary emotions. She contains multitudes. In the final image of the poem, children look to the woman for strength and guidance. She provides the model, the "chart" by which they learn "to live their lives."

Forms and Devices

Images of power abound in "Woman Me." The images cluster around traditional male power figures and female representations of power. These powers are not pitted against one another in the poem but coexist with some degree of harmony because of woman's wisdom.

The powerful male authority figures of the day, the "Beggar-Kings," "red-ringed Priests" as well as the Pharaohs, are all embroiled in political struggles or revolutions. In the poem, the kings and priests are represented in the violent image of the lion, the king of the jungle. The woman is represented as the lamb in whose lap the lion rests. Yet it is not the females in the poem who seek shelter from these seemingly powerful males, but the males who seek comfort and solace in women. More than in the revolutions they fight, these men seek "glory" by "conquering" a woman sexually. This kind of victory, a sexual one, is more potent than any military victory for these men. In the poem, all traditional symbols of power—both political and religious—are overturned. The poem represents women as the true sources of power.

The power of woman is not manifested only in her ability to comfort kings. She also has the power to mold the lives of children. The image of traditional male power in the final stanza of the poem is the church. The power of the mother to guide the lives of those around her, however, is portrayed as being stronger than the power of the church to guide its flock. The cathedrals depicted in this last stanza are "ruined," powerless. It is woman to whom the children must look to lead the way.

Themes and Meanings

In "Woman Me," Angelou addresses her subject (everywoman) directly through the use of the personal pronoun "you." In so doing, the poet achieves a sense of intimacy. Yet this sense of intimacy is directed, as previously mentioned, not at one particular woman, but at all women. The poet writes to women of women. The title of the poem, "Woman Me," indicates that in addition to addressing other women. Angelou is both writing about and addressing herself in the "you" of the poem.

The major theme of Angelou's poem is woman's strength. The poet begins the first line of each of the three stanzas with one of the three features that she believes constitute the essence of woman's strength. The first stanza opens with the phrase "Your smile." This smile is woman's sign of reconciliation with herself and with man. It is a sign that she acknowledges but does not accept the traditional authority of men; she must trust in her own power, even though this power is unrewarded by society's standards. Woman's smile is represented as a sign of peace, not of resignation or passivity. It is a sign that she can acknowledge the males in authority while knowing that it is to her that these men look for strength and comfort. Woman is depicted as smiling on the outside despite the revolutions that stir within her spirit.

The second stanza opens with the phrase "Your tears." Woman's pain becomes the focus of this stanza. The tears, however, like the smile, are an indicator not of weakness but of power. The significance of the tears lies in the fact that woman's power lies in her capacity not only to feel but also to show her feelings without shame; this is the power that caused kings and pharaohs to both desire and fear her.

"Your laughter" opens the final stanza. In praising the capacity of women to regard the pain and tragedy of life not with bitterness but with humor, Angelou focuses upon that quality that allows women not only to survive, but also to affect the lives of the people around them, particularly children. In the closing stanza of the poem, woman's laughter is heard ringing out even louder than the bells of "ruined cathedrals," implying that woman is a source of strength and authority even more powerful than the traditional and established authority of the church.

Genevieve Slomski

THE WOODSPURGE

Author: Dante Gabriel Rossetti (1828-1882)
Type of poem: Lyric
First published: 1870, in *Poems*

The Poem

Dante Gabriel Rossetti's "The Woodspurge" is a sixteen-line poem divided into four-line stanzas of iambic tetrameter that describe an unidentified grief-stricken narrator in an outdoor setting, who experiences a vivid heightening of sense perception during a time of intense psychic stress. In his depressed state, the narrator undergoes an unforeseen and unbidden, but clear and intense, visual experience of the woodspurge, a species of weed that has a three-part blossom.

The poem's first stanza presents a countryside that is geographically unspecified—an area of trees and hills—and begins to suggest the narrator's state of mind. The narrator is not walking toward a specific destination; he moves in the direction the wind is blowing, and, once the wind ceases, he stops and sits in the grass. The fact that his walking and stopping are guided merely by the wind indicates aimlessness, passivity, and apathy.

The narrator's posture in the second stanza indicates that he feels exceedingly depressed, although there is no explanation given for his emotional state. Sitting on the grass he is hunched over with his head between his knees. His depression is so severe that he cannot even groan aloud or speak a work of grief ("My lips . . . said not Alas!"). His head is cast down, as is his soul—so much so that his hair is touching the grass. His physical state reflects his psychic paralysis as he remains motionless in this position for an unspecified length of time, but long enough so that he "hear[s] the day pass."

Although he is not trying to look around and seems oblivious to the country setting as a whole, the narrator remarks in the third stanza that his eyes are "wide open," and this important fact becomes the inadvertent cause for his ensuing visual experience. From his seated position, he says there are "ten weeds" that his eyes can "fix upon." Out of that group, a flowering woodspurge captures his complete attention, and he is dramatically impressed by the detail that it flowers as "three cups in one."

The narrator attributes his depressed state to "perfect grief" in the final stanza, but there is still no elaboration as to its cause. He then comments, first, that grief may not function to bring wisdom or insight and may not even be remembered, and, second, implies that he himself learned nothing from his grief that day and can no longer remember its cause. However, "One thing then learnt remains": He had been visually overwhelmed by the shape of the woodspurge, and, consequently, its image and the fact that "The woodspurge has a cup of three" have been vividly burned into his memory forever.

Forms and Devices

The short, simple lyric, focusing on sadness of some kind, was a popular genre for Victorian poets, as it had been earlier for the Romantic poets at the beginning of the nineteenth century. For Rossetti, it was a genre that suited his ideal of simplicity in poetry.

Rossetti's choice of imagery, diction, rhythm, and rhyme demonstrates a simplicity that mirrors—and therefore underscores—the narrator's state of mind. The images are simple; the tree, hill, grass, weeds, and sun have no descriptors of any kind. There are no metaphors, similes, or other figures of speech; nature is presented in broad brushstrokes without ornamentation. It is only when the narrator accidentally fixes his gaze upon the woodspurge that any specific details come forth, and, even then, it is only the shape of the flower that is of any concern. Rossetti's use of nature tends to the particular, not the universal; the experience of his narrator, thus, occurs through an interplay with a very narrow, concentrated, and specific part of nature.

Rossetti's unadorned presentation of nature mutes the setting, forcing it into the background, and causes the narrator's mental and emotional state to emerge as the central focus. The bare minimum of description functions to signal to the reader that the narrator himself is oblivious to the details of his surroundings because his mind is focused elsewhere. The only record of his awareness of his environment, before his dramatic visual experience of the woodspurge, is that he walked when the wind was blowing and that he sat when that external impetus ceased. His reference in the first stanza to the wind having been "Shaken out dead from tree and hill" introduces the thought of death, establishing a negative tone that suggests that the narrator's internal state is negative.

Another poetic device that maintains simplicity in the poem—and yet functions to express sadness or sorrow—includes Rossetti's use of monosyllabic words. All but one word in the first stanza are monosyllables, causing the movement to be slowed to a plodding pace to initially signal a rhythmic parallel for the narrator's inner state. With each of the next three stanzas consisting primarily of monosyllabic words, the poem's tempo continues to be retarded. This consistently slowed rhythm throughout the poem creates a dirge-like effect that mirrors the narrator's mood.

There is one common end rhyme in each stanza (*aaaa, bbbb, cccc*), suggesting a dullness, a lack of variety, or a paralysis in the rhyme that reflects the paralysis in the narrator resulting from his psychic state. The word "wind" is repeated four times in the first stanza, and the end rhyme for the first and fourth lines of this stanza repeats the same word, "still." This deliberate repetition of words and of simple rhymes also functions to maintain the simplicity of the poem and is consistent with its simple imagery and vocabulary.

Themes and Meanings

In September, 1848, Rossetti, along with other fellow painters such as John Everett Millais and William Holman Hunt, founded the Pre-Raphaelite brotherhood, whose goal was a return to simplicity, to a direct presentation of nature, and to faithfulness and accuracy in detail. The name was derived from the Italian Renaissance painter Raphael, who was a symbol for them of a departure from the simplicity of presentation and the use of bright colors, which produced a direct emotional effect in pre-Renaissance paintings. The ideals of this group were applied to poetry as well as to painting: simplicity of syntax, imagery, and diction, with themes that concentrated on the experience of sense perception and created emotional resonance.

Although "The Woodspurge" has a plant's name as its title, the poem does not have nature, or even the woodspurge itself, as its subject. Nature does play an indirect role in the poem, but it is not the focus here or in other works by Rossetti. Both in his painting and in his poetry, the function of nature is to act as a background for the presentation of human action and emotion. The depiction of details from nature, although precise and accurate, is not meant to draw attention to nature itself but to mirror a psychic state or inner experience.

"The Woodspurge" does not tell a story or embody an ethical or moral lesson; it does not deal with contemporary issues or events. It is removed from any cultural or historical context and—more concerned with emotion than ideology—aims to express a universal human experience, the paradox of intense sense perception during times of emotional numbness.

The possibility that the three-in-one nature of the woodspurge—which could recall the Christian concept of the Trinity or the concept of unity in diversity—might symbolize a higher truth and thus be a consolation for the speaker's grief is not given any space in the poem. The woodspurge's shape is a botanical fact, of interest particularly to a painter's eye, but it points to no significance beyond its sheer existence in the material realm. It functions as an example of a detail or image that can remain vivid after emotional stress has been left behind and forgotten. Rossetti's tendency to focus on intense sensual experience rather than to illustrate truth or meaning is evident here.

Although the cause of the narrator's sorrow is never specified, the poem was written in the spring of 1856 when Rossetti was in an anguished state. He was experiencing intense strife with Elizabeth ("Lizzie") Siddal, the chief model he had used for many of his paintings since 1850, over the issue of her desire for marriage. (He eventually married her in 1860.) Rossetti was also tormented at that time about relationships with other women and with what he perceived as lost artistic opportunities. However, nothing in the poem points to these specific issues. By leaving the cause of the narrator's depression unspecified, Rossetti gives universal expression to the psychological phenomenon of acute mental awareness and heightened sensation simultaneous with mental and emotional distress.

Although Rossetti's later poetry is more ornate, complex, and difficult both in style and in content, "The Woodspurge" concentrates on sense perception, accuracy of detail (including botanical accuracy), and the use of nature as a framework for the expression of the mental and emotional state of the narrator. Its simplicity in theme and poetic devices makes it a superb demonstration of the tenets of Pre-Raphaelite poetry.

Marsha Daigle-Williamson

WORDS

Author: Sylvia Plath (1932-1963)
Type of poem: Meditation
First published: 1965, in *Ariel*

The Poem

"Words" is a short poem in four stanzas of five lines each. It is written in an open form with irregular meter and only occasional rhyme. Because the poem is written entirely in metaphor, the title serves as an important clue to meaning. For the reader, the knowledge that the poem is about "words" (and by inference, poetry) becomes a fixed star in the journey through the poem's metaphoric landscape.

Because the landscape of "Words" is mental rather than physical, its effect on the reader can be disorienting. There is no hand on the axe that strikes, no riders on the horses, no eyes behind the welling tears. One does not encounter the narrator until near the end of the third stanza. At this point, one sees that the poem is written in the first person, and it becomes clearer that preceding stanzas are the thoughts of the poet as she meditates on her subject, words.

"Words" is structured as a series of stanza-paragraphs, each exploring a different aspect of the subject. Distinct but interlocking images unify the ideas and reveal a progression of perceptions about the nature of the poetic utterance. The dominant image pattern of movement radiating from a center is established immediately. The juxtaposition of the title and the one-word first line, "Axes," links the two ideas. Words set to paper ring out like an ax set to wood. The lack of a discernible narrator here allows the reader to enter the poem and feel the physical sensation of impact. (This is a particularly apt image for Sylvia Plath's poetic style, which is frequently sharp and biting.)

The almost physical sense of vibration coupled with the repetition of the word "echoes" links the ax image to that of horses galloping. Plath often uses horse imagery to denote creative energy. In an earlier poem, "Elm," she says, "All night I shall gallop thus, impetuously," and in "Years," "What I love is/ The piston in motion—// And the hooves of the horses,/ Their merciless churn." Similarly, "Words" begins with a vibrant sense of purpose, of statements made and messages sent.

In the second stanza, the mood changes, becoming quieter. Welling sap ties this stanza to the preceding ax imagery, and likening sap to tears places the imagery in a human context. Poets, particularly those of the confessional school to which Plath belongs, often use their work as catharsis, as a way of healing. Certainly there is a sense of attempted healing in the sap that tries to seal the wounded flesh of the tree and tears that can release psychic pain. Paradoxically, however, healing occurs only after a wound has been opened.

In the middle of the second stanza, the imagery changes to water into which a stone has been dropped. Because of the similarity of the images, one expects a continuation of the healing idea. The implication here shifts subtly from healing to concealing, however; the stone that caused the disturbance has submerged, and the breach is being sheeted over; that which lies beneath is covered up.

Up to this point, the language of the poem, though metaphoric, has been grounded in concrete easily identifiable imagery. As one moves into the third stanza, the poetic landscape changes almost imperceptibly from the real to the surreal. As the stone sinks beneath the surface of the water, it drops and turns, changing to a skull. One has seen that echoes from ax strokes, galloping horses, and ripples represent words. Like the "axe," the "rock" is the initiator of echoes, but the mood has shifted. The ringing power of the "axe" has given way to the inertness of the "rock," which in its tumbling, changes into a macabre remnant of creative energy, a bleached skull.

The idea of lifelessness is reinforced by the next lines. The reader is jerked back to the surface world, but the boundaries of reality are still blurred. In a reversal of the usual metaphoric technique in the first stanza where horses represented words, words are now spoken of as if they were horses. The power and purpose behind the words is gone, however; they are "dry and riderless." The words seem to have taken on a power of their own, outside the control of their creator. They have become as strangers one might meet on the road.

Finally, as if to escape those "indefatigable hoof-taps," the poem, like the skull, sinks to the bottom of the pool, away from the energy, the pain, and the nightmarish confusion, to a place of certainty.

Forms and Devices

Metaphor is the overriding device of "Words." Because there is no narrative framework, even a superficial reading requires some interpretation of its metaphor. Plath does not make the reader's task easy, but she does supply the clues. The interlocking nature of the metaphors unifies the poem and leads the reader to understanding. In the first stanza, Plath links two seemingly disparate images, axes and horses. By emphasizing the common ground of echoing sound, movement out from the center, and energy, these images restate the central image. When, in the third stanza, words are spoken of specifically as horses, one understands "words" also to be the referent of the earlier metaphors. Because Plath is a poet and this is a poem, words imply poetry.

Plath uses metaphor as more than a device for seeing experience in a new light. In this poem, she uses progressive linking of subtly changing imagery to mirror a changing mental state. Ax strokes are an image of power and controlled force. Galloping horses are exhilarating but imply the potential for loss of control. In stanza 2, the welling sap and tears suggest a reaction to the preceding violent energy, a wounded state. In stanza 3, the descent of the rock into the pool mirrors a mental descent into a nightmarish world where stones become skulls and the creative mind is a dead and empty shell. Using similar imagery in "Paralytic," which was written only a few days before "Words," Plath says, "My mind a rock,/ No fingers to grip, no tongue." The imagery of "Words" lets the reader into the trapped nightmare world of that mind, a world unseen by the outside observer because the water has smoothed over and is now a mirror that hides the depths.

In the last two lines of the third stanza and the first two of the last, the poet rises briefly from the depths and sees her past work. Now, "years later," her words seem meaningless. "Dry and riderless," they have lost the urgency of their creation. Finally, the effort of creativity seems too much. The exhilaration has given way to the relentless demands of the "indefatigable hoof-taps," and the mood is of surrender to inevitability.

The metaphoric movement is from energy to stasis, from manic creative energy to pain, to madness, to brief barren lucidity, and finally to quiescence, the still certainty of the bottom of the pool. The ultimate quiescence is death. The movement toward death is a pervasive theme in Plath's poetry, and she has used similar imagery elsewhere. For example, in "Getting There," she speaks of the longing for death: "Is there no still place/ Turning and turning in the middle air." At the end of "Words," the poet has surrendered to the "fixed star" of death that has pervaded her life and her work. There is no escaping this inference, given the fact that "Words" was written only ten days before Sylvia Plath's death by suicide.

Themes and Meanings

Few poets have resisted the impulse to, at some point, write about the nature of poetry. Sylvia Plath was no exception, and "Words" is such a poem. Most poems of this type take as their theme the enduring nature of poetry and its ability to immortalize the poetic vision. They are essentially a praise of the power of poetry. Plath too acknowledges the enduring nature of poetry. Her poetic utterances travel out in all directions from the center of her creation. The poems exist as a separate entity, to be met by any traveler on the road of life. For Plath, though, the poems seem to lose importance once they are out of her control. Met with later, they are "dry and riderless," seemingly without relevance to the person who has gone on down the road.

The act of writing seems to be both what Plath celebrates and what in the end fails her. For Plath more than for most writers, her writing is her life. Her writing as a whole reveals a continuing effort to control the conflicts and obsessions of her life through the tight structure of her craft. In the twenty carefully crafted lines of "Words," Sylvia Plath lays bare the emotional journey of her life, from creative power to despair and death.

Sherrill Keller

WORDS FOR MY DAUGHTER

Author: John Balaban (1943-   )
Type of poem: Lyric
First published: 1989; collected in *Words for My Daughter,* 1991

The Poem

"Words for My Daughter" is a six-stanza poem written in free verse directed to the poet's daughter. Although the poem tells several brief stories of the poet's past, it is not truly a narrative poem. Rather, it is the poet's first-person voice recalling events to his daughter in order to account for the violence that adults direct at children. The poem opens with scenes from John Balaban's childhood in the rough neighborhood of a Philadelphia housing project. In the opening stanza, the reader learns the story of a boy named Reds, "fourteen, huge/ as a hippo." The scene of idyllic childhood fort building is interrupted by screams from Reds's mother, and Reds rushes to rescue her from his father's brutality. The litany of violence continues in the second stanza, in which another of Balaban's friends attacks the milkman who is raping his mother. The poem then turns to a girl "with a dart in her back, her open mouth/ pumping like a guppy's, her eyes wild." It can be surmised that the girl's brother has caused her pain because later the neighborhood kids, with their rough justice, try to hang him.

The third stanza, only three lines long, shifts abruptly back to Reds: "Reds had another nickname you couldn't say/ or he'd beat you up: Honeybun.'/ His dad called him that when Reds was little." This stanza further addresses the source of Reds's hatred for his father. The sexual connotation of the nickname suggests that Reds himself had been abused by his father. The next stanza is set off from the rest of the poem not only by stanzaic white space but also by asterisks. Here, Balaban addresses his daughter, directing his words to some future time when she will be able to read. In addition, the reader finds the first of three things Balaban wants his daughter to know: "I want you to know about their pain/ and about the pain they could loose on others." The stanza ends with the assertion that "children suffer worse." This statement catapults the poet and the reader into a memory of the Vietnam War. The two stanzas are connected by the word "worse," which closes the previous stanza and starts the next. In addition, the two stanzas are connected by the idea of children suffering. In this nine-line stanza, Balaban recalls a nine-year-old Vietnamese boy on an operating table screaming and "thrashing in his pee" while Balaban tries to identify the source of his pain. The child, however, is deaf. "Forget it. His ears are blown," is the surgeon's comment to the poet.

The next scene describes Balaban and his infant daughter on Halloween. For the poet, the smell of her "fragrant peony head" launches him back to a Vietnamese orphanage filled with screaming infants. At that moment, a young trick-or-treater dressed as a Green Beret arrives with his father, who is also dressed in camouflage. That the father would put his son in such clothing infuriates Balaban, and the memories of Vietnam and his daughter's infancy merge. In the last stanza, Balaban concludes the lesson: "I want you to know the worst and be free from it./ I want you to know the worst and still find good." After presenting images of his daughter laughing and interacting with friendly adults, Balaban suddenly seems to realize that while he protects his daughter, his daughter also protects him.

Forms and Devices

Balaban uses images to great effect throughout the poem. By providing the reader with specific detail, he is able to recount the violence done to and by children. In addition, Balaban combines visual, auditory, kinesthetic, olfactory, and tactile images so that all of the reader's senses are engaged in the poem. In the first stanza, for example, pastoral visual images such as a "mulberry grove" and "the thick swale/ of teazel and black-eyed susans" are interspersed with the auditory images of the screeches of Reds's mother, "thumps like someone beating a tire/ off a rim," and the sound of Reds yelling profanities "at the skinny drunk/ stamping around barefoot and holding his ribs." In the fifth stanza, the reader is absorbed by Balaban's description of his infant daughter and her fragrance. These images, endearing and comforting, are interrupted by a memory from Vietnam of "Sœur Anicet's orphans writhing in their cribs." Again, through this device, Balaban is able to convey his primary concern of violence done to children.

Another device that Balaban uses effectively to introduce and develop his themes is juxtaposition. That is, the poet carefully places his memories in a particular order to create a particular atmosphere. In the opening scene, he layers examples of adult brutality to children and the children's brutal retaliation. In the final three-line stanza of this section, he only needs to hint at the sexual abuse of Reds for the reader to make the connection. Perhaps the most important juxtaposition, however, is the connection of his memories of children in Vietnam with his memories of his own childhood friends and with his own infant daughter. The memories, initially divided by stanzas, ultimately become one memory in the fifth stanza, in which he holds his infant daughter, hears Sœur Anicet's orphans in his mind, and sees the "tiny Green Beret" trick-or-treating at his door. Balaban is able to convey the traumatic nature of his memory by inserting that trauma into the happiest of his moments. Even in these long years after the war, his memories of his daughter are inextricably tied to his memories of injured Vietnamese children. The juxtaposition, then, serves to underscore his theme.

Themes and Meanings

"Words for My Daughter" is a poem about the damage adult violence does to children. It is also, however, a poem of adult redemption made possible by a child. Balaban's background provides some clues to his themes and meanings in "Words for My Daughter." In his book *Remembering Heaven's Face: A Moral Witness in Vietnam* (1992), Balaban recounts his days as a conscientious objector who volunteered to go to Vietnam. As a Quaker, Balaban committed his life to nonviolence and opposition to war. While in Vietnam, Balaban worked for the Quaker and Mennonite Committee of Responsibility to Save War-Burned and War-Injured Children as a field representative. His knowledge, then, of the damage done to children is born out of firsthand experience. It is also clear from reading Balaban's memoir that he roots his poetry in his own experience. "Words for My Daughter," for example, grew out of an actual incident he details in *Remembering Heaven's Face*.

When Balaban writes of his early memories of life in Philadelphia, he thematically connects incidents that concern abusive relationships among family members. Children are not only abused themselves, but they are also called upon to rescue other members of their family who are being abused, or they turn to abuse themselves. What should be loving, protective relationships are instead violent and painful. Certainly, one of Balaban's primary themes in this poem is what happens when "desperate loves" are "twisted in shapes of hammer and shard." However, even if the pain is dreadful in Philadelphia, it is worse in Vietnam. There Balaban's recollections turn to orphaned children who have no family members to protect them and who find themselves abused by members of the human family at large. In these instances, Balaban tries to protect the children just as he finds himself in a protective position with his own daughter as he faces the father and son dressed as Green Berets. The confrontation is ironic: Balaban the pacifist finds that his own love for his daughter twists his response to the other father, whom he curses. Thus Balaban arrives at another important theme: Violence can shape and twist the experience of love.

In the last stanza, the reader is introduced to yet another theme, and perhaps it is here that the meaning of the poem seems most clear. What Balaban says he wants for his daughter is, ultimately, what he wants for himself: "I want you to know the worst and be free from it./ I want you to know the worst and still find good." The ease with which traumatic memories intrude into Balaban's life suggests that he may never "be free" from them. It does seem, however, that he knows the worst and still finds some good. The last stanza, with its description of the poet and his daughter, corrects the early vision of family violence. In the last full sentence, the poem turns around. Suddenly, it is no longer Balaban who is the protector of children; rather, it is his child who redeems him. For Balaban, who often finds himself wandering in the memories of violence and despair, his daughter represents hope. She pulls him from the past and into the future, her birth a regeneration of the world.

Diane Andrews Henningfeld

WORDS FOR THE WIND

Author: Theodore Roethke (1908-1963)
Type of poem: Lyric
First published: 1954; collected in *Words for the Wind*, 1958

The Poem

"Words for the Wind" is a love poem in four parts. In it, Theodore Roethke demonstrates his characteristic concern for and sense of union with nature, his questing curiosity about the meaning of things, and finally his belief that meaning is ultimately discovered through feeling and intuition, not through rationality. Yet what really helps the speaker to become one with all and to answer the questions he asks (or, really, to recognize the unimportance of the questions or the answers) is love felt for and returned by another person.

There appears to be no progression in the various parts of the poem, but there is a pattern. The speaker repeats verses (apparently addressed to no one) that resemble snatches of old songs ("Love, love, a lily's my care") or nonsense rhymes ("She's sweeter than a tree"). He also notes events in nature: "The shallow stream runs slack;/ The wind creaks slowly by." He has questions about what he observes: "Are flower and seed the same?" Sometimes, there are answers that defy common sense: "Whatever was, still is,/ Says a song tied to a tree." The speaker also describes his own contented condition: "Mad in the wind I wear/ Myself as I should be." He believes that nature is favorably disposed toward him because "the birds came down/ And made my song their own." The poet's beloved appears from time to time, raising no conflicts, as accepting and pleasant with the poet as the rest of nature is: "She likes wherever I am."

The first three parts of the poem repeat these elements, but in the fourth there is a difference, as the poet's love comes near, dominates the lines, physically embraces the poet, and finally leads him out of himself into a larger and fuller life. The activities of the two become one, as he does "what she does." His lover transcends ordinary categories; her skin is not merely beautiful or smooth or soft, but "hilarious," a word that also indicates the happiness that she has brought him.

In an image very familiar to Roethke's poetry, the two dance, expressing at once their vitality, their singularity, and their union. The poet is happily able to say, "I . . . see and suffer myself/ In another being, at last." "Suffer" carries both the modern meaning, "endure the pain of," and the older one, "allow." Because his lover accepts him, because his life means as much to her as it does to him, she feels his hurts and his sorrows, and she also excuses and tolerates those elements of his personality that neither he nor she admires. A further meaning of these lines is that because the two lovers now share a life, the poet can see and understand both his triumphs and his shortcomings more clearly because he sees them with and through the eyes of another. Perhaps the most powerful words in the poem are the final ones, "at last," with their implied message that the search for love, the attempt to find this quiet, restful place and time in nature and in life, has been a long and sorrowful one.

In the last section of the poem, one sees that there has indeed been a progression in the poem, as the poet draws closer and closer to his lover, whose presence and emotion overwhelm the poet and the poem at the end. "Progression" may be the wrong word to describe this change, for that word is too logical and orderly. The movement of the poem has been rather like that of the wind to which it is addressed: moving sometimes forward and sometimes backward, swirling without apparent purpose, but ultimately informing and directing life itself.

Forms and Devices

Roethke married his wife, Beatrice, in January, 1953, and "Words for the Wind" was published the next year, so while it is clearly a celebration of his love for her, it is more specifically an epithalamium, or wedding song. The tradition of the epithalamium, a poem in celebration of a marriage, began in antiquity and reached what many regard as its finest expression in Edmund Spenser's "Epithalamion" (1595). Such a poem is usually set in a pastoral environment in which the poet not only praises his bride but also invokes the tender elements of nature and asks for divine blessings on the nuptials. Roethke performs all these traditional poetic tasks but with a modern twist: The poet and his love are not only in nature but also a part of it; not only the bride's beauty is noted but also her sensuality; and, finally, there is no need to ask the blessings of God because love itself is a confirmation of and experience of divinity.

A number of images and metaphors appear in this poem and connect it to the rest of Roethke's work, which makes use of the same devices. Most notable among these are the images of the stone, the rose, the tree, light, and the vine as well as the metaphor of the dance, which Roethke often used as a way of describing life lived properly, with a sense of regard for other life. Foremost among the metaphors for life, though, is wind, for not only does the word "wind" appear in the title of the poem, but also the poem itself is the title poem for the volume in which it was collected.

In Roethke's poetry, as in Percy Bysshe Shelley's "Ode to the West Wind" (1819), wind represents not only the vitality of life itself but also the confusion of that life. The wind not only reminds one that the world itself is alive but also upsets, confuses, and disorients. Wind appears several times in the poem, but equally important is the poet's relationship with the wind. At the end of "In a Dark Time" (1960), the poet is "free in the tearing wind," a statement that indicates that although the poet has achieved a kind of release, he is still in the middle of a maelstrom. In "Words for the Wind," however, the love that the poet shares with another brings genuine and lasting peace: "I get a step beyond/ The wind, and there I am,/ I'm odd and full of love." Even though the poet is "odd," he does not feel strange, for love sustains and nurtures him.

Themes and Meanings

Several of Roethke's previously stated themes not only appear but also are further developed in "Words for the Wind." In "The Waking" (1954), a poem that also celebrates the sheer joy of existence and the knowledge that one finds by living one's life intensely, Roethke wrote, "Great Nature has another thing to do/ To you and me," meaning that death will come to all living things and therefore one must enjoy the miracle of life as much as possible. In "Words for the Wind," however, these rather grim thoughts are balanced by the line, "Love has a thing to do," which suggests that life is more than merely an inevitable decline to the grave and that it may be expanded and enlarged by the emotion of love.

Also in "The Waking," Roethke wrote, "What falls away is always. And is near," a line that suggests that the mind or spirit retains what the senses no longer have and that nothing is irrevocably lost. The echoing lines in "Words for the Wind" are "What falls away will fall;/ All things bring me to love." This pair of lines suggest that it does not even matter if what is lost is permanently lost, because everything leads the poet back to the supreme experience, love. It is not necessary to dwell on or to retain the past if the present is informed by this ennobling and defining condition.

In "The Waking," Roethke's line "We think by feeling. What is there to know?" might be considered at worst nonsensical, since there seem to be many things to know, and at best anti-intellectual, a strange contention for a poet who was also a university professor. Roethke's point, however, is that knowledge that leads to depression or confusion is worse than no knowledge at all. The human body persists in believing that it is good to be alive, in spite of the threat of war, poverty, nuclear disaster, or other horrors. Roethke's poetry implies that one need know no more than that it feels good to be alive. In "Words for the Wind," Roethke amplifies the lines in "The Waking," with "Wisdom, where is it found?—/ Those who embrace, believe." These lines unite and relate love, belief, and not merely knowledge but wisdom.

Sometimes, the intensity with which Roethke lived life led him into a manic-depressive cycle that dipped into psychosis. Yet, Roethke's philosophy seems to hold that one can trust one's possibly self-destructive feelings because love leads one out of one's self and confirms that one's single impressions and feelings are not merely solipsistic madness but also shared by and thereby confirmed by others: "I bear, but not alone,/ The burden of this joy." In receiving love's embrace, one is also helping another to live and understand, so that love is not something one selfishly receives but something through which one enlarges the life of the world and the other beings in it.

Jim Baird

THE WORLD

Author: Henry Vaughan (1622-1695)
Type of poem: Meditation
First published: 1650, in *Silex Scintillans*

The Poem

"The World" is a sixty-line poem in four fifteen-line stanzas in iambic pentameter, with a rhyme scheme *aaa, bb, cc, dd, ee, ff, gg*. The title is purposefully ambiguous and reflects the dual focus of the poem: the earthly world, the here and now; and the world to come, heaven and eternity. The four stanzas develop the idea that unless mortals shed their concern for the values of this world they are doomed. True value lies in belief in God and in the search for salvation.

In the first stanza, Henry Vaughan presents the powerful image of the ring of light, which embodies for him the idea of eternity and salvation. This image represents a transcendent state of enlightenment for humankind, a center of calm and peace. In contrast to this image, Vaughan projects the earthly world as a world in shadow, a Platonic world in which mortals grasp illusions, with reality forever beyond their reach. The figure of the lover is the vehicle for expressing this view. Surrounded by the attributes of earthly love—the lute and his fanciful and witty poems or lyrics—the lover is trapped in silly pursuits of vain and ephemeral pleasures. His attention is fixed on earthly rather than spiritual beauty.

In the second stanza, Vaughan turns to another facet of earthly existence, power and politics. He attacks the statesman for false goals and priorities, delivering his condemnation in images of darkness and subterranean life. In worse circumstances than those of the lover, the politician lives underground, like a mole, and is fed by public policy and the tribute paid by the churches. In metaphoric terms, Vaughan tells the reader that the great cost of such an existence is in human misery, specifically in blood and tears. The exercise of political power is necessarily an act of violence against people.

In the third stanza, Vaughan excoriates life devoted to accumulation of wealth. He gives the image of the miser, afraid of his condition, afraid to show his wealth for fear that it might be stolen. Attached to his wealth—his seat of "rust," his pile of "dust"—the miser is the victim of his own accumulation, which dominates and enslaves him. The kingdom of heaven is beyond his reach. Worse, blinded by his concern for wealth, he does not recognize the source of his misery. Like the ancient Epicureans, who lived for their own pleasure, the miser knows only himself and lives only for himself.

In the fourth stanza, Vaughan returns to the possibility of salvation. "Some" mortals are capable of rising into the ring of light, thereby transcending the limitations of mortality. Such a transcendence reflects the value of light over darkness, of salvation and eternal life. Those who cannot see the value of light are condemned to live in "grots" and "caves" in this "dead and dark abode."

The poem ends with a curious statement intended to hit the reader with an ironic wallop. The poet writes of one mortal whispering in his ear that this ring of light, this salvation, was not intended for anyone but the "bride," an allusion to Christ. This comment explains why mortals do not believe in God's ultimate salvation.

Although the poem properly ends at this point, Vaughan adds a postscript that is characteristic of his religious poetry. His quotation from the Bible, John 2:16-17, epitomizes the poem's message and emphasizes its didactic religious purpose: Salvation awaits those who relinquish the pleasures of the flesh and the false values of the material world.

Forms and Devices

Metaphors of light and dark dominate the poem and are the basis for its structure. To understand this metaphoric pattern, one should first consider the poem's title. The meaning of the title is ambiguous: To what "world" does it refer? The reader learns quickly that the title refers to both the earthly and the heavenly worlds. More important, earth and heaven are not separate worlds but two dimensions of one world. The concept of "the world" combines earth and heaven in the same way that the person of Jesus combines human and divine. He is neither one nor the other, but both.

Light and dark are similarly two parts of one world. A condition of dark is necessary to the condition of light. Both worlds exist as contrast, but exist as yin and yang, two parts of a whole.

In the first stanza, the image of the ring of light is an encircling metaphor, both in its own dimension as circle or ring and as a frame for the poem. The image serves to establish the ultimate dimension toward which the entire poem moves and as the basis for development of the poem. Light is contrasted to darkness. The light is the light of heaven, the center of "calm" and peace. In contrast is the magnificent image of the "shadow" of time which covers the earth; this "shadow" is also "round." In the light there is a state of calm, while in the dark everything is "hurl'd" and "driven."

In the second stanza all that is not part of the light is "weighted" and full of "woe," which, like a "thick midnight-fog," hinders movement. The image of darkness takes on even starker proportions in the image of the mole burrowing underground. Human enterprise, particularly human political enterprise, is equated with the underground life of an animal. The political animal burrows in the dark.

In the third stanza, the image of light and dark is muted in a lightless, colorless world of avarice. The miser's hoard is described as a "heap of rust" and pile of "dust," which the miser manages in a state of fear, trusting only himself. Although this state of being is not wrought in terms of explicit images of light and dark, it is the equivalent of a moral and spiritual darkness.

The bright image of the ring of light appears in the fourth stanza, where explicit comparisons of the world of light and the world of dark appear. Vaughan speaks of the "dark night" in contrast to the "true light," the dark world of "caves" and "grottos," life on earth as a "dead and dark abode," beyond which is the "Sun." In the terms of this poem, that sun—partly an allusion to Plato's allegory of the cave, in which the sun stands for ultimate truth and reality—is God. In the light, which represents the world of God, is salvation, eternal life, peace, and fulfillment. All the rest, earthly life, is darkness, death, and misery.

Themes and Meanings

The theme of "The World" is religious and didactic. Readers need not search long to understand Vaughan's intention, as he employs hard-hitting imagery of salvation and damnation. The postscript from John 2 reiterates the poem's meaning.

Vaughan's theme is that salvation and eternal life, peace and happiness, exist only through God. Life not devoted to God is ruined now and forever. The way to salvation is evident: The vain pursuits of this life must be abandoned. At issue for Vaughan are lives devoted to the pursuit of pleasure, exemplified by the lover; the pursuit of power, embodied in the "darksome States-man"; and the pursuit of wealth, represented by the miser. Vaughan derides these figures, their activities and values, as false, destructive, and ultimately futile.

The central problem in all these ungodly pursuits is that they fail to address the main purpose of living, the worship of God. Lives that do not address this end become bogged down in search of other ends that have no lasting significance and are therefore worthless. The power seeker, the money worshiper, even the lover, fail, not only in terms of their own personal happiness and possible redemption, but also by inflicting their desires on others, to whom they cause harm because their activities are not informed with God-centered values.

Those who do not understand this fundamental religious and moral truth are blind and doomed to live in a moral, spiritual, and religious darkness. In the terms of the poem, the mass of humanity is bound to suffer this fate. Only the enlightened few who recognize the promise of salvation are capable of freeing themselves from this ultimate condition of desolation. The poet seems to say, "Reader, wake up. Salvation awaits those who repent as surely as eternal damnation awaits those who do not."

Richard Damashek

THE WORLD IS TOO MUCH WITH US

Author: William Wordsworth (1770-1850)
Type of poem: Sonnet
First published: 1807, in *Poems in Two Vols.*

The Poem

In "The World Is Too Much with Us," William Wordsworth offers his reader a sonnet, albeit an idiosyncratic one that deliberately ignores or adapts the traditional sonnet conventions to convey its theme. The sonnet is typically a poem composed of fourteen lines that features two "movements": an octave, or opening set of eight lines, that presents a dilemma or conflict, the resolution to which is offered in the closing sestet, or set of six lines. Besides this structural convention, the traditional Italian sonnet, which is the basic form the poet builds upon, also features an *abba, abba, cde, cde* rhyme scheme, in which each letter represents a new end rhyme for each line.

Wordsworth elects, however, to manipulate both conventions and substitute his own formula instead. Rather than the traditional octave and sestet, there is only a brief break, or caesura, in line 9 to distance the previous lines from those that follow; the effect is that the reader immediately is transported into the climactic declaration of line 9. Similarly, the poet also posits his own rhyme scheme, beginning with the traditional *abba* form, but ending ostentatiously with three rhymed couplets.

These decisions to forgo convention are part of the poet's Romantic temperament and his thematic tendencies. In effect, the form of the sonnet embodies the poet's theme. Wordsworth—the most respectful of tradition among the clan of "rebel spirits" whose poetic company includes George Gordon, Lord Byron, John Keats, Percy Bysshe Shelley, and Samuel Taylor Coleridge—nevertheless is concerned with creating his own form and promoting it.

The poet begins with a straightforward declaration, "The world is too much with us," then proceeds to explicate the meaning of this maxim. First offered is a comment upon the maxim's scope: "late and soon." Comprehensively, totally, utterly, the poet opines, people are captives of the world they seek to understand or control.

The reader is implicated with the poet ("us") in "getting and spending" and laying "waste our powers" to see in "Nature" what is "ours." "World" as cosmos, as debilitating "system" that robs people of their perceptions, is contrasted with "Nature," the benevolent teacher through which one might learn of his or her inner nature and thus be free of deceit and cunning. The poet concludes, "We have given our hearts away," and this is a "sordid boon!"

Wordsworth follows this assessment with a series of images from nature that underscores one's ignorance and leads one to an abrupt denouement. The sea and the winds that might liberate one from world-weariness are depicted as singers or musicians with whose song people "are out of tune." The reader is then startled by the poet's sudden, aggressive "anti-confession": "Great God! I'd rather be/ A Pagan suckled in a creed outworn."

One looks for the "than," the syntactic particle that would complete the comparison—the poet would rather be a pagan than what? The implied answer is "a citizen of Christian civilization," one who has too quickly been dulled to the glories and lessons of "the pleasant lea" on which he stands.

He feigns, in conclusion, to prefer the ancient mythology, so dated, yet so contemporary, that would bring him "glimpses" of "Proteus rising from the sea" or "old Triton blow[ing] his wreathed horn." From beginning to end, the sonnet is seen as an unrelenting attack on superficiality and conventionality in faith and in human motivation promoted by the fixed contours of "the world."

Forms and Devices

Wordsworth's *Lyrical Ballads* (1798) set forth a manifesto of poetic insight that shook the nineteenth century poetic establishment. Decrying tradition and classicism for their own sake, the poet undertook to write poetry "in the real language of men" and to defend his new techniques as a more authentic response to the world at large.

Wordsworth and his fellow Romantics sought nothing less than the revitalization of poetry and literature in the lives of common men and women, not just the aristocracy, while at the same time hoping for a more prestigious place for himself in the arbitration of taste, virtue, and religion in the public square.

"The World Is Too Much with Us" exemplifies both the proud, buoyant spirit and the dark undertones of his endeavor. In the poem, Wordsworth simultaneously employs and flaunts the traditional form as it has come to him. The sonnet serves as a bridge between the arrant traditionalism in which he was nurtured and the emancipated imagination of a new age, an age in which "the spontaneous overflow of emotion" would define poetic achievement.

The first eight lines are constructed with the expected metric and rhyme schemes; as readers arrive at what appears to be a conventional octave-sestet structural split, they are struck by the abrupt shift in tone, marked by the caesura, and the auspicious launch into rhymed couplets. The latter device, the equivalent of a "jingle" in twentieth century advertising, jars the reader's poetic sensibilities and, further, undermines his or her confidence in interpreting the poem aright at first glance.

These conventions broken, the poet proceeds to navigate new thematic territory as well. Faithful to his self-confessed predilections for "common language," the diction of the sonnet is unpretentious, if graphically sensuous. The poet's ploy of depicting the pre-Christian worldview as a nursing mother to be suckled surely shocked its original audience. This rather indelicate juxtaposition of "Pagan creed" and, by implication, "Mother Church" foregrounds Wordsworth's—and, more commonly, the Romantics'—disdain for organized religion and what he regarded as its untoward effect upon the appreciation of nature as a source of spiritual enlightenment.

Themes and Meanings

This sonnet comprises an apt summary of many of the themes Wordsworth pursued throughout his tumultuous career. Primarily, "The World Is Too Much with Us" is a poem about vision, about lines of sight, about the debris of history that prevents the observer from seeing through to the real meaning and purpose of human life.

Throughout the first eight lines of the sonnet, two competing worldviews are silently compared before the poet explicitly declares in line 9 his allegiance to a modified paganism that preserves nature's autonomy and authority apart from human control or divine manipulation. In short, the poet seeks to divorce Christian vice from pagan virtue and form a hybrid ethic that permits the soul to return to its spiritual moorings.

The poet's intellectual vista envisions a decadent West poised on utter industrialization and eventually ruin. The incipient "environmentalism" found in the sonnet undergirds most of Wordsworth's other works, especially his long narrative poem, *The Prelude* (published posthumously in 1850), and his verse drama, *The Borderers* (1842). Nature is conceptualized as a willing teacher, a personified, secularized "Holy Spirit," who will "guide us into all truth."

The "world" that is "too much with us" is the world as stylized, fixed, unmalleable—the world of a sovereign deity who has placed humankind in a cosmos of his and not their making. Echoed here, then, is the poet's rebellion against this fixedness. The sonnet is thus a call to arms, a rallying cry to cease "getting and spending" with the coinage of heaven and to turn to a "creed outworn" for sustenance and guidance.

In this, the sonnet reflects the poet's quite explicit preoccupation with expressing the nature and consequences of self-consciousness for an appreciation of nature's role in forming the human spirit. In commenting upon his poetics, Wordsworth offered that "the study of human nature suggests this awful truth, that, as in the trials to which life subjects us, sin and crime are apt to start from their very opposite qualities." In other words, whatever merits Christian civilization may have presented, its excesses breed the very behaviors and social conditions that cause its dissolution.

This sentiment is in line with the sonnet's poetic form and theme, and with the poet's own testimony about his life in the autobiographical work, *The Prelude*. Therein Wordsworth suggests that he had sought a rudder for the future by attaining a clear sense of his own past, and not merely the historian's pseudo-objective reconstruction of the past.

That past, the past of each person, is available for introspection, and thus evaluation, in the poet's view only to the extent that one breaks free of the "world" as a prison house. To regain "our powers," people must get "in tune" with nature's melodies. The alternative—from the perspective of the sonnet and the poet himself—is to reap captivity of spirit and poverty of soul. Hence, "The World Is Too Much with Us" is a prototypical Romantic anthem, impishly prodding readers to reconsider the basis of their transcendent faith and their despair at reclaiming nature for their own purposes.

Bruce L. Edwards

THE WOUND-DRESSER

Author: Walt Whitman (1819-1892)
Type of poem: Dramatic monologue
First published: 1865, as "The Dresser," in *Drum-Taps*; as "The Wound-Dresser," in
  Leaves of Grass, 1876

The Poem

Walt Whitman's "The Wound-Dresser" is a sixty-five-line free-verse poem in four sections describing the suffering in the Civil War hospitals and the poet's suffering, faithfulness to duty, and developing compassion as he tended to soldiers' physical wounds and gave comfort. Published at war's end, the poem opens with an old veteran speaking, imaginatively suggesting some youths gathered about who have asked him to tell of his most powerful memories. The children request stories of battle glory, but the poet quickly dismisses these as ephemeral. He then narrates a journey through a military hospital such as Whitman experienced in Washington, D.C., during the second half of the war.

In three lines added in 1881 (lines 5-8, previously the epigraph to "Drum-Taps") he admits he was at first "[a]rous'd and angry" and "urge[d] relentless war," but soon relinquished his war-as-glory stance to dress wounds of soldiers both Northern and Southern, to "sit by the wounded and soothe them, or silently watch the dead." The poem then takes the reader into his "dreams' projections," the horrors of the hospitals that vividly haunt him while others around him are happy and busy making money on the economic recovery.

The vision from the past proceeds in the present tense as a scene projected before the poet's eyes. The majority of the lines set the details of the military hospitals before the reader's senses, with Whitman leading the reader onward as he confronts agony, comforts and bandages the wounded, and watches some die. The soldiers' agony is agony to him as well, but he moves on "with hinged knees," humbled and barely able to continue at times.

Section 2 gives a view of the wound dresser as a soldier, steadfastly pressing "onward" through the hospital tending the wounded amid horrible conditions and despite the unbearable pain he witnesses—row after row of cots, some soldiers without cots lying on the ground bleeding into the dirt, row after row of amputations, gangrene, fevers, crazed minds, bloody rags, open wounds. Seeing the look of death coming upon one soldier, the poet wishes he could die in the boy's place, but he cannot and so he asks for merciful death to hurry.

Section 3 develops this dutiful faithfulness and expands on the poet's experience of loving compassion as he witnesses the suffering and suffers himself to see others in such pain, as he can do little to relieve them. Detailing more specific and terrible wounds, the poet stays firm, calm, "impassive" on the surface, "yet in [his] breast a fire, a burning flame." The final section summarizes his actions and their profound effect on him, that the complex "experience sweet and sad" continues, relived "in silence in dreams' projections."

Forms and Devices

Whitman earned his place as the father of modern American poetry by developing a capacious free-verse style, voice, and imaginative content capable of expressing the country's expansive democratic spirit. Among his chief devices are long lines of rhythmic cadences, catalogues rich with detail, syntactic repetition, and a voice that is bold and mastering yet casually intimate, inviting the reader to see and share his experience of reality. In most poems, these devices advance experiences of celebration, wonder, and joy. In this poem syntactic, cataloguing, and rhythmic repetition concentrates the deep suffering, piles detail upon detail, portrays the relentlessness of the appalling conditions, and underlines strong emotional content—the wound-dresser's shock, humility, and loving compassion—as he moves through the hospital doing his work. Long lines of flowing rhythms interrupted by pauses and short phrases modulate the emotional content of a consciousness that can stand to witness the horror of amputations, crazed minds, and dying boys and still remain open enough to feel deep compassion. A hushed, awed quietude is advanced by long cadences and in the lines of accurate, honest details as the reader follows his eyes:

> From the stump of the arm, the amputated hand,
> I undo the clotted lint, remove the slough, wash off the matter and blood;
> Back on his pillow the soldier bends, with curv'd neck, and side-falling head;
> His eyes are closed, his face is pale, (he dares not look on the bloody stump,
> And has not yet look'd on it.)

The visual and psychological power of the poem owes much to the unflinching rendering of bloody details delivered by the voice of a person who not only does not turn away but also allows himself to feel deep tenderness for those to whom he ministers. The poet notices the specific way each head is laid on a pillow and intuits a soldier's horror at the loss of his hand.

The poem is characteristic of Whitman's belief that experience, not logic, convinces, and he gives the reader raw experience, causing one to cringe and look away, as the soldier did, as the speaker wanted to but did not. Metaphor is rare, but when it appears is used to dismiss, as early in the poem in a quick figure—"like a swift-running river they fade." Metaphor is also transformed into a complex of pervasive and profound meaning, as in the central figure of the wound-dresser as soldier, going without fail to the work of binding wounds and comforting despite horror, unbearable pain, and death surrounding him on all sides. Humbled, the poet gives the reader twice the marvelous rich image of his going with "hinged knees," suggesting in its complex symbolism a physical, emotional, and spiritual door where quaking fear, petition, utter weariness, humility, love, strength, and courage to go on, are all fused—the whole powerful mix of thought and feeling that marked his experience as a nurse.

Themes and Meanings

As a tale told to the young, the poet's memories act as an offering of wisdom and future direction for healing the nation: not to remember the glory of battles won, but to remember the pain that soldiers on both sides suffered, their sacrificial deaths, and the war wounds that need loving healing. The nation's people should not pass by the wounded because they are too difficult to look at; instead they are to become wound-dressers, whose function is a holy one. A few but clear allusions are made to the divine nature of the soldiers as Christ-like: the soldiers' "priceless blood," the poet dressing "a wound in the side, deep, deep," the dying arms "cross'd" on the wound-dresser's neck. The soldiers are sacrificial soldiers like the dying Christ, the suffering servant, except that they have died to preserve the unity of the nation. The wound-dresser is also a servant, the one who attends faithfully and humbly to the greater suffering of the soldiers. The wound-dresser's love goes as deep as that of the soldiers' love for country, for he desires to die in a boy's stead. The image of the dying soldiers with their arms crossed on the nurse's neck and kissing, which closes the poem, is fully earned through the nurse's deep compassion and humble service.

"The Wound-Dresser" occupies a central place in the "Drum-Taps" group. It not only is one of Whitman's finest poems but also marks a shift from Whitman's call to war of the early poems to the later poems' distressed assessment of the human costs on both sides with its implicit injunction to heal the broken nation through wound-binding love. This poem expresses the powerful effect direct exposure to the war had on Whitman, resulting in the late poems' powerful treatment of the pain and sacrifice endured by the soldiers and their families, who were left to grieve unconsoled. This and other poems in "Drum-Taps" constitute the first modern war poetry, which turns away from celebrating the glories of battle to render starkly, even brutally, the physical and emotional realities of war and its costs to human individuals.

In this context, the image of "hinged knees" suggests that the nation choose the path of humility, not glory; prayer for the end of hardship; and awareness of the divinity of all people, North and South, to bind the broken nation with loving, unflagging service in spite of personal suffering. Thus, personal suffering is recognized for its true weight, but it is to be turned to the recognition of shared pain and loss, and from thence to the shared work of rebuilding the nation. The war experience has been both "sweet and sad," bringing profound harm but with it the means necessary for healing. The poem's ending, with the strong memory of the loving kisses of dying soldiers on the poet's lips, promotes the power of loving union. The soldiers in Whitman's care have gone into death with loving arms about them, a theme that is continued in other poems, such as "When Lilacs Last in the Dooryard Bloom'd." It is left to the listeners—especially the young—to take up the message and continue the example of healing at war's end.

Rosemary Gates Winslow

A WREATH FOR TOM MOORE'S STATUE

Author: Patrick Kavanagh (1904-1967)
Type of poem: Satire
First published: 1944, as "Statue, Symbol, and Poet"; collected in *A Soul for Sale*, 1947

The Poem

Patrick Kavanagh's "A Wreath for Tom Moore's Statue" is a four-verse satire in which the poet voices his anger and disillusionment with the cultural hypocrisy, narrow-mindedness, and materialism of post-revolutionary Ireland. Identified with the urban middle classes, Dublin corrupts and stifles the creative originality of its contemporary poets while raising upon a pedestal a false image of the heroic past. This means that Irish society has lost its ideals, joyful vitality, and vision and has reverted its gaze toward idolizing a reusable past, molding and manipulating it so that it fits perfectly the rather insular and practical interests of the rising Catholic bourgeoisie.

The title and the first verse of the poem introduce Thomas Moore, a prominent figure of the Irish cultural and national revival, and use his monument as a tool to satirize the current state of affairs in Ireland. To a certain extent, Moore's monument comes to represent a horde of national poets and heroes whose achievements are gradually narrowed down to and categorized in one single expression and image. Having petrified and, thus, appropriated them for a cause different from, and even opposite to, their original ones, the Catholic middle class has dishonored these public figures of the past, Kavanagh's lyric persona claims: "The cowardice of Ireland is in his statue,/ No poet's honoured when they wreathe this stone."

Moreover, in doing so, the bourgeoisie brings equal dishonor upon itself and its country. Having identified the driving force behind such a desecrating act, "An old shopkeeper," a "bank-manager," the first verse specifies their motivation: mediocre "passion" and "shallow, safe sins." The result is revealed through the middle-class attitude toward Moore's statue: The heroic ideals of the past find their present-day monetary or material equivalence and substitute, corruption and lack of clear vision of morality are veiled by veneration of a stone idol, and financial security takes over spiritual matters. Eventually, this stifles human vitality; confuses one's notions of high and low; and, like a "vermin," reduces the human spirit to a low state of existence, similar to that of "lice."

The second verse elaborates on this idea by revealing the utilitarian rationale of deception: Dead heroes are very useful because they are helpless; they cannot defend their ideals and their image. Therefore, they are easy to manipulate. Like puppets, they are forced to participate in masquerades of dishonesty: "The corpse can be fitted out to deceive—/ Fake thoughts, fake love, fake ideal." At this point the poem introduces the persona of the contemporary poet, who, alive and aware of his own worth and honor, refuses to be molded in the shape of the appropriated image of his dead counterpart. Yet it is his vitality of creative originality, and the resultant unpredictability, that sentence the poet to neglect and poverty, social isolation, and "death." The "rogues" and "lice," who dominate contemporary society, simply cannot tolerate the danger of poetic irrationality.

In the second part of the third verse and especially in the fourth, the satiric voice in the poem drops its indignation with Ireland's cultural and spiritual backwardness and introduces, instead, the idea that improvement is possible. It is poetic creativity that is to revitalize the spirit of Ireland by raising it above bourgeois utilitarianism, by constructing a "new city high above lust and logic." It is poetic imagination alone, the poet claims, that can reverse the process of "annihilation of the flesh-rotted word," revive the "magic" and laughter of language, and restore Ireland to a former state of heavenly purity and innocence.

Forms and Devices

"A Wreath for Tom Moore's Statue" is built upon a series of oppressive contrasts, which demonstrate a tendency to develop from immediate and specific to more general images. Thus, it is significant that when the poem was first published in 1944 in *The Irish Times*, below the original title, "Statue, Symbol, and Poet," there stood a note saying: "Not concerning Thomas Moore." To many critics this is an indication that the erection of Thomas Moore's statue and the subsequent attitudes of the middle class are concrete indications of a more general, ongoing process of cultural backwardness as a result of which the heroic ideals of the past, twisted and corrupted, become subject to public exploitation targeting material gains.

The initial contrast between the dead poet and urban Dublin, represented respectively by the statue and its worshippers, leads through scathing irony to a similarly constructed opposition: the contemporary poet and the Catholic bourgeoisie. In both cases poetic individuality faces "death": The dead poet's honor is desecrated through a huckster's type of worship, while the living poet is physically neglected and forced to become a social outcast. In either case, individuality and human nobility, and especially originality and creative irrationality of thought, are suppressed by utilitarian values and symbols of the modern bourgeois class. It is the wreath that turns Thomas Moore's statue into one such symbol.

The reader also can feel the undercutting effects of irony in the characterization of contemporary society. Religious imagery associated with the Catholic Church—"god," "confession," "passion," "sin," "flood"—is employed in ways that undermine its original purity and demonstrate a decline in religious morality among the bourgeoisie. Thus, in the context of the first verse, "god" finds its negation in the statue—a stone idol—via extreme worship; "confession," bought in a literal sense, is debased to monthly monetary transactions; "passion" loses its purifying effects and turns into "mediocrity"; "sins" enter an oxymoronic relationship with the adjective "safe."

Continuing this train of thought brings the reader to a more subtle allusion: the "wreath" on Thomas Moore's statue, contrasted with Christ's wreath of thorns, brings up the horrifying idea of useless sacrifice. As a result of the total reversal of religious and humanistic values, the low is worshiped while the high is trampled upon and made to crawl; the soil loses its vitality to become "seven-deadened clay." Similarly, the idea of religious desecration introduced in the first verse finds its continuation in the second in the total desecration of the human body, in the utter objectification and dehumanization of heroism. Thus, the image of the "statue" is replaced by that of a "corpse." The latter is denied any agency whatsoever as death does not allow it to "contradict the words some liar has said."

The rhythmic pace of "A Wreath for Tom Moore's Statue" is regular in the first eight lines of stanzas 1 and 2, with a rhyme scheme of *abba cddc*. However, it shifts to a series of interlocking rhymes or near rhymes, whose effect is to slow down the pace of reading as they imitate the speaker's escalating anger, disillusionment, and confusion of emotions. For example, the last six lines of the first stanza's end rhyme (or nearly rhyme), following the scheme *efgefg*, while the last six lines of the next stanza produce the rather confusing *efegfg*. The third stanza returns to the regularity of *abba cddc*, while the last one follows the interlocking scheme of the first verse: *efgefg*. A closer look at the specific text of the poem reveals that the rhythmically tense and confusing six lines in stanza 2 correspond exactly to the first mention in the poem of the contemporary "poet," who refuses to be pliable and insists on preserving his individual, poetic creativity and unpredictability.

Themes and Meanings

Although in "A Wreath for Tom Moore's Statue" the speaker insists upon the poet's individuality and originality of creation, Kavanagh himself is aware of the Irish literary tradition before him. Moreover, through a number of overt and subtle allusions to earlier literary works, he not only situates his poem within this tradition, relying upon it as a source of rich and complex imagery, but also builds upon this imagery. For example, James Joyce explores the theme of Dublin's intellectual decay and spiritual paralysis in his collection of short stories *Dubliners* (1914) and later in his novel *A Portrait of the Artist as a Young Man* (1916).

In a critical study of Kavanagh's work and life titled *Patrick Kavanagh: Born-Again Romantic* (1991), Antoinette Quinn examines the way Kavanagh's speaker in "A Wreath for Tom Moore's Statue" builds upon Joyce's metaphor of Dublin. Stephen Dedalus, Joyce's young artist, views the city as well as Moore's statue as a symbol of Irish paralysis: "sloth of the body and of the soul" creeps "over it like unseen vermin." Almost thirty years later, Kavanagh's speaker alludes to this metaphor but takes it further by giving it clear vision: The nature of the "vermin"—the parasitic, predominantly Catholic, bourgeois class—is identified with great precision. Having lost the republican ideals of pre-independent Ireland and having embraced instead modern standards of popular culture, the Irish bourgeoisie of the 1940's attempts to silence its national conscience, still heard in the voice of some active literary men, by requiring artists to meet its standards of "lust and logic."

"A Wreath for Tom Moore's Statue" contains another, rather subtle, allusion: Its roots lie in the poem "September 1913" by William Butler Yeats, one of the key figures of the Irish literary Renaissance. Although sharing a similar indignation at Irish middle-class culture, its materialistic and commercial attitudes toward Ireland's Romantic national ideals and art, eventually Kavanagh's speaker manages to pull himself out of the bitter disillusionment and, having overcome his anger, ends an a constructive, positive note: "The sense is over-sense. No need more/ To analyse." Although the dead can no longer defend their ideals and aspirations, for the living there is still hope. Because the Catholic bourgeoisie has desecrated God's creation, now it is the poet's mission to save Ireland by an act of active imagination. It is art and literature, therefore, that can produce a purer self, culture, and future.

Miglena Ivanova

X/SELF

Author: Edward Kamau Brathwaite (1930-   )
Type of poem: Poetic sequence
First published: 1987

The Poem

X/Self is a book-length work divided into five parts, which are further divided into individual, closely connected poems. The thematic and stylistic connection among these shorter poems is so strong that the work is best thought of as a single, unified poem. As such, it is also the final third of a larger sequence that Edward Brathwaite began with the publication of *Mother Poem* (1977), continued in *Sun Poem* (1982), and concluded in *X/Self.*

The title of the poem has a complex meaning. The figure of an "X" within the poem implies the crossing of cultures, such as the crossing of an imperialist European culture with African and Native American cultures, which is the collective legacy of the Caribbean peoples with whom Brathwaite, a native of Barbados, identifies. Because of the confusion that such a legacy can cause within an individual, the "X" also has a second meaning as the "X" in a mathematical formula, the unknown element that the mathematician—or in this case, the poet—is trying to identify. As a whole, the title *X/Self* implies that the self of the person born into a colonized state is, to an extent, an unknown element. Further, it becomes clear throughout the poem that Brathwaite is writing not only about Caribbean people but also about people from colonized and Third World nations throughout the world.

Two lines repeated throughout the poem are "Rome burns/ and our slavery begins." By this, Brathwaite implies a connection between the fall of the Roman Empire and the enslavement of various peoples around the world. In his many references to such things as slave revolts against Rome, the re-enslavement of a Brazilian republic of ex-slaves by the Portuguese in 1696, and the slaughter of children by South African forces during the Soweto uprising of 1976, it becomes apparent that Brathwaite views the fall of the Roman Empire as an event that made future empires feel justified in resorting to slavery to suppress "others" whose independence might threaten the might of the empire. That is, the devaluation of women that Brathwaite writes about, as well as the enslavement of African and Native American peoples, have been politically justified throughout the ages as a means of maintaining political order.

Brathwaite conveys this idea through an astounding array of poetic techniques, among them, a facility with words that seems to decompose language even as it composes with it. Thus, many visual and verbal puns are apparent in his writing: "Cincinnati" becomes "sin/cinnati," "hallelujah" becomes "hellelluia," and in a pun that has to be read aloud to be appreciated, Christopher Columbus's first name becomes a question when written as "Christ/opher who?"

Similarly, just as he tries to re-envision language by looking at it differently, so he tries to reimagine history and culture by looking at familiar figures in a new light. Christopher Columbus, for example, appears many times throughout the poem, not as the brave explorer of legend, but as the man who began the process of enslaving and destroying the people of the new world. Prospero, from William Shakespeare's *The Tempest* (1611), also appears, but envisioned as a plantation owner rather than a benevolent magician, while Caliban, from the same play, appears as a native who has been enslaved and forced to speak his master's tongue. Similarly, Richard Nixon appears as Augustus Caesar, while a character in a 1960's television situation comedy, *Julia*, is compared with a daughter of Caesar, also named Julia.

These elaborate references and jokes are part of what Brathwaite himself, in notes that follow the poem, refers to as "magical montage." Taken together, such images have a jazzy feel to them in that, much like jazz, they provide what seems to be a freshly improvised version of old tunes. More than simply a spirit of play, however, is being conveyed. Brathwaite is also deliberately trying to subvert traditional views of culture and history by improvising his own views from his own perspective. That is, the rapid, freewheeling associations that are made in his poetry are a way of saying that European culture and history belong to him, as a member of a society that has been shaped by European imperialism, as much as it does to the Europeans. He has a right to provide his own interpretations.

Because his references are so wide ranging—from the Greek philosopher Socrates to the black actress Diahann Carroll, and from T. S. Eliot to the Martinican poet of negritude Aimé Césaire—many readers will find his poetry quite dense and difficult. As an aid to readers, the poet includes eighteen pages of notes at the end of the poem, explaining and commenting on many of his references. In a brief introductory comment to these notes, Brathwaite admits that he provides these notes with "great reluctance," afraid that some readers will be misled by them into reading his poem as an academic exercise built around these notes. Perhaps because of this reluctance, the notes have an idiosyncratic flavor all their own. They do not read as dry, academic notes, nor as mere comments, but often as an integral part of the poem, which not only clarifies but extends the type of interpretation of history that is going on in the main poem.

Forms and Devices

Without a doubt, the most important poetic device employed by Brathwaite in this poem is his use of historical and cultural allusion. Brathwaite, however, relies on allusion so heavily that this allusion becomes cultural and historical revision.

Although the poem does not adhere to a strict outline, the reader will notice a general progression throughout the poem. The earlier sections, sections 1 and 2 especially, focus on the rise and fall of the Roman Empire. His view of the Empire, though, is not of a unifying force throughout the world but of one that spreads death and destruction. Not only does he call attention to many revolts against the Empire, but he also associates these with later revolts against other empires, such as (in the section entitled "Salt") a Haitian rebel, Toussaint Louverture who, near the turn of the eighteenth century, led a successful revolt against France. Similarly, later wars and battles, such as (in the section entitled "Nix") the 1961 United States-sponsored Bay of Pigs invasion of Fidel Castro's Cuba, are compared to battles waged by the leaders of Rome to maintain the Roman Empire.

As the poem develops, however, it becomes clear that at least as much as the poem is interested in reinterpreting the grand sweep of history, it is interested in the human cost of individual battles and revolutions and other such mayhem.

In the section entitled "Edge of the Desert," for example, he writes:

> rome burns
> the desert multiplies its drought into this child
> whose only drying water is his pools of singing eyes there . . .
>
> chad sinks
> and forest trees crash down.

The relation between the destruction of these empires and of the land is not purely a metaphorical one. Empire building and empire destruction has a very real ecological cost.

Among the most important allusions the reader of *X/Self* encounters are the allusions to William Shakespeare's *The Tempest*, particularly to the characters of Prospero and Caliban. In the section entitled "X/Self's Xth Letters from the Thirteen Provinces," a character writes (in a dialect characteristic of Barbados) to his mother on a computer. In the references to Prospero in this letter, he is recast as a plantation owner, while Caliban, his unwilling servant, is seen as an enslaved native of the island whose attempt at rebellion failed. Readers who recall that Shakespeare's Caliban appreciates language only because it allows him to curse will appreciate the pun Brathwaite makes when he says "for not one a we should responsible if prospero get curse/ wid im own/ curser"; even others will appreciate the wordplay in the footnote that describes a "curser" as the "tongue of the computer." The wit, however, should not overshadow the meaning: Use a man as a machine, and the "machine" that is created will rebel, if only in language.

Not the least important echo within this poem is that of T. S. Eliot. Not only might a long, footnoted poem remind one of Eliot's *The Waste Land* (1922), but the title of the last section, named "Xango" after an African god of thunder, recalls the final section of Eliot's poem, entitled "What the Thunder Said"; more important, Brathwaite's poem comments on *The Waste Land* by re-envisioning it. That is, Brathwaite's poem (like Eliot's) traces the descent of Western civilization. It does so, however, not through tracing its devaluation of art—a common reading of Eliot's poem—but by tracing the destruction this Western tradition has caused by looking at its sometimes devastating effects on peoples' lives.

Themes and Meanings

X/Self has two main themes unifying the poem. One involves an examination of how the imperialistic tradition of European civilization has led to a devaluation of those defined as "other"—blacks, Native Americans, women. The second involves an attempt to find a self-defined identity as an Other—as an "X."

An example of how the first of these themes is played out can be found in the section entitled "Phalos," which discusses the plight of women in three Third World cities (Addis, Actium, and Kumas) that have been overrun by European powers by saying,

> And since that day at addis at actium at kumas
> our women have forshook their herbs forshorn their naked saviours
> . . . .
> they have straightened their nostrils where they would flare.

The reference to straightening nostrils is a reference to the type of cosmetic surgery that women of African descent can have to hide African features. More generally, though, the poem is concerned with the long-term distortion of sensibilities that has resulted from European imperialism. Local standards of beauty tend to be forcefully adapted to the European standards of beauty—standards to which women of the occupied race do not conform and which thus compel them and their descendants in modern times to resort to surgery and fashion so as not to be thought of as "ugly."

If, however, the poem were nothing more than a critique, it might be a rather somber affair—which it is not. Much of the liveliness of the poem comes from its attempt to assert an identity based not only on the poet's own African Caribbean identity but also on its relations (as, if nothing else, fellow outsiders) to other groups that have often been denied their cultural identity. Thus, for example, a footnote points out the "black, African, slave, brown, Creole, Latin, Asian, Alexandrine, or Byzantine" identity of figures who appear in the poem, such as Muhammad, Aesop, Herod, Moses, and Ho Chi Minh (among many others), not so much to posit a cultural identity common to all those various groups and people but to point out the diversity of the different cultural strands that constitute the weave of any kind of modern (or postmodern) cultural identity.

From this context, his references to such people as jazz great Sonny Rollins and reggae star Bob Marley have a strong thematic connection to his references to such things as Aananse, the West African and Caribbean spider trickster who appears briefly at the end of the section entitled "Citadel," and his own style of magical montage poetry. In the music of Sonny Rollins he finds an artistic conscience dedicated to avoiding jazz cliches, and in the music of Bob Marley he finds a singer who can exhort his audience to "get up/ stand up/ stand up for your rights," and in both a view of artistic creation which, like a spider, weaves something new from available materials. The poem emphasizes Third World, African, Latin, and black figures as if to say that these artistic traditions offer a technique of reworking common cultural elements in uncommon ways to create something new—especially a new, and potentially liberating, way of looking at the dominant culture.

Finally, then, the poem comments on its own style of artistic creativity through the allusions it makes. That is to say, the poem itself situates its magical montage writing (which Brathwaite also at one point refers to as "magical realism," a term often used to describe the works of writers as diverse as Gabriel García Márquez and Gloria Naylor) within this discourse of what the French philosopher Michel Foucault called a counter-memory—cultural discourse that tries to re-envision the traditions and history that have influenced it, rather than simply maintaining or extending them.

Thomas J. Cassidy

THE YACHTS

Author: William Carlos Williams (1883-1963)
Type of poem: Lyric
First published: 1935, in *An Early Martyr and Other Poems*

The Poem

The title of William Carlos Williams's "The Yachts" serves as the first two words of the poem. Making the title and the poem continuous in this manner is a technique he uses elsewhere, in poems such as "To a Poor Old Woman" and "The Raper from Passenack." It calls into question the separability of the poem's subject and its expression. Yachts have always been an emblem of wealth, but beginning in the 1890's they became particularly strongly identified with American business magnates who did battle for the America's Cup in races off Newport, Rhode Island. Seeking both to retain the cup and to avoid being the first American to lose, J. P. Morgan, the Vanderbilts, and other tycoons sailed against foreign contenders such as Sir Thomas Lipton in huge racing craft that were aesthetic and engineering wonders driven by acres of canvas.

The poem is descriptive and narrative through the first eight stanzas but becomes nightmarish in the final three stanzas. Sea and harbor are very different domains, and the yachts that "contend" in stanza 1 do so with one another and not directly with the "ungoverned ocean." Here, the yachts seem fragile and face outside the harbor an inimical force that "sinks them pitilessly." Their implied delicacy of construction is confirmed when the yachts are described as "Mothlike in mists" and "scintillant in the minute brilliance of cloudless days"—a phrase that gives the entire scene the shimmer of a pointillist painting. "Ant-like," the insignificant crew serves the yacht, "grooming" it like a queen insect, even while the yacht tacks to windward. The race marker—presumably the starting line buoy—is upwind from this regal object. Since boats cannot sail directly into the wind, motion toward the mark is accomplished with a technique called tacking. The boat sails at an angle into the wind, leaning away from it, and then is turned onto another tack, leaning the opposite way; it repeats this zigzagging until the goal upwind has been reached.

More of the scene comes into view in stanza 5. The eye now takes in the smaller craft, which, rather like the crew, are fawning admirers of the great craft. Invested with youth, beauty, and freedom, the yachts are personified and idealized. Stanza 9 marks a shift in the quality of the scene's imagery and changes the relation of the yachts, the human figures, and the sea. Now, the waves, rather than the yacht, are fully personified, described as broken beings whose arms and hands seem oddly distinct and whose bodies are cut by the sharp bow of the yachts. Grotesque images of contorted faces on corpses awash in the waves coupled with sounds of desperate cries seem borrowed from the inferno of Dante's damned or the paintings of purgatory by Hieronymus Bosch. The yachts have become powerful and indifferent.

Forms and Devices

"The Yachts" is composed in terza rima, a series of three-line stanzas that was used by Dante in the fourteenth century as the stanza form of the *The Divine Comedy* (c. 1320), and by the English Romantic poet Percy Bysshe Shelley in "Ode to the West Wind." In a fully realized terza rima, the three-line stanzas are in iambic pentameter rhythm and are linked by a complex overlapping rhyme scheme: *aba, bcb, cdc,* and similar patterns. Williams gestures toward this pattern of rhyme by making the first four lines conform to it. The rhyme is soon abandoned, however, with the loose rhythm of blank unrhymed verse used throughout the rest of the poem. Aside from making "The Yachts" unusual—Williams rarely borrowed traditional poetic forms— the terza rima recalls the theme of creation and destruction in the Dante and Shelley poems. Still, the lapsed interlace rhyme and Williams's use of blank verse mark the poem's origin in the twentieth century, and the reader might expect that the handling of its themes will similarly reflect a modern sensibility.

The relation between the sentence units and the individual lines and stanzas in "The Yachts" shows the strain Williams places on the traditional terza rima form. Lines and stanzas in the poem do not usually end with one of the natural breaks within the sentences. The first sentence ends partway through the second stanza, and within the sentence the phrases "blows of an ungoverned ocean" and "the best man knows to pit" are broken over two lines. This technique, enjambment, can be used to draw attention to the words at the line ends. In "The Yachts," however, it mainly works in company with the many asides in the sentences to give the first six stanzas of "The Yachts" some of the improvised quality of speech. As a result, the image of the boats, not the poetic medium, is the center of the reader's attention.

Short, terse sentences mark a shift in tone in the last line of stanza 7, at which point the race starts. Even expressions not formally set off as sentences—"they slip through . . . they take in canvas"—are independent. Stanza 9, in which the violent images are dominant, consists of sharply drawn lines, each a complete unit of meaning and perception. As the "horror of the race dawns" (perhaps the human race), the tidily punctuated images of action are replaced by the distortion and wandering focus of nightmare. Phrase is piled on phrase as the poem slows in the final three lines.

Williams was an exponent of poetic theories—first of Imagism and later Objectivism—that advocated the use of simple language to create clear, compressed images of objects. Poetic language was to be renewed by avoiding abstract or sentimental language, conventional poetic devices, and the insistent presence of the poet's views in the poem. The yachts and their setting are described with precision; images, not commentary, are the basis of this poem. Yet, the language is occasionally sophisticated— "scintillant" and "sycophant," for example—and abstract: "all that is fleckless, free and naturally to be desired." Moreover, the human qualities of the yachts and the sea can be read as the projections of the poet's own mood into these objects, giving him a tangible presence in the poem. Despite the poem's success with his readers, therefore, Williams himself thought that "The Yachts" was consciously "imitative" and worried that he had forgotten to make the poem's language and form characteristically American.

Themes and Meanings

"The Yachts" is about the conflict between that which has form and that which lies outside it. Looking at the yachts, the poet takes note of both their beauty and their apparent indifference to the forces whirling about them. Williams makes so much of the grace of their hulls and their tall rigs that they seem works of art immune to time and the violence of human life. As John Keats shows in "Ode on a Grecian Urn," art seems not to be subject to cycles of creation and destruction. As art, Keats's urn has a special sort of permanence. The danger exists, however, of forgetting that the very beauty of art that sets it apart from life's formlessness and uncertainty is an impossible ideal. Thus, the yachts in Williams's poem that escape the grasping hands of time and change also sail over the cries of pain.

Form and structure are not merely characteristic of works of art. Social and economic institutions also serve as structures, order and define the roles that people will perform, and allocate power. The strong identification between the yachts and the industrialists who, in Williams's time, were the fairest bloom of capitalism suggests that the form and disorder represented by the yachts and the sea have social significance. Like monopolies and trusts protected from the "ungoverned" world of real free enterprise, the yachts sail serenely and seem to bear testimony to all that is attractive in capitalism—the products of its industry and the lives of the wealthy class. The outward beauty of the yachts, however, is akin to the illusion constructed by F. Scott Fitzgerald's hero in *The Great Gatsby* (1925), whose fine manners and largesse did not come without a price, for the social structures of capitalism demand competition between classes. As the race starts between the poetic symbols of American enterprise, their blindness to the world below them is conveyed in the violent images and accelerated phrases of the final stanzas. The powers of industry "pass over" in an ironic echo of the Old Testament angels who deign to save a select few in their flight over biblical Egypt. Upton Sinclair's novel *The Jungle* (1906) portrays in more realistic terms the sea of jobless men and women from which Chicago's bosses rescue a fortunate few.

The poem finally makes the struggle between form and disorder fundamental to all human experience. "The Yachts" also insists that the mutual definition of form and disorder or of object and ground is not stable. For while the image of the yacht holds the reader's attention in the first part of the poem, it is the disorder of the sea that does so as the poem closes.

Peter Lapp

YELLOW LIGHT

Author: Garrett Kaoru Hongo (1951-   )
Type of poem: Narrative
First published: 1980; collected in *Yellow Light*, 1982

The Poem

Garrett Kaoru Hongo's "Yellow Light" is unrhymed free verse of five unequal stanzas, the longest one opening the poem and the shortest one closing it. The tone of the poem is conversational; its syntax, diction, rhythms, and lilt are those of contemporary conventional speech.

On its surface, "Yellow Light" is at once a poem about a community that is specifically identified and about an individual, who is not specifically identified. Its setting is inner-city Los Angeles, a "J-Town" barrio a few blocks from the intersection of Olympic Boulevard and Figueroa Street. This is a struggling, racially mixed, working-class neighborhood whose social and economic anxieties, it is evident, erupt regularly in domestic abuse and street brawls. The poem, both wistfully and indignantly, describes the tawdry setting in sensory detail. This is a busy, crowded, and volatile environment where Japanese, Koreans, Hawaiians, and Chicanos exist in close proximity and not always harmoniously.

The poem's bare narrative focuses on a female adult's homeward trek at the end of a tiring day's work. The reader is given no personal information about the woman, but one determines in the course of the poem that she is either poor or frugal (perhaps both), that her job is probably office work or sales (she wears high heels), and that she lives on the second floor of an apartment building. It is dusk; she gets off the bus and walks uphill three blocks to her home. She is carrying ingredients for the evening's supper: spinach, fish, bread. She passes "gangs of schoolboys playing war" and angry "young couples . . . yelling at kids." Reaching her home, she walks up two flights of steps and fishes her keys out of her messy purse, poised to unlock her door. The narrative leaves her at this point, turning attention toward the moon for the poem's final few lines.

A fourth-generation Japanese American, Hongo was born in Volcano, Hawaii, which his family left when he was six months old, settling in a small city south of Los Angeles called Gardena. At that time, Gardena boasted the largest community of Japanese Americans on mainland United States, though it was bordered on the north by the predominantly African American towns of Watts and Compton and on the southwest by Torrance and Redondo Beach, white towns.

Growing up in a working-class neighborhood with a variety of ethnic groups sensitized Hongo early to issues of race relations, cultural alienation, and urban street life, themes that figure prominently in many of his poems, including "Yellow Light." He knows intimately the environment through which his female heroine makes her way: its disputes, its loneliness, and its frustrations. There seems little comfort here to be gleaned from community or family; the only note of guarded optimism is the image of the full moon that ends the poem.

Forms and Devices

The name Hongo means "homeland," and in ways either subtle or overt, Hongo's poetry is intimately tied up with his ethnicity. At the same time that his poetry is written in honor and in memory of his Japanese ancestors, it exhibits full awareness of the assimilation necessary for Asian Americans to live in the United States. Assimilation is taken to a higher level in "Yellow Light" as Japanese must not only acclimatize to American culture but also live side by side with Hawaiians, Koreans, and Chicanos in a true melting pot. The idea of the melting pot is emphasized by Hongo's decision to set the poem at suppertime, when apartments are "just starting to steam with cooking."

The apartments may be steaming with cooking, but the neighborhood is steaming with racial unrest. The fights broadcast from loud televisions and the adults yelling at their children signal the conflict, both domestically and socially, that plagues this working-class community. Hongo's concrete imagery gives the anger and the hostility a sharp edge. The bus from which the woman departs is "hissing," the schoolboys she passes are "playing war," the televisions are not being turned on but "flick[ed]" on.

After the initial paragraph, which sets the volatile mood, Hongo pauses for wistful reflection of a past season, presumably a more peaceful time. "If it were May. . . . ," stanza 2 begins, then late spring flowers would be blooming, despite the smog; the monkey flowers obscuring the trash would be "tangled in chain-link fences" and buzzing with butterflies, mosquitoes, and moths. It was a more idyllic, even carefree time.

The poem, however, is set in October, at the tail end of a hot summer, the end of a long day, when the city is not blooming with fresh possibility but is "seeth[ing] like a billboard" and patience wears thin. Hongo's sharp, concrete images sharply delineate the tensions between ethnic cultures despite their forced proximity. The sharpness extends to the woman in the poem, whose spike heels click "like kitchen knives" as she ascends the stairs.

Hongo's sharp imagery is reinforced by his clear and conventional grammar. There is no evocative, elusive poetic language or diction here, but rather clear-headed declarative sentences, some long and complex, others shorter. There are no sentence fragments. The first, fourth, and fifth stanzas are composed of a single sentence; the second and third stanzas have three sentences each. The well-crafted, complete sentences glide along seamlessly and rhythmically, some with initial modifying clauses, others beginning right off with the subject.

Themes and Meanings

Hongo's earliest volume of collected poems, *Yellow Light* was extremely well received. The collection earned Hongo the Discovery/*The Nation* award and a National Endowment for the Arts Fellowship in 1982. The title poem, "Yellow Light," as the lead poem in the collection, is indicative of the quality and concerns of the remaining twenty poems in its precision, its detail, its emphasis on ethnicity and assimilation, on tensions that humanity wreaks versus the peace and harmony that nature can bestow.

In addition to ethnic disharmony, a rift in economic classes is implied in the poem, subtly but importantly. Although there are hints that the woman and her community are not well-off financially, their poverty does not really come into play until the middle of the poem, when the barrio is contrasted with the parts of the city that are some distance away, geographically and economically. The woman's community houses used car lots and side streets from which greasy yellow kitchen lights emanate. Other, "better" parts of Los Angeles, "whole freeways away," have movie houses from which "long silver sticks of light probe the sky." The "fluorescence" of these wealthier sections of the city is "brilliant" in contrast to weaker lights in the woman's neighborhood. In fact, the glamour of the wealth there "makes war" with the dim kitchen bulbs in the barrio. There is no indication that the population in the moneyed neighborhoods is even aware of the woman's poor community, but lights from those entertainment complexes probing into their space remind the barrio of what they are deprived of and will never attain.

The reader is not informed whether the woman lives alone or with others. Tellingly, she must climb two flights of stairs to reach her apartment. This is important because it builds a trajectory of ascent, physical and psychological. As the woman steps up and up and is left poised to unlock the door to her home, the reader's mind keeps ascending, skyward to the moon. This is an optimistic gesture, one of faith and spirit in times of adversity—one looks to the heavens in prayer or supplication for deliverance.

The moon, embodiment of both the natural world and a higher power, is contrasted with the bitterness and pettiness of human struggle and divisiveness. The moon is "cruising," taking its own sweet, sublime time. It "covers everything"—the neighborhoods that have and the neighborhoods that have not—treating all alike in conferring its cosmic light. What it offers humankind in the final stanza is tantamount to a blessing that is substantial ("heavy") and that bends down to meet people in the place where they are (its light is like the "yellow onions" cooking in the barrio). Importantly, the moon as a symbol of nature connects with the remembered May flowers in stanza 2, which bring a natural order and harmony to the disorder, havoc, and decay that humanity generates ("smog" and "trash"). Thus, Hongo's poem implies a greater truth, one that transcends the individual and even the community and points significantly to the harmony that is the natural world.

Jill B. Gidmark

"YES" AND "NO"

Author: Yevgeny Yevtushenko (1933-   )
Type of poem: Dramatic monologue
First published: 1965, as " 'Da' i 'net' "; English translation collected in *The New Russian Poets, 1953-1968*, 1968

The Poem

Like many of Yevgeny Yevtushenko's poems, "'Yes' and 'No'" is a kind of dramatic monologue. The poem is subtitled "From the Verses about Love," and it can be seen also as a lyric poem. Its eighty-two lines are all in one uninterrupted stanza, lined up in a cascading fashion, a form that Yevtushenko inherited from Vladimir Mayakovsky.

" 'Yes' and 'No' " is about a dilemma in which the poet finds himself. He sees himself shuttling like a train for years between the two cities that he has named Yes and No. He is torn between these two cities, and his nerves are strained like the telegraph wires. He first describes the city of No as being loveless, resembling a room upholstered with anguish and full of scowling objects; the sofas are made of spurious material and the walls of misfortune. In such an environment, it is impossible to experience love, let alone get good counsel. Instead, all the persona finds is constant rejection (hence the name of the city). It is so depressing that when the lights are switched off, ghosts in the room dance a somber ballet. It is also extremely difficult to travel away from this "black city of 'No'."

In contrast, the city of Yes is like a bird's song; there are no walls, and the stars beg to make friends. Instead of rejection, acceptance and embrace are offered by lips begging to be kissed, or plucked, as the poet puts it. The herds offer their milk gratis, and there is no suspicion in anyone. Most important, freedom reigns supreme wherever, whenever, and however one wishes to go. Instead of a constant "no," in the city of Yes even the water whispers an alluring "yes-yes-yes."

Finally, the poet seems to tire of everything that is given to him on a platter, as it were, in the "multicolored,/ brightly lit/ city of 'Yes'." Unable to appreciate things for which he does not exert himself, he concludes that it is better to shuttle between the two cities forever, even if it costs him heartache and strained nerves.

Forms and Devices

"'Yes' and 'No,'" even though it is written in one stanza, has four distinct parts. In the first, the poet presents himself as a person torn between two cities: the city of Yes and the city of No. In the second, the city of No is described in a few bold strokes. In the third, its opposite is described by means of several telling details. In the concluding part, the poet, being unable to choose between the two cities, returns to shuttling between them instead.

The main devices Yevtushenko uses in " 'Yes' and 'No' " are allegory, metaphor, and images. There are two possible interpretations of the allegory. The subtitle "From the Verses about Love" leads one to assume that the poet is alluding to a love affair. The metaphor of a city of No fits the description of unrequited love. The constant rebuke the poet gets from the object of his love precludes any happiness, even a simple welcome. To emphasize the depth of his unhappiness, he paints everything in bleak images: The floors are polished with bile, and objects scowl at him. His plight is personified by ghosts dancing a somber ballet in a dark room.

To contrast this picture of gloom, the poet experiences exactly the opposite in the city of Yes—another metaphor. Here, presumably, his prospects of happiness are much brighter. Fittingly, they are enhanced by cheerful images. Life here is a song of a thrush, and the suffocating room of the city of No becomes an open, friendly nest, from which, figuratively, any train, plane, or ship can take him to even wider horizons as soon as he wishes. The multicolored, brightly lit city of Yes reflects the cornucopia of bliss, in contrast to the restricting walls of misfortune of the city of No. At the end, however, even such unrestricted bliss is too much for the poet, and he wishes to return to the constant tension of strained nerves.

Another possible allegory lies in the area of politics. The metaphors of the two cities in " 'Yes' and 'No' " may allegorically represent the two states between which the poet is forced to choose. The images in the city of No, in particular, conform to the conditions of daily life in Yevtushenko's country. A loveless city resembling a room upholstered with anguish, the parquet polished with bile, and silently scowling objects are some of the images that clearly reflect conditions in the poet's Russian homeland. The inability to travel abroad, particularly, points out the restrictions placed on people, especially on freedom-loving individuals like the poet. On the other hand, the images depicting life in the city of Yes correspond to the life of freedom: no walls, the sky brightly lit by stars, lips that offer themselves, milk flowing in the streets, no suspicion anywhere, and unrestricted freedom to travel. With such distinct images, the poet delineates the two worlds in which the allegory is placed.

Themes and Meanings

Thematically, " 'Yes' and 'No' " is a relatively simple poem, with two main themes already hinted at in the preceding discussion of the poem as an allegory.

The first of these is the age-old theme of love between a man and a woman. Considering the fact that Yevtushenko has written many poems concerning this human emotion, love as a primary theme in this poem imposes itself. It is interesting that the lover (most likely a man, although it is not explicit, and does not need to be) does not even mention the object of his love, let alone describe her. He is more concerned about where his love either languishes (in the city of No) or triumphs (in the city of Yes). It is as though both he and his lover are victims of invisible external forces and restrictions that have been imposed upon them. These restricting forces compel the woman to behave like a robot, giving the same negative answer again and again. Thus the rejected lover places all the blame on the circumstances.

For a time, he seems to be compensated in the city of Yes, where everything is the opposite. Yet even though he thinks he has satisfied his emotional needs with other women, instead of enjoying the bliss of the plenty, he returns to the site of his defeat, only to move to easier conquests in the city of Yes when he is rejected again. It is as though he has become a prisoner of his own feelings, unable to extricate himself, resigning himself willingly and knowingly to the indefinite rejection in the belief that what is gained without pain and strain is not worth having.

It is here that the other theme, the striving of an individual for freedom and dignity, offers itself. It should be kept in mind that Yevtushenko has always been a man of politics, not merely a man of letters; for that very reason, every work of his allows at least the possibility of a dual interpretation. Throughout his career he has been locked in a duel with the powers that be. It is therefore conceivable that he is using Aesopian language and allegory to pretend to write about love while in fact the city of No is the portrait of the state in which he has to live, and the city of Yes is the Arcadia of all his dreams, wishes, and hopes. When he has a chance to partake of the delights of the city of Yes, however, he tires of them quickly, undoubtedly remembering that the city of No is his own city, after all, and that it is there that he should work to create conditions like those in the city of Yes. Once again, he becomes a prisoner of his own noble feelings as he resigns himself to a constant shuttling between the two worlds. These two worlds can easily be seen as the East and the West, and Yevtushenko's oscillation between them as his desire to reside in both worlds with equal right and goodwill.

Vasa D. Mihailovich

YET DO I MARVEL

Author: Countée Cullen (1903-1946)
Type of poem: Sonnet
First published: 1925, in *Color*

The Poem

Like all true sonnets, "Yet Do I Marvel" is a fourteen-line poem written in iambic pentameter. Its seven rhymes are arranged in two quatrains, *abab* and *cdcd*, and one sestet, *eeffgg*. The two quatrains not only use a similar metrical pattern but also form a single grammatical unit, in which the poet makes several observations and poses his problem. In the sestet, the poet draws a general conclusion from these observations. The final couplet of the poem offers a dramatic, personal turn, in which the poet transforms this general observation into a statement about his own position in the world. The title, taken from the thirteenth line of the poem, reflects the theme of wonder and amazement around which the poem moves.

The poem is a first-person monologue in which a black poet, indistinguishable from Countée Cullen, voices doubt and confusion about the world, about the relationship between God and man, and about this particular poet's place in the world. No audience is addressed directly.

The poet begins by professing his belief in a God who is all-good, good-intentioned and almighty. He also affirms that God has reasons for everything that happens in the world, even if these reasons are often difficult for humans to understand. In particular, the poet wonders why such an all-good Supreme Being could allow things like physical disabilities and death.

In the two quatrains, the poet observes several examples of worldly imperfection. He mentions the blindness of the mole and the mortality of human flesh. He also refers to the never-ending punishments of two figures from Greek mythology: Tantalus, plagued by hunger and thirst but prevented from reaching food and drink; and Sisyphus, faced with the impossible task of rolling up a hill a rock that continuously slips back to the starting point before the task is finished.

In the sestet, the poet wonders whether there is any way to explain the blindness of the mole, the punishments of Tantalus and Sisyphus, or the deaths of human beings, and decides that only God has a satisfactory explanation for these worldly imperfections. The ways of God are beyond understanding, and human beings are too distracted by the everyday cares of life to see reason behind the mighty hands of God.

The poet does not mention that he is black until the final couplet. The "I" at the beginning of the poem is an anonymous human. At the end of the poem, this "I" proudly reveals himself to be not only a poet, but a black poet. This revelation transforms the poem from a general comment upon the human experience to personal reflection. Of all the incomprehensible actions of God, the most amazing for the poet to understand is that God made him both a poet and black.

Forms and Devices

The language of this sonnet is highly polished. The meter, iambic pentameter, offers a steady rhythm, which reiterates the poet's own fixed belief in God. The end rhyming couplets create a list of significant words that resonate throughout the poem. In the first quatrain, the pairs contrast the nature of God and the plight of humankind ("kind" versus "blind"), and echo the poem's essential question ("why" and "die"). Later in the poem, "immune" and "strewn" also contrast the conditions of God and human. The role of Tantalus and Sisyphus in the poem is also emphasized by their coupling in rhyme.

An important literary device in the poem is the catalog, or list, which Cullen employs in the first line to describe three qualities of God ("good, well-meaning, kind"). Lists also appear throughout the two quatrains, in which the poet not only offers a list of God's mysteries—including the mole's blindness, the mortality of humans, and the punishments of Tantalus and Sisyphus—but also uses a string of synonyms ("could tell," "make plain," and "declare") to affirm God's ability to provide explanations for these mysteries.

Anthropomorphism is a dominant feature of this poem. Tantalus's fruit is associated with human characteristics through words like "fickle" and "baits." God's humanity is also very strong. Cullen's Supreme Being is not only identified with traditional masculine personal pronouns and adjectives like "He" and "His," but also said to "stoop" and to have a brain and a hand.

Two important areas of allusion in the poem are classical mythology and the Bible. The mythological references center around Sisyphus and Tantalus, two great sinners of ancient Greece. In the poem, Cullen ignores ancient accounts of the crimes of Tantalus, who tried to outwit the gods by feeding them the flesh of his own son, and Sisyphus, who tried to escape death. Instead, Cullen presents their eternal punishments in the afterlife as essentially inexplicable. Humankind simply does not possess sufficient perspective to understand why Sisyphus must eternally roll that rock up the hill, or why Tantalus must forever thirst. In this way, both sinners become symbols of the pathos, the meaningless suffering, of the human condition.

Cullen's biblical allusion turns especially on the book of Genesis, in which Adam, the first man, is made in the image and likeness of God. In the Judeo-Christian tradition, this divine element in humans is a source of hope and even a promise of life after death. For Cullen, however, the divine image of God within mortals is also another example of the frustrating plight of human existence. Although made in God's image, the human body must die. Irony, an intense sense of contradiction, thus pervades the poem. Although their human flesh is godlike, Tantalus and Sisyphus experience incomprehensible suffering, and their condition reflects the ironic condition of every mortal, poised between God and death.

Themes and Meanings

The strong mood of religious reflection in "Yet Do I Marvel" stems in large part from the central position of the Christian church in the culture of African Americans.

Intensity of religious fervor and a vivid sense of divine anthropomorphism are common themes in the poetry of black American poets.

A second important theme for Cullen is his race. Blackness is a focal point of the poem. It is the last of a series of imponderables of the human condition. On the one hand, the poet's black skin is included in the same category as the blindness of the mole or the punishments of Tantalus and Sisyphus. It is another example of the mysterious ways of a God who inexplicably made humans of different skin color. On the other hand, the blackness of the poet is a source of pride, a gift of that almighty Creator whose ways are always right. Thus, Cullen, a poet of the Harlem Renaissance in the early part of the twentieth century, was asserting the beauty of black skin long before the Civil Rights movement made black pride more widespread later in the century.

At the same time, Cullen's experience as a black man is set in the context of his role as a poet. He is a poet made black, not a black man made a poet. Like his black skin, Cullen's poetic talent is a mysterious source of both pain and joy. This poet who fashions a highly polished poem filled with sophisticated allusion is, at the same time, a member of an oppressed race often denied the opportunity to acquire such erudition and poetic skill.

Indeed, Cullen emphasizes the involuntary nature of his poetry. He did not choose to be a poet any more than he chose to be black. It was God who made him both. It is God who commands him to sing. The poet cannot help himself any more than he could change the color of his skin. The source of his poetic power is divine and lies outside him. While some poets locate this source in nature or in the personal subconscious, Cullen attributes this power to the Supreme Being who dominates this poem. Cullen's insistence upon the divine inspiration of the poet is appropriate in a poem that combines themes from classical and biblical sources, for both traditions affirm the ability of supernatural beings to speak through humans. The Greeks called these deities of inspiration Muses, while the biblical God inspires prophets with warnings for humans.

Thomas J. Sienkewicz

YOU, ANDREW MARVELL

Author: Archibald MacLeish (1892-1982)
Type of poem: Meditation
First published: 1930, in *New Found Land: Fourteen Poems*

The Poem

"You, Andrew Marvell" is a short, meditative poem in nine four-line stanzas, with a simple rhyme scheme. The title refers to a seventeenth century poet, one of whose best-known poems is a *carpe diem* lyric entitled "To His Coy Mistress." *Carpe diem* means "seize the day" in Latin, and in a *carpe diem* poem the poet (or speaker) reminds his audience (usually either a lover or the reader himself) of life's brevity and the prospect of inevitable, impending death, as he urges his audience to "seize the day" and make the most of what life and its pleasures still afford. Andrew Marvell's "To His Coy Mistress" invokes images of death and decay and of "Time's wingèd chariot hurrying near" as the speaker attempts to convince his beloved to be more receptive to his advances. Strictly speaking, "You, Andrew Marvell" is not a *carpe diem* poem, because it does not explicitly urge one to act or to reflect on one's own life's short span, but Archibald MacLeish's choice of title is a deliberate suggestion of the *carpe diem* genre.

The speaker, who is not distinguished from the poet, identifies himself at the poem's opening as lying "face down beneath the sun" at noon, though he does not specify a geographical location. He describes how he can "feel the always coming on/ The always rising of the night," literally, the dark shadow of nightfall moving slowly across the earth from east to west.

The speaker then moves, in imagination, from his own location to the other side of the globe, to the "curving east," where at noontime in the speaker's own land night is falling. He describes the darkness of night spreading across places such as Persia, Baghdad, Arabia, Lebanon, and Crete. He imagines the details of the landscape—trees, mountains, and rivers—fading from view in the darkness of night. He envisions the shadow of evening moving westward over Spain and Africa and, finally, across the sea. By the final stanza, he has returned to his own starting point, the place where he is still "face downward in the sun," and the poem ends almost like the closing of a circle as the final stanza echoes the first.

Forms and Devices

"You, Andrew Marvell" has virtually no punctuation. The poet sets off his point of departure (in the first stanza, in which he describes his prone position) from the rest of the poem with a colon; thenceforth the description of night falling across the earth flows in an unbroken stream of images. In this way the structure helps evoke a sense of the constant, inexorable approach of the night. In the final stanza, another colon sets the long description of nightfall apart from the poet's own noontime location as he returns to his point of departure.

The poem is rich with images that not only create a vivid landscape of evening, but also suggest level of meaning beneath the poem's surface. The visual images alternate in perspective as the poet moves back and forth between minute details and sweeping overviews of the landscape. In the third stanza, for example, he describes how in Ecbatan "the trees take leaf by leaf the evening," then abruptly pulls back to describe the darkness flooding over an entire mountain range in Persia. In other stanzas, the poet shifts from a lone bridge in Baghdad to the entire land of Arabia, and from a street in Palmyra to the huge vista of all of Lebanon and Crete. This shifting of perspective gives a sense of the all-pervasiveness of nightfall, which does not miss even one leaf of a tree, as well as a sense of its vast scope as it closes over entire continents.

MacLeish peppers "You, Andrew Marvell" with images of death. A vague suggestion of death is connected with the rising of the night through the connotations of "the earthly chill of dusk and slow," a suggestion that is strengthened by later images of empty gates, withered grass, and ruined stone. The whole landscape seems to drown in the "flooding dark" that rises over trees, mountains, and continents like a relentless tide. Some of the hints of death are so subtle as to be almost imperceptible and may depend on the reader's own associations. Some readers may find that the "ever-climbing shadow" that creeps up the "under-lands" is reminiscent of the "valley of the shadow of death" in the Twenty-third Psalm; others may believe it connotes the poetic sense of a shadow as a ghost.

Even the few references to a human presence have a vaguely deathly quality in that they suggest a bygone era, rather than a modern one. "The wheel rut in the ruined stone" in Palmyra's street is certainly an image of an ancient city. Ships glimpsed in the twilight show "sails above the shadowy hulls"; perhaps modern sailboats, but within the context appearing as symbols of an older way of life. Scattered travelers hurrying through a mountain pass, a disappearing bridge across a silent river, and an empty gate overgrown with withered grass suggest, not a vital, modern society, but a civilization from the past.

The places themselves support this sense of an ancient land in decline. All the cities and countries mentioned are places that at one time were homes to advanced ancient civilizations which have disappeared or gone into decline. The once-thriving lands the poet envisioned are now in a kind of civilizational as well as literal twilight.

Themes and Meanings

"You, Andrew Marvell" is about the passage of time and its attendant decline and death. The poem operates on several levels. The immediate surface of the poem describes the passage of time in a literal, limited sense: the end of another day and the beginning of another night. By stressing the constant, irresistible approach of night ("the always coming on/ The always rising of the night"), the poet removes his reflections on the night from the realm of the literal. In the real world, night is followed by morning; if night is a kind of figurative ending, each new dawn is a new beginning. In this poem, however, the approach of night eclipses all sense of day, all ideas of new beginnings. Even at noon, the brightest part of the day, the poet is keenly aware of the night, far away on the other side of the earth, swiftly stealing toward him like a dark flood.

Though the poet does not explicitly link the rising of the night with individual human aging and death, the poem reverberates with suggestions of death. The analogy of a human life as a single day is a common one in literature, from the riddle which compares man to a creature that walks on four legs in the morning (crawling in infancy), two legs at noon (walking upright in adulthood), and three legs in the evening (walking with a cane in old age), to Dylan Thomas's well-known poem about death, "Do Not Go Gentle into That Good Night" ("Old age should burn and rave at close of day;/ Rage, rage against the dying of the light"). In MacLeish's poem, the titular reference to Andrew Marvell and, by association, the suggestion of Marvell's famous *carpe diem* lyric, are in themselves enough to spur the reader who is familiar with Marvell's poem to make the connection between MacLeish's "ever climbing shadow" and death, but images such as the withered grass and the ruined stone amply reinforce the inference.

References to the homes of dead civilizations widen the suggestion of death from the individual to society or to the whole world. As night falls, so people age and die; so, too, do societies decline and fall. The poet's vision of the darkness rising over the whole earth places his analogy of night in the widest possible context: As he describes himself "upon earth's noonward height (literally the point of the globe closest to the sun) and envisions the "curving east," the reader can picture the earth as a globe, spinning inexorably away from the sun into darkness. As the "flooding dark" rises to swallow up mountains and oceans, the reader may even be reminded of Noah's flood and thus make a poetic leap of imagination from night to individual death, to the fall of civilizations, to, finally, the end of the world.

Catherine Swanson

YOU ARE IN BEAR COUNTRY

Author: Maxine Kumin (1925-   )
Type of poem: Satire
First published: 1982; collected in *The Long Approach*, 1985

The Poem

"You Are in Bear Country" is a poem of seventy-three lines parodying a bureaucratic guidebook with futile warnings about bear attacks, which, for some reason, seem much more frightening to people than the threat of mass human violence such as nuclear annihilation. Maxine Kumin is a teacher, wife, mother, and author residing in Newton, Massachusetts; a collection of her poems, *Up Country: Poems of New England* (1973), won a Pulitzer Prize. Whether writing in verse or in prose, Kumin strives for the precise image, a lucidity of insight, and an economy of language.

The epigraph of "You Are in Bear Country" sums up the humorous content of the first sixty-five lines, which provide a satirical exemplum for the poem's concluding message; according to the epigraph, it is "advice from a pamphlet published by the Canadian Minister of the Environment."

What follows is a tongue-in-cheek parody of the Canadian pamphlet's directives to avoid contact with bears, even to the point of stifling the sound of one's own whistling, which it claims is too much like the siren sounds of bears mating. The implicit advice may be, ironically, to steer clear of joy and beauty springing from an unguarded immersion in nature.

The next verse paragraph continues the nonsensical advice and makes the vaguest of distinctions between grizzly and black bears—so vague, in fact, that it renders the advice useless and makes the bureaucratic speaker a fool. The third and fourth verse paragraphs express ironically the culminating stupidity of bureaucratic advice about ensuring one's safety around bears. Nothing ultimately guarantees safety: Running away does not work; climbing a tree will not help; playing dead might not protect one against mauling or worse.

The final stanza is the poem's reductio ad absurdum—the climactic absurdity of the previous catalog of tidy and futile advice. It is a moral commentary on the absurd fears of human beings. Death in nature is far less of a threat than death by human inventions that by the early 1980's (when this poem was published) had created a nuclear capability of killing every man, woman, and child on Earth.

Forms and Devices

"You Are in Bear Country" is a satire with four verse paragraphs that waver between irregular iambic meter and free verse. The use of curt, staccato lines with insistent end rhymes (many of which are feminine, or weak, rhymes) and approximate end rhymes (the repeated final sounds being inexact but musically close) are reminiscent of the Renaissance satiric techniques of John Skelton, whose "Skeltonic line" capitalizes on short iambic beats and on insistent ingenious rhyming for comic effect. Like Skelton, Kumin uses a cascading catalog of absurdities in this poem to drive home the overwhelming absurdity of humanity's creation of nuclear weaponry capable of humanity's destruction.

There is a severe economy of language. The diction ranges from the simplicity of "your clatter" to the scientific bureaucratese of "a small *horribilis*/ is difficult to distinguish/ from a large *americanus*" to the final eloquence of "Cherish/ your wilderness." By omitting the word "the" before any use of the word "bear," Kumin interjects the humor of primitive childlike intimacy into the vapid voice of the bureaucratic speaker ("bear may not hear your clatter," "Bear can outrun a racehorse"). The delicious irony of this linguistic anomaly is that the bureaucrat is warning against making the primitive contact with nature that is captured in his own childlike expressions of familiarity with "bear."

The poem is a satire, a literary form ridiculing human vice and folly for the sake of providing humanity with moral instruction. Crucial to this poem's success is the pervasive use of irony in having the bureaucratic speaker make a series of stupid statements when, in fact, the opposite is true. Contact with nature, however dangerous, is a much safer option than confrontation with artificial implements of violence and annihilation.

Themes and Meanings

"You Are in Bear Country" is about the absurdity of humanity's primal fears of nature's dangers, such as bear attacks, when these fears are contrasted with humanity's nonchalance about the threat of violence and annihilation in the nuclear age.

The bureaucrat intent on offering guidelines that promise safety shows only an inability to set forth definite or effective advice to keep readers out of trouble. This vapid civil servant may be a model for the kind of inept government bureaucrat in charge of supervising a country's nuclear arsenal and, therefore, in charge of the preservation of the human race. The thought is not comforting.

What Kumin ultimately demonstrates is the extent of human ignorance about threats to human survival. She also demonstrates the grave limitations in the ability to ensure and promote human survival. Her tongue-in-cheek parody of a bureaucrat's futile warnings becomes, in the end, bitter gallows humor of terrifying seriousness.

Thomas M. Curley

YOU, WALKING PAST ME

Author: Marina Tsvetayeva (1892-1941)
Type of poem: Lyric
First published: 1976, as "Vy, idushchiye mimo menya," in *Neizdannye: Stikhi, teatr, proza*; English translation collected in *Three Russian Women Poets*, 1983

The Poem

Marina Tsvetayeva's "You, walking past me," written in 1913 but unpublished until 1976, is a short lyric poem of sixteen lines divided into four stanzas. Like many of the poems written during Tsvetayeva's twenties, it evokes a mood of loneliness and estrangement from the world. The title of the poem, which is also its first line, addresses a stranger who is to remain largely unaware of the narrator's state of mind. This indifferent crossing of paths sets the tone for the rest of the poem.

The first-person narrator speaks directly to an unidentified "You," a device that Tsvetayeva uses in many of her poems. The second-person pronoun refers to a stranger walking past the narrator, but it could also easily refer to the reader. This identification of the reader with the stranger through the word "you," which is sustained throughout the poem, gives it a special appeal, making the reader aware of his or her immutable estrangement from the poet's condition. Like the stranger who remains untouched by the pain and loss that the narrator has experienced, the reader, although reading about this experience, will never really know the poet's anguish.

The stranger who walks *past* the narrator—not toward her—merely passes through her orbit, blind to a life that has expended itself on nothing, just as he is unaware of her "dubious witchcraft." There is an unnamed energy and intensity in her thoughts that perhaps the passerby completely misses.

In the second stanza, the "heroic passion" arouses a tone of regret as the narrator recalls a passion that has been spent in casual movements, chance encounters. Having burnt away, this life, lived so intensely, has left her with an "incinerated" heart.

The stranger who has been the addressee of the first two stanzas disappears from the narrator's orbit of perception as her attention turns to the train flying away into the darkness. The train carries away "the sleep at the station," perhaps by waking passengers asleep at the station with its noise, or by carrying away sleeping passengers. Like the stranger, the train is in the position of the indifferent interlocutor, a fleeting presence that is incapable of gaining any knowledge about the narrator. These two images—of the passing stranger and the speeding train—seem to encompass a certain element of urban life that many people have experienced: brief encounters and ephemereal moments when one is keenly aware of one's estrangement from those who are so physically close.

The wish expressed in the first stanza—"if you only knew"—is rearticulated in the last two lines of the third. This time, however, it is directed toward the train, and the narrator adds that even if her interlocutor "knew" something about her, he would not be able to comprehend exactly her true situation. There is, thus, at once a desire to invoke the other's curiosity and draw attention to the self, and a resignation to the fact of the other's limitations.

With this statement, which links the third stanza with the fourth, the reader realizes that the poet is making a distinction between knowing and experiencing. Although one can approach and gain knowledge about the other, one will remain ultimately cut off from her or his innermost experiences. The stranger will never know what causes the narrator's speech to be abrupt or why there is so much "menacing" pain within her.

Forms and Devices

Tsvetayeva is known for her unique use of imagery. In this poem, the images are, if not unusual, certainly crucial to the meaning of the poem. It is through images and metaphors, rather than verbs, that the poem achieves a progression of meaning. It is possible to isolate two groups of images, both of which are built around certain types of contrasts. The first group evokes sensations of the heating and cooling of passion, as well as a contrast between light and dark: images, that is, of fire, ash, incineration, smoke, and the dark night. The second group is constructed around the contrast between movement and stasis: a passerby, a train, a rustle, the movement of the smoke, and sleep.

The image of fire adds to the mystique of the narrator's "dubious witchcraft" in the first stanza. The sorcery of the female narrator, although enigmatic, is, like the metaphor of the fire that represents it, a "wasted" energy. Images of intense energy continue into the second stanza, where the narrator tells us of her "heroic passion." The fire that was introduced in the first stanza now turns to cool ash as it is transformed into the "incinerated" heart of the narrator. In the third stanza, heat has been replaced by the cool of the night, although the presence of the speeding train does something to disturb that cool stillness. In the final stanza, the fire and the ash have eventually given way to smoke: The smoke rising from the narrator's cigarettes curls like the light-colored hair on her head, but fills the inside of her head with dark pain. These contrasts between outside and inside, dark and light, tie together other contrasting images and ideas, such as those of fire and the night, heroic passion and ravishing charms, on the one hand, and a life full of "nothing" on the other.

The second group of contrasting metaphors originates in the movement of the stranger walking past the narrator. The words "walking past" in the first line of the poem seem to suggest a contrast between the movement of the passerby and the stasis of the narrator. The "chance shadow" and the "rustle" in the next stanza stir up memories of past affairs that have stopped, like the heart, on "nothing." In the third stanza, the "train flying in the night" moves away from the "sleep" at the station, duplicating the earlier movement of the stranger away from the narrator, as well as his ignorance of the deep passion that marks her life. Finally, the "perpetual" movement of the cigarette smoke sharpens, through contrast, the "abrupt" endings of her speech.

Through thus adding layer upon layer of sharp contrasting images, the poem arrives at a meaning caught amid these oppositions. The gap between the "you" and the "me" of the poem's title is given multiple representations through these various contrasting metaphors, moving the reader toward the suggestion that the meanings of the poem are to be found in the seams between these metaphorical edges.

Themes and Meanings

The pervasive theme of alienation that becomes apparent through the images and metaphors of the poem reminds the reader that this poem was written during the early twentieth century. The modernist angst—whether it is caused by urbanization and industrialization or by dehumanizing wars and political persecutions—is as present here as it is in the poetry of T. S. Eliot or Edward Thomas. The poet expresses a sentiment of estrangement from the world—even from her immediate surroundings. As in Eliot's poetry, in the twentieth century, the fires of passion seem wasted on casual encounters, leaving behind only ash and incineration.

Tsvetayeva's style is, however, much more personal than Eliot's. The expression of regret for a past spent too quickly and in a rush of intensity is not intended to encapsulate the meaning of an entire civilization or culture, but rather folds inward toward the particular situation of one woman's isolation. This is perhaps the poet's strength—that she is able to draw the reader inward into the workings of an individual female psyche to embrace specific sensations.

An awareness of evanescence is characteristic of the poet's vision. The link between the fleeting moment and the theme of alienation consists in the fact that chance encounters, being transitory, never seem to provide enough time or space for any tangible connections between human beings. Like the loss of the past, these brief contacts are fugitive events that disappear into the distance beyond the narrator's field of vision. Although romantic brushes are ephemeral, however, the anguish that remains in the heart seems to last, leaving behind a desire—or perhaps an affinity—for sleep, a temporary or permanent rest in the heart of ash.

The spells that the female narrator has cast in the past now leave those who cross her path unenchanted. Her seductive, bewitching charms, which were earlier realized in action, now seem to blow away with the smoke of her cigarette. The narrator remains alone with her "abrupt" speeches, her language cut short by the absence of communication. This is perhaps always at the heart of a poet's anguish—the fear that the poem will fail to touch the listener, that the poet's speech is empty of any communicable content.

In early twentieth century life, as addressed in Tsvetayeva's poem, there is a saturation of superficial knowledge without a concomitant experience of essences. The two interlocutors of the poem—the passerby and the train—epitomize the theme of alienation in their concrete but fleeting presence in the sphere of the narrator's experience. Like the stranger and the train, which rush away from the meaning of the narrator's existence without ever arriving at full comprehension, perhaps the position of the reader toward the poem (this or any other) will always be one of a motion toward and then away from it. The estrangement that the poet desires to express is something in which the reader, too, unwittingly participates.

Anu Aneja

YOU WERE WEARING

Author: Kenneth Koch (1925-   )
Type of poem: Lyric
First published: 1962, in *Thank You and Other Poems*

The Poem

"You Were Wearing" is a free-verse lyric poem consisting of thirteen long lines divided into two stanzas. Most of Kenneth Koch's lines appear to be two or three lines long on the page, but each one is considered a single poetic line. The title is taken from the first line of the poem: "You were wearing your Edgar Allan Poe printed cotton blouse." What follows is a series of scenes of family life and innocent adolescent flirtations between the speaker and a "cute" girl addressed in the poem as "you," with incongruous references to figures from American history and literature. These imply that the place of the poem is a resort, possibly in New England, the region of the United States that fostered both American revolutionary fervor and served as the cradle of American literature. However, the allusions are meant to be out of place and comic in their effect. To emphasize this, Koch's historical and literary references are often intentionally artificial and grammatically awkward, as in the last line of the first stanza: "And ran around in an attic, so that a little of the blue enamel was scraped off my George Washington, Father of His Country, shoes."

Though the poem does not pinpoint a specific setting, one cannot doubt that the characters appearing in the poem are all Americans, and the reader may well recognize the nationalism that celebrates all things American. This overly patriotic impulse is satirized by the poem, especially when it describes objects with unlikely adornments such as teacups "painted with pictures of Herman Melville" that depict scenes from his works. Yet such objects might well be found in tourist shops, and the American trait of making commodities out of all aspects of its culture—that is, finding ways to sell that which Americans hold dear—is likewise an object of Koch's satire.

The speaker is also a character in the poem, a young male who acts as a wry observer of this commodified world. Since his father wears a "Dick Tracy necktie" and his mother wears a "Strauss Waltzes comb" (the only non-American allusion), readers may surmise that his upbringing has been influenced both by his father's popular culture leanings and his mother's preference for European high culture. These influences, combined with the nationalistic fervor that pervades American life through the sale of these objects in the marketplace, convey a sense of the components of American culture: Comic strips and remnants of European influence commingle in a land in which respect of culture is conveyed through the surreal appearance of cultural icons on everyday objects.

Forms and Devices

Koch is most frequently associated with the New York School poets, which include Frank O'Hara, John Ashbery, and James Schuyler. They, like Koch, frequently write poems that mix high and low culture, employ surrealistic techniques (unusual or even impossible juxtapositions designed to mimic dream states rather than directly lived reality), and, especially in the case of O'Hara, utilize a kind of chatty poetic line that may not seem like poetry at all to readers more accustomed to metrically ordered lines. The New York School poets do not completely eliminate rhyme and meter, but they do want to free poets from the necessity of using these devices in every poem as a *sine qua non* without which a poem cannot exist.

The reason for this abandonment of the more formal qualities of poetry or even of traditional free verse (there is also very little in the way of metaphor or lyric imagery in this poem) is that the New York School poets want to write a more immediate kind of poetry, one that reflects modern American life and escapes the academic formalism of backward-looking poetic devices. (Koch's poem "Fresh Air" lampoons these contemporary conservative academic poets.) Koch is more interested in mimicking the odd juxtapositions the past creates for contemporary lives than he is in commenting upon the past itself.

Comedy is a technique used by all the New York School poets, and, in the final lines of the poem, the clash between historical allusion and contemporary utility becomes most farcical when the narrator and his girl sits on an "Abraham Lincoln" swing: "You sat on the eyes, mouth, and beard part, and I sat on the knees." From this vantage point, they see "a snowman holding a garbage can lid smashed into a likeness of the mad English king, George the Third." At first, this might strike the reader as departing from the American context until one remembers it was this king against whom the colonists staged their rebellion. That a trash can lid would resemble such a figure becomes an additional step in the transformation of the American locale: This is not a manufactured image painted or printed on an object but one that is imagined by the speaker of the poem as one might describe the shapes that clouds appear to resemble. Yet there is no distinction made in the poem between this imagined historical reference and the overt likenesses on blouses, neckties, and teacups elsewhere in the poem. This suggests that the inhabitants of this place—this American place—have come to perceive the world through eyes that have been structured by their environment. This is not a reflective engagement with the past that allows people to apply history's lessons to contemporary life but rather a fetishization of icons from the past that allows people to believe they are learned and in tune with their history and literature simply through the act of using an object, drinking tea, or sitting on a swing.

Themes and Meanings

Koch identifies a kind of "lifestyle history" as part of the American character, and though Americans surround themselves with references to the past, Koch suggests that this is merely commodity fetishism masquerading as an understanding of their literature and history and its importance to contemporary life. While his examples, designed for comic effect, might not seem familiar to the reader (who has probably never seen a blouse divided into squares with a picture of Edgar Allan Poe in each one), every reader is likely to be able to identify similar objects in American culture. Koch suggests that Americans seem to think that by wearing a T-shirt embossed with the image of a famous person they can take a shortcut to true knowledge and understanding. However, a certain malaise results from practicing blind reverence toward surface details of American history rather than attending to actual meanings. When the narrator smells the hair of the girl he is with, he gets a whiff of "the mould of [her] seaside resort hotel bedroom," suggesting the moldiness of the lives that pass through historical resort locales as well.

Readers see very little of substance in any of the characters in the poem; thus the "You Were Wearing" title acts as an indicator of practically everything the narrator remembers about the young girl he may have met at the resort. While there is something of a nostalgic tone conveyed by the past-tense description of the happy details of this carefree summer holiday life, there is also the suggestion of lost opportunity: The boy and girl are so immersed in the images of the past they are expected to unreflectingly revere that they discover little about each other or about history, literature, or life. Koch's poem thus acts as a caution to readers to not blindly accept what is alleged to be significant in the past but to dig toward more meaningful experiences of the past's legacy. Everyone has been in crowds of half-alert people walking through national monument sites acting reverent because they are expected to do so. While Koch's juxtaposition of important figures from American culture seems at first to detract from their importance, the final lesson of the poem is otherwise: It serves as an instruction to appreciate the significance of American cultural history, which, paradoxically, is the way people can best take possession of their own place within the culture and live lives that do not dote on icons of the past.

This is consistent with what Koch and the New York School poets are also attempting to do in poetry. Their forsaking of traditional poetic practices does not occur in a vacuum; rather, Koch is very conscious of literary history throughout his work. However, he suggests that the best way to honor the past is to live in the present. One is reminded that historical figures who are honored today were usually people who attempted to find new forms through which to convey the experiences of their own time. Blind reverence was not something that motivated Washington, Melville, or any of the other figures who appear in the poem. A true appreciation of the American national legacy demands that Americans live in their own moment, conscious of, but not trapped within, their own history.

Ted Pelton

THE YOUNG HOUSEWIFE

Author: William Carlos Williams (1883-1963)
Type of poem: Narrative
First published: 1916; collected in *The Complete Collected Poems of William Carlos Williams, 1906-1938*, 1938

The Poem

A short poem in free verse, "The Young Housewife" consists of three stanzaic units of four, five, and three lines each. The poem is told by a first-person narrator who seems to be William Carlos Williams himself, although one has no way of knowing that this is the case. The title identifies a woman who is the object of attention of the poem's narrator, indicating that she is young, recently married, and identified in relation to the house in which she and her husband live.

These motifs are elaborated in the poem's first sentence, the emotional high point of which is the narrator's fantasy of the woman "in negligee." Clearly, the narrator knows her and is attracted to her. He apparently does not have access to the woman, however, and his story becomes a humorous variation on the theme that unrequited love (or lust) soon becomes a bore. The first four words of stanza 2 ("Then again she comes") and the multiple indefinite objects of the woman's calling ("the ice-man, fish-man") suggest that stanza 1—indeed, the whole poem—does not describe a one-time event but rather recurrent events that happen fairly frequently. Perhaps the narrator drives by the woman's house every day "at ten A.M." on his way to work. The woman's coming "to the curb" and the other events of stanzas 2 and 3 are repeated, too, though less frequently than his driving by her house.

Altogether, the poem is a generalized depiction of the narrator's attraction to, sightings of, thoughts about, and actions toward a young married woman with whom he has limited contact—restricted, perhaps, to these chance encounters when he passes her in his car.

His attraction is apparent—as are his playfulness, humor, and cheerfulness—in his repeated actions: imagining her "in negligee," comparing her to "a fallen leaf," and bowing and passing smiling. If his fantasy suggests that he is a bit of a rogue, his transformation of the woman into "a fallen leaf" that he is a poet, and his running over her and the other "leaves" that he is a male chauvinist, his bowing and smiling nevertheless suggest that he is also a gentleman. Every time he sees her, he pays genuinely cheerful and friendly homage. The narrator's behavior appears to be in conformity with Williams's own remark about this poem to John Thirlwall: "Whenever a man sees a beautiful woman it's an occasion for poetry—compensating beauty with beauty."

Forms and Devices

Parallelism may be the central principle informing the poem's technique, form, and content. While the poem can be described as free verse, it nevertheless plays with the possibility of metrical and formal regularity. Many of its lines are four-and five-stress, eight-and nine-syllable lines. There are frequent stretches of regular meter among the lines. The poem is "almost" in quatrains. All of this parallels, without really adhering to, conventional English and American versification.

More specific parallelisms exist. The content of the three stanzaic units is arranged in a parallel manner: In each of them, the narrator first treats the woman, then himself. Stanza 1 initially sums up his fantasies of her as being "in negligee," while stanza 2 initially sums up his perceptions of her, and stanza 3 initially sums up his imagined, metaphorical rendering of her fate. These are parallel modes of his conceiving of her, describing her, and imagining her. Still more local parallelisms occur in this material: For example, stanzas 1 and 2 begin with a time reference, which is followed by a reference to the woman herself, followed in turn by an account of her actions that contains a reference to her clothing and, implicitly, her body. A kind of grammatical parallelism (a synthetic parallelism), built on the subject-predicate repetitions ("I pass," "I compare," "I bow and pass"), closes each of the three stanzas. In stanza 1, this grammatical figure is the heart of a complete, simple sentence; in stanza 2, it is the heart of an independent clause; and in stanza 3, it is the heart of a dependent clause. Grammatically, these subject-predicate constructions become less and less independent as they undergo a kind of shifting among parallel grammatical forms; at the same time, the narrator draws closer and closer to the woman in his car.

Parallelism also occurs among the sonic features of the poem. The main sonic event in the poem is the sound made by the narrator's car as it rides over the dried leaves and crushes them. This event and sound should be understood as occurring throughout the poem, for, whether they are mentioned or not, the leaves are there in all three stanzas. The linguistic, sonic parallel to this event and sound is the onomatopoeia maintained throughout the poem, primarily by the repetitions of the hard *c* sound (as in "car" and "crackling"), but also by hard *s* sounds (as in "moves" and "leaves"), soft *s* sounds (as in "pass solitary" and "pass smiling"), and *sh* sounds (as in "she" and "rush")—all of which can be heard in the noise a car's wheels make crushing dried leaves.

Finally, the woman's poetic fate parallels her "real" fate. In her role as a "young housewife," she is defined in terms of her relationship with her husband; she is the caretaker of her husband's house. She seems to have tucked away her individuality as casually as she tucks in her "stray ends of hair." She fares no better in her role as the object of the narrator's admiration. She is one fallen leaf among many—something to be swept away and forgotten.

Themes and Meanings

Even though Williams had only recently begun the poetic career that would last more than fifty years when he wrote "The Young Housewife," the poem embodies at least two elements with which, like the aforementioned parallelism, he would work throughout his life.

One of these is a stylistic feature that impinges strongly on the poem's interpretation and meaning: the sense of the poem's being literally autobiographical—an effect that is characteristic of much of Williams's poetry. Although some critics identify the poem's narrator as Williams himself, one cannot do this with any certainty, since the poem may be partly or entirely fictional. The most one can say with certainty is that the narrator possesses the skills of a poet and storyteller.

The second element is a thematic one: "The Young Housewife" is about women—a subject that is often at the heart of Williams's poetry. The poem is an early, successful rendering of several themes relating to women that Williams treated throughout his career, all of which can be summed up under the theme of how a lustful man sometimes behaves in response to a desirable but unobtainable woman.

The interior monologue that makes up the poem represents the way in which a man might transform his sexual attraction to an unobtainable woman into a personally and publicly acceptable gesture of homage to her. Psychologically known as sublimation, this activity informs not only the plot of the story but also the poem's diction. The effect is that the narrator appears to speak on two levels: a conscious and public level, on which he tells an acceptable story, and an unconscious and private level, on which his thinly concealed libido (or sexual drive), perhaps along with his conscience, reveals itself.

Thus, his mind jumps from the image of the woman "in negligee" immediately to the highly suggestive word "behind," and throughout the poem he seems to speak in a kind of Freudian language containing buried words and hidden meanings. In this view, the poem suggests that, public appearances notwithstanding, some women do not fare well at the hands (or in the stories) of some men—a universal truth that Williams knew well and about which he wrote often.

Jerrald Ranta

THE YOUNG WOMAN OF BEARE

Author: Austin Clarke (1896-1974)
Type of poem: Dramatic monologue
First published: 1929, in *Pilgrimage and Other Poems*

The Poem

"The Young Woman of Beare" is based on a tenth century Irish poem, "The Old Woman of Beare." In both poems the woman recollects her love of the world and of men. Though both are presumed to be dramatic monologues, neither poet indicated the identity of the person who does not speak; again, presumably, the other person does not share the speaker's passions and may even disapprove. In the tenth century original, the speaker is at the end of her life, defiantly rejecting the admonitions she has heard from clerics. In "The Young Woman of Beare," the speaker is in the fullness of youth, so caught up in her delights that such admonitions as she hears are of no consequence. She is luxuriously describing her life, not justifying it.

"The Young Woman of Beare" is a long poem written in ten-line stanzas that contain a variety of repeated sounds: rhyme, assonance, consonance. The repetitions are irregular, and they give the poem a musical, dreamy air. The young woman is in her room, comfortable and drowsy, reflecting on her lovers and rejecting any moral, religious, or political concerns that might lessen or censure her life of pleasure. She is content to consider herself "the bright temptation" the clergy censures.

As the poem develops her character, she emerges as a woman committed to seizing the day, rather than living for an uncertain future, either in this life or the afterlife. She recalls a lover: "Sin-fast—we can enjoy/ What is allowed in marriage." She continues with this meditation by describing herself in metaphors usually reserved for the clergy's use in condemning sinners, calling herself "the dark temptation" and acknowledging the clergy's view.

As she daydreams into nightfall, she mentions her foreign face, though does not indicate whether she is from another country or simply of another moral view. By taking the terms of admonition as recognition of her power, she establishes a moral order separate and different from that of Ireland in the late sixteenth century, the setting for the poem. Such a rejection of Christian ethical codes appears throughout the poetry and prose of Austin Clarke.

Forms and Devices

"The Young Woman of Beare" is a first-person meditation on life, with an assumed listener. The listener is quite likely a society with values that differ from those of the young woman, rather than an actual person. She repeats religious references in the poem, delighting in her lack of concern with their admonitions. "Judgment," "Sin," and "shining orders/ Of clergy" appear regularly in the poem, as do references to political events, such as "That Ormond's men are out/ And the Geraldine is in." The reference is to forces that contended for dominance in Ireland between 1564 and 1632. Regularly mentioned, as well, are her lovers, among them MacWilliam, a Flemish merchant. Place names give the poem added detail. She left Beare because she got a bad name there, wandered with men to the islands, Limerick, to the Curragh (Ireland's ancient race course).

Set in place as it is, the poem uses metaphors to contrast the beauty of the young woman with the bleakness of those who condemn her: "as from a lathe/ My polished body turning," "the silver knots of sleep." The language used to describe her is luxurious, sensuous. By contrast, those who condemn her are described with words that evoke a lack of beauty and pleasure: clergy with "staven hands upraised," a "black archway" where "praying people hurry."

The imaginative reconstruction of an ancient being and experience is representative of Clarke's writing. Placing the tenth century original of his young woman some centuries later, he was able to make both a political and a moral statement relevant to his own time, though translations from Gaelic of "The Old Woman of Beare" show that a similar social commentary was intended in the earlier work. Clarke's poem is an ironic equation of the present government and church of Ireland with the earlier ones, which today are regarded as repressive.

Themes and Meanings

"The Young Woman of Beare" is a poem praising the unstinted pleasure of the flesh, in a country that has tended to regard the flesh as servant of both church and state. As such, it has much in common with the literature of the Irish Literary Revival, which praised the growth of the spirit and of the body frequently, without the restrictions of religion and politics. Like the poems of the revival, "The Young Woman of Beare" is based on an Irish experience and was produced as a result of the poet's familiarity with the indigenous literature of Ireland.

As are many of the poems of this period, "The Young Woman of Beare" is consciously antagonistic to the Catholic church. Unlike most of the poems, this one does not strike a political note that is antagonistic to the rule of Ireland by the English and by the Anglo-Irish, the descendants of English landowners who live in Ireland. The young woman has lovers from these ruling groups and cannot even be troubled to know what armies are at war.

The poet here praises life itself above all that would compromise its pleasure, and he gives no indication that the young woman should be other than she is. For the poet, as he explains in a note to the poem in his *Collected Poems of Austin Clarke* (1936), the woman expresses an understanding of life that was part of Gaelic culture, and was not known to many of Clarke's contemporaries because they were not acquainted with the literature "first-hand."

The purpose of the poem, then, is threefold: to praise life, to re-create a character from the Gaelic past, and to make a social comment. Clarke experienced difficulties with official censors, as did other poets at this time. In his note, he states that he is aware that officials will disapprove of his poem and that it might well be condemned from the pulpit on the basis that it is immodest and liable "to incite passions."

The strength of this poem is its graceful challenge to whatever laws or customs would restrict life. Though committed to the culture of Ireland, past and present, Clarke prized the life that he saw as essential to the culture, a life in direct opposition to compromise and moderation.

Frank L. Kersnowski

THE YOUNGEST DAUGHTER

Author: Cathy Song (1955-   )
Type of poem: Dramatic monologue
First published: 1980; collected in *Picture Bride*, 1983

The Poem

"The Youngest Daughter" is a monologue in fifty-two lines of delicately cadenced verse divided into five stanzas of differing lengths. The speaker of the poem is the youngest daughter of her family, and she is burdened with caring for her aging parent. Her monologue reveals a conflict of emotions within her: Love and pity for her invalid mother clash with feelings of resentment and entrapment for having to deny herself.

In the first stanza, Cathy Song evokes the effects of aging upon both women. The housebound daughter describes her skin becoming "damp/ and pale," while her mother's skin is "parched" from having labored in the fields. Both images are joined referentially by sunlight or the lack of it. The daughter's condition results from being cloistered and kept in the "dark/ for many years," whereas her mother's condition results from spending too much time in the "drying sun." Thus one of the paradoxes in this poem emerges: The sufferings of mother and daughter, though different, are also similar. Another contradiction rests on the reversal of roles that continually takes place. The mother and daughter switch back and forth between being the caregiver and the cared for, the soother of pain and its cause. In stanza 2, the daughter's eyes are burning with frustration. Ironically, it is suggested that the mother, who tries to soothe her daughter's "migraine," is also the cause of it.

In stanza 3, the daughter describes an instance of her role as caregiver and reflects on her mother's plight. She attends her mother, bringing her in a wheelchair to her morning bath. As the daughter washes her mother's breasts, the imagery not only reveals the daughter's understanding that her mother's body has been used to pleasure her husband and suckle her children but also suggests the daughter's revulsion at such a fate. Song proceeds, in stanza 4, to express the odd tenderness the daughter feels toward her mother. The daughter pities the mother's diabetic body scarred by insulin injections. She realizes that the two of them have always been trapped together in the same "sunless" room in a futile unity. Neither has a choice but to be there for the other.

The last stanza describes a reversal of roles as the mother prepares a meal for the daughter. As they eat, there is an unspoken understanding between the two. The daughter thinks, "She knows I am not to be trusted,/ even now planning my escape." In the final irony of the poem, the daughter toasts her mother's health, although it is her mother's longevity that prevents the daughter from having a life of her own. Song ends enigmatically, however, with the daughter's wistful (or perhaps ominous) description of the "thousand cranes" pictured on the window curtains that "fly up," presumably to a freedom that may yet be hers.

Forms and Devices

The cadences of Song's verse are as unobtrusive as breathing. They ripple and eddy in her speaker's stream of thought that seemingly proceeds from the very heart of her being. Upon this introspective stream, Song launches intricately contrasting images that create the poem's irony and paradox. Light and heat, food, and the body are the primary sources of Song's imagery. The poem begins by contrasting mother and daughter in terms of sunlight and skin. For the speaker-daughter, "The sky has been dark/ for many years," a powerful image of long-term deprivation that suggests a seed with arrested germination. Expressed in terms of the body, her "skin has become as damp/ and pale as rice paper": overly delicate, pallid, and friable. The daughter's sunless state contrasts starkly with the mother's overexposure to the sun that has parched her skin in the fields. The mother's experience of the exterior heat and light of the sun is, in turn, contrasted with an internal fever and pain that sears the daughter's body. The daughter says that when she touches her eyelids, they feel "hot enough to burn"; her "skin, aspirin colored,/ tingles with migraine"; and "pain flares up" on her face.

These two initial stanzas intimate the long-term situation of the two women. The rest of the poem describes two specific scenes, a morning bath and an afternoon meal, that are symmetrically balanced and contrasted: In the morning, the daughter is the caregiver bathing her mother; in the afternoon, the mother is the cook making their meal. Both situations are replete with painful body images. In the morning scene, the mother is an invalid who must be "wheeled . . . into her bath." Her skin is "freckled" with mementos of pain, the "blue bruises" of thirty years of insulin injections. However, the commanding body image is of the mother's breasts "floating in the milky water/ like two walruses,/ flaccid and whiskered around the nipples." Startling and unsavory as this image is, its effect is heightened by the gustatory image that follows: "I scrubbed them with a sour taste/ in my mouth, thinking:/ six children and an old man/ have sucked from these brown nipples."

Gustatory and food imagery fills the lines describing the afternoon meal. In this scene, the women's roles are reversed, the mother becoming the cook and the daughter the diner. This role reversal completes Song's construction of the two women's relationship as a paradoxically life-giving and life-sapping one, at once symbiotic, parasitic, and codependent. Song's food imagery takes on symbolic overtones when the daughter thinks of "a slice of pickled turnip" as a "token" for her "white body." The women's "ritual" meal, then, is a communion approaching cannibalism wherein the communicants feed off the daughter's body, consuming her opportunities for life. Hence the daughter toasts her mother's health with tea, a bitter cup. At the same time, the mother knows the daughter is planning escape like the thousand cranes of the window curtain that "fly up in a sudden breeze."

Themes and Meanings

In "The Youngest Daughter," Song, a Hawaii-born daughter of a Korean American father and a Chinese American mother, elaborates upon the universal feminist theme of mother-daughter relationships and puts an Asian American spin on it. Both situation and imagery in Song's poem have Asian overtones. In traditional Asian families, it is customary for the unmarried daughter to remain with the parents and care for them as they age. In many cases, this will be the youngest daughter's lot. The title of Song's poem carries resonances of this social and familial phenomenon, the speaker being the youngest of six siblings. Of Asian provenance, too, are several of the poem's images and symbols. The ingredients of the women's meal, for instance, are Asian: tea, rice, gingered fish, and pickled turnip, the last probably being the Japanese daikon, which is blanched white in color like the speaker's pallid skin. The crane image is also a common Asian symbol that connotes health and longevity, a connotation that Song employs enigmatically at the end of the poem: "As I toast to her health// a thousand cranes curtain the window,/ fly up in a sudden breeze." Clearly, the daughter longs to take flight from this sick relationship and achieve her freedom. Readers may wonder how she envisions this happening: through her mother's recovery, her longevity, or her death?

The relationship between mothers and daughters is an enduring theme of much literature written by or about women. Filiality, which shows itself in reverence for one's parents and respect for one's elders, is also a cardinal virtue of Confucianism and a widespread subject of writing in East Asia. The Asian overlay to a fundamental element of the human experience gives Song's situation a special piquancy. The mother-daughter relationship in Song's poem is depicted through the point of view of the daughter, the speaker of the poem. Through her, Song portrays a complex and rending mix of love and hate, of gratitude and resentment. It is a relationship that sustains and destroys, nourishes and devours, emphasized by the poem's use of food and gustatory imagery. The mother has brought the daughter into life by giving birth to her, has sustained her by nursing her at the breast, and continues to nurture her by soothing her migraine and preparing her food. However, now that age is taking its course, the women's roles are reversing. The daughter increasingly plays the role of nurse and caregiver, wheeling her diabetic mother about, bathing her, and companioning her. In this role, the daughter feels trapped, deprived of the freedom to be what she wants, and is keenly aware that her filial duties are atrophying her vital energies. Since it is unlikely that the mother can recover from her thirty-year-old diabetes or arrest the process of aging, the daughter is presumably trapped in her role until her mother's death can provide a final solution to her filial bondage. Hence the poem's closing irony and ambiguity are wrought by the daughter's bitter toast to the mother's health juxtaposed against the image of the cranes escaping in flight.

C. L. Chua and Keisha Blakely

ZONE

Author: Guillaume Apollinaire (Guillaume Albert Wladimir Alexandre Apollinaire de Kostrowitzky, 1880-1918)
Type of poem: Lyric
First published: 1913, as "Zone," in *Alcools*; English translation collected in *Selected Writings*, 1950

The Poem

"Zone," an exemplary modernist work, is a fairly long poem of 159 lines divided into thirty-four irregular sections; a section may contain only two words or be as long as twenty-nine lines. The title of the poem is as enigmatic as the poem itself. It most likely refers to the region just outside Paris where the indigent and homeless lived during Guillaume Apollinaire's time. The poem's form and content similarly inhabit a region just outside the normal boundaries for poetry.

The poem begins in the morning, a traditional starting place for narrative poems, but Apollinaire immediately indicates that something different is happening here: The Eiffel tower, in his eyes, becomes a shepherdess "whose flock of bridges bleats at the morning." The bizarre image is followed by another, more typical allusion to a shepherd with a flock—the pope and his church. Apollinaire explains that the "most modern European is you Pope Pius X," and the reader can only guess why or whether the poet is being sarcastic. Clarity does not come easily in this poem.

The sixth section moves away from the world of religion into the very secular world of work. The poet admires a "pretty street" where typists, laborers, and directors pass back and forth to work four times a day. There is a certain "gracefulness to this industrial street" which the poet loves. Unlike a more typical poem, which might speak of lovers beginning their day, "Zone" acknowledges Apollinaire's love in the morning for a street, and a type of street not normally admired by poets.

In section 7, the poem returns to the religious theme and becomes a poem set in memory rather than the present. Apollinaire, remembering his own pious childhood, when he prayed "all night in the school chapel" with his friend René Dalize, begins a litany in honor of the "flaming glory of Christ." The litany, however, ends with a reference to Christ that compares his Ascension to an airplane's flight. Irreverently, Apollinaire suggests that Christ holds the "world altitude record."

The mixture of religion and technology, the sacred and profane, is continued in the eighth and longest section. Here the progress of the twentieth century, epitomized by the invention of the airplane, is praised. The century "soars like Jesus," and angels fly around the "pretty flyer" of the first airplane. The distance that one would expect between the ancient world of myth and the modern era of scientific advancement is nullified by Apollinaire's conflation of various biblical and classical images: The third person of the Trinity, the Dove, joins with Icarus, the phoenix, and Elijah in fraternizing "with the flying machine" of the modern era.

Leaving this extended meditation, the poet returns to the present time of the poem, the morning, and his walk through Paris "among the crowds/ And herds of autobuses." He recalls the pain or grief he is feeling because of a personal loss of love and anxiously thinks that he is "never going to be loved again." Sections 12 through 20 record generally positive memories the poet has of his travels on the Riviera, in Prague, Marseilles, Koblenz, Rome, and Amsterdam. The travelogue ends, however, with an odd summation: "I have lived like an idiot," and "I feel like sobbing/ Over you over the girl and over everything that has terrified you."

The poem, once again, shifts back to the present, which by this time is evening. The poet sees "the eyes of those emigrants which are brimming with tears" and drinks coffee and then spirits in a "crapulous bar . . . among the unfortunates." He feels pity for the outcasts, perhaps seeing a mirror of himself in them.

In the end, the poem returns to its beginning. Night "passes away," and morning arrives with the milkman. The poet completes his sojourn, wants to return to sleep among his idols, his "minor Christs," and notices the sun coming up, a "corseless head."

Forms and Devices

The principal technique Apollinaire employs in this poem that travels through time and space, moods and tones, is juxtaposition. At the simplest level, he is combining two normally antithetical devices: rhyming couplets and free verse. This union of modern and traditional forms serves the poem well, since it in many ways celebrates the twentieth century's innovations as well as the power of the mythic past.

The powerful and, some might say, sacrilegious union of Christianity and aviation is the most glaring example of juxtaposition in the poem. Within the space of six lines, angels gather around the heroic flyer, making way from time to time "for those whom the Eucharist transports," while "host-elevating priests ascend endlessly" and "the airplane alights at last without folding its wings." Science and religion, usually opposed, are here combined; the upward spiritual journey is conflated with the soaring possibilities of the plane. The fact that Apollinaire uses no punctuation whatsoever in the poem allows these separate worlds to glide into each other more easily.

Apollinaire also brings together specific images that are normally kept apart. Sections 9 through 11, while they move from private grief over love lost to religious passion, are joined by the image of blood. Apollinaire walks the streets in despair, thinking that he will "never be loved again," and sees that all the "women are covered with blood," perhaps because of the violence implicit in love, or the failure of love. Two lines later, the bloodstained women are temporarily replaced by "the blood of the Sacred Heart drown[ing]" the poet in Montmartre. The lost love for a woman, the painter Marie Laurencin according to biographers, has been juxtaposed with the overwhelming love the speaker feels for Christ, or the love he remembers feeling for Christ in his youth.

What makes this poem particularly modern is not only this discordant joining together of images but also Apollinaire's playing with the conventional subject matter for poems. Poets often reminisce about the romantic adventures they had while traveling, and Apollinaire remembers an affair with a pretty girl in Amsterdam. Then he adds that she was actually ugly and already engaged. He also focuses on a Parisian woman's chapped hands and scarred belly. The symbol of beauty about which poets often write, the rose, Apollinaire transforms as well; instead of admiring the color or aroma of the rose (only the odor of the emigrants is noted in this poem), the poet concentrates on the rosebug asleep in the heart of the rose."

Themes and Meanings

Despite its playfulness and humor, the poem focuses generally on loss. By interchangeably referring to himself as *tu*, or "you," and as *je*, or "I," Apollinaire demonstrates the disjointed nature of the modern consciousness. It can be assumed that the poet in his youth felt a sense of wholeness and well-being when he devoutly worshiped God in the church; this is reflected in the consistency with which the poet sometimes addresses himself as "you," especially in section 7. This unity is lost over time, however, because of his failure in love and his loss of faith. Toward the poem's end, the narrator is as dislocated as the poem itself: "You no longer dare look at your hands and every minute I feel like sobbing/ Over you and over the girl I love and over everything that has terrified you."

The loss of faith haunts the poet. As a boy, nothing delighted him "more than church ceremony," but as an adult he can only say, "You are ashamed when you catch yourself saying a prayer/ You laugh at yourself." His shame also keeps him from "entering a church and confessing [his] sins." He ends the poem walking toward his home to sleep among fetishes and idols, "Which are Christs of another form . . ./ Minor Christs of dim expectancies." They do not offer the consolation the youthful faith provided; when the sun rises, often a symbol of hope, of possible resurrection or rebirth, the poet sees it instead as a severed head.

The progress of the twentieth century seems to offer some form of salvation to the poet. He genuinely exults, particularly in section 8, in the tremendous advances in technology; the mythic world is temporarily reborn because humans are able to fly. Yet this amazingly eclectic section, which euphorically joins the natural and supernatural, the East and West, and the biblical and classical worlds, really can not sustain the poet. Without human love ("The love I endure is like a syphilis") or divine intervention in his life, the poet feels displaced, disjointed, and ill at ease in the contemporary world. Memory, working like the "hands on the clock in the Jewish quarter that go backward," comforts him somewhat, but it also unnerves him by showing what he has lost and the years he has wasted. Only art, an art true to the dislocations of the period, can offer recompense for what is gone.

Kevin Boyle

GLOSSARY

Accented syllable: See *Stressed syllable*

Accentual meter: One of four base meters used in English (accentual, accentual-syllabic, syllabic, and quantitative), accentual meter is the system in which the occurrence of a syllable marked by a *stress* determines the basic unit, regardless of the number of unstressed syllables. In other words, it is the stresses that determine the metrical base. An example from modern poetry is "Blue Moles" by Sylvia Plath, the first line of which scans: "They're out of the dark's ragbag, these two." Because there are five stressed syllables in this accentually based poem, the reader can expect that many of the other lines will also contain five stresses. (See also *Scansion*)

Accentual-syllabic meter: By far the most common base meter for English poetry, accentual-syllabic meter measures the pattern of stressed syllables relative to the unstressed ones. In the first line of William Shakespeare's Sonnet 130, "My mistress' eyes are nothing like the sun," there is a pattern of alternating unstressed with stressed syllables, although there is a *substitution* of an unstressed syllable for a stressed syllable at the word "like." In the accentual-syllabic system, stressed and unstressed syllables are grouped together into *feet.*

Allegory: One of the "figures of speech," allegory represents an abstract idea in concrete imagery, almost always in the form of a humanized character. Gluttony, for example, might be allegorized by a character who eats all the time, while Christian love might be allegorized by a character who does charitable deeds. The traditional use for allegory is to make it possible for the poet to show how abstract ideas affect real people who are in contact with them, or how abstract emotions affect each other within a human being.

Alliteration: When consonant repetition is focused at the beginning of syllables, the repetition is called alliteration, as in: "Large mannered motions of his mythy mind." Alliteration is used when the poet wishes to focus on the details of a sequence of words and to show relationships between words within a line. Because a reader cannot easily skim over an alliterative line, it is conspicuous and demands emphasis.

Allusion: When a reference is made to a historical or literary event whose story or outcome adds dimension to the poem, then poetical allusion occurs. "Fire and Ice" by Robert Frost, for example, alludes to the biblical account of the flood and the prophecy that the next destruction will come by fire, not water. Without recognizing the allusion and understanding the biblical reference to Noah and the surrounding associations of hate and desire, the reader cannot fully appreciate the poem.

Anacrusis: The opposite of *truncation,* anacrusis occurs when an extra unstressed syllable is added to the beginning or end of a *line,* as in the line: "their shoul/ders held the sky/suspended." This line is described as iambic tetrameter with terminal anacrusis. Anacrusis is used to change a rising meter to falling, and vice versa, in order to change the reader's emotional response to the subject.

Anapest: One of six standard rhythmic units in English poetry, the anapestic foot associates two unstressed syllables with one stressed syllable, as in the line, "With the sift/ed, harmón/ious pause." The anapestic foot is one of the three most common in English poetry and is used to create a highly rhythmical, usually emotional, line.

Anaphora: Anaphora occurs when successive phrases or lines begin with the same word or words. Timothy Steele's "Sapphics Against Anger" uses anaphora in the repetition of the phrase "May I."

Approximate rhyme: The two categories of approximate rhyme are assonance and half rhyme (or slant rhyme). Assonance occurs when words with identical vowel sounds but different consonants are associated. "Stars," "arms," and "park" all contain identical *a* (and *ar*) sounds, but because the consonants are different the words are not *full rhymes.* Half rhyme or slant rhymes contain identical consonants but different vowels, as in "fall" and "well." "Table" and "bauble" constitute half rhymes; "law," "cough," and "fawn" assonate.

Assonance: See *Approximate rhyme*

Aubade: An aubade is a type of poem welcoming or decrying the arrival of the dawn. Often the dawn symbolizes the separation of two lovers. An example is William Empson's "Aubade."

Ballad: The ballad stanza, a type of *quatrain,* may alternate its rhyme scheme as *abab* or *abcb.* If all four lines contain four feet each (*tetrameter*), the stanza is called a "long ballad"; if one or more of the lines contain only three feet (trimeter), it is called a "short ballad." Ballad stanzas, which are highly *mnemonic,* originated with verse adapted to singing. For this reason, the poetic ballad is well suited for presenting stories. Popular ballads are songs or verse which tell tales, usually impersonal, and they usually impart folk wisdom. Supernatural events, courage, and love are frequent themes, but any experience which appeals to people is acceptable material. A famous use of the ballad form is *The Rime of the Ancient Mariner* (1798), by Samuel Taylor Coleridge.

Ballade: The French "ballade," a popular and sophisticated form, is commonly (but not necessarily) composed of an eight-line stanza rhyming *ababbcbc.* Early ballades usually contained three stanzas and an *envoy,* commonly addressed to a nobleman, priest, or the poet's patron, but no consistent syllable count. Another common characteristic of the ballade is a refrain that occurs at the end of each stanza.

Base meter (or metrical base): Poems in English and in most European languages which are not *free verse* are written in one of four base meters (*accentual, accentual-syllabic, syllabic,* or *quantitative*), measured by the number, pattern, or duration of the syllables within a line or stanza. Rhythm in verse occurs because of *meter,* and the use of meter depends upon the type of base into which it is placed.

Blank verse: Although many variations can occur in the *meter* of blank verse, its *base meter* is iambic pentameter. Blank verse lines are unrhymed, and are usually arranged in *stichic* form (that is, not in stanzas). Most of Shakespeare's plays are written in blank verse; in poetry it is often used for subject matter that requires much narration or reflection. In both poetry and drama, blank verse elevates emotion and gives a dramatic sense of importance. Although the base meter of blank verse is iambic pentameter, the form is very flexible, and *substitution, enjambment,* feminine endings, and extra syllables can relax the rigidity of the base. The flexibility of blank verse gives the poet an opportunity to use a formal structure without seeming unnecessarily decorous. T. S. Eliot's "Burnt Norton" is a modern blank-verse poem.

Cadence: The rhythmic speed or tempo with which a line is read is its cadence. All language has cadence, but when the cadence of words is forced into some pattern, it then becomes *meter,* thus distinguishing poetry from prose. A *prose poem* may possess strong cadence, combined with poetic uses of imagery, symbolism, and other poetic devices.

Caesura: When the poet imposes a pause or break in the poem, with or without punctuation marks, a caesura has occurred. The comma, question mark, colon, and dash are the most common signals for pausing, and these are properly termed "caesuras"; pauses may also be achieved through syntax, *lines, meter, rhyme,* and the sound of words. The type of punctuation determines the length of the pause. Periods and question marks demand full stops; colons take almost a full stop; semicolons take a long pause; commas a short pause. The end of a line usually demands some pause even if there is no punctuation.

Cinquain: Any five-line stanza, including the *mad-song* and the *limerick,* is a cinquain. Cinquains are most often composed of a *ballad* stanza with an extra line added to the middle.

Conceit: One of several types of *metaphor,* the term "conceit" is used for comparisons which are highly intellectualized. A conceit may therefore be said to be an extended, elaborate, or complex metaphor. The term is frequently applied to the work of the Metaphysical poets, notably John Donne.

Connotation: Words convey meaning through their sound, through their formal, *denotative* definitions, through their use in context, and through connotation. When a word takes on an additional meaning other than its denotative one, it achieves connotation. The word "mercenary," for example, simply means a soldier who is paid to fight in an army not of his own region, but connotatively a mercenary is an unprincipled scoundrel who kills for money and pleasure, not for honor and patriotism. Connotation is one of the most important devices for achieving *irony,* and readers may be fooled into believing a poem has one meaning because they have missed connotations which reverse the poem's apparent theme.

Consonance: When the final *consonants* of stressed syllables agree but the preceding vowels are different, consonance occurs. "Chair/star" is an example of consonance, since both words end with *r* preceded by different vowels. Terminal consonance creates half or slant rhyme (see *Approximate rhyme*). Consonance differs from *alliteration* in that the final consonants are repeated rather than the initial consonants. In the twentieth century consonance became one of the principal rhyming devices, used to achieve formality without seeming stilted or old-fashioned.

Consonants: Consonants (all letters except the vowels, *a, e, i, o, u,* and sometimes *y*) are among the most important sound-producing devices in poetry. There are five basic effects that certain consonants will produce: resonance, harshness, plosiveness, exhaustiveness, and liquidity. Resonance, exhaustiveness, and liquidity tend to give words—and consequently the whole line if several of these consonants are used—a soft effect. Plosiveness and harshness, on the other hand, tend to create tension. Resonance is the property of long duration produced by nasals, such as *n* and *m,* and by voiced fricating consonants such as *z, v,* and the voiced *th,* as in "them." Exhaustiveness is created by the voiceless fricating consonants and consonant combinations, such as *h, f,* and the voiceless *th* and *s.* Liquidity results from using the liquids and semivowels *l, r, w,* and *y,* as in the word "silken." Plosiveness occurs when certain consonants create a stoppage of breath before releasing it, especially *b, p, t, d, g, k, ch,* and *j.*

Controlling image/controlling metaphor: Just as a poem may include as structural devices form, theme, action, or dramatic situation, it may also use imagery for structure. When an image runs throughout a poem, giving unity to lesser images or ideas, it is called a "controlling image." Usually the poet establishes a single idea and then expands and complicates it; in Edward Taylor's "Huswifery," for example, the image of the spinning wheel is expanded into images of weaving until the reader begins to see life as a tapestry. Robert Frost's "The Silken Tent" is a fine example of a controlling image and *extended metaphor.*

Couplet: Any two succeeding lines that rhyme form a couplet. Because the couplet has been used in so many different ways, and because of its long tradition in English poetry, various names and functions have been given to types of couplets. One of the most common is the decasyllabic (ten-syllable) couplet. When there is an *end-stop* on the second line of a couplet, it is said to be "closed"; an *enjambed* couplet is "open." An end-stopped decasyllabic couplet is called a "heroic couplet," because the form has often been used to sing the praise of heroes. The heroic couplet was widely used by the neoclassical poets of the eighteenth century. Because it is so stately and sometimes pompous, the heroic couplet invites satire, and many poems have been written in "mock heroic verse," such as Alexander Pope's *The Rape of the Lock* (1712). Another commonly used couplet is the octasyllabic (eight-syllable) couplet, formed from two lines of iambic tetrameter, as in "L'Allegro" by John Milton: "Come, and trip as we go/ On the light fantastic toe." The light, sing-song tone of the octasyllabic couplet also invited satire, and in the seventeenth century Samuel Butler wrote one of the most famous of all satires, *Hudibras*, in this couplet. When a couplet is used to break another rhyme scheme, it generally produces a summing-up effect and has an air of profundity. Shakespeare found this characteristic particularly useful when he needed to give his newly invented Shakespearean *sonnet* a final note of authority and purpose.

Dactyl: The dactyl, formed of a stress followed by two unstressed syllables (´ᵛᵛ), is fairly common in isolated words, but when this pattern is included in a line of poetry, it tends to break down and rearrange itself into components of other types of feet. Isolated, the word "meaningless" is a dactyl, but in the line "Polite/meaning/less words," the last syllable becomes attached to the stressed "words" and creates a *split foot,* forming a *trochee* and an *iamb.* Nevertheless, a few dactylic poems do exist. "After the/pangs of a/desperate/lover," is a dactyllic line.

Denotation: The explicit formal definition of a word, exclusive of its implications and emotional associations (see *Connotation*), is its denotation or denotative meaning.

Depressed foot: Occasionally, two syllables occur in a pattern in such a way as to be taken as one syllable without actually being an *elision,* thus creating a depressed foot. In the line: "To each the boul/ders (that have)/fallen/to each" the *base meter* consists of five iambic feet, but in the third foot there is an extra syllable which disrupts the meter but does not break it, so that "that have" functions as the second half of the iambic foot.

Diction: John Dryden defined diction concisely as the poet's "choice of words." In Dryden's time, and for most of the history of English verse, the diction of poetry was elevated, sharply distinct from everyday speech. Since the early twentieth century, however, the diction of poetry has ranged from the banal and the conversational to the highly formal, and from obscenity and slang to technical vocabulary, sometimes in the same poem. The diction of a poem often reveals its persona's values and attitudes.

Dieresis: Caesuras which come after the foot (see *Split foot* for a discussion of caesuras which break feet), called "dieresis" (although the technical name is seldom used), can be used to create long pauses in the *line*, and they are often used to prepare the line for *enjambment*.

Dramatic dialogue: When two or more personae speak to each other in a poem or a play, they engage in dramatic dialogue. Unlike a *dramatic monologue*, both characters speak, and in the best dramatic dialogues, their conversation leads to a final resolution in which both characters and the reader come to the same realization at the same time.

Dramatic irony: See *Irony*

Dramatic monologue: In dramatic monologue, the narrator addresses a silent persona who never speaks but whose presence greatly influences what the narrator tells the reader. The principal reason for writing in dramatic monologue form is to control the speech of the major persona through the implied reaction of the silent one. The effect is one of continuing change and often surprise. In Robert Browning's "My Last Duchess," for example, the duke believes that he is in control of the situation, when in fact he has provided the emissary with terrible insights about the way he treated his former duchess. The emissary, who is the silent persona, has asked questions which the duke has answered; in doing so he has given away secrets. Dramatic monologue is somewhat like hearing one side of a telephone conversation in which the reader learns much about both participants.

Duration: The measure of quantitative meter is the duration or length of the syllables. Duration can alter the tone and the *relative stress* of a line and influence meaning as much as the *foot* can.

Elegy: The elegy and pastoral elegy are distinguishable by their subject matter rather than their form. The elegy is usually a long, rhymed, *strophic* poem whose subject is meditation upon death or a lamentable theme, while the pastoral elegy uses the natural setting of a pastoral scene to sing of death or love. Within the pastoral setting the simplicity of the characters and the scene lends a peaceful air despite the grief the narrator feels.

Elision: The two types of elision are synaeresis and syncope; they occur when a poet who is attempting to maintain a regular *base meter* joins two vowels into a single vowel or omits a vowel altogether. In the line "Of man's first disobedience, and the fruit" the "ie" in "disobedience" is pronounced as a "y" ("ye") so that the word reads dis/o/bed/yence, thereby making a five-syllable word into a four-syllable word. This process of forming one vowel out of two is synaeresis. When a vowel is dropped altogether, rather than combining two into one, it is called "syncope," as when "natural" becomes "nat'ral" and "hastening" becomes "hast'ning." Less frequent uses of elision are to change the sound of a word, to spell words as they are pronounced, and to indicate dialect.

Emphasis: Through a number of techniques, such as *caesura,* the *line, relative stress, counterpointing,* and *substitution,* poets are able to alter the usual emphasis or meaning of words. Whenever the meter of a poem is intentionally altered through one of these techniques, certain words or an entire line will be highlighted or emphasized for the purpose of calling attention to the most important parts of the poem.

End rhyme: See *Rhyme*

End-stop: When a punctuated pause occurs at the end of a line, the line is said to be "end-stopped." The function of end-stops is to show the relationship between lines and to create *emphasis* on particular words or lines. End-stopping in rhymed poems creates more emphasis on the rhyme words, which already carry a great deal of emphasis by virtue of their rhymes. *Enjambment* is the opposite of end-stopping.

Enjambment: When a line is not *end-stopped*—that is, when it carries over to the following line—the line is said to be "enjambed," as in John Milton's: "Avenge, O Lord, thy slaughtered saints, whose bones/ Lie scattered on the Alpine mountains cold." Enjambment is used to change the natural emphasis of the *line,* to strengthen or weaken the effect of *rhyme,* or to alter *meter.*

Envoy: Generally, an envoy (or envoi) is any short poem or stanza addressed to the reader as a beginning or end to a longer work. Specifically, the envoy is the final stanza of a sestina or a *ballade* in which all the rhyme words are repeated or echoed.

Extended metaphor: When *metaphors* are added to one another so that they run in a series, they are collectively called an "extended metaphor." Robert Frost's poem "The Silken Tent" uses an extended metaphor; it compares the "she" of the poem to the freedom and bondage of a silken tent. (See also *Controlling image/controlling metaphor*)

Eye rhyme: Words that appear to be identical because of their spelling but that sound different are known as "eye rhymes." "Bough/enough/cough" and "ballet/pallet" are examples. Because of changes in pronunciation, many older poems appear to use eye rhymes but do not. For example, "wind" (meaning moving air) once rhymed with "find." Eye rhymes which are intentional and do not result from a change in pronunciation may be used to create a disconcerting effect.

Fabliau: A fabliau is a bawdy medieval verse, such as many found in Geoffrey Chaucer's *Canterbury Tales.*

Falling rhyme: Rhyme in which the correspondence of sound comes only in the final unstressed syllable, which is preceded by another unstressed syllable, is known as a "falling rhyme." T. S. Eliot rhymes "me-tic-u-lous" with "ri-dic-u-lous" and creates a falling rhyme. (See also *Feminine rhyme*; *Masculine rhyme*)

Falling rhythm: A line in which feet move from stressed to unstressed syllables (*trochaic* or *dactyllic*) is said to "fall," as in this line from "The Naming of Parts": "Glistens/like cor/al in/all of the/neighboring/gardens." Because English and other Germanic-based languages naturally rise, imposing a falling rhythm on a rising *base meter* creates *counterpointing*.

Feminine rhyme: Feminine rhyme occurs when (1) a line's final accented syllable is followed by a single unaccented syllable and (2) the accented syllables rhyme, while the unaccented syllables are phonetically identical, as with "flick-er/snick-er " and "fin-gers/ma-lin-gers." Feminine rhymes are often used for lightness in tone and delicacy in movement.

First person: This *point of view* is particularly useful in short lyrical poems, which tend to be highly subjective, taking the reader deep into the narrator's thoughts. First-person poems normally, though not necessarily, signal the use of the first person through the pronoun "I," allowing the reader direct access to the narrator's thoughts or providing a character who can convey a personal reaction to an event. (See also *Third person*)

Foot/feet: The natural speech pattern in English and other Germanic-based languages is to group syllables together in family units. In English, the most common of these rhythmic units is composed of one unstressed syllable attached to one stressed syllable (an *iamb*). When these family groups are forced into a line of poetry, they are called "feet" in the *accentual-syllabic* metrical system. In the line "My mis/tress' eyes/ are noth/ing like/ the sun" there are four iambic feet (˘′) and one pyrrhic foot (˘ ˘), but in the line "There where/ the vines/ cling crim/son on/ the wall" there are three *substitutions* for the iamb—in the first, third, and fourth feet. The six basic feet in English poetry are the iamb (˘′), *trochee* (′˘), *anapest* (˘˘′), *dactyl* (′˘˘), *spondee* (″), and *pyrrhus* (˘˘).

Form: The form of a poem is determined by its arrangement of lines on the page, its base meter, its rhyme scheme, and occasionally its subject matter. Poems which are arranged into *stanzas* are called "strophic," and because the strophic tradition is so old a large number of commonly used stanzas have evolved particular uses and characteristics. Poems which run from beginning to end without a break are called *stichic*. The form of "pattern poetry" is determined by its visual appearance rather than by lines and stanzas, while the definition of *free verse* is that it has no discernable form. Some poem types, such as the sestina, *sonnet*, and *ode*, are written in particular forms and frequently are restricted to particular subject matter.

Found poetry: Found poetry is created from language which is "found" in print in nonliterary settings—on menus, tombstones, fire extinguishers, even on shampoo bottles. Any language which is already constructed, but especially language which appears on artifacts that characterize society, such as cereal boxes, provides the material from which the found poem is created. The rules for writing a found poem vary, but generally the found language is used intact or altered only slightly.

Free verse: A poem that does not conform to any traditional convention, such as meter, rhyme, or form, and that does not establish any pattern within itself, is said to be a free verse poem. There is, however, great dispute over whether "free" verse actually exists. Eliot said that by definition poetry must establish some kind of pattern, and Frost said that "writing free verse is like playing tennis with the net down." However, some would agree with Carl Sandburg, who insisted that "you can play a better game with the net down." Free verse depends more on cadence than on meter.

Ghazal: The ghazal is a poetic form based on a type of Persian poetry. A ghazal is composed of couplets, often unrhymed, that function as individual images or observations but that also interrelate in sometimes subtle ways.

Gnomic verse: Gnomic verse typically includes many proverbs or maxims.

Haiku: Haiku is a Japanese form which appeared in the sixteenth century and is still practiced in Japan. A haiku consists of three lines of five, seven, and five syllables each; in Japanese there are other conventions regarding content which are not observed in Western haiku. The traditional haiku took virtually all of its images from nature, using the natural world as a *metaphor* for the spiritual.

Half rhyme: See *Approximate rhyme*

Heroic couplet: See *Couplet*

Hymn stanza: See *Ballad*

Hyperbole: When the poet deliberately overstates in order to heighten the reader's awareness, he is using hyperbole. As with *irony*, hyperbole works because the reader can perceive the difference between the importance of the dramatic situation and the manner in which it is described.

Iamb: The basic *foot* of English speech, the iamb associates one unstressed syllable with one stressed (˘´). The line "So long/as men/can breathe/or eyes/can see" is composed of five iambs. In the line "A cold/coming/we had/of it," a trochaic foot (a *trochee*) has been substituted for the expected iamb in the second foot, thus emphasizing that this is a "coming" rather than a "going," an important distinction in T. S. Eliot's "The Journey of the Magi."

Iambic pentameter: Iambic pentameter is a very common type of poetic *line* in English. It consists of five iambic feet together in a line (a foot is a two-syllable grouping). The following two lines by Thomas Wyatt are in iambic pentameter: "I find no peace and all my war is done,/ I fear and hope, I burn and freeze like ice." (See also *foot*; *iamb*)

Identical rhyme: Identical rhyme occurs when the entire final stressed syllables contain exactly the same sounds, such as "break/brake," or "bear" (noun), "bear" (verb), "bare" (adjective), "bare" (verb).

Imagery: Imagery is traditionally defined as the verbal simulation of sensory perception. Like so many critical terms, "imagery" betrays a visual bias: it suggests that a poetic image is necessarily visual, a picture in words. In fact, however, imagery calls on all five senses, although the visual is predominant in many poets. In its simplest form, an image re-creates a physical sensation in a clear, literal manner, as in Robert Lowell's lines, "A sweetish smell of shavings, wax and oil/ blows through the redone bedroom newly aged" ("Marriage"). Imagery becomes more complex when the poet employs *metaphor* and other figures of speech to re-create experience, as in Seamus Heaney's lines, "Right along the lough shore/ A smoke of flies/ Drifts thick in the sunset" ("At Ardboe Point"), substituting a fresh metaphor ("A smoke of flies") for a trite one (a cloud of flies) to help the reader visualize the scene more clearly.

Interior monologue: A first-person representation of a persona's or character's thoughts or feelings. It differs from a *dramatic monologue* in that it deals with thoughts rather than spoken words or conversation.

Internal rhyme: See *Rhyme*

Irony: Irony is among the three or four most important concepts in modern literary criticism. Although the term originated in classical Greece and has been in the vocabulary of criticism since that time, only in the nineteenth and twentieth centuries has it assumed central importance. The term is used in many different contexts with an extraordinary range of meanings, eluding precise definition. In its narrowest sense, irony is a figure of speech in which the speaker's real meaning is different from (and often exactly opposite to) the apparent meaning. In Andrew Marvell's lines, "The Grave's a fine and private place,/ But none I think do there embrace" ("To His Coy Mistress"), the speaker's literal meaning—in praise of the grave—is quite different from his real meaning. This kind of irony, the easiest to define, is often called "verbal irony." Another kind of irony is found in narrative and dramatic poetry. In the *Iliad* (c. 800 B.C.), for example, the reader is made privy to the counsels of the gods, which greatly affect the course of action in the epic, while the human characters are kept in ignorance. This discrepancy between the knowledge of the reader and that of the character (or characters) is called "dramatic irony." Beyond these narrow, well-defined varieties of irony are many wider applications.

Limerick: The limerick is a comic five-line poem rhyming *aabba* in which the third and fourth lines are shorter (usually five syllables each) than the first, second, and last lines, which are usually eight syllables each. The limerick's *anapestic* base makes the verse sound silly; modern limericks are almost invariably associated with bizarre indecency or with ethnic or anticlerical jokes.

Line: A line has been defined as a poetical unit characterized by the presence of *meter,* and lines are categorized according to the number of feet (see *Foot/feet*) they contain. A pentameter line, for example, contains five feet. This definition does not apply to a great deal of modern poetry, however, which is written in *free verse.* Ultimately, then, a line must be defined as a typographical unit on the page that performs various functions in different kinds of poetry.

Lyric poetry: The two ancient roots of poetry are the narrative and lyric traditions. Narrative poetry, such as the *Iliad,* relates long stories, often historical, which preserve information, characters, and values of a culture. Lyric poetry developed when music was accompanied by words, and although the "lyrics" were later separated from the music, the characteristics of lyric poetry have been shaped by the constraints of music. Lyric poems are short, adaptable to metrical variation, and usually personal compared with the cultural functions of narrative poetry. Lyric poetry sings of the self, exploring deeply personal feelings about life.

Mad-song: The mad-song—verse uttered by the presumably insane—usually expresses a happy, harmless, inventive sort of insanity. The typical rhyme scheme of the mad-song is *abccb,* and the unrhymed first line helps to set a tone of oddity and unpredictability, since it controverts the expectation that there will be a rhyme for it. The standard mad-song has short lines that help suggest benign madness, since "simple" people are associated with uncomplicated sentence patterns.

Masculine rhyme: Masculine rhyme occurs when rhyme exists in the stressed syllables. "Men/then" constitute masculine rhyme, but so do "af-ter-noons/spoons." Masculine rhyme is generally considered more forceful than *feminine rhyme,* and while it has a variety of uses, it generally gives authority and assurance to the line, especially when the final syllables are of short duration.

Metaphor: Metaphor, like *irony,* is one of a handful of key concepts in modern literary criticism. Like irony, the term "metaphor" is used in such a wide variety of contexts that a precise, all-encompassing definition is impossible. In its narrowest sense, metaphor is a figure of speech in which two strikingly different things are identified with each other, as in "the waves were soldiers moving" (Wallace Stevens). A metaphor contains a "tenor" and a "vehicle." The tenor is the subject of the metaphor, and the vehicle is the *imagery* by which the subject is presented. In D. H. Lawrence's lines, "Reach me a gentian, give me a torch/ let me guide myself with the blue, forked torch of this flower" ("Bavarian Gentians"), the tenor is the gentian and the vehicle is the torch. This relatively restricted definition of metaphor by no means covers the usage of the word in modern criticism. Some critics argue that metaphorical perception underlies all figures of speech. Others dispute the distinction between literal and metaphorical description, saying that language is essentially metaphorical. The term "metaphor" has become widely used to identify analogies of all kinds in literature, painting, film, and even music.

Meter: Meter is the pattern of language when it is forced into a *line* of poetry. All language has rhythm; when that rhythm is organized and regulated in the line so as to affect the meaning and emotional response to the words, then the rhythm has been refined into meter. Because the lines of most poems maintain a similar meter throughout, poems are said to have a *base meter.* The meter is determined by the number of syllables in a line and by the relationship between them.

Metonymy: When an object which is closely related to an idea comes to stand for the idea itself, such as saying "the crown" to mean the king, "metonymy" is being used. The use of a part of an object to stand for the entire object, such as using "heart" to mean a person, is called "synecdoche." Metonymy and synecdoche are used to emphasize a particular part of the whole or one particular aspect of it.

Mnemonic verse: Poetry in which rhythmic patterns aid memorization but are not crucial to meaning is called "mnemonic verse." Ancient bards were able to remember long poems partly through the use of stock phrases and other mnemonic devices.

Mock-heroic: See *Couplet.*

Narrator: The terms "narrator," "persona," and "speaker" are roughly synonymous. They all refer to who is doing the talking—or observing or thinking—in a poem. Lyric poetry most often consists of the poet expressing his or her own personal feelings directly. Other poems, however, may involve the poet adopting the *point of view* of another person entirely. In some poems—notably in a *dramatic monologue*—it is relatively easy to determine that the narrative is being related by a fictional (or perhaps historical) character, but in others it may be more difficult to identify the "I."

Occasional verse: Broadly defined, occasional verse includes any poem written for a specific occasion, such as a wedding, a birthday, a death, or a public event. Edmund Spenser's *Epithalamion* (1595), which was written for his marriage, and John Milton's "Lycidas," which commemorated the death of his schoolmate Edward King, are examples of occasional verse, as are W. H. Auden's "September 1, 1939" and Frank O'Hara's "The Day Lady Died."

Octave: An octave is a poem in eight lines. Octaves may have many different variations of meter, such as ottava rima.

Ode: The ode is a *lyric* poem which treats a unified subject with elevated emotion, usually ending with a satisfactory *resolution*. There is no set *form* for the ode, but it must be long enough to build intense emotional response. Often the ode will address itself to some omnipotent source and will take on a spiritual hue. When explicating an ode, readers should look for the relationship between the narrator and some transcendental power to which the narrator must submit in order to find contentment. Modern poets have used the ode to treat subjects which are not religious in the theological sense but which have become innate beliefs of society.

Ottava rima: Ottava rima is an eight-line *stanza* of *iambic* pentameter, rhyming *abababcc*. Probably the most famous English poem written in ottava rima is Lord Byron's *Don Juan* (1819-1824), and because the poem was so successful as a spoof, the form has come to be associated with poetic high jinks. However, the stanza has also been used brilliantly for just the opposite effect, to reflect seriousness and meditation.

Oxymoron: Closely related to *paradox*, an oxymoron occurs when two paradoxical words are placed in juxtaposition, such as "wise fool" or "devilish angel."

Pantoum: A French form of four quatrains in which entire lines are repeated in a strict pattern of 1234, 2546, 5768, 7183. Peter Meinke's "Atomic Pantoum" is an example.

Paradox: A paradox is a statement that contains an inherent contradiction. It may be a statement that at first seems true but is in reality contradictory. It may also be a statement that appears contradictory but is actually true or that contains an element of truth that reconciles the contradiction.

Pentameter: A type of rhythmic pattern in which each line consists of five poetic feet. (See also *Accentual-syllabic meter*; *Foot/feet*; *Iamb*; *Iambic pentameter*; *Line*)

Periphrasis: Periphrasis is the use of a wordy phrase to describe something that could be described simply in one word.

Persona: See *Narrator*

Point of view: Point of view may be simply defined as the eyes and other senses through which readers experience the situation of a poem. As with fiction, poems may be related in the *first person*, second person (unusual), or *third person*. (The presence of the words "I" or "we" indicates singular or plural first-person narration.) Point of view may be limited or omniscient. A limited point of view means that the narrator can see only what the poet wants him or her to see, while from an omniscient point of view the narrator can know everything, including the thoughts and motives of others.

Prose poem: The distinguishing feature of the prose poem is its typography: It appears like prose on the page, with no line breaks. There are no formal characteristics by which a prose poem can be distinguished from a piece of prose. Many prose poems employ rhythmic repetition and other poetic devices not normally found in prose, but others use such devices sparingly if at all. Prose poems range in length from a few lines to three or four pages; most prose poems occupy a page or less.

Pun: A pun occurs when words which have similar pronunciations have entirely different meanings. By use of a pun the speaker establishes a connection between two meanings or contexts that the reader would not ordinarily make. The result may be a surprise recognition of an unusual or striking connection, or, more often, a humorously accidental connection.

Pyrrhus: When two unstressed syllables comprise a foot, it is called a pyrrhus or a pyrrhic foot, as in the line "Appéar/and dis/appéar/in the/blúe depth/of the ský," in which foot four is a pyrrhus.

Quatrain: Any four-line stanza is a quatrain; aside from the *couplet,* it is the most common stanza type. The quatrain's popularity among both sophisticated and unsophisticated readers suggests that there is something inherently pleasing about the form. For many readers, poetry and quatrains are almost synonymous. Balance and antithesis, contrast and comparison not possible in other stanza types are indigenous to the quatrain.

Regular meter: A *line* of poetry that contains only the same type of *foot* is said to be regular. Only the dullest of poems maintains a regular meter throughout, however; skillful poets create interest and *emphasis* through *substitution*.

Relative stress: When more emphasis is placed on one syllable in a pattern than on another, that syllable is said to be "stressed." Once the dominant stress in the line has been determined, every other syllable can be assigned a stress factor relative to the dominant syllable. The stress factor is created by several aspects of prosody: the position of the syllable in the *line,* the position of the syllable in its word, the surrounding syllables, the type of vowels and consonants which constitute the syllable, and the syllable's relation to the *foot, base meter,* and *caesura.* Since every syllable will have a different stress factor, there could be as many values as there are syllables, although most prosodists *scan* poems using primary, secondary, and unstressed notations. In the line "I am thĕre likĕ thĕ deád, or thĕ beást" the anapestic base meter will not permit "I" to take a full stress, but it is a more forceful syllable than the unstressed ones, so it is assigned a secondary stress. Relative to "dead" and "beast," it takes less pressure; relative to the articles in the line, it takes much more.

Resolution: Generally, a resolution is any natural conclusion to a poem, especially to a short *lyric* poem which establishes some sort of dilemma or conflict that the narrator must solve. Specifically, the resolution is the octave stanza of a Petrarchan *sonnet* or the couplet of a Shakespearean sonnet in which the first part of the poem presents a situation which must find balance in the resolution.

Rhyme: Rhyme is a correspondence of sound between syllables within a line or between lines whose proximity to each other allows the sounds to be sustained. Rhyme may be classified in a number of ways: according to the sound relationship between rhyming words, the position of the rhyming words in the line, and the number and position of the syllables in the rhyming words. Sound classifications include full rhyme and approximate rhyme. Full rhyme is defined as words that have the same vowel sound, followed by the same consonants in their last stressed syllables, and in which all succeeding syllables are phonetically identical. "Hat/cat" and "laughter/after" are full rhymes. Categories of *approximate rhyme* are *assonance, slant rhyme, alliteration, eye rhyme,* and *identical rhyme.*

Rhyme classified by its position in the line includes end, internal, and initial rhyme. End rhyme occurs when the last words of lines rhyme. Internal rhyme occurs when two words within the same line or within various lines recall the same sound, as in "Wet, below the snow line, smelling of vegetation" in which "below" and "snow" rhyme. Initial rhyme occurs when the first syllables of two or more lines rhyme. (See also *Masculine rhyme; Feminine rhyme*)

Rhyme scheme: Poems that establish a pattern of rhyme have a "rhyme scheme," designated by lowercase (and often italicized) letters. The letters stand for the pattern of rhyming sounds of the last word in each line. For example, the following A. E. Housman quatrain has an *abab* rhyme scheme.

> Into my heart an air that kills
> From yon far country blows:
> What are those blue remembered hills,
> What spires, what farms are those?

As another example, the rhyme scheme of the poetic form known as *ottava rima* is *abababcc.* Traditional stanza forms are categorized by their rhyme scheme and *base meter.*

Rime royal: The only standard seven-line stanza in English prosody is rime royal, composed of iambic pentameter lines rhyming *ababbccc*. Shakespeare's *The Rape of Lucrece* (1594) is written in this form. The only variation permitted is to make the last line hexameter.

Rondeau: One of three standard French forms assimilated by English prosody, the rondeau generally contains thirteen lines divided into three groups. A common stanzaic grouping rhymes *aabba, aabR, aabbaR*, where the *a* and *b* lines are tetrameter and the *R* (refrain) lines are dimeter. The rondel, another French form, contains fourteen lines of trimeter with alternating rhyme (*ababab babab*) and is divided into two stanzas. The rondeau and rondel forms are always light and playful.

Rondel: See *Rondeau*

Scansion: Scanning is the process of assigning *relative stresses* and meter to a line of poetry, usually for the purpose of determining where variations, and thus emphasis, in the *base meter* occur. Scansion can help explain how a poem generates tension and of-fer clues as to the key words. E. E. Cummings's "singing each morning out of each night" could be scanned in two ways: (1) singing/each morn/ing out/of each night or (2) sing/ing each/morning/out of/each night. Scansion will not only affect the way the line is read aloud but will also influence the meaning of the line.

Secondary stress: See *Relative stress*

Seguidilla: Like the Japanese haiku, the Spanish seguidilla is a mood or imagistic poem whose success hinges on the reader's emotional recognition or spiritual insight. Although there is no agreement as to what form the English seguidilla should take, most of the successful ones are either four or seven lines with an alternating *rhyme scheme* of *ababcbc*. Lines 1, 3, and 6 are trimeter; lines 2, 4, 5, and 7 dimeter.

Sestet: A sestet is a six-line stanza. A Petrarchan or Italian sonnet is composed of an octave followed by a sestet, as in John Milton's Sonnet XIX and William Words-worth's "The World Is Too Much with Us."

Sestina: A sestina is composed of six six-line stanzas followed by a three-line envoy. The words ending the lines in the first stanza are repeated in different order at the ends of lines in the following stanzas as well as in the the middle and end of each line of the envoy. Elizabeth Bishop's "Sestina" is a good example.

Shakespearean sonnet: See *Sonnet*

Simile: Loosely defined, a simile is a type of *metaphor* that signals a comparison by the use of the words "like" or "as." Shakespeare's line "My mistress' eyes are nothing like the sun" is a simile that establishes a comparison between the woman's eyes and the sun.

Slant rhyme: See *Approximate rhyme*

Sonnet: The most important and widely used of traditional poem types, the sonnet is almost always composed of fourteen lines of iambic pentameter with some form of alternating rhyme, and it contains a turning point that divides the poem into two parts. The two major sonnet types are the "Petrarchan" (or "Italian") sonnet and the "Shakespearian" sonnet. The original sonnet form, the Petrarchan (adopted from the poetry of Petrarch), presents a problem or situation in the first eight lines, the "octave," then resolves it in the last six, the "sextet." The octave is composed of two *quatrains* (*abbaabba*), the second of which complicates the first and gradually defines and heightens the problem. The sestet then diminishes the problem slowly until a satisfying resolution is achieved.

During the fifteenth century, the Italian sonnet became an integral part of the courtship ritual, and most sonnets during that time consisted of a young man's description of his perfect lover. Because so many unpoetic young men had generated a nation full of bad sonnets by the end of the century, the form became an object of ridicule, and the English sonnet developed as a reaction against all the bad verse being turned out in the Italian tradition. When Shakespeare wrote "My mistress' eyes are nothing like the sun," he was deliberately negating the Petrarchan conceit, rejoicing in the fact that his loved one was much more interesting and unpredictable than nature. Shakespeare also altered the sonnet's formal balance. Instead of an octave, the Shakespearean sonnet has three quatrains of alternating rhyme and is resolved in a final couplet. During the sixteenth century, long stories were told in sonnet form, one sonnet after the next, to produce "sonnet sequences." Although most sonnets contain fourteen lines, some contain as few as ten (the curtal sonnet) or as many as seventeen.

Speaker: See *Narrator*

Split foot: A split foot occurs when the natural division of a word is altered as a result of being forced into a metrical base. For example, the words "point/ed," "lad/der," and "stick/ing" have a natural falling rhythm, but in the line "My long/two-point/ed lad/der's stick/ing through/a tree" the syllables are rearranged so as to turn the falling rhythm into a rising meter. The result of splitting feet is to create an uncertainty and delicate imbalance in the line.

Spondee: When two relatively stressed syllables occur together in a foot, the unit is called a "spondee" or "spondaic foot," as in the line "Appear/and dis/appear/in the/blue depth/of the sky."

Sprung rhythm: If *accentual meter* is taken to its extreme, one can never predict the patterns of succeeding stresses: It is possible only to predict a prescribed number of stresses per line. This unpredictability characterizes sprung rhythm, first described near the end of the nineteenth century by Gerard Manley Hopkins. In sprung rhythm "any two stresses may either follow one another running, or be divided by one, two, or three slack syllables."

Stanza: When a certain number of lines are meant to be taken as a unit, that unit is called a "stanza." Although a stanza is traditionally considered a unit that contains rhyme and recurs predictably throughout a poem, the term is also sometimes applied to nonrhyming and even irregular units. Poems that are divided into fairly regular and patterned stanzas are called "strophic"; poems that appear as a single unit, whether rhymed or unrhymed, or that have no predictable stanzas, are called "stichic." Both strophic and stichic units represent logical divisions within the poem, and the difference between them lies in the formality and strength of the interwoven unit. Stanza breaks are commonly indicated by a line of space.

Stichic verse: See *Stanza*

Stress: See *Relative stress*

Strophic verse: See *Stanza*

Substitution: Substitution, one of the most common and effective methods by which the poet can emphasize a foot, occurs when one type of foot is replaced by another within a *base meter.* For example, in the line "Thy life/a long/ dead calm/of fixed/ repose," a spondaic foot (″) has been substituted for an iambic foot (‿′). Before substitution is possible, the reader's expectations must have been established by a base meter so that a change in those expectations will have an effect. (See also *Foot/feet; iamb; spondee*)

Syllabic meter: The system of meter which measures only the number of syllables per line, without regard to stressed and unstressed syllables, is called syllabic meter.

Symbol: Loosely defined, a symbol is any sign that a number of people agree stands for something else. Poetic symbols cannot be rigidly defined; a symbol often evokes a cluster of meanings rather than a single specific meaning. For example, the rose, which suggests fragile beauty, gentleness, softness, and sweet aroma, has come to symbolize love, eternal beauty, or virginity. The tide traditionally symbolizes, among other things, time and eternity. Modern poets may use personal symbols; these take on significance in the context of the poem or of a poet's body of work, particularly if they are reinforced throughout. For example, through constant reinforcement swans in William Butler Yeats's poetry come to mean as much to the reader as they do to the narrator.

Synaeresis: See *Elision*

Synecdoche: See *Metonymy*

Tenor: See *Metaphor*

Tercet: A tercet is any form of a rhyming triplet. Examples are *aaa bbb*, as used in Thomas Hardy's "Convergence of the Twain"; *aba cdc*, in which *b* and *d* do not rhyme; *aba bcb*, also known as terza rima.

Terza rima: Terza rima is a three-line stanzaic form in which the middle line of one stanza rhymes with the first line of the following stanza, and whose rhyme scheme is *aba bcb cdc*, and so on. Since the rhyme scheme of one stanza can be completed only by adding the next stanza, terza rima tends to propel itself forward, and as a result of this strong forward motion it is well suited to long narration.

Theme: Loosely defined as "what a poem means," theme more specifically refers to recurring elements. The term is sometimes used interchangeably with "motif." A motif is any recurring pattern of images, symbols, ideas, or language and is usually restricted to the internal workings of the poem. Thus, one might say that there is an animal motif in William Butler Yeats's poem "Sailing to Byzantium." Theme, however, is usually more general and philosophical, so that the theme of "Sailing to Byzantium" might be interpreted as the failure of human attempts to isolate oneself within the world of art.

Third person: Third-person narration exists when a poem's narrator, or speaker, has not been part of the events described and is not probing his or her own relationship to them; rather, the speaker is describing what happened without the use of the word "I" (which would indicate first-person narration). A poet may use a third-person *point of view*, either limited or omniscient, to establish a distance between the reader and the subject, to give credibility to a large expanse of narration, or to allow the poem to include a number of characters who can be commented on by the narrator.

Tone: Strictly defined, tone is the expression of a poet's attitude toward the subject and persona of the poem as well as about him- or herself, society, and the poem's readers. If the ultimate aim of art is to express and control emotions and attitudes, then tone is one of the most important elements of poetry. Tone is created through the denotative and connotative meanings of words and through the sound of language (principally, *rhyme, consonants,* and *diction*). Adjectives such as "satirical," "compassionate," "empathetic," "ironical," and "sarcastic" are used to describe tone.

Trochee: One of the most common feet in English poetry, the trochee associates one stressed syllable with one unstressed syllable (´˘), as in the line: "Double/double toil and/trouble." Trochaic lines are frequently *substituted* in an iambic *base meter* in order to create counterpointing. (See also *Foot/feet*; *iamb*)

Truncation: Truncation occurs when the last, unstressed syllable of a falling line is omitted, as in the line: "Tyger,/tyger/burning/bright," where the "ly" has been dropped from bright."

Vehicle: See *Metaphor*

Verse: The term "verse" has two or three different applications. It is a generic term for poetry, as in *The Oxford Book of English Verse* (1939). Verse also refers in a narrower sense to poetry that is humorous or superficial, as in "light verse" or "greeting-card verse." Finally, "verse" is sometimes used to mean *stanza* or *line*.

Verse drama: Drama which is written in poetic rather than ordinary language and which is characterized and delivered by the *line* is called "verse drama." Verse drama flourished during the eighteenth century, when the *couplet* became a standard literary form.

Verse paragraph: A division created within a stichic poem (see *Stanza*) by logic or syntax, rather than by form, is called a "verse paragraph." These are important for determining the movement of a poem and the logical association between ideas.

Villanelle: The villanelle, like the *rondeau* and the rondel, is a French verse form that has been assimilated by English prosody. It is usually composed of nineteen lines divided into five tercets and a quatrain, rhyming *aba*, *bba*, *aba*, *aba*, *abaa*. The third line is repeated in the ninth and fifteenth lines. Dylan Thomas's "Do Not Go Gentle into That Good Night" is a modern English example of a villanelle.

BIBLIOGRAPHY

General Works: Critical and Theoretical

Abrams, M. H. *A Glossary of Literary Terms*. 7th ed. Fort Worth, Tex.: Harcourt Brace College, 1999. An indispensable handbook, containing concise essays on a large number of topics—some basic, some advanced. Many entries are supplemented by a bibliography.

_____. *The Mirror and the Lamp: Romantic Theory and the Critical Tradition*. 1953. Reprint. New York: Oxford University Press, 1976. A landmark study examining the development of Romantic literary theory. Abrams shows how the expressive poetic theory of the Romantics (symbolized by the lamp) differed sharply from traditional mimetic theory (symbolized by the mirror); covers many related topics.

Alden, Raymond Macdonald. *English Verse: Specimens Illustrating Its Principles and History*. 1911. Reprint. New York: AMS Press, 1970. Standard reference work that provides all the materials necessary for a complete study of English verse forms.

Allen, Gay Wilson. *American Prosody*. New York: American Book Company, 1934. A historical introduction, from Philip Freneau to Emily Dickinson. Its purpose is to trace the theories of the American poets regarding techniques and to analyze their practice of them.

Attridge, Derek. *Poetic Rhythm: An Introduction*. New York: Cambridge University Press, 1995. Focuses on accentual-syllabic verse in Middle and modern English; includes survey of traditional and linguistic approaches to meter, with chapters on rhythm in the English language, metrical conventions, and critical implications of rhythmic forms.

_____. *The Rhythms of English Poetry*. London: Longman, 1982. This has won universal praise as one of the best books in the field. Summarizes traditional approaches, then provides detailed analysis of rhythm and meter, focusing on the tradition of regular accentual-syllabic verse in Middle and modern English.

_____. *Well-Weighed Syllables: Elizabethan Verse in Classical Metres*. London: Cambridge University Press, 1974. Comprehensive study of Elizabethan knowledge of, and attempts to write in, quantitative meter. Concludes with a survey of Elizabethan quantitative poets and theorists including Sidney, Spenser, and Campion.

Barfield, Owen. *Poetic Diction: A Study of Meaning*. 3d ed. Middletown, Conn.: Wesleyan University Press, 1973. Frequently cited theoretical study; includes an influential chapter on metaphor.

Baum, Paull Franklin. *The Principles of English Versification*. Cambridge, Mass.: Harvard University Press, 1922. Standard work, concise and clearly written; very helpful for the beginner.

Bloom, Harold. *The Anxiety of Influence: A Theory of Poetry.* 2d ed. New York: Oxford University Press, 1997. Influential theory about how one poet influences another. Bloom argues that poets deliberately misread their predecessors in order to carve out a space in which their own creative imaginations can flourish.

_____. *A Map of Misreading.* New York: Oxford University Press, 1975. Bloom's theory of the anxiety of influence is applied to a variety of poetic texts, including those written in the shadow of Milton and Emerson.

Bodkin, Maud. *Archetypal Patterns in Poetry: Psychological Studies of Imagination.* 1934. Reprint. New York: AMS Press, 1978. The first book to apply Jungian psychology, particularly the concept of archetypes, to the study of poetry. Bodkin's thoughtful approach still remains useful and can shed light on aspects of Coleridge, Shakespeare, Dante, Milton, and T. S. Eliot.

Booth, Wayne C. *A Rhetoric of Irony.* Chicago: University of Chicago Press, 1974. More advanced treatment than Hodgart or Muecke, but witty and engaging. Booth describes it as "a book about how we manage to share ironies and why we often do not."

Brooks, Cleanth. *The Well-Wrought Urn: Studies in the Structure of Poetry.* New York: Reynal & Hitchcock, 1947. Very influential book by one of the leading practitioners of the New Criticism. Essays on poems by Milton, Gray, Donne, Pope, Wordsworth, Keats, Tennyson, Yeats. Emphasis is on paradox and ambiguity.

Brooks, Cleanth, and Robert Penn Warren. *Understanding Poetry.* 4th ed. New York: Harcourt Brace Jovanovich, 1988. Ten essays on such topics as metaphor, wit, Metaphysical and Symbolist poetry, and the poetry of Frost, T. S. Eliot, and Yeats.

Chatman, Seymour. *A Theory of Meter.* The Hague: Mouton, 1965. Important work using structural linguistics to develop a theory of meter. Not easy reading, but the analysis of eleven recorded readings of Shakespeare's Sonnet 18 in chapter 6 is very stimulating.

Christ, Carol T. *Victorian and Modern Poetics.* Chicago: University of Chicago Press, 1984. Examines similarities between Victorian and modernist poets (especially Yeats, Pound, and T. S. Eliot) and their common reactions against aspects of the Romantic tradition.

Curtis, Tony. *How to Study Modern Poetry.* London: Macmillan, 1990. Designed to develop critical skills; gives practical advice on writing about modern poetry. Includes chapters on the poetry of each decade from the 1940's to the 1980's.

Davie, Donald. *Purity of Diction in English Poetry.* London: Routledge & Kegan Paul, 1952. An attempt to define the principles underlying what Davie calls "purity" of diction. Concentrates on English poetry of the eighteenth and nineteenth centuries.

Deutsch, Babette. *Poetry Handbook: A Dictionary of Terms.* 4th ed. New York: Funk & Wagnalls, 1974. A classic but still useful guide to poetry terms, with examples drawn from a wide range of poets.

Eagleton, Terry. *Literary Theory: An Introduction.* 2d ed. Minneapolis: University of Minnesota Press, 1996. Readable introduction to literary theory intended for those with little or no previous knowledge. Covers phenomenology, hermeneutics, reception theory, structuralism, semiotics, post-structuralism, and psychoanalysis.

Easthope, Antony. *Poetry as Discourse.* New York: Methuen, 1983. Treats poetry as a form of discourse that is marked by giving precedence to the signifier; focuses on British poetry.

Empson, William. *Seven Types of Ambiguity.* 1930. Rev. ed. New York: New Directions, 1947. Influential essays on ambiguity, classified under seven different headings. Ambiguity is defined as "any verbal nuance, however, slight, which gives room for alternative reactions to the same piece of language." Includes stimulating discussions of Chaucer, Shakespeare, Donne, Marvell, Pope, Wordsworth, Hopkins, and Eliot.

Ferry, Anne. *The Title to the Poem.* Stanford, Calif.: Stanford University Press, 1996. Innovative study of the conventions and complex functions of the titles of poems, illustrated by examples from poetry of Britain and the United States.

Fletcher, Angus. *Allegory: The Theory of a Symbolic Mode.* Ithaca, N.Y.: Cornell University Press, 1964. A wide-ranging theoretical analysis of the literary elements of allegory; employs concepts drawn from psychoanalysis, comparative religion (particularly religious ritual and symbolism), and anthropology. Includes thirty-two illustrations of allegorical paintings.

Fraser, G. S. *Metre, Rhyme, and Free Verse.* London: Methuen. 1970. A primer that is distinguished by the author's informal style and good critical sense. Explains basic principles and uses a wide range of literature as examples. Annotated bibliography.

Frye, Northrop. *Anatomy of Criticism: Four Essays.* 1957. Reprint. Princeton, N.J.: Princeton University Press, 2001. Extremely influential work that attempts to encompass the entire range of literature in a comprehensive theory. Emphasis is on archetypal criticism and recurring mythic patterns in literature.

————, ed. *Sound and Poetry.* New York: Columbia University Press, 1957. Collection of six theoretical essays, with an introduction by Frye on rhythm in poetry and music.

Fussell, Paul, Jr. *Poetic Meter and Poetic Form.* Rev. ed. New York: Random House, 1979. One of the most useful of short introductions. Chapters on meter, scansion, metrical variations, the sonnet, and the various forms of the English stanza. Annotated bibliography.

Graff, Gerald. *Poetic Statement and Critical Dogma.* Evanston, Ill.: Northwestern University Press, 1980. Useful for its critique of the New Criticism, and of myth critics such as Frye and Wheelwright.

Gross, Harvey, ed. *The Structure of Verse: Modern Essays on Prosody.* Rev. ed. New York: Ecco Press, 1979. Wide-ranging collection of fifteen essays. Part 1 deals with the function of sound in literary structure and the psychological effects of rhythmic organization. Part 2 is on metrical theory; in this section, Northrop Frye's "The Rhythm of Recurrence: Epos" and Yvor Winters's "The Audible Reading of Poetry" should especially be noted. Part 3 deals with literary criticism.

Hall, Donald, ed. *Claims for Poetry*. Ann Arbor: University of Michigan Press, 1982. Anthology in which forty-three contemporary American poets discuss their ideas about poetry. Poets represented include A. R. Ammons, Robert Bly, Denise Levertov, W. S. Merwin, Adrienne Rich, Gary Snyder, and Richard Wilbur.

Hamburger, Michael. *The Truth of Poetry: Tensions in Modernist Poetry Since Baudelaire*. 1968. Reprint. London: Anvil Press Poetry, 1996. An attempt to understand the nature and function of modern poetry and the ways in which it differs from other poetry. Poets discussed include Yeats, Pound, Eliot, Crane, García Lorca, Neruda, Mallarmé, Valery, Rilke, Marianne Moore, and William Carlos Williams. With updated postscript.

Hartman, Charles O.. *Free Verse: An Essay on Prosody*. Princeton, N.J.: Princeton University Press, 1980. Important study that seeks to explain the prosody of free verse, with a brief historical introduction, survey of responses to free verse, and numerous examples. Analyzes poems by William Carlos Williams and T. S. Eliot and comments on developments in the prosody of contemporary verse.

Haublein, Ernst. *The Stanza*. New York: Methuen, 1978. Concise introduction that includes chapters on stanza form, stanzaic unity, and stanza and poetic structure. Annotated bibliography.

Hodgart, Matthew. *Satire*. New York: McGraw-Hill, 1969. Concise, well-illustrated introduction to literary satire. Covers origins, techniques, and forms of satire; topics of satire (with chapters on politics and women); and satire in drama and in the novel.

Hollander, John. *Rhyme's Reason*. 3d ed. New Haven, Conn.: Yale University Press, 2001. Witty and ingenious short guide by a poet renowned for his mastery of prosody. Students and others will enjoy Hollander's many original examples, which embody the forms and variations he wishes to illustrate.

_____. *Vision and Resonance: Two Senses of Poetic Form*. 2d ed. New Haven, Conn.: Yale University Press, 1985. Collection of essays by a leading poet and critic on the structure of verse. Includes analysis of a variety of poetic texts, from Donne and Ben Jonson to Wallace Stevens and William Carlos Williams. Particularly useful insights into the relation of verse to music.

Hosek, Chaviva, and Patricia Parker, eds. *Lyric Poetry: Beyond New Criticism*. Ithaca, N.Y.: Cornell University Press, 1985. A collection of essays intended to introduce students to criticism and theory as it has developed after the influential school of New Criticism. Useful for undergraduates.

Ing, Catherine. *Elizabethan Lyrics: A Study in the Development of English Metres and Their Relation to Poetic Effect*. 1951. Reprint. New York: Barnes & Noble, 1971. This study of the development of English meters includes a very useful chapter on Renaissance theories of meter and detailed analysis of the lyrics of Thomas Campion, as well as a survey of lyrics by Shakespeare, Spenser, Donne, and others.

Jones, R. T. *Studying Poetry: An Introduction*. London: Edward Arnold, 1986. Useful brief study that employs various approaches to understanding what constitutes a poem and what a poem is about. Examples drawn from a wide range, including

Shakespeare, Marvell, Blake, Stevens, and Hopkins. The aim is to encourage readers to find their own ways of reading.

Jump, John. *The Ode*. New York: Methuen, 1974. Brief introductory study, covering classical models of the ode, the development of the ode in English literature, and examples of odes from the nineteenth and twentieth centuries. Annotated bibliography.

Ker, William Paton. *Form and Style in Poetry*. Edited by R. W. Chambers. 1928. Reprint. New York: Russell & Russell, 1966. Most useful here are the twenty-four "London lectures" on form and style, which succinctly cover a wide range of topics.

Kirby-Smith, H. T. *The Origins of Free Verse*. Ann Arbor: University of Michigan Press, 1996. Situates modern free verse in a broader historical context of "cycles" of nonmetrical poetry that begin as early as the Renaissance. An important study.

Kreuzer, James R. *Elements of Poetry*. New York: Macmillan, 1955. Each chapter is devoted to one or more of the major elements of poetry. Useful for the student because each chapter is followed by exercises consisting of poems for analysis.

Lambropoulos, Vassilis, and David Neal Miller, eds. *Twentieth Century Literary Theory: An Introductory Anthology*. New York: State University of New York Press, 1987. Organized around ten topics and containing thirty essays, this is an ideal anthology for anyone interested in modern literary theory. Includes chronology and list of supplementary readings.

Leech, Geoffrey N. *A Linguistic Guide to English Poetry*. London: Longman, 1969. Intended as an introduction to stylistics for students of English. Leech provides a framework for the interpretation of the linguistic aspects of poetry.

Lindley, David. *Lyric*. New York: Methuen, 1985. Introductory study that discusses categories and definitions, the relation between lyric and music, and the lyric "I." Annotated bibliography.

MacQueen, John. *Allegory*. New York: Methuen, 1970. One of the best introductions to allegory; suitable for the beginner. Covers Greek, Roman, and biblical allegory, medieval theories of allegory, allegory and the individual, and allegory and satire.

Miles, Josephine. *Eras and Modes in English Poetry*. 1964. Reprint. Westport, Conn.: Greenwood Press, 1976. Concerned with basic traits or structures of language and how they change over a long period of time. Covers English poetry from 1500 in terms of eras of emphasis, then covers the seventeenth to nineteenth centuries in terms of single modes and their developments.

Muecke, D. C. *The Compass of Irony*. London: Methuen, 1969. One of the best introductions to irony. Analyzes and classifies the principal forms of irony; includes an important chapter on Romantic irony. Bibliography.

Murray, Gilbert. *The Classical Tradition in Poetry*. 1927. Reprint. New York: Russell & Russell, 1968. The essence and spirit of the Greco-Roman literary tradition is defined; Murray holds that the greatest English poetry throughout the ages is that which embodies the classical spirit.

Olson, Elder. *Aristotle's "Poetics" and English Literature: A Collection of Critical Essays*. Chicago: University of Chicago Press, 1965. Fourteen essays, ranging from the eighteenth to the twentieth century, that show the influence of Aristotle on English literature.

Parini, Jay, ed. *The Columbia History of American Poetry.* New York: Columbia University Press, 1993. A collection of essays by various scholars on poets, movements, and genres in American poetry from its beginnings to the present. Coverage is somewhat uneven, especially for ethnic and women writers.

Paulson, Ronald, ed. *Satire: Modern Essays in Criticism.* Englewood Cliffs, N.J.: Prentice-Hall, 1971. Twenty essays forming a representative collection of criticism from 1912 to 1968. Includes important work by Maynard Mack, W. H. Auden, Northrop Frye, and Alvin P. Kernan.

Perkins, David. *A History of Modern Poetry: From the 1890's to the High Modernist Mode.* Vol. 1 in *A History of Modern Poetry.* 2 vols. Cambridge, Mass.: Belknap Press of Harvard University Press, 1976.

_____. *A History of Modern Poetry: Modernism and After.* Vol. 2 in *A History of Modern Poetry.* 2 vols. Cambridge, Mass.: Belknap Press of Harvard University Press, 1987. Valuable and thorough history of modern English and American poetry. Inclusion of lesser-known writers and historical detail places the contributions of important poets, journals, and genres in contemporary context.

Piper, William Bowman. *The Heroic Couplet.* Cleveland: Press of Case Western Reserve University, 1969. A history of the development of the heroic couplet that concentrates on the period between 1585 and 1785, when nearly every English poet employed the form. Includes forty-eight brief essays on the use made of the heroic couplet by individual poets from Chaucer to Keats.

Preminger, Alex, and T. V. F. Brogan, eds. *New Princeton Encyclopedia of Poetry and Poetics.* 3d ed. Princeton, N.J.: Princeton University Press, 1993. Comprehensive handbook with more than one thousand individual entries that deal with the history, theory, technique. and criticism of poetry from earliest times to the present.

Rhys, Ernest. *Lyric Poetry.* 1913. Reprint. New York: AMS Press, 1973. Many later scholars have been indebted to this fine study, which is a history of the English lyric from earliest times to the Victorian age.

Ruthven, K. K. *The Conceit.* London: Methuen. 1969. Concise study dealing with the theoretical basis of conceits, some common types of conceit, and the decline of the conceit from the middle of the seventeenth century.

Sacks, Peter M. *The English Elegy: Studies in the Genre from Spenser to Yeats.* Baltimore: The Johns Hopkins University Press, 1985. Sacks puts forward an interpretive approach to the genre, followed by close readings of individual works, including those by Spenser, Milton, Jonson, Dryden, Gray, Shelley, Tennyson, Swinburne, Hardy, and Yeats.

Saintsbury, George. *A History of English Prosody, from the Twelfth Century to the Present Day.* 2d ed. 3 vols. New York: Russell & Russell, 1961. Exhaustive treatment, probably in more detail than the average student requires. Much of the most useful material was reprinted in Saintsbury's *Historical Manual of English Prosody* (1910. Reprint. New York: Schocken Books, 1966).

Scully, James, ed. *Modern Poetics*. New York: McGraw-Hill, 1965. Fifteen modern poets write about their own theories of poetry: Yeats, Pound, Frost, Eliot, William Carlos Williams, Hopkins, John Crowe Ransom, Marianne Moore, E. E. Cummings, Wallace Stevens, Hart Crane, Auden, Dylan Thomas, David Jones, and Robert Lowell.

Shafer, Robert. *The English Ode to 1660: An Essay in Literary History*. 1918. Reprint. New York: Haskell House, 1966. Examines the odes of Pindar and Horace and the development of the English ode in the work of Drayton, Milton, Ben Jonson, and Jonson followers Lovelace, Marvell, and Cowley.

Shapiro, Karl, and Robert Benn. *A Prosody Handbook*. New York: Harper & Row, 1965. A concise and useful manual intended for the general reader of poetry. Includes a glossary and extensive bibliography, covering 171 items ranging from Aristotle to works published in 1963.

Shuster, G. N. *The English Ode from Milton to Keats*. 1940. Reprint. Gloucester, Mass.: Peter Smith, 1964. Studies the English ode from the middle of the seventeenth century to the middle of the nineteenth. Considers the development of the form and the use to which it was put by poets such as Milton, Crashaw, Cowley, Dryden, Collins, Gray, and Keats. Emphasizes the relationship between poetry and music.

Smith, Barbara. *Poetic Closure: A Study of How Poems End*. Chicago: University of Chicago Press, 1968. A highly praised, fascinating, and very readable study of how poems end, ranging from Elizabethan lyrics to modern poetry. Smith's fundamental point is that the effects of closure depend mostly on the reader's experience of the structure of the whole poem. Particularly interesting on the development of a sense of "anticlosure" in the modern poem.

Spearing, A. C. *Medieval to Renaissance in English Poetry*. New York: Cambridge University Press, 1985. Examines English poetry from Chaucer through Spenser. Seeing Chaucer as having introduced ideas that would continue through the Renaissance, Spearing traces the Chaucerian tradition though later writers.

Spiller, Michael R. G. *The Development of the Sonnet: An Introduction*. New York: Routledge, 1992. Historical survey of the sonnet form from its Italian origins through its use by English Renaissance writers from Wyatt and Surrey through Milton.

_____. *The Sonnet Sequence: A Study of Its Strategies*. Studies in Literary Themes and Genres 13. New York: Twayne, 1997. Offers a concise introduction to the history of the sonnet form and the sonnet sequence, then treats various kinds of sequences (formal, topographical, narrative, lyric, and philosophical). Includes a bibliographical essay for further study.

Steele, Tim. *Missing Measures: Modern Poetry and the Revolt Against Meter.* Fayetteville: University of Arkansas Press, 1990. Examines the ideas and conditions that led to the rise of modern free verse poetry. Focuses on the cultural and intellectual environment of the late nineteenth and early twentieth century, and on British and American poets.

Symonds, John Addington. *Blank Verse*. 1895. Reprint. New York: AMS Press, 1970. Three short essays, including a history of blank verse and an analysis of the blank verse of Milton.

Thompson. John. *The Founding of English Metre*. 1961. Reprint. New York: Columbia University Press, 1989. Examines the development of the iambic line in Elizabethan literature. From this narrow focus, Thompson develops a theory of what meter is and how it developed. Very highly recommended.

Tindall, William York. *The Literary Symbol*. Bloomington: Indiana University Press, 1965. Engaging and undogmatic, this study covers a wide range of modern Symbolist poetry, including Yeats, Stevens, Baudelaire, Hopkins, Eliot, Auden, Dylan Thomas, and Lawrence.

Tuve, Rosemond. *Allegorical Imagery: Some Mediaeval Books and Their Posterity*. 1966. Reprint. Princeton, N.J.: Princeton University Press, 1977. On the uses and meanings of allegory in medieval texts, and how allegorical imagery stemming from those texts was used by English poets of the sixteenth century. Particularly illuminates the poetry of Spenser.

Wells, H. W. *Poetic Imagery*. New York: Columbia University Press, 1924. General study of imagery in Elizabethan literature, analyzed under eight types of poetic metaphor. Includes analyses of Sidney, Daniel, Kyd, Spenser, Bacon, Marlowe, Nash, and Shakespeare.

Welsh, Andrew. *Roots of Lyric: Primitive Poetry and Modern Poetics*. Princeton, N.J.: Princeton University Press, 1978. Fascinating study of the roots of lyric poetry as found in riddles, charms, and chants of primitive and folk poetry. Welsh traces further developments through Renaissance emblem books, Japanese haiku, and the satires of John Skelton, and finds the roots of the lyric still present in modern poets such as Pound, Williams, Yeats, and Hopkins.

Wheelwright, Philip. *The Burning Fountain: A Study in the Language of Symbolism*. Rev. ed. Gloucester, Mass.: Peter Smith, 1982. Influential book that applies myth and archetypal criticism to literature and art; includes an excellent chapter on T. S. Eliot's *Four Quartets*.

Wimsatt, William K. *The Verbal Icon: Studies in the Meaning of Poetry*, 1954. Reprint. Lexington: University Press of Kentucky, 1989. A collection of seventeen essays. Topics include the kind of meaning that literature has and how this is embodied in concepts such as metaphor and symbol; the relation of literary value to moral value; style viewed as a level of meaning; and the relation of literature to other arts.

_____, ed. *Versification: Major Language Types*. New York: New York University Press, 1972. Sixteen essays on the principles of versification in different languages, including classical Chinese, classical Greek and Latin, Germanic, Italian, Spanish, French, and English. Rae Ann Nager has contributed a very useful annotated bibliography covering English versification.

Woodring, Carl, and James Shapiro, eds. *The Columbia History of British Poetry*. New York: Columbia University Press, 1993. A useful overview of British poetry from Old English through 1990. Bibliographies for further reading follow each chapter.

Works on Individual Authors
Anna Akhmatova

Amert, Susan. *In a Shattered Mirror: The Later Poetry of Anna Akhmatova.* Stanford, Calif.: Stanford University Press, 1992.

Driver, Sam N. *Anna Akhmatova.* New York: Twayne, 1972.

Haight, Amanda. *Anna Akhmatova: A Poetic Pilgrimage.* 1976. Reprint. New York: Oxford University Press, 1990.

Reeder, Robert. *Anna Akhmatova: Poet and Prophet.* New York: St. Martin's Press, 1994.

Rosslyn, Wendy, ed. *The Speech of Unknown Eyes: Akhmatova's Readers on Her Poetry.* Nottingham, England: Astra Books, 1990.

A. R. Ammons

Bloom, Harold, ed. *A. R. Ammons.* New York: Chelsea House, 1987.

Holder, Alan. *A. R. Ammons.* Boston: Twayne, 1978.

Kirschten, Robert, ed. *Critical Essays on A. R. Ammons.* New York: G. K. Hall, 1997.

Schneider, Steven Paul. *A. R. Ammons and the Poetics of Widening Scope.* Rutherford, N.J.: Fairleigh Dickinson University Press, 1994.

Guillaume Apollinaire

Bates, Scott. *Guillaume Apollinaire.* Boston: Twayne, 1989.

Berry, David C. *The Creative Vision of Guillaume Apollinaire: A Study of Imagination.* Saratoga, Calif.: Anma Libri, 1982.

Bohn, Willem. *Apollinaire and the International Avant-Garde.* Albany: State University of New York Press, 1997.

Mathews, Timothy. *Reading Apollinaire: Theories of Poetic Language.* New York: St. Martin's Press, 1988.

Matthew Arnold

Bloom, Harold, ed. *Matthew Arnold.* New York: Chelsea House, 1987.

Buckler, William. *On the Poetry of Matthew Arnold: Essays in Critical Reconstruction.* New York: New York University Press, 1982.

Bush, Douglas. *Matthew Arnold: A Survey of His Poetry and Prose.* New York: Macmillan, 1971.

Culler, Dwight. *Imaginative Reason: The Poetry of Matthew Arnold.* New Haven, Conn.: Yale University Press, 1966.

Pratt, Linda Ray. *Matthew Arnold Revisited.* New York: Twayne, 2000.

Stange, Robert. *Matthew Arnold: The Poet as Humanist.* Princeton, N.J.: Princeton University Press, 1967.

John Ashbery
Bloom, Harold, ed. *John Ashbery.* New York: Chelsea, 1985.
Lehman, David, ed. *Beyond Amazement: New Essays on John Ashbery.* Ithaca, N.Y.: Cornell University Press, 1980.
Schultz, Susan M., ed. *The Tribe of John: Ashbery and Contemporary Poetry.* Tuscaloosa: University of Alabama Press, 1995.
Shoptaw, John. *On the Outside Looking Out: John Ashbery's Poetry.* Cambridge, Mass.: Harvard University Press, 1994.

W. H. Auden
Bahlke, George W. *Critical Essays on W. H. Auden.* New York: G. K. Hall, 1991.
Bloom, Harold, ed. *W. H. Auden.* New York: Chelsea House, 1986.
Fuller, John. *W. H. Auden: A Commentary.* Princeton, N.J.: Princeton University Press, 1998.
Rodwav, Allan. *A Preface to Auden.* New York: Longman, 1984.
Smith, Stan. *W. H. Auden.* New York: Basil Blackwell, 1985.
Wright, George T. *W. H. Auden.* Boston: Twayne, 1981.

Charles Baudelaire
Bloom, Harold, ed. *Charles Baudelaire.* New York: Chelsea House, 1987.
Chesters, Graham. *Baudelaire and the Poetics of Craft.* Cambridge, England: Cambridge University Press, 1988.
Hyslop, Lois. *Charles Baudelaire Revisited.* New York: Twayne, 1992.
Peyer, Henri. *Baudelaire: A Collection of Critical Essays.* Englewood Cliffs, N.J.: Prentice-Hall, 1967.
Turnell, Martin. *Baudelaire: A Study of His Poetry.* New York: New Directions, 1972.

John Berryman
Bloom, Harold, ed. *John Berryman.* New York: Chelsea House, 1989.
Conarroe, Joel. *John Berryman: An Introduction to the Poetry.* New York: Columbia University Press, 1977.
Haffenden, John. *John Berryman: A Critical Commentary.* New York: New York University Press, 1980.
Martz, William J. *John Berryman.* Minneapolis: University of Minnesota Press, 1969.
Thomas, Harry, ed. *Berryman's Understanding: Reflections on the Poetry of John Berryman.* Boston: Northeastern University Press, 1988.

Elizabeth Bishop
Bloom, Harold, ed. *Elizabeth Bishop.* New York: Chelsea House, 1986.
Millier, Brett C. *Elizabeth Bishop: Life and the Memory of It.* Berkeley: University of California Press, 1993.
Parker, Robert D. *The Unbeliever: The Poetry of Elizabeth Bishop.* Champaign: University of Illinois Press, 1988.

Schwartz, Lloyd, and Sybil P. Estess, eds. *Elizabeth Bishop and Her Art*. Ann Arbor: University of Michigan Press, 1983.

Travisiano, Thomas J. *Elizabeth Bishop: Her Artistic Development*. Charlottesville: University Press of Virginia, 1988.

William Blake

Adams, Hazard, ed. *Critical Essays on William Blake*. Boston: G. K. Hall, 1991.

Blackstone, Bernard. *English Blake*. 1949. Reprint. Hamden, Conn.: Archon Books, 1966.

Bloom, Harold. ed. *William Blake*. New York: Chelsea House, 1985.

Erdman, David E. *Prophet Against Empire: A Poet's Interpretation of the History of His Own Times*. 1954. 3d ed. Princeton, N.J.: Princeton University Press, 1977.

Frye, Northrop. *Fearful Symmetry: A Study of William Blake*. Princeton. N.J.: Princeton University Press, 1947.

Hagstrum, Jean. *William Blake, Poet and Painter: An Introduction to the Illuminated Verse*. Chicago: University of Chicago Press, 1964.

Larrissy, Edward. *William Blake*. Oxford, England: Basil Blackwell, 1985.

Punter, David. *William Blake*. New York: St. Martin's Press, 1996.

Robert Bly

Davis, William V. *Robert Bly: The Poet and His Critics*. Columbia, S.C.: Camden House, 1994.

_____. *Understanding Robert Bly*. Columbia: University of South Carolina Press, 1988.

_____, ed. *Critical Essays on Robert Bly*. New York: G. K. Hall, 1992.

Nelson, Howard. *Robert Bly: An Introduction to the Poetry*. New York: Columbia University Press, 1984.

Sugg, Richard P. *Robert Bly*. Boston: Twayne, 1986.

Joseph Brodsky

France, Peter. *Poets of Modern Russia*. New York: Cambridge University Press, 1982.

Polukhina, Valentina. *Joseph Brodsky: A Poet for Our Time*. New York: Cambridge University Press, 1989.

Elizabeth Barrett Browning

Cooper, Helen. *Elizabeth Barrett Browning, Woman and Artist*. Chapel Hill: University of North Carolina Press, 1988.

Leighton, Angela. *Elizabeth Barrett Browning*. Bloomington: Indiana University Press, 1986.

Mermin, Dorothy. *Elizabeth Barrett Browning: The Origins of a New Poetry*. Chicago: University of Chicago Press, 1989.

Radley, Virginia L. *Elizabeth Barrett Browning*. Boston: Twayne, 1972.

Stone, Marjorie. *Elizabeth Barrett Browning*. New York: St. Martin's Press, 1995.

Robert Browning

Bloom, Harold, ed. *Robert Browning*. New York: Chelsea House, 1985.

Drew, Philip. *The Poetry of Browning: A Critical Introduction*. London: Methuen, 1970.

_____, ed. *Robert Browning: A Collection of Critical Essays*. London: Methuen, 1966.

Gibson, Mary Ellis, ed. *Critical Essays on Robert Browning*. New York: G. K. Hall, 1992.

Jack, Ian. *Browning's Major Poetry*. Oxford, England: Clarendon Press, 1973.

Roberts, Adam. *Robert Browning Revisited*. New York: Twayne, 1996.

Tracy, Clarence, ed. *Browning's Mind and Art*. New York: Barnes & Noble Books, 1970.

George Gordon, Lord Byron

Blackstone, Bernard. *Byron: A Survey*. London: Longman, 1975.

Bloom, Harold, ed. *George Gordon, Lord Byron*. New York: Chelsea House, 1986.

Gleckner, Robert F. *Byron and the Ruins of Paradise*. Baltimore: The Johns Hopkins University Press, 1967.

_____., ed. *Critical Essays on Lord Byron*. New York: G. K. Hall, 1991.

Graham, Peter W. *Lord Byron*. New York: Twayne, 1998.

McGann, Jerome J. *Fiery Dust: Byron's Poetic Development*. Chicago: University of Chicago Press, 1968.

John Clare

Barrell, John. *The Idea of Landscape and the Sense of Place, 1730-1840: An Approach to the Poetry of John Clare*. London: Cambridge University Press, 1972.

Chilcott, Tim *"A Real World and Doubting Mind": A Critical Study of the Poetry of John Clare*. Hull, England: Hull University Press, 1985.

Haughton, Hugh, Adam Phillips, and Geoffrey Summerfield, eds. *John Clare in Context*. Cambridge, England: Cambridge University Press, 1994.

Howard, William. *John Clare*. Boston: Twayne, 1981.

Storey, Mark. *The Poet of John Clare: A Critical Introduction*. New York: Macmillan, 1974.

Samuel Taylor Coleridge

Bate, Walter Jackson. *Samuel Taylor Coleridge*. New York: Macmillan, 1968.

Beer, J. B. *Coleridge the Visionary*. London: Chatto & Windus, 1959.

Holmes, Richard. *Coleridge: Early Visions*. New York: Viking Press, 1990.

Orr, Leonard, ed. *Critical Essays on Samuel Taylor Coleridge*. New York: G. K. Hall, 1994.

Prickett, Stephen. *Coleridge and Wordsworth: The Poetry of Growth*. New York: Cambridge University Press, 1970.

Yarlott, Geoffrey. *Coleridge and the Abyssinian Maid*. London: Methuen, 1967.

Hart Crane

Bloom, Harold, ed. *Hart Crane.* New York: Chelsea House, 1986.

Clark, David R,. ed. *Critical Essays on Hart Crane.* Boston: G. K. Hall, 1982.

Leibowitz, Herbert A. *Hart Crane: An Introduction to the Poetry.* New York: Columbia University Press, 1968.

Lewis, R. W. B. *The Poetry of Hart Crane: A Critical Study.* Princeton, N.J.: Princeton University Press, 1967.

Trachtenberg, Alan, ed. *Hart Crane: A Collection of Critical Essays.* Englewood Cliffs, N.J.: Prentice-Hall, 1982.

Uroff, M. D. *Hart Crane: The Patterns of His Poetry.* Chicago: University of Illinois Press, 1974.

Robert Creeley

Edelberg, Cynthia Dubin. *Robert Creeley's Poetry: A Critical Introduction.* Albuquerque: University of New Mexico Press, 1978.

Ford, Arthur L. *Robert Creeley.* Boston: Twayne, 1978.

Sor Juana Inés de la Cruz

Ackerman, Diane. *Reverse Thunder.* New York: Lumen, 1988.

Flynn, Gerard C. *Sor Juana Inés de la Cruz.* New York: Twayne, 1971.

E. E. Cummings

Friedman, Norman. *E. E. Cummings: The Art of His Poetry.* Baltimore: The Johns Hopkins University Press, 1960.

————. *(Re)Valuing Cummings: Further Essays on the Poet, 1962-1993.* Gainesville: University Press of Florida, 1996.

Kennedy, Richard S. *E. E. Cummings Revisited.* New York: Twayne, 1994.

Kidder, Rushworth. *E. E. Cummings: An Introduction to the Poetry.* New York: Columbia University Press, 1979.

Marks, Barry A. *E. E. Cummings.* New York: Twayne, 1964.

Rotella, Guy, ed. *Critical Essays on E. E. Cummings.* Boston: G. K. Hall, 1984.

Wagner, Robert. *The Poetry and Prose of E. E. Cummings: A Study in Appreciation.* New York: Harcourt, Brace & World, 1965.

James Dickey

Baugham, Ronald. *Understanding James Dickey.* Columbia: University of South Carolina Press, 1985.

Bloom, Harold, ed. *James Dickey.* New York: Chelsea House, 1987.

Calhoun, Richard J., and Robert W. Hill. *James Dickey.* Boston: Twayne, 1983.

Kirschten, Robert, ed. *"Struggling for Wings": The Art of James Dickey.* Columbia: University of South Carolina Press, 1997.

Emily Dickinson
Blake, Caesar R., and Carlton F. Wells. *The Recognition of Emily Dickinson: Selected Criticism Since 1890*. Ann Arbor: University of Michigan Press, 1964.
Farr, Judith, ed. *Emily Dickinson: A Collection of Critical Essays*. Englewood Cliffs, N.J.: Prentice-Hall, 1996.
Ferlazzo, Paul J., ed. *Critical Essays on Emily Dickinson*. Boston: G. K. Hall, 1984.
Gelpi, Albert J. *Emily Dickinson: The Mind of the Poet*. New York: W. W. Norton, 1965.
Keller, Karl. *The Only Kangaroo Among the Beauty: Emily Dickinson and America*. Baltimore: The Johns Hopkins University Press, 1979.
Miller, Ruth. *The Poetry of Emily Dickinson*. Middletown, Conn.: Wesleyan University Press, 1968.

John Donne
Leishman, J. B. *The Monarch of Wit: An Analytical and Comparative Study of the Poetry of John Donne*. London: Hutchinson University Library, 1951.
Marotti, Arthur, ed. *Critical Essays on John Donne*. New York: G. K. Hall, 1994.
_____. *John Donne, Coterie Poet*. Madison: University of Wisconsin Press, 1986.
Mousley, Andrew, ed. *John Donne*. New York: St. Martin's Press, 1999.
Roston, Murray. *The Soul of Wit: A Study of John Donne*. Oxford, England: Clarendon Press, 1974.
Sanders, Wilbur. *John Donne's Poetry*. Cambridge, England: Cambridge University Press, 1971.
Wanke, Frank J. *John Donne*. Boston: Twayne, 1987.
Winny, James. *A Preface to Donne*. New York: Longman, 1981.

John Dryden
Bloom, Harold, ed. *John Dryden*. New York: Chelsea House, 1987.
Hopkins, David. *John Dryden*. New York: Cambridge University Press, 1986.
Miner, Earl. *Dryden's Poetry*. Bloomington: Indiana University Press, 1967.
Myers, William. *Dryden*. London: Hutchinson University Library, 1973.
Winn, James Anderson. *John Dryden and His World*. New Haven, Conn.: Yale University Press, 1987.

T. S. Eliot
Bergonzi, Bernard. *T. S. Eliot*. New York: Macmillan, 1972.
Bloom, Harold, ed. *T. S. Eliot*. New York: Chelsea House, 1985.
Frye, Northrop. *T. S. Eliot: An Introduction*. Chicago: University of Chicago Press, 1963.
Gardner, Helen. *The Art of T. S. Eliot*. London: Cresset, 1949.
Headings, Philip R. *T. S. Eliot*. Rev. ed. Boston: Twayne, 1982.
Kenner, Hugh, ed. *T. S. Eliot: A Collection of Critical Essays*. Englewood Cliffs, N.J.: Prentice-Hall, 1962.

Moody, A. David. *Thomas Stearns Eliot*. New York: Cambridge University Press, 1979.

————, ed. *The Cambridge Companion to T. S. Eliot*. New York: Cambridge University Press, 1994.

Robert Frost

Barry, Elaine. *Robert Frost*. New York: Frederick Ungar, 1973.

Gerber, Philip L. *Robert Frost*. Rev ed. Boston: Twayne, 1982.

————, ed. *Critical Essays on Robert Frost*. Boston: G. K. Hall, 1982.

Oster, Judith. *Toward Robert Frost: The Reader and the Poet*. Athens: University of Georgia Press, 1991.

Poirier, Richard. *Robert Frost: The Work of Knowing*. New York: Oxford University Press, 1977.

Federico García Lorca

Barea, Arturo. *Lorca, the Poet and His People*. London: Faber & Faber, 1944.

Campbell, Roy. *Lorca: An Appreciation of His Poetry*. New Haven. Conn.: Yale University Press, 1952.

Duran, Manuel, ed. *Lorca: A Collection of Critical Essays*. Englewood Cliffs, N.J.: Prentice-Hall, 1962.

Havard, Robert, ed. *Lorca: Poet and Playwright*. Cardiff: University of Wales, 1992.

Higginbotham, Virginia. *The Comic Spirit of Federico García Lorca*. Austin: University of Texas Press, 1976.

Allen Ginsberg

Hyde, Lewis, ed. *On the Poetry of Allen Ginsberg*. Ann Arbor: University of Michigan Press, 1984.

Merrill, Thomas F. *Allen Ginsberg*. Boston: Twayne, 1988.

Portuges, Paul. *The Visionary Poetics of Allen Ginsberg*. Santa Barbara, Calif.: Ross-Erikson, 1978.

Oliver Goldsmith

Bloom, Harold, ed. *Oliver Goldsmith*. New York: Chelsea House, 1987.

Gwynn, Stephen L. *Oliver Goldsmith*. Reprint. New York: Haskell House, 1976.

Kirk, Clara M. *Oliver Goldsmith*. New York: Twayne, 1967.

Thomas Gray

Bloom, Harold, ed. *Thomas Gray's "Elegy Written In a Country Churchyard."* New York: Chelsea House, 1987.

Golden, Morris. *Thomas Gray*. Boston: Twayne, 1988.

Hutchings, W. B. *Thomas Gray: Contemporary Essays*. Liverpool, England: Liverpool University Press, 1993.

H.D.

Bloom, Harold, ed. *H. D.* New York: Chelsea House, 1989.

Friedman, Susan Stanford. *Psyche Reborn: The Emergence of H. D.* Bloomington: Indiana University Press, 1981.

Guest, Barbara. *Herself Defined : The Poet H. D. and Her World.* New York: Quill, 1984.

Hollenberg, Donna Krolik, ed. *H. D. and Poets After.* Iowa City: University of Iowa Press, 2000.

Quinn, Vincent. *H. D. (Hilda Doolittle).* New York: Twayne, 1967.

Thomas Hardy

Buckler, William E. *The Poetry of Thomas Hardy: A Study in Art and Ideas.* New York: New York University Press, 1983.

Butler, Lance St. John. *Thomas Hardy.* New York: Cambridge University Press, 1978.

Cullen, Joanna. *A Journey into Thomas Hardy's Poetry.* London: W. H. Allen, 1989.

Davie, Donald. *With the Grain: Essays on Thomas Hardy and Modern British Poetry.* Edited by Clive Wilmer. Manchester, England: Carcanet, 1998.

Page, Norman. *Thomas Hardy.* Boston: Routledge & Kegan Paul, 1977.

Pinion, F. B. *A Commentary on the Poems of Thomas Hardy.* New York: Barnes & Noble Books, 1977.

Zietlow, Paul. *Moments of Vision: The Poetry of Thomas Hardy.* Cambridge, Mass.: Harvard University Press, 1974.

Seamus Heaney

Andrews, Elmar. *The Poetry of Seamus Heaney.* Basingstoke, England.: Macmillan, 1988.

Bloom, Harold, ed. *Seamus Heaney.* New York: Chelsea House, 1986.

Foster, Thomas C. *Seamus Heaney.* Boston: Twayne, 1989.

Garratt, Robert F., ed. *Critical Essays on Seamus Heaney.* New York: G. K. Hall, 1995.

Vendler, Helen. *Seamus Heaney.* Cambridge, Mass.: Harvard University Press, 1998.

George Herbert

Stewart, Stanley. *George Herbert.* Boston: Twayne, 1986.

Strier, Richard. *Love Known: Theology and Experience in George Herbert's Poetry.* Chicago: University of Chicago Press, 1983.

Summers, Joseph H. *George Herbert: His Religion and Art.* Cambridge, Mass.: Harvard University Press, 1954.

Tuve, Rosemond. *A Reading of George Herbert.* Chicago: University of Chicago Press, 1952.

Vendler, Helen. *The Poetry of George Herbert.* Cambridge, Mass.: Harvard University Press, 1975.

Robert Herrick
Rollin, Roger B. *Robert Herrick*. Rev. ed. New York: Twayne, 1992.
Scott, George W. *Robert Herrick*. New York: St. Martin's Press, 1974.

Geoffrey Hill
Bloom, Harold, ed. *Geoffrey Hill*. New York: Chelsea House, 1986.
Hart, Henry. *The Poetry of Geoffrey Hill*. Carbondale: Southern Illinois University Press, 1986.
Sherry, Vincent. *The Uncommon Tongue: The Poetry and Criticism of Geoffrey Hill*. Ann Arbor: University of Michigan Press, 1987.

Gerard Manley Hopkins
Bergonzi, Bernard. *Gerard Manley Hopkins*. New York: Macmillan, 1977.
Bump, Jerome. *Gerard Manley Hopkins*. Boston: Twayne, 1982.
Johnson, Margaret. *Gerard Manley Hopkins and Tractarian Poetry*. Brookfield, Vt.: Ashgate, 1997.
Mariani, Paul L. *A Commentary on the Complete Poems of Gerard Manley Hopkins*. Ithaca, N.Y.: Cornell University Press, 1969.
Sulloway, Alison G., ed. *Critical Essays on Gerard Manley Hopkins*. Boston: G. K. Hall, 1990.

A. E. Housman
Haber, Tom Burns. *A. E. Housman*. New York: Twayne, 1967.
Leggatt, B. J. *The Poetic Art of A. E. Housman: Theory and Practice*. Lincoln: University of Nebraska Press, 1978.
Ricks, Christopher, ed. *A. E. Housman: A Collection of Critical Essays*. Englewood Cliffs, N.J.: Prentice-Hall, 1968.

Langston Hughes
Bloom, Harold, ed. *Langston Hughes*. New York: Chelsea House, 1989.
Miller, R. Baxter. *The Art and Imagination of Langston Hughes*. Lexington: University Press of Kentucky, 1989.
Mullen, Edward J., ed. *Critical Essays on Langston Hughes*. Boston: G. K. Hall, 1986.
Onwuchekwa, Jemie. *Langston Hughes: An Introduction to the Poetry*. New York: Columbia University Press, 1976.
Trotman, C. James, ed. *Langston Hughes: The Man, His Art, and His Continuing Influence*. New York: Garland, 1995.

Ted Hughes
Sagar, Keith. *The Laughter of Foxes: A Study of Ted Hughes*. Liverpool, England: Liverpool University Press, 2000.
Scigaj, Leonard M. *The Poetry of Ted Hughes: Form and Imagination*. Iowa City: University of Iowa Press, 1986.

_____. *Ted Hughes*. Boston: Twayne, 1991.
_____, ed. *Critical Essays on Ted Hughes*. New York: G. K. Hall, 1992.
West, Thomas. *Ted Hughes*. New York: Methuen, 1985.

Robinson Jeffers
Brophy, Robert. *Robinson Jeffers: Dimensions of a Poet*. New York: Fordham University Press, 1995.
Carpenter, Frederic I. *Robinson Jeffers*. New York: Twayne, 1962.
Coffin, Arthur B. *Robinson Jeffers: Poet of Inhumanism*. Madison: University of Wisconsin, 1971.
Karman, James, ed. *Critical Essays on Robinson Jeffers*. Boston: G. K. Hall, 1990.
Zaller, Robert. *The Cliffs of Solitude: A Reading of Robinson Jeffers*. New York: Cambridge University Press, 1983.

Ben Jonson
Bloom, Harold, ed. *Ben Jonson*. New York: Chelsea House, 1987.
Leggatt, Alexander. *Ben Jonson: His Vision and His Art*. New York: Methuen, 1981.
Summers, Claude J., and Ted-Larry Pebworth. *Ben Jonson*. Boston: Twayne, 1979.
Trimpi, Wesley. *Ben Jonson's Poems: A Study of the Plain Style*. Stanford, Calif.: Stanford University Press, 1962.

John Keats
Bate, Walter Jackson. *John Keats*. Cambridge, Mass.: Harvard University Press, 1963.
Bloom, Harold, ed. *John Keats*. New York: Chelsea House, 1985.
_____, ed. *The Odes of Keats*. New York: Chelsea House, 1987.
Bush, Douglas. *John Keats: His Life and Writings*. New York: Macmillan, 1966.
De Almeida, Hermione, ed. *Critical Essays on John Keats*. Boston: G. K. Hall, 1990.
Dickstein, Morris. *Keats and His Poetry: A Study in Development*. Chicago: University of Chicago Press, 1971.
Evert, Walter H. *Aesthetic and Myth in the Poetry of Keats*. Princeton, N.J.: Princeton University Press, 1965.
Sperry, Stuart M. *Keats the Poet*. Princeton, N.J.: Princeton University Press, 1973.
Van Ghent, Dorothy. *Keats: The Myth of the Hero*. Princeton, N.J.: Princeton University Press, 1983.
Waldoff, Leon. *Keats and the Silent Work of Imagination*. Urbana: University of Illinois Press, 1985.

Philip Larkin
Martin, Bruce K. *Philip Larkin*. Boston: Twayne, 1978.
Motion, Andrew. *Philip Larkin*. New York: Methuen, 1982.
Regan, Stephen, ed. *Philip Larkin*. New York: St. Martin's Press, 1997.

Rossen, Janice. *Philip Larkin: His Life's Work*. Iowa City: University of Iowa Press, 1990.

Salwak, Dale, ed. *Philip Larkin: The Man and His Work*. Iowa City: University of Iowa Press, 1988.

Whalen, Terrence. *Philip Larkin and English Poetry*. Basingstoke, England: Macmillan, 1988.

D. H. Lawrence

Becket, Fiona. *D. H. Lawrence: The Thinker as Poet*. New York: St. Martin's Press, 1997.

Draper, Ronald P. *D. H. Lawrence*. New York: Grosset and Dunlap, 1964.

Gilbert, Sandra M. *Acts of Attention: The Poems of D. H. Lawrence*. Ithaca, N.Y.: Cornell University Press, 1972.

Murfin, Ross C. *The Poetry of D. H. Lawrence: Texts and Contexts*. Lincoln: University of Nebraska Press, 1983.

Denise Levertov

Marten, Harry. *Understanding Denise Levertov*. Columbia: University of South Carolina Press, 1988.

Rodgers, Audrey T. *Denise Levertov: The Poetry of Engagement*. Rutherford, N.J.: Fairleigh Dickinson University Press, 1993.

Wagner-Martin, Linda. *Denise Levertov*. Albany, N.Y.: New College and University Press, 1967.

_____, ed. *Critical Essays on Denise Levertov*. Boston: G. K. Hall, 1990.

Li Bo

Lancashire, Douglas. *Li Po-vuan*. Boston: Twayne, 1981.

Waley, Arthur. *The Poetry and Career of Li Po*. Cambridge, Mass.: Unwin Hyman, 1951.

Robert Lowell

Axelrod, Steven Gould, and Helen Deese, eds. *Robert Lowell: Essays on the Poetry*. Cambridge, England: Cambridge University Press, 1986.

Bloom, Harold, ed. *Robert Lowell*. New York: Chelsea House, 1987

Hobsbaum, Philip. *A Reader's Guide to Robert Lowell*. New York: Thames and Hudson, 1988.

Price, Jonathan, ed. *Critics on Robert Lowell*. Coral Gables, Fla.: University of Miami Press, 1972.

Raffel, Burton. *Robert Lowell*. New York: Frederick Ungar, 1981.

Rudman, Mark. *Robert Lowell: An Introduction to the Poetry*. New York: Columbia University Press, 1983.

Stéphane Mallarmé
Bloom, Harold, ed. *Stéphane Mallarmé*. New York: Chelsea House, 1987.
Lloyd, Rosemary. *Mallarmé: The Poet and His Circle*. Ithaca, N.Y.: Cornell University Press, 1999.
St. Aubyn, Frederic C. *Stéphane Mallarmé*. Boston: Twayne, 1989.

Osip Mandelstam
Brown, Clarence. *Mandelstam*. New York: Cambridge University Press, 1973.
Harris, Jane Gary. *Osip Mandelstam*. Boston: Twayne, 1988.
Hingley, Ronald. *Nightingale Fever: Russian Poets in Revolution*. New York: Alfred A. Knopf, 1981.

Andrew Marvell
Bloom, Harold, ed. *Andrew Marvell*. New York: Chelsea House, 1989.
Colie, Rosalie. *My Echoing Song: Andrew Marvell's Poetry of Criticism*. Princeton, N.J.: Princeton University Press, 1970.
Leishman, J. B. *The Art of Marvell's Poetry*. London: Hutchinson University Library, 1966.
Wheeler, Thomas. *Andrew Marvell Revisited*. New York: Twayne, 1996.
Wilcher, Robert. *Andrew Marvell*. New York: Cambridge University Press, 1985.

James Merrill
Labrie, Ross. *James Merrill*. Boston: Twayne, 1982.
Lehman, David, and Charles Berger, eds. *James Merrill: Essays in Criticism*. Ithaca, N.Y.: Cornell University Press, 1983.
Moffett, Judith. *James Merrill: An Introduction to the Poetry*. New York: Columbia University Press, 1984.
Rotella, Guy L., ed. *Critical Essays on James Merrill*. New York: Twayne, 1996.
Yenser, Stephen. *The Consuming Myth: The Work of James Merrill*. Cambridge, Mass.: Harvard University Press, 1987.

W. S. Merwin
Davis, Cheri. *W. S. Merwin*. Boston: Twayne, 1981.
Hix, H. L. *W. S. Merwin*. Columbia: University of South Carolina Press, 1997.
Nelson, Cary, and Ed Folsom. *W. S. Merwin: Essays on the Poetry*. Urbana: University of Illinois Press, 1987.

Czesław Miłosz
Davie, Donald F. *Czesław Miłosz and the Insufficiency of Lyric*. Knoxville: University of Tennessee Press, 1986.
Fuit, Aleksander. *The Eternal Moment: The Poetry of Czesław Miłosz*. Translated by Theodosia S. Robertson. Berkeley: University of California Press, 1989.

Nathan, Leonard, and Arthur Quinn. *The Poet's Work: An Introduction to Czesław Miłosz.* Cambridge, Mass.: Harvard University Press, 1991.

John Milton

Allen, Don Cameron. *The Harmonious Vision: Studies in Milton's Poetry.* Enlarged ed. Baltimore: The Johns Hopkins University Press, 1970.

Bloom, Harold, ed. *John Milton.* New York: Chelsea House, 1986.

Martz, Louis. *Milton, Poet of Exile.* 2d ed. New Haven, Conn.: Yale University Press, 1986.

Miller, David M. *John Milton: Poetry.* Boston: Twayne, 1978.

Nicolson, Marjorie. *John Milton: A Reader's Guide to His Poetry.* New York: Farrar, Straus & Giroux, 1963.

Patrides, C. A., ed. *Milton's "Lycidas": The Tradition and the Poem.* Columbia: University of Missouri Press, 1983.

Woodhouse, A. S. P. *The Heavenly Muse: A Preface to Milton.* Toronto: University of Toronto Press, 1972.

Zunder, William, ed. *Paradise Lost.* New York: St. Martin's Press, 1999.

Marianne Moore

Bloom, Harold, ed. *Marianne Moore.* New York: Chelsea House, 1986.

Costello, Bonnie. *Marianne Moore: Imaginary Possessions.* Cambridge, Mass.: Harvard University Press, 1981.

Engel, Bernard F. *Marianne Moore.* Rev. ed. Boston: Twayne, 1989.

Philips, Elizabeth. *Marianne Moore.* New York: Frederick Ungar, 1982.

Tomlinson, Charles, ed. *Marianne Moore: A Collection of Critical Essays.* Englewood Cliffs, N.J.: Prentice-Hall, 1969.

Pablo Neruda

Agosin, Marjorie. *Pablo Neruda.* Translated by Lorraine Ross. Boston: Twayne, 1986.

Bloom, Harold, ed. *Pablo Neruda.* New York: Chelsea House, 1989.

De Costa, René. *The Poetry of Pablo Neruda.* Cambridge, Mass.: Harvard University Press, 1979.

Durán, Manuel, and Margery Salk. *Earth Tones: The Poetry of Pablo Neruda.* Bloomington: Indiana University Press, 1981.

Charles Olson

Bollobas, Eniko. *Charles Olson.* New York: Twayne, 1992.

Merrill, Thomas F. *The Poetry of Charles Olson: A Primer.* Newark: University of Delaware Press, 1982.

Von Haltberg, Robert. *Charles Olson: The Scholars Art.* Cambridge, Mass.: Harvard University Press, 1978.

Octavia Paz
Chiles, Frances. *Octavio Paz: The Mythic Dimension*. New York: Peter Lang, 1987.
Fein, John M. *Toward Octavia Paz: A Reading of His Major Poems*. Lexington: University Press of Kentucky, 1986.
Quiroga, Jose. *Understanding Octavio Paz*. Columbia: University of South Carolina Press, 1999.
Wilson, James. *Octavio Paz*. Boston: Twayne, 1986.

Sylvia Plath
Alexander, Paul, ed. *Ariel Ascending: Writings About Sylvia Plath*. New York: Harper & Row, 1984.
Barnard, Caroline King. *Sylvia Plath*. Boston: Twayne, 1978.
Bloom, Harold, ed. *Sylvia Plath*. New York: Chelsea House, 1989.
Lane, Gary. *Sylvia Plath: New Views on the Poetry*. Baltimore: The Johns Hopkins University Press, 1979.
Rosenblatt, Jon. *Sylvia Plath: The Poetry of Initiation*. Chapel Hill: University of North Carolina Press, 1979.
Wagner, Linda W., ed. *Critical Essays on Sylvia Plath*. Boston: G. K. Hall, 1984.

Edgar Allan Poe
Halliburton, David. *Edgar Allan Poe: A Phenomenological View*. Princeton, N.J.: Princeton University Press, 1973.
Levine, Stuart. *Edgar Allan Poe: Seer and Craftsman*. Deland, Fla.: Everett/Edwards, 1972.
Peeples, Scott. *Edgar Allan Poe Revisited*. New York: Twayne, 1998.

Alexander Pope
Bloom, Harold, ed. *Alexander Pope*. New York: Chelsea House, 1985.
Brower, Reuben A. *Alexander Pope: The Poetry of Allusion*. New York: Oxford University Press, 1968.
Clark, Donald B. *Alexander Pope*. New York: Twayne, 1967.
Edwards, Thomas R. *This Dark Estate: A Reading of Pope*. Berkeley: University of California Press, 1963.
Gooneratne, Yasmine. *Alexander Pope*. New York: Cambridge University Press, 1976.
Jackson, Wallace, and R. Paul Yoder, eds. *Critical Essays on Alexander Pope*. New York: G. K. Hall, 1993.
Weinbrot, Howard D. *Alexander Pope and the Traditions of Formal Verse Satire*. Princeton, N.J.: Princeton University Press, 1982.

Ezra Pound
Alexander, Michael J. *The Poetic Achievement of Ezra Pound*. Berkeley: University of California Press, 1979.

Bloom, Harold, ed. *Ezra Pound*. New York: Chelsea House, 1987.

Davie, Donald. *Ezra Pound*. New York: Viking Press, 1976.

Dembo, L. S. *The Confucian Odes of Ezra Pound: A Critical Appraisal*. Berkeley: University of California Press, 1963.

Durant, Alan. *Ezra Pound, Identity in Crisis: A Fundamental Reassessment of the Poet and His Work*. Totowa, N.J.: Barnes & Noble Books, 1981.

Grieve, Thomas F. *Ezra Pound's Early Poetry and Poetics*. Columbia: University of Missouri Press, 1997.

John Crowe Ransom

Parsons, Thornton H. *John Crowe Ransom*. New York: Twayne, 1969.

Stewart, John Lincoln. *John Crowe Ransom*. Minneapolis: University of Minnesota Press, 1962.

Williams, Miller. *The Poetry of John Crowe Ransom*. New Brunswick, N.J.: Rutgers University Press, 1972.

Kenneth Rexroth

Bartlett, Lee. *Kenneth Rexroth*. Boise, Idaho: Boise State University Press, 1988.

Gibson, Morgan. *Revolutionary Rexroth: Poet of East-West Wisdom*. Hamden, Conn.: Shoe String, 1986.

Gutierrez, Donald. *"The Holiness of the Real": The Short Verse of Kenneth Rexroth*. Madison, N.J.: Associated University Presses, 1996.

Adrienne Rich

Altieri, Charles. *Self and Sensibility in Contemporary American Poetry*. New York: Cambridge University Press, 1984.

Cooper, Jane R., ed. *Reading Adrienne Rich: Reviews and Re-Visions*. Ann Arbor: University of Michigan Press, 1984.

Keyes, Claire. *The Aesthetics of Power: The Poetry of Adrienne Rich*. Athens: University of Georgia Press, 1986.

Rainer Maria Rilke

Baron, Frank, Ernst S. Dick, and Warren R. Maurer, eds. *Rilke: The Alchemy of Alienation*. Lawrence: The Regents Press of Kansas, 1980.

Brodskv, Patricia P. *Rainer Maria Rilke*. Boston: G. K. Hall, 1988.

Casey, Timothy. *Rainer Maria Rilke: A Centenary Essay*. London: Macmillan, 1976.

Graf, W. L. *Rainer Maria Rilke: Creative Anguish of a Modern Poet*. Princeton, N.J.: Princeton University Press, 1956.

Ryan, Judith. *Rilke, Modernism, and Poetic Tradition*. Cambridge, England: Cambridge University Press, 1999.

Arthur Rimbaud
Bloom, Harold, ed. *Arthur Rimbaud*. New York: Chelsea House, 1987.
Chadwick, Charles. *Rimbaud*. Atlantic Highlands, N.J.: Humanities Press, 1979.
Hackett, C. A. *Rimbaud: A Critical Introduction*. New York: Cambridge University Press, 1981.
Miller, Henry. *The Time of the Assassins: A Study of Rimbaud*. New York: New Directions, 1962.
St. Aubyn, Frederic C. *Arthur Rimbaud*. Boston: Twayne, 1978.
Starkie, Enid. *Arthur Rimbaud*. Rev. ed. New York: New Directions, 1968.

Theodore Roethke
Bloom, Harold, ed. *Theodore Roethke*. New York: Chelsea House, 1987.
Kalaidjian, Walter B. *Understanding Theodore Roethke*. Columbia: University of South Carolina Press, 1987.
Malkoff, Karl. *Theodore Roethke: An Introduction to the Poetry*. New York: Columbia University Press, 1966.
Parini, Jay. *Theodore Roethke: An American Romantic*. Amherst: University of Massachusetts Press, 1979.
Wolff, George. *Theodore Roethke*. Boston: Twayne, 1981.

Christina Rossetti
Arseneau, Mary, Antony H. Harrison, and Lorraine Janzen Kooistra, eds. *The Culture of Christina Rossetti: Female Poetics and Victorian Contexts*. Athens: Ohio University Press, 1999.
Kent, David A., ed. *The Achievement of Christina Rossetti*. Ithaca, N.Y.: Cornell University Press, 1987.
Smulders, Sharon. *Christina Rossetti Revisited*. New York: Twayne, 1996.

Anne Sexton
George, Diana. *Oedipus Anne: The Poetry of Anne Sexton*. Urbana: University of Illinois Press, 1987.
Hall, Caroline King. *Anne Sexton*. Boston: Twayne, 1989.
Middlebrook, Diane Wood. *Anne Sexton: A Biography*. Boston: Houghton Mifflin, 1991.
Morton. Richard E. *Anne Sexton's Poetry of Redemption: The Chronology of a Pugrimage*. Lewiston, N.Y.: Edwin Mellen Press, 1988.
Wagner-Martin, Linda, ed. *Critical Essays on Anne Sexton*. Boston: G. K. Hall, 1989.

William Shakespeare
Bloom, Harold, ed. *Shakespeare's Sonnets*. New York. Chelsea House, 1987.
_____, ed. *William Shakespeare: Histories and Poems*. New York: Chelsea House, 1986.

Booth. Stephen. *An Essay on Shakespeare's Sonnets.* New Haven, Conn.: Yale University Press, 1969.

Dubrow, Heather. *Captive Victors: Shakespeare's Narrative Poems and Sonnets.* Ithaca, N.Y.: Cornell University Press, 1987.

Hubler, Edward. *The Sense of Shakespeare's Sonnets.* Princeton. N.J.: Princeton University Press, 1952.

Krieger, Murray. *A Window to Criticism: Shakespeare's Sonnets and Modern Poetics.* Princeton, N.J.: Princeton University Press, 1964.

Leishman, J. B. *Themes and Variations in Shakespeare's Sonnets.* 2d ed. New York: Harper & Row, 1966.

Schiffer, James, ed. *Shakespeare's Sonnets: Critical Essays.* New York: Garland, 1999.

Smith, Hallett. *The Tension of the Lyre: Poetry in Shakespeare's Sonnets.* San Marino, Calif.: Huntington Library, 1981.

Percy Bysshe Shelley

Allott, Miriam, ed. *Essays on Shelley.* Totowa, N.J.: Barnes & Noble Books, 1982.

Bloom, Harold, ed. *Percy Bysshe Shelley.* New York: Chelsea House, 1985.

Cameron, Kenneth Neill. *Shelley: The Golden Years.* Cambridge, Mass.: Harvard University Press, 1974.

Chernaik, Judith. *The Lyrics of Shelley.* Cleveland: Press of Case Western Reserve University, 1972.

Holmes, Richard. *Shelley: The Pursuit.* London: Weidenfeld & Nicolson, 1974. Reprint. London: Quartet Books, 1976.

Sperry, Stuart M. *Shelley's Major Verse: The Narrative and Dramatic Poetry.* Cambridge, Mass.: Harvard University Press, 1988.

Wasserman, Earl R. *Shelley: A Critical Reading.* Baltimore: The Johns Hopkins University Press, 1971.

Gary Snyder

Molesworth, Charles. *Gary Snyder's Vision: Poetry and the Real Work.* Columbia: University of Missouri Press, 1983.

Murphy, Patrick D., ed. *Critical Essays on Gary Snyder.* Boston: G. K. Hall, 1990.

Steuding, Bob. *Gary Snyder.* Boston: Twayne, 1976.

Edmund Spenser

Bloom, Harold, ed. *Edmund Spenser.* New York: Chelsea House, 1986.

Heale, Elizabeth. *The Faerie Queene: A Reader's Guide.* Cambridge, England: Cambridge University Press, 1999.

Hieatt, A. Kent. *Short Time's Endless Monument: The Symbolism of the Numbers in Edmund Spenser's "Epithalamion."* New York: Columbia University Press, 1960.

King, John N. *Spenser's Poetry and the Reformation Tradition.* Princeton, N.J.: Princeton University Press, 1990.

Oram, William Allan. *Edmund Spenser.* New York: Twayne, 1997.

Wallace Stevens
Baird, James. *The Dome and the Rock: Structure in the Poetry of Wallace Stevens.* Baltimore: The Johns Hopkins University Press, 1968.
Bates, Milton J. *Wallace Stevens: A Mythology of Self.* Berkeley: University of California Press, 1985.
Bloom, Harold, ed. *Wallace Stevens.* New York: Chelsea House, 1985.
Kesler, Edward. *Images of Wallace Stevens.* New Brunswick, N.J.: Rutgers University Press, 1972.
McCann, Janet. *Wallace Stevens Revisited: The Celestial Possible.* New York: Twayne, 1995.
Morris, Adalaide Kirby. *Wallace Stevens: Imagination and Faith.* Princeton, N.J.: Princeton University Press, 1974.

Alfred, Lord Tennyson
Bloom, Harold, ed. *Alfred Lord Tennyson.* New York: Chelsea, 1985.
Culler, A. Dwight. *The Poetry of Tennyson.* New Haven, Conn.: Yale University Press, 1977.
Hellstrom, Ward. *On the Poems of Tennyson.* Gainesville, Fla.: University of Florida Press, 1972.
Ricks, Christopher. *Tennyson.* New York: Macmillan, 1972.
Smith, Elton E. *The Two Voices: A Tennyson Study.* Lincoln: University of Nebraska Press, 1964.
Tucker, Herbert F., ed. *Critical Essays on Alfred Lord Tennyson.* New York: G. K. Hall, 1993.

Dylan Thomas
Emery, Clark. *The World of Dylan Thomas.* London: J. M. Dent & Sons, 1971.
Gaston, Georg, ed. *Critical Essays on Dylan Thomas.* New York: G. K. Hall, 1989.
Korg, Jacob. *Dylan Thomas.* Updated ed. New York: Twayne, 1992.
Maud, Ralph. *Entrances to Dylan Thomas's Poetry.* Pittsburgh: University of Pittsburgh Press, 1963.
Olson, Elder. *The Poetry of Dylan Thomas.* Chicago: University of Chicago Press, 1954.
Tindall, William York. *A Reader's Guide to Dylan Thomas.* New York: Farrar, Straus and Cudahy, 1962.

Thomas Traherne
Day, Malcolm M. *Thomas Traherne.* Boston: Twayne, 1982.
Salter, Keith W. *Thomas Thaherne: Mystic and Poet.* New York: Barnes & Noble Books, 1965.

Georg Trakl
Detsch, Richard. *Georg Trakl's Poetry: Toward a Union of Opposites.* University Park: Pennsylvania State University Press, 1983.

Sharp, Francis M. *The Poet's Madness: A Reading of Georg Trakl*. Ithaca, N.Y.: Cornell University Press, 1981.

Williams, Eric, ed. *The Dark Flutes of Fall: Critical Essays on Georg Trakl*. Columbia, S.C.: Camden House, 1991.

Marina Tsvetayeva

Feinstein, Elaine. *A Captive Lion: The Life of Marina Tsvetayeva*. London: Hutchinson University Library, 1987.

Karlinsky, Simon. *Marina Tsvetaeva: The Woman, Her World, and Her Poetry*. Cambridge, England: Cambridge University Press, 1985.

Paul Verlaine

Porter, Laurence M. *The Crisis of French Symbolism*. Ithaca, N.Y.: Cornell University Press, 1980.

Zweig, Stefan. *Paul Verlaine*. Translated by O. F Theis. 1913. Reprint. New York: AMS Press, 1980.

Robert Penn Warren

Bloom, Harold, ed. *Robert Penn Warren*. New York: Chelsea House, 1986.

Bohner, Charles H. *Robert Penn Warren*. Rev. ed. Boston: G. K. Hall, 1981.

Madden, David, ed. *The Legacy of Robert Penn Warren*. Baton Rouge: Louisiana State University Press, 2000.

Strandberg, Victor H. *A Colder Fire: The Poetry of Robert Penn Warren*. Westport, Conn.: Greenwood, 1975.

Walt Whitman

Allen, Gay Wilson. *A Reader's Guide to Walt Whitman*. New York: Farrar, Straus & Giroux, 1970.

Aspiz, Harold. *Walt Whitman and the Body Beautiful*. Urbana: University of Illinois Press, 1980.

Bloom, Harold, ed. *Walt Whitman*. New York: Chelsea House, 1985.

Chari, V. K. *Whitman in the Light of Vedantic Mysticism*. Lincoln: University of Nebraska Press, 1964.

Loving, Jerome. *Walt Whitman: The Song of Himself*. Berkeley: University of California Press, 1999.

Marx, Leo, ed. *The Americanness of Walt Whitman*. Boston: D. C. Heath, 1960.

Miller, James Edwin, Jr. *Walt Whitman*. Updated ed. Boston: Twayne, 1990.

Woodress, James, ed. *Critical Essays on Walt Whitman*. Boston: G. K. Hall, 1983.

Richard Wilbur

Edgecombe, Rodney Stenning. *A Reader's Guide to the Poetry of Richard Wilbur*. Tuscaloosa: University of Alabama Press, 1995.

Michelson, Bruce. *Wilbur's Poetry: Music in a Scattering Time*. Amherst: University of Massachusetts Press, 1991.

Salinger, Wendy, ed. *Richard Wilbur's Creation*. Ann Arbor: University of Michigan Press, 1983.

William Carlos Williams

Bloom, Harold, ed. *William Carlos Williams*. New York: Chelsea House, 1986.

Cushman, Stephen. *William Carlos Williams and the Meanings of Measure*. New Haven, Conn.: Yale University Press, 1985.

Guimond, James. *The Art of William Carlos Williams: A Discovery and Possession of America*. Urbana: University of Illinois Press, 1968.

Miller, J. Hillis, ed. *William Carlos Williams: A Collection of Critical Essays*. Englewood Cliffs, N.J.: Prentice-Hall, 1962.

Ostrom, Alan. *The Poetic World of William Carlos Williams*. Carbondale: Southern Illinois University Press, 1966.

Rodgers, Audrey T. *Virgin and Whore: The Image of Women in the Poetry of William Carlos Williams*. Jefferson, N.C.: McFarland, 1987.

William Wordsworth

Bloom, Harold, ed. *William Wordsworth*. New York: Chelsea House, 1985.

Ferry, David. *The Limits of Mortality*. Middeletown, Conn.: Wesleyan University Press, 1959.

Hartman, Geoffrey H. *Wordsworth's Poetry, 1787-1814*. 1964. Reprint. New Haven, Conn.: Yale University Press, 1971.

Jacobus, Mary. *Tradition and Experiment in Wordsworth's "Lyrical Ballads" (1798)*. Oxford, England: Clarendon Press, 1976.

Lindenberger, Herbert. *On Wordsworth's "Prelude."* Princeton, N.J.: Princeton University Press, 1963.

Noyes, Russell. *William Wordsworth*. New York: Twayne, 1971.

O'Donnell, Brennan. *The Passion of Meter: A Study of Wordsworth's Metrical Art*. Kent, Ohio: Kent State University Press, 1995.

Pine, David P. *William Wordsworth: The Poetry of Grandeur and Tenderness*. New York: Methuen, 1982.

Rader, Melvin R. *Wordsworth: A Philosophical Approach*. Oxford. England: Clarendon Press, 1967.

William Butler Yeats

Bloom, Harold, ed. *William Butler Yeats*. New York: Chelsea House, 1986.

Ellman, Richard. *The Identity of Yeats*. 2d ed. New York: Oxford University Press, 1964.

Finneran, Richard J., ed. *Critical Essays on W. B. Yeats*. Boston: G. K. Hall, 1986.

Henn, T. R. *The Lonely Tower: Studies in the Poetry of Yeats*. 2d ed. London: Methuen, 1965.

Jeffares, A. Norman. *A New Commentary on the Poems of W B. Yeats.* Stanford, Calif.: Stanford University Press, 1984.

Meir, Cohn. *The Ballads and Songs of W. B. Yeats: The Anglo-Irish Heritage in Subject and Style.* New York: Barnes & Noble Books, 1974.

Peterson, Richard F. *William Butler Yeats.* Boston: Twayne, 1982.

Rosenthal, M. L. *Running to Paradise: Yeats's Poetic Art.* New York: Oxford University Press, 1994.

Unterecker, John. *A Reader's Guide to William Butler Yeats.* Syracuse, N.Y.: Syracuse University Press, 1996.

Bryan Aubrey; updated by Maura Ives

Poetry Titles in *Masterplots, Revised Second Edition*

NOTE: The titles listed below are covered not in *Masterplots II: Poetry Series, Revised Edition* but in the twelve-volume *Masterplots, Revised Second Edition* (1996).

Absalom and Achitophel—John Dryden
Aeneid—Vergil
Afternoon of a Faun, The—Stéphane Mallarmé
Age of Anxiety, The—W. H. Auden
Alcools—Guillaume Apollinaire
Amores—Ovid
Amoretti—Edmund Spenser
Anabasis—Saint-John Perse
Annie Allen—Gwendolyn Brooks
Ariel—Sylvia Plath
Arme Heinrich, Der—Hartmann von Aue
Art of Poetry, The—Horace
Ash Wednesday—T. S. Eliot
Astrophil and Stella—Sir Philip Sidney
Atalanta in Calydon—Algernon Charles Swinburne
Aurora Leigh—Elizabeth Barrett Browning

Bells in Winter—Czesław Miłosz
Beowulf—Unknown
Bevis of Hampton—Unknown
Biglow Papers, The—James Russell Lowell
Book of Songs—Heinrich Heine
Book of the Duchess—Geoffrey Chaucer
Book of Theseus, The—Giovanni Boccaccio
Boris Godunov—Alexander Pushkin
Borough, The—George Crabbe
Bride's Tragedy, The, and *Death's Jest-Book*—Thomas Lovell Beddoes
Bridge, The—Hart Crane
Bronze Horseman, The—Alexander Pushkin
Brut—Layamon

Cane—Jean Toomer
Canterbury Tales, The—Geoffrey Chaucer
Canto General—Pablo Neruda
Cantos—Ezra Pound
Carmina—Catullus
Cawdor—Robinson Jeffers

Faerie Queene, The—Edmund Spenser
Far Field, The—Theodore Roethke
Faust—Johann Wolfgang von Goethe
Fêtes Galantes and Other Poems—Paul Verlaine
Filostrato, Il—Giovanni Boccaccio
Finn Cycle—Unknown
First Poetic Works and *New Poetic Works*—Alfred de Musset
Flowers of Evil—Charles Baudelaire
For the Union Dead—Robert Lowell
Four Quartets—T. S. Eliot
Frithiof's Saga—Esaias Tegnér

Gaucho Martín Fierro, The—José Hernández
Georgics—Vergil
Gilgamesh Epic, The—Unknown
Goblin Market—Christina Rossetti
Great Testament, The—François Villon
Guy of Warwick—Unknown

Harmonium—Wallace Stevens
Harp-Weaver and Other Poems, The—Edna St. Vincent Millay
Havelok the Dane—Unknown
Heroides—Ovid
Hesperides—Robert Herrick
Holy Sonnets—John Donne
Homage to Mistress Bradstreet—John Berryman
Homeward—Æ
House of Life, The—Dante Gabriel Rossetti
Howl—Allen Ginsberg
Hudibras—Samuel Butler
Hugh Selwyn Mauberley—Ezra Pound
Huon of Bordeaux—Unknown
Hymns—Callimachus

Idylls—Theocritus
Idylls of the King—Alfred, Lord Tennyson
Iliad, The—Homer
In Memoriam—Alfred, Lord Tennyson
Inundación castálida—Sor Juana Inés de la Cruz
Irish Melodies—Thomas Moore

Jerusalem Delivered—Torquato Tasso
John Brown's Body—Stephen Vincent Benét

Kalevala—Elias Lönnrot
King Horn—Unknown

Lady of the Lake, The—Sir Walter Scott
Lais of Marie de France, The—Marie de France
Lalla Rookh—Thomas Moore
Lancelot—Chrétien de Troyes
Lay of Igor's Campaign, The—Unknown
Lay of the Last Minstrel, The—Sir Walter Scott
Leaves of Grass—Walt Whitman
Legend of Good Women, The—Geoffrey Chaucer
Longing for the Light, A—Vicente Aleixandre
Lost World, The—Randall Jarrell
Lucasta Poems—Richard Lovelace
Lusiads, The—Luís de Camões

Mac Flecknoe—John Dryden
Mahabharata, The—Unknown
Manfred—George Gordon, Lord Byron
Marmion—Sir Walter Scott
Maud—Alfred, Lord Tennyson
Maximus Poems, The—Charles Olson
Men and Women—Robert Browning
Metamorphoses—Ovid
Metamorphosis—Edith Sitwell
Milton—William Blake
Miscellanies—Abraham Cowley
Modern Love—George Meredith
Mölna Elegy, A—Gunnar Ekelöf
Mother Hubberd's Tale—Edmund Spenser
Mr. Cogito—Zbigniew Herbert

Narrow Road to the Deep North, The—Matsuo Bashō
New Life, The—Dante Alighieri
Nibelungenlied, The—Unknown
North & South—Elizabeth Bishop
North of Boston—Robert Frost
Novice, The—Mikhail Lermontov

Ode to Aphrodite—Sappho
Odes—Pindar
Odyssey, The—Homer

Odyssey, The—Nikos Kazantzakis
On Sepulchres—Ugo Foscolo
On the Nature of Things—Lucretius
Orlando furioso—Ludovico Ariosto
Orlando innamorato—Matteo Maria Boiardo

Paradise Lost—John Milton
Paradise Regained—John Milton
Parlement of Foules—Geoffrey Chaucer
Parzival—Wolfram von Eschenbach
Passions and Ancient Days—Constantine P. Cavafy
Paterson—William Carlos Williams
People, Yes, The—Carl Sandburg
Personae and Other Poems—Ezra Pound
Pharsalia—Lucan
Piers Plowman—William Langland
Pilgrimage of Charlemagne, The—Unknown
Platero and I—Juan Ramón Jiménez
Poem of the Cid—Unknown
Poems—Sidney Lanier
Poems—Sir Walter Ralegh
Poems and Ballads—Algernon Charles Swinburne
Poems, Chiefly in the Scottish Dialect—Robert Burns
Poetic Edda—Unknown
Poetical Meditations—Alphonse de Lamartine
Poetry of Campion—Thomas Campion
Poetry of Carducci—Giosuè Carducci
Poetry of Carew—Thomas Carew
Poetry of Clare—John Clare
Poetry of Du Bellay—Joachim du Bellay
Poetry of Stefan George—Stefan George
Poetry of Laforgue—Jules Laforgue
Poetry of Machado—Antonio Machado
Poetry of Mörike—Eduard Mörike
Poetry of Skelton—John Skelton
Poetry of Traherne—Thomas Traherne
Poetry of Vaughan—Henry Vaughan
Poly-Olbion—Michael Drayton
Porto sepolto, Il—Giuseppe Ungaretti
Prelude, The—William Wordsworth
Preludes for Memnon—Conrad Aiken
Princess, The—Alfred, Lord Tennyson
Profane Hymns—Rubén Darío

Prometheus Unbound—Percy Bysshe Shelley
Prophet, The—Kahlil Gibran

Ramayana, The—Valmiki
Rape of Lucrece, The—William Shakespeare
Rape of the Lock, The—Alexander Pope
Requiem—Anna Akhmatova
Rhymes, The—Gustavo Adolfo Bécquer
Rhymes—Petrarch
Rime of the Ancient Mariner, The—Samuel Taylor Coleridge
Ring and the Book, The—Robert Browning
Roan Stallion—Robinson Jeffers
Rubáiyát of Omar Khayyám—Edward FitzGerald
Ruslan and Lyudmila—Alexander Pushkin

Satires—Nicolas Boileau-Despréaux
Satires—Juvenal
Satires—Persius
Sea Garden—H. D.
Season in Hell, A—Arthur Rimbaud
Seasons, The—James Thomson
Seatonian Poems and *A Song to David*—Christopher Smart
Seeing Things—Seamus Heaney
Shepheardes Calender, The—Edmund Spenser
Shih Ching, The—Confucius
Shropshire Lad, A—A. E. Housman
Sir Gawain and the Green Knight—The Pearl-Poet
Snow-Bound—John Greenleaf Whittier
Sohrab and Rustum—Matthew Arnold
Solitudes, The—Luis de Góngora y Argote
Song of Hiawatha, The—Henry Wadsworth Longfellow
Song of Roland, The—Unknown
Songs of Innocence and of Experience—William Blake
Sonnets, The—Michelangelo
Sonnets for Helen—Pierre de Ronsard
Sonnets from the Portuguese—Elizabeth Barrett Browning
Sonnets of Shakespeare, The—William Shakespeare
Sonnets to Orpheus—Rainer Maria Rilke
Spain, Take This Cup from Me—César Vallejo
Spoon River Anthology—Edgar Lee Masters
Steps to the Temple—Richard Crashaw

Tala—Gabriela Mistral
Tales of Ise—Unknown
Tamar—Robinson Jeffers
Task, The—William Cowper
Temple, The—George Herbert
Thanatopsis—William Cullen Bryant
Thebaid, The—Statius
These Jaundiced Loves—Tristan Corbière
To His Coy Mistress—Andrew Marvell
To Urania—Joseph Brodsky
Tower, The—William Butler Yeats
Tristan and Isolde—Gottfried von Strassburg
Tristia—Osip Mandelstam
Tristram—Edwin Arlington Robinson
Troilus and Criseyde—Geoffrey Chaucer
Twelve, The—Aleksandr Blok

Venus and Adonis—William Shakespeare

War of the Mice and the Crabs, The—Giacomo Leopardi
Waste Land, The—T. S. Eliot
Weary Blues, The—Langston Hughes
Whitsun Weddings, The—Philip Larkin
Works and Days—Hesiod
Wreck of the Deutschland, *The*—Gerard Manley Hopkins

Yvain—Chrétien de Troyes

MASTERPLOTS II

POETRY SERIES
REVISED EDITION

TITLE INDEX

AUTHOR INDEX

GEOGRAPHICAL AND ETHNIC INDEX

CATEGORIES

TYPE OF POEM INDEX

CATEGORIES

BALLAD
- American Primitive (Smith, W.), I-108
- Arrest of Oscar Wilde at the Cadogan Hotel, The (Betjeman), I-210
- Ballad of an Old Cypress (Du Fu), I-349
- Ballad of Birmingham (Randall), I-352
- *Ballad of Reading Gaol, The* (Wilde), I-355
- Ballad of Rudolph Reed, The (Brooks), I-359
- Ballad of the Landlord (Hughes, L.), I-362
- Barbara Frietchie (Whittier), I-368
- Belle Dame sans Merci, La (Keats), IV-2112
- Bird, The (Simpson), I-453
- Blessed Damozel, The (Rossetti), I-494
- Connachtman, A (Colum), II-798
- Fight (García Lorca), III-1349
- Goblet, The (Mistral), III-1550
- Hand That Signed the Paper, The (Thomas, D.), III-1634
- Hard Rock Returns to Prison from the Hospital for the Criminal Insane (Knight), III-1646
- *Hunting of the Snark, The* (Carroll), IV-1798
- In mourning wise since daily I increase (Wyatt), IV-1960
- Lament by the River, The (Du Fu), IV-2144
- Lament for the Makaris (Dunbar, W.), IV-2151
- *Mask of Anarchy, The* (Shelley), V-2422
- Raven, The (Poe), VI-3139
- Sir Patrick Spens (Unknown), VI-3404
- Skipper Ireson's Ride (Whittier), VII-3419
- Somnambule Ballad (García Lorca), VII-3472
- Telling the Bees (Whittier), VII-3766
- Transfer (Brown), VII-3974
- Ulalume (Poe), VIII-4062
- Village Blacksmith, The (Longfellow), VIII-4121
- We Are Seven (Wordsworth), VIII-4193

DRAMATIC MONOLOGUE
- Aeneas at Washington (Tate, A.), I-28
- Ancestor (Baca), I-117
- Andrea del Sarto (Browning, R.), I-132
- Animals Are Passing from Our Lives (Levine), I-154
- Babii Yar (Yevtushenko), I-333
- Bishop Orders His Tomb at Saint Praxed's Church, The (Browning, R.), I-456
- Bomb (Corso), I-523
- Collar, The (Herbert, G.), II-775
- Corinna's Going A-Maying (Herrick), II-833
- Country Walk, A (Kinsella), II-860

TYPE OF POEM INDEX